AD Non
346.730   W9-CKT-269

Stewart, Marcia, author. Every landlord's legal
guide   9001201137

DISCARDED BY
MEAD PUBLIC LIBRARY

Download Forms on Nolo.com

You can download the forms in this book at:

 www.nolo.com/back-of-book/ELLI.html

We'll also post updates whenever there's an important change to the law affecting this book—as well as articles and other related materials.

More Resources
from Nolo.com

 Legal Forms, Books, & Software

Hundreds of do-it-yourself products—all written in plain English, approved, and updated by our in-house legal editors.

 Legal Articles

Get informed with thousands of free articles on everyday legal topics. Our articles are accurate, up to date, and reader friendly.

 Find a Lawyer

Want to talk to a lawyer? Use Nolo to find a lawyer who can help you with your case.

NOLO
LAW for ALL

⚖ NOLO

The Trusted Name
(but don't take our word for it)

"In Nolo you can trust."
THE NEW YORK TIMES

"Nolo is always there in a jam as the nation's premier publisher of do-it-yourself legal books."
NEWSWEEK

"Nolo publications…guide people simply through the how, when, where and why of the law."
THE WASHINGTON POST

"[Nolo's]…material is developed by experienced attorneys who have a knack for making complicated material accessible."
LIBRARY JOURNAL

"When it comes to self-help legal stuff, nobody does a better job than Nolo…"
USA TODAY

"The most prominent U.S. publisher of self-help legal aids."
TIME MAGAZINE

"Nolo is a pioneer in both consumer and business self-help books and software."
LOS ANGELES TIMES

16th Edition

Every Landlord's Legal Guide

Marcia Stewart & Attorneys Janet Portman & Ann O'Connell

SIXTEENTH EDITION	MAY 2022
Cover & Book Design	SUSAN PUTNEY
Proofreading	SUSAN CARLSON GREENE
Index	THERESA DURAN
Printing	SHERIDAN

ISSN 2576-7186 (print)
ISSN 2576-7194 (online)

ISBN 978-1-4133-2975-9 (paperback)
ISBN 978-1-4133-2976-6 (ebook)

This book covers only United States law, unless it specifically states otherwise.

Copyright © 1996, 1997, 1998, 2000, 2001, 2003, 2004, 2006, 2008, 2010, 2012, 2014, 2016, 2018, 2020, and 2022 by Nolo. All rights reserved. The NOLO trademark is registered in the U.S. Patent and Trademark Office. Printed in the U.S.A.

No part of this publication may be reproduced, stored in a retrieval system, or transmitted in any form or by any means, electronic, mechanical, photocopying, recording, or otherwise without prior written permission. Reproduction prohibitions do not apply to the forms contained in this product when reproduced for personal use. For information on bulk purchases or corporate premium sales, please contact tradecs@nolo.com.

Please note

Accurate, plain-English legal information can help you solve many of your own legal problems. But this text is not a substitute for personalized advice from a knowledgeable lawyer. If you want the help of a trained professional—and we'll always point out situations in which we think that's a good idea—consult an attorney licensed to practice in your state.

About the Authors

Marcia Stewart is the coauthor of *Every Tenant's Legal Guide, Renters' Rights, First-Time Landlord,* and *Nolo's Essential Guide to Buying Your First Home.* Marcia received a Master's degree in Public Policy from the University of California at Berkeley.

Janet Portman, an attorney and Nolo's Executive Editor, received undergraduate and graduate degrees from Stanford and a law degree from Santa Clara University. She is an expert on landlord-tenant law and the coauthor of *Every Tenant's Legal Guide, Every Landlord's Guide to Finding Great Tenants, First-Time Landlord, Renters' Rights, The California Landlord's Law Book: Rights and Responsibilities, California Tenant's Rights, Leases & Rental Agreements,* and *Negotiate the Best Lease for Your Business.* As a practicing attorney, she specialized in criminal defense before joining Nolo.

Ann O'Connell, an attorney and editor at Nolo, received an undergraduate degree from Boston College and a law degree from U.C. Berkeley School of Law. She is also a licensed Colorado real estate broker, and is a coauthor of *Renters' Rights, Every Tenant's Legal Guide, Leases & Rental Agreements, Saving the Family Cottage,* and *Nolo's Essential Guide to Buying Your First Home.* Before joining Nolo, Ann focused on real estate and business matters as a practicing attorney, and represented both sellers and buyers as a real estate agent.

Table of Contents

Appendixes

Introduction: Your Landlord Companion

Whether you own one rental property or a hundred, you want to run a profitable business, protect your investment, and avoid legal hassles. Your success depends heavily on knowing and complying with dozens of state, federal, and local laws. Fortunately, you don't need a law degree—just this book.

We'll take you step by step through everything from accepting rental applications to returning security deposits when tenants move out. Learn how to prepare a lease, handle repairs, and deal with tenants who pay rent late, make too much noise, or cause other problems. This book covers not only straightforward procedures (such as how to legally reject a prospect) but also advises you on how to deal with more complicated situations (like what to do when a tenant threatens to withhold rent until you make certain repairs). This book also provides:

State-specific legal info. Use the comprehensive State Landlord-Tenant Law Charts in Appendix A to find your state's laws on: security deposits, required landlord disclosures, rent withholding, abandoned property, unconditional quit terminations, and much more.

Legal forms and letters. This book includes dozens of forms, letters, notices, checklists, and agreements you can use in your landlord business. Each form is easy to complete and has comprehensive instructions. You'll find filled-in samples in the text and downloadable forms on the companion page for this book on the Nolo website (see below for details). With these forms, you'll be able to create your own rental applications, leases, letters to tenants, and much, much more.

Getting Expert Help

Throughout this book, we'll alert you to situations in which it's wise to get expert help beyond this book, including:

- **Preparing eviction papers.** We explain how to terminate a tenancy, but if you need to pursue an eviction lawsuit, get more help. Evictions are governed by very specific state and local laws and procedures.
- **Rentals in mobile home parks and marinas.** In most states, completely different sets of laws govern these rentals.
- **Renting out a condo or town house.** Many owners will find this book helpful, but be sure to also review your homeowners' association's CC&Rs (covenants, conditions, and restrictions). Sometimes CC&Rs clash with or go beyond, federal, state, or local laws. An attorney can help you evaluate which rules the judges in your area are most likely to uphold.
- **Live-work units.** You'll find this book helpful if you're renting out live-work units, but be aware that local zoning regulations we don't cover in this book might apply.
- **Section 8 housing.** If you participate in the Section 8 rent assistance program, you'll find most of the day-to-day recommendations of this book usable, but you'll need to use the lease addendum supplied by the housing authority that administers the program.
- **Short-term rentals.** Many of the landlord-tenant laws discussed in this book specifically exclude short-term, hotel-like rentals. If you offer short-term rentals as part of your business, check with your local government. Many municipalities require registration, limit the number of short-stay days per year, or otherwise restrict short-term rentals. See Chapter 8 for more on the subject.

Time-tested and timely information. This book, which first appeared in 1996, has been updated many times since to keep up with the constantly changing world of residential landlording. Ours is the only book on the shelf that combines current, comprehensive legal information and practical advice usable by landlords in every state. In addition, when important laws change during the life of this edition, you'll find updates on this book's companion page (described below).

We believe that finding and retaining good tenants is the key to running a successful residential rental business. Our approach will guard your legal and financial interests and, at the same time, make your customers—your tenants—feel that your practices are fair and reasonable.

In a nutshell: By choosing tenants carefully; keeping good tenants happy; teaching mediocre tenants how to improve; getting rid of bad tenants by applying policies that are strict, fair, and legal; and backing up everything with detailed records, you can run a business that's both satisfying and profitable.

Get Legal Updates, Forms, and More on This Book's Companion Page on Nolo.com

This book includes three dozen useful forms and worksheets, including a lease, a rental application, and security deposit itemizations. You can download any of the forms and worksheets in this book at:

www.nolo.com/back-of-book/ELLI.html

When there are important changes to the information in this book, we'll post updates on this same dedicated page (what we call the book's companion page). See Appendix B, "How to Use the Downloadable Forms on the Nolo Website," for a list of forms available on Nolo.com.

Other Helpful Nolo Books and Resources for Landlords

Nolo publishes a comprehensive library of books for landlords and property managers. Besides *Every Landlord's Legal Guide*, Nolo offers:

- ***Every Landlord's Guide to Finding Great Tenants,*** by Janet Portman. Focuses solely on advertising and showing your rental, evaluating prospects, and choosing and rejecting tenants. Includes over 40 forms, including a credit report evaluation, marketing worksheets, and departing tenant's questionnaire. Especially useful for landlords who own multiunit properties or have a lot of tenant turnover.

- ***Every Landlord's Guide to Managing Property***, by Michael Boyer. Provides practical and legal compliance advice for small-time landlords who manage property and tenants on the side (while holding down a day job). Includes do-it-yourself advice on handling day-to-day issues, such as nitty-gritty maintenance and conflicts with tenants regarding late rent, pets, and unauthorized occupants. Explains how to manage and grow a successful rental property business with minimal hassle and cost.

- ***Every Landlord's Tax Deduction Guide,*** by Stephen Fishman. Includes all the information you need to take advantage of tax deductions and write-offs available to landlords, such as depreciation, legal services, travel, and insurance. Includes instructions on filling out Schedule E.

- ***Leases & Rental Agreements,*** by Janet Portman and Ann O'Connell. Includes a lease, rental agreement, and several other basic forms. If you own *Every Landlord's Legal Guide*, you don't need *Leases and Rental Agreements*.

- ***The California Landlord's Law Book: Rights & Responsibilities,*** by Nils Rosenquest and Janet Portman, and ***The California Landlord's Law Book: Evictions***, by Nils Rosenquest. Contain all the information California landlords need to run their business and handle an eviction in court by themselves. *Every Landlord's Legal Guide* covers residential landlord-tenant law in all 50 states, including California, but these books provide more details, including rent control rules and step-by-step instructions on how to file and handle an eviction lawsuit.

- ***First-Time Landlord: Your Guide to Renting Out a Single-Family Home***, by Janet Portman, Ilona Bray, and Marcia Stewart. Covers the basic information that first-time or "accidental" landlords need to rent and manage a single-family home or condo, such as how to determine if a property will turn a profit, things to consider when renting out a room in an owner-occupied house, and how to use a lease-option-to-buy contract.

You can order these books from Nolo's website (Nolo.com) or by phone (800-728-3555). You can also find Nolo books at public libraries and bookstores.

In addition to these books, Nolo offers many interactive online forms of interest to landlords, such as state-specific leases and rental agreements.

Also, be sure to check out the Landlords section of Nolo.com for a wide variety of articles of interest to landlords, including state eviction rules. Nolo's website includes other useful resources, including legal updates on this book's companion page (described above).

Screening Tenants:
Your Most Important Decision

FORMS IN THIS CHAPTER

Chapter 1 includes instructions for and samples of the following forms:

- Rental Application
- Consent to Contact References and Perform Credit Check
- Tenant References
- Notice of Denial Based on Credit Report or Other Information
- Notice of Conditional Acceptance Based on Credit Report or Other Information
- Receipt and Holding Deposit Agreement

The purchase of this book includes free downloadable and customizable copies of all of these forms. See Appendix B for the download link and instructions.

Choosing tenants is the most important decision any landlord makes, and to do it well you need a reliable system. Follow the steps in this chapter to maximize your chances of selecting tenants who will pay their rent on time, keep their units in good condition, and not cause you any legal or practical problems later.

How Landlords' Associations Can Help

This chapter provides all the legal and practical information and forms you need to choose tenants. You can also get a lot of advice from talking with other landlords. Also, many local or state rental property associations and landlords' associations provide the following:

- legal information and updates through newsletters, publications, seminars, and blogs
- tenant screening and credit check services
- training and practical advice on compliance with legal responsibilities, and
- a place to meet other rental property owners and exchange information and ideas.

If you can't find an association of rental property owners online, ask other landlords for references. You can also contact the National Apartment Association (NAA), an organization whose members include many individual state associations (NAAHQ.org), and the National Multifamily Housing Council (NMHC.org), which provides useful networking opportunities and research.

Avoiding Fair Housing Complaints and Lawsuits

Federal and state antidiscrimination laws limit what you can say and do in the tenant selection process. Because the topic of discrimination is so important, we devote a whole chapter to it (Chapter 5). You should read Chapter 5 before you run an ad or interview prospective tenants. For now, keep in mind four important points:

- **You are legally free to choose among prospective tenants as long as your decisions are based on legitimate business criteria.** You are entitled to reject applicants with bad credit histories, income that you reasonably regard as insufficient to pay the rent, or past behavior— such as property damage or consistent late rent payments—that makes someone a risk. A valid occupancy limit that is clearly tied to health and safety or legitimate business needs can also be a legal basis for refusing tenants. And it's always legal to refuse to rent to someone who can't come up with the security deposit or meet another condition of the tenancy.

- **Fair housing laws specify illegal reasons to refuse to rent to a tenant.** Federal law prohibits discrimination on the basis of race, color, religion, national origin, sex, familial status, or physical or mental disability (including recovering alcoholics and people with a past drug addiction). Many states and cities also prohibit discrimination based on marital status or sexual orientation.

- **Anybody who deals with prospective tenants must follow fair housing laws.** This includes owners, landlords, managers, and real estate brokers, and all of their employees. As the property owner, you could be held legally responsible for your employees' discriminatory statements or conduct, including sexual harassment. "Your Liability for a Manager's Acts," in Chapter 6, explains how to protect yourself from your employees' illegal acts.

- **Consistency is crucial when dealing with prospective tenants.** If you don't treat all tenants more or less equally—for example, if you arbitrarily set tougher standards for renting to a member of a racial minority— you are violating federal laws and opening yourself up to lawsuits.

How to Advertise Rental Property

You can advertise rental property in many ways:

- posting a notice online
- using an "Apartment for Rent" sign
- taking out ads in a local newspaper
- posting flyers on neighborhood bulletin boards
- listing with a local real estate broker
- hiring a property management company that will advertise your rentals as part of the management fee, or
- posting a notice with university, alumni, or corporate housing offices.

The kind of advertising that will work best depends on a number of factors, including the characteristics of the particular property (such as rent, size, amenities), its location, your budget, and how quickly you need to rent. Many smaller landlords find that instead of advertising widely and having to screen many potential tenants in an effort to sort the good from the bad, it makes better sense to market their rentals through word of mouth—telling friends, colleagues, neighbors, and current tenants, and by posting on social media.

Avoid getting into legal hot water by following these rules:

Describe the rental unit accurately. Avoid abbreviations and real estate jargon in your ad. Be enthusiastic but honest! Include basic details, such as:

- rent and deposit
- room size (particularly number of bedrooms and baths)
- location (either the general neighborhood or street address)
- move-in date and term (lease or month-to-month rental agreement)
- special features
- pets (whether you allow them and any restrictions, such as dog breeds your insurance prohibits)

- your nonparticipation in the Section 8 program (assuming you have the choice—see Chapter 5 for details)
- phone number, website, and/or email for more details (unless you're going to show the unit only at an open house and don't want to take calls), and
- date and time of any open house.

Keep in mind that even if you aren't prosecuted for breaking fraud laws, false advertising can still come back to haunt you. A tenant who is robbed or attacked in what you advertised as a "high-security building" could sue you for medical bills, lost earnings, and pain and suffering.

If you have important rules (legal and nondiscriminatory), such as no smoking, put them in your ad. Letting prospective tenants know your policies can save you from talking to a lot of people who wouldn't qualify.

Be sure your ad can't be construed as discriminatory. The best way to do this is to focus only on the rental property—not on any particular type of tenant. Ads should never mention sex, race, religion, disability, or age (unless your rental is legally recognized senior citizens' housing). And ads should never imply through words, photographs, or illustrations that you prefer to rent to (or won't rent to) people because of their age, sex, or race. For example, an ad that says the property is "close to the XYZ Church" could be construed as your preference for people of that religion.

Quote an honest price and stick to it. If an applicant meets all your good-tenant requirements and agrees to the terms in your ad, you might violate false advertising laws if you arbitrarily raise the price. This doesn't mean you are always legally required to rent at your advertised price, however. If an applicant asks for more services or different lease terms that you feel require more rent, it's fine to bargain and raise your price, as long as your proposed increase doesn't violate local rent control laws.

Don't advertise a property that isn't actually available. Some landlords advertise units that aren't really available in order to produce a large number of applicants who could then be directed to higher-priced or inferior units. Such bait-and-switch advertising is illegal under consumer fraud laws.

Craigslist and Online Apartment Listing Services

Online services make it easy to reach potential tenants.

Online community posting boards allow you to list your rentals at no or low charge and are a good place to start. Craigslist (craigslist.org), the most established community board, has local sites for every major metropolitan area. Many neighborhoods and zip codes also have local groups for posting rentals on Facebook and Nextdoor.

Local online services might also be available, particularly in large urban areas.

National apartment listing services encompass millions of apartment units. Some of the most established are:

- Apartments.com
- Zillow.com
- Rentals.com
- Rent.com
- ApartmentGuide.com
- ForRent.com, and
- Zumper.com.

These national sites offer a wide range of services, from simple ads that provide basic information on your rental (such as the number of bedrooms) to full-scale virtual tours and floor plans of the rental property. Services typically include mobile apps, too. Prices vary widely depending on the type of ad, how long you want it to run, and any services you purchase (some websites provide tenant screening services).

Before you use any online apartment rental service, make sure it's reputable. Find out who owns it, how long the company has been in business, and how they handle problems with apartment listings. Search online for consumer complaints and ratings.

Consider Tenants Who Are Advertising Themselves

Because good rental properties are so hard to find, many people post "rental wanted" ads.

Apartment seekers who post online ads describe their property needs and their price range, hoping that a landlord in the area will see their post and contact them.

Craigslist is chock-full of posts that run the gamut from sophisticated to self-defeating. If you decide to peruse these listings, keep these tips in mind:

- The ad should reveal relevant information about the tenant's needs and rental history, so that you don't call someone who isn't suited for your rental.
- The ad should describe a seeker who is stable, clean, and honest. Of course, the words on the page don't make it true. If you encounter information that raises red flags (a history of short-term rentals), take heed.
- The ad should explain what the tenant is looking for but not be too demanding. Be wary of requirements that, if you meet them, could involve you in a fair housing problem (such as, "Looking for a quiet, adult community").
- Look carefully at the writer's jobs, interests, and hobbies. Activities that spell "property damage" or "party animal" should put you on notice.
- Beware the post that plays the sympathy card. Although it's admirable to work with in-place tenants who have hit a rough patch, it's risky to begin a landlord-tenant relationship based on charity.

Renting Property That's Still Occupied

Ideally, you'll be able to wait until the old tenant moves out to show a rental unit to prospective tenants. This gives you the chance to refurbish the unit and avoids problems such as promising the place to a new tenant, only to have the existing tenant not move out on time or leave the place a mess.

To eliminate any gap in rent, however, you might need to show an occupied rental. In most states, you have a right to show the property to prospective tenants, but your current tenants are still entitled to their privacy. To minimize disturbing current tenants, follow these guidelines:

- Before advertising, discuss your plans and needs with the outgoing tenants, so you can be as accommodating as possible.
- Give the current tenants as much notice as possible before entering and showing a rental unit to prospective tenants. State law usually requires at least one or two days. (See Chapter 13 for details.)
- Limit the number of times you show the unit in a given week, and make sure your current tenants agree to any evening and weekend visits.
- Consider reducing the rent slightly for the existing tenants if showing the unit really will be an imposition.
- If possible, avoid putting a sign on the rental property itself, because this almost guarantees that your existing tenants will be bothered by strangers. Or, if you can't avoid using a sign, make sure it warns against disturbing the occupants and includes contact information. "For Rent: Shown by Appointment Only. Call 555-1700. DO NOT DISTURB OCCUPANTS" should work fine.

If, despite your best efforts to protect their privacy, the current tenants are uncooperative, wait until they leave before showing the unit. Also, if the current tenants are complete slobs or have damaged the place, you'll be far better off fixing it before trying to rerent it.

Dealing With Prospective Tenants and Accepting Rental Applications

It's good business, as well as a sound way to protect yourself from future legal problems, to carefully screen prospective tenants.

Tell Prospective Tenants Your Basic Requirements and Rules

It's best to describe all your general requirements—rent, deposits, pet policy, move-in date, maximum number of occupants, and the like—and any special rules and regulations up front. This helps screen out poor matches for your rental, and can also help avoid charges of discrimination, which can occur when members of a protected class are told key facts so late in the process that it appears you've made up new requirements just to keep them out.

Also be sure to tell prospective tenants about the kind of personal information they'll be expected to supply on an application, including phone numbers of previous landlords and credit and employment references.

CAUTION

Show the property to and accept applications from everyone who's interested. Even if, after talking to someone on the phone, you doubt that a particular tenant can qualify, it's best to politely take all applications. Refusing to take an application might unnecessarily anger a prospective tenant, and might result in the applicant's looking into the possibility of filing a discrimination complaint. Show the property to and accept applications from anyone who's interested and make decisions about who will rent the property later. Be sure to keep copies of all applications. (See discussion of record keeping below.)

Ask Interested Tenants to Complete a Rental Application

Ask all prospective tenants to fill out a written rental application. A sample is shown below, and the Nolo website includes a downloadable copy. See Appendix B for the link to the forms in this book.

Before giving prospective tenants a rental application, complete the box at the top. Here are some basic rules for accepting rental applications:

Give an application to each adult applicant. Each prospective tenant—everyone age 18 or older—should completely fill out a written application.

Insist on a completed application. Always make sure that prospective tenants complete the entire rental application, including Social Security number (SSN) or Individual Taxpayer Identification Number (ITIN) (explained below), driver's license number (or other identifying information such as a passport number), current employment, and emergency contacts. You might need this information later to track down a tenant who skips town leaving unpaid rent or abandoned property. Also, you might need the Social Security number or other identifying information to request an applicant's credit report.

> **CAUTION**
> **Don't ask for applicant's date of birth.** This rental application doesn't ask for date of birth (DOB). Doing so is risky: A disappointed applicant could attempt to challenge your rejection as an instance of age discrimination. However, although you should be able to order a credit report and a screening report using only the applicant's Social Security number, some credit reporting companies request DOBs. If you run across this issue, you have a valid reason to request the applicant's DOB at that point.

You might encounter an applicant who does not have an SSN (only citizens or immigrants authorized to work in the United States can obtain one). For example, someone with a student visa usually won't have an SSN. If you categorically refuse to rent to applicants without SSNs, and these applicants happen to be foreign students, you're courting a fair housing complaint.

Fortunately, nonimmigrant aliens (such as people lawfully in the United States who don't intend to stay here permanently, and even those who are here illegally) can obtain an alternate piece of identification that will suit your needs as well as an SSN. It's called an Individual Taxpayer Identification Number (ITIN), and is issued by the IRS to people who expect to pay taxes. Most people who are here long enough to apply for an apartment will also be earning income while in the United States and should therefore have an ITIN. Consumer reporting agencies and tenant screening companies can use an ITIN to find the information they need to effectively screen an applicant. On the rental application, use the line "Other Identifying Information" for an applicant's ITIN.

> **CAUTION**
> **Do not consider an ITIN number as proof of legal status in the United States.** The IRS does not research the taxpayer's immigration status before handing out the number.

Check for a signature and consider getting a separate credit check authorization. Be sure all potential tenants sign the rental application, authorizing you to verify the information, call references, and run a credit report. You might also want to prepare a separate authorization, signed and dated by the applicant, that you can provide to a bank or an employer that wants proof that the tenant authorized you to verify the information. A sample Consent to Contact References and Perform Credit Check is shown below, and the Nolo website includes a downloadable copy. (See Appendix B for the link to the forms in this book.)

Rental Application

A separate application is required from each applicant age 18 or older.

Date and time received by Landlord _____

THIS SECTION TO BE COMPLETED BY LANDLORD

Address of property to be rented: ___178 West 81st St., Apt. 4F___

Rental Term: ☐ month-to-month ☑ lease from ___March 1, 20xx___ to ___February 28, 20xx___

Amounts Due Prior to Occupancy

First month's rent	$ 3,000
Security deposit	$ 3,000
Credit check fee	$ 38
Other (specify): ___Broker's fee___	$ 3,000
TOTAL..	$ 9,038

Applicant

Full Name—include all names you use or have used in the past: ___Hannah Silver___

Home Phone: ___609-555-3789___   Work Phone: ___609-555-4567___

Cell Phone: ___609-987-6543___   Email: ___hannah@coldmail.com___

Social Security Number: ___123-00-4567___   Driver's License Number/State: ___D123456/New Jersey___

Other Identifying Information: _____

Vehicle Make: ___Toyota___   Model: ___Corolla___   Color: ___White___   Year: ___2015___

License Plate Number/State: ___NJ1234567/New Jersey___

Additional Occupants

List everyone, including minor children, who will live with you:

Full Name	Relationship to Applicant
Dennis Olson	Husband

Rental History

FIRST-TIME RENTERS: INSTEAD ATTACH A DESCRIPTION OF YOUR HOUSING SITUATION FOR THE PAST FIVE YEARS.

Current Address: ___39 Maple St., Princeton, NJ 08540___

Dates Lived at Address: ___May 2011 – date___   Rent $ ___2,000___   Security Deposit $ ___4,000___

Landlord/Manager: ___Jane Tucker___   Landlord/Manager's Phone: ___609-555-7523___

Reason for Leaving: ___New job in NYC___

Previous Address: 1215 Middlebrook Lane, Princeton, NJ 08540

Dates Lived at Address: June 2008 – May 2011   Rent $ 1,800   Security Deposit $ 1,000

Landlord/Manager: Ed Palermo   Landlord/Manager's Phone: 609-555-3711

Reason for Leaving: Better apartment

Previous Address: 1527 Highland Dr., New Brunswick, N.J. 08444

Dates Lived at Address: Jan. 2007 – June 2008   Rent $ 800   Security Deposit $ 800

Landlord/Manager: Millie and Joe Lewis   Landlord/Manager's Phone: 609-555-9999

Reason for Leaving: Wanted to live closer to work

Employment History

EMPLOYEES: ATTACH TAX RETURNS FROM THE MOST RECENT TWO YEARS, PLUS PAY STUBS FROM THE PAST SIX MONTHS

SELF-EMPLOYED APPLICANTS: INSTEAD ATTACH TAX RETURNS FOR THE PAST TWO YEARS

Name and Address of Current Employer: Argonworks, 54 Nassau St., Princeton, NJ

Phone: 609-555-2333

Name of Supervisor: Tom Schmidt   Supervisor's Phone: 609-555-2333

Dates Employed at This Job: 2008 – date   Position or Title: Marketing Director

Name and Address of Previous Employer: Princeton Times

13 Junction Rd., Princeton, NJ   Phone: 609-555-1111

Name of Supervisor: Dory Krossber   Supervisor's Phone: 609-555-2366

Dates Employed at This Job: Jan. 2007 – June. 2008   Position or Title: Marketing Associate

Income

1. Your gross monthly employment income (before deductions): $ 8,000

2. Average monthly amounts of other income (specify sources): $
    Note: This does not include my husband's income. $
    See his application. $

                                          TOTAL: $ 8,000

Bank/Financial Accounts

	Account Number	Bank/Institution	Branch
Savings Account:	1222345	N.J. Federal	Trenton, NJ
Checking Account:	789101	Princeton S&L	Princeton, NJ
Money Market or Similar Account:	234789	City Bank	Princeton, NJ

Credit Card Accounts

Major Credit Card: ☑ VISA ☐ MC ☐ Discover Card ☐ Am Ex ☐ Other: _____

Issuer: _City Bank_____ Account No. _1234 5555 6666 7777_

Balance $ _1,000_____ Average Monthly Payment: $ _1,000_

Major Credit Card: ☐ VISA ☐ MC ☐ Discover Card ☐ Am Ex ☑ Other: _Dept. Store_

Issuer: _City Bank_____ Account No. _2345 0000 9999 8888_

Balance $ _500_____ Average Monthly Payment: $ _500_

Loans

Type of Loan (mortgage, car, student loan, etc.)	Name of Creditor	Account Number	Amount Owed	Monthly Payment

Other Major Obligations (such as child support, alimony, tax liens, etc.)

Type	Payee		Amount Owed	Monthly Payment

Pets

Type	Breed	Sex	Age	Neutered/ spayed?	Weight	Years owned

Miscellaneous

Describe water-filled furniture you want to have in the rental property: _None_

Do you smoke? ☐ yes ☑ no

Have you ever:

Filed for bankruptcy?	☐ yes	☑ no	How many times	_____
Been sued?	☐ yes	☑ no	How many times	_____
Sued someone else?	☐ yes	☑ no	How many times	_____
Been evicted?	☐ yes	☑ no	How many times	_____

Explain (include dates) any "yes" listed above: _____

References and Emergency Contact

Personal Reference: _Joan Stanley_   Relationship: _Friend, coworker_

Address: _785 Spruce St., Princeton, NJ 08540_

Email: _joan@joan.com_   Phone: _609-555-4578_

Personal Reference: _Marnie Swatt_   Relationship: _Friend_

Address: _82 East 59th St., #128, NYC_

Email: _marnie@marnie.com_   Phone: _212-555-8765_

Contact in Emergency: _Connie & Martin Silver_   Relationship: _Parents_

Address: _7852 Pierce St., Somerset, NJ 08321_

Email: _connie@connie.com_   Phone: _609-555-7878_

Source

marnie@marnie.com

Where did you learn of this vacancy? _Ryan Cowell, Broker_

I certify that all the information given above is true and correct and understand that my lease or rental agreement may be terminated if I have made any material false or incomplete statements in this application. I authorize verification of the information provided in this application from my credit sources, credit bureaus, current and previous landlords and employers, and personal references. This permission will survive the expiration of my tenancy.

Hannah Silver   _February 15, 20xx_

Applicant   Date

Notes (Landlord/Manager): _____

Consent to Contact References and Perform Credit Check

I authorize ___Jan Gold_____ to obtain information about me from my credit sources, current and previous landlords, employers, and personal references, to enable ___Jan Gold_____ to evaluate my rental application.

I give permission for the landlord or its agent to obtain a consumer report about me for the purpose of this application, to ensure that I continue to meet the terms of the tenancy, for the collection and recovery of any financial obligations relating to my tenancy, or for any other permissible purpose.

_Hannah Silver_____
Applicant signature

Hannah Silver_____
Printed name

39 Maple St., Princeton, NJ 08540_____
Address

609-555-3789_____
Phone Number

February 2, 20xx_____
Date

Request Proof of Identity and Immigration Status

Many landlords ask prospective tenants to show their driver's license or other government photo ID as a way to verify that applicants are using their real names.

Except in California (Cal. Civ. Code § 1940.3), and New York City (N.Y.C. Admin. Code § 8-107(5)(a)), you may also ask applicants for proof of identity and eligibility to work under U.S. immigration laws, such as a work permit, a U.S. passport, or a naturalization certificate. Do so using Form I-9 (*Employment Eligibility Verification*) from the U.S. Citizenship and Immigration Services, or USCIS (a bureau of the U.S. Department of Homeland Security). This form and its instructions are available at www.uscis.gov/i-9, or by phone at 800-375-5283. Remember that an Individual Taxpayer Identification Number (ITIN) is not proof of legal status in the United States—it is merely a way for the IRS to identify a taxpayer.

Some people who have the right to be in the United States, such as some students and other temporary visa holders, might not have the right to work, which is the focus of the I-9 form. To confirm their right to be in the United States, ask for their I-94 or other document describing their status.

Under federal fair housing laws, you may not selectively ask for such immigration information— that is, you must ask all prospective tenants, not just those you suspect might be in the country illegally. It is illegal to discriminate on the basis of national origin, although you may reject someone on the basis of immigration status, as discussed in Chapter 5.

RELATED TOPIC

For a related discussion on security issues regarding suspected terrorists, see "Cooperating With Law Enforcement in Terrorism Investigations" in Chapter 13.

CAUTION

Take your time to evaluate applications. Landlords are often faced with anxious, sometimes desperate people who need a place to live immediately. Don't fall for it. People who have planned so poorly that they will literally have to sleep in the street if they don't rent your place that day are likely to present similar stories when it's time to pay the rent.

Never, never let anyone stay in your property on a temporary basis. Even if you haven't signed a rental agreement or accepted rent, anyone to whom you give a key or allow to move in might gain the legally protected status of a tenant. Then, if the person doesn't leave voluntarily when you want them to, you will have to file an eviction lawsuit.

When and How to Check References, Credit History, and More

If an application looks good, your next step is to dig deeper. The time and money you spend checking out applicants are some of the most cost-effective expenditures you'll ever make.

CAUTION

Be consistent in your screening. You risk a charge of illegal discrimination if you screen certain categories of applicants more stringently than others. Make it your policy, for example, to always require credit reports; don't get a credit report for just single parents or older applicants.

Here are six steps of a very thorough screening process. You should always go through at least the first three to check out the applicant's previous landlords, income, and employment, and run a credit check.

Check With Current and Previous Landlords and Other References

Always call current and previous landlords or managers for references—even if you have a written letter of reference from them. (A prior landlord might be a better source of information than a current one, because a past landlord has no motive to give a falsely glowing report on a troublemaker.) Also call employers and personal references.

To organize the information you gather from these calls, use the Tenant References form, which lists key questions to ask landlords and other references. A sample is shown below and the Nolo website includes a downloadable copy. See Appendix B for the link to the forms in this book.

> **TIP**
>
> **Check out pets, too.** If the prospective tenant has a dog or cat, be sure to ask previous landlords if the pet caused any damage or problems for other tenants or neighbors. It's also a good idea to meet the dog or cat, so you can make sure that it's well-groomed and well-behaved, before you make a final decision. You must, however, accommodate a disabled applicant whose pet serves as an assistance animal. For more information on renting to tenants with pets, see Chapter 2, Clause 14.

Be sure to take and keep notes of all your conversations. You can note your reasons for refusing an individual on the Tenant References form. You'll want to record this information so that you can survive a fair housing challenge if a disappointed applicant files a discrimination complaint against you.

Occasionally, you might encounter a former landlord who is unwilling to discuss the applicant. This reluctance might have nothing to do with the prospective tenant, but instead reflects an exaggerated fear of lawsuits. When a former landlord seems hesitant to talk, try to keep the person on the line long enough to verify the dates of the applicant's tenancy. If you get minimal cooperation, you might say something like this: "I assume your reluctance to talk about Julie has to do with one or more negative things that occurred while she was your tenant." If the former landlord doesn't say anything, you have all the answer you need. If you hear instead, "No, I don't talk about any former tenants—actually, Julie was fairly decent," you can probably follow up with a few general questions.

Verify Income and Employment

Make sure that all tenants have the income to pay the rent each month. Call the prospective tenant's employer to verify income and length of employment.

Before providing this information, some employers require written authorization from the employee. You'll need to send them a signed copy of the release included at the bottom of the Rental Application form, or the separate Consent to Contact References and Perform Credit Check form shown above. If for any reason you question the income information you get by telephone, you could also ask applicants for copies of recent paycheck stubs.

It's also reasonable to require documentation of other sources of income, such as Social Security, disability, workers' compensation, public assistance, child support, or alimony. To evaluate the financial resources of a self-employed person or someone who's not employed, ask for copies of recent tax returns or bank statements.

> **TIP**
>
> **How much income is enough?** Think twice before renting to applicants if the rent will take more than one-third of their gross income, especially if they have a lot of debts.

Tenant References

Name of Applicant: _____ Michael Clark _____

Address of Rental Unit: _____ 123 State Street, Chicago, Illinois _____

Previous Landlord or Manager

Contact (name, property owner or manager, address of rental unit): _Kate Steiner, 345 Mercer St., Chicago,_
_____Illinois; (312) 555-5432_____

Date: _____ February 4, 20xx _____

Questions

When did tenant rent from you (move-in and move-out dates)? _____ December 2012 to date _____

What was the monthly rent? _____ $1,250 _____   Did tenant pay rent on time?   ☐ Yes ☑ No

If rent was not paid on time, did you have to give tenant a legal notice demanding the rent?   ☐ Yes ☑ No

If rent was not paid on time, provide details _____ He paid rent a week late a few times _____

Did you give tenant notice of any lease violation for other than nonpayment of rent?   ☐ Yes ☑ No

If you gave a lease violation notice, what was the outcome? _____

Was tenant considerate of neighbors—that is, no loud parties and fair, careful use of common areas?
_____ Yes, considerate _____

Did tenant have any pets?   ☑ Yes ☐ No   If so, were there any problems? _He had a cat in violation_
_____ of the rental agreement_____

Did tenant make any unreasonable demands or complaints?   ☐ Yes ☑ No   If so, explain: _____

Why did tenant leave? _____ He wants to live someplace that allows pets _____

Did tenant give the proper amount of notice before leaving?   ☑ Yes ☐ No

Did tenant leave the place in good condition? Did you need to use the security deposit to cover damage?
_____ No problems _____

Any particular problems you'd like to mention? _____ No _____

Would you rent to this person again? _____ Yes, but without pets _____

Other comments: _____
_____
_____

Employment Verification

Contact (name, company, position): _Brett Field, Manager, Chicago Car Company_

Date: _February 5, 20xx_   Salary: $ _80,000 + bonus_

Dates of Employment: _March 2011 to date_

Comments: _No problems. Fine employee. Michael is responsible and hard-working._

Personal Reference

Contact (name and relationship to applicant): _Sandy Cameron, friend_

Date: _February 5, 20xx_   How long have you known the applicant? _Five years_

Would you recommend this person as a prospective tenant? _Yes_

Comments: _Michael is very neat and responsible. He's reliable and will be a great tenant._

Credit and Financial Information

Mostly fine — see attached credit report

Notes, Including Reasons for Rejecting Applicant

Applicant had a history of late rent payments and kept a cat, contrary to the rental
agreement.

Obtain a Credit Report

Private credit reporting agencies collect and sell credit files and other information about consumers. It's common to check a prospective tenant's credit history with at least one credit reporting agency to see how responsible the person is managing money.

 TIP

Get the applicant's consent to run a credit report. Because many people think that you must have their written consent before you pull their credit report, we have included it in our consent forms (at the end of the Rental Application and in the separate Consent to Contact References and Perform Credit Check form). But there's another reason for doing this: A written consent will help if you later decide that you need an updated credit report. For example, you might want to consult a current report in order to help you decide whether to sue a tenant who has skipped out and owes rent. Without a broadly written consent, your use of a credit report at that time might be illegal (see the "Advisory Opinion to Long (07-06-00)," on the FTC website at FTC.gov).

How to Get a Credit Report

A credit report contains a gold mine of information. You can usually find out if a particular person has ever filed for bankruptcy or has been:

- late or delinquent in paying rent or bills, including student or car loans
- convicted of a crime, or, in many states, even arrested
- evicted (your legal right to get information on evictions, however, might vary among states)
- involved in another type of lawsuit such as a personal injury claim, or
- financially active enough to establish a credit history.

Depending on the type of report you order, you might also get an applicant's credit score, the most popular being the "FICO" score. This number,

ranging from 300 to 850, purports to indicate the risk that an individual will default on payments. High credit scores indicate less risk. Generally, any score above 670 is considered a medium risk or less. Don't put too much value in a high credit score, because this number does not reflect the many other good-tenant characteristics (such as ability to take good care of your property) that are very important.

Credit report information covers the past seven to ten years. To run a credit check, you'll need a prospective tenant's name, address, and Social Security number or ITIN (Individual Taxpayer Identification Number). Three credit bureaus have cornered the market on credit reports:

- Equifax (Equifax.com)
- TransUnion (TransUnion.com), and
- Experian (Experian.com).

All three bureaus also offer tenant screening services on their websites (as do many property management websites, such as Avail (Avail.co) and TurboTenant (TurboTenant.com)).

Using these screening services has pros and cons. On the plus side, the information they provide is geared to the rental housing context (whereas a credit score was designed to predict whether the applicant would repay a loan). The method also protects applicants' credit scores, in that the report counts only as a "soft inquiry" to the applicant's file (multiple requests for credit reports can lower a credit score). Importantly, SSNs are not revealed to the landlord. Either the landlord or the applicant can pay for the service.

Applicants initiate the screening process by filling out an application to generate a report. The report contains a recommendation on whether to rent to this applicant, based on credit, criminal, and eviction history. (Note that some states and cities limit how and when landlords can consider applicants' criminal histories. See "Criminal Records," below.) For a bit more money, landlords can ask for a credit score, too.

On the negative side, some states do not post criminal data, so landlords who are evaluating applicants who have lived in those states will be paying for a service that isn't available (not to mention that one doesn't have to live in a particular state to commit a crime there). In addition, the service requires some work on the part of the applicants (they must complete an authentication form, to deter identity theft). This step will deter some applicants (but an applicant who isn't serious enough to complete the process arguably is not the one for you, either).

Your state or local apartment association might also offer credit reporting services. Fees depend on the type of service you select. Often, you can request the provider to contact—and collect payment from—the applicant directly, saving you the hassle of having to collect a screening fee.

If negative information in a credit report causes you to not rent to someone or charge higher rent, you must give the prospective tenant the name and address of the agency that reported the negative information. This is a requirement of the federal Fair Credit Reporting Act. (15 U.S.C. §§ 1681 and following.) You must also inform the applicant of the right to obtain a copy of the file from the agency that reported the negative information, by requesting it within 60 days of being told that the rejection was based on the individual's credit report.

Tenants who are applying for more than one rental might try to avoid multiple fees by obtaining their own report, making copies, and asking you to accept their copy. Federal law does not require you to accept an applicant's copy—that is, you may require applicants to pay a credit check fee for you to run a new report. Wisconsin and Washington are exceptions: State law in Wisconsin forbids landlords from charging for a credit report if, before the landlord asks for a report, the applicant offers one from a consumer reporting agency and the report is less than 30 days old. (Wis. Adm. Code § ATCP

134.05(4)(b).) And in Washington, landlords must advise prospective tenants whether they will accept a screening report provided by the applicant done by a consumer reporting agency (in which case you may not charge the tenant a fee for a screening report). Landlords who maintain a website that advertises residential rentals must include this information on the home page. (Wash. Rev. Code Ann. § 59.18.257.)

Credit Check Fees

It's legal in most states to charge prospective tenants a fee for the cost of the credit report itself and your time and trouble. Any credit check fee should be reasonably related to the cost of the credit check—$30 to $50 is common.

Some landlords don't charge credit check fees, preferring to absorb the cost as they would any other cost of business. For low-end units, charging an extra fee can be a barrier, and an applicant who pays such a fee but is later rejected is likely to be annoyed and possibly more apt to try to concoct a discriminatory reason for the denial.

Our Rental Application form informs applicants of your credit check fee. Be sure they know the purpose of a credit check fee and understand that this fee is not a holding deposit and does not guarantee the rental unit. (We discuss holding deposits below.)

Also, if you expect a large number of applicants, you'd be wise not to accept fees from everyone. Instead, read over the applications first and do a credit check only on those who are genuine contenders. That way, you won't waste your time (and prospective tenants' money) collecting fees from unqualified applicants.

CAUTION

It is illegal to charge a credit check fee if you do not use it for the stated purpose and pocket it instead. Return any credit check fees you don't use for that purpose.

Investigative or Background Reports

Some credit reporting companies and tenant screening companies also gather and sell background reports about a person's character, general reputation, personal characteristics, or mode of living. If you order a background check, it will be considered an "investigative consumer report" under federal law (the Fair Credit Reporting Act, 15 U.S.C. §§ 1681 and following, as amended by the Fair and Accurate Credit Transactions Act of 2003) and you must tell the applicant, within three days of requesting the report, that the report might be made and that it will contain information about the applicant's character, reputation, personal characteristics, and criminal history. You must also tell the applicant that more information about the nature and scope of the report will be provided upon request; and, if asked, you must provide said information within five days.

If you turn down the applicant based wholly or in part on information in the report, you must tell the applicant that the application was denied based on information in the report, and give the applicant the credit or tenant screening agency's name and address.

What You're Looking For

In general, be leery of applicants with lots of debts—so that their monthly payments plus the rent obligation exceed 40% of their gross income. Also, look at the person's bill-paying habits, and, of course, pay attention to lawsuits and evictions.

Sometimes, your only choice is to rent to someone with poor or fair credit. If that's your situation, you might condition acceptance on:

- good references from previous landlords and employers
- a creditworthy cosigner to cosign the lease (Chapter 2 includes a cosigner agreement)
- a good-sized deposit, as much as you can collect under state law (see Chapter 4), and

- proof of steps taken to improve credit—for example, enrollment in a debt counseling group.

If the person has no credit history—for example, a student or recent graduate—you might reject them or consider requiring a cosigner before agreeing to rent to them.

> **CAUTION**
>
> **Handle credit reports carefully.** Federal law requires you to keep only needed information, and to discard the rest. See "How to Handle Credit Reports," in Chapter 7 for precise information.

Verify Bank Account Information

If an individual's credit history raises questions about financial stability, you might want to double-check the bank accounts listed on the rental application. You'll probably need an authorization form such as the one included at the bottom of the Rental Application, or the separate Consent to Contact References and Perform Credit Check (discussed above). Banks differ as to the type of information they will provide over the phone. Generally, banks will at most only confirm that an individual has an account there and that it is in good standing.

> **CAUTION**
>
> **Be wary of an applicant who has no checking or savings account.** Tenants who offer to pay cash or with a money order should be viewed with extreme caution. Perhaps the individual bounced so many checks that the bank dropped the account or the income comes from an illegitimate source—such as drug dealing.

Review Court Records

If your prospective tenants have lived in the area, you might want to review local court records to see if collection or eviction lawsuits have been filed against them. Checking court records is not a violation of antidiscrimination laws as long as you check the records of every applicant who reaches this stage of your screening. Because court records are kept for many years, this kind of information can supplement references from recent landlords. Call the local court that handles eviction cases for details, including the cost of checking court records.

Use Megan's Law to Check State Databases of Sexual Offenders

Not surprisingly, most landlords do not want tenants with criminal records, particularly convictions for violent crimes or crimes against children. Checking a prospective tenant's credit report, as we recommend above, might give you information about a person's criminal history.

"Megan's Law" might assist you in confirming some of the information provided in a credit report. This 1996 federal crime prevention law charged the FBI with keeping a nationwide database of names and whereabouts of persons convicted of sexual offenses against minors and violent sexual offenses against anyone. Every state has its own version of Megan's Law. These laws require certain convicted sexual offenders to register with local law enforcement officials.

How Megan's Law Works

Unfortunately, how states use and distribute database information varies. Depending on the law where you live, your right to access the information and receive notifications might be restricted.

For information about Megan's Law in your state, contact your local law enforcement agency. To learn how to access your state's sex offender registry, you can also contact the 24 Hour National Megan's Law Helpline at 888-ASK-PFML or visit www.parentsformeganslaw.org.

The Limitations of Megan's Law Searching

Landlords should be aware of the following issues with the Megan's Law databases:

- **Accuracy.** Megan's Law databases are notoriously inaccurate—entries often are incomplete, contain old data, or even mistake one person for another.
- **Relevance.** The criminal offense you discover on the database might not be relevant to whether this applicant is likely to be a threat to you, your tenants, or your property. For example, in some states consensual intercourse between minors (statutory rape) is an offense for which a person must register.
- **Misleading "clean" reports.** Some registerable crimes result in nonregisterable convictions. For example, someone charged with a serious and registerable offense might end up with a simple assault conviction—perhaps because the prosecutor couldn't prove the charge, or because a chief witness disappeared. That simple assault conviction won't appear on a Megan's Law database.

Tenants Will Be Checking You Out, Too

While you're checking out a potential tenant (asking for references and getting a credit report), don't be surprised if the tenant is checking you out, too.

Several websites provide tenants with background information about you and your property. One of the major ones is ApartmentRatings.com. This comprehensive website has close to three million reviews of individual apartments and property managers nationwide. It includes other information useful to new tenants, such as noise and safety ratings for each rental.

- **Expectations you create in other tenants.** You should let applicants know if you plan to search for them on the database (this will allow applicants to opt out of the application process, and might spare you a charge of invading their privacy). However, one drawback to making it known that you run Megan's Law searches is that tenants will assume that you have not rented to anyone on a Megan's Law list. This might cause residents to relax their guard—for example, a family might assume it's okay for their children to be home alone after school. Suppose you've rented to someone who should have been on the list but mistakenly wasn't, and he assaults one of the children. The family could argue in court that they relied on your implied promise that the building was safe, and that you bear some of the responsibility because you rented to someone who posed a risk of harm.
- **Loss of other tenants.** Ironically, if you decide to rent to an applicant with a past offense, you might have to disclose the new tenant's record to other tenants (to save you from the fate described just above). Other tenants might leave due to concerns about their new neighbor. Before you know it, your only tenant will be the one you least want to keep.
- **Illegal in some states.** Finally, it's illegal in some states and cities to reject an applicant based on information derived from a Megan's Law database.

Many landlord associations and landlords' lawyers have concluded that the problems associated with Megan's Law searches are simply not worth the questionable results you'll get when you run them.

Their advice is to stick to the tried-and-true methods of thoroughly checking references and examining the applicant's credit report for unexplained gaps (which could be the result of time in prison).

Choosing—And Rejecting—An Applicant

After you've collected applications and done some screening, you can start narrowing down the pool of potential tenants. Begin by using the legal, nondiscriminatory reasons discussed here to eliminate applicants who pose the biggest risks to your property and profitability. You'll want to arrange and retain all applications for two reasons: to be ready to survive a fair housing challenge, and to comply with any laws requiring you to divulge your reasons for rejecting an applicant.

Legal Reasons for Rejecting a Rental Applicant

While narrowing down the pool of applicants, you need to focus on making sure that your screening process does not precipitate a costly charge of discrimination.

You are free to choose tenants based on "legitimate business interests"—criteria that are reasonably related to running your business in a competent, legal, and profitable manner. Only certain kinds of discrimination in rental housing are illegal. For example, you may legally reject an applicant with bad credit, unsteady employment, or an income that you reasonably regard as insufficient to pay the rent.

Sometimes, you will reject an applicant who happens to be a member of a protected group, but you've done so for legitimate business reasons.

Judges, tenants' lawyers, and government agencies that administer and enforce fair housing laws know full well that some landlords try to cover up their discriminatory reasons for rejecting applicants by inventing (and trying to document) a legitimate reason. So, when you refuse to rent to someone, make it a practice to always:

- Be consistent in your screening and treat all applicants more or less equally.
- Avoid applying a generalization about people of a certain group to an individual.
- Document your legal reasons for not renting to a prospective tenant.

This section discusses some of the common legally acceptable reasons for turning down an applicant. A valid occupancy limitation (such as overcrowding) can also be a legal basis for a refusal, but because this issue is fairly complicated, we have devoted a separate section to the subject.

What Are Objective Tenant Selection Criteria?

"Objective criteria" are tenancy requirements you establish before you begin accepting applications, and are unaffected by your personal value judgments. For example, a requirement that an applicant must never have been evicted for nonpayment of rent is "objective" because whether the eviction happened is not open to differing interpretations.

"Subjective criteria," on the other hand, must be assessed and assigned value. Questions that call for subjective answers have no "correct" answer, and every person evaluating the responses might interpret them differently.

Subjective criteria are always suspicious in a housing context because they can be used to mask deliberate illegal discrimination.

Here are a few examples of relevant, objective criteria for choosing tenants:

- no prior bankruptcies
- two positive references from previous landlords
- sufficient income to pay the rent—for example, an income that is at least three times the rent
- signed waiver allowing you to investigate applicant's credit history, and
- a minimum credit score.

Poor Credit Record or Income

You can legitimately refuse to rent to an applicant whose credit check raises red flags or whom you reasonably believe would be unable to pay rent in the future.

Here's some advice on how to avoid charges of discrimination when choosing tenants on the basis of income or credit history:

- **Check the credit of every applicant who has passed your initial screening process, and base your selection on the results of that credit check.** Selecting tenants based on objective criteria tied to a credit report is the best way to protect yourself against an accusation that you're using a bad credit history as an excuse to illegally discriminate against certain prospective tenants. For example, if you establish rules saying you won't rent to someone with bad credit or who was evicted by a previous landlord for nonpayment of rent (information commonly found in credit reports), be sure you apply this policy to all tenants.
- **Always consider the income of all tenants.** When you receive an application from a married couple, be sure to consider the income of both people. This will help avoid an accusation of marital status discrimination or sex discrimination.
- **Don't give too much weight to years spent at the same job.** Some states prohibit discrimination on the basis of personal characteristics or traits. Included in this category is a ban on discriminating against certain occupations. Because people employed in some industries (like tech) change jobs more often than others, using the time spent at the same job as one of your criteria can be discriminatory.

Negative References From Previous Landlords

You can legally refuse to rent to someone based on what a previous landlord or manager has to say— for example, that the tenant was consistently late paying rent, broke the lease, or left the place a shambles.

Evictions and Civil Lawsuits Involving a Tenant

Credit reports typically indicate whether the applicant has been involved in civil lawsuits, such as an eviction or breach of contract suit. For many landlords, an eviction lawsuit is a red flag. Can you reject a tenant on this basis? It depends.

If a former landlord has filed—and won—an eviction lawsuit against the applicant, you have solid grounds to reject this person. Be careful, though, when the credit report indicates that the applicant, not the former landlord, won the eviction suit: A tenant who has been vindicated in a court of law has not done anything wrong, even though you might suspect that the person is a troublemaker who just got lucky. If you reject applicants simply because an eviction lawsuit was filed against them, and if you live in a state that prohibits discrimination on the basis of someone's personal characteristic or trait, you are risking a charge that you are discriminating. In most situations, however, when the applicant is truly a poor prospect, the information you get from prior landlords and employers will confirm your suspicions, and you'll then have solid grounds for rejecting the applicant.

The credit report might also indicate that the applicant is or has been involved in another type of civil lawsuit—for example, a custody fight, or a personal injury claim. If the legal matter has nothing to do with the applicant's rental history, ability to pay the rent, or your other tenancy requirements, you might be on shaky ground if it's the reason for your rejection.

Criminal Records

Understandably, many landlords wish to check an applicant's criminal history, and credit reports sometimes include this information. Can you reject an applicant because of a conviction for drunk driving, or murder, or drug use? What if there was an arrest but no conviction?

The answer to these questions depends on where your rental is located. A growing trend in states and cities is to "ban the box" (the check box next to the question about arrests and convictions). These laws limit landlords' ability to ask about and use criminal histories in their tenant screening. For example, under New Jersey's recently passed Fair Chance in Housing Act, a landlord cannot consider an applicant's criminal history (unless the applicant is a registered sex offender or was convicted for making meth in federally assisted housing) until after the landlord has made a conditional offer of housing to the applicant. After making a conditional offer, the landlord can consider certain convictions depending on how long ago the conviction occurred.

Before you ask applicants about their criminal history, check both your state's and city's laws about how landlords can use criminal histories to screen tenants.

Convictions. So long as there is no "ban the box" law where your rental is located, you can usually reject applicants who have been convicted of a criminal offense. After all, a conviction indicates that the applicant was not, at least in that instance, a law-abiding individual, which is a legitimate criterion for prospective tenants or managers. In most areas—even those that have "ban the box" laws—you can refuse to rent to persons who are registered sex offenders.

One exception, however, involves convictions for past drug use. As explained below, past drug addiction is a disability under the Fair Housing Amendments Act, and you may not refuse to rent to someone on that basis—even if the addiction resulted in a conviction. People with convictions for the sale or manufacture of drugs, or current drug users are not, however, protected under federal law.

Arrests. A more difficult problem is posed by the person who has an arrest record but no conviction. Under our legal system, a person is presumed not guilty until the prosecution proves its case or the arrestee pleads guilty. So, is it illegal to deny housing to someone whose arrest did not result in a conviction?

"Arrestees" are not, unlike members of a race or religion, protected under federal or state law. However, the U.S. Department of Housing and Urban Development (HUD) issued an opinion in 2016 stating that the fact of a prior arrest is not a "reliable basis" for rejecting applicants, as a prior arrest shows nothing more than that the person was suspected of doing something illegal. (HUD's Office of General Counsel guidance memo dated April 4, 2016.)

Because the law is not clear, your safest practice would be to not use a history of one or more arrests as your sole basis for rejecting an applicant. So how should you ensure you're not accepting dangerous characters as tenants? Chances are that a previously arrested applicant who is *truly* a bad risk will have plenty of other facts in his or her background (like poor credit or negative references) that will justify your rejection. In short, if you do a thorough check on each applicant, you'll get enough information on which to base your decision.

Incomplete or Inaccurate Rental Application

A carefully designed rental application form is a key tool in choosing tenants, and we include a rental application in this book. This (or any other) application will do its job only when applicants provide all the necessary information.

You can reject applicants who don't allow you to run a background check, as well as anyone you catch in a lie concerning an important fact.

Inability to Meet Legal Terms of Lease or Rental Agreement

You may legally refuse to rent to someone who can't come up with the security deposit or meet another valid condition of the tenancy, such as being able to stay for the length of the lease.

Pets

You can legally refuse to rent to people with pets, and you can restrict the types or size of pets you accept. In fact, your insurance might prohibit renting to tenants with certain breeds of dogs. If the rental is part of a homeowners' association, additional pet restrictions might also apply.

You can also, strictly speaking, let some tenants keep a pet and say no to others—because pet owners, unlike members of a religion or race, are not as a group protected by antidiscrimination laws. However, from a practical point of view, an inconsistent pet policy is a bad idea, because it can result in angry, resentful tenants. Also, if the pet owner you reject is someone in a protected category and you let someone outside of that category rent with a pet, you are courting a discrimination lawsuit.

Keep in mind that you cannot refuse to rent to someone with an animal if that animal is a service or companion animal—for example, a properly trained dog for a person with disability. (42 U.S.C. § 3604(f)(3)(B).) Clause 16 of the form lease and rental agreements in Chapter 2 discusses pet policies and legal issues.

What Information Should You Keep on Rejected Applicants?

Be sure to note your reasons for rejection—such as poor credit history, pets (if you don't accept pets), or negative references—on the Tenant References form or in any other record-keeping system you use. Keep organized files of applications, credit reports, and other materials and notes on prospective tenants for at least three years after you rent a particular unit. Keep in mind that if a rejected applicant files a complaint with a fair housing agency or files a lawsuit, your file will be made available to the applicant's lawyers. Knowing that, choose your words carefully, avoid slurs and exaggerations, and be scrupulously truthful.

CAUTION
Be careful handling credit reports. Under the federal "Disposal Rule" of the Fair and Accurate Credit Transactions Act of 2003, you must store credit reports in a secure place where only those who "need to know" have access. For advice on handling credit reports and other personal information on applicants, see "How to Handle Credit Reports" in Chapter 7.

How to Reject an Applicant

The Fair Credit Reporting Act, as amended by the Fair and Accurate Credit Transactions Act of 2003, requires you to give certain information to applicants whom you reject as the result of a report from a credit reporting agency (credit bureau) or from a tenant screening or reference service. (15 U.S.C. §§ 1681 and following.) These notices are known as "adverse action reports." The federal requirements do not apply if your decision is based on information that the applicant furnished or that you or your employee learned on your own.

If you reject someone because of negative information contained in (or missing from) the credit report or their credit score (even if other factors also played a part in your decision), you must give the applicant the name and address of the agency that provided the credit report. Tell applicants they have a right to obtain a copy of the file from the agency that reported the negative information, by requesting it within the next 60 days or by asking within one year of having asked for their last free report. You must also tell rejected applicants that the credit reporting agency did not make the decision to reject them and cannot explain the reason for the rejection. Finally, tell applicants that they can dispute the accuracy of their credit report and add their own consumer statement to their report.

Use the Notice of Denial Based on Credit Report or Other Information form for this purpose. A sample is shown below and the Nolo website includes a downloadable copy. See Appendix B for the link to the forms in this book.

Assuming you choose the best-qualified candidate, you have no legal problem. But what if you have a number of more or less equally qualified applicants? The best response is to use an objective tie-breaker: Accept the person who applied first. If you cannot determine who applied first, strive to find some aspect of one applicant's credit history or references that objectively establishes that person as the best applicant. Be extra careful not to always select a person of the same age, sex, or ethnicity.

Conditional Acceptances

If you want to accept an applicant but have legitimate concerns, you might want to offer a conditional acceptance. For example, you might feel more comfortable if the new tenant pays a higher rent or security deposit (one that's within any legal limits, of course), supplies a cosigner, or agrees to a different rental term than you originally advertised. If your decision to impose the condition resulted from information you gained from a credit report or a report from a tenant screening service, you have to accompany the offer with an adverse action letter (described above). Use the Notice of Conditional Acceptance Based on Credit Report or Other Information, shown below. The Nolo website includes a downloadable copy. See Appendix B for the link to the forms in this book.

Finder's Fees and Holding Deposits

Almost every landlord requires tenants to give a substantial security deposit. The laws concerning how much can be charged and when deposits must be returned are discussed in Chapters 4 and 15. Here we discuss some other fees and deposits.

Finder's Fees

You may legitimately charge a prospective tenant for the cost of performing a credit check. Less legitimate, however, is the practice of collecting a nonrefundable "finder's fee" or "move-in fee" just for renting the place to a tenant. Whether it's a flat fee or a percentage of the rent, we recommend against finder's fees. First, finder's fees are illegal in some cities and states (particularly those with rent control). Second, it's just a way of squeezing a little more money out of the tenant—and tenants will resent it. If you think the unit is worth more, raise the price.

Holding Deposits

If you make a deal with a tenant but don't actually sign a lease or rental agreement, you might want a cash deposit to hold the rental unit while you do a credit check or call the tenant's references. Or, if the tenant needs to borrow money (or wait for a paycheck) to cover the rent and security deposit, you might want a few hundred dollars cash to hold the place. And some tenants might want to reserve a unit while continuing to look for a better one.

Although accepting a deposit to hold a rental unit is legal in some states, it's almost always unwise. Holding deposits do you little or no good from a business perspective, and all too often result in misunderstandings or even legal fights.

Rating Applicants on a Numerical Scale

To substantiate your claim that you are fair to all applicants, you might be tempted to devise a numerical rating system—for example, ten points for an excellent credit report, 20 points for an excellent past landlord reference, and the like. While this type of rating system can simplify screening, it has two significant drawbacks:

- Every landlord is entitled to rely on gut feelings regarding a potential tenant (as long as these are not illegally discriminatory—see Chapter 5). You can decline to rent to an applicant who creeps you out—regardless of stellar recommendations or solid finances. Using a numerical rating system could interfere with your trusting your instincts.
- If a rejected tenant sues you, you will have to hand over your rating sheet. It will be easier to explain your decision by referring to the whole picture, rather than defending every "point" allocated in your system. While you'll want to be able to refer to the specific background checks you used to arrive at your decision, you don't want to lock yourself into a numerical straitjacket that you'll have to defend.

EXAMPLE: A landlord, Jim, takes a deposit of several hundred dollars from a prospective tenant, Michael. What exactly is Jim promising Michael in return? To rent him the apartment? To rent Michael the apartment only if his credit checks out to Jim's satisfaction? To rent to Michael only if he comes up with the rest of the money before Jim rents to someone who offers the first month's rent and deposit? If Jim and Michael disagree about the answers to any of these questions, it can lead to needless anger and bitterness and result in a small claims court lawsuit alleging breach of contract.

Another prime reason to avoid holding deposits is that the laws of most states are unclear as to what portion of a holding deposit you can keep when—for whatever reason—you don't sign a lease or rental agreement with the applicant.

In California, for example, the basic rule is that a landlord can keep an amount that bears a "reasonable" relation to the landlord's costs—for example, to cover additional advertising costs or prorated rent during the holding period. A landlord who keeps a larger amount might be sued for breach of contract. A few states require landlords to provide a receipt for any holding deposit and a written statement of the conditions under which it is refundable.

If, contrary to our advice, you decide to take a holding deposit, it is essential that both you and your prospective tenant have a clear, written agreement that includes:

- the amount of the holding deposit
- your name and that of the applicant
- the address of the rental property
- the dates you will hold the rental property vacant
- the term of the potential rental agreement or lease
- conditions under which you will rent the unit to the applicant—for example, satisfactory references and credit history and full payment of first month's rent and security deposit
- when the conditions must be satisfied

- what happens to the holding deposit when the applicant signs the rental agreement or lease (it's usually applied to the first month's rent), and
- the amount of the holding deposit you'll keep if the applicant doesn't sign a rental agreement or lease—for example, an amount equal to the prorated daily rent for each day the rental unit was off the market plus a small charge to cover your inconvenience.

A sample Receipt and Holding Deposit Agreement that covers each of these items is shown below and the Nolo website includes a downloadable copy. See Appendix B for the link to the forms in this book.

What to Do When You Have a Hard-to-Rent Property

When you have a problem filling vacancies, resist the temptation to relax your screening requirements. In the long run, you're better off having a vacant rental than a tenant who causes problems. Instead of taking a chance on a risky applicant, evaluate your rent: Is it comparable to what landlords in your market are charging for similar properties?

If not, lower it. Also, make sure the condition of the rental isn't turning applicants off.

You could also implement a resident referral program, which rewards existing tenants for bringing in applicants who become tenants. A common incentive is a free month's rent.

Notice of Denial Based on Credit Report or Other Information

To: ___Ryan Paige_____
Applicant

___1 Mariner Square_____
Street Address

___Seattle, Washington 98101_____
City, State, and Zip Code

Your rights under the Fair Credit Reporting Act and Fair and Accurate Credit Transactions (FACT) Act of 2003. (15 U.S.C. §§ 1681 and following.)

THIS NOTICE is to inform you that your application to rent the property at ___75 Starbucks Lane, Seattle,___ ___WA 98108_____

has been denied because of [*check all that apply*]:

☑ Insufficient information in the credit report provided by:

Credit reporting agency: ___ABC Credit Bureau_____

Address, phone number, URL: ___310 Griffey Way, Seattle, WA 98140; Phone: 206-555-1212;___

___www.abccredit.com_____

☐ Negative information in the credit report provided by:

Credit reporting agency: _____

Address, phone number, URL: _____

_____

☑ The credit score supplied on the credit report, ___511___, was used in whole or in part when making the decision.

☑ The consumer credit reporting agency noted above did not make the decision not to offer you this rental. It only provided information about your credit history. You have the right to obtain a free copy of your credit report from the consumer credit reporting agency named above, if your request is made within 60 days of this notice or if you have not requested a free copy within the past year. You also have the right to dispute the accuracy or completeness of your credit report. The agency must reinvestigate within a reasonable time, free of charge, and remove or modify inaccurate information. If the reinvestigation does not resolve the dispute to your satisfaction, you may add your own "consumer statement" (up to 100 words) to the report, which must be included (or a clear summary) in future reports.

☐ Information supplied by a third party other than a credit reporting agency or you and gathered by someone other than myself or any employee. You have the right to learn of the nature of the information if you ask me in writing within 60 days of the date of this notice.

___Jason McGuire_____   ___10-01-20xx_____
Landlord/Manager   Date

Notice of Conditional Acceptance Based on Credit Report or Other Information

To: _William McGee_
Applicant
1257 Bay Avenue
Street Address
Anytown, FL 12345
City, State, and Zip Code

Your application to rent the property at _37 Ocean View Drive, #10-H, Anytown, FL 12345_

_____ has been accepted, conditioned on your willingness and

ability to: _Supply a cosigner that is acceptable to the landlord_

_____

Your rights under the Fair Credit Reporting Act and Fair and Accurate Credit Transactions (FACT) Act of 2003. (15 U.S.C. §§ 1681 and following.)

Source of information prompting conditional acceptance

My decision to conditionally accept your application was prompted in whole or in part by:

☑ Insufficient information in the credit report provided by:

Credit reporting agency: _Mountain Credit Bureau_

Address, phone number, URL: _75 Baywood Drive, Anytown, FL 12345. 800-123-4567._

www.mountaincredit.com

☐ Negative information in the credit report provided by:

Credit reporting agency: _____

Address, phone number, URL: _____

☑ The consumer credit reporting agency noted above did not make the decision to offer you this conditional acceptance. It only provided information about your credit history. You have the right to obtain a free copy of your credit report from the consumer credit reporting agency named above, if your request is made within 60 days of this notice or if you have not requested a free copy within the past year. You also have the right to dispute the accuracy or completeness of your credit report. The agency must reinvestigate within a reasonable time, free of charge, and remove or modify inaccurate information. If the reinvestigation does not resolve the dispute to your satisfaction, you may add your own "consumer statement" (up to 100 words) to the report, which must be included (or a clear summary) in future reports.

☐ Information supplied by a third party other than a credit reporting agency or you and gathered by someone other than myself or any employee. You have the right to learn of the nature of the information if you ask me in writing within 60 days of the date of this notice.

Jane Thomas   _May 15, 20xx_
Landlord/Manager   Date

Receipt and Holding Deposit Agreement

This will acknowledge receipt of the sum of $ ___500___ by ___Jim Chow_____

_____ "Landlord" from ___Hannah Silver_____

_____ "Applicant" as a holding deposit to hold vacant

the rental property at _178 West 81st St., #4F, New York City_____

_____ ,

until ___February 20, 20xx_____ at ___5 P.M._____ . The property will be rented to Applicant

on a ___one-year_____ basis at a rent of $ ___3,000___ per month, if Applicant signs

Landlord's written ___lease_____ and pays Landlord the first month's rent and a

$ ___3,000_____ security deposit on or before that date, in which event the holding deposit will be

applied to the first month's rent.

Applicant's rental of the rental property depends upon Landlord receiving a satisfactory report of Applicant's references and credit history. Landlord and Applicant agree that if Applicant fails to sign the lease or rental agreement and pay the remaining rent and security deposit, Landlord may retain of this holding deposit a sum equal to the prorated daily rent of $ ___100_____ per day plus a $ ___50_____ charge to compensate Landlord for time and labor.

Hannah Silver	_February 16, 20xx_
Applicant	Date
Jim Chow	_February 16, 20xx_
Landlord/Manager	Date

Preparing Leases and Rental Agreements

FORMS IN THIS CHAPTER

Chapter 2 includes instructions for and samples of the following forms:

- Month-to-Month Residential Rental Agreement
- Month-to-Month Residential Rental Agreement (Spanish Version) (online download only)
- Fixed-Term Residential Lease (online download only)
- Fixed-Term Residential Lease (Spanish Version) (online download only)
- Cosigner Agreement

The purchase of this book includes free downloadable and customizable copies of all of these forms. See Appendix B for the download link and instructions.

Interactive Online Forms

You can download and customize all the rental forms in this book for no additional charge—see Appendix B for the download link and instructions. These forms are good in all 50 states. To tailor them to your state's laws, use the charts included in this book's appendix.

If you prefer, you can purchase (at Nolo.com) a year-long subscription to use an interactive lease or rental agreement form where you will receive step-by-step instructions while you fill out the form. An interactive form that works for all 50 states, as well as state-specific interactive forms for many states, are available. There's a special discount for purchasers of this book: Just use coupon code **ELLIBOB16**.

The rental agreement or lease that you and your tenant sign forms the contractual basis of your relationship. Together with the laws of your state—and, in a few areas, local and federal laws—it sets out almost all the legal rules you and your tenant must follow.

Your rental agreement or lease is also a blueprint for the tenancy, full of crucial and practical details, such as how long the tenant can occupy your property and the amount of the rent.

Because your lease or rental agreement governs so much of your relationship with your tenant, it's important to get it right. This chapter shows you how to prepare clear, fair, and effective leases and rental agreements, and provides explanations of each clause (some clauses get their own chapter later).

You can easily tailor our forms to fit your own situation. Throughout the chapter, we suggest modifications to reflect your circumstances. We also caution you about common clauses that get landlords into legal hot water.

> **CAUTION**
> **Don't use our forms if the rent is subsidized by the government.** You might need to use a special government lease if you rent subsidized housing, such as Section 8.

Which Is Better, a Lease or a Rental Agreement?

Although leases and rental agreements are both contracts that establish tenancies, they are legally (and practically) very different. You'll need to understand how leases and rental agreements differ before you decide which one to use.

Month-to-Month Rental Agreements

A rental agreement creates a short-term tenancy, typically month-to-month. Many states refer to rental agreements as "periodic" tenancy agreements, and allow them to govern tenancies for other time periods (for example, biweekly rentals). You can change the form month-to-month rental agreement provided with this book to reflect a rental period of your choosing.

A month-to-month tenancy automatically self-renews each month. To end a month-to-month tenancy, you or your tenant gives the other the legal amount of written notice (usually 30 days).

Month-to-month rental agreements are more flexible than leases, because they allow landlords to:

- increase the rent or change other terms of the tenancy on relatively short notice (subject to any local rent control restrictions), and
- end the tenancy at any time (again, subject to any rent control restrictions) after giving the required amount of notice.

Because of this flexibility, many landlords in tight rental markets with plenty of tenants and rising rents prefer to rent on a month-to-month basis.

On the flip side, month-to-month tenancies often result in more tenant turnover. Tenants who make a short-term commitment are more likely to move than those who have signed a long-term lease. If your rental business strategy is based on having high-quality, long-term renters (or if you live where it's difficult to fill vacancies), you'll probably want tenants to commit for a longer period. But, as discussed below, although a fixed-term lease might encourage tenants to stay longer, it doesn't guarantee you won't have turnover.

Fixed-Term Leases

A lease binds both you and the tenant to all of its terms for a fixed period of time—usually a year. During the lease term, you can't raise the rent or change other terms of the tenancy unless the lease itself allows you to make a described change (such as a rent increase after the first year) or the tenant agrees to your proposed changes in writing.

In addition, you usually can't terminate a tenancy or prevail in an eviction lawsuit before the lease term expires, unless the tenant fails to pay the rent or significantly violates the lease. Being locked in by a lease can be problematic if you have a tenant you would like to be rid of but don't have sufficient cause to evict.

For example, if you wish to sell the property halfway into the lease, the existence of long-term tenants—especially if they pay less than the market rate—can deter some potential buyers. The new owner usually purchases all the obligations of the previous owner, including those created by existing leases. Of course, the opposite can also be true—a property with quality, long-term tenants who pay market rent might be attractive to potential new owners who want to use the property as an investment, not a home for themselves.

At the end of the lease term, you have several choices. You can:

- decline to renew the lease (this might not be an option in areas with rent control)
- sign a new lease for a set period, or
- do nothing (under most states' laws, if you continue to collect monthly rent, you've created a month-to-month tenancy).

Chapter 14 discusses in detail how fixed-term leases end.

Although leases restrict your flexibility, having long-term tenants can be beneficial. Some tenants make a serious personal commitment when they enter into a long-term lease, in part because they think they'll be liable for several months' rent if they leave early. And people who plan to be with you over the long term are often more likely to respect your property and the rights of other tenants, making your job easier and more enjoyable.

> **CAUTION**
>
> **A lease guarantees less income security than you think.** As experienced landlords know well, it's usually not hard for a determined tenant to break a lease and avoid paying rent for the unused portion of the lease term. A few states allow tenants to break a lease without penalty when certain circumstances arise, such as needing to move to a nursing home. In addition, tenants who enter military service or who receive activation orders are entitled to break a lease. And most states require landlords to "mitigate" (minimize) the loss they suffer as a result of a broken lease—meaning that if a tenant moves out early, you must use reasonable efforts to find another suitable tenant at the same or a greater rent. If you rerent the unit immediately (or if a judge believes it could have been rerented with reasonable effort), the lease-breaking tenant is off the hook—except, perhaps, for rent for the days or weeks the unit was vacant plus (sometimes) any costs of rerenting it.

Landlords typically prefer leases in areas with a lot of vacancies or where it's difficult to find tenants for one season of the year. For example, if your rental is near a college that closes in the summer or in a seasonal vacation area, you can secure year-round rent income by requiring renters to sign a lease. If you can charge a large security deposit, you'll have additional insurance: A tenant who wants to leave early will have a strong incentive to find someone to take over the tenancy.

TIP
Always put your agreement in writing.
Oral leases or rental agreements are perfectly legal for month-to-month tenancies and, in most states, for leases of a year or less. If you have an oral lease for a term exceeding one year, it becomes an oral month-to-month agreement after the first year is up. While oral agreements are easy and informal, it is never wise to use one. Oral leases are dangerous because they require that both parties accurately remember one important term—the length of the lease—over a considerable time. As time passes, people's memories (even yours) have a funny habit of becoming unreliable. And other issues, like how deposits may be used, probably aren't covered at all. If something goes wrong with an oral rental agreement or lease, you and your tenants are all too likely to end up in court, arguing over who said what to whom, when, and in what context.

Leases and Rental Agreements in a Nutshell

Leases	Rental Agreements
You can't raise the rent or change other terms of the tenancy until the lease ends.	You can increase rent or change other terms of the tenancy on relatively short notice (subject to any rent control restrictions).
You usually can't end the tenancy before the term expires, unless the tenant doesn't pay rent or violates another term of the lease.	You or the tenant can end the tenancy at any time (subject to any rent control restrictions), by giving the required amount of written notice, typically 30 days.

Clause-by-Clause Instructions for Completing the Lease or Rental Agreement Form

This section:
- explains each clause in the lease and rental agreement forms provided in this book

- gives instructions on how to fill in the blanks, and
- directs you to the chapters that discuss important issues relating to each clause.

Before you complete any clause for the first time, read the discussion about it in the chapters noted under "Required Reading."

Except for the length of the term of the tenancy (see Clause 4 in the forms), leases and written rental agreements are so similar that they are sometimes hard to tell apart. Both cover the basics of the tenancy (such as amount of rent and date due). Except where indicated below, the clauses in the lease and rental agreement are identical.

A filled-in sample rental agreement is included at the end of this chapter. This book's online companion page (see Appendix B for the link and more info) includes copies of the Month-to-Month Residential Rental Agreement and the Fixed-Term Residential Rental Lease. Both are in English and Spanish.

Tips for Landlords Taking Over Rental Property

If you've recently bought (or inherited) property, you might be taking on tenants with existing rental agreements or leases. Be sure the last owner gives you copies of all tenant and property files, including leases and rental agreements, details on deposits (location and amounts), house rules, maintenance and repair records, and all other paperwork and records relevant to the property. Make sure that the former owner transfers ownership and control of all financial accounts to you. If you want to change any of the terms of the lease or rental agreement, follow our advice in the first part of Chapter 14.

How to Modify the Lease or Rental Agreement Form

You might want to modify our lease and rental agreement forms in some situations. The instructions suggest possible modifications for some of the clauses. If you make extensive changes, however, consider having a local landlord-tenant attorney review your work.

Don't be tempted to try to cram too many details into the lease or rental agreement. Instead, send new tenants a move-in letter that dovetails with the lease or rental agreement and highlights important terms of the tenancy—for example, how and where to report maintenance problems. You can also use a move-in letter to cover issues not included in the lease or rental agreement—for example, rules for use of a pool or laundry room or procedures for returning security deposits.

 RENT CONTROL

You might need to modify the forms to comply with local or state law. Local and state rent control ordinances might require that your lease or rental agreement include specific information—for example, the address of the local rent control board. Check your ordinance for more information, and modify our forms accordingly.

Clause 1. Identification of Landlord and Tenant

This Agreement is between _____

_____ ("Tenant") and

_____ ("Landlord").

Each Tenant is jointly and severally liable for the payment of rent and performance of all other terms of this Agreement.

Every lease or rental agreement must identify the tenant and the landlord or the property owner—often called the "parties" to the agreement. The term "Agreement" (a synonym for contract) refers to either the lease or rental agreement.

The last sentence of Clause 1 states that if you have more than one tenant, they (the cotenants) are all "jointly and severally" liable for paying rent and abiding by the terms of the agreement. This means that each tenant is legally responsible for the whole rent and complying with the agreement. You can legally seek full compensation from any one of the cotenants should another skip out or fail to pay rent. You can also evict all of the tenants even if just one violates the lease.

How to Fill in Clause 1:

Fill in the names of all adults who will live in the premises, including each member of a couple, regardless of their marital status. Any competent adult—at least 18 years of age—may be a party to a lease or rental agreement. A teenager who is slightly under age 18 and who has achieved legal status through a court order (called emancipation), military service, or marriage may also be a party to a lease in most states.

Make sure the tenants' names match their driver's license or another form of identification, such as a passport.

In the last blank, list the names of all landlords or property owners—that is, the names of every person who will be signing the lease or rental agreement. If you are using a business name, enter your name followed by your business name.

Required Reading:

- Chapter 5
- Chapter 8

Clause 2. Identification of Premises

Subject to the terms and conditions set forth in this Agreement, Landlord rents to Tenant, for residential purposes only, the premises located at _____ _____ ("Premises").
Rental of the Premises also includes: _____ _____ . Rental of the Premises excludes: _____ .

Clause 2 identifies the address of the property being rented (the "Premises") and provides details about other items that are included, such as furnishings or a parking space. The words "for residential purposes only" are to prevent a tenant from using the property for conducting a business that might affect your insurance, violate zoning laws, or burden other tenants or neighbors.

How to Fill in Clause 2:

Fill in the street address of the unit or house you are renting. If there is an apartment or building number, specify that as well as the city and state.

Add as much detail as necessary to clarify what's included in the rental premises. For example, describe other areas that the tenant has exclusive access to, such as an assigned parking space or storage in the garage. If the unit has only a few basic furnishings, list them here. If the rental unit is fully furnished, state that here and provide detailed information on the Landlord-Tenant Checklist included in Chapter 7 or in a separate room-by-room list.

In the exclusions line, note parts of the rental property that might be assumed to be included that are *not* being rented, such as a garage or storage shed you wish to use yourself or rent to someone else.

Required Reading:

- Chapter 7

Clause 3. Limits on Use and Occupancy

The Premises are to be used only as a private residence for Tenant(s) listed in Clause 1 of this Agreement, and their minor children: _____ _____
Occupancy by guests for more than is prohibited without Landlord's written consent and will be considered a breach of this Agreement.

Clause 3 states that the rental unit is the residence of the tenants and their minor children only. It lets the tenants know they may not move anyone else in as a permanent resident without your consent. The value of this clause is that a tenant who tries to move in a relative or friend for a longer period has clearly violated a defined standard, which gives you grounds for eviction. (New York landlords, however, are subject to the "Roommate Law," RPL § 235-f, which allows tenants to move in relatives and other qualified individuals. The number of total occupants is still restricted, however, by any local statutes governing overcrowding.)

Clause 3 also allows you to set a time limit for guest stays. Even if you don't plan to strictly enforce guest restrictions, this provision will be very handy if a tenant tries to move in a friend or relative for a month or two, calling that person a guest. Chapter 8 discusses guests in more detail.

How to Fill in Clause 3:

In the first blank, list the full names of the Tenant's minor children, if any, who will live at the rental.

In the second blank, fill in the number of days you allow guests to stay within a given time period without your consent. We suggest up to ten consecutive days in any six-month period, but, of course, you can modify this based on your own preferences.

Required Reading:

- Chapter 5
- Chapter 8

Investigate Before Letting a Tenant Run a Home Business

Millions of Americans run a business from their house or apartment. If a tenant asks you to modify Clause 2 to allow a home-based business, you have some checking to do—even if you're inclined to say yes.

For one, you'll need to check local zoning laws for restrictions on home-based businesses, including the type of businesses allowed (if any), the amount of car and truck traffic the business can generate, outside signs, on-street parking, the number of employees, and the percentage of floor space devoted to the business. And if your rental unit is in a planned unit or a condominium development, check the CC&Rs of the homeowners' association.

You'll also want to consult your insurance company as to whether you'll need a different policy to cover potential liability caused by a tenant's employees or guests. In many situations, a home office for occasional use will not be a problem. But if the tenant wants to operate a business, especially one with people and deliveries coming and going, you should seriously consider whether to expand or add coverage.

You might also want to require that the tenant maintain certain types of liability insurance, so that you won't wind up paying if someone gets hurt on the rental property—for example, a business customer who trips and falls on the front steps.

Finally, be aware that if you allow a residence to be used as a commercial site, your property might need to meet the accessibility requirements of the federal Americans with Disabilities Act (ADA). For more information on the ADA contact the U.S. Department of Justice, 950 Pennsylvania Ave., NW, Civil Rights Division, Disability Rights Section, Washington, DC 20530, call 800-514-0301 (800-514-0383 TTY), or check the ADA website at ADA.gov.

CAUTION
You might not be able to restrict a child care home business. A tenant who wants to do child care in the rental might be entitled to do so, despite your general prohibition against businesses. In California and New York, for example, legislators and courts have declared a strong public policy in favor of home-based child care and have limited a landlord's ability to say no. (Cal. Health & Safety Code § 1597.40; *Haberman v. Gotbaum*, 698 N.Y.S.2d 406 (N.Y. City Civ. Ct. 1999).) If you're concerned, check with your state's office of consumer protection for information on laws that cover in-home child care in residential properties.

If you allow a tenant to run a business from your rental property, you might want to provide details in Clause 24 (Additional Provisions) of your lease or rental agreement.

CAUTION
Don't discriminate against families with children. You can legally establish reasonable space-to-people ratios, but you cannot use overcrowding as an excuse for refusing to rent to people with children. Discrimination against families with children is illegal, except in housing reserved for senior citizens only. Chapter 5 covers discrimination and occupancy standards.

Clause 4. Term of the Tenancy (Lease)

The term of the rental will begin on _____ , and end on _____ .

This clause sets out the key difference between a lease and a rental agreement: how long a rent-paying tenant is entitled to stay.

The lease form sets a definite date for the beginning and expiration of the lease and obligates both you and the tenant for a specific term.

Chapter 14 discusses a tenant's liability for breaking a lease, what exactly happens at the end of a lease, monetary consequences if a tenant "holds over" or fails to leave after the lease ends, termination of fixed-term leases, and your duty to mitigate damages. It also covers notice requirements. You might want to address some of these issues in the lease or rental agreement or in a move-in letter you send new tenants.

How to Fill in Clause 4 (Lease):

In the blanks, fill in the starting date and the expiration date. The starting date is the date the tenant has the right to move in. This date does not have to be the date that you and the tenant sign the lease. The lease-signing date is simply the date that you're both bound to the terms of the lease. If the tenant moves in before the regular rental period—such as the middle of the month and you want rent due on the first of every month—you will need to prorate the rent for the first partial month as explained in Clause 5 (Payment of Rent).

Possible Modifications to Clause 4 (Lease):

If you want to provide for a periodic rent increase, such as a $50 increase as of specific dates, you'll need to add language to this effect. Without this type of built-in increase, you can't increase the rent until the lease ends.

We recommend that you not provide for a periodic increase that is tied to a change in the Consumer Price Index, which is surprisingly hard to nail down. It's a lot easier to simply choose a specific dollar amount.

Likewise, avoid pegging increases to your added operating expenses (a common approach by commercial landlords). If challenged by a tenant who refuses to pay the increased rent (and whom you have to evict), you'll need to open your books to prove your increase. No residential landlord wants to do that.

> ⚠ **CAUTION**
>
> **Avoid liquidated damages provisions.** Some preprinted forms (not ours) include what lawyers call a "liquidated damages" clause that requires tenants who move out before the lease expires to pay you a predetermined amount of money (damages). Unless the amount of liquidated damages is close to the landlord's actual out-of-pocket costs resulting from the tenant's early departure, this approach is likely illegal. Chapter 14 provides more detail on what to do when a tenant breaks a lease.

Required Reading:

- Chapter 1
- Chapter 7
- Chapter 14

Clause 4. Term of the Tenancy (Rental Agreement)

The rental will begin on _____ , and continue on a month-to-month basis. Landlord may terminate the tenancy or modify the terms of this Agreement by giving the Tenant ____ days' written notice. Tenant may terminate the tenancy by giving the Landlord ____ days' written notice.

The rental agreement provides for a month-to-month tenancy. It specifies how much written notice you must give a tenant to change or end a tenancy, and how much notice the tenant must provide you before moving out. Chapter 14 discusses changing or ending a month-to-month tenancy.

How to Fill in Clause 4 (Rental Agreement):

In the first blank, fill in the date the tenancy will begin. The date the tenancy will begin is the date the tenant has the right to move in, such as the first of the month. This date does not have to be the date that you and the tenant sign the rental agreement. The agreement signing date is simply the date that you're both bound to the terms of the rental agreement. If the tenant moves in at a time other than the beginning of the regular rental period—such as the middle of the month—and you want rent due on the first of every month, you will need to prorate the rent for the first partial month as explained in Clause 5 (Payment of Rent).

In the next two blanks, fill in the amount of written notice you'll need to give tenants to end or change a tenancy, and the amount of notice tenants must provide to end a tenancy. In most states, the law requires both landlords and tenants to give 30 days' notice to end a month-to-month tenancy. See "State Rules on Notice Required to Change or Terminate a Month-to-Month Tenancy" in Appendix A for details.

Possible Modifications to Clause 4 (Rental Agreement):

This rental agreement is on a month-to-month renewal period, but you can change it to a different interval as long as you don't go below the minimum notice period required by your state's law. Your state's notice requirements for changing or ending a tenancy for a term other than month to month might be different from those required for standard month-to-month rental agreements.

RENT CONTROL

Your right to terminate or change the terms of a tenancy, even one from month to month, can be limited by a rent control law or ordinance. These laws and ordinances not only limit rent and other terms of tenancies, but often require the landlord to have a good reason to terminate a tenancy.

Required Reading:

- Chapter 1
- Chapter 7
- Chapter 14
- Appendix A Chart: State Rules on Notice Required to Change or Terminate a Month-to-Month Tenancy

Clause 5. Payment of Rent

Regular monthly rent.

Tenant will pay to Landlord a monthly rent of $_____, payable in advance on the first day of each month, except when that day falls on a weekend or legal holiday, in which case rent is due on the next business day. Rent will be paid as follows, or in another manner as Landlord designates from time to time:

Delivery of payment.

Rent will be paid:

- ☐ by mail, to _____
- ☐ in person, at _____
- ☐ electronically, to _____

Form of payment.

Landlord will accept payment in the form of:

- ☐ cash
- ☐ personal check made payable to _____
- ☐ certified funds or money order payable to _____
- ☐ credit or debit card
- ☐ electronic funds transfer _____

Prorated first month's rent.

- ☐ On signing this Agreement, Tenant will pay to Landlord for the period of _____ through _____ the sum of $_____ as rent, payable in advance of the start of the tenancy.
- ☐ Upon move-in, Tenant will owe as rent the prorated rent specified above, plus one full month's rent in the amount designated above, for a total of $_____.

This clause states the monthly rent amount and gives details about payment. It requires the tenant to pay rent monthly on the first day of the month, unless the first day falls on a weekend or a legal holiday, in which case rent is due on the next business day. (Extending the rent due date for holidays is legally required in some states and is an industry practice.)

How to Fill in Clause 5:

Regular monthly rent. In the first blank, state the amount of monthly rent. Unless your rental is subject to rent control, you can legally charge as much rent as you want.

Delivery of payment. Next, specify how to pay rent. If allowing payment by mail, give the mailing address. If allowing payment in person, list the drop-off address, and specify the days and hours that the location is open.

If allowing payment to be made electronically, list who will receive the funds. For example, you'd put your full name here or the name of your management company.

Form of payment. Note all the forms of payment you'll accept:

- **Cash.** Although it's an option, it's generally not a good one; checks are safer.
- **Personal check.** Be sure to note the full name on your deposit account (the recipient can be an individual or an entity).
- **Certified funds or money order.** You can also accept certified funds such as a money order or cashier's check. Be sure to note the full name on your deposit account.
- **Credit or debit card.** For credit card payments, follow the instructions issued by the card's issuer.
- **Electronic funds transfer.** An electronic funds transfer (EFT) is the computer-based exchange of money from one account to another, either within a single financial institution or across multiple institutions. The parties involved decide whether the transfers will be automatic or manual.

Electronic funds transfers require little effort when all is going well, are not that difficult to set up, and are easy to monitor online.

Describe any electronic means of payment you will accept (such as direct deposit, wire transfer, and digital payment platforms or apps) and include any information the tenant will need from you in order to successfully transfer the funds.

(Note that in California, you cannot require that rent be paid only by cash or electronic funds transfer.)

Prorated first month's rent. If the tenant moves in before the regular rental period—let's say in the middle of the month, and you want rent due on the first of every month—you can specify the prorated amount due for the first partial month. To figure out prorated rent, divide the monthly rent by 30 days and multiply by the number of days in the first (partial) rental period. That will avoid confusion about what you expect to be paid. Enter the move-in date, such as "June 21, 20xx," and the amount of prorated monthly rent.

If you will collect the prorated rent at the time the tenant signs, check the first box. If you want to wait until the first day of the tenancy (move-in), and collect the prorated rent plus the first month's rent, check the second box.

EXAMPLE: Meg rents an apartment for $2,100 per month with rent due on the first of the month. She moves in on June 21, so she should pay ten days' prorated rent of $700 when she moves in. ($2,100 ÷ 30 = $70 × 10 days = $700.) Beginning with July 1, Meg's full $2,100 rent check is due.

If the tenant is moving in on the first of the month or the same day rent is due, don't check either of the boxes or delete this section of the clause.

Possible Modifications to Clause 5:

Here are a few common ways to modify Clause 5:

Rent due date. You can establish a rent due date different from the first of the month, such as the day of the month on which the tenant moves in. For example, if the tenant moved in on July 10, rent would be due on the tenth of each month, a system that of course saves the trouble of prorating the first month's rent.

Frequency of rent payments. You are not legally required to have your tenant pay rent on a monthly basis. You can modify the clause and require that the rent be paid twice a month, each week, or by whatever schedule suits you.

Required Reading:

- Chapter 3
- Appendix A Chart: State Rent Rules

Clause 6. Late Charges

Because Landlord and Tenant agree that actual damages for late rent payments are very difficult or impossible to determine, Landlord and Tenant agree to the following:

- Tenant will pay Landlord a late charge if Tenant fails to pay the rent in full within _____ days after the date it is due.
- The late charge will be $_____, plus $_____ for each individual day that the rent continues to be unpaid. The total late charge for any one month will not exceed $_____.

Landlord does not waive the right to insist on payment of the rent in full on the date it is due.

Subject to any restrictions and requirements in your state's law, it is your legal right to charge a late fee when rent is not paid on time. This clause spells out details on your policy on late fees. Charging a late fee does not mean that you give up your right to insist that rent be paid on the due date. To bring this point home, Clause 6 states that you do not waive the right to insist on full payment of the rent on the date it is due. A late fee is simply one way to motivate tenants to pay on time. Many states put precise limits on the amount of late fees or when they can be collected. For advice on setting a late charge policy, see Chapter 3.

How to Fill in Clause 6:

In the first blank, specify when you will start charging a late fee. You can charge a late fee the first day rent is late, but many landlords don't charge a late fee until the rent is two or three days late.

Next, fill in details on your late rent fee, such as the daily charge and any maximum fee.

Possible Modifications to Clause 6:

If you decide not to charge a late fee (something we consider highly unwise), you can delete this clause. If you delete this clause, you'll need to renumber the remaining clauses.

Required Reading:

- Chapter 3
- Appendix A Chart: State Rent Rules

Clause 7. Returned Check and Other Bank Charges

If any check offered by Tenant to Landlord in payment of rent or any other amount due under this Agreement is returned for lack of sufficient funds, a "stop payment," or any other reason, Landlord will make a demand for payment and otherwise pursue remedies as allowed by law.

As with late charges, any bounced-check charges you demand must be reasonable. Some states regulate the amount you can charge; in the absence of such regulation, you should seek no more than the amount your bank charges you for a returned check, probably $25 to $50 per returned item, plus a few dollars for your trouble.

How to Fill in Clause 7:

You do not need to add anything to this clause.

Possible Modifications to Clause 7:

If you won't accept checks, or you are not charging a returned check fee (something we consider unwise), you may delete this clause from your lease or rental agreement (in which case, you'll need to renumber the remaining clauses).

Required Reading:

- Chapter 3
- Appendix A Chart: State Rent Rules

Clause 8. Security Deposit

> On signing this Agreement, Tenant will pay to Landlord the sum of $_____ as a security deposit. Tenant may not, without Landlord's prior written consent, apply this security deposit to the last month's rent or to any other sum due under this Agreement. Within _____ after Tenant has vacated the Premises, returned keys, and provided Landlord with a forwarding address, Landlord will return the deposit in full or give Tenant an itemized written statement of the reasons for, and the dollar amount of, any of the security deposit retained by Landlord, along with a check for any deposit balance.

The use and return of security deposits is a frequent source of disputes between landlords and tenants. To avoid confusion and legal hassles, this clause is clear on the subject, including:

- the dollar amount of the deposit
- the fact that the deposit may not be used for the last month's rent without your prior written approval, and
- when the deposit will be returned, along with an itemized statement of deductions.

Chapters 4 and 15 (and the chart "State Security Deposit Rules" in Appendix A) cover the basic information you need to complete Clause 8.

How to Fill in Clause 8:

Once you decide how much security deposit you can charge, fill in the amount in the first blank. Unless there's a lower limit, we suggest charging about the equivalent of two months' rent as your deposit, assuming your potential tenants can afford that much.

Next, fill in the time period when you will return the deposit. If there is no statutory deadline for returning the deposit, we recommend three to four weeks as a reasonable time to return a tenant's deposit. Establishing a fairly short period (even if the law of your state allows more time) will discourage anxious tenants from repeatedly bugging you or your manager for their refund.

Possible Modifications to Clause 8:

The laws of several states require you to give tenants written information on various aspects of the security deposit, including where the security deposit is being held, interest payments, and the terms of and conditions under which the security deposit may be withheld. The "State Security Deposit Rules" chart in Appendix A gives you information on disclosures you might need to add to Clause 8. This chart also includes a list of states that require separate accounts for deposits or interest payments on deposits.

Nonrefundable Fees

We don't recommend nonrefundable fees—for one thing, they are illegal in many states. If you do collect a nonrefundable fee—for example, for cleaning or pets—be sure your lease or rental agreement is clear on the subject.

Even if it's not required, you might want to provide additional details on security deposits in your lease or rental agreement. Here are optional clauses you could add to the end of Clause 8.

> The security deposit will be held at: (*name and address of financial institution*).

> Landlord will pay Tenant interest on all security deposits at the prevailing bank rate.

> Landlord may withhold only that portion of Tenant's security deposit necessary to: (1) remedy any default by Tenant in the payment of rent; (2) repair damage to the premises, except for ordinary wear and tear caused by Tenant or Tenant's guests; (3) clean the premises if necessary; and (4) compensate Landlord for any other losses as allowed by state law.

Required Reading:

- Chapter 4
- Chapter 15
- Appendix A Chart: State Security Deposit Rules

Clause 9. Utilities

> Tenant will pay all utility charges, except for the following, which will be paid by Landlord: _____
>
> _____
>
> _____ .

This clause clarifies who's responsible for paying utilities. Normally, landlords pay for garbage (and sometimes water, if there is a yard). Tenants usually pay for other services, such as phone, gas, electricity, Internet access, and cable TV.

How to Fill in Clause 9:

In the blank, fill in the utilities you—not the tenants—will be responsible for paying. If you

will not be paying for any utilities, delete the last part of the clause so that the clause simply reads, "Tenant will pay all utility charges."

Required Reading:

- Appendix A Chart: Required Landlord Disclosures

Consider Water Submetering

Making tenants pay for their water usage has become a popular way for landlords to recoup their water costs and increase their profits (studies have also shown that when tenants are billed directly, a property's overall water usage drops considerably). You can use one of three ways to go about this:

- Have the water company install meters for each unit, so that each household pays the utility directly.
- Contract with a submetering company to install submeters, which transmit a unit's water usage to the company digitally. The company bills each household directly, and the landlord pays an administrative fee.
- Estimate each unit's usage by using the "RUBS" method (Ratio Utility Billing System), in which you estimate each unit's usage and share of the total bill based on the unit's square footage or number of occupants. The landlord pays the utility directly, then bills each household for its share.

All of these approaches have their limitations—be sure to do your homework before proceeding further. Your state might disallow submetering altogether, and your local laws might have something to say, too.

Start by talking with your local water company. For more information on the issue of submetering, check out the website of the Utility Management & Conservation Association, at www.utilitymca.org.

Disclose Shared Utility Arrangements

If your property does not have separate gas and electric meters for each unit, or if a meter measures gas or electricity used in more than one area (such as a water heater that serves several apartments or lighting in a common area), you should disclose this in your lease or rental agreement. Simply add details to Clause 22, Disclosures. This type of disclosure is required by law in some states (see "Required Landlord Disclosures," in Appendix A), and is only fair in any case. The best solution is to put in a separate meter for the areas served outside the tenant's unit. If you don't do that, you should:

- pay for the utilities measured by the tenant's meter yourself, by placing that utility in your name (and possibly upping the rent a little bit; do this before advertising the rental)
- reduce rent to compensate for payment of utility usage outside of the tenant's unit (this will probably cost you more in the long run than if you either added a new meter or simply paid for the utilities yourself), or
- sign a separate written agreement with the tenant, under which the tenant specifically agrees to pay for others' utilities, too.

Clause 10. Prohibition of Assignment and Subletting

Tenant will not sublet any part of the Premises or assign this Agreement without the prior written consent of Landlord. Violating this clause is grounds for terminating the tenancy.

☐ a. Tenant will not sublet or rent any part of the Premises for short-term stays of any duration, including but not limited to vacation rentals.

☐ b. Short-stay rentals are prohibited except as authorized by law. Any short-stay rental is expressly conditioned upon the Tenant's following all regulations, laws, and other requirements as a condition to offering a short-stay rental. Failure to follow all laws, ordinances, regulations, and other requirements, including any registration requirement, will be deemed a material, noncurable breach of this Agreement and will furnish cause for termination.

Clause 10 is an antisubletting clause, breach of which is grounds for eviction. It prevents tenants from subleasing during a vacation—letting someone stay in their place and pay rent while they're gone for an extended period of time— or renting out a room to someone unless you specifically agree.

Clause 10 is also designed to prevent assignments, a legal term for when tenants transfer their entire tenancy to someone else. Practically, you need this clause to prevent your tenant from leaving in the middle of the month or lease term and moving in a replacement—maybe someone you wouldn't choose to rent to—without your consent.

By including Clause 10 in your lease or rental agreement, you have the option to not accept the person your tenant proposes to take over the lease. Under the law of most states, however, you should realize that if a tenant who wishes to leave early provides you with another suitable tenant, you can't both unreasonably refuse to rent to this person and hold the tenant financially liable for breaking the lease.

Subletting and Short-Term Stays (Airbnb)

Online businesses such as Airbnb act as clearing-houses for short-term (or "short-stay") rentals (less than 30 days) for use by vacationers or visiting businesspersons. Tenants using these platforms sublet their rentals and pocket the rent, turning your property into a hotel. Although landlords are universally opposed to allowing tenants to offer short-term stays, many have chosen to convert their own properties into short-term rentals.

If you want to restrict tenants from running a short-term rental business, be sure your lease is clear on this. First, however, check local law: Bowing to political pressure, many municipalities are changing their laws concerning short-stay tenancies, by requiring registration and limiting the number of short-stay days per year.

How to Fill in Clause 10:

After you have determined whether any local ordinances regulate short-term rentals, choose the appropriate alternative language for Clause 10. Alternate (a) flatly prohibits such rentals, while Alternate (b) advises tenants that they must follow the short-term stay law or risk termination of their tenancies.

Required Reading:

- Chapter 8
- Chapter 14

Clause 11. Tenant's Maintenance Responsibilities

Tenant agrees to: (1) keep the Premises clean, sanitary, and in good condition and, upon termination of the tenancy, return the Premises to Landlord in a condition identical to that which existed when Tenant took occupancy, except for ordinary wear and tear; (2) immediately notify Landlord of any defects or dangerous conditions in and about the Premises of which Tenant becomes aware; and (3) reimburse Landlord, on demand by Landlord, for the cost of any repairs to the Premises, including Landlord's personal property therein, damaged by Tenant or Tenant's guests or business invitees through misuse or neglect.

Tenant has examined the Premises, including appliances, fixtures, carpets, drapes, and paint, and has found them to be in good, safe, and clean condition and repair, except as noted in the Landlord-Tenant Checklist.

Clause 11 makes the tenant responsible for keeping the rental premises clean and sanitary. This clause also makes it clear that if the tenants damage the premises or the landlord's personal property, it's their responsibility to pay for the damage.

It is the law in some states (and wise in all) to notify tenants in writing of procedures for making complaints and repair requests. Clause 11 requires the tenant to alert you to defective or dangerous conditions.

Clause 11 also states that the tenant has examined the rental premises, including appliances, carpets, and paint, and found them to be safe and clean, except as noted in a separate form (the Landlord-Tenant Checklist, described in Chapter 7). Before the tenant moves in, you and the tenant should inspect the rental unit and fill out the Landlord-Tenant Checklist in Chapter 7, describing what is in the unit and noting any problems. Doing so will help you avoid disputes over security deposit deductions when the tenant moves out.

Chapter 9 provides details on landlords' and tenants' repair and maintenance responsibilities, recommends a system for tenants to request repairs, and offers advice on maintaining your rental property. Chapter 9 also covers tenant options (such as rent withholding) should you fail to maintain your property and keep it in good repair.

How to Fill in Clause 11:

You do not need to add anything to this clause.

Required Reading:

- Chapter 7
- Chapters 9–12

Clause 12. Repairs and Alterations by Tenant

a. Except as provided by law, or as authorized by the prior written consent of Landlord, Tenant will not make any repairs or alterations to the Premises, including nailing holes in the walls or painting the rental unit.

b. Tenant will not, without Landlord's prior written consent, alter, rekey, or install any locks to the Premises or install or alter any security alarm system. Tenant will provide Landlord with a key or keys capable of unlocking all such rekeyed or new locks as well as instructions on how to disarm any altered or new security alarm system.

Clause 12 makes it clear that the tenant may not make alterations and repairs without your consent, including painting the unit or making holes in the walls.

And to make sure you can take advantage of your legal right of entry in an emergency situation, Clause 12 specifically forbids the tenant from rekeying the locks or installing a security alarm system without your consent. If you do grant permission, make sure your tenant gives you duplicate keys and the name and phone number of the alarm company, as well as instructions on how to disarm the security system so that you can enter in case of emergency.

The "except as provided by law" language in Clause 12 refers to the fact that, in certain situations and in certain states, tenants have a narrowly defined right to alter or repair the premises, regardless of what you've said in the lease or rental agreement. Examples include:

- alterations by a person with a disability, such as lowering countertops for a wheelchair-using tenant
- use of the "repair and deduct" procedure
- installation of satellite dishes and antennas
- specific alterations allowed by state statutes. Some states permit tenants to install specific equipment, often when the landlord has refused to do so. Examples include energy conservation measures, burglary prevention devices, and door and window locks (notably when the tenant has a restraining order against a domestic abuser). Check your state statutes or call your local rental property association for more information on these types of laws.

How to Fill in Clause 12:

If you do not want the tenant to make any repairs without your permission, you do not need to add anything to this clause.

You might, however, want to go further and specifically prohibit certain repairs or alterations by adding details in Clause 12. For example, you might want to make it clear that any "fixtures"—a legal term that describes anything attached to the structure, such as bolted-on bookcases or built-in dishwashers—are your property and may not be removed by the tenant without your permission.

If you do authorize the tenant to make repairs, provide enough detail so that the tenant knows exactly what is expected, how much repairs can cost, and who will pay. For example, if you decide to allow the tenant to take over the repair of broken windows, routine plumbing jobs, or landscaping, give specific descriptions of and limits on the tasks. Chapter 9 includes a detailed discussion of delegating repair and maintenance responsibilities, a sample agreement form regarding tenant alterations and improvements, and an overview of legal issues regarding fixtures.

> ! **CAUTION**
>
> **If you want the tenant to perform maintenance work for you in exchange for reduced rent, don't write it into the lease or rental agreement.** Instead, use a separate agreement and pay the tenant for the services. That way, if there's a problem with the work, you still have the full rent, and you can simply terminate the contract.

Required Reading:

- Chapter 5
- Chapter 9
- Chapter 12
- Chapter 13
- Appendix A Chart: State Laws on Rent Withholding and Repair and Deduct Remedies

Clause 13. Violating Laws and Causing Disturbances

Tenant is entitled to quiet enjoyment of the Premises. Tenant and guests or invitees will not use the Premises or adjacent areas in such a way as to: (1) violate any law or ordinance, including laws prohibiting the use, possession, or sale of illegal drugs; (2) commit waste (severe property damage) or cause or tolerate a nuisance; or (3) interfere with the quiet enjoyment and peace and quiet of or annoy, disturb, or inconvenience any other tenant or nearby resident.

This type of clause is found in most leases and rental agreements. It prohibits tenants (and their guests) from violating the law, damaging your property, or disturbing other tenants or nearby residents. Although this clause contains legal jargon like waste and nuisance, it's probably best to leave it as is, because courts have experience with these terms (defined below).

Waste and Nuisance: What Are They?

In legalese, committing **waste** means causing severe damage to real estate, including a house or an apartment unit—damage that goes way beyond ordinary wear and tear. Punching holes in walls, pulling out sinks and fixtures, and knocking down doors are examples of waste.

Nuisance means behavior that prevents tenants and neighbors from fully enjoying the use of their homes and results in a substantial danger to their health and safety. Continuous loud noise and foul odors are examples of legal nuisances that can disturb neighbors and affect their "quiet enjoyment" of the premises. So, too, are selling drugs or engaging in other illegal activities that disturb neighbors.

This clause also refers to tenants' right to "quiet enjoyment" of the premises. As courts define it, the "covenant of quiet enjoyment" amounts to an implied promise that you will not act (or fail to act) in a way that seriously interferes with or destroys the ability of the tenant to use the rented premises—for example, by allowing garbage to pile up, tolerating a major rodent infestation, or failing to control a tenant whose constant loud music makes it impossible for other tenants to sleep.

If you want more specific rules—for example, no loud music played after midnight—add them to Clause 20: Tenant Rules and Regulations, or to Clause 24: Additional Provisions.

How to Fill in Clause 13:

You do not need to add anything to this clause.

Required Reading:

- Chapter 12
- Chapter 16

Clause 14. Damage to the Premises

In the event the Premises are partially or totally damaged or destroyed by fire or other cause, the following will apply:

a. Premises totally damaged and destroyed. Landlord will have the option to: (1) repair such damage and restore the Premises, with this Agreement continuing in full force and effect, except that Tenant's rent will be abated while repairs are being made; or (2) give written notice to Tenant terminating this Agreement at any time within thirty (30) days after such damage, and specifying the termination date; in the event that Landlord gives such notice, this Agreement will expire and all of Tenant's rights pursuant to this Agreement will cease.

b. Premises partially damaged by fire or other cause. Landlord will attempt to repair such damage and restore the Premises within thirty (30) days after such damage. If only part of the Premises cannot be used, Tenant must pay rent only for the usable part, to be determined by Landlord. If Landlord is unable to complete repairs within thirty (30) days, this Agreement will expire and all of Tenant's rights pursuant to this Agreement will terminate at the option of either party. Whether the Premises are totally or partially destroyed will be decided by Landlord, in the exercise of its sole discretion.

c. In the event that Tenant, or Tenant's guests or invitees, in any way caused or contributed to the damage of the Premises, Landlord will have the right to terminate this Agreement at any time, and Tenant will be responsible for all losses, including, but not limited to, damage and repair costs as well as loss of rental income.

d. Landlord will not be required to repair or replace any property brought onto the Premises by Tenant.

This clause outlines what will happen if all or part of the premises is destroyed or damaged. Because there's no way of knowing the exact situation under which you might need to use this clause, it has a lot of flexibility: As the landlord, you'll have the option to try to repair or rebuild or terminate the lease. If the tenant or tenant's guests damage or destroy your property, you'll be able to hold the tenant responsible.

How to Fill in Clause 14:

You do not need to add anything to this clause.

Clause 15. Renters' Insurance

Tenant acknowledges that Landlord's property insurance policy will not cover damage to or loss of Tenant's personal property. Tenant will obtain a renters' insurance policy that will:

- reimburse Landlord for cost of fire or water damage caused by Tenant or Tenant's guests, and vandalism to the Premises
- indemnify Landlord against liability to third parties for any negligence on the part of Tenant, Tenant's guests, or invitees; and
- cover damage to Tenant's personal possessions to a minimum of $100,000.

Tenant will provide Landlord with proof of such policy by giving Landlord a certificate of insurance issued by the insurance company within fifteen (15) days of _____. The policy will name Landlord as an "additional insured." Tenant will provide Landlord with a certificate of insurance upon every renewal. Tenant will not allow such policy to expire during the rental term. Failure to obtain and maintain a renters' insurance policy will be treated as a material breach of this Agreement.

This clause requires the tenant to obtain a renters' insurance policy. The policy will insure the tenant's personal property, and the liability portion will cover loss or damage to your rental property caused by the tenant's carelessness. Tenants must give you proof that they have purchased a policy within 15 days after the tenancy begins. Be sure to ask for it, and stay on top of any renewals.

This clause warns tenants that if they fail to buy and maintain a renters' policy, they will have materially breached the agreement. This will entitle you to terminate the agreement if you wish.

Renters' insurance covers losses to the tenant's belongings as a result of fire or theft, as well as injury to other people or property damage caused by the tenant's negligence. Besides protecting the tenant from personal liability, renters' insurance benefits you, too: If damage caused by the tenant could be covered by either the tenant's insurance policy or yours, a claim made on the tenant's policy will affect the tenant's premiums, not yours. Renters' insurance will not cover intentional damage by the tenant.

Be advised that it might not be legal for you to require your tenants to carry renters' insurance (in particular, liability insurance). Judges in some states (including Oklahoma) have held that tenants are by implication coinsureds under the landlord's property policy, because their rent helps pay the landlord's premiums, and that it's unfair to require them to buy duplicate insurance.

Landlords subject to rent control might not be able to require renters' insurance, because a court might consider the premiums as a rent overcharge. Before requiring tenants to carry renters' insurance, you'll need to check with your agent or lawyer on the legality of such a requirement in your state or locality.

How to Fill in Clause 15:

In the blank, type in the date that the tenancy begins—refer back to the date you wrote into Clause 4. Keep in mind that this date might be different from the date you signed the agreement, and it might also be different from the date the tenant actually moves in.

If you decide to not require a tenant to obtain renters' insurance, delete this clause, and renumber the following clauses.

Clause 16: Pets

> No animal may be kept on the Premises, without Landlord's prior written consent, except animals needed by tenants who have a disability, as that term is understood by law, and _____
> under the following conditions: _____
> _____
> _____ .

This clause prevents tenants from keeping pets without your written permission. If you want, you can have a flat "no pets" rule, though many landlords report that pet-owning tenants are more appreciative, stable, and responsible than the norm. Without this sort of provision, there's little to prevent your tenant from keeping multiple, dangerous, or nonhousebroken pets, except for city ordinances prohibiting exotic animals and animal cruelty laws.

With the exception of trained dogs and some other animals used by people who have a mental or physical disability, you have the right to prohibit all pets, or to restrict the types of pets or dog breeds you allow. Your pet policy should cover not only pets the tenant may have, but also pets of guests. When creating your pet policy, be sure to check any insurance or homeowners' association restrictions as to breeds of dog, weight, number of pets, and species allowed.

How to Fill in Clause 16:

If you don't allow pets, simply delete the words "and _____ under the following conditions."

If you allow pets, identify the type and number of pets in the first blank—for example, "one cat" or "one dog under 20 pounds." Spell out your pet

rules in the second blank, or in an attachment—for example, that the tenants will keep the grounds and street free of animal waste; and that cats and dogs be spayed or neutered, licensed, and up-to-date on vaccinations.

It is also important to inform tenants from the start that you will not tolerate dangerous or even apparently dangerous pets; and that as soon as you learn of a worrisome situation, you have the option of insisting that the tenant get rid of the pet (or move). You might want to advise tenants that their pets must be well-trained and nonthreatening in the second blank of Clause 16. Your policy might look something like this:

> Tenant's pet(s) will be well-behaved and under Tenant's control at all times and will not pose a threat or apparent threat to the safety of other tenants, their guests, or other people on or near the Premises. If, in the opinion of Landlord, tenant's pet(s) pose such a threat, Landlord will serve Tenant with the appropriate notice to terminate the tenancy.

Rules prohibiting dangerous pets are effective only if they're enforced. To limit your liability if a tenant's pet injures someone on or even near your property, you or your manager must keep an eye on your tenants' pets, and listen to and act on complaints from other tenants or neighbors. In general, if you know a tenant has breached the lease or rental agreement (for example, by keeping a pet) and you do nothing about it for a long time, you risk having legally waived your right to object.

If your pet policy is too long to put in Clause 16, include it in your Tenant Rules and Regulations. See Clause 20. Note in the Clause 16 blank that tenants should refer to the attached Tenant Rules and Regulations.

Required Reading:

- Chapter 4
- Chapter 5
- Chapter 10
- Chapter 16

Should You Require a Separate Deposit for Pets?

Some landlords allow pets but require tenants to pay a separate deposit to cover damage caused by the pet. The laws of a few states specifically allow separate, nonrefundable pet deposits. In other states, charging a designated pet deposit is legal only if the amount you charge, plus any other deposits (like security deposits) does not exceed the state maximum for deposits. (See Chapter 4 for details on security deposits.)

Even where allowed, separate pet deposits can be a bad idea because they limit how you can use that part of the security deposit. For example, if the pet is well-behaved, but the tenant trashes your unit, you can't use the pet portion of the deposit to clean up after the human. If you want to protect your property from damage done by a pet, you are probably better off charging a slightly higher rent or security deposit to start with (assuming you are not restricted by rent control or the security deposit upper limit).

It is illegal to charge an extra pet deposit for people with trained service or companion animals.

Clause 17. Landlord's Right to Access

Landlord or Landlord's agents may enter the Premises in the event of an emergency, to make repairs or improvements, or to show the Premises to prospective buyers or tenants. Landlord may also enter the Premises to conduct an annual inspection to check for safety or maintenance problems. Except in cases of emergency, Tenant's abandonment of the Premises, court order, or where it is impractical to do so, Landlord will give Tenant _____ notice before entering.

Clause 17 tells the tenant that you have a legal right of access to the property to make repairs or to show the premises for sale or rental, provided you give the tenant reasonable notice. In most states,

24 hours is presumed to be a reasonable amount of notice. A few states require a longer notice period.

How to Fill in Clause 17:

In the blank, indicate the amount of notice you will provide the tenant before entering, at least the minimum required in your state. If your state law simply requires "reasonable" notice or has no notice requirement, we suggest you provide at least 24 hours' notice.

Required Reading:

- Chapter 13
- Appendix A Chart: State Laws on Landlord's Access to Rental Property

Clause 18. Extended Absences by Tenant

Tenant will notify Landlord in advance if Tenant will be away from the Premises for _____ or more consecutive days. During such absence, Landlord may enter the Premises at times reasonably necessary to maintain the property and inspect for damage and needed repairs.

This clause requires that the tenants notify you when leaving your property for an extended time. It gives you the authority to enter the rental unit during the tenant's absence to maintain the property as necessary and to inspect for damage and needed repairs.

How to Fill in Clause 18:

In the blank, fill in the minimum amount of time the tenant will be gone that will require the tenant to notify you of an extended absence. Ten or 14 days is common.

Required Reading:

- Chapter 13

Clause 19. Possession of the Premises

a. Tenant's failure to take possession.

If, after signing this Agreement, Tenant fails to take possession of the Premises, Tenant will still be responsible for paying rent and complying with all other terms of this Agreement.

b. Landlord's failure to deliver possession.

If Landlord is unable to deliver possession of the Premises to Tenant for any reason not within Landlord's control, including, but not limited to, failure of prior occupants to vacate or partial or complete destruction of the Premises, Tenant will have the right to terminate this Agreement upon proper notice as required by law. In such event, Landlord's liability to Tenant will be limited to the return of all sums previously paid by Tenant to Landlord.

The first part of this clause (Part a) explains that a tenant who chooses not to move in (take possession) after signing the lease or rental agreement will still have to pay rent and satisfy other conditions of the agreement. This does not mean, however, that you can sit back and expect to collect rent for the entire lease or rental agreement term—in most states you must take reasonably prompt steps to rerent the premises, and you must credit the rent you collect against the first tenant's rent obligation.

The second part of the clause (Part b) protects you if you're unable, for reasons beyond your control, to turn over possession after having signed the agreement or lease—for example, if a fire destroyed the premises. It limits your financial liability to the return of any prepaid rent and security deposits (the "sums previously paid in the language of the clause).

CAUTION

Clause 19 might not limit your liability if you cannot deliver possession because the old tenants are still on the premises—even when they are the subject

of an eviction that you ultimately win. When a holdover tenant prevents the new tenant from moving in, landlords are often sued by the new tenant for not only the return of any prepaid rent and security deposits, but also the costs of temporary housing, storage costs, and other losses. In some states, an attempt in the lease to limit the new tenant's recovery to the return of prepaid sums alone would not hold up in court. If the old tenants gave written notice of their decision to move out, you'll have some basis for shifting the liability for these expenses to the old tenants. (See Clause 4, above, which requires written notice.)

How to Fill in Clause 19:

You do not need to add anything to this clause.

TIP

Don't rerent until you are positive that the unit will be available. If you have any reason to suspect that your current tenant will not vacate when the lease or rental agreement is up, think twice before signing a new lease or agreement, or even promising the rental unit to the next tenant. If you declined to renew the old tenants' lease or rental agreement and there are bad feelings between you, or you suspect that the tenants have fallen on hard times and have not obtained replacement housing—and certainly if they are the subject of an eviction—you are asking for trouble if you promise the unit to someone else before it's actually vacant.

Required Reading:

- Chapter 14
- Appendix A Chart: Landlord's Duty to Rerent.

Clause 20. Tenant Rules and Regulations

☐ Tenant acknowledges receipt of, and has read a copy of, the Tenant Rules and Regulations, which are labeled Attachment ____ and attached to and incorporated into this Agreement by this reference. Tenant understands that serious or repeated violations of the rules may be grounds for termination.

Many landlords don't worry about detailed rules and regulations, especially when they rent single-family homes or duplexes. However, in large multitenant buildings, rules are usually important to control the use of common areas and equipment—both for the convenience, safety, and welfare of the tenants and as a way to protect your property from damage. Rules and regulations also help avoid confusion and misunderstandings about day-to-day issues, such as garbage disposal, use of recreation areas, and lost key charges.

Not every minor rule needs to be incorporated in your lease or rental agreement. But it is a good idea to specifically incorporate important ones (especially those that are likely to be ignored by some tenants), such as no smoking in individual units or common areas. Doing so gives you the authority to evict a tenant who seriously or repeatedly violates your rules and regulations.

To avoid charges of illegal discrimination, apply rules and regulations equally to all tenants in your rental property. And make sure your tenants know that the rules apply to guests as well.

Because tenant rules and regulations are often lengthy and might be revised occasionally, we suggest you prepare a separate attachment. Be sure the rules and regulations (including any revisions) are dated on each page and signed by both you and the tenant.

You can usually change your rules and regulations without waiting until the end of the rental (for leases) or without giving proper notice (for rental agreements)—but only if the change is minor and not apt to affect the tenants' use and enjoyment of their tenancies. Shortening the pool hours in the winter months is an example of a minor change. Major changes, such as closing all laundry facilities in an attempt to save on water and electrical bills, should be the subject of a proper notice for month-to-month tenants. To make a major, building-wide change when your tenants have leases, you likely will have to wait until the longest lease is up for renewal.

What's Covered in Tenant Rules and Regulations

Tenant rules and regulations typically cover issues such as:

- elevator use
- pool rules, including policies on guest use
- garbage and recycling pickups
- vehicles and parking regulations—for example, restrictions on making repairs at the premises, types of vehicles allowed (such as no RVs), and guest parking
- lock-out and lost key charges
- pet rules
- security system use
- specific details on what's considered excessive noise and rules to limit noise—for example, carpets or rugs required on hardwood floors
- dangerous materials—nothing flammable or explosive should be on the premises
- storage of bikes, baby strollers, and other equipment in halls, stairways, and other common areas
- specific landlord and tenant maintenance responsibilities
- use of the grounds
- maintenance and use of balconies and decks
- display of signs in windows
- laundry room rules, and
- waterbeds.

Resist the temptation to place significant rules in your rules and regulations. Some landlords, realizing that rules and regulations can be changed without notice and wanting to be able to take advantage of this flexibility, place important restrictions in them, rather than in the lease. For example, they might place smoking restrictions in the rules, so that they can change them as needed. But a smoking policy is a big deal, and should be something that tenants agree to before signing the lease. Put another way, a policy belongs in the lease when a candid evaluation of its importance suggests that it would probably play a part in a tenant's decision to rent the unit in the first place.

How to Fill in Clause 20:

If you have a rules and regulations document, check the box and attach it. Fill in the blank with the label you assign to the attachment. For example, if this is the first attachment referenced in the lease, you could call it Attachment A. If it's the second or third, label it "B," "C," and so on. Do the same if your rental is in a community with homeowners' association or condo rules. If you do not have a separate set of tenant rules and regulations, delete this clause (renumber the remaining clauses).

Clause 21. Payment of Court Costs and Attorneys' Fees in a Lawsuit

> In any action or legal proceeding to enforce any part of this Agreement, the prevailing party ☐ will not / ☐ will recover reasonable attorneys' fees and court costs.

Many landlords assume that if they sue a tenant and win (or prevail, in legalese), the court will order the losing tenant to pay the landlord's court costs (filing fees, service of process charges, deposition costs, and so on), as well as attorneys' fees. In some states and under certain conditions, this is true. For example, an Arizona landlord who wins a contested eviction lawsuit is eligible to receive costs and fees even if the lease does not have a "costs and fees" clause in it. (Ariz. Rev. Stat. Ann. §§ 33-1315, 12-341.01.) But in most states, a court will order the losing tenant to pay your attorneys' fees and court costs only if a written agreement specifically provides for it.

If you have an "attorneys' fees" clause in your lease, and you hire a lawyer to bring or defend a lawsuit concerning the lease and win, the judge will order your tenant to pay your court costs and attorneys' fees. (In rare instances, a court will order the loser to pay costs and fees even though there's no "attorneys' fees" clause in the lease, if it finds that the behavior of the losing party was particularly outrageous—for example, filing a totally frivolous lawsuit.)

By law in many states, an attorneys' fees clause in a lease or rental agreement works both ways —even if you haven't written it that way. This means that even if the lease states that only *you* are entitled to attorneys' fees, your tenants will be entitled to collect their attorneys' fees from you if they prevail. The amount each would be ordered to pay is whatever the judge decides is reasonable.

Give some thought to whether you want to bind both yourself and the tenant to paying for the winner's costs and fees—especially if you live in a state that will read a "one-way" attorneys' fees clause as a two-way street. If you can't actually collect a judgment containing attorneys' fees from an evicted tenant (which often happens), the clause won't help you. Including the clause could actually hurt you, because if the tenant prevails, you'll be stuck paying the tenant's court costs and attorneys' fees. In addition, the presence of a two-way clause will make it easier for a tenant to secure a willing lawyer for even a doubtful claim, because the source of the lawyer's fee (you, if you lose) will often appear more financially solid than the client.

Also, if you intend to do all or most of your own legal work in any potential eviction or other lawsuit, you will almost surely be better off not to allow for attorneys' fees. Why? Because when you represent yourself, the clause benefits only the tenant: If the tenant wins, you will have to pay the tenant's attorneys' fees; but if you win, the tenant won't owe you any fees, because you didn't hire an attorney. You can't even recover for the long hours you spent preparing for and handling the case.

How to Fill in Clause 21:

If you don't want to allow for attorneys' fees, check the box before the words "will not."

If you want to be entitled to attorneys' fees and costs if you win—and you're willing to pay them if you lose—check the box before the words "will recover."

 CAUTION
Check your state's laws about attorneys' fees clauses. Many states do not allow attorneys' fees requirements in leases and rental agreements. See "State Laws on Attorneys' Fees and Court Costs Clauses" in Appendix A for the rules in your state.

 CAUTION
Attorneys' fees clauses don't cover all legal disputes. They cover fees only for lawsuits that concern the meaning or implementation of a rental agreement or lease—for example, disputes about rent, security deposits, or a landlord's right to access (assuming that the rental document includes these subjects). An attorneys' fees clause would not apply in a personal injury or discrimination lawsuit.

Clause 22. Disclosures

Tenant acknowledges that Landlord has made the following disclosures regarding the Premises:

☐ Disclosure of Information on Lead-Based Paint and/ or Lead-Based Paint Hazards and the pamphlet *Protect Your Family From Lead in Your Home*

☐ Other disclosures: _____

_____

_____

_____

Under federal law, you must disclose any known lead-based paint hazards in rental premises constructed prior to 1978.

State and local laws might require you to make other disclosures before a new tenant signs a lease or rental agreement or moves in.

 RENT CONTROL
Rent control ordinances typically include additional disclosures, such as the name and address of the government agency or board that administers the ordinance, and details on tenants' rights. (Chapter 3 discusses rent control.)

How to Fill in Clause 22:

If your rental property was built before 1978, you must meet federal lead disclosure requirements, so check the first box and follow the advice in Chapter 11.

If you are legally required to make other disclosures as described above, check the second box and provide details in the blank space, adding additional details or pages as necessary.

 CAUTION
Some problems need to be fixed, not merely disclosed. Warning your tenants about a hidden defect does not absolve you of legal responsibility if the condition makes the dwelling uninhabitable or unreasonably dangerous. For example, you are courting liability if you rent an apartment with a gas heater that you know might blow up, even if you warn the tenant that the heater is faulty. Nor can you simply warn your tenants about prior crime on the premises and then fail to take reasonable steps to promote safety (like installing deadbolts or an alarm system). Chapters 10, 11, and 12 discuss problems that are proper subjects of warnings and those that ought to be fixed.

Required Reading:

- Chapter 3
- Chapter 7
- Chapters 10–12
- Chapter 14
- Appendix A Chart: Required Landlord Disclosures

Clause 23. Authority to Receive Legal Papers

The Landlord, any person managing the Premises, and anyone designated by the Landlord are authorized to accept service of process and receive other notices and demands, which may be delivered to:

The Landlord, at the following address: _____

_____

The manager, at the following address: _____

_____

The following person, at the following address: _____

_____

It's the law in many states—and a good idea everywhere—to give your tenants information about everyone you have authorized to receive notices and legal papers, such as notices to end the tenancy, requests for maintenance, or court documents regarding an eviction. You can designate yourself or delegate to a manager or management company. The person you designate to receive legal papers should almost always be available to receive tenant notices and legal papers. In some states, nonresident owners must designate an in-state agent to receive papers and notices.

Notify your tenants in writing whenever there is a change to this information.

How to Fill in Clause 23:

If you will receive notices and legal documents, provide your name and street address. If you've designated a manager or someone else, list their names and addresses.

 CAUTION

Do you trust the person you've designated? If your agent for receiving notices and legal papers doesn't pay attention by forwarding important notices, you could be sued in a lawsuit and not even know it. When defendants don't respond to a lawsuit, the court can enter judgment against them and the winner can place a lien against their property. For this and many other reasons, you must hire a trusted manager or agent. For more information on using property managers, see Chapter 6.

Required Reading:

- Chapter 6

Clause 24. Additional Provisions

Additional provisions are as follows: _____

_____

_____

_____ .

In this clause, list any additional provisions or agreements that are unique to this particular tenancy.

If you don't have a separate Tenant Rules and Regulations clause (see Clause 20, above), you can spell out a few rules under this clause—for example, lost key charges or pool access hours.

How to Fill in Clause 24:

List additional provisions or rules here or in an attachment. If you have no additional provisions, delete this clause and renumber the other clauses accordingly.

 TIP

No legal or practical imperative requires that you put every small detail you want to communicate to the tenant into your lease or rental agreement. Instead, prepare a welcoming, but no-nonsense, "move-in letter" that dovetails with the lease or rental agreement and any rules and regulations, and highlights important terms of the tenancy—for example, how and where to report maintenance problems. In the absence of a separate set of rules and regulations, you could also use a move-in letter to cover issues not included in the lease or rental agreement—for example, rules for use of a laundry room. Chapter 7 covers move-in letters.

> CAUTION
>
> **Do not include exculpatory clauses or hold-harmless clauses.** Many form leases include provisions that attempt to absolve you in advance from responsibility for all damages, injuries, or losses, including those caused by your legal misdeeds. These clauses come in two varieties:
> - Exculpatory: "If there's a problem, you won't hold me responsible," and
> - Hold-harmless: "If there's a problem traceable to me, you're responsible."
>
> Many exculpatory clauses are blatantly illegal and will not be upheld in court (Chapter 10 discusses exculpatory clauses). If a tenant is injured because of a dangerous condition you knew about but failed to fix for an unreasonably long time, no boilerplate lease language will protect you from civil and possibly even criminal charges.

Required Reading:

- Chapter 7
- Chapter 9
- Chapter 10

Clause 25. Validity of Each Part

If a court holds any portion of this Agreement to be invalid, its invalidity will not affect the validity or enforceability of any other provision of this Agreement.

This clause is known as a "savings" clause, and found in many contracts. It means that, in the unlikely event that a court finds one of the other clauses in this lease or rental agreement to be invalid, the remainder of the agreement will remain in force.

How to Fill in Clause 25:

You do not need to add anything to this clause.

Clause 26. Grounds for Termination of Tenancy

The failure of Tenant or Tenant's guests or invitees to comply with any term of this Agreement, or the misrepresentation of any material fact on Tenant's Rental Application, is grounds for termination of the tenancy, with appropriate notice to Tenant and procedures as required by law.

This clause states that any violation of the lease or rental agreement by the tenant, or by the tenant's business or social guests, is grounds for terminating the tenancy, according to the procedures established by your state or local laws. Making tenants responsible for the actions of their guests can be extremely important. For example, this clause would allow you to terminate the tenancy if you discover that the tenants' family or friends are dealing illegal drugs on the premises, have damaged the property, or have brought a dog to visit a no-pets apartment. Chapter 17 discusses terminating tenancies and evicting tenants for lease or rental agreement violations.

This clause also tells tenants that if they made false statements on the rental application concerning an important fact—such as prior evictions—you may terminate the tenancy and evict if necessary.

How to Fill in Clause 26:

You do not need to add anything to this clause.

Required Reading

- Chapter 17

Clause 27. Entire Agreement

This document constitutes the entire Agreement between the parties, and no promises or representations, other than those contained here and those implied by law, have been made by Landlord or Tenant. Any modifications to this Agreement must be in writing signed by Landlord and Tenant.

This clause establishes that the lease or rental agreement and any attachments (such as rules and regulations) constitute the entire agreement between you and your tenant. It means that oral promises (by you or the tenant) to do something different with respect to any aspect of the rental are not binding. Any changes or additions must be in writing. Chapter 14 discusses how to modify signed rental agreements and leases.

How to Fill in Clause 27:

You do not need to add anything to this clause.

Required Reading

- Chapter 14

Signing the Lease or Rental Agreement

Prepare two identical copies of the lease or rental agreement to sign, including all attachments.

You and each tenant should sign both copies. The end of the lease or rental agreement has space to include your signature, street address, phone number, and email; or that of the person you authorize as your agent, such as a property manager. There's also space for the tenants' signatures and phone numbers. Again, as stressed in Clause 1, make sure all adults living in the rental unit sign, including both members of a couple. And check that the tenants' names and signatures match what's in their driver's licenses or other legal documents.

If the tenant has a cosigner, you'll need to add a line for the cosigner's signature or use a separate form. Cosigners are discussed below.

If you alter our form after you have printed it by writing in changes, you and all tenants should initial the changes when you sign the document, which will defeat a claim that you unilaterally inserted changes after everyone signed.

Give one copy of the signed document to the tenant(s) and keep the other one for yourself. If you are renting to more than one tenant, you don't need to make additional copies for each cotenant. After you all have signed the agreement, cotenants can make their own copies of the signed document.

 CAUTION

Don't sign a lease until all terms are final. All of your expectations should be written into the lease or rental agreement (or its attachments, such as Rules and Regulations) before you and the tenant sign. Never sign an incomplete document assuming last-minute changes can be made later. If necessary, help your tenant understand the lease or rental agreement before signing (this might mean you'll need to review it clause by clause).

Some states require landlords who discuss the lease or rental agreement in a language other than English to provide a written translation. For example, California requires landlords who discuss the lease primarily in Spanish, Chinese, Tagalog, Vietnamese, or Korean to give the applicant an unsigned, translated version of the lease before asking the applicant to sign. (This law doesn't apply when tenants supply their own translator—someone who is not a minor and can fluently read and speak both languages.) (Cal. Civil Code § 1632.)

Even when a translation's not legally required, it's in your interest for your tenants to know and follow the rules. If most or all of your communications with the tenant about the lease or rental agreement are in a language other than English, you should give the tenant a written translation. (We include Spanish versions of our lease and rental agreement forms on Nolo's website. See Appendix B for the link to the forms in this book.)

Month-to-Month Residential Rental Agreement

Clause 1. Identification of Landlord and Tenant

This Agreement is between _____ Marty Nelson _____ ("Tenant") and

_____ Alex Stevens _____ ("Landlord").

Each Tenant is jointly and severally liable for the payment of rent and performance of all other terms of this Agreement.

Clause 2. Identification of Premises

Subject to the terms and conditions set forth in this Agreement, Landlord rents to Tenant, for residential purposes only, the premises located at ___ 137 Howell St., Philadelphia, Pennsylvania _____

_____ ("Premises").

Rental of the Premises also includes: _____

_____ .

Rental of the Premises excludes: _____

_____ .

Clause 3. Limits on Use and Occupancy

The Premises are to be used only as a private residence for Tenant(s) listed in Clause 1 of this Agreement, and their minor children: ___ N/A ___ . Occupancy by guests for more than ___ ten days every six months ___ is prohibited without Landlord's written consent and will be considered a breach of this Agreement.

Clause 4. Term of the Tenancy

The rental will begin on _____ September 15, 20xx _____ , and continue on a month-to-month basis. Landlord may terminate the tenancy or modify the terms of this Agreement by giving the Tenant _____ 30 _____ days' written notice. Tenant may terminate the tenancy by giving the Landlord _____ 30 _____ days' written notice.

Clause 5. Payment of Rent

Regular monthly rent.

Tenant will pay to Landlord a monthly rent of $_____ 900 _____ , payable in advance on the first day of each month, except when that day falls on a weekend or legal holiday, in which case rent is due on the next business day. Rent will be paid as follows, or in another manner as Landlord designates from time to time:

Delivery of payment.

Rent will be paid:

☑ by mail, to _____ Alex Stevens, 28 Franklin St., Philadelphia, Pennsylvania 19120 _____

☐ in person, at _____

☐ electronically, to _____

Form of payment.

Landlord will accept payment in the form of:

☐ cash

☑ personal check made payable to ___Alex Stevens___

☑ certified funds or money order

☐ credit or debit card

☑ other electronic funds transfer: _____

Prorated first month's rent.

☑ On signing this Agreement, Tenant will pay to Landlord for the period of ___September 15, 20xx___ through ___September 15, 20xx___ the sum of $___450___ as rent, payable in advance of the start of the tenancy.

☐ Upon move-in, Tenant will owe as rent the prorated rent specified above, plus one full month's rent in the amount designated above, for a total of $_____.

Clause 6. Late Charges

Because Landlord and Tenant agree that actual damages for late rent payments are very difficult or impossible to determine, Landlord and Tenant agree to the following:

- Tenant will pay Landlord a late charge if Tenant fails to pay the rent in full within ___three___ days after the date it is due.
- The late charge will be $___10___, plus $___5___ for each individual day that the rent continues to be unpaid. The total late charge for any one month will not exceed $___45___.

Landlord does not waive the right to insist on payment of the rent in full on the date it is due.

Clause 7. Returned Check and Other Bank Charges

If any check offered by Tenant to Landlord in payment of rent or any other amount due under this Agreement is returned for lack of sufficient funds, a "stop payment," or any other reason, Landlord will make a demand for payment and otherwise pursue remedies as allowed by law.

Clause 8. Security Deposit

On signing this Agreement, Tenant will pay to Landlord the sum of $___1,800___ as a security deposit. Tenant may not, without Landlord's prior written consent, apply this security deposit to the last month's rent or to any other sum due under this Agreement. Within ___30 days___ after Tenant has vacated the Premises, returned keys, and provided Landlord with a forwarding address, Landlord will return the deposit in full or give Tenant an itemized written statement of the reasons for, and the dollar amount of, any of the security deposit retained by Landlord, along with a check for any deposit balance.

[optional clauses here, if any]

The security deposit of $1,800 will be held at:

Federal Bank

1 Federal Street

Philadelphia, PA 19120

Clause 9. Utilities

Tenant will pay all utility charges, except for the following, which will be paid by Landlord:

garbage and water

Clause 10. Prohibition of Assignment and Subletting

Tenant will not sublet any part of the Premises or assign this Agreement without the prior written consent of Landlord. Violating this clause is grounds for terminating the tenancy.

☐ a. Tenants will not sublet or rent any part of the Premises for short-term stays of any duration, including but not limited to vacation rentals.

☐ b. Short-stay rentals are prohibited except as authorized by law. Any short stay-rental is expressly conditioned upon the Tenant's following all regulations, laws, and other requirements as a condition to offering a short-stay rental. Failure to follow all laws, ordinances, regulations, and other requirements, including any registration requirement, will be deemed a material, noncurable breach of this Agreement and will furnish cause for termination.

Clause 11. Tenant's Maintenance Responsibilities

Tenant agrees to: (1) keep the Premises clean, sanitary, and in good condition and, upon termination of the tenancy, return the Premises to Landlord in a condition identical to that which existed when Tenant took occupancy, except for ordinary wear and tear; (2) immediately notify Landlord of any defects or dangerous conditions in and about the Premises of which Tenant becomes aware; and (3) reimburse Landlord, on demand by Landlord, for the cost of any repairs to the Premises, including Landlord's personal property therein, damaged by Tenant or Tenant's guests or business invitees through misuse or neglect.

Tenant has examined the Premises, including appliances, fixtures, carpets, drapes, and paint, and has found them to be in good, safe, and clean condition and repair, except as noted in the Landlord-Tenant Checklist.

Clause 12. Repairs and Alterations by Tenant

a. Except as provided by law, or as authorized by the prior written consent of Landlord, Tenant will not make any repairs or alterations to the Premises, including nailing holes in the walls or painting the rental unit.

b. Tenant will not, without Landlord's prior written consent, alter, rekey, or install any locks to the Premises or install or alter any security alarm system. Tenant will provide Landlord with a key or keys capable of unlocking all such rekeyed or new locks as well as instructions on how to disarm any altered or new security alarm system.

Clause 13. Violating Laws and Causing Disturbances

Tenant is entitled to quiet enjoyment of the Premises. Tenant and guests or invitees will not use the Premises or adjacent areas in such a way as to: (1) violate any law or ordinance, including laws prohibiting the use, possession, or sale of illegal drugs; (2) commit waste (severe property damage); or cause or tolerate a nuisance; or (3) annoy, disturb, inconvenience, or interfere with the quiet enjoyment and peace and quiet of any other tenant or nearby resident.

Clause 14. Damage to the Premises

In the event the Premises are partially or totally damaged or destroyed by fire or other cause, the following will apply:

a. Premises totally damaged and destroyed. Landlord will have the option to: (1) repair such damage and restore the Premises, with this Agreement continuing in full force and effect, except that Tenant's rent will be abated while repairs are being made; or (2) give written notice to Tenant terminating this Agreement at any time within thirty (30) days after such damage, and specifying the termination date; in the event that Landlord gives such notice, this Agreement will expire and all of Tenant's rights pursuant to this Agreement will cease.

b. Premises partially damaged by fire or other cause. Landlord will attempt to repair such damage and restore the Premises within thirty (30) days after such damage. If only part of the Premises cannot be used, Tenant must pay rent only for the usable part, to be determined by Landlord. If Landlord is unable to complete repairs within thirty (30) days, this Agreement will expire and all of Tenant's rights pursuant to this Agreement will terminate at the option of either party. Whether the Premises are totally or partially destroyed will be decided by Landlord, in the exercise of its sole discretion.

c. In the event that Tenant, or Tenant's guests or invitees, in any way caused or contributed to the damage of the Premises, Landlord will have the right to terminate this Agreement at any time, and Tenant will be responsible for all losses, including, but not limited to, damage and repair costs as well as loss of rental income.

d. Landlord will not be required to repair or replace any property brought onto the Premises by Tenant.

Clause 15. Renters' Insurance

Tenant acknowledges that Landlord's property insurance policy will not cover damage to or loss of Tenant's personal property. Tenant will obtain a renters' insurance policy that will:

- reimburse Landlord for cost of fire or water damage caused by Tenant or Tenant's guests, and vandalism to the Premises
- indemnify Landlord against liability to third parties for any negligence on the part of Tenant, Tenant's guests, or invitees; and
- cover damage to Tenant's personal possessions to a minimum of $100,000.

Tenant will provide Landlord with proof of such policy by giving Landlord a certificate of insurance issued by the insurance company within fifteen (15) days of September 15, 20xx. The policy will include Landlord as an "additional insured." Tenant will provide Landlord with a certificate of insurance upon every renewal. Tenant will not allow such policy to expire during the rental term. Failure to obtain and maintain a renters' insurance policy will be treated as a material breach of this Agreement.

Clause 16. Pets

No animal may be kept on the Premises without Landlord's prior written consent, except animals needed by tenants who have a disability, as that is a term is understood by law, and one dog under 20 pounds under the following conditions: Tenant complies with Pet Rules set out in separate Attachment A to this Agreement.

Clause 17. Landlord's Right to Access

Landlord or Landlord's agents may enter the Premises in the event of an emergency, to make repairs or improvements, or to show the Premises to prospective buyers or tenants. Landlord may also enter the Premises to conduct an annual inspection to check for safety or maintenance problems. Except in cases of emergency, Tenant's abandonment of the Premises, court order, or where it is impractical to do so, Landlord will give Tenant 24 hours' notice before entering.

Clause 18. Extended Absences by Tenant

Tenant will notify Landlord in advance if Tenant will be away from the Premises for seven or more consecutive days. During such absence, Landlord may enter the Premises at times reasonably necessary to maintain the property and inspect for damage and needed repairs.

Clause 19. Possession of the Premises

a. *Tenant's failure to take possession.*

If, after signing this Agreement, Tenant fails to take possession of the Premises, Tenant will still be responsible for paying rent and complying with all other terms of this Agreement.

b. *Landlord's failure to deliver possession.*

If Landlord is unable to deliver possession of the Premises to Tenant for any reason not within Landlord's control, including, but not limited to, failure of prior occupants to vacate or partial partial or complete destruction of the Premises, Tenant will have the right to terminate this Agreement upon proper notice as required by law. In such event, Landlord's liability to Tenant will be limited to the return of all sums previously paid by Tenant to Landlord.

Clause 20. Tenant Rules and Regulations

☐ Tenant acknowledges receipt of, and has read a copy of, the Tenant Rules and Regulations, which are labeled __Attachment B__ and attached to and incorporated into this Agreement by this reference. Tenant understands that serious or repeated violations of the rules may be grounds for termination.

Clause 21. Payment of Court Costs and Attorneys' Fees in a Lawsuit

In any action or legal proceeding to enforce any part of this Agreement, the prevailing party

☐ will not / ☐ will recover reasonable attorneys' fees and court costs.

Clause 22. Disclosures

Tenant acknowledges that Landlord has made the following disclosures regarding the Premises:

☐ Disclosure of Information on Lead-Based Paint and/or Lead-Based Paint Hazards and the pamphlet *Protect Your Family From Lead in Your Home*

☑ Other disclosures: ___A copy of the "City of Philadelphia Partners for Good Housing"___ ___brochure and supplement, and a Certificate of Rental Suitability___

_____

_____ .

Clause 23. Authority to Receive Legal Papers

The Landlord, any person managing the Premises, and anyone designated by the Landlord are authorized to accept service of process and receive other notices and demands, which may be delivered to:

☑ The Landlord, at the following address: __28 Franklin St., Philadelphia, Pennsylvania 19120__

_____ .

☐ The manager, at the following address: _____

_____ .

☐ The following person, at the following address: _____

_____ .

Clause 24. Additional Provisions

Additional provisions are as follows: _____

_____

_____

_____

_____

_____

_____

_____

Clause 25. Validity of Each Part

If a court holds any portion of this Agreement to be invalid, its invalidity will not affect the validity or enforceability of any other provision of this Agreement.

Clause 26. Grounds for Termination of Tenancy

The failure of Tenant or Tenant's guests or invitees to comply with any term of this Agreement, or the misrepresentation of any material fact on Tenant's Rental Application, is grounds for termination of the tenancy, with appropriate notice to Tenant and procedures as required by law.

Clause 27. Entire Agreement

This document constitutes the entire Agreement between the parties, and no promises or representations, other than those contained here and those implied by law, have been made by Landlord or Tenant. Any modifications to this Agreement must be in writing signed by Landlord and Tenant.

Sept. 1, 20xx	*Alex Stevens*	Landlord	
Date	Landlord or Landlord's Agent	Title	

28 Franklin Street				
Street Address				

Philadelphia	Pennsylvania	19120	215-555-1578	
City	State	Zip Code	Phone	Email

Sept. 1, 20xx	*Marty Nelson*		215-555-8751
Date	Tenant		Phone

Date	Tenant		Phone

Date	Tenant		Phone

About Cosigners

Some landlords require cosigners (sometimes known as guarantors), especially when renting to students who are financially dependent on their parents.

Cosigners sign either the lease or rental agreement itself or a separate agreement. By signing, the cosigner becomes jointly and severally liable with the tenant for the tenant's obligations. In other words, you can look to the cosigner to cover any rent the tenant fails to pay or the costs of repairing any damage the tenant causes (Clause 1 discusses the concept of joint and several liability). The cosigner retains responsibility regardless of whether the tenant sublets or assigns the agreement. Clause 10 discusses sublets and assignments, and Chapter 8 covers these issues in detail.

In practice, a cosigner's promise to guarantee the tenant's rent obligation might have less value than you think. This is because the threat of eviction is the primary factor that motivates a tenant to pay the rent, and obviously you cannot evict a cosigner. Also, seeking payment from the cosigner might be more trouble than it's worth: The cosigner must be sued separately in either a regular civil lawsuit or in small claims court.

Clause 5 of the cosigner agreement designates the tenant as the cosigner's "agent for service of process." This bit of legal jargon will save you some time and aggravation if you decide to sue the cosigner—it means that you won't have to serve the cosigner personally with notification of your lawsuit. Instead, you can serve the legal papers meant for the cosigner on the tenant (who will be easier to locate). It's then up to the tenant to get in touch with the cosigner. If the cosigner fails to show up, you will be able to win by default. Of course, you still have to collect, and that might involve hiring a lawyer (particularly if the cosigner lives in another state). You can always assign the judgment to a collection agency and resign yourself to giving the agency a cut of any recovery.

Overall, the benefits of having a lease or rental agreement cosigned by someone who won't be living on the property (particularly someone who lives out of state) are largely psychological. But these benefits are still worth something: A tenant who thinks you can (and will) sue the cosigner—who is usually a relative or close friend—might be less likely to default on the rent. Similarly, a cosigner who's ultimately responsible for the tenant's defaults (and whose credit score is on the line) might monitor the tenant's payments, and even provide financial assistance if necessary.

Because of the practical difficulty of collecting from cosigners, many landlords refuse to consider them, which is legal in every situation but one: If a tenant with a disability who has insufficient income (but is otherwise suitable) asks you to accept a cosigner who will cover the rent if needed, you must relax your blanket rule at least to the extent of investigating the suitability of the proposed cosigner. If that person is solvent and stable, federal law requires you to accommodate the applicant by accepting the cosigner, in spite of your general policy. (*Giebeler v. M & B Associates*, 343 F.3d 1143 (9th Cir. 2003).)

If you decide to accept a cosigner, you have that person fill out a separate rental application and agree to a credit check. Should the tenant and prospective cosigner object to these inquiries and costs, consider it a warning sign: They might not be serious about the guarantor's willingness to stand behind the tenant. Once you are satisfied that the cosigner can back up the tenant, add a line at the end of the lease for the dated signature, phone, email, and address of the cosigner; or use the cosigner agreement form we provide here.

If your lease or rental agreement requires the prevailing party in a lawsuit to pay for attorneys' fees and court costs, check the box in Clause 6 of the Cosigner Agreement.

Cosigner Agreement

1. Parties

This Cosigner Agreement ("Agreement") is entered into on September 1 , 20xx , between
 Marty Nelson ("Tenant"),
 Alex Stevens ("Landlord"),
and Sandy Cole ("Cosigner").

2. Underlying Lease or Rental Agreement

Tenant has leased from Landlord the premises located at 137 Howell Street, Philadelphia, PA
 ("Premises").

Landlord and Tenant signed a lease or rental agreement specifying the terms and conditions of this rental

on September 1 , 20xx . A copy of the lease or rental agreement is attached to this Agreement.

3. Cosigner's Responsibility

Cosigner agrees to be jointly and severally liable with Tenant for Tenant's obligations arising out of the lease or rental agreement described in Paragraph 2, including but not limited to unpaid rent, property damage, and cleaning and repair costs. Cosigner further agrees that Landlord will have no obligation to give notice to Cosigner should Tenant fail to abide by the terms of the lease or rental agreement. Landlord may demand that Cosigner perform as promised under this Agreement without first using Tenant's security deposit.

4. Assignment or Subleasing

If Tenant assigns or subleases the Premises, Cosigner will remain liable under the terms of this Agreement for the performance of the assignee or sublessee, unless Landlord relieves Cosigner by written termination of this Agreement.

5. Service of Process

Cosigner appoints Tenant as his or her agent for service of process in the event of any lawsuit arising out of this Agreement.

6. Payment of Legal Fees and Costs

☐ If Landlord, Tenant, and Cosigner (or any combination of them) are involved in any legal proceeding arising out of this Agreement, the prevailing party will recover reasonable attorneys' fees, court costs, and any costs reasonably necessary to collect a judgment.

Alex Stevens	September 1, 20xx
Landlord/Manager	Date
Marty Nelson	September 1, 20xx
Tenant	Date
Sandy Cole	September 1, 20xx
Cosigner	Date

_____

Cosigner's address

_____   _____

Cosigner's phone number   Cosigner's email

A sample Cosigner Agreement is shown above, and the Nolo website includes a downloadable copy. See Appendix B for the link to the forms in this book. Simply fill in your name and your tenant's and cosigner's names, the address of the rental unit, and the date you signed the agreement with the tenant.

CAUTION

If you later amend the rental agreement or lease (a topic discussed in Chapter 14), have the cosigner sign the new version. Generally speaking, cosigners are bound only to the terms of the exact lease or rental agreement they cosign.

Basic Rent Rules

 FORMS IN THIS CHAPTER

Chapter 3 includes instructions for and a sample of the following form:

• Agreement for Delayed or Partial Rent Payments

The purchase of this book includes a free downloadable and customizable copy of this form. See Appendix B for the download link and instructions.

One of your foremost concerns as a landlord is receiving your rent—on time and without hassle. This chapter outlines basic state and local rent laws affecting how much you can charge, as well as where, when, and how rent is due. It also covers rules regarding grace periods, late rent, returned check charges, and rent increases.

Avoiding Rent Disputes

Here are three guidelines that can help you and your tenants have a smooth relationship when it comes to rent:

- Clearly spell out rent rules in your lease or rental agreement as well as in a move-in letter to new tenants.
- Be fair and consistent about enforcing your rent rules.
- If rent isn't paid on time, follow through with a legal notice telling the tenant to pay or move —the first legal step in a possible eviction— as soon as possible.

 RELATED TOPIC
Related topics covered in this book include:

- Lease and rental agreement provisions relating to rent: Chapter 2
- Collecting deposits and potential problems with calling a deposit "last month's rent": Chapter 4
- Compensating a manager with reduced rent: Chapter 6
- Highlighting rent rules in a move-in letter to new tenants and collecting the first month's rent: Chapter 7
- Cotenants' obligations for rent: Chapter 8
- Rent withholding and other tenant options when a landlord fails to maintain the premises in good condition: Chapter 9
- Tenants' obligation to pay rent when breaking a lease: Chapter 14
- Accepting rent after a 30-day notice is given: Chapter 14
- Evicting a tenant for nonpayment of rent: Chapter 17
- State rent rules: Appendix A
- State rent control laws: Appendix A.

How Much Can You Charge?

In most states, the law doesn't limit how much rent you can charge—you are free to charge what the market will bear at the beginning of the tenancy, and increase the rent accordingly throughout the tenancy. However, in some states, cities, and counties, rent control ordinances and laws closely govern how much rent a landlord can legally charge existing tenants. And in Connecticut, which does not have rent control, tenants in some cities may challenge an initial rent or a rent increase that they believe is excessive. (Conn. Gen. Stat. Ann. §§ 7-148b and following.)

For a new tenancy, it's up to you to determine how much your rental unit is worth. To do this, check rents of comparable properties in your area, and visit a few places that sound similar to yours. Local property management companies, real estate offices that handle rental property, and online ads can also provide useful information. In addition, local apartment associations—or other landlords you meet at association functions—are a good source of pricing information.

Many wise landlords choose to charge just slightly less than the going rate as part of a policy designed to find and keep excellent tenants. As with any business arrangement, it usually pays in the long run to have your tenants feel they are getting a good deal. In exchange, you hope the tenants will be responsive to your business needs. This doesn't always work, of course, but tenants who feel their rent is fair are less likely to complain over trifling matters and more likely to stay for an extended period.

Rent Control

 SKIP AHEAD
Unless you own property in California, Oregon, the District of Columbia; or in certain cities in Maryland, New Jersey, or New York, you aren't affected by rent control and can skip this section. To find out if your state has statewide rent control or allows cities to have rent control, see the "State Rent Control Laws" chart in Appendix A.

Communities in only some states—such as California and New York—have laws that limit the amount of rent landlords may charge. Typically, only a few cities or counties in each of these states have enacted local rent control ordinances (also called rent stabilization, maximum rent regulation, or a similar term), but often these are some of the state's largest cities. California has *both* statewide rent control and numerous local ordinances.

RESOURCE
California rent control. California landlords should consult *The California Landlord's Law Book: Rights & Responsibilities*, by Nils Rosenquest and Janet Portman and *The California Landlord's Law Book: Evictions*, by Nils Rosenquest. These books are published by Nolo and are available at bookstores and public libraries. They can also be ordered directly from Nolo's website, Nolo.com, or by calling 800-728-3555.

The Rent Control Board

In most cities, rent control rests in the hands of a rent control board of five to ten people. Board members often decide annual rent increases, fines, and other important issues. (In many areas, the law itself limits how and when the rent may be raised.)

The actual rent control ordinance is a product of the city council or county board of supervisors. But the rent control board is in charge of interpreting the provisions of the law, which can give the board significant power over landlords and tenants.

(Neither California's nor Oregon's statewide rent control laws provide for a rent control board.)

Rent control laws commonly regulate much more than rent. For example, owners of rent-controlled properties must follow specific eviction procedures. Because local ordinances are often quite complicated and vary widely, this book cannot provide details on each city's program.

Instead, we provide a general description of what rent control laws and ordinances cover.

If you own rental property in a state or city that has rent control, you should always have a current copy of the law or ordinance and any regulations interpreting it. And be sure to keep up to date; rent control laws change frequently, and court decisions also affect them. It's a good idea to subscribe to publications of the local property owners' association, and pay attention to local politics to keep abreast of changes in your rent control ordinance.

CAUTION
Know the law or pay the price. Local governments typically levy fines—sometimes heavy ones—for rent control violations. Violation of a rent control law might also give tenants a legal ground on which to win an eviction lawsuit—and even sue you.

Property Subject to Rent Control

Not all rental housing within a rent-controlled state or city is subject to rent control. Generally, new buildings as well as owner-occupied buildings with two (or sometimes even three or four) units or fewer are exempt from rent control. Some cities also exempt single-family rental houses and luxury units that rent for more than a certain amount.

Rent Increases for Existing Tenants

Rent control laws and ordinances have mechanisms for limiting, or capping, rent increases for existing tenants. Here are just a few common examples.

Annual increases. This approach allows a specific percentage rent increase each year. The amount of the increase can be a fixed percentage or a percentage tied to a local or national Consumer Price Index.

Increased expenses. Some rent control boards have the power to adjust rents of individual units based on certain cost factors, such as increased taxes, maintenance expenses, or capital improvements.

The landlord might need to request permission from the rent control board before upping the rent.

Tenant consent. In some cities, landlords may increase rent under certain circumstances only if the tenants voluntarily agree to the increase—or don't protest it.

A word of caution: Even if you are otherwise entitled to raise the rent under the terms of your rent control ordinance, the rent board might be able to deny you permission if you haven't adequately repaired and maintained your rental units.

Where to Get Information About Rent Control

- **Online at your city's rent control board's website.** It will post the current ordinance, and might also have FAQs and a brochure explaining the ordinance.
- **Your state or local apartment owners' association.** Virtually every city with a rent control ordinance has an active property owners' association. The New York City Rent Stabilization Association, for example, gives members information and help on rent matters and tenant screening.
- **Local attorneys who specialize in landlord-tenant law.** Search online or ask another landlord for recommendations. Chapter 18 discusses how to find and work with a lawyer.

Increasing Rent When a Tenant Moves

In most rent control areas, landlords may raise rent—either as much as they want or by a specified percentage—when a tenant voluntarily moves out (or is removed for cause). This feature, called "vacancy decontrol," "vacancy rent ceiling adjustment," or a similar term, is built into many local ordinances.

In practice, it means that rent control applies to a particular rental unit only as long as a particular tenant (or tenants) stays there. If that tenant voluntarily leaves or, in some cities, is evicted for a legal or "just" cause (discussed below), the rental

unit is subject to rent control again after the new (and presumably higher) rent is established.

> **EXAMPLE:** Marla has lived in Edward's apartment building for seven years. During that time, Edward has been allowed to raise the rent only by the modest amount authorized by the local rent board each year. Meanwhile, the market value of the apartment has gone up significantly. When Marla finally moves out, Edward is free to charge the next tenant the market rate. But once set, that tenant's rent will also be subject to the rent control rules, and Edward will again be limited to small annual increases as approved by the rent control board.

In some areas, no rent increase is allowed at all, even when a tenant moves out. Check your ordinance.

Legal or "Just Cause" Evictions

Because landlords may increase the rent to market rates when new tenants move in, the law must place some restrictions on tenancy terminations. Otherwise, landlords who wanted to create a vacancy so they could raise the rent would be free to throw out tenants, undermining the whole system. Recognizing this, many laws and ordinances require landlords to have a legal or just cause—that is, a good reason—to terminate and, if the tenants don't leave, evict.

Just cause is usually limited to a few specific situations described in the law or ordinance. If you need to evict a tenant for a valid business reason, you should have no problem finding your reason on the approved list. Here are a few typical examples of legal or just cause to evict:

- The tenant violates a significant term of the lease or rental agreement—for example, by failing to pay rent or causing substantial damage to the premises. However, in many situations, you're legally required to first give the tenant a chance to correct the problem.
- The landlord wants to move into the rental unit or give it to an immediate family member.

- The landlord wants to substantially remodel the property, and the type of work needed requires the tenant to move out.
- The tenant creates a significant nuisance— for example, by repeatedly disturbing other tenants or engaging in illegal activity, such as drug dealing, on the premises.

Just cause restrictions affect renewals as well as terminations midway through the tenancy. Unless you have just cause to not renew, you might have to continue renting to tenants you don't like until they decide to leave on their own.

Registration of Rental Units

Some rent control ordinances require landlords to register their properties with the local rent control agency. This allows the rent board to keep track of the city's rental units, and the registration fees provide operating funds. (California's state law and Oregon's law do not require registration.)

Deposits and Notice Requirements

Rent control laws and ordinances might impose rules regarding security deposits, interest payments, and the type of notice you must give tenants when you want to raise the rent or terminate a tenancy. Local ordinance requirements are in addition to any state law requirements. For example, state law might require a 30-day notice for a rent increase. A local rent control law might also require the notice to tell the tenant that the rent control board can verify that the new rental amount is legal under the ordinance.

When Rent Is Due

Most leases and rental agreements, including the ones in this book, call for rent to be paid monthly, in advance, on the first day of the month. See Clause 5 of the form agreements in Chapter 2.

First Day, Last Day, or In-Between?

The first of the month is a customary and convenient due date for rent, in part because many tenants get their paychecks on the last workday of the month. Also, the approach of a new month can, in itself, help remind people of monthly bills due on the first.

Your Right to Go Out of Business

It's not uncommon for landlords in rent-controlled areas to decide to get out of the residential rental business entirely. To do so, however, they must evict tenants, who will protest that the eviction violates the rent control rules.

No rent control law or ordinance can force you to continue with your business against your will. However, if you withdraw rental units from the market, you must typically meet strict standards regarding the necessity of doing so. Rent control boards do not want landlords to use going out of business as a ruse for evicting long-term tenants, only to start up again with a fresh batch of tenants whose rents will invariably be substantially higher.

If you decide to go out of business and must evict tenants, check your law or ordinance carefully. It might require you to give tenants a lengthy notice period or offer relocation assistance, and might impose a minimum time period during which you can't resume business. If you own multiple units, the rent control ordinance might prohibit you from withdrawing more than a specified number of units; and if the premises are torn down and new units constructed, you might have to offer former tenants a right of first refusal. Contact your local landlords' association or rent control board for details on the specifics.

It is perfectly legal to require rent to be paid on a different day of the month, and might make sense if the tenant gets paid at odd times. Some landlords make the rent payable each month on the date the tenant first moved in. Generally, it's easier to prorate rent for a short first month and then require that rent be paid on the first of the next month. But if you have only a few tenants, and don't mind having tenants paying you on different days of the month, it makes no legal difference.

Special rules for tenants who receive public assistance. Some states make special due date accommodations for public assistance recipients. Public assistance recipients in Hawaii, for example, may change the rent due date to within three business days (excluding Saturdays, Sundays, and holidays) after the mailing date of public assistance checks. The tenants need to make a one-time prorated payment to cover the period between the original due date in the rental agreement and a newly established due date. (Haw. Rev. Stat. § 521-21 (2021).)

Whatever rent due date you choose, be sure to put it in your lease or rental agreement. If you don't, state law might do it for you. In several states, for month-to-month rental agreements, rent is due in equal monthly installments at the beginning of each month, unless otherwise agreed.

In a few states, however, rent is not due until the end of the term unless the lease or rental agreement says otherwise. You would probably never deliberately allow a tenant who moved in on the first day of the month to wait to pay rent until the 31st. Nor would you want tenants to continue to pay at the end of the month. Avoid this possibility by specifying that rent is due on the first of the month in your lease or rental agreement.

Collecting Rent More Than Once a Month

If you wish, you and the tenant can agree that the rent be paid twice a month, each week, or on whatever schedule suits you. The most common variation on the standard monthly payment arrangement is having rent paid twice a month. This is a particularly good idea if you have tenants who have relatively low-paying jobs and get paid twice a month, because they might have difficulty saving the needed portion of their midmonth check until the first of the month.

When the Due Date Falls on a Weekend or Holiday

The lease and rental agreements in this book state that when the rent due date falls on a weekend day or legal holiday, the tenant must pay it by the next business day. See Clause 5 of the form agreements in Chapter 2.

This is legally required in some states, and is the general rule in most. If you want to insist that tenants always get rent checks to you on the first, no matter what, you'll have to check the law in your state to make sure it's allowed. It's probably not worth the trouble.

Grace Periods for Late Rent

Lots of tenants are absolutely convinced that if rent is due on the first, but they pay by the fifth (or sometimes the seventh or even the tenth) of the month, they have legally paid their rent on time because they are within a legal grace period. This is simply not true.

In practice, many landlords do not get upset about late rent or charge a late fee (discussed below) until the rent is a few days past due. Additionally, your state law might require you to give tenants a few days to come up with the rent before you can send a termination notice.

Regardless, it is your legal right to insist that rent be paid on the day it is due, and you should make it clear in your lease or rental agreement and move-in letter that there is no grace period other than what's stated in writing or required by state law. Your best approach is to consistently stress to tenants that rent must be paid on the due date.

CAUTION

If you wait more than three or five days to collect your rent, you are running your business unwisely, and just extending the time a nonpaying tenant can stay. Be firm, but fair. Any other policy will get you into a morass of special cases and exceptions and will cost you a bundle in the long run. If you allow exceptions only in extreme circumstances, tenants will learn to not waste your (and their) time with frequent sob stories.

Evictions for Nonpayment of Rent

Failure to pay rent on time is by far the most common reason landlords go to court and evict tenants. Before going to court, though, a landlord must give the tenant a written notice, demanding that the tenant either pay within a few days or move out. How long the tenant is allowed to stay depends on state law; in most places, it's about three to five days.

In most instances, the tenant who receives this kind of notice pays up, and that's the end of it. But if the tenant doesn't pay the rent (or move), you can (in most circumstances) file an eviction lawsuit. The only real exception is if your state or city has an eviction ban in place due to the coronavirus pandemic or another disaster, such as flooding. Chapter 17 explains the kinds of termination notices that landlords must use when tenants are behind on the rent, and includes a brief summary of evictions. Appendix A includes details on state laws on termination for nonpayment of rent, as well as directions on how to research whether these evictions might be on hold due to the coronavirus pandemic or another emergency.

If you find yourself delivering too many pay-the-rent-or-leave notices to a particular tenant, you might want to end the tenancy if you can—even if the tenant always comes up with the rent at the last minute.

Where and How Rent Is Due

You should specify in your lease or rental agreement where the tenant should pay the rent and how you want it paid—for example, by check or money order only. See Clause 5 of the form agreements in Chapter 2.

CAUTION

Landlords should take special care to inform tenants of where and how rent is paid. Many states require landlords to notify tenants (either in a separate writing or in a written rental agreement or lease) of the name and street address of the owner or manager responsible for collection of rent, how rent is to be paid, and who is available for service of notices.

Where Rent Must Be Paid

You have several options for where the tenant pays you rent, assuming you will receive cash or checks (see below for electronic alternatives).

By mail. You can allow tenants to mail you the rent check. However, consider building in a day or two of extra time to receive the check in the event mail delivery is delayed due to weather, emergency, or post office delays.

At home. You can send someone to each unit, every month, to pick up the rent. But this more old-fashioned way of collecting the rent isn't well-suited to modern life, when most people aren't at home during the day.

At your office. Requiring the rent to be paid personally at your place of business or manager's office is feasible (and, in some states, legal) only if you have an on-site office. Although this approach does have some advantages, in most cases asking tenants to travel across town is both unreasonable and counterproductive, because inevitably some of them just won't get around to it.

If your lease or rental agreement doesn't specify where you want tenants to pay you rent, state law might decide. Under statutes in several states, the default rule is that rent is payable at the dwelling unit unless otherwise agreed. This is yet another reason to specify in your rental agreement or lease that your tenant should pay by mail or at your on-site office.

Form of Rent Payment

You should also specify in your lease or rental agreement how rent must be paid: by cash, check, credit card, money order, or electronic transfer. See Clause 5 of the form agreements in Chapter 2.

For most landlords, checks are routine. If a tenant doesn't have a checking account or has bounced too many checks, you might want to require a certified check or money order (note that some state laws prohibit landlords from requiring rent to be paid only in cash).

You should never accept postdated checks. You have absolutely no assurance that necessary funds will ever be deposited in the account. In addition, a postdated check may legally be considered a "note" promising to pay on a certain date. In some states, if you accept such a note (check), you have no right to bring an eviction action while the note is pending. Far better to tell the tenant that rent must be paid in full on time and to give the tenant a late notice if it isn't.

> **CAUTION**
> **Don't accept cash unless you have no choice.**
> You are a likely target for robbery if word gets out that you are taking in large amounts of cash once or twice a month. And if you accept cash knowing that the tenant earned it from an illegal act, such as drug dealing, the government could seize it from you under federal and state forfeiture laws. If you do accept cash, be sure to provide a written, dated receipt stating the tenant's name and rental unit and the amount of rent and time period for which rent is paid. Such a receipt is required by law in a few states, and it's a good idea everywhere.

Easy Ways to Pay the Rent

Other quick and reliable ways to ensure timely rent payments are:

Online banking. Tenants with bank accounts that they know will always have enough money on deposit to handle the rent might be willing to set up an automatic transfer. On the day they specify, the rent funds are electronically transferred to your account. Every major bank offers this service, some for a small fee.

Credit card. If you have enough tenants to make it worthwhile, explore the option of accepting credit cards. You must pay a percentage of the amount charged for the privilege, but the cost might be justified if it results in more on-time payments and less hassle for you and your tenants. You can either have someone in your on-site office process the credit card payments and give tenants receipts, or accept credit card payments through one of the many online property management services available. And if your tenant population is affluent enough, consider requiring automatic credit card debits.

Electronic billing. Many property management apps and software offer billing services, where the tenant receives a bill via email and can pay using an electronic service such as PayPal, Apple Pay, or direct credit card payment. Often, tenants can also set up automatic payments via whatever method they prefer.

Changing Where and How Rent Is Due

If you've been burned by bounced checks from a particular tenant, you might want to decree that, from now on, you'll accept nothing less than a certified check or money order, and that rent may be paid only during certain hours at the manager's office.

Be careful. It might be illegal to suddenly change your practice for payment of rent without proper notice to the tenant.

If your lease or rental agreement doesn't say where and how rent is to be paid, your past practice might legally control how rent is paid until you properly notify the tenant of a change. If you want to require tenants to pay rent at your office, for example, you must formally change a month-to-month rental agreement, typically with a written 30-day notice. If you rent under a lease, you will have to wait until the lease runs out.

Late Charges and Discounts for Early Payments

If you're faced with a tenant who hasn't paid rent on the due date, you probably don't want to immediately hand out a formal notice telling the tenant to pay the rent or leave. After all, it's not going to do anything positive for your relationship with the tenant, who might have just forgotten to drop the check in a mailbox. But how else can you motivate tenants to pay rent on time?

A fairly common and sensible practice is to charge a reasonable late fee and highlight your late fee policy in your lease or rental agreement and move-in letter to new tenants. See Clause 6 of the form agreements in Chapter 2.

Some states have statutes that put precise limits on late fees (see the "Late Fees" column in the "State Rent Rules" chart in Appendix A). But even if your state doesn't have specific rules, you are still bound by general legal principles that prohibit unreasonably high fees. Courts in some states have ruled that contracts that provide for unreasonably high late charges are not enforceable—which means that if a tenant fights you in court (either in an eviction lawsuit or a separate case brought by the tenant), you could lose.

 RENT CONTROL

Some rent control laws and ordinances also regulate late fees. Check any rent control ordinances applicable to your properties.

Unless your state regulates late fees, you should be on safe ground if you adhere to these principles:

The late fee should not apply until at least three to five days after the due date. Imposing a stiff late charge if the rent is only one or two days late might not be upheld in court.

The total late charge should not exceed 4%–5% of the rent. That's $44 to $55 on a $1,100-per-month rental. Even in states with no statutory limits, a higher late charge might not be upheld in court.

If the late fee increases each day the rent is late, it should be moderate and have an upper limit. A late charge that increases without limit each day could be considered interest charged at an illegal (usurious) rate. State laws set the maximum allowable rate of interest, typically less than 10%, that may be charged for a debt. (Ten dollars a day on a $1,000-per-month rent is 3,650% annual interest.) A more acceptable late charge would be $10 for the first day rent is late, plus $5 for each additional day, up to a maximum of 5% of the rental amount.

Don't try to disguise excessive late charges by giving a "discount" for early payment. For one thing, this kind of "discount" is illegal in some states. One landlord we know concluded he couldn't get away with charging a $100 late charge on an $850 rent payment, so, instead, he designed a rental agreement calling for a rent of $950 with a $100 discount if the rent was not more than three days late. Ingenious as this ploy sounds, it is unlikely to stand up in court, unless the discount for timely payment is very modest. Giving a relatively large discount is in effect the same as charging an excessive late fee, and a judge is likely to see it as such.

Anyway, fooling around with late charges is wasted energy. If you want more rent for your unit, raise the rent (unless you live in a rent control area). If you are concerned about tenants paying on time—and who isn't?—put your energy into choosing responsible tenants.

If you have a tenant with a month-to-month tenancy who drives you nuts with late rent payments, and a reasonable late charge doesn't resolve the situation, terminate the tenancy with the appropriate notice.

> ⚠ **CAUTION**
>
> **Don't try to disguise late fees as "additional rent."** In many leases and rental agreements, the late fee clause contains a statement like this: "Late fees are deemed 'additional rent.'" Landlords insert this statement in case they have to evict for rent nonpayment, and are limited to asking the judge to award them only unpaid rent. By describing the late fee as "rent," they are trying to shoehorn that fee into their damage award. But not all states allow this ploy. And in rent control areas, bumping the rent by adding the late fee will probably result in an illegal monthly rent. Use this trick at your peril.

Returned Check Charges

It's legal to charge the tenant an extra fee if a rent check bounces (see Clause 7 of the form agreements in Chapter 2). If you're having a lot of trouble with bounced checks, you might want to change your policy to accept only money orders for rent.

Most states regulate the amount you can charge for a bounced check. $25 to $40 is common for the first check; some states allow escalating charges for subsequent checks. Some states allow you to charge the stated flat fee or a specific percent of the check's amount, whichever is greater. Check with your state's consumer protection bureau or agency to learn the rule that applies to you.

If your state does not impose limits on bounced check fees, be sure that you do not impose an unreasonably high fee. Like late charges, bounced check charges must be reasonable. You should charge no more than the amount your bank charges you for a returned check charge, plus a few dollars for your trouble.

It is a poor idea to let your bank redeposit rent checks that bounce. Instead, tell the bank to return bad checks to you immediately. Getting a bounced check back quickly alerts you to the fact that the rent is unpaid much sooner than if the check is resubmitted and returned for nonpayment a second time. You can use this time to ask the tenant to make the check good immediately. If the tenant doesn't come through, you can promptly serve the necessary paperwork to end the tenancy.

If tenants habitually give you bad checks, give them a notice demanding that they pay the rent or move. When they don't make the check good by the deadline, you can start eviction proceedings.

Partial or Delayed Rent Payments

On occasion, a tenant suffering a temporary financial setback will offer something less than the full month's rent, with a promise to catch up as the month proceeds, or at the first of the next month. Although agreeing to this plan is generally a bad business practice, you might nevertheless wish to make an exception when the tenant's financial problems truly appear to be temporary and you have reason to trust the tenant.

If you do give a tenant a little more time to pay some or all of the rent, establish a schedule, in writing, for when the rent will be paid. Then monitor the situation carefully. Otherwise, the tenant might try to delay payment indefinitely, or make such small and infrequent payments that the account is never brought current. A signed agreement—say for a one-week extension—lets both you and the tenant know what's expected. If you give the tenant two weeks to catch up and the tenant doesn't follow through, the written agreement precludes any argument about what you agreed to. A sample Agreement for Delayed or Partial Rent Payments is shown below, and the Nolo website includes a downloadable copy. See Appendix B for the link to the forms in this book.

If the tenant doesn't pay the rest of the rent when promised, you can—and should—follow through with the appropriate steps to terminate the tenancy.

Agreement for Delayed or Partial Rent Payments

This Agreement is made between ___Betty Wong_____ ("Tenant")

and __John Lewis_____ ("Landlord").

1. Tenant has paid _one-half of her $1,000 rent for apartment #2 at 111 Billy St., Phoenix, Arizona_

   on _____March 1, 20xx_____. The rent due date is _March 1, 20xx_____.

2. Landlord agrees to accept all the remainder of the rent on or before _March 15, 20xx_____,

   and to hold off on any legal proceeding to evict Tenant until that date.

____John Lewis_____   ____March 2, 20xx_____
Landlord   Date

____Betty Wong_____   ____March 2, 20xx_____
Tenant   Date

_____   _____
Tenant   Date

_____   _____
Tenant   Date

Raising the Rent

Except in cities and states with rent control, your freedom to raise rent depends primarily on whether the tenant has a lease or a month-to-month rental agreement.

When You Can Raise Rent

For the most part, a lease fixes the terms of tenancy for the length of the lease. You can't change the terms of the lease until the end of the lease period unless the lease itself allows it or the tenant agrees. When the lease expires, you can present the tenant with a new lease that has a higher rent or other changed terms. It's always safest to give tenants at least a month or two notice of any rent increase before negotiating a new lease.

In contrast, you can raise the rent in a periodic tenancy just by giving the tenant proper written notice, typically 30 days for a month-to-month tenancy. State law might override these general rules, however. In a few states, landlords must provide 45 or 60 days' notice to raise the rent for a month-to-month tenancy. See "State Rules on Notice Required to Change or Terminate a Month-to-Month Tenancy" in Appendix A and the Chapter 14 discussion of changing terms during the tenancy. You'll need to consult your state statutes for the specific information you must provide in a rent increase notice, how you must deliver it to the tenant, and any rights tenants have to dispute rent increases.

How Much Can You Raise the Rent?

Areas without rent control or rent regulation do not limit the amount by which you can increase the rent of a month-to-month or other periodic tenant. Similarly, there is no restriction on the period of time between rent increases. You can legally raise the rent as much and as often as good business dictates. Of course, common sense should tell you that if your tenants think your increases are unfair, you might end up with vacant units or hostile tenants.

Avoiding Tenant Charges of Retaliation or Discrimination

You can't legally raise a tenant's rent as retaliation —for example, in response to a legitimate complaint or rent-withholding action—or in a discriminatory manner. The laws in many states actually presume retaliation if you increase rent soon—typically, within three to six months— after a tenant's complaint of defective conditions. See the Chapter 16 discussion of general ways to avoid tenant charges of retaliation. "State Laws Prohibiting Landlord Retaliation" in Appendix A lists state-by-state details.

One way to protect yourself from charges that ordinary rent increases are retaliatory or discriminatory is to adopt a sensible rent increase policy and stick to it.

For example, many landlords raise rent once a year in an amount that more or less reflects the increase in the regional Consumer Price Index. Other landlords use a more complicated formula that takes into account other rents in the area, as well as factors such as increased costs of maintenance or rehabilitation. They make sure to inform their tenants about the rent increase in advance and apply the increase uniformly to all their tenants. Usually, this protects the landlord against any claim of a retaliatory rent increase by a tenant who recently made a complaint about the condition of the premises.

EXAMPLE: Lois owns two multiunit complexes. In one of them, she raises rents uniformly, at the same time, for all tenants. In the other apartment building, where she fears tenants hit with rent increases all at once will organize and generate unrest, Lois does things differently: She raises each tenant's rent in accordance with the Consumer Price Index on the yearly anniversary of the date each tenant moved in. Either way, Lois is safe from being judged to have increased rents for retaliatory reasons, even if a rent increase to a particular tenant follows on the heels of a complaint from that tenant.

Of course, any rent increase given to a tenant who has made a complaint should be reasonable—in relation to the previous rent, what you charge other similarly situated tenants, and rents for comparable property in the area—or you are asking for legal trouble.

EXAMPLE: Lonnie has no organized plan for increasing rents in his 20-unit building, but simply raises them when he needs money. On November 1, he raises the rent for one of his tenants, Teresa, without remembering her recent complaint about her heater. Teresa is the only one to receive a rent increase in November. She has a strong retaliatory rent increase case against Lonnie, simply because an increase that seemed to single her out coincided with her exercise of a legal right. If the increase made her rent higher than those for comparable units in the building, she will have an even better case.

Security Deposits

Most landlords quite sensibly ask for a security deposit before entrusting hundreds of thousands of dollars' worth of real estate to a tenant. But it's easy to get into legal trouble over deposits, because they are strictly regulated by state law, and sometimes also by city ordinance.

The law of most states dictates how large a deposit you can require, how you can use it, when you must return it, and more. Many states require you to put deposits in a separate account and pay interest on them. You cannot escape these requirements by putting different terms in a lease or rental agreement. This chapter explains how to set up a clear and fair system of setting, collecting, and holding deposits.

 RELATED TOPIC

Related topics covered in this book include:

- Charging prospective tenants credit check fees, finder's fees, or holding deposits: Chapter 1
- Writing clear lease and rental agreement provisions on security deposits: Chapter 2
- Highlighting security deposit rules and procedures in move-in and move-out letters to the tenant: Chapters 7 and 15
- Returning deposits and deducting for cleaning, damage, and unpaid rent; how to handle legal disputes involving deposits: Chapter 15
- State Security Deposit Rules: Appendix A.

Purpose and Use of Security Deposits

The purpose of a security deposit is to provide funds for the landlord to use if the tenant fails to pay the rent or leaves the property in a damaged condition. Rent you collect in advance for the first month is not part of the security deposit.

State laws control the amount you can charge and how and when you must return security deposits. When a tenant moves out, you will have a set amount of time (usually from 14 to 30 days, depending on the state) to either return the tenant's entire deposit or provide an itemized statement of deductions and refund any deposit balance.

Although state laws vary, you can generally withhold all or part of the deposit to pay for:

- unpaid rent
- repairing damage to the premises (except for "ordinary wear and tear") caused by the tenant, a family member, or a guest
- cleaning necessary to restore the rental unit to its level of cleanliness at the beginning of the tenancy (taking into consideration ordinary wear and tear), and
- restoring or replacing rental unit property taken or destroyed by the tenant.

States typically also allow you to use a deposit to cover the tenant's obligations under the lease or rental agreement, which might include paying utility charges.

You don't necessarily need to wait until tenants move out to tap into their security deposits. You may, for example, use some of the security deposit during the tenancy if the tenant broke something and didn't fix it or pay for it. In this case, you should require the tenant to replenish the security deposit.

> **EXAMPLE:** Millie pays her landlord Maury a $1,000 security deposit when she moves in. Six months later, Millie goes on vacation, leaving the water running. By the time Maury is notified, the overflow has damaged the paint on the ceiling below. Maury repaints the ceiling at a cost of $250, taking the money out of Millie's security deposit. Maury is entitled to ask Millie to replace that money, so that her deposit remains $1,000.

To protect yourself and avoid misunderstandings with tenants, make sure your lease or rental agreement is clear on the use of security deposits and the tenant's obligations. See Clause 8 of the form agreements in Chapter 2.

TIP

A few states exempt some landlords from security deposit rules. For details, see the "State Security Deposit Rules" chart in Appendix A.

Dollar Limits on Deposits

Many states limit the amount you can collect as a deposit to an amount equal to one or two months of rent. And the limit within each state might vary depending on:

- the age of the tenant (senior citizens may have a lower deposit ceiling)
- whether the rental unit is furnished
- whether you have a month-to-month rental agreement or a long-term lease, and
- whether the tenant has a pet or waterbed.

For details, see "State Security Deposit Rules," in Appendix A.

CAUTION

An inconsistent security deposit policy is an invitation to a lawsuit. Even if your motives are good—for example, you require a smaller deposit from a student tenant—you risk a charge of illegal discrimination by other tenants who did not get the same break.

How Much Deposit Should You Charge?

Normally, the best advice is to charge as much as the market will bear, within any legal limits. The more the tenant has at stake, the better the chance the tenant will respect your property. And, the larger the deposit, the more financial protection you will have if a tenant leaves owing you rent or you have repair damage beyond wear and tear.

Sometimes, the market rate of deposits is lower than the maximum allowed by law. Here are some suggestions for how to determine a reasonable security deposit amount:

- **Charge the full limit in high-risk situations.** For example, you're more likely to have to use the security deposit when there's a lot of tenant turnover, when you allow a pet, or when you rent to a tenant with poor credit.

- **Consider the psychological advantage of a higher rent rather than a high deposit.** Many tenants would rather pay a slightly higher rent than an enormous deposit. Also, many acceptable, solvent tenants have a hard time coming up with a hefty deposit, especially if they are still in a rental and are awaiting the return of a previous security deposit. And remember, unlike the security deposit, the extra rent is not refundable.

  EXAMPLE: Lenora rents out a three-bedroom furnished house in San Francisco for $6,000 a month. Because total deposits on furnished property in California can legally be three times the monthly rent, Lenora could charge up to $18,000. This is in addition to the first month's rent of $6,000 that Lenora can (and should) insist on before turning the property over to a tenant. But, realistically, Lenora would probably have difficulty finding a tenant if she insisted on receiving an $18,000 deposit plus the first month's rent, for a total of $24,000. So she decides to charge only one month's rent for the deposit but to increase the monthly rent. That gives Lenora the protection she feels she needs without imposing an enormous initial financial burden on her tenants.

- **Single-family homes call for a bigger deposit.** Unlike multiunit residences, where close-by neighbors or a manager can spot, report, and quickly stop any destruction, the single-family home is somewhat of an island. The condition of the interior and even the exterior might be hard to assess. And, of course, the cost of repairing damage to a house is likely to be higher than for an apartment.

- **Gain a marketing advantage by allowing a deposit to be paid in installments.** If rentals are plentiful in your area, with comparable units renting at about the same price, you might give yourself a competitive edge by allowing tenants to pay the deposit in several installments over a few months, rather than one lump sum.

TIP

Renters' insurance will cover the cost to repair your property when the tenant has damaged it. If you're worried about damage but don't think you can raise the deposit any higher, require renters' insurance. Clause 15 of the lease and rental agreement in this book requires the tenant to maintain renters' insurance, and Chapter 2 explains the legal limitations that might apply in your state or locality. While you're at it, evaluate your own insurance policy to make sure it is adequate. If the tenant's security deposit is inadequate to cover any damage and the tenant doesn't have renters' insurance (or it won't cover the loss), you might be able to collect from your own carrier.

Last Month's Rent

It's a common—but often unwise—practice to collect a sum of money called "last month's rent" from a tenant who's moving in. Landlords tend to treat this money as just another security deposit, and use it to cover not only the last month's rent but also other expenses such as repairs or cleaning.

Problems can arise when you:

- try to use the last month's rent to cover repairs or cleaning, or
- have raised the rent during the tenancy —and you want to top off the last month's rent.

We'll look at these situations below.

Applying Last Month's Rent to Damage or Cleaning

If you have collected a sum of money labeled last month's rent, a departing tenant won't need to write a rent check for the last month. But surprisingly, many tenants do pay for the last month anyway, often forgetting that they have prepaid. Can you use that "last month's rent" to cover damage?

Some states allow you to use it as part of the security deposit or for cleaning and repair costs.

EXAMPLE: Katie required her tenant Joe to pay a security deposit of one month's rent, plus last month's rent. Her state law allowed a landlord to use all advance deposits to cover a tenant's unpaid rent or damage, regardless of what the landlord called the deposit. When Joe moved out, he didn't owe any back rent, but he left his apartment a shambles. Katie was entitled to use the entire deposit, including that labeled last month's rent, to cover the damage.

Many states restrict the use of money labeled as "last month's rent" to its stated purpose: the rent for the last month of your occupancy. In these states, if you use any of the last month's rent to repair the cabinet the tenant broke, you're violating the law.

EXAMPLE: Mike collected a security deposit of one month's rent, plus last month's rent, from his tenant Amy. Mike's state required that landlords use money collected for the last month as last month's rent only, not for cleaning or repairs. When Amy moved out, she didn't owe any rent but she left her apartment a mess. Mike had to refund Amy's last month's rent and, when the remaining security deposit proved too little to cover the damage Amy had caused, Mike had to sue Amy in small claims court for the excess.

In general, it's a bad idea to call any part of the deposit "last month's rent." Why? Because if your state restricts your use of the money, you've unnecessarily hobbled yourself. And if your state considers last month's rent part of the security deposit, your label is useless anyway. You might even have put yourself at a disadvantage, because you've given the tenant the impression that the last month's rent is taken care of. You would be better off if the tenant paid the last month's rent when it came due, leaving the entire security deposit available to cover cleaning and repairs.

How a Rent Increase Affects Last Month's Rent

Avoiding the term "last month's rent" also keeps things simpler if you raise the rent, but not the deposit, before the tenant's last month of occupancy.

At the end of the term, does the tenant owe you for the difference? If so, can you take money from the tenant's security deposit to make it up?

Unfortunately, there are no clear answers. But because landlords in every state are allowed to ask tenants to top off the last month's rent at the time they increase the rent, judges would probably allow you to go after it at the end of the tenancy, too. Whether you get the difference from your security deposit or sue the tenant in small claims court is somewhat academic.

> **EXAMPLE:** When Rose moved in, the rent was $1000 a month, and she paid this much in advance as last month's rent, plus an additional $1000 security deposit. Over the years the landlord, Artie, has raised the rent to $1,500. Rose does not pay any rent during the last month of her tenancy, figuring that the $1000 she paid up front will cover it. Artie, however, thinks that Rose should pay the $500 difference. Artie and Rose could end up in small claims court fighting over who owes what.

How to Avoid Problems With Last Month's Rent

To minimize confusion and disputes, avoid labeling any part of the security deposit last month's rent and get issues involving last month's rent straight with your tenant at the outset.

Clause 8 of the form agreements in Chapter 2 makes it clear that the tenant may not apply the security deposit to the last month's rent. Even with this type of clause, a tenant who's leaving might ask you to use the security deposit for the last month's rent. Chapter 15 discusses how to handle these types of requests.

Interest and Accounts on Deposit

In many states, you can't just put the tenant's security deposit in your personal bank account—you have to place it in a separate account. And,

depending on your state or local law, you might have to pay interest on the deposit—even if your bank isn't paying *you* any interest.

See "State Security Deposit Rules," in Appendix A, for details on which states have rules regarding interest on and separate accounts for deposits.

Separate Accounts

If your state requires you to keep security deposits separate from your personal or business account, you might have to put the deposit in a "trust" account. Some states require landlords to give tenants information on the location of this separate trust account at the start of the tenancy, usually as part of the lease or rental agreement. The idea is that by isolating these funds, you're more likely to have the money available whenever tenants move out and become entitled to it. In addition, keeping security deposits separate from other funds makes it easier to trace them in the event you face claims of mishandling deposits. You are not required to set up separate accounts for every tenant. If you keep one account, be sure to maintain careful records of each tenant's contribution.

Interest

Several states require landlords to pay tenants interest on security deposits. Even if interest payments aren't legally required, consider offering them as a way to boost relationships with your tenants.

A few states exempt small landlords from having to pay interest. Other states allow landlords to keep any interest earned during the early period of the tenancy.

State laws on interest typically dictate:
- **The rate to be paid.** Usually it's a little lower than what the bank pays, so the landlord's costs and trouble of setting up the account are covered.
- **When payments must be made.** The most common laws require annual payments, as well as a final payment when the tenancy ends.

- **Landlord disclosures.** Many laws require landlords to inform tenants in writing about where and how the security deposit is being held, and the rate of interest.

Chicago, Los Angeles, San Francisco, and several other cities (typically those with rent control) require landlords to pay or credit tenants with interest on security deposits, even when state law does not impose this duty. A few cities require that the funds be kept in separate interest-bearing accounts.

Nonrefundable Deposits and Fees

State laws are often unclear on the subject of nonrefundable deposits and fees. A few states explicitly prohibit landlords from charging any fee or deposit that is not refundable. Some states specifically allow landlords to collect a fee that is not refundable—such as for pets or cleaning (see "State Security Deposit Rules" in Appendix A). While most of these permissive states don't require terms to be spelled out in the lease or rental agreement, it's still a good idea to do so, in order to avoid disputes with your tenant.

The best way to avoid legal uncertainties is to not collect any nonrefundable fees from tenants. It's much simpler just to consider the expenses these fees cover as part of your overhead, and figure them into the rent.

If you have a specific concern about a particular tenant—for example, you're afraid a tenant's pet will damage the carpets or furniture—just ask for a higher security deposit. That way, you're covered if the pet causes damage, and, if it doesn't, the tenant won't have to shell out unnecessarily.

> **CAUTION**
>
> **Don't charge a "redecoration fee" if you're already collecting the maximum allowed security deposit.** A judge is likely to view the redecoration fee as an additional (illegal) security deposit.

How to Increase Deposits

If you rent to a tenant for many years, you might want to increase the amount of the security deposit. The legality of doing this depends on the situation:

- **Leases.** If you have a fixed-term lease, you may not raise the security deposit during the term of the lease, unless the lease allows it. You can increase a security deposit, though, when the lease is renewed or becomes a month-to-month tenancy.
- **Written rental agreements.** With a month-to-month tenancy, you can increase a security deposit the same way you raise the rent, typically by giving the tenant a written notice 30 days in advance of the change. You also have the option of increasing the security deposit without also increasing the rent as long as you don't exceed the maximum legal amount.

 RENT CONTROL

State and local rent control ordinances typically cover your right to raise deposits as well as to raise rents.

Handling Deposits When You Buy or Sell Rental Property

When you sell rental property, what should you do with the deposits you've already collected? When tenants move out after the sale, who owes them the money? In most states, whoever happens to be the landlord at the time a tenancy ends is legally responsible for complying with state security deposit laws. That means that you might need to hand over the deposits to the new owner. Read your state's statutes carefully to learn how to handle this transfer, and note any requirements that tenants be notified of the new owner's name, address, and phone number.

If you buy rental property, make sure you get accurate and complete records of how much you're acquiring in security deposits, and how much is allocated to each tenant.

Discrimination

FORMS IN THIS CHAPTER

Chapter 5 includes instructions for and a sample of the following form:

- Verification of Disabled Status

The purchase of this book includes a free downloadable and customizable copy of this form. See Appendix B for the download link and instructions.

So that all Americans would have the right to live where they chose, Congress and state legislatures passed laws prohibiting housing discrimination. Most notable of these are the federal Fair Housing Acts, which outlaw discrimination based on race or color, national origin, religion, sex, familial status, or disability. Many states and cities have laws making it illegal to discriminate based on additional factors, such as marital status or sexual orientation. Courts play a role, too, by interpreting and applying antidiscrimination laws.

The discussion in this chapter is intended not only to explain the law, but to steer you away from hidden discrimination traps. It explains:

- protected categories (such as race and religion) identified by federal and state laws prohibiting housing discrimination
- precautions to ensure that managers don't violate housing discrimination laws
- legal penalties for housing discrimination, including tenant lawsuits in state and federal courts, and
- whether your insurance policy is likely to cover the cost of defending a discrimination claim, and the cost of the judgment if you lose the case.

RELATED TOPIC

Chapter 1 also discusses how to avoid discrimination in advertising your property, accepting applications, and screening potential tenants, as well as how to document why you chose—or rejected—a particular tenant.

Sources of Antidiscrimination Laws

This section reviews the following sources of antidiscrimination laws:

- the federal Fair Housing Act of 1968 and the federal Fair Housing Amendments Act of 1988 (throughout this chapter, we refer to these laws collectively as the FHA)
- the 1866 Civil Rights Act, and
- state and local antidiscrimination laws.

The Federal Fair Housing Acts

The Fair Housing Act and Fair Housing Amendments Act (42 U.S.C. §§ 3601–3619, 3631), which are enforced by the U.S. Department of Housing and Urban Development (HUD), address many types of housing discrimination. They apply to all aspects of the landlord-tenant relationship throughout the United States.

Types of Discrimination Prohibited

The FHA prohibits discrimination on the following grounds (called protected categories):

- race or color or religion
- national origin
- familial status—includes families with children under the age of 18 and pregnant women and elderly persons
- disability or handicap, and
- sex.

Although the FHA uses certain words to describe illegal discrimination (such as "national origin"), HUD's and the courts' enforcement is not limited to the precise language used in the FHA. For instance, sexual harassment is a form of illegal discrimination on the basis of sex—even though the term "sexual harassment" is not used in the text of the law itself.

Aspects of Landlord-Tenant Relationship Covered

The FHA essentially prohibits landlords from taking any of the following actions:

- indicating a bias against or preference for any protected category in advertising
- falsely telling a member of a protected class that no rentals are available
- using more restrictive criteria to screen applicants in protected categories
- refusing to rent to people in certain protected groups
- before or during the tenancy, setting different terms, conditions, or privileges for rental of a dwelling unit, such as requiring larger

deposits of some tenants, or adopting an inconsistent policy of responding to late rent payments

- during the tenancy, providing different housing services or facilities, such as making a community center or other common area available only to selected tenants, or
- terminating a tenancy because a tenant is a member of a protected category.

How Fair Housing Groups Uncover Discrimination

Landlords who turn away prospective tenants on the basis of race, ethnic background, or other group characteristics rarely come out and admit what they're doing. More often, a landlord falsely tells a person who's a member of a racial minority that no rentals are available, or that the prospective tenant's income and credit history aren't good enough.

From a legal point of view, this is a dangerous—and potentially expensive—tactic. Here's why: Fair housing groups (often backed by HUD) as well as the U.S. Department of Justice, are adept at uncovering these ruses by having "testers" apply to landlords for vacant housing. Typically, a tester who is African-American or Hispanic will fill out a rental application, listing certain occupational, income, and credit information. Then, a white tester will apply for the same housing, listing information very similar to—or sometimes not as good as—that given by the minority applicant.

A landlord who offers to rent to a white tester, and rejects—without valid reason—a minority applicant who has the same (or better) qualifications, is very likely to be found to be guilty of discrimination. Such incidents have resulted in many hefty lawsuit settlements. You can avoid the morass of legal liability for discrimination by adopting tenant screening policies that don't discriminate, and applying them evenhandedly.

An individual who suspects discrimination can file a complaint with HUD or a state or local fair housing agency, or sue in federal or state court. Guests of tenants can also sue landlords for housing discrimination under the FHA. (*Lane v. Cole*, 88 F.Supp.2d 402 (E.D. Pa., 2000).) (Landlords are always free, however, to impose reasonable restrictions on guest stays.)

CAUTION

Failure to stop a tenant from making discriminatory or harassing comments to another tenant might also get you into legal trouble. If one tenant reports that another is making ethnic or racial slurs or threatening violence because of their race, religion, ethnicity, or other characteristic that is considered a protected category, act promptly. If an oral warning doesn't stop the problem, you'll want to follow up with a warning letter (see Chapter 16 for advice on writing warning letters). Also, depending on the situation, you might be able to evict the offending tenant for violating your lease or rental agreement's "quiet enjoyment of the premises" clause. If you're reasonably worried about violence or the threat of violence, you'll need to act quickly and call the police. As with all tenant complaints, keep good records of conversations and correspondence related to the matter. Such documentation is necessary in the event you have to defend yourself against a tenant complaint that you acted illegally by failing to stop discrimination or harassment or that you illegally evicted the harassing tenant.

Exempt Property

The following types of property are exempt from the federal ban against discrimination in housing, as long as their rental is accomplished without the use of discriminatory advertising (42 U.S.C. §§ 3603(b), 3607):

- owner-occupied buildings with four or fewer units (this is called the "Mrs. Murphy" exemption)

- single-family housing, as long as the owner owns no more than three such houses at any one time
- certain types of housing operated by religious organizations and private clubs that limit occupancy to their own members, and
- with respect to age discrimination only, housing geared toward seniors. See "Seniors' Housing," below.

Seniors' Housing

If you have a multifamily property and decide you'd like to rent exclusively to seniors, you can do so as long as you follow federal guidelines. You have two options:

1. **80% of the units must have at least one occupant who is 55 or older.** You must make it known to the public, through your advertising, that you offer senior housing, and must verify applicants' ages. Once you've reached the 80% mark, you can set any other age restriction as long as it does not violate any state or local bans on age discrimination. For example, you could require the remaining 20% of tenants to be over 18 years of age, as long as no state or local law forbids such a policy.

OR:

2. **All of your residents must be 62 or older.** This includes spouses and adult children, but excludes caregivers and on-site employees.

CAUTION

State and local laws might cover federally exempt units. Even if your property is exempt under federal law, similar state or local anti-housing-discrimination laws might nevertheless cover your rental units. For example, owner-occupied buildings with four or fewer units are exempt under federal law, but not under California law.

More Information From HUD and State Agencies

For more information about the FHA, free copies of federal fair housing posters, and technical assistance on accessibility requirements, contact HUD's Office of Fair Housing and Equal Opportunity (FHEO). FHEO's website has a wealth of information at www. hud.gov/program_offices/fair_housing_equal_opp. You can also call the agency's Housing Discrimination Hotline at 800-669-9777 (or 800-927-9275 TTY).

FHEO's website also contains information about how to contact state and local fair housing agencies; you'll find contact information under the "FHEO Programs and Initiatives" tab.

The 1866 Civil Rights Act

Passed at the end of the Civil War, the 1866 Civil Rights Act also bans discrimination in housing on the basis of a person's race or color. (42 U.S.C. § 1981.) Importantly, unlike the federal Fair Housing Acts, the Civil Rights Act does not exempt the "Mrs. Murphy" situation, in which the owner lives on premises that consist of four or fewer units. This means that all landlords, no matter the size of their properties or whether they live in them, may not lawfully discriminate for or against someone on the basis of race or color.

State and Local Antidiscrimination Laws

Most state and local housing laws echo federal antidiscrimination law: They outlaw discrimination based on race or color, national origin, religion, familial status, disability, and sex. (If your state law doesn't track federal law group by group, it makes little difference—you're still bound by the more-inclusive federal law.) But state and local laws often forbid additional kinds of discrimination, such as discrimination based on marital status, sexual orientation, or military status.

Display Fair Housing Posters in Rental Office

Federal regulations require you to put up special fair housing posters wherever you normally conduct housing-related business. You must display a HUD-approved poster saying that you rent apartments in accordance with federal fair housing law (24 Code of Federal Regulations (CFR) §§ 110 and following). Many state laws have similar requirements.

Hang the fair housing posters in a prominent spot in the office or area where you greet prospective tenants and take applications. If you have a model apartment, it's a smart idea to hang a poster there, too. To get free posters (available in English and Spanish) contact HUD.

Types of Illegal Discrimination

In this section, we'll look at some of the categories of illegal discrimination and explore their obvious—and sometimes not-so-obvious—meanings. You'll find the following categories covered here:

- race, color, or religion
- national origin
- familial status
- disability
- sex and sexual harassment
- age
- marital status
- sexual orientation and gender identity/expression
- source of income, and
- arbitrary discrimination.

Keep in mind that your state or local laws might prohibit additional forms of discrimination not covered here.

Race, Color, or Religion

Racial and religious housing discrimination is often subtle, as the amount of overt discrimination has lessened over the last several decades. Unfortunately, both forms still occur.

Most landlords honestly believe that they would never engage in illegal discrimination. However, a significant percentage of all discrimination cases start with landlords who are unaware of how their unconscious personal biases can ultimately result in harmful—and illegal—actions. We'll discuss some examples of both intentional and unintentional discrimination here. Learning how certain actions have led to claims of discrimination can bring awareness to your own practices, and help you avoid getting yourself into a sticky situation.

Intentional, Subtle Discrimination

Overtly treating tenants differently because of their race or religion—for example, advertising that you'll accept only renters who belong to a certain religion—is clearly illegal. Less direct, subtle forms of intentional discrimination, such as that discussed in the examples below, are just as illegal as blatant discrimination. Consider the following scenarios.

EXAMPLE 1: Creekside Apartments received several applications for a 2-bedroom apartment vacancy. In an effort to narrow down the field of applicants, the property manager skimmed the applications, looking quickly at only the names and current addresses listed. He moved applications from Maria Gonzalez, Javier de Jesus, and Reza Ibim into the "reject" pile. By making a decision based solely on the applicant's names (and apparently their race), the manager is likely engaging in illegal discrimination. If HUD were investigating this matter, it would look at the manager's files to see if there is a pattern of rejections based on the apparent race or national origin of the applicants.

EXAMPLE 2: Apex Property Management advertises current apartment vacancies in the window of its office on Main Street. Anureet Singh stepped into the office to apply for an apartment he saw posted. When he approached the agent inside, she exclaimed that she'd just rented the unit—she'd just forgotten to remove the listing sheet from the window. Anureet walked by the office the next week and saw the listing still up. He suspects that the agent lied about the status after seeing his turban. When Anureet filed a complaint with his state's fair housing agency, he learned that he was not the first member of a protected class to be lied to about a vacancy.

> ! **CAUTION**
>
> **Don't discriminate on the basis of how applicants sound over the phone.** Academic studies have shown that people can often identify a person's ethnic background based on short phone conversations. Researchers have tested this theory on unsuspecting landlords, some of whom rejected large numbers of qualified Black applicants (when compared to the number of times they rejected equally qualified non-Black callers). Fair housing advocacy groups, described in "How Fair Housing Groups Uncover Discrimination," above, sometimes compare a landlord's reaction to Black and non-Black undercover callers in an effort to weed out this form of discrimination.

Unintended Discrimination

In Chapter 1, we discussed the unintended discriminatory messages that are conveyed when advertisements feature statements such as "safe Christian community" or "Sunday quiet times enforced." (Both ads might be interpreted as suggesting that only Christians are welcome as tenants.) The same considerations apply to your dealings with your tenants after they have moved in. Conscientious landlords should carefully review tenant rules, signs, newsletters, and all communications to make sure that they cannot be construed in any way to benefit, support, or discriminate against any racial or religious group.

The examples and advice we give below are based on actual fair housing complaints and deserve to be taken seriously:

- The apartment complex newsletter invites everyone to a "Christmas party" held by the management. Non-Christian tenants might feel that this event is not intended for them and therefore that they have been discriminated against. A better approach: Call it a "Holiday Party."

- Management allows tenants to use the common club room for "birthday parties, anniversaries, and Christmas and Easter parties." A better idea: Invite your tenants to use the common room for special celebrations, rather than list specific Christian holidays.

- In an effort to accommodate your Spanish-speaking tenants, you translate your move-in letter and house rules into Spanish. Regarding the use of alcohol in the common areas, the Spanish version begins, "Unlike Mexico, where drinking is practiced in public places, alcoholic beverages may not be consumed in common areas…." Because to many people this phrase implies an ethnic generalization (not to mention the fact that it ignores the fact many Spanish speakers come from countries other than Mexico), it could become the basis for a fair housing complaint.

- The metropolitan area where you own residential rental property contains large numbers of both Spanish-speaking and Cantonese-speaking people. Advertising only in Spanish, or translating your lease only into Cantonese, and stating that you prefer to rent to people who speak that language, could constitute a fair housing violation because it likely indicates a preference for renters of a certain race.

National Origin

Like discrimination based on race or religion, discrimination based on national origin is illegal, no matter the intent.

When you choose tenants in a way that singles out people of a particular nationality, you are illegally discriminating—even if your reason for doing so is purportedly based on business considerations. For example, deciding to conduct credit checks only on people from Mexico based on the fact that two tenants from Mexico recently failed to pay rent is illegal. Creating different screening policies for persons from certain countries is just one example of a national-origin-based policy that will get you in trouble.

On the other hand, if you create screening policies that require all prospective tenants to consent to a credit check (and to meet any other objective criteria as discussed above), you will get the information you need to make wise business decisions in a nondiscriminatory way.

Discriminatory comments and behavior—not just policies—can get you in trouble, too, as one New York landlord learned the hard way. The landlord told a Honduran applicant that she couldn't rent an apartment because "Spanish people … like to have loud music." The applicant sued the landlord for the discriminatory statement. A federal court ordered the landlord to pay $24,847 in damages: $7,000 to compensate her for her losses; $9,736 for attorneys' fees; $2,111 for court costs; and $6,000 to penalize the landlord for making the discriminatory comment. (*Gonzales v. Rakkas*, 1995 WL 451034 (E.D. N.Y., 1995).)

TIP

If you ask one person a question, ask everyone. It cannot be emphasized enough that questions on a prospective tenant's legal status must be put to all applicants, not just the ones whom you suspect are illegal, and not just the ones who are applying to live in one of your buildings in a certain part of town.

Discrimination on the Basis of Immigration Status

Landlords often ask whether it's legal to refuse to rent to people residing in the United States illegally. In other words, can landlords require tenants to demonstrate that they are citizens, permanent residents, visa holders, or otherwise here legally?

Landlords refusing to rent to illegal residents might have legitimate business reasons for their policy. For example, they might believe that people without legal status are more likely to move suddenly and break a lease, due to being deported or having concerns about being apprehended.

However, requiring verification from only some applicants is almost always an instance of race, color, or national origin discrimination. When landlords require documentation from only applicants whom they suspect are in the United States illegally, they're usually making a call based on the applicant's skin color, accent, or other characteristic that suggests foreign origins. And therein lies the problem.

HUD has addressed this issue with great care. Because "immigration status" is not a protected category under the federal fair housing laws, it is not illegal to require that all applicants provide "identity documents" to meet rental criteria (which, presumably, can include legal residency). However, HUD states that "a person's ability to pay rent or fitness as a tenant is not necessarily connected to his or her immigration status." (See HUD's publication titled, "Immigration Status and Housing Discrimination Frequently Asked Questions") And HUD makes it very clear that landlords cannot require only certain applicants to supply residence verification—they must require it from all applicants.

Familial Status

Discrimination on the basis of familial status typically occurs when landlords want to prevent children from living in a rental. For example, some landlords might refuse to rent to families with children or to pregnant women. Familial status discrimination can also be more subtle—for example, when landlords set overly restrictive occupancy rules (limiting the maximum number of people permitted to occupy a rental unit), thereby preventing families with children from occupying smaller units.

We discuss how to establish reasonable occupancy standards later in this chapter. The fact that you can legally adopt occupancy standards, however, doesn't mean you can use "overcrowding" as a euphemism for refusing to rent to tenants with children, if you would rent to the same number of adults. A few landlords have adopted criteria that for all practical purposes forbid children under the guise of preventing overcrowding—for example, allowing only one person per bedroom, with a couple counting as one person. Under these criteria, a landlord would rent a two-bedroom unit to a husband and wife and their one child, but would not rent the same unit to a mother with two children. This practice, which has the effect of keeping all (or most) children out of a landlord's property, would surely be found illegal in court and would result in monetary penalties.

It is also illegal to restrict where children can live. For example, rules prohibiting children from occupying certain floors of an apartment building, or designating certain apartments or buildings within an apartment community as "family" units, would constitute familial status discrimination.

It is essential to maintain a consistent occupancy policy. If you allow three adults to live in a two-bedroom apartment, you need to allow a couple with a child (or a single mother with two children) to live in the same type of unit. Otherwise, tenants (or rejected applicants) might have a strong argument that you are illegally discriminating.

> **EXAMPLE:** Jackson owned and managed two identical one-bedroom units in a duplex, one of which he rented out to three flight attendants who were rarely there at the same time. When the other unit became vacant, Jackson advertised it as a one-bedroom, two-person apartment. Harry and Sue Jones and their teenage daughter were turned away because they exceeded Jackson's occupancy limit of two people. The Jones family, learning that the companion unit was rented to three people, filed a complaint with HUD, whose investigator questioned Jackson regarding the inconsistency of his occupancy policy. Jackson realized that his policy was discriminatory, and agreed to rent to the Jones family and to compensate them for the humiliation they had suffered as a result of being refused.

Finally, do not inquire as to the age and sex of any children who will be sharing the same bedroom. This is their parents' business, not yours.

Disability

The FHA prohibits discrimination against people who:

- have a physical or mental disability that substantially limits one or more major life activities—including, but not limited to, hearing, mobility and visual impairments, chronic alcoholism (but only if it is being addressed through a recovery program), mental illness, HIV positive, AIDS, AIDS-Related Complex, and intellectual disability
- have a history or record of such a disability, or
- are regarded by others as though they have such a disability.

The law also protects those who are "associated with" someone who has a disability, such as a family member, cotenant, or caregiver who lives with the tenant or makes house visits.

It isn't always easy to determine what is—and what is not—considered a disability. For example, alcoholism is classed as a protected disability. Does this mean that you must rent to all people who suffer from alcohol addiction? What about past, and current, drug addiction? Let's look at each of these issues.

Recovering Alcoholics

You might encounter an applicant, let's call him Ted, who passes all your tenant selection criteria, but whose personal history includes a disquieting note: Employers and past landlords let you know that Ted has a serious drinking problem that he is dealing with by attending AA meetings. As far as you can tell, Ted has not lost a job or a place to live due to his drinking problem. Can you refuse to rent to Ted for fear that he will drink away the rent, exhibit loud or inappropriate behavior, or damage your property?

No, you can't—unless you can point to specific acts of misbehavior or financial shakiness that would sink any applicant, regardless of the underlying cause. Your fear about Ted's potential for bad behavior alone is not a legal reason to refuse to rent to him.

In a nutshell, an applicant's status as what HUD calls a "recovering alcoholic" cannot be your sole reason for turning the person away.

> **EXAMPLE:** Patsy applied for an apartment one morning and spoke with Carol, the manager. Patsy said she would have to return that afternoon to complete the application form because she was due at her regular Alcoholics Anonymous meeting. Carol decided on the spot that she did not want Patsy for a tenant, and she told Patsy that the unit "had just been rented," which was a lie. (Patsy continued to see the unit advertised online.) Patsy filed a complaint with HUD, alleging that she was an alcoholic who had been discriminated against. Because Carol could not point to any reason for turning Patsy away other than her assumption that Patsy, as a recovering alcoholic, would be a bad tenant, the judge awarded Patsy several thousand dollars in damages.

Unfortunately, HUD has not been very helpful in explaining what steps an alcoholic must take in order to qualify as "recovering." Regular attendance at AA meetings and counseling probably qualify, but an alcoholic who is less conscientious might not make the grade. So how can you choose tenants without risking a violation of law?

The answer lies in putting your energies into thorough reference checking that will yield information that can unquestionably support a rejection at the rental office. If the applicant, recovering or not, is truly a bad risk, you'll discover facts (like job firings, bad credit, or past rental property damage) independent of the thorny problem of whether the person has entered the "recovery" stage of alcoholism.

If you suspect a current tenant is an alcoholic, use the same approach: Focus on the tenant's objective behavior, regardless of whether it's caused by intoxication. You are entitled to terminate any tenancy—regardless of the tenant's status—if the tenant damages your property, doesn't pay rent, or otherwise violates the lease.

> **EXAMPLE:** Same facts as above, except that Carol went ahead and took an application from Patsy later that day and checked her references. Patsy's former landlord told Carol that Patsy had refused to pay for damage from a fire she had negligently caused. On top of that, Patsy's employment history showed a pattern of short-lived jobs and decreasing wages. Carol noted this information on Patsy's application form and, as she would have done for any applicant with a similar background, Carol rejected Patsy. Patsy filed a complaint with HUD, again claiming discrimination on the basis of her alcoholism. When the HUD investigator asked to see Patsy's application and questioned Carol about her application criteria for all applicants, he concluded that the rejection had been based on legally sound business reasons and was not, therefore, a fair housing violation.

Drug Users

Under the FHA, having a past drug addiction is considered a disability. Therefore, you cannot discriminate against applicants or tenants on the basis that they used to be addicted to drugs—even if they have felony convictions for drug use. Put another way, it's illegal to reject an applicant based on your fear that the person will resume using illegal drugs. However, if your screening reveals a rental or employment history that would disqualify any applicant, you can reject the person for that reason.

On the other hand, someone who currently uses illegal drugs is breaking the law. Current illegal activity is a legitimate, nondiscriminatory basis for refusing an applicant.

A history of selling or manufacturing illegal drugs is also a legal reason to reject an applicant. For example, if the applicant has felony convictions for dealing or manufacturing illegal drugs (rather than just convictions for possession of drugs for personal use), you can use that history as a basis of refusal.

Mental or Emotional Impairments

Applicants and tenants who had, or have (or appear to have) mental or emotional impairments are protected by fair housing laws. Landlords cannot reject applicants because of their mental health status. Unless you can point to specific instances of past behavior that would disqualify any applicant regardless of mental health, such as assaults on tenants or destruction of property, a refusal to rent or a special requirement such as cosigner on the lease could result in a fair housing complaint.

No "Approved List" of Disabilities

The FHA protects persons with physical and mental disabilities of all sorts—even disabilities that are not readily apparent to others. For example, discriminating against someone who is HIV positive on the basis of their illness is illegal.

The list of disabilities covered by the law is not, however, definitive. For example, tenants with hypertension (which can lead to more serious medical problems) have been known to ask for protection under the fair housing laws, as have tenants suffering from "building material sensitivity" (sensitivities to vapors emitted from paint, upholstery, and rugs).

Similarly, tenants who have a sensitivity or problem that is widespread throughout the population, such as asthma or allergies, might also win coverage under the fair housing laws. What might seem to you like an individual's hypochondria or personal quirk might become a legally recognized disability if tested in court.

Contact your local HUD office to find out whether the courts have extended fair housing protections to a situation you're dealing with.

Questions and Actions to Avoid

Unfortunately, even the most innocuous, well-meaning question or remark can get you into trouble, especially if you decide not to rent to the person. What you might consider polite conversation can be interpreted as a probing question designed to discourage an applicant.

> **EXAMPLE:** Sam, an Iraq War veteran, was the owner of Belleview Apartments. Jim, who appeared to be the same age as Sam and who used a wheelchair, applied for an apartment. Thinking that Jim might have been injured in the Iraq War, Sam questioned Jim about the circumstances of his disability, intending only to pass the time and put Jim at ease. When Jim was not offered the apartment—he did not meet the financial criteria that Sam applied to all applicants—he filed a complaint with HUD, alleging discrimination based on his disability. Sam was unable to convince the HUD investigator that his questions were not intended to be discriminatory, and, on the advice of his attorney, Sam settled the case for several thousand dollars.

Your well-intentioned actions, as well as your words, can become the basis of a fair housing complaint. You are not allowed to "steer" applicants to units that you, however innocently, think would be more appropriate. For example, if you have two units for rent—one on the ground floor and one three stories up—do not fail to offer to show both units to the applicant who is movement impaired, however reasonable you think it would be for the person to consider only the ground floor unit.

The Rights of Tenants With Disabilities to Enter and Live in an Accessible Place

The physical layout of your leasing office and other areas open to the public (where applicants will go to inquire about vacancies, for example) must be wheelchair accessible.

You also have legal responsibilities towards tenants with disabilities. Under the FHA, landlords must:

- make **accommodations** for the needs of tenants with disabilities, at the landlord's own expense (42 U.S.C. § 3604(f)(3)(B)), and
- allow tenants with disabilities to make reasonable **modifications** of their living unit or common areas at their expense if that is what is needed for the person to comfortably and safely live in the unit. (42 U.S.C. § 3604(f)(3)(A).)

We'll look briefly at each of these requirements.

Accommodations. You are expected to adjust your rules, procedures, or services in order to give a person with a disability an equal opportunity to use and enjoy a dwelling unit or a common space. Frequently, landlords make accommodations regarding:

- parking—if you provide tenants with parking, provide a close-in, spacious parking space for a tenant who uses a wheelchair
- service or companion animals—allowing a guide dog, hearing dog, or service dog in a residence that otherwise disallows pets
- rent payment—crafting a unique rent payment plan for a tenant whose finances are managed by someone else or by a government agency
- communications—arranging to read all communications from management to a blind tenant, and
- phobias—for example, providing a tub and clothesline for a tenant whose clinically diagnosed anxiety about machines makes her unable to use the washer and dryer.

Does your duty to accommodate tenants with disabilities mean that you must bend every rule and change every procedure at the tenant's request? Generally speaking, the answer is no. You are expected to accommodate "reasonable" requests, but need not undertake changes that would seriously impair your ability to run your business (or that would result in a dangerous situation for other residents). For example, if an applicant who uses a wheelchair prefers the third-story apartment in a walk-up building constructed in 1926 to the one on the ground floor, you do not have to rip the building apart to install an elevator.

Modifications. Where your duty to accommodate the needs of tenants with disabilities ends, your obligation to allow the tenant to modify living space likely begins. A person with disabilities has the right to modify the living space to the extent necessary to make it safe and comfortable, as long as the modifications will not make the unit unacceptable to the next tenant. Alternatively, the tenant with a disability can agree to undo the modifications at the end of the tenancy.

Tenants with disabilities don't have the right to modify their units at will, though—you are entitled to ask for a reasonable description of the proposed modifications, proof that they will be done in a professional manner, and evidence that the tenant is obtaining any necessary building permits.

Unless the property is federally financed or is a dwelling with ten or more units located in Massachusetts, tenants must pay for their modifications. (But if your building opened for occupancy on or after March 13, 1991, and the modification is needed because the building doesn't comply with HUD's accessibility requirements (see "New Buildings and Tenants With Disabilities," below), you must pay for the modification.) If a tenant proposes to modify the unit in such a way that will require restoration when the tenant leaves (such as the repositioning of lowered kitchen counters), you can require that the tenant pay into an interest-bearing escrow account the amount estimated for the restoration. (The interest belongs to the tenant.)

Do You Need to Accommodate Tenants With Disabilities Who Are Dangerous?

You do not have to accommodate a tenant with a disability who poses a direct threat to others' safety, or who is likely to commit serious property damage. You must rely on objective evidence, such as current conduct or a recent history of disruptive behavior, before concluding that someone poses a threat. In particular, consider the following:

- The nature, severity, and duration of the risk of injury. For example, someone whose behavior is merely annoying is not as worrisome as someone who is prone to physical confrontations.
- The probability that injury will actually occur. Here, you must take into account the likelihood the person will go too far with their actions.
- Whether there are any reasonable accommodations that will eliminate the direct threat. For example, you might have to change a rule or procedure if doing so will diffuse a high-risk situation.

Making a decision when faced with these situations can be challenging. For example, suppose residents tell you about a tenant who has threatened them with a baseball bat on several occasions. In keeping with your policy to enforce your "no threats" policy, you terminate the tenant's lease. The tenant's lawyer contacts you and suggests that as soon as his client resumes appropriate medication, the behavior will stop. Must you give this a try?

The answer is yes, though you can ask for satisfactory assurance that the tenant will receive appropriate counseling and periodic medication monitoring. To be sure, receiving such assurances, such as periodic letters from counselors or therapists, puts you uncomfortably in the thick of your tenant's personal problems, but there is no other way to meet your obligations to other tenants (to maintain a safe environment). You'd be on solid ground to continue with the termination if the tenant refused to work with you in this way.

CAUTION

Your duty to evaluate any request begins when you learn of it, even if it's oral or communicated through a third party, such as an applicant's friend or family member.

New Buildings and Tenants With Disabilities

The Fair Housing Amendments Act (42 U.S.C. §§ 3604(f)(3)(C) and 3604(f)(7)) imposes requirements on new buildings of four or more units that were first occupied after March 13, 1991. All ground floor units and every unit in an elevator building must be designed or constructed so that:

- There is an accessible route from the public right of way outside the building (such as the sidewalk) to all units and common areas.
- The "primary entrance" of each rental unit is accessible.
- Any stair landing shared by more than one rental unit is handicapped accessible (*U.S. v. Edward Rose & Sons*, 384 F.3d 258 (6th Cir. 2004)).
- The public and common areas are "readily accessible to and usable by" people with disabilities, including parking areas (a good rule of thumb is to reserve 2% of the spaces).
- Entryway doorways have 36" of free space *plus* shoulder and elbow room; and interior doorways are at least 32" wide.
- Interior living spaces have wheelchair-accessible routes throughout, with changes in floor height of no more than ¼".
- Light switches, outlets, thermostats, and other environmental controls are within the legal "reach range" (15" to 48" from the ground).
- Bathroom walls are sufficiently reinforced to allow the safe installation of "grab bars."
- Kitchens and bathrooms are large enough to allow a wheelchair to maneuver within the room (40" turning radius minimum) and have sinks and appliances positioned to allow side or front use.

For more information on accessibility requirements, see HUD's informative website, HUD.gov (search "fair housing accessibility guidelines").

Verification of Disabled Status

When it is obvious that someone has a disability—for example, the person is in a wheelchair or is blind—it is illegal to ask for documentation of the disability or to inquire how severely that person is disabled. But certain disabilities are not observable, particularly those that often form the basis for a request for an emotional support animal. In these instances, landlords may ask for information about the disability and the disability-related need for the animal.

In January 2020, HUD released a guidance memo that addresses how landlords should obtain verification of a person's non-obvious disability. The information you may ask for can include:

- A determination of disability from a federal, state, or local government agency.
- Receipt of disability benefits or services (Social Security Disability Income (SSDI)), Medicare or Supplemental Security Income (SSI) for a person under age 65; veterans' disability benefits, services from a vocational rehabilitation agency, or disability benefits or services from another federal, state, or local agency.
- Eligibility for housing assistance or a housing voucher received because of disability.
- Information confirming disability from a health care professional, such as a physician, optometrist, psychiatrist, psychologist, physician's assistant, nurse practitioner, or nurse. (*FHEO Notice 2020-01*.)

Many prospects and tenants will turn to a health care professional to provide documentation. Although you can certainly leave it up to that professional to provide the written documentation in a letter, you can also give the "Verification of Disabled Status By Health Care Professional" form (see sample below) to your tenants, asking them to give it to their doctors or other professionals. Using this form is a convenient and safe way to elicit the information you need (and keep unwanted details out of the picture). **However, understand that you cannot require your tenants or applicants to use our form (the form's cover sheet makes this clear).** You must, for example, accept a letter written by the health care professional.

Although you cannot require anyone to use our form, offering it is beneficial, because it:

- **Evidences your willingness to entertain the tenant's request.** When you give the form to your tenant, make a dated note in the prospect's or tenant's file. This note might come in handy should you later be accused of discouraging (or even outright denying) the request.
- **Educates the third party as to the legal standard for being considered to have a disability.** By placing the federal definition of "disabled" right on the form, you're reminding the signer of the standard to keep in mind when verifying status.
- **Identifies the precise modification or accommodation.** When you give the form to your tenant, fill in the accommodation or modification that's been requested. If you leave it blank, you risk the insertion of irrelevant or extra requests that you and the tenant have not discussed. Of course, it's possible that the third party will have additional suggestions, and if so, there's room for those suggestions (which will be subject to the same "reasonableness" standard as are all modification and accommodation requests, as explained in "How to Respond to Unreasonable Requests for Accommodations or Modifications," below).
- **Eliminates the chance that the third party will give you details of the tenant's disability.** You don't need these details, and you don't want to know them, either (you never want to enable an accusation of having misused this information). A third party might nevertheless think you require the full picture and might include it in a letter. There's no place on this form for these details.

Give tenants at least ten days to return the form or provide the information in another format.

A sample Verification of Disabled Status By Health Care Professional form is shown below and the Nolo website includes a downloadable copy, including the cover sheet. See Appendix B for the link to the forms in this book.

Verification of Disabled Status by Health Care Professional

Dr. Harold Smith
Health care professional's name

4720 Main Street, Anytown, CA
Address

123-456-7890
Phone number

drhsmith@coldmail.com
Email

May 3, 20xx
Date

Dear ___Roger Jones_____ [*Landlord or manager's name*],

I am a ___licensed medical doctor_____ [*describe health care professional's work or occupation*).

I have a personal and professional relationship involving the provision of health care or disability-related

services with ___Terry Tenant_____ [*patient's name*].

In my opinion, ___Terry Tenant_____ [*patient's name*] is *legally disabled*,

as that term is defined by federal law (Fair Housing Amendments Act, 42 United States Code section 3602(h)):

> A disabled person is someone who
>
> (1) has a physical or mental impairment that substantially limits one
>
> or more of such person's major life activities, or
>
> (2) has a record of having such an impairment, or
>
> (3) is regarded as having such an impairment.

I understand that ___Terry Tenant_____ [*patient's name*] has requested the

following accommodation or modification for your rental property: ___Mr. Tenant would like to live___

___with his support animal, Rex, a 4-year old golden retriever.___

_____ [*describe proposed accommodation or modification*].

To the best of my personal knowledge and consistent with my professional obligations, I can say that this proposed

accommodation or modification is needed in order for___Terry Tenant_____ [*patient's name*]

to live safely and comfortably at the rental premises.

Dr. Harold Smith   May 3, 20xx
Signature   Date

Dr. Harold Smith
Print name

Medical Board of California, License C 80705
Licensing information (if applicable)

How to Respond to Unreasonable Requests for Accommodations or Modifications

The law requires you to agree to "reasonable" requests for accommodations or modifications. You don't have to go along with unreasonable ones, but you can't simply say "No" and shut the door. You must engage in what HUD calls an "interactive process" with the tenant. In essence, this means you have to get together and try to reach an acceptable compromise. For example, suppose you require tenants to pay rent in person at the manager's office. A tenant with a disability asks that the manager collect the rent at her apartment. Because this would leave the office unstaffed, you suggest instead that the tenant mail the rent check. This might be a reasonable compromise.

Assistance Animals: Service Animals and Support Animals (Including Emotional Support Animals)

You might be asked by an applicant or a tenant with a legal disability to allow that person to live with a dog or another assistance animal. In legal lingo, "assistance animals" are either "service animals" or "support animals:"

- **Service animals** are dogs (and miniature horses, if qualified), who are *trained* to do work, perform tasks, or assist persons with disabilities.
- **Support animals** are animals commonly kept in households, such as a dog, cat, small bird, rabbit, hamster, gerbil, other rodent, fish, turtle, or other small, domesticated animal that is traditionally kept in the home for pleasure rather than for commercial purposes. Importantly, reptiles (other than turtles), barnyard animals, monkeys, kangaroos, and other nondomesticated animals are not common household animals (though they can sometimes qualify as helpers, see below). Support animals are trained or *untrained*

animals that do any or all of the following: perform work or tasks, provide assistance, and provide therapeutic emotional support for individuals with disabilities.

These definitions are followed by the federal government (the U.S. Department of Housing and Urban Development). States might have more expansive definitions. You can find HUD's January 2020 complete guidance by searching online for "Assessing a Person's Request to Have an Animal as a Reasonable Accommodation Under the Fair Housing Act."

You are entitled to learn whether the service animal proposed by your applicant or tenant has been trained to deliver the required assistance. In the case of a service dog, it's often apparent, as when the dog provides assistance to someone who is visually impaired, or pulls a wheelchair, or provides assistance with stability. If the help is not apparent, you may ask what work the animal has been trained to perform. As for support animals, emotional and otherwise, you are entitled to ask for information that shows that the animal does work, performs tasks, provides assistance, or provides therapeutic emotional support that is related to the person's disability.

In rare situations, animals that are not commonly kept in households can qualify as assistance animals. For example, a health care professional might certify that a trained capuchin monkey, who can retrieve items from a refrigerator and serve them to the tenant, is unique and provides substantial support not possible from a dog. When dealing with unique, noncommon animals, you may ask that the health care professional inform you of:

- the date of the tenant's last consultation
- any unique circumstances justifying the tenant's need for the particular animal(s), and
- whether the provider has reliable information about this specific animal or whether the provider specifically recommended this type of animal.

Tenants might attempt to satisfy the requirement that they provide proof of training by showing you a "certificate" that they obtained online, supposedly attesting to the animal's qualifications as a service or support animal. HUD's January 2020 guidance states that attestations purchased online, without more, will not provide proof of training. The notice acknowledges, on the other hand, that many legitimate therapists deliver services via the internet.

Fraudulent Assistance Animal Claims

Well over half the states make it a crime to fraudulently claim that an animal is an assistance animal in an area of public accommodation (such as a restaurant or shop). When it comes to fraudulent claims in housing, only a handful have similar laws, but the number has been growing (those states include California, Florida, Indiana, Kentucky, Missouri, North Dakota, Oklahoma, Pennsylvania, South Dakota, and Tennessee). For more information, search online for "States with Laws on Fraudulent Assistance Animals."

Sex and Sexual Harassment

You may not refuse to rent to a person on the basis of gender—for example, you cannot refuse to rent to a single woman solely because she is female. Neither may you impose special rules on people because of their gender—for example, limiting upper-story apartments to single females.

Illegal sex discrimination also includes sexual harassment. Sexual harassment in housing usually takes one of the following two forms:

- **Hostile environment.** A pattern of persistent, unwanted attention of a sexual nature, including the making of sexual remarks and physical advances, or a single instance of highly egregious behavior. A manager's persistent requests for social contact, or constant remarks concerning a tenant's appearance or behavior, could constitute sexual harassment, as could a single extraordinarily offensive remark.

- **Quid pro quo.** A situation in which a tenant's rights are conditioned upon the acceptance of the owner's or manager's attentions. For example, a manager who refuses to fix the plumbing until the tenant agrees to a date is guilty of sexual harassment. Just one incident of this type can establish harassment.

EXAMPLE: Oscar, the resident manager of Northside Apartments, was attracted to Martha, his tenant, and asked her repeatedly for a date. Martha always turned Oscar down and asked that he leave her alone. Oscar didn't back off, and began hanging around the pool whenever Martha used it. Oscar watched Martha intently and made suggestive remarks about her to the other tenants. Martha stopped using the pool and filed a sexual harassment complaint with HUD, claiming that Oscar's unwanted attentions made it impossible for her to use and enjoy the pool and even to comfortably live at Northside. Oscar refused to consider a settlement when the HUD investigator spoke to him and Martha about his actions. As a result, HUD pursued the case in court, where a federal judge ordered Oscar to leave Martha alone and awarded several thousand dollars in damages to Martha.

> **CAUTION**
> **Sexual harassment awards under the Civil Rights Acts have no limits.** Owners and managers who engage in sexual harassment risk being found liable under either the FHA or Title VII of the 1964 Civil Rights Act, which also prohibits sexual discrimination. The Fair Housing Act limits the dollar amount of damages that can be levied against the defendant, but there are no limits to the amount of punitive damages that can be awarded in Title VII actions. Punitive damages are generally not covered by insurance, and it is far from clear whether even actual damages in a discrimination case (that is, nonpunitive damages such as pain and suffering) will be covered, either.

Age

Although the federal fair housing laws don't expressly use the word "age," discrimination on the basis of age is included within the ban against discrimination on the basis of familial status. Additionally, many states and localities have laws that directly ban age discrimination.

Can you, as the landlord, refuse to rent to an older person solely because you fear that the person's frailty or dimming memory will pose a threat to the health or safety of the rest of your tenants? Or, can you favor younger tenants over equally qualified elderly tenants because you would like your property to have a youthful appearance?

The answer to these questions is no. Unless you can point to an actual incident or to facts that will substantiate your concern, you cannot reject an elderly applicant on the basis of your fears alone. For example, you could turn away an older applicant if you learned from a prior landlord or employer that the person regularly forgot to lock the doors or pay rent, or demonstrated an inability to undertake basic housekeeping chores. In other words, if the applicant has demonstrated an inability to live alone, your regular and thorough background check should supply you with those facts, which are legally defensible reasons to refuse to rent.

As for your stylistic preference for youthful tenants, this is age discrimination in its purest form, and it will never survive a fair housing complaint.

EXAMPLE: Nora's 80-year-old mother Ethel decided that it was time to find a smaller place and move closer to her daughter. Ethel sold her home and applied for a one-bedroom apartment at Coral Shores. Ethel had impeccable references from neighbors and employers and an outstanding credit history. Nonetheless, Mike, the manager of Coral Shores, was concerned about Ethel's age. Fearful that Ethel might forget to turn off the stove, lose her key, or do any number of other dangerous things, Mike decided on the spot not to rent to her. Ethel filed a fair housing complaint, which she won on the basis of age discrimination.

Learning from his experience with Ethel, Mike, the manager at Coral Shores, became more conscientious in screening tenants. The following example shows how he avoided another lawsuit on age discrimination.

EXAMPLE: William was an elderly gentleman who decided to sell the family home and rent an apartment after his wife passed away. He applied for an apartment at Coral Shores. Since William had no "prior rental history," Mike, the manager, drove to William's old neighborhood and spoke with several of his former neighbors. Mike also called William's personal references. From these sources, Mike learned that William had been unable to take care of himself the last few years, having been completely dependent on his wife. Mike also learned that, since his wife's death, William had made several desperate calls to neighbors and family when he had been unable to extinguish a negligently started kitchen fire, find his keys, and maintain basic levels of cleanliness in his house. Mike noted these findings on William's application and declined to rent to him on the basis of these specific facts.

The issue of age discrimination might also arise during a well-established tenancy, such as a tenant who has lived alone competently for years but who, with advancing age, appears to be gradually losing the ability to live alone safely.

Renting to Minors

You might wonder whether the prohibition against age discrimination applies to minors (in most states, people under age 18). A minor applicant who is legally "emancipated"—is legally married, or has a court order of emancipation or is in the military—has the same status as an adult. This means you will need to treat the applicant like any other adult. In short, if the applicant satisfies the rental criteria that you apply to everyone, a refusal to rent to a minor could form the basis of a fair housing complaint. On the other hand, an applicant who is not emancipated lacks the legal capacity to enter into a legally binding rental agreement with you.

You cannot take action merely on the basis of the person's age or because you fear what that person might do. You must be able to point to real, serious violations of the criteria that apply to all tenants before you can evict or take action against an elderly tenant.

> **CAUTION**
>
> **Elderly tenants might also qualify as disabled tenants, who are entitled to accommodation under the law.** An elderly tenant who, because of her age, cannot meet one of your policies might be entitled to special treatment because she also qualifies as a disabled person. In other words, just because an elderly tenant cannot abide by one of the terms of the tenancy does not mean you can evict her. Rather, you might be required to adjust your policy in order to accommodate her disability. For example, an elderly tenant who is chronically late with the rent because of her sporadic disorientation might be entitled to a grace period, or a friendly reminder when the rent is due; whereas a nondisabled tenant who is chronically late with the rent is not entitled to such special treatment. And if an elderly tenant can't negotiate the stairs, the legal solution is a ramp (assuming the cost is not unreasonable), not an eviction notice.

Marital Status

Federal law does not prohibit discrimination on the basis of marital status (oddly, being married isn't included within the federal concept of "familial status"). Consequently, in most states you can legally refuse to rent to applicants on the grounds that they are (or are not) married. The issue comes up when a landlord chooses a married couple over a single applicant, or when an unmarried couple applies for a rental (or a current tenant wants to move in a romantic partner).

Some states have addressed these situations. About half the states, plus the District of Columbia ban discrimination on the basis of marital status, but most of these extend protection to married couples only. In these states, landlords cannot legally prefer single, platonic roommates (or one-person tenancies)

over married couples. What about the reverse—preferring married couples over single roommates or a single tenant? Courts in some states, such as Maryland, Minnesota, New York, and Wisconsin, have ruled that the term "marital status" only protects married people from being treated differently from single people, not vice versa.

Now then, what about the remaining possibility—an unmarried couple? Only a few states—such as Alaska, California, Massachusetts, Michigan, and New Jersey—protect unmarried couples under the umbrella of "marital status." If you own rental property in these states, can you reject unmarried couples solely because they aren't married? It depends on your reasons. For example, if you refuse to rent to unmarried couples on the grounds that cohabitation violates your religious beliefs, the answer is no.

> **TIP**
>
> **Local ordinances prohibiting discrimination on the basis of sexual orientation might protect unmarried couples.** Although usually passed to protect the housing rights of gay and lesbian tenants, most city and county laws forbidding discrimination based on sexual orientation also protect unmarried heterosexual couples. In addition, unmarried people might be able to challenge a landlord's refusal to rent to them on the basis of sex discrimination, which is covered by the FHA.

Sexual Orientation and Gender Identity/Expression

The federal fair housing laws do not ban discrimination on the basis of sexual orientation or gender identity or expression. However, their ban on discrimination on the basis of sex can apply when landlords make decisions based on notions of gender conformity—regardless of the orientation or identity of the tenant or applicant. For example, a landlord's rejection of a prospective tenant because she wears traditionally masculine clothes and engages in other physical expressions that are typically male might qualify as discrimination on the basis of sex.

Several states do address discrimination on the basis of orientation and identity/expression, banning both or only sexual orientation. For a comprehensive list (and other information), search for "identifying as LGBTQ" on HUD.gov. Many cities also forbid these practices; contact your city attorney's office for information.

Source of Income

In several states, including California, Colorado, Connecticut, the District of Columbia, Maine, Massachusetts, New Jersey, New York, North Dakota, Oklahoma, Oregon, Utah, Vermont, and Washington (subject to some conditions), you may not refuse to rent to applicants based simply on their receipt of public assistance (many localities in other states have similar law). You may, however, refuse to rent to persons whose available incomes fall below a certain level, as long as you apply that standard across the board.

Understand that the prohibition against discriminating on the basis of source of income does not necessarily mean that you must participate in the Section 8 program. In the states that ban discrimination based on the source of income, tenants' lawyers have argued that the ban supports their theory that landlords should not be free to decline to participate in government-subsidized programs; but these cases have not been universally successful. As noted in "Section 8 and Low-Income Housing Programs," below, if you don't want to participate in a Section 8 program, seek legal counsel.

Arbitrary Discrimination

Just because a form of discrimination isn't mentioned by name in a state or federal law does not mean it's legal. For example, even though discriminating against men with beards or long hair isn't specifically prohibited by a civil rights law, there might be instances where such behavior violates the law.

For example, California's Unruh Civil Rights Act (Cal. Civ. Code §§ 51–53.7, 54.1–54.8) specifically lists only "sex, race, color, religion, ancestry, national origin, disability, medical condition, genetic information, marital status, gender identity, citizenship, primary language, or sexual orientation" as types of illegal discrimination. However, courts in California have ruled that these categories are just examples: All discrimination based on personal characteristics or traits is prohibited by the Unruh Civil Rights Act.

Even if you live in a state that does not specifically outlaw arbitrary discrimination, there is a very strong practical reason why you should not engage in arbitrary discrimination—for example, based on obesity, occupation, or style of dress. Because fair housing law includes numerous protected categories—race, sex, religion, and so on—chances are that disappointed applicants can fit themselves into at least one of the protected categories and file a discrimination claim. Even if the claim is unsuccessful, you'll spend significant time and money defending yourself.

> **EXAMPLE:** Jane, a lawyer, applied for an apartment and returned her application to Lee, the landlord. Lee had spent the better part of the last year fighting a frivolous lawsuit brought by a former tenant (who was also a lawyer), and the thought of renting to another lawyer was more than Lee could bear. Jane's credit, rental, and personal references were excellent, but Lee rejected her application.
>
> One of Lee's tenants told Jane that Lee had refused her solely because she was a lawyer. This made Jane angry, and she decided to get even. Although her state did not have a law prohibiting arbitrary discrimination, that didn't stop Jane. She filed a fair housing complaint alleging that she had been turned away because she was single, female, and Jewish. The complaint was ultimately dismissed, but not before it had cost Lee a bundle of time and energy to defend.

Valid Occupancy Limits

Landlords' ability to limit the number of people living in a rental unit is one of the most hotly debated issues in the rental housing industry. No one disputes the wisdom of enforcing building codes that specify minimum square footage per occupant for reasons of health and safety. But it is another matter altogether when even relatively small families—especially those with children—are excluded from a large segment of the rental market because landlords set unreasonable occupancy policies.

The law allows you to establish an occupancy policy based on genuine health and safety considerations. In addition, you can adopt standards that are driven by a legitimate business reason, such as the capacity of your plumbing system. Your personal goals (such as reducing wear and tear by capping the number of occupants, or ensuring a quiet, upscale environment for older tenants), however, are not valid reasons for limiting occupancy.

Placing illegitimate limits on how many tenants can live in your rental exposes you to accusations of familial status discrimination, discussed above.

The federal government has taken the lead in establishing occupancy standards through passage of the Fair Housing Amendments Act. But states and localities may also set their own occupancy standards, and many have. And this is where things get tricky.

Ordinarily, when the federal government legislates on a particular subject, states and localities can also pass laws on the subject, as long as they're equally (or more) protective of the targeted group. But the federal government's guidance (a mere memo to regional HUD directors) specifically reminded its readers that Congress didn't intend to develop "a national occupancy code." ("Fair Housing Enforcement—Occupancy Standards Notice of Statement of Policy," C.F.R. Vol. 63, No. 243, Dec. 18, 1998.) The memo practically invited states and localities to set their own occupancy standards, and didn't make it clear whether those standards had to be at least as generous (to tenants) as the federal guidance. As a result, some states developed occupancy standards that, when applied, resulted in fewer people allowed in a rental.

Landlords were perplexed: Which standard did they need to follow? Their policy might be legal when examined in a state court, using state occupancy standards, but illegal when tested in a federal court, using the HUD guidance. And some states, like California, developed standards that resulted in more occupants than the federal guidance.

The way out of this morass is, fortunately, rather commonsense. To avoid lawsuits, you need to adopt an occupancy policy that is at least as generous as the federal standard, which is explained just below. And if your state or locality has legislated more generous standards, you'll have to follow them. If they're less generous, don't take a chance, because you risk that a tenant's lawyer will choose to sue you using the federal standard.

Minimum and Maximum Numbers of Occupants

Two kinds of laws affect your occupancy standards:

- **Minimum occupancy standards.** Federal, state, and local occupancy standards establish the minimum number of occupants you must allow in a particular unit. If you set a lower occupancy limit, you might be accused of violating a fair housing law.
- **Maximum occupancy limits.** State and local health and safety codes might set maximum limits on the number of tenants, based purely on the size of the unit and number of bedrooms and bathrooms.

Finding out whether your occupancy policy is legal is not always easy. You must answer three questions for each rental situation:

- How many people must you allow in that particular unit under the federal standard?
- How many people must you allow in that unit under the state standard?
- How many people must you allow in that unit under the local standard?

Once you know the answers to each of these questions, the rest is easy: To avoid a federal, state, or local fair housing complaint, simply apply the occupancy standard that is the least restrictive—that is, the one that allows the most people. If you don't follow the least restrictive standard, be prepared to show that your policy (allowing fewer people) is motivated by reasons of health or safety or a legitimate business reason.

Unfortunately, getting the answers to the three questions is often difficult. This section will attempt to guide you through the process. It covers:

- federal occupancy standards
- common state and local occupancy standards
- how to calculate the number of occupants that must be allowed for each rental unit, and
- "legitimate business reasons" that might support a more restrictive policy than the law allows.

The Federal Occupancy Standard

Federal law allows you to establish "reasonable" restrictions on the number of persons per dwelling. These restrictions must be motivated by legitimate business reasons or the need to preserve the health and safety of the occupants.

HUD interprets federal law by means of memos, guidelines, and regulations. Unfortunately, HUD has never been very helpful when it comes to explaining what a "reasonable" restriction on persons per dwelling might be. HUD has simply said that a policy of two persons per bedroom is, as a general rule, reasonable, but that other factors will also be considered when investigating claims of landlord discrimination. As such, the federal test is known as the "two-per-bedroom-plus" standard, and considers:

- the size of the bedrooms and rental unit—if the unit or the bedrooms are small, you may take that into account
- age of the children—for example, babies do not have the same space requirements as teenagers
- configuration of the rental unit—if a room could serve as a bedroom, but there is no access to a bathroom except through another bedroom, you might be able to designate that room a "nonbedroom" and limit the number of occupants accordingly
- physical limitations of the building—for example, a septic tank that can't handle use from more than three people
- state and local building codes that impose their own set of minimum space requirements per occupant, and
- prior discrimination complaints—if you must respond to a fair housing complaint, you will be at a disadvantage if you are known to repeatedly violate antidiscrimination laws.

The flexibility of the federal standard helps landlords because it takes into account unique circumstances. But it can also be frustrating: Landlords cannot set an occupancy limit for a unit and know for certain that it will pass the federal test, as the legal maximum might change depending on the applicant.

For example, if you decide that the family with a newborn needs less space than one with a teenager, the occupancy limit for the same unit will be different for each family.

As you might imagine, a federal "standard" that changes according to the makeup of every applicant has proven very difficult and confusing to apply. However, you can do your best to apply it conscientiously by using these guidelines.

Section 8 and Low-Income Housing Programs

Many tenants with low incomes qualify for federally subsidized housing assistance, the most common being HUD's tenant-based Section 8 program. ("Section 8" refers to Section 8 of the United States Housing Act of 1937, 42 U.S.C. § 1437f.) Tenants then pay a designated percentage of their income to the landlord while the housing agency pays the difference between the tenant's contribution and what it determines is the market rent each month.

The Pros and Cons of Section 8 Participation

Section 8 is a mixed bag for landlords. It offers several advantages:

- The housing agency pays the larger part of the rent on time every month. The tenant's responsibility is low enough that they shouldn't have too much trouble paying on time, either.
- If the tenants don't pay the rent and you have to evict them, the housing agency guarantees you'll receive any unpaid rent as well as compensation for any tenants-caused damages, up to a certain limit.
- If your neighborhood or area is popular with low-income tenants you won't have a shortage of potential tenants.

Section 8's disadvantages are legion, however. They include:

- Housing agencies often lowball market rent, and the program caps the security deposit (which might be lower than your state's maximum).
- You are locked into a tenancy agreement for one year, and can only terminate it for nonpayment of rent or another serious breach of the lease. (Evictions based on other grounds are difficult.)
- When HUD experiences a budget crunch, it cuts the public housing agencies' budgets. As a result, the housing agencies are likely to lower the landlords' allotments. Though this practice is legally iffy, it's done anyway.
- To qualify, new Section 8 landlords must often wait up to a month or longer for a mandatory inspection—during which they see no rent. These inspections often reveal picky, minor violations that state inspectors wouldn't cite for.

Call your local public housing agency if you wish to participate in the Section 8 program. They will refer eligible applicants to you, arrange for an inspection of the rental property, and prepare the necessary documents (including the lease addendum) if you decide to rent to an eligible applicant. Be sure to get a copy of the Section 8 rules and procedures that all participating landlords must use. Often, they vary significantly from your state or local law.

Must Landlords Participate in Section 8?

Landlords have traditionally been able to choose not to participate in the Section 8 program without fear of violating federal fair housing laws. However, as the federal government's ability to provide sufficient low-income housing diminishes, this is changing in some localities. In New Jersey, for example, if an existing tenant becomes eligible for Section 8 assistance, you may not refuse to accept the vouchers—you must participate in the program as to this tenant, at least. (*Franklin Tower One, L.L.C. v. N.M.*, 157 N.J. 602; 725 A.2d 1104 (1999).) In Connecticut, Maryland, and Massachusetts, landlords may not refuse to rent to existing or new tenants who will be paying with Section 8 vouchers. (*Comm' on Human Rights and Opportunities v. Sullivan Assoc.*, 250 Conn. 763; 739 A.2d 238 (1999); Mass. Gen. Laws ch. 151B, § 4(10); *Montgomery County v. Glenmont Hills Associates Privacy World at Glenmont Metro Centre*, 936 A.2d 325 (2007).)

Some states have required landlord participation in Section 8 by way of their ban on discrimination on the basis of source of income ("SOI"). These states make Section 8 vouchers one of the protected sources. Localities in other states can pass laws that include Section 8 as a protected SOI even though there is no statewide protection in those states.

Begin by multiplying the number of bedrooms times two, and then think about the factors listed above. For example, is one of the bedrooms so small as to be unsuitable for two people? On the other hand, could the den be usable as another bedroom? Could a couple with a baby in a bassinet comfortably occupy a bedroom that would be unsuitable for three adults? In situations such as these, using the federal two-per-bedroom-plus standard sometimes yields different results from applying a general rule of multiplying the number of bedrooms by two.

> **EXAMPLE:** Murray owned a large, old house that had been remodeled into two apartments. The upstairs unit had large rooms, two bedrooms, and two bathrooms. The lower apartment was considerably smaller, with one bedroom and one bath.
>
> *The Upstairs.* Murray was approached by a family of five: three young children and two adults. He realized that the large bedroom could safely sleep three children, so he figured that the five people in this family came within the federal standards.
>
> *The Downstairs.* The first applicants for the lower apartment were three adults. Murray told them that the occupancy limit was two. Later, a couple with a newborn applied for the apartment. Realizing that a bassinet could easily fit into the bedroom, Murray adjusted his occupancy limit and rented to the couple.

Common State and Local Occupancy Standards

Even if your limit meets the federal standard, you can't relax just yet. Remember, states and localities can set their own occupancy standards, as long as they are more generous than the federal government. You must comply with any state or local standard or (if a complaint is filed) risk prosecution by the state or local agency that administers the standard.

New York landlords, for example, must comply with the "Unlawful Restrictions on Occupancy" law, commonly known as the "Roommate Law." (N.Y. Real Prop. Law § 235-f.) The Roommate Law prohibits New York landlords from limiting occupancy of a rental unit to just the tenant named on the lease or rental agreement. It permits tenants to share their rental units with their immediate family members, and, in many cases, with unrelated, nontenant occupants, too, so long as a tenant (or tenant's spouse) occupies the unit as a primary residence.

The number of total occupants is still restricted, however, by local laws governing overcrowding.

It is crucial to check whether any state or local standard applies to you. Contact your local and state housing authority for information, or the U.S. Department of Housing and Urban Development (HUD) office.

> ⓘ CAUTION
> **Remember, you must apply the most generous standard—federal, state, or local—in determining how many people may occupy a particular rental unit.** If you are unsure, it is always safer to err on the side of more, rather than fewer, occupants.

Legitimate Reasons for a More Restrictive Occupancy Policy

What if you decide that your particular rental unit ought to be occupied by fewer than the most generous number allowed by federal, state, and local laws? If you set an occupancy limit that is lower than the legal standard, you must be prepared to defend it with a legitimate business reason. This term is impossible to describe in the abstract, because legitimate reasons vary depending on the circumstances of every rental property. Here are some examples of legitimate business reasons that have justified occupancy limits lower than the government standard:

- **Limitations of the infrastructure.** The plumbing or electrical systems cannot, without extensive and expensive upgrades, accommodate more than a certain amount of use. (*U.S. v. Weiss*, 847 F.Supp 819 (1994).)
- **Limitations of the facilities.** Common areas and facilities (such as laundry rooms and hallways) would be overcrowded if more occupants were allowed.

- **Dilapidation that common sense tells you would result from more people living in the structure.** The house is so small that allowing more occupants would result in unreasonable wear and tear. (*Pfaff v. U.S. Dep't of Hous. and Urban Dev.*, 88 F.3d 739 (1996).)

If your occupancy policy is lower than the most generous applicable legal standard, be prepared for an uphill fight. It is very difficult to establish a "winning" legitimate business reason that justifies a lower occupancy standard. You'd be wise to hire a neutral professional, such as an engineer, to evaluate and report on the limiting factor in light of your community's needs (for example, you'll want a report that measures your boiler's limited hot water delivery against the number of residents who you think should reasonably live there). Get that report *before* imposing a restrictive occupancy policy, and make sure it truly justifies your decision to use more restrictive occupancy standards.

You will need to carefully assess whether it's worth your time and money to fight a fair housing complaint. In order to establish that your lower occupancy policy is based upon legitimate business reasons and is therefore legal, you'll need to convince a fair housing judge that:

- changing the limiting factor (such as rewiring the rental unit's electrical system to accommodate more use) is impractical from a business perspective, or
- common sense, your business experience, and the practice of landlords in your area support your lower number, or
- limiting the number of occupants is the only practical way to address the limiting factor.

Here are some examples of situations in which landlords argued that the limitations of their septic systems justified a more restrictive occupancy standard. In the first example, the landlord prevailed. In the second example, the landlord failed to establish that his occupancy policy was based upon legitimate business reasons.

EXAMPLE 1: John and Mary Evans advertised the small two-bedroom cottage on their property as suitable for two people only. Their occupancy limit was based on the limitations of the septic system, which could legally accommodate no more than four people (the Evanses and two tenants in the cottage). John and Mary declined to rent to a family of four, who then filed a fair housing complaint. At the conciliation meeting arranged by the housing authority, John and Mary presented an engineer's estimate that it would cost many thousands of dollars to expand the septic system to accommodate more than four residents. The hearing officer accepted the Evanses' explanation and decided not to take the complaint further.

EXAMPLE 2: The occupancy policy for all the units at Westside Terrace was three persons per apartment, even for the two-bedroom units. A family of four applied for one of the two-bedrooms and was turned down. When the family filed a complaint with HUD, the owner of Westside Terrace justified the policy on the grounds that the building's infrastructure—its sewage capacities, pipes, and common areas—could not support as many people as would result from allowing four persons in the two-bedroom apartment units. Westside also presented evidence that it would be prohibitively expensive to upgrade these facilities. The judge heard evidence from structural and sanitary engineers which indicated that these facilities were capable of handling that number of people and had done so many times in the past. HUD decided that Westside's restrictive occupancy policy was not based on legitimate business needs, and ruled against it.

Managers and Discrimination

Because you are liable for your employees' actions, you must ensure that any manager you hire—especially one who selects tenants—fully understands and abides by antidiscrimination laws. On the other hand, if you use an independent management company (which is a true independent contractor, rather than an employee), the possibility that you will be liable for its discriminatory acts is greatly decreased. (See Chapter 6 on landlord liability for a manager's conduct and strategies for avoiding problems in this area.)

You should always let your tenants know that you and your manager intend to abide by the law, and that you want to know about and will address any fair housing concerns. While this will not shield you from liability for your manager's conduct, it might (if you are lucky) result in a tenant's contacting you before complaining to a fair housing agency. If you hear about a manager's discriminatory act and can resolve a complaint before it gets into "official channels," you will have saved yourself a lot of time, trouble, and money.

One way to alert your tenants and prospective tenants to your commitment to the fair housing laws is to write all ads, applications, and other material given to prospective tenants to include a section containing your antidiscrimination stance. Prepare a written policy statement as to the law and your intention to abide by it. See the sample statement below.

Also, be sure to display fair housing posters on the premises, as described earlier in the chapter.

Sample Statement on Equal Opportunity in Housing

FROM: Mesa Village Apartments

TO: All Tenants and Applicants

It is the policy of the owner and manager of Mesa Village Apartments to rent our units without regard to a person's race, ethnic background, sex, age, religion, marital or family status, physical disability, gender identity, or sexual orientation. As part of our commitment to provide equal opportunity in housing, we comply with all federal, state, and local laws prohibiting discrimination. If you have any questions or complaints regarding our rental policy, call the owner at [phone number].

If, despite your best efforts, you have the slightest suspicion your manager might use unlawful discriminatory practices to select or deal with tenants—whether on purpose or inadvertently—you should immediately and personally take control of the situation. Once the coast is clear, it might be the opportunity to shield yourself from potential liability in the future by engaging the services of an independent management company, which in most cases will be responsible for its employees' actions.

> **CAUTION**
> **Never give managers or rental agents the authority to offer their own rent concessions or "deals" to selected tenants or applicants.** If you want to offer inducements—a discount for signing an extended lease or one free month for tenants who begin renting in the month of March—be consistent. Make sure offers are available to all tenants who meet the requirements of the special deal. Otherwise, for example, a tenant who finds out he didn't get as good a deal as his identically situated neighbor is sure to complain. If he is a member of a group protected by fair housing laws, he's got the makings of a case against you.

Unlawful Discrimination Complaints

A landlord accused of unlawful discrimination can end up in a state, federal, or local administrative proceeding, or in a state or federal lawsuit. According to the most recent HUD data (covering fiscal year 2020), about 45% of complaints alleged disability discrimination, and about 20% alleged race-based discrimination. ("U.S. Department of Housing and Urban Development State of Fair Housing Annual Report to Congress, FY 2020.") This section gives you a brief description of the legal process involved in each arena and the consequences of discrimination charges.

SEE AN EXPERT

Get expert help to defend a housing discrimination lawsuit. With the exception of a suit brought in small claims court, you should see an attorney if a tenant sues you or files an administrative complaint against you for discrimination. For advice on finding and working with an attorney or doing your own legal research, see Chapter 18.

When a Tenant Complains to a Fair Housing Agency

A prospective or current tenant may file a discrimination complaint with either HUD (by phone, mail, or online) or the state or local agency charged with overseeing fair housing complaints. A federal HUD complaint must be filed within one year of the alleged violation. State statutes or local ordinances might set shorter time periods for filing nonfederal complaints. If the complaint is filed with HUD, the agency should (but doesn't always) conduct an investigation within 180 days. (Time periods for state housing agencies vary.)

After HUD investigates the complaint, it will either dismiss the complaint or attempt to reach a conciliation agreement (compromise) between you and the person filing the complaint. (This is also the procedure in most state agencies, as well.) For example, an aggrieved applicant might agree to drop his complaint in exchange for a sum of money or your written promise to rent him an apartment.

If conciliation is unsuccessful, the fair housing agency will hold an administrative hearing (a trial before a judge but without a jury) to determine whether discrimination has occurred. If the administrative law judge decides that a fair housing violation occurred, the judge will direct that the violation be corrected in the ways described below.

HUD litigation is typically long and laborious. It is not unusual for cases to take up to ten years before they are concluded.

When a Tenant Sues in Federal or State Court

Complainants may also file suit in federal court or state court. This can be done even after filing an administrative complaint (as long as there is no signed conciliation agreement or pending HUD administrative hearing). A federal housing discrimination lawsuit must be filed within two years of the alleged violation.

In a typical federal lawsuit, the aggrieved tenant (or would-be tenant) goes to a private lawyer immediately after the alleged discriminatory incident. The attorney prepares and files a complaint, and also asks the court for an expedited hearing, hoping to get an order from the court directing the landlord to cease the discriminatory practice. Courts issue these "temporary restraining orders," when plaintiffs (the tenant) demonstrate that they have a good chance of ultimately winning their lawsuit, and will suffer irreparable harm if immediate relief isn't granted. The order remains in place until a more formal hearing is held. Open-and-shut cases of discrimination often settle at the temporary restraining order stage.

Penalties for Discrimination

If a state court, federal court, or housing agency finds that discrimination has taken place, it may order you to do one or more of the following:

- rent a particular unit to the person who was discriminated against
- pay for "actual" or "compensatory" damages the victim incurred, such as additional rent paid elsewhere as a result of being turned down, as well as damages for humiliation or emotional distress
- pay punitive damages (extra money as punishment for especially outrageous discrimination) and the victim's attorneys' fees

- in the case of a disability violation, retrofit your property or set up an escrow fund to be used for retrofitting in the future, and
- pay a civil penalty to the federal government. The maximum penalty under the federal Fair Housing Acts is $21,663 for a first violation, $54,157 for a second violation within five years of the first, and $108,315 for a third violation within seven years. (24 CFR § 180.671 (2021).) Many states have comparable penalties.

Even if you are ultimately vindicated, the costs of defending a discrimination claim can be devastating. Your insurance policy might cover the monetary costs, but it cannot compensate you for lost time and aggravation. Careful attention to the discrimination rules described in this chapter and Chapter 1 will, we hope, save you from this fate.

CAUTION

If you are the subject of a fair housing complaint, do not take the matter "into your own hands." It is illegal to retaliate against, threaten, coerce, intimidate, or interfere with anyone who either files a complaint with HUD, cooperates in the investigation of such a complaint, or exercises a fair housing right.

Insurance Coverage in Discrimination Claims

Even the most conscientious landlords sometimes find themselves facing a fair housing claim or a discrimination lawsuit. If this happens to you, will your insurance policy cover the cost of defending the claim and, if you lose, the cost of the settlement or judgment? The answers to these questions depend entirely on two highly variable factors: the wording of your insurance policy and how courts in your area have decided similar cases.

In short, there are no answers that will apply to everyone, but we can alert you to the issues that arise in every situation. At the very least, knowing how insurance companies approve or deny defense and judgment costs in discrimination claims should help you as you evaluate your own policy.

RELATED TOPIC

Chapter 10 discusses broad types of liability insurance, coverage for managers and other employees, and coverage for injuries suffered as a result of defective conditions on the property. The advice in that chapter on choosing property insurance is also relevant to choosing liability coverage for discrimination claims.

Most owners of residential rental property carry comprehensive liability insurance, which typically includes business liability coverage. In these policies, the insurance company agrees to pay on your behalf all damages "for bodily injury, property damage, or personal injury caused by an occurrence to which this insurance applies" that you are ordered to pay. The policy will usually define the three key terms "bodily injury," "occurrence," and "personal injury." Whether the insurance company will help you with a discrimination claim depends on these definitions.

CAUTION

Find out if your policy covers administrative claims (complaints to fair housing agencies such as HUD). Insurance companies in several states have successfully argued that their duties to defend and cover you extend only to lawsuits, not fair housing agency claims. Ask your agent.

Definition of "Bodily Injury"

Discrimination complaints rarely include a claim that the victim suffered a physical injury at the hands of the landlord or manager. It is far more likely that the tenant or applicant will sue for the emotional distress caused by the humiliation of the discriminatory act.

The Insurance Company's Duty to Defend: Broader Than the Duty to Cover

When you purchase liability insurance, you buy two things: the promise of the insurance company to defend you if you are sued for an act that arguably falls within the coverage of the policy, and its promise to pay the settlement or damage award if you lose. But sometimes (as is the case in fair housing claims) it is unclear whether, assuming you lose the case, your policy covers the conduct that gave rise to the claim. When this happens, your insurance company will usually defend you, but it might reserve the right to argue about whether it is obligated to pay the damages if you lose the case. For example, if a court requires you to pay punitive damages, although your policy might cover civil fines, it might not cover sums you're required to pay as punishment for egregious behavior. Before you purchase insurance, find out exactly what's covered.

"Bodily injury" usually doesn't include emotional distress. Courts in a few states, however, have held that bodily injury does include emotional distress. If your state doesn't include emotional distress in the concept of bodily injury, an insurance company might be able to successfully decline coverage.

Definition of "Personal Injury"

Most insurance policies also provide coverage for "personal injury" that arises out of the conduct of your business. Personal injury typically includes false arrest, libel, slander, and violation of privacy rights; it might also include "wrongful entry or eviction or other invasions of the right of private occupancy." As you can see from this definition, personal injury includes items that are neither bodily injuries nor accidental. And the definition includes some offenses, like libel, that seem somewhat similar to discrimination.

Nevertheless, an insurance company might argue that a discrimination claim isn't covered under a policy's definition of "personal injury."

Very few courts have faced this issue, let alone decided it. However, the few opinions that courts have voiced on the matter vary. For example, coverage has been denied on the grounds that "discrimination" is a specific wrong and, as such, it would've been specifically listed in the policy if the insurance company intended to cover it. Coverage for discrimination claims by prospective tenants (such as applicants who have been turned away) has been denied on the theory that "the right of private occupancy" is a right enjoyed only by current, not would-be, tenants. Other courts, when faced with unclear language in insurance policies, give the insured the benefit of the doubt, and have ordered the insurance company to at least defend the lawsuit.

Definition of "Occurrence"

Your insurance company will defend and pay out on a claim if it is caused by an occurrence to which the policy applies. An "occurrence" is typically defined as an accident, whose results are neither expected nor intended from the standpoint of the insured (the property owner).

It doesn't take much brainwork to see how an insurance company can argue that an act of discrimination—like turning away a minority applicant—is intentional, and therefore not a covered "occurrence." Courts in a few states have ruled in favor of insurance companies on this issue, and courts in other states have ruled similarly when the question has come up in employment discrimination cases.

A Policy Specifically for Discrimination Claims and Lawsuits

As you've just learned, when you're sued for discrimination, it can be difficult (or impossible) to get coverage under your commercial general liability (CGL) policy.

Another type of policy will offer you narrow, but certain coverage. This coverage is called "Tenant Discrimination Insurance," and it works a bit differently than your CGL policy. A CGL policy supplies the defense attorney and all resources to defend against the claim, and pays for any judgment, up to the limits of your policy. When using discrimination insurance, however, you find your own lawyer and, once a lawsuit or claim is filed (with HUD or any state or local fair housing agency), you get reimbursed for legal costs from that point on, and the amount of any judgment.

The discrimination policy does not present any of the thorny issues encountered with a CGL policy—even intentional, blatant acts of discrimination will be covered. The policy will exclude class actions, suits by employees, any legal work and settlement that occurred without the other side having filed a lawsuit or a claim; and it might exclude punitive damages or fines, depending on state law. One definite drawback is that you must initiate the request for reimbursement, and if the carrier balks, you have to take action (with your CGL, the insurance company in most instances will at least step up on notice of the claim and defend you).

Discrimination insurance is not well known. It is relatively inexpensive. If you are interested, contact your insurance agent or broker and ask for information. You might have to mention that Tokio Marine HCC is the underwriter. For more information, visit www.tmhcc.com/en-us/products/tenant-discrimination.

Discrimination and Public Policy

An insurance company will occasionally argue that it should not have to cover a landlord's intentional acts of discrimination because discrimination is an evil act that someone should not be able to insure against. While this argument has some persuasive aspects—discrimination is, indeed, contrary to public policy—it falls apart when you acknowledge that all sorts of other intentional bad acts (like libel and slander) are perfectly insurable. Courts have not been persuaded by the "public policy" argument. Be sure to check with your insurance broker whether your policy covers intentional acts of discrimination.

Review Insurance, and Act Wisely

In sum, there are at least three ways that insurance companies can deny coverage, if not also the defense of a fair housing claim and award by arguing that:

- The discriminatory act didn't result in a covered bodily injury (when emotional distress is the only physical injury claimed).
- Discrimination is not a type of business-related personal injury that the policy intended to cover.
- Only accidental "occurrences" are covered, and discrimination is an intentional act.

We suggest that you consider the details of discrimination coverage when choosing a broker and negotiating your policy. But the best use of your energy—by far—is to make sure that your business practices don't expose you to these claims in the first place.

Property Managers

FORMS IN THIS CHAPTER

Chapter 6 includes instructions for and a sample of the following form:

- Property Manager Agreement

The purchase of this book includes a free downloadable and customizable copy of this form. See Appendix B for the download link and instructions.

Many landlords hire a resident manager to handle the day-to-day details of running an apartment building, including fielding tenants' routine repair requests and collecting rent. Landlords who own several rental properties (large or small) often contract with a property management firm in addition to, or in place of, a resident manager. Hiring a manager can free you from many of the time-consuming (and tiresome) aspects of being a residential landlord.

But it can also create some headaches of its own: lots of paperwork for the IRS; worries about liability for a manager's acts; and the responsibility of finding, hiring, and supervising an employee.

This chapter explains how to weigh all these factors and how to minimize complications if you decide to get some management help.

In some states, you might not have a choice— you might be required by law to hire a manager. California, for example, requires a resident manager on the premises of any apartment complex with 16 or more units. (Cal. Code of Regulations, Title 25, § 42.) New York City has similar requirements for buildings with nine or more units. Check with your state or local rental property owners' association, or do your own research, to see if your state requires resident managers.

RESOURCE
Several other Nolo books provide useful information on hiring, managing, and firing employees:

- *The Essential Guide to Federal Employment Laws*, by Lisa Guerin and Sachi Barreiro, has extensive discussions on relevant federal laws, including the Fair Labor Standards Act, Americans with Disabilities Act, Equal Pay Act, Immigration Reform and Control Act, Fair Credit Reporting Act, and Occupational Safety and Health Act, as well as state and federal employment discrimination laws.

- *Dealing With Problem Employees*, by Lisa Guerin and Amy DelPo, includes chapters on hiring, evaluating, disciplining, and firing employees.
- *The Essential Guide to Workplace Investigations*, by Lisa Guerin, gives employers practical information on how to investigate and resolve workplace problems.
- *The Employer's Legal Handbook*, by Fred S. Steingold, is a complete guide to the latest workplace laws and regulations. It covers everything you need to know about hiring and firing employees, drug tests of employees, personnel policies, employee benefits, discrimination, and other legal issues affecting small business practices.

These books are available at bookstores and public libraries. They may also be ordered directly from Nolo's website, Nolo.com, or by calling 800-728-3555.

For free general information on employment law, from discrimination to workers' compensation, see Nolo's articles in the Employment Law Center at Nolo.com.

Property Managers and Building Supers

The focus in this chapter is on property managers, not supers. While there aren't any hard and fast rules, here's the difference between a building superintendent (super) and a manager.

Property managers usually have more tenant-relations responsibilities than supers do, such as taking apartment applications, accepting rent, and responding to tenant problems and complaints. You might also authorize a trusted manager to purchase building supplies and hire outside contractors for specialized repairs.

Building supers, on the other hand, usually concentrate on building repairs and maintenance tasks. They often have special skills and are experienced at running complicated heating plants and air conditioning systems. Customarily, supers don't collect rent or take rental applications.

The legal issues as to hiring and compensating managers and supers are generally the same.

Hiring Your Own Resident Manager

If you put some thought into writing a job description, and some effort into recruiting and hiring a good manager, you'll avoid problems down the road. Don't hurry the process, or jump into an informal arrangement with a tenant who offers to help out if you'll take a little off the rent—you'll almost surely regret it.

Decide the Manager's Duties, Hours, and Pay

Why do you want to hire a manager? You need to answer this question in some detail, as well as the following:

What are the manager's responsibilities? The Property Manager Agreement included in this book lists duties you might want to delegate, such as selecting tenants, collecting rents, and hiring and paying repair people. Finding an on-site manager who can handle all these aspects of the job, however, is a tall order—so tall that many owners restrict the on-site manager's job to handling routine repairs and maintenance chores.

Is the job full or part time? How many hours do you anticipate the manager working? What hours do you expect the manager to be on the rental property or on call?

Will the manager live on the rental property or off? Someone who just collects rent and handles minor repairs doesn't necessarily need to live at the rental.

How much do you plan to pay the manager? You may pay an hourly wage, generally ranging from $20 to $35 per hour, or a flat salary. How much you pay depends on the manager's responsibilities, the number of hours, time of day and regularity of the schedule, benefits, and the going rate in your community. You can get an idea how much managers are paid by asking other landlords or checking want ads for managers. Offering slightly above the going rate in your area should allow you to hire the best, most experienced candidates. If you do this, you might want to try and tap into the local grapevine of experienced managers to see if you can snag someone who wants to move up.

> ### Illegal Discrimination in Hiring
>
> Federal, state, and local laws prohibit many kinds of discrimination in hiring. The Equal Pay Act applies to every employer, regardless of size; the Immigration Reform and Control Act of 1986 (IRCA) applies to employers with four or more employees. Title VII of the Civil Rights Act and the Americans with Disabilities Act apply only if you employ 15 or more people. Some state laws apply even if you have only one employee, such as California's prohibition on worker harassment.
>
> Pay attention to these laws even if they do not directly bind your business. Doing so will not hinder you from making a decision based on sound business reasons: skills, experience, references. The laws only forbid making a decision based on a factor that isn't reasonably related to the applicant's ability to do the job. Following them will protect you from accusations of discrimination.
>
> Here are some of the bases on which these laws make it illegal to discriminate: race, color, gender, religious beliefs, national origin, age (if the person is 40 or older), and disability. Several states and cities also prohibit discrimination based on marital status, sexual orientation, or other factors. Contact your state fair employment office for details.
>
> Much of the advice in Chapter 5, which deals with illegal discrimination against tenants, will also be of help when you're hiring a manager.

Should you give the manager reduced rent? Some landlords prefer giving a resident manager reduced rent in exchange for management services, rather than paying a separate salary. This isn't a good idea—for one thing, reduced rent alone won't work for a full-time manager. Reduced rent in exchange for being a manager can be a particular problem in rent control areas, because you might not be able to adjust rent easily. If you later have to fire a manager who is compensated by reduced rent, you might run into problems when you insist that the ex-manager go back to paying the full rent. But if the tenant-manager pays the full rent and receives a separate salary, there will be no question that you are entitled to the full rent if you have to fire the manager. (Note that firing the manager doesn't mean you can expect the person to leave the rental; you'll need to follow proper termination rules for that.)

Your obligations as an employer are the same whether you compensate the manager with reduced rent or a paycheck. For example, you must still pay Social Security and payroll taxes, as discussed below. However, paying the manager by reducing rent can create problems under wages and hours and overtime laws.

Advertise the Job

Some landlords find great managers primarily via word of mouth: by talking to tenants, friends, and relatives; or getting the word out through Facebook or other social media. Others run an online ad, use an employment agency, or advertise elsewhere. If you place an ad somewhere, keep it simple: Stick to the job skills needed and the basic responsibilities. For example, "Fifty-unit apartment complex seeks full-time resident manager with experience in selecting tenants, collecting rent, and apartment maintenance."

Interview Strong Candidates

Limit your in-person interviews to people you're really interested in hiring as manager. Ask candidates to bring a résumé with relevant experience and names and phone numbers of four or five references.

Before you begin interviewing, write down questions focusing on the job duties and the applicant's skills and experience. To avoid potential charges of discrimination, ask everyone the same questions, and don't ask questions that are not clearly job related—for example, the applicant's health status, religion, or plans for having children.

Here are some examples of questions that are appropriate to ask potential managers:
- "Tell me about your previous jobs managing rental properties."
- "How much experience do you have collecting rents? Doing general repairs? Keeping records of tenants' complaints or repair problems?"
- "What have you liked most about previous manager jobs? What have you liked least?"
- "What kinds of problems have you encountered as a property manager? How did you solve them?"
- "Why do you want this job?"
- "Are the job's proposed pay and schedule in keeping with your expectations?"

You might also ask some more direct questions, like:
- "What would you do if a tenant who had paid rent on time for six months asked for a ten-day extension because money was short as a result of a family problem?"
- "What would you do if a tenant called you at 11 p.m. with a complaint about a clogged sink?"

Get a Completed Rental Application

If your manager will also be a tenant, make sure the applicant completes a rental application (as discussed in Chapter 1) and that you check references and other information carefully. Be sure the applicant signs a form authorizing you to check credit history and references, such as the Consent to Contact References and Perform Credit Check form in Chapter 1.

CAUTION

When you check a prospective manager's application or résumé, look for holes—dates when the person didn't indicate an employer. The applicant might be covering up a bad reference. Insist that the applicant explain any gaps in employment history.

Check References

No matter how wonderful someone appears in person or on paper, it's essential to contact former employers. Ideally, you should talk with at least two former employers or supervisors with whom the applicant held similar positions.

Before calling, make a list of questions to ask the references. Ask about the applicant's previous job responsibilities, character and personality traits, strengths and weaknesses, and reasons for leaving the job. Also, review your notes from interviewing the applicant for issues you want to explore more—for example, if you sense that the potential manager doesn't seem organized enough to handle all the details of the manager's job, ask about it.

Employers are often reluctant to say anything negative about a former employee for fear of being hit with a defamation lawsuit. Many will refuse to give any information other than the dates the person worked and the position held. It might be helpful to send the former employer a copy of the applicant's signed consent to disclosure of employment information. When a former employer is not forthcoming, you'll need to read between the lines. When former employers are neutral, offer only faint praise, or overpraise a person for a minor aspect of a job—"Always nicely dressed!"—they might be hiding negative information. Ask former employers: "Would you hire this person back if you could?" The response could be telling. When a reference isn't glowing and doesn't cover all aspects of the job, check several other references—or hire someone else.

Check Credit History and Background

Checking an individual's credit history is especially important if you want a manager to handle money. Someone with large debts might be tempted to skim money from your business. And a prospective manager with sloppy personal finances is not a good choice for managing rental property. Before you order a credit report, get the applicant's consent.

You might also wish to ask a credit bureau or tenant screening company to do an investigative or background report, similar to the one some landlords run on tenants (see Chapter 1 for details).

> **CAUTION**
>
> **Handle credit reports carefully.** Federal law requires you to keep only needed information, and to discard the rest. See "How to Handle Credit Reports," in Chapter 7 for precise information.

Character Traits of a Good Manager

Look for a person who is:

- **Honest and responsible.** This is especially important if the manager will be entitled to receive legal documents and papers on your behalf.
- **Patient.** Dealing with tenants, repairpeople, and guests has its share of hassles. A person with a short fuse is a definite liability.
- **Financially responsible.** This quality should be demonstrated by a good credit history.
- **Personable yet professional.** Good communication skills are a must, with you and your current and prospective tenants and any other workers the manager might supervise (for example, a cleaning crew).
- **Fastidious.** One of the manager's responsibilities will be to keep the building and common areas neat, clean, and secure.
- **Meticulous about maintaining records.** This is particularly important if collecting rent will be part of the job.
- **Fair and free of biases.** A manager who will be showing apartments, taking rental applications, or selecting tenants must be able to steer clear of fair housing mistakes.
- **Unafraid of minor confrontations with tenants.** A degree of fortitude is particularly important if the manager will be collecting overdue rents, delivering termination notices, and handling disputes between tenants (for example, complaints over noise).

Check Criminal and Driving Records

A property manager occupies a position of trust, often having access to tenants' apartments as well as to your money. Check an applicant's criminal history; credit reports often include this information. Depending on your state's laws concerning use of Megan's Law databases, you might want to use the database to check for registered sex offenders, as explained in Chapter 1.

Another reason for thoroughness is your personal liability—if a manager commits a crime, you might be held responsible as discussed in "Protect Tenants From Your Employees" in Chapter 12.

Our best advice is check carefully and consider the type, seriousness, and dates of any prior convictions and how they relate to the job. *The Employer's Legal Handbook*, by Fred S. Steingold (Nolo), includes information about state laws on obtaining and using information on arrest and conviction records when making employment decisions.

If a manager will be driving your car or truck, be sure your insurance covers someone driving your vehicle as part of their employment.

Offer the Position and Put Your Agreement in Writing

Once you make your decision and offer someone the manager's job, you might need to do some negotiating. The potential employee might, for example, want a higher salary, different hours, more vacation, a different rental unit, or a later starting date than you offer.

When all terms and conditions of employment are agreed upon, you and the manager should complete a Property Manager Agreement (discussed below) that covers manager responsibilities, hours, and pay. Importantly, the agreement states that the job can be terminated at any time for any reason by either party.

We recommend that when you hire a tenant as a manager, you also sign a separate month-to-month rental agreement that can be terminated by either of you with the amount of written notice, typically 30 days, as required under state law. If your new hire insists on a lease, realize that if you decide to terminate the employment part of the relationship, you will not be able to get the ex-manager off your property until the lease is up (unless a term and condition of the lease is that it will terminate within a specified number of days following the tenant's loss of the manager's job).

How to Reject Applicants for the Manager's Job

It used to be a matter of simple courtesy to reject unsuccessful applicants by sending a quick but civil letter, which cut down on postinterview calls, too. You didn't owe them an explanation, however, and were usually better off saying as little as possible.

Is this approach still legal? It depends on why you have rejected the applicant. If your reasons come from information that the applicant has provided, or if the applicant doesn't have the qualifications for the job, you can still use the courteous-but-minimalist approach. For example, if the applicant tells you that she has never managed a large real estate property, or if the interview reveals that the applicant doesn't have the necessary "people skills," you can simply say that someone more qualified got the job.

However, if your rejection is based on information from a credit reporting agency that collects and sells credit files or other information about consumers, you must comply with the Fair Credit Reporting Act (15 U.S. Code §§ 1681 and following). See "How to Reject an Applicant" in Chapter 1 for more details, including a sample Notice of Denial Based on Credit Report or Other Information form.

! CAUTION

Don't promise long-term job security. When you hire someone, don't give assurances that you might not be able to honor or that give an applicant a false sense of security. Your best protection is to make sure your Property Manager Agreement emphasizes your right to fire the employee at will—and have the applicant acknowledge this in writing (see Clause 7 of the agreement shown below). This means you'll have the right to terminate the employment at any time for any reason that doesn't violate the law.

Why Do You Need a Written Agreement?

Landlords and resident managers often agree orally on the manager's responsibilities and compensation, never signing a written agreement.

Even though oral agreements are usually legal and binding, they are not advisable. Memories fade, and you and your employee might have different recollections of what you've agreed to. If a dispute arises, the exact terms of an oral agreement are difficult or impossible to prove if you end up arguing about them in court.

It is a far better business practice to put your understanding in writing.

How to Prepare a Property Manager Agreement

Below is an example of a written agreement that spells out the manager's responsibilities, hourly wage or salary, hours, schedule, and other terms. The step-by-step instructions that follow take you through the process of completing your own agreement.

The Nolo website includes a downloadable copy of the Property Manager Agreement. See Appendix B for the link to the form in this book.

Clause 1. Parties

Here, insert your name or your business' name as landlord. List your manager's full legal name.

Clause 2. Property

Insert the full address of the rental property in the first blank. The second sentence applies if your manager will be living at the rental property, and notes that the rental agreement is a separate arrangement and document. In the first blank, note the unit number the manager will live in (if applicable). If your manager will not be living at the property, simply cross out or delete the second sentence.

Clause 3. Beginning Date

Fill in the month, day, and year of the manager's first day of work.

Clause 4. Responsibilities

This form includes a broad checklist of managerial duties, such as rent collection, maintenance, and repair. Check all the boxes that apply to your situation. In the space provided, spell out what is required, with as much detail as possible, particularly regarding maintenance responsibilities.

To help your manager follow relevant laws, prepare a more detailed set of instructions to give to the manager when work starts. We show a sample below, which you can tailor to reflect the circumstances of your situation, as well as any relevant state or local laws.

Clause 5. Hours and Schedule

Before filling this section in, check with your state department of labor or employment for wage and hour laws that might affect the number of hours you can schedule a manager to work in a day or days in a week. Don't expect a manager to be on call 24 hours a day. In most circumstances, you must pay overtime after 40 hours per week.

Should You Pay Benefits?

No law requires you to provide paid vacation, paid holidays, or premium pay for weekend or holiday work (unless it's for overtime). While most states do not require paid sick leave either, a handful of states require employers to provide at least a few paid sick days each year. Fringe benefits are not required, although larger employers (those with 50 or more full-time employees) might need to provide health insurance under the Affordable Care Act.

Clause 6. Payment Terms

In this clause, state how much and when you pay your manager. Specify the interval and dates on which you will pay the manager. For example, if the payment is weekly, specify the day. If payment is once each month, state the date, such as "the first of the month." If the payment is twice each month, indicate the dates, such as "the 15th and the 30th, or the last previous weekday if either date falls on a weekend."

Clause 7. Ending the Manager's Employment

This clause gives you the right to fire a manager any time for any legal reason. It makes clear that you are not guaranteeing a year's, or even a month's, employment to your new hire. You can legally fire your manager any time for any or no reason—as long as your actions aren't motivated by illegal reasons, such as racial or religious discrimination or in retaliation for the manager's legally protected acts. Your manager can quit at any time, for any reason—with or without notice.

Clause 8. Additional Agreements and Amendments

In this clause, you provide details about any areas of the manager's employment that weren't covered elsewhere in the agreement, such as the number of vacation or sick days, any annual paid holidays, or how you plan to reimburse any of the manager's out-of-pocket costs for repairs or other expenses.

The last part of this section is fairly standard in written agreements. It states that this is your entire agreement about the manager's employment, and that any changes to the agreement must be in writing.

Together, these provisions prevent you or your manager from later claiming that additional oral or written promises were made, but just not included in the written agreement.

CAUTION
Make changes in writing. If you later change the terms of your agreement, write the new terms down and have each person sign.

Clause 9. Place of Execution

Here you specify the city and state in which you signed the agreement. If there's any legal problem with the agreement later, it can be resolved by the courts where it was signed. Be advised, however, that the laws where the work is to be performed might be applied instead. So if, for example, you sign the Property Manager Agreement at your office in Maryland, but your rental property and the manager's workplace is in nearby Washington, D.C., the Maryland court hearing your case might use Washington, D.C.'s laws to decide the outcome.

Your Legal Obligations as an Employer

Whether you compensate a manager with reduced rent or a regular salary, you have specific legal obligations as an employer, such as following minimum wage and overtime laws. If you don't pay Social Security and meet your other legal obligations as an employer, you might face substantial financial penalties.

RESOURCE
Start out by getting IRS Publication 15 (Circular E), *Employer's Tax Guide,* **which provides details about your tax and record-keeping obligations.** Visit IRS.gov (or, a direct link to the form pops up if you search for "IRS Publication 15") to obtain a free copy of this and other IRS publications and forms. *Tax Savvy for Small Business,* by Frederick W. Daily (Nolo), covers strategies that will help you minimize taxes and stay out of legal trouble, including how to deduct business expenses, write off or depreciate long-term business assets, keep the kinds of records that will satisfy the IRS, get a tax break from business losses, and handle a small business audit.

Most Resident Managers Are Employees, Not Independent Contractors

No matter how you label your arrangement with your resident manager, the IRS and other government agencies will probably consider the manager to be your employee, not an independent contractor. Under the law, you must provide employees with a number of workplace rights that you would not be required to provide to an independent contractor.

To be considered an independent contractor, a person must offer services to the public at large and work under an arrangement in which the worker (rather than the hiring party) controls the means and methods of accomplishing a job. Most tenant-managers are legally considered to be employees because they work for only one property owner who hires them, sets the hours and responsibilities, and determines the particulars of the job. Managers who work for several different landlords and exercise extensive control over how they perform their tasks, on the other hand, might qualify for independent contractor status.

Employer Identification Number

As an employer, you need a federal identification number for tax purposes. If you don't already have one, you need to get an "employer identification number" (EIN) from the IRS. To obtain an EIN, you can apply online at the IRS website (go to IRS.gov and search for "EIN"), or complete IRS Form SS-4, *Application for Employer Identification Number* and send it to the IRS.

Income Taxes

The IRS considers the manager's compensation as taxable income to the manager. For that reason, when beginning work, your manager must fill out IRS Form W-4, *Employee's Withholding Allowance Certificate*. You must deduct federal income, Social Security, and Medicare taxes from each paycheck (and state taxes if required), and turn over the withheld funds to the IRS and the appropriate state tax agency. If your payroll taxes for either the current quarter or preceding quarter are less than $2,500, you can remit them quarterly to the IRS along with Form 941, *Employer's Quarterly Federal Tax Return*. Otherwise, small employers generally make payroll tax payments monthly. You must also provide the manager with IRS Form W-2, *Wage and Tax Statement*, for the previous year's earnings by January 31. The W-2 form lists the employee's gross wages and provides a breakdown of any taxes that you withheld.

Social Security and Medicare Taxes ("FICA")

Federal Insurance Contributions Act (FICA) taxes go toward the employee's future Social Security and Medicare benefits. Every employer must pay the IRS a "payroll tax," equal to 7.65% of the employee's gross compensation— that is, the paycheck amount before deductions (6.2% goes to Social Security, 1.45% goes to Medicare). You must also deduct an additional 7.65% from the employee's wages and turn it over (with the payroll tax) to the IRS along with the employee's withheld income taxes. For updated information on payroll taxes, including additional Medicare taxes for employees who earn more than $200,000 in a calendar year, see the most current edition of Publication 15, Circular E (*IRS Employer's Tax Guide*).

If you compensate your manager with reduced rent, you must still pay the FICA payroll tax, unless you meet certain conditions, explained below. For example, an apartment owner who compensates a manager with a rent-free $500/month apartment must pay 7.65% of $500, or $38.25, in payroll taxes each month. The manager is responsible for paying another 7.65% ($38.25) to the IRS.

Property Manager Agreement

1. Parties

This Agreement is between ___Jacqueline Marsh_____ ("Landlord"),

and Manager of the property ___Bradley Finch_____ ("Manager").

2. Property

Manager agrees to manage the property located at _175 Donner Avenue, Syracuse, New York_ ("Property")

in accordance with the terms of this Agreement. Manager will be renting unit _Number 5_ of the Property

under a separate written rental agreement that is in no way contingent upon or related to this Agreement.

3. Beginning Date

Manager will begin work on _____April 10, 20xx_____.

4. Responsibilities

Manager agrees to lawfully and with due diligence perform the duties indicated below:

Renting Units

☑ advertise vacancies

☑ respond promptly to all inquiries about vacancies

☑ show vacant units

☐ accept rental applications

☐ select tenants

☑ accept initial rents and deposits

☐ other (specify) _____

☐ _____

☐ _____

Vacant Apartments

☑ inspect unit when tenant moves in and document condition of rental

☑ inspect unit when tenant moves out and document condition of rental

☐ clean unit after tenant moves out, including:

    ☐ floors, carpets, and rugs

    ☐ walls, baseboards, ceilings, lights, and built-in shelves

    ☐ kitchen cabinets, countertops, sinks, stove, oven, and refrigerator

    ☐ bathtubs, showers, toilets, and plumbing fixtures

    ☐ doors, windows, window coverings, and miniblinds

    ☑ other (specify) _Hire and supervise cleaning service to clean rental unit when a tenant moves out._

    ☐ _____

Rent Collection

☑ collect rents when due

☑ sign rent receipts

☑ maintain rent collection records

☑ collect late rents and charges

☑ inform Landlord of late rents

☑ prepare late rent notices

☑ serve late rent notices on tenants

☑ serve rent increase and tenancy termination notices

☑ deposit rent collections in bank

☐ other (specify) _____

☐ _____

Maintenance

☑ vacuum and clean hallways and entryways

☑ replace lightbulbs in common areas

☑ drain water heaters

☑ clean stairs, decks, patios, facade, and sidewalks

☐ clean garage oils on pavement

☐ mow lawns

☐ rake leaves

☑ trim bushes

☑ clean up garbage and debris on grounds

☑ shovel snow from sidewalks and driveways or arrange for snow removal

☐ other (specify) _____

☐ _____

Repairs

☑ accept tenant complaints and repair requests

☑ inform Landlord of maintenance and repair needs

☑ maintain written log of tenant complaints

☑ handle routine maintenance and repairs, including:

    ☑ plumbing stoppages

    ☑ garbage disposal stoppages/repairs

    ☑ faucet leaks/washer replacement

☑ toilet tank repairs

☑ toilet seat replacement

☑ stove burner repair/replacement

☑ stove hinges/knobs replacement

☑ dishwasher repair

☑ light switch and outlet repair/replacement

☐ heater thermostat repair

☐ window repair/replacement

☐ painting (interior)

☐ painting (exterior)

☑ replacement of keys

☐ other (specify) _____

☐ _____

Other Responsibilities

_____

_____

_____

_____

_____

_____

_____

5. Hours and Schedule

Manager will be available to tenants during the following days and times: ___monday through Friday,___ ___1 p.m. – 6 p.m (on the property) and by phone other times___. If Manager believes that the hours required to carry out any duties in a given week might reasonably exceed _____30_____ hours, Manager shall notify Landlord and obtain Landlord's consent before working such extra hours, except in the event of an emergency. Extra hours worked due to an emergency must be reported to Landlord within 24 hours.

6. Payment Terms

a. Manager will be paid:

☐ $ _____ per hour

☐ $ _____ per week

☑ $ ___2,500___ per month

☐ Other: _____

b. Manager will be paid on the specified intervals and dates:

☐ Once a week on every _____

☑ Twice a month on _the first and the 15th of the month_

☐ Once a month on _____

☐ Other (specify) _____

7. Ending the Manager's Employment

This Agreement creates an "at will" employment arrangement: Landlord may terminate Manager's employment at any time, for any reason that isn't unlawful, with or without notice. Manager may quit at any time, for any reason, with or without notice.

8. Additional Agreements and Amendments

a. Landlord and Manager additionally agree that: _manager will be available to consult with_ _Landlord's attorney as needed, and will provide sworn testimony if necessary._

_____

_____

_____

_____

_____

_____

_____

_____

b. All agreements between Landlord and Manager relating to the work specified in this Agreement are incorporated in this Agreement. Any modification to the Agreement must be in writing and signed by both parties.

9. Place of Execution

Signed at __Syracuse_____, __New York_____
City   State

_Jacqueline Marsh_____   _April 3, 20xx_____
Landlord   Date

_Bradley Finch_____   _April 3, 20xx_____
Manager   Date

You do not have to pay FICA taxes on the value of the reduced rent if all the following conditions are met:

- The manager's unit is on your rental property.
- You provide the unit for your convenience (or to comply with a state law that requires on-site managers for properties of a certain size).
- Your manager actually works as a manager.
- The manager accepts the unit as a condition of employment—in other words, the manager must live in the unit in order to be your resident manager.

Help With Paperwork

Employers are responsible for a certain amount of paperwork and record keeping, such as time and pay records. If you hate paperwork, your accountant or bookkeeper can probably handle it for you. Or, a reputable payroll tax service that offers a tax notification service will calculate the correct amount of Social Security, unemployment, workers' compensation, and other taxes due; produce the check to pay your manager; and calculate the taxes and notify you when the taxes are due.

Payroll services can be cost-effective even if you employ only one or two people. But when you look for one, it pays to shop around. To get cost quotes, search the Internet for "payroll service" or "bookkeeping service." Avoid services that charge set-up fees—basically, a fee for putting your information into the computer—or extra fees to prepare W-2 forms or quarterly and annual tax returns.

CAUTION
Always pay payroll taxes on time. If you don't, the IRS will fine you—and you could be forced out of business by the huge penalties and interest charges it will add to the delinquent bill. And unlike most other debts, you must pay back payroll taxes even if you go through bankruptcy.

Unemployment Taxes

A manager who is laid off, quits for good reason, or is fired for reasons other than misconduct is probably entitled to unemployment benefits. These benefits are financed by unemployment taxes paid by employers. You must pay a federal unemployment tax (FUTA) at a rate of 6% of the first $7,000 of the employee's wages for the year. (The actual FUTA tax rate is usually 0.6% because you get a 5.4% credit if you pay state unemployment taxes for your employee.) Once each year, you must file IRS Form 940, *Employer's Annual Federal Unemployment Tax Return*. In addition to contributing to FUTA, you might also be responsible for contributing to an unemployment insurance fund in your state.

RESOURCE
Contact the IRS for information on Form 940 (used for unemployment tax returns) and FUTA. For information on state tax requirements, contact a local office of your state department of labor or employment or the government agency that oversees your state income tax program.

Minimum Wage and Overtime

However you pay your manager—by the hour, with a regular salary, or by a rent reduction—you should monitor the number of hours worked to make sure you're complying with the federal Fair Labor Standards Act (FLSA; 29 U.S.C. §§ 201 and following) and any state minimum wage laws.

The federal minimum hourly wage for 2022 is $7.25 an hour.

If your state's (or city's) minimum wage is higher than the federal rate, you must pay the higher rate. The Economic Policy Institute maintains a helpful tracker of each state's minimum wage—visit EPI.org and search for "minimum wage tracker" in the search box.

If part or all of your manager's compensation is in the form of a rent reduction, you might not be able to count the full amount of the rent reduction in complying with minimum wage laws. For example, in California, the maximum reduction in rent that can be credited toward the minimum wage owed a resident manager is $734.21 per month for a single manager and $1,086.07 per month for a couple. This problem is avoided by not providing a resident manager a rent reduction. Instead, pay the manager cash for all hours worked and charge market rates for the manager's rental through a separate rental agreement.

Federal wage and hour laws also require employers to pay time-and-a-half if an employee works more than 40 hours a week (with a few exceptions). Some states (most notably California) require you to pay overtime if an employee works more than eight hours in a day, even if the employee works less than 40 hours in a week.

RESOURCE

For information on minimum wage laws, overtime rules, and record-keeping requirements, see the U.S. Department of Labor's website at DOL.gov. Also see IRS Publication 15-B, *Employer's Tax Guide to Fringe Benefits*, available at IRS.gov. You can also contact the nearest office of the U.S. Labor Department's Wage and Hour Division or a local office of your state's department of labor or employment.

Equal Pay for Equal Work

You must provide equal pay and benefits to all persons who do the same job or jobs that require substantially equal skills, effort, and responsibility—regardless of sex. This is required by the Equal Pay Act (29 U.S.C. § 206(d)), an amendment to the FLSA.

Workers' Compensation Insurance

Workers' compensation provides some replacement income and pays medical expenses for employees who are injured or become ill as a result of their jobs. It's a no-fault system—an injured employee is entitled to receive benefits whether or not you provided a safe workplace and whether or not the manager's own carelessness contributed to the injury. (You are, of course, required by federal and state laws to provide a reasonably safe workplace.) But you, too, receive some protection for having provided workers' compensation insurance, because the manager, in most cases, cannot sue you for damages. In addition, the manager is limited to fixed types of compensation—basically, partial wage replacement and payment of medical bills. Injured employees might also receive compensation and vocational training when they're left with a permanent impairment and unable to return to the same line of work. The manager can't get paid for pain and suffering or mental anguish.

To cover the costs of workers' compensation benefits for employees, you'll need to purchase a special insurance policy—either through a state fund or a private insurance company. Each state has its own workers' compensation statute. Many states require all employers to get coverage; however, some states set a minimum number of employees (generally between three and five) before requiring coverage.

Most wise landlords obtain workers' compensation insurance, whether or not it's required. A lawsuit over a manager's injuries could bankrupt your business.

CAUTION

Workers' comp doesn't apply to intentional acts. Workers' compensation typically won't cover you from employee lawsuits for injuries caused by *your* intentional or reckless behavior—for example, if you know of a dangerous condition but refuse to fix it, and it results in an injury.

RESOURCE

Contact your state workers' compensation office for information on coverage and costs. The U.S. Department of Labor maintains the names and contact information of each state's office at www.dol.gov/agencies/owcp/wc.

Immigration Laws

When you hire someone—even someone who was born and raised in the same city as your rental—you must review documents such as a passport or birth certificate that prove the employee's identity and employment eligibility. You and each new employee must complete USCIS Form I-9, *Employment Eligibility Verification.* These rules come from the Immigration Reform and Control Act (IRCA), a federal law that prohibits hiring undocumented workers. The law, administered by the U.S. Citizenship and Immigration Services (USCIS), prohibits hiring workers who don't have government authorization to work in the United States.

RESOURCE

For more information, visit USCIS.gov.

New Hire Reporting Form

Within a short time after you hire someone—20 days or less—you must file a New Hire Reporting form with a designated state agency. The information on the form becomes part of the National Directory of New Hires, used primarily to locate parents so that child support orders can be enforced. Government agencies also use the data to prevent improper payment of workers' compensation and unemployment benefits or public assistance benefits. For more information, check out the website of the federal Office of Child Support Enforcement, www.acf.hhs.gov/programs/css; click "Employers."

Management Companies

Owners of large apartment complexes and absentee owners often use property management companies. Property management companies generally take care of renting units, collecting rent, taking tenant complaints, arranging repairs and maintenance, and evicting troublesome tenants. Of course, some of these responsibilities can be shared with or delegated to resident managers who, in some instances, might work for the management company.

A variety of relationships between owners and management companies is possible, depending on your wishes and how the particular management company chooses to do business. For example, if you own one or more big buildings, the management company will probably recommend hiring a resident manager. But if your rental property has only a few units, or you own a number of small buildings spread over a good-sized geographical area, the management company will probably suggest simply responding to tenant requests and complaints from its central office.

Pros and Cons of Management Companies

One advantage of working with a management company is that you avoid all the legal hassles of being an employer: paying payroll taxes, buying workers' compensation insurance, withholding income tax. The management company is an independent contractor, not an employee. It hires and pays the people who do the work. Typically, you sign a contract spelling out the management company's duties and fees. Most companies charge a fixed percentage—about 5% to 10%—of the total rent collected. (This does not include the cost of a resident manager whom you employ.) Tying the pay to the total collected rent gives the company a good incentive to keep the building filled with rent-paying tenants.

The primary disadvantage of hiring a management company is the expense. For example, if you pay a management company 10% of the $14,000 you collect in rent each month from tenants in a 12-unit building, this amounts to $1,400 a month and $16,800 per year. While many companies charge less than 10%, it's still quite an expense. Also, if the management company works from a central office with no one on-site, tenants might feel that management is too distant and unconcerned with their day-to-day needs.

Questions to Ask When You Hire a Management Company

- Who are its clients: owners of single-family houses, small apartment buildings, or large apartment complexes? Look for a company with experience handling property like yours. Also ask for client references, and check to see whether other landlords are satisfied with the management company. (Don't forget to ask these landlords how their tenants feel about the service they get. Unhappy tenants are bad for business.)
- What services are provided?
- What are the costs? What services cost extra?
- Will the management company take tenant calls 24 hours a day, seven days a week?
- Will there be an individual property manager assigned to your property? How frequently will the property manager visit and inspect your building?
- Is the company located fairly close to your property?
- Are employees trained in landlord-tenant law? Will the company consult an attorney qualified in landlord-tenant matters if problems arise, such as disputes over rent?
- Does the company handle evictions when necessary? If so, ask them to describe the process and any additional costs and fees involved.
- Has the company been sued for fair housing violations, or been named in an administrative complaint?
- If your property is under rent control, are company personnel familiar with the rent control law?
- Can you terminate the management agreement without cause on reasonable notice?

Management Company Contracts

Management companies have their own contracts, which you should read thoroughly and understand before signing. But don't sign anything that you'd like to see changed. Negotiate the company's fee, as well as any extra charges you can expect to pay during the length of the contract. You might also specify spending limits for ordinary repairs. And if you are picky about who works on your property, you might be able to specify that certain repairpersons or firms should be called before others are used.

It's a good idea to write down these understandings and attach them to the contract as an addendum or attachment.

Special Issues Involving Leases and Insurance

The contract with your management company will usually address the issues of leases and insurance.

Leases

Many management companies will insist on using their own leases. You might find that the company's lease is acceptable— but you might also find that it is not. For example, it's common to see late-fee policies that exceed a fair and legal limit. No surprise—the more money collected by the management company, the more money it earns for itself.

If the management company uses a lease that is legally amiss, it's a clear sign to look elsewhere. Now, what about other clauses in the company lease that are legal but not to your liking, such as a prohibition against pets? Again, no surprise—most management companies assume that pets equal more work, and they prefer not to have to deal with them. If the company will not negotiate with you over changing its "standard" lease, you might want to talk to other management companies that will be more flexible.

Insurance

All landlords need comprehensive liability insurance. Special issues arise when you hire a management company. Most important, both you and the management company need to show proof that you are each insured—and you each should be added to the other's policy as an "additional insured." Here's how it works.

You should require proof that the management company is insured under a comprehensive general liability policy, with extra coverage for "errors and omissions" and employee dishonesty. When you are added as an "additional insured," you get the benefit of that policy. If you are named in a lawsuit over something that the management company allegedly did or didn't do, you will be covered by the management company's insurer. They will defend you and pay out any settlement or verdict that results against you. Your insurance broker should be able to recommend how much insurance is adequate.

The management company will demand proof that you, too, carry adequate amounts of liability insurance, and they will also want to be named as an additional insured in your policy. If you don't currently have enough insurance coverage, the management company might refuse to take your business or require you to obtain additional coverage.

Fortunately, adding a landlord or a management company as an additional insured is not a big deal. Insurance companies do it all the time, generally at no additional cost. Simply contact your broker and request that the management company be added. Ask the broker to send a certificate of insurance to the management company. And don't forget to demand the same of the management company— you, too, want a certificate of insurance stored safely in your files.

Your Liability for a Manager's Acts

Depending on the circumstances, you could be legally responsible for the acts of a manager or management company. For example, you might be sued and found liable if your manager or management company:

- refuses to rent to a qualified tenant for discriminatory reasons, or otherwise violates antidiscrimination laws
- sexually harasses a tenant
- makes illegal deductions from the security deposit of a tenant who has moved out, or does not return the departing tenant's deposit within the time limit set by law
- ignores a dangerous condition, such as substandard wiring that results in an electrical fire, causing injury or damage to a tenant, or dismisses security problems that result in a criminal assault on a tenant
- invades a tenant's privacy by flagrant and damaging gossip or trespass, or
- commits a crime such as assaulting a tenant.

In short, a landlord who knows the law but has a manager (or management company) who doesn't could wind up in a lawsuit brought by prospective or former tenants.

Protect your tenants and yourself by:

Choosing your manager carefully. Legally, you have a duty to protect your tenants from injury caused by employees you know or should know pose a risk of harm to others. If someone gets hurt or has property stolen or damaged by a manager whose law-breaking background you didn't check, you could be sued.

Ensuring that your manager is familiar with the basics of landlord-tenant law. This is especially important if your manager will be selecting tenants or serving eviction notices. One approach is to give your manager a copy of this book to read and refer to.

Sample Instructions to Manager

Dear New Manager:

Welcome to your new position as resident manager. Here are important instructions to guide you as you perform your duties under our management agreement. Please read them carefully and keep them for future reference.

1. Discrimination in rental housing on the basis of race, religion, sex, familial status, age, national or ethnic origin, or disability is illegal—whether you are accepting rental applications for vacant apartments or dealing with current residents. Your duties are to advertise and accept rental applications in a nondiscriminatory manner. This includes allowing all individuals to fill out applications and offering the unit on the same terms to all applicants. After you have collected all applications, please notify me. I will sort through the applications, set up interviews, and decide whom to accept.

2. Tenants have a right to feel comfortable and relaxed in and near their homes. To be sure all do, please avoid any comments, actions, or physical contact that could be considered offensive, even by those whom you might see as being overly sensitive on the issue. Harassment is against the law and will not be tolerated.

3. Do not issue any rent increase or termination notices without my prior approval.

4. Treat all tenants who complain about defects, even trivial defects or ones you believe to be nonexistent, with respect. Enter all tenant complaints into the log I have supplied to you on the day they are made. Respond to tenant complaints about the building or apartment units immediately in emergencies or if the complaint involves security; and respond to other complaints within 24 hours. If you cannot correct (or arrange to correct) any problem or defect yourself, please telephone me immediately.

5. Except in serious life- or property-threatening emergencies, never enter (or allow anyone else to enter) a tenant's apartment without the tenant's consent or in the tenant's absence, unless you have given written notice at least 24 hours in advance, either delivered personally or, if that's not possible, posted on the door. If you have given the tenant 24-hour written notice, you may enter in the tenant's absence during ordinary business hours (9 a.m. to 5 p.m., M-F) to do repairs or maintenance work, unless the tenant objects. If the tenant objects, do not enter, but instead call me.

6. When tenants move in, and again when they move out, inspect the unit. If possible, have the tenants accompany you. On each occasion, both you and the tenants should complete and sign a Landlord-Tenant Checklist form. Take pictures on your phone or make a video during both walkthroughs.

7. If you think a tenant has moved out and abandoned the apartment, do not enter it. Call me first.

Sample Instructions to Manager (continued)

8. Once a tenant has vacated an apartment and given you the key, keep track of all costs necessary to repair damages in excess of ordinary wear and tear. Give me a copy of this list, along with a notation of the amount of any back rent; the "before" and "after" Landlord-Tenant Checklist, and the departing tenant's forwarding address. Please make sure I see this material within a week after the tenant moves out, preferably sooner. I will mail the itemization and any security deposit balance to the tenant.

9. If you have any other problems or questions, please do not hesitate to call or text me. Leave a message if I am not available.

Sincerely,

Terry Herendeen

Terry Herendeen, Owner

1111 Maiden Lane, Omaha, Nebraska 54001

402-555-1234 (cell phone)

402-555-5678 (work)

terry@terrylandlord.com

I have received a copy of this memorandum and have read and understood it.

Dated: ___April 7, 20xx___

Barbara Louis

Barbara Louis, Manager

In addition, you'll want to provide detailed instructions that cover likely trouble areas, such as the legal rules prohibiting antidiscrimination in tenant selection. Above is a sample set of instructions for a manager with fairly broad authority; you can tailor it to fit your situation. You'll also need to add any requirements that are imposed by the laws in your state—for example, stricter discrimination laws or notice requirements for entering rental property than are outlined in the sample instructions. Make two copies and have the manager sign one of them and give it to you.

Keeping an eye on your manager, and listening to tenants' concerns and complaints. Don't discourage tenants from reporting problems to you directly, even if your manager is designated as the primary contact. If you hear about or suspect problems, do your own investigating. Try to resolve problems and get rid of a bad manager before problems accelerate and you end up having to defend tenants' legal claims.

Emergency Contacts and Procedures for Your Employees

It's an excellent idea to prepare written emergency guidance for the manager, including:

- your name and emergency phone number (along with the owner's, if different), along with directions on when it's appropriate to use them
- names and phone numbers of nearest hospital and poison control center
- a reminder to call 9-1-1 or local ambulance, police, and fire departments when needed
- names and phone numbers of contractors who can respond to a building emergency on a 24-hour basis, including any licensed plumber, electrician, locksmith, boiler mechanic, elevator service company, and air conditioner maintenance company with whom you have set up an account, and
- procedures to follow in case of a fire, flood, earthquake, hurricane, tornado, or other disaster, including how to safely shut down elevators, water, electricity, and gas.

Making sure your insurance covers illegal acts of your employees. No matter how thorough your precautions, you might still be liable for your manager's illegal acts—even if your manager commits an illegal act in direct violation of your instructions. To really protect yourself, purchase a good landlord's insurance policy.

Notifying Tenants of the Manager

In many states, you are legally required to give tenants the manager's name and address and tell them that the manager is authorized to accept legal documents on your behalf, such as termination of tenancy notices or court documents in an eviction lawsuit.

We recommend that you give tenants this information in writing, whether or not it's required by law. A section for this information is included in our lease and rental agreements (see Clause 23 "Authority to Receive Legal Papers," discussed in Chapter 2), but don't forget to also notify tenants who moved in before you hired the manager.

You should also post a copy of the written notice you provided to tenants in a prominent place in the building.

Be sure your Property Manager Agreement, discussed above, notes the manager's authority in this regard. You can put details in the last section, Additional Agreements and Amendments.

Firing a Manager

Unless you have an oral or written contract to employ a manager for a specific period of time, you have the right to terminate employment at any time. But you cannot do it for an illegal reason, such as:

- race, age, gender, or other prohibited forms of discrimination, or
- retaliation against the manager for calling your illegal acts to the attention of authorities.

EXAMPLE: You order your manager to dump 20 gallons of fuel oil at the back of your property. Instead, the manager complains to a local environmental regulatory agency, which fines you. If you now fire the manager, you will be vulnerable to a lawsuit for illegal termination.

The High Cost of a Bad Manager: Sexual Harassment in Housing

If tenants complain about illegal acts by a manager, pay attention. The owners of a Fairfield, California, apartment complex learned this lesson the hard way—by paying more than a million dollars to settle a lawsuit.

The tenants, mostly single mothers, were tormented by an apartment manager who spied on them, opened their mail, and sexually harassed them. They were afraid to complain, for fear of eviction. When they did complain to the building's owners, the owners refused to take any action—and the manager stepped up his harassment in retaliation.

Finally, the tenants banded together and sued, and the details of the manager's outrageous and illegal conduct were exposed. The owners settled the case before trial for $1.6 million.

To head off the possibility of a wrongful termination lawsuit, be prepared to show a good business-related reason for the firing. If the manager's behavior poses a threat to health, safety, or property, immediate termination is justified. Use your best judgment, and back up all firings with written records documenting your reasons.

Reasons that might support a firing include:

- performing poorly on the job
- refusing to follow instructions
- possessing a weapon at work
- being dishonest or stealing money or property from you or your tenants
- endangering the health or safety of tenants
- engaging in criminal activity
- arguing or fighting with tenants

- behaving violently at work, or
- unlawfully discriminating against or harassing prospective or current tenants.

If the manager's poor performance doesn't justify immediate termination, give your manager ongoing feedback about job performance and impose progressive discipline, such as an oral or written warning, before termination. Do a six-month performance review (and more often, if necessary) and keep notes about the review and copies of any written evaluations. Solicit comments from tenants twice a year (as mentioned earlier) and keep records of the comments.

Handling Requests for References

One of your biggest problems after a manager quits or has been fired might be what to tell other landlords or employers who inquire about the former manager. You might be tugged in several directions:

- You want to tell the truth—good, bad, or neutral—about the former manager.
- You want to help the former manager find another, more suitable, job.
- You don't want to be sued for libel or slander because you say something negative.

Legally, you're better off saying as little as possible, rather than saying anything negative. Just say that it's your policy not to comment on former managers. Many callers will assume that if you politely say, "I would rather not discuss Mr. Jones," you've implicitly given a negative reference.

Firing a Property Management Company

If you find that your arrangement with your independent contractor management company isn't working out, read over your contract with the company. It likely contains a termination clause. Unless you have reason to fire the company immediately, the contract probably requires you to give the company a 30-day notice before ending the relationship.

Evicting a Manager

When you fire a manager, you might want the ex-employee to move out of your property, particularly if there is a special manager's unit or the firing has generated (or resulted from) ill will. How easy it will be to get the fired manager out depends primarily on whether you have separate management and rental agreements.

![briefcase icon] SEE AN EXPERT

In many cases, you'll want the eviction of a former manager to be handled by an attorney who specializes in landlord-tenant law. See Chapter 18 for advice on finding a qualified lawyer.

If you and the tenant-manager signed separate management and rental agreements, firing the manager does not affect the tenancy. The ex-manager will have to keep paying rent but will no longer work as manager. Evicting the former manager is just like evicting any other tenant. You will have to give a normal termination notice, typically 30 days for month-to-month tenancies, subject to any applicable rent control restrictions. If the tenant has a separate fixed-term lease, you cannot terminate the tenancy until the lease expires.

If you are evicting the manager for not paying rent or for violating a lease or rental agreement term (for example, by damaging rental property), you might be able to provide less notice. See Chapter 17 for details.

We do not recommend combining a tenant-manager's management and rental agreements. Doing so makes it especially difficult to evict an ex-manager, and adds unnecessary complexity to the relationship. Keeping the two agreements separate allows you to deal with each one in its own time and without excessive concern over how taking action regarding one will affect the other.

Getting the Tenant Moved In

 FORMS IN THIS CHAPTER

Chapter 7 includes instructions for and samples of the following forms:

- Landlord-Tenant Checklist
- Move-In Letter

The purchase of this book includes free downloadable and customizable copies of both of these forms. See Appendix B for the download link and instructions.

A clearly written lease or rental agreement, signed by all adult occupants, is the foundation of a strong tenancy. But establishing a dispute-free relationship based on mutual understanding requires more. In addition to signing a solid lease or rental agreement, you'll want to:

- inspect the property with the tenant and fill out a Landlord-Tenant Checklist, and
- prepare a move-in letter highlighting important terms of the tenancy and your expectations.

> ### States That Require a Landlord-Tenant Checklist
>
> To find out if your state requires a landlord-tenant checklist documenting the unit's condition, check the "Required Landlord Disclosures" chart in Appendix A.

Inspect the Rental Unit

To reduce the potential for future arguments, you (or your representative) and the new tenants (together, if possible) should inspect the rental for damage and obvious wear and tear before the tenants move in.

During the inspection, document what you see. Using a Landlord-Tenant Checklist, discussed below, is one of the most straightforward ways of recording the unit's condition.

In some states, the law requires you to give new tenants a written statement on the condition of the premises at move-in time, including a comprehensive list of existing damage.

Tenants in many of these states have the right to inspect the premises after receiving the landlord's list, and to note any problems or disagreements.

Even if a move-in inspection with documentation isn't legally required, you should consider it an essential part of creating a thorough file on the tenancy.

Use a Landlord-Tenant Checklist

When the tenant moves out, if you discover damage, you'll want to use the tenant's security deposit to cover the repair costs. Without thorough documentation, it will be difficult to prove that the tenant caused the damage—how will you show that the damage didn't exist when the tenant moved in?

A Landlord-Tenant Checklist provides the written record you'll need to support charging a tenant for damages to the rental. It can also serve as a key piece of evidence in the event you find yourself in a court battle over the security deposit. Our form includes a recital at the end that documents the presence of working smoke detectors and carbon monoxide detectors, along with an acknowledgment that you may enter to inspect and maintain them.

Coupled with a system to regularly keep track of the rental property's condition, the checklist will also be extremely useful if a tenant withholds rent, breaks the lease and moves out, or sues you outright based on a claim that the unit needs substantial repairs or isn't habitable. See Chapter 9 for instructions and forms that will let you stay updated on the condition of your rental properties.

A portion of our Landlord-Tenant Checklist is shown below, and the Nolo website includes free, customizable downloads for furnished and unfurnished property. See Appendix B for the link to the forms in this book.

Landlord-Tenant Checklist

Property Address: _____ 572 Fourth St., Apt. 11, Washington, D.C. _____

General Condition of Rental Unit and Premises

	Move-In Condition Date of Walk-Through: May 1, 20xx	Move-Out Condition Date of Walk-Through:
Living Room		
Flooring	OK, slight wearing from normal use	
Walls & Ceilings	OK	
Light Fixtures	OK	
Windows & Screens	miniblinds on both windows discolored	
Doors & handles/locks	OK	
Fireplace	OK	
...ector & CO detector		

How to Fill Out the Checklist

You and the tenants should fill out the checklist together. If that's impossible, complete the form and give it to the tenants to review. The tenant should note any disagreement and return it to you within a few days.

The checklist is in two parts: the General Condition of Rental Unit and Premises, and Checklist for Furnished Property. If your rental is not furnished, you can delete the second part. If your rental is fully or significantly furnished, you'll want to use this part of the checklist to inventory and describe the included items.

You can delete items that aren't present in your rental, or you can place "N/A" in the applicable box. You can also add as many items or rooms to the checklist as you need.

You will be filling out the first column—*Move-In Condition*—on or before the tenant's move-in date. You'll fill out the second column—*Move-Out Condition*—when the tenant moves out and you inspect the unit again.

You can change the entries by adding or deleting rows and columns. You can also delete sections and items if they are not included with your property.

General Condition of Rental Unit and Premises

In the *Move-In Condition* column, make detailed notes about items that aren't working or are dirty, scratched, or in poor condition. For example, don't simply note that the refrigerator "needs fixing" if the ice maker doesn't work—it's just as easy to write "ice maker broken, should not be used." If the tenants use the ice maker anyway and cause water damage, they cannot claim that they weren't aware it wasn't working properly.

You should remedy any mold, pest, or other habitability issues before new tenants move in. However, if you weren't aware of the problem before the move-in inspection, describe it in the checklist and note that you will be repairing it within a certain time frame.

Mark "OK" next to items that are in satisfactory condition—basically, clean, safe, sanitary, and in good working order.

> ### CAUTION
> **Make repairs and clean thoroughly before showing a rental unit.** To get the tenancy off to the best start and avoid hassles over repairs, handle problems before the start of a new tenancy. You must fix certain defects—such as a broken heater or leaking roof—under state and local housing codes. If you discover that the outgoing tenant is responsible for a problem, you might be able to cover your repair and cleaning costs by deducting from the outgoing tenant's security deposit.

Sign the Checklist

After you and your new tenants have made entries on the checklist, each of you should sign and date every page, including any attachments. Keep the original and give the tenants a copy. If the tenants filled out the checklist on their own, make sure you review their comments, note any disagreement, and return a copy to them.

You should make the checklist part of your lease or rental agreement, as we recommend in Chapter 2, Clause 11.

Be sure the tenants also check the boxes stating that the smoke detectors and carbon monoxide detectors—required for new occupancies in many states and cities—were tested in their presence and shown to be in working order. A check next to these boxes also signifies that the tenants agree to notify the landlord of any malfunctioning or broken smoke detector.

> ### TIP
>
> **Update the checklist if you repair, replace, add, or remove items or furnishings after the tenant moves in.** Both you and the tenant should initial and date any changes.

Photograph or Video the Rental Unit

Taking photos or videos of the unit before new tenants move in (and out) is another excellent way to record the initial condition of the rental. You'll be able to compare your "after" pictures at the end of the tenancy with the "before" pictures, as well as refer to the written record you created via the checklist. If tenants claim that damage was present when they moved in, you can show them the records to refresh their memory.

If you end up in mediation or court for not returning the full security deposit, having a visual record of the unit's condition will be invaluable. In addition, photos or a video can also help if you have to sue a former tenant for cleaning and repair costs that end up being more than the deposit amount.

Whether you take photos or a video with your phone or use a separate camera, date- and time-stamp them. Provide tenants with a copy of (or a link to) the photos and videos.

Send New Tenants a Move-In Letter

A move-in letter supplements the lease or rental agreement and provides basic information such as the manager's phone number and office hours. You can also use a move-in letter to explain any procedures and rules that are too detailed or numerous to include in your lease or rental agreement—for example, how and where to report maintenance problems. Consider including a brief list of maintenance dos and don'ts as part of the move-in letter—for example, how to avoid overloading circuits and proper use of the garbage disposal. Alternatively, some landlords provide a set of rules and regulations to cover some of these issues. (See Clause 20 of the form agreements in Chapter 2.)

A sample move-in letter is shown below, and the Nolo website includes a downloadable copy (see Appendix B for the link to the forms in this book). You should tailor this move-in letter to your needs—for example, alter it if you don't employ a resident manager or if your property is subject to rent control.

We recommend asking tenants to sign the last page of your move-in letter to indicate that they have read it. After everyone has signed, keep a copy for your records and give one to the tenants. (As an extra precaution, ask tenants to initial each page.)

Review your move-in letter before you provide it to a new tenant, and update it as needed.

Cash Rent and Security Deposit Checks

Every landlord's nightmare is a new tenant whose deposit or first rent check bounces.

To avoid this, never sign a lease or rental agreement until you have the tenant's cash, certified check, or money order for the first month's rent and security deposit. Alternatively, deposit the tenant's check at the bank and make sure it clears before the move-in date. (While you have the tenant's first check, photocopy it for your records. The information on it can be helpful if you need to sue to collect a judgment from the tenant.) Give the tenant a signed receipt for the deposit.

Clause 5 of the form lease and rental agreements in Chapter 2 requires tenants to pay rent on the first day of each month. If the move-in date is other than the first day of the month, rent is prorated between that day and the end of that month.

Organize Your Tenant Records

Develop a system for recording all significant tenant complaints and repair requests, as well as your responses. This will provide a valuable paper trail should disputes develop later. Without good records, the outcome of a dispute might come down to your word against your tenant's—always a precarious situation.

How to Establish a Filing System

Set up a file—paper or electronic—on each property for each tenant. Include the following documents in each tenant's file:

- tenant's rental application, references, credit report, and background information (but see the below discussion of disposing of this information eventually)
- information about any cosigners
- the signed lease or rental agreement, plus any changes or addenda
- the Landlord-Tenant Checklist plus photos or video made at move-in, and
- the signed move-in letter.

After a tenant moves in, add these documents to the individual's file:

- your written requests for entry
- rent increase notices
- records of repair requests, and details of how and when they were handled (if you have a master system to record all requests and complaints in one log, you would save that log separately, not necessarily put it in every tenant's file)
- safety and maintenance updates
- inspection reports, and
- correspondence, including copies of important emails and texts.

See "Using Email for Notices or Other Communications with Tenants," at the end of this chapter.

Move-In Letter

September 1, 20xx
Date

Frank O'Hara
Tenant

139 Porter Street
Street Address

Madison, Wisconsin 53704
City and State

Dear Frank ,
Tenant

Welcome to Apartment 45 B at Happy Hill Apartments

(address of rental unit). We hope you will enjoy living here.

This letter is to explain what you can expect from the management and what we'll be looking for from you.

Rent: Rent is due on the first day of the month. There is no grace period for the payment of rent. (See Clauses 5 and 6 of your rental agreement for details, including late charges.) Also, we don't accept postdated checks.

New Roommates: If you want someone to move in as a roommate, please contact us first. If your rental unit is big enough to accommodate another person, we will arrange for the new person to fill out a rental application. If it's approved, all of you will need to sign a new rental agreement. Depending on the situation, there might be a rent increase to add a roommate.

Notice to End Tenancy: To terminate your month-to-month tenancy, you must give at least 28 days' written notice. We have a written form available for this purpose. We may also terminate the tenancy, or change its terms, on 28 days' written notice. If you give less than 28 days' notice, you will still be financially responsible for rent for the balance of the 28-day period.

Deposits: Your security deposit will be applied to costs of cleaning, damages, or unpaid rent after you move out. You may not apply any part of the deposit toward any part of your rent in the last month of your tenancy. (See Clause 8 of your rental agreement.)

Manager: Sophie Beauchamp (Apartment #15, phone 555-1234, email Sophie@sophie.com) is your resident manager. You should pay your rent to her and promptly let her know of any maintenance or repair problems (see below) and any other questions or problems. She's in her office every day from 8 a.m. to 10 a.m. and from 4 p.m. to 6 p.m. and can be reached by phone at other times.

Landlord-Tenant Checklist: By now, Sophie Beauchamp should have taken you on a walk-through of your apartment to check the condition of all walls, drapes, carpets, and appliances and to test the smoke alarms and fire extinguisher. These are all listed on the Landlord-Tenant Checklist, which you should have reviewed carefully and signed. When you move out, we will ask you to check each item against its original condition as described on the Checklist.

Maintenance/Repair Problems: We are determined to maintain a clean, safe building in which all systems are in good repair. To help us make repairs promptly, we will give you maintenance/Repair Request forms to report any problems in your apartment. (Extra copies are available from the manager.) In an emergency, or when it's not convenient to use this form, please call the manager at 555-1234.

Semiannual Safety and Maintenance Update: To help us keep your unit and the common areas in excellent condition, we'll ask you to fill out a form every six months updating any problems on the premises or in your rental unit. This will allow you to report any potential safety hazards or other problems that otherwise might be overlooked.

Annual Safety Inspection: Once a year, we will ask to inspect the condition and furnishings of your rental unit and update the Landlord-Tenant Checklist. In keeping with state law, we will give you reasonable notice before the inspection, and you are encouraged to be present for it.

Insurance: Under the terms of your rental agreement, you are required to purchase renters' insurance. The building property insurance policy will not cover the replacement of your personal belongings if they are lost due to fire, theft, or accident. In addition, you could be found liable if someone is injured on the premises you rent as a result of your negligence. If you damage the building itself — for example, if you start a fire in the kitchen and it spreads — you could be responsible for large repair bills.

Moving Out: It's a little early to bring up moving out, but please be aware that we have a list of items that should be cleaned before we conduct a move-out inspection. If you decide to move, please ask the manager for a copy of our Move-Out Letter, explaining our procedures for inspection and returning your deposit.

Changes to Your Contact Information Please notify us if your phone number(s) change(s), so we can reach you promptly in an emergency.

Please let us know if you have any questions.

Sincerely,

Tom Guiliano
_____
Landlord/Manager

September 1, 20xx
_____
Date

I have read and received a copy of this statement.

Frank O'Hara
_____
Tenant

September 1, 20xx
_____
Date

Several property management software programs allow you to electronically track every aspect of your business, from the receipt of rents to the follow-up on repair requests. Purchasing one of these programs is well worth the cost, especially if you own multiple rental properties. Alternatively, you can set up your own database for each tenant containing the following information:

- address or unit number
- move-in date
- phone number (cell, home, work)
- name, address, and phone number of employer
- credit information, and up-to-date banking information
- monthly rent amount and rent due date
- amount and purpose of deposits plus any information your state requires on location of deposit and interest payments
- vehicle make, model, color, year, and license plate number
- emergency contacts, and
- whatever else is important to you.

Once you enter the information into your database, you'll be able to sort the list by address or other variables and easily print labels for rent increases or other notices.

How to Handle Credit Reports

Under federal law, you must store credit reports (and any information that is derived from credit reports) in a secure place where only those who "need to know" have access. ("Disposal Rule" of the Fair and Accurate Credit Transactions Act of 2003, known as the FACT Act, 69 Fed. Reg. 68690.) In addition, you must dispose of such records when you're done with them, by burning them or using a shredder. The goal of the Disposal Rule is to prevent identity theft. It applies to every landlord who pulls a credit report, no matter how small your operation. You should also safeguard and dispose of *any* record that contains a tenant's or applicant's personal or financial information, once you no longer need it. This would include the rental application itself, as well as any notes you make that include such information.

Implementing the Disposal Rule will require some effort and follow-through. Follow these suggestions:

- **Restrict access to applicant, tenant, and employee files.** Password-protect electronic files, and keep paper files in a locked cabinet or locked room. This is a good practice for many reasons. Only you and your manager should have access to these files.

- **Determine when you no longer have a legitimate business reason to keep an applicant's credit report.** The Disposal Rule requires you to dispose of credit reports or any information taken from them when you no longer need them. Unfortunately, you might need these reports long after you've rejected or accepted an applicant—they might be essential in refuting a fair housing claim. Under federal law, such claims must be filed within two years of the claimed discrimination, but some states set longer periods. Keep the records at least two years, and longer if your state gives plaintiffs more time to file suits.

- **Establish a system for purging old credit reports.** Don't rely on haphazard file purges to keep you legal when it comes to destroying old reports. Establish a purge date for every applicant for whom you pull a report, and use a reminder system.

- **Choose an effective purging method.** The Disposal Rule requires you to choose a level of document destruction that is reasonable in the context of your business. For example, a landlord with a few rentals would do just fine with an inexpensive shredder, but a multi-property operation might want to contract with a shredding service.

- **Don't forget computer files.** Reports stored on your computer or phone, or information derived from them, must also be kept secure and deleted when no longer needed. Purchase a utility that will "wipe" the data completely—that is, a program that will delete not only the directory, but the text as well.

The Disposal Rule comes with teeth for those who willfully disregard it—that is, for those who know about the law and how to comply but who deliberately refuse to do so. You could be liable for a tenant's actual damages resulting from identity theft (say, the cost of covering a portion of a credit card's unauthorized use), or damages per violation of between $100 and $1,000, plus the tenant's attorneys' fees and costs of suit, plus punitive damages. The Federal Trade Commission and state counterparts can also enforce the act and impose fines.

How to Respond to Security Breaches

If you lose a laptop, are hacked, or suffer the consequences of a dishonest employee, sensitive identifying information about residents and applicants in the wrong hands might result in identify theft.

Every state has laws on the books concerning security breaches. These laws cover who should comply, define the information that's at issue ("personal information"), define what constitutes a breach, provide notice requirements, and note any exemptions. To find the law in your state, go to the website of the National Conference of State Legislatures (NCSL.org) and enter "security breach notification laws" in the search box.

Organize Income and Expenses for Schedule E

If you pay taxes on your rental income via your personal return (IRS Form 1040), you will be used to reporting your income and expenses on

Schedule E. The schedule is relatively simple. For each address (which might include multiple rental units), you report the year's rent and list enumerated expenses (the first page of Schedule E is reproduced below). You can download a fillable version of Schedule E from IRS.gov.

Many landlords find it easiest to use *QuickBooks* or another accounting software package to track their income and expenses. You can buy programs designed specifically for completing Schedule E, notably *Quicken Home & Business,* which allows you to track income, expenses, and tax deductions; and converts the information into a Schedule E at tax time. You can also design your own spreadsheet using Microsoft *Excel, Google Sheets,* or a similar program, to keep track of rental income and expenses.

Finally, there's always the old-fashioned way of making your own paper ledger of income and expenses.

Of course, the system you use to track income and expenses is only as good as the information you enter. To maximize tax deductions, keep receipts and records of all rental-property-related costs and income.

RESOURCE
For detailed information on completing Schedule E and valuable tax advice for landlords, see *Every Landlord's Tax Deduction Guide,* **by Stephen Fishman (Nolo).** For personalized advice, consult an accountant or a tax professional. (The cost of this book and a tax pro's bill are both tax-deductible expenses.)

Using Email for Notices or Other Communications With Tenants

Often, the lease or rental agreement contains a clause that describes how landlords and tenants should deliver "notices and demands."

Unfortunately, most of the time you'll see a generic requirement that they be delivered "in writing"—and it will be unclear whether email or text is acceptable.

If communicating by email and text will work for you and your tenants, it's best to put a clear statement in your lease or rental agreement that these methods are acceptable ways to communicate. If you don't have such a clause, your email and texts might not be legally acceptable ways to send important notices.

Even when you and your tenant agree to communicate by text and email, you might still have a problem if you end up in a legal dispute. Suppose, for example, that you want to give notice terminating a tenant's month-to-month rental agreement, and do so by sending an email that's 30 days in advance of the termination date (your state's notice period). If you end up in a legal dispute, you'll need confirmation that your tenant received the email—and if the tenant claims to have never received it, you might have no way of proving otherwise.

On the One Hand: Electronic Notice Is Acceptable in Most Situations

Two laws confirm the acceptability in court of electronic notices: "UETA" (the Uniform Electronic Transactions Act), adopted in some form by 49 states and the District of Columbia (New York didn't adopt UETA, but instead passed a functional equivalent), and "ESIGN" (Electronic Signatures in Global and National Commerce Act), a federal law. Unless some other law prohibits it, UETA and ESIGN permit the use of electronic signatures and electronic notices. Put another way,

under each of these laws, a legal notice cannot be denied admission in court simply because it is electronic (and not on paper).

On the Other Hand: Emails and Texts Might Be Legal, But Demonstrating Their Receipt Might Not Be Easy

While it might be legally permissible to introduce emails as evidence in court, first you'll have to prove that the tenant received your email.

Although some email providers and services allow you to receive receipts that your email was received, they're not always reliable. The recipient can often decline to allow a receipt to be sent or might simply not open an email from you. Also, electronic glitches happen, and email can get stuck in your outbox or lost in limbo. Even when you use the most reliable email system possible, the recipients can always claim a problem on their end—and it's a very involved and expensive process to run the forensics to prove they actually did receive the message.

Getting an accurate record of text messages is even more difficult. Many phones and messaging programs allow you to communicate via the user's phone number or email address—and many of us have multiple numbers and email addresses. Keeping track of what was sent and when gets complicated quickly, and printing out a complete record of the conversation can be nearly impossible. On top of that, texts are prone to misspellings, autocorrect disasters, emoji use, and internet shorthand—all of which can lead to a very confusing record.

Other than sending an occasional note or hello, it's best to avoid communicating with your tenants in this manner.

SCHEDULE E
(Form 1040)

Department of the Treasury
Internal Revenue Service (99)

Supplemental Income and Loss

(From rental real estate, royalties, partnerships, S corporations, estates, trusts, REMICs, etc.)

▶ **Attach to Form 1040, 1040-SR, 1040-NR, or 1041.**
▶ **Go to** *www.irs.gov/ScheduleE* **for instructions and the latest information.**

OMB No. 1545-0074

2021

Attachment
Sequence No. **13**

Name(s) shown on return

Your social security number

Part I   **Income or Loss From Rental Real Estate and Royalties**   **Note:** If you are in the business of renting personal property, use **Schedule C.** See instructions. If you are an individual, report farm rental income or loss from **Form 4835** on page 2, line 40.

A Did you make any payments in 2021 that would require you to file Form(s) 1099? See instructions . . . . . ☐ Yes ☐ No
B If "Yes," did you or will you file required Form(s) 1099? . . . . ☐ Yes ☐ No

1a Physical address of each property (street, city, state, ZIP code)

A

B

C

1b	Type of Property (from list below)	**2**	For each rental real estate property listed above, report the number of fair rental and personal use days. Check the **QJV** box only if you meet the requirements to file as a qualified joint venture. See instructions.		**Fair Rental Days**	**Personal Use Days**	**QJV**
A				A			☐
B				B			☐
C				C			☐

Type of Property:

1 Single Family Residence   3 Vacation/Short-Term Rental   5 Land   7 Self-Rental
2 Multi-Family Residence   4 Commercial   6 Royalties   8 Other (describe)

Income:	**Properties:**		**A**	**B**	**C**
3 Rents received		**3**			
4 Royalties received		**4**			
Expenses:					
5 Advertising		**5**			
6 Auto and travel (see instructions)		**6**			
7 Cleaning and maintenance		**7**			
8 Commissions.		**8**			
9 Insurance		**9**			
10 Legal and other professional fees		**10**			
11 Management fees		**11**			
12 Mortgage interest paid to banks, etc. (see instructions)		**12**			
13 Other interest.		**13**			
14 Repairs.		**14**			
15 Supplies		**15**			
16 Taxes		**16**			
17 Utilities		**17**			
18 Depreciation expense or depletion		**18**			
19 Other (list) ▶ _____		**19**			
20 Total expenses. Add lines 5 through 19		**20**			
21 Subtract line 20 from line 3 (rents) and/or 4 (royalties). If result is a (loss), see instructions to find out if you must file **Form 6198**		**21**			
22 Deductible rental real estate loss after limitation, if any, on **Form 8582** (see instructions)		**22**	( )	( )	( )

23a	Total of all amounts reported on line 3 for all rental properties	**23a**	
b	Total of all amounts reported on line 4 for all royalty properties	**23b**	
c	Total of all amounts reported on line 12 for all properties	**23c**	
d	Total of all amounts reported on line 18 for all properties	**23d**	
e	Total of all amounts reported on line 20 for all properties	**23e**	

24	**Income.** Add positive amounts shown on line 21. **Do not** include any losses	**24**	
25	**Losses.** Add royalty losses from line 21 and rental real estate losses from line 22. Enter total losses here .	**25**	( )
26	**Total rental real estate and royalty income or (loss).** Combine lines 24 and 25. Enter the result here. If Parts II, III, IV, and line 40 on page 2 do not apply to you, also enter this amount on Schedule 1 (Form 1040), line 5. Otherwise, include this amount in the total on line 41 on page 2 .	**26**	

For Paperwork Reduction Act Notice, see the separate instructions.   Cat. No. 11344L   Schedule E (Form 1040) 2021

The Bottom Line: Stick With a Traditional Mail or Delivery Service

The postal service is far from perfect, but it's still the most foolproof and easily tracked way of sending important notices to tenants.

Before you mail an important notice, make a copy of the document. You could also take a date-stamped photo of the letter next to the stamped envelope you're sending it in—in some situations, a court will accept this as evidence of mailing (and might presume that it was delivered as intended).

When you mail the letter, consider asking for a tracking number and proof of delivery. (In most situations, you won't want to require a signature for delivery—the post office might hold the notice until the tenant is available to sign—which might be never.) Once you receive proof of delivery, save it in your tenant file, as it will be the best evidence that your tenant received the notice.

Cotenants, Sublets, and Assignments

FORMS IN THIS CHAPTER

Chapter 8 includes instructions for and samples of the following forms:

- Landlord-Tenant Agreement to Terminate Lease
- Consent to Assignment of Lease
- Letter to Original Tenant and New Cotenant

The purchase of this book includes free downloadable and customizable copies of all of these forms. See Appendix B for the download link and instructions.

You go through a lot of trouble to screen prospective tenants. However, all your precautions won't matter if unapproved tenants simply move in at the invitation of existing tenants. Not only is it possible that you'll have difficulty getting these tenants to pay rent or maintain the rental unit, but if they fail to do so, you might have an extra tough time evicting them.

This chapter helps you analyze your options when your tenant asks questions like these:

- "Can I sublet my apartment?"
- "May I get someone else to take over the rest of my lease?"
- "Is it okay if I move in a roommate?"

We also advise you on what to do when your tenant attempts to do any of the above *without* consulting you. Because the best defense is a good offense, we'll help you protect your interests from the outset by suggesting lease clauses that limit occupants and require your permission for subleasing or assigning.

RELATED TOPIC

Related topics covered in this book include:

- Limiting how long tenants' guests may stay: Chapter 2 (Clause 3)
- Requiring your written consent in advance for any sublet or assignment of the lease or rental agreement, or for any additional people to move in: Chapter 2 (Clauses 1, 3, and 10)
- Your duty to rerent the property if a tenant neither sublets nor assigns, but simply breaks the lease: Chapter 14, and
- Returning security deposits when one tenant leaves but the others stay: Chapter 15.

CAUTION

New York tenants have special rights. By virtue of New York's Roommate Law (RPL § 235-f), New York tenants have the right to bring in certain additional roommates without obtaining the landlord's prior approval and subject only to any applicable local laws on overcrowding. If you own rental property in New York, be sure you understand this law before setting restrictions on tenants and roommates.

Cotenants

When two or more people rent property together, and all sign the same rental agreement or lease—or enter into the same oral rental agreement and move in at the same time—they are cotenants. Each cotenant shares the same rights, and each is legally responsible to the landlord to abide by the terms of the lease.

Obligation for Rent

Cotenants can agree among themselves to split the rent equally or unequally. However, any cotenant who signs a lease or rental agreement with you is independently liable for the total rent. Landlords often remind cotenants of this obligation by inserting into the lease a chunk of legalese that says the tenants are "jointly and severally" liable for paying rent and adhering to terms of the agreement (see "Joint and Several Liability," below).

> **EXAMPLE:** James and Helen sign a month-to-month rental agreement for a $1,200 apartment rented by Blue Oak Properties. They agree between themselves to each pay half of the rent. After three months, James moves out without notifying Helen or Blue Oak. As one of two cotenants, Helen is still legally obligated to pay Blue Oak all the rent (although she might be able to recover James's share by suing him).
>
> Blue Oak has four options if Helen can't pay the rent:
>
> - Blue Oak can give Helen a written notice to pay up or leave (called a Notice to Pay Rent or Quit in most states), and follow through with an eviction lawsuit if Helen fails to pay the entire rent or move within the required amount of time (usually three to seven days).
> - If Helen offers to pay part of the rent, Blue Oak can legally accept it, but should make it clear that Helen is still responsible for the entire rent.
> - If Helen wants to stay and finds a new cotenant with a decent credit history, Blue Oak might not be able to withhold its approval of the new person and still hold Helen to her obligation to pay 100% of the rent. If Blue Oak accepts Helen's proposed roommate, it should, however, have the person become a cotenant by signing a rental agreement (as discussed below).

- If Helen wants to stay and proposes a cotenant who proves to be unacceptable to Blue Oak (because the applicant does not meet Blue Oak's usual credit or income specifications for every new tenant), Blue Oak may say "No" and evict Helen if Helen is unable to pay the entire rent.

Joint and Several Liability

"Joint and several" refers to the sharing of obligations and liabilities among two or more people—both as a group and as individuals. When two or more tenants are "jointly and severally liable," you can choose to hold all of them, or just one of them, responsible to pay rent and to abide by the rules of the tenancy.

That means you may demand the entire rent from just one tenant should the others skip out, or evict all of the tenants even when just one has broken the terms of the lease.

Even if your lease or rental agreement doesn't include this clause, cotenants are jointly and severally liable for rent and other obligations. Nonetheless, we recommend you include a "jointly and severally liable" clause to alert tenants to this responsibility. Clause 1 of both the lease and rental agreement in Chapter 2 makes cotenants jointly and severally liable.

Violations of the Lease or Rental Agreement

In addition to paying rent, each tenant is responsible for any cotenant's action that violates any term of the lease or rental agreement—for example, every cotenant is liable if one of them seriously damages the property or gets a dog despite a no-pets policy in the lease or rental agreement. Serious law-breaking by one tenant (such as dealing drugs) is also grounds for evicting all cotenants. In all of these situations, you can hold all cotenants responsible and can terminate the entire tenancy with the appropriate notice.

If only one tenant has broken the law or violated the lease, you might be inclined to get rid of the troublemaker but keep the others. There's a way

to do that: Terminate the lease for everyone, as explained above, and immediately sign a new one with the blameless cotenants.

Pay special attention to a situation involving domestic violence: In some states, laws allow the landlord to "bifurcate" the lease (evict only the violent cotenant) without terminating the lease of the victim cotenant.

See "State Laws in Domestic Violence Situations," in Appendix A, for state rules.

Special Rules for Married Couples

We strongly recommend requiring everyone who lives in a rental unit—including both members of a married couple or domestic partnership—to sign the lease or rental agreement. This underscores your expectation that each individual is responsible ("jointly and severally liable") for the rent and the proper use of the rental property.

If, however, you neglect to have one individual sign the lease, that person might still be directly responsible to you. That's because, in some states, a spouse or domestic partner is financially responsible for the necessities of life of the other, including rent.

Don't count on your state's law for protection, though—just put both names on the lease or rental agreement and make them each cotenants. And, if one of your tenants gets married or enters into a domestic partnership during the lease term, prepare a new agreement and have both spouses sign it.

Disagreements Among Cotenants

Usually, cotenants make only an oral agreement among themselves concerning how they will split the rent, occupy bedrooms, and generally share their joint living space. For all sorts of reasons, roommate arrangements sometimes go awry. If the situation gets bad enough, the tenants might start arguing about who should leave, whether one cotenant can kick another out of the apartment, or who is responsible for what part of the rent.

The best practical and legal advice we can give landlords who face serious disagreements among cotenants is this: Don't get involved, as a mediator or otherwise.

On the practical side, you probably don't have the time to get to the bottom of financial or personal disputes; and, even if you do, you don't have the ability to enforce any decisions among your tenants.

You won't be much help on the legal side, either. For example, you cannot threaten eviction if a tenant violates an agreement with the other tenant and occupies the larger bedroom, unless that particular "offense" is in the lease as a ground for eviction. And because it's impossible to design a lease that will list every possible roommate disagreement, attempting to use a legal solution will be of little help.

If one or more cotenants approach you about a dispute, explain that they must resolve any disagreements among themselves. Remind them that they are each legally obligated to pay the entire rent, and that you are not affected by any rent-sharing agreements they have made among themselves. If one cotenant asks you to change the locks to keep another cotenant out, tell the tenant that you cannot legally do that—unless a court has issued an order that the particular tenant stay out.

The advice to stay out of tenants' squabbles doesn't apply when you fear for the physical safety of one of your tenants. Call the police immediately if you hear or see violence between tenants, or if a reliable source tells you about it. In fact, if you have any reasonable factual basis to believe that a tenant intends to harm another tenant, you might have a legal duty to warn the intended victim and begin proceedings to evict the aggressor. Failure to sensibly intervene when violence is threatened might result in a finding of liability if the aggressor carries through with the threat. (The fact that the parties are cotenants instead of tenants in different rental units wouldn't matter to a court when determining liability.)

In the meantime, if one tenant fears violence from a cotenant, consider taking the following steps:

- Suggest mediation if you think they might be able to reasonably (and safely) resolve the dispute.
- Contact the local police department or court clerk's office on behalf of the potential victim for information on obtaining a temporary restraining order, and urge the victim to apply for one. A judge who decides that the situation merits it will issue an order forbidding the aggressor tenant from coming near the other.
- Evict the aggressor or all cotenants. If you choose to allow a blameless tenant to stay, keep in mind that the remaining tenant might not be able to pay the rent without a paying cotenant.

EXAMPLE: Andy and his roommate Bill began their tenancy on friendly terms. Unfortunately, it became clear that their personal habits were completely at odds. Their arguments regarding housekeeping, guests, and their financial obligations to contribute to the rent escalated to a physical fight. As a result, they each asked their landlord, Anita, to evict the other.

After listening to Andy's and Bill's complaints, Anita referred them to a local mediation service, and they agreed to participate. The mediator's influence worked for a while, but Andy and Bill were soon back at loud, unpleasant shouting matches. Anita initiated eviction proceedings against both, on the grounds that their disruptive behavior interfered with the rights of the other tenants to the quiet enjoyment of their homes.

Domestic Violence Situations

Many states extend special protections to victims of domestic violence. If you are responding to a problematic rental situation that involves domestic violence, proceed cautiously and check with local law enforcement or a battered women's shelter to find out if any special laws apply. Your state might have rules like the following (see "State Laws in Domestic Violence Situations," in Appendix A, for specific laws):

When Couples Separate or Divorce

Landlords need to be alert to the special emotional and possibly legal situations presented by a couple who rents the premises but later breaks up or goes through a divorce. Here are some issues to consider:

- Divorcing couples typically go through a period of separation before they get a final decree of divorce. When one spouse moves out, that spouse is still jointly and severally liable for the rent, though surprisingly many departing spouses feel differently. Likewise, the final divorce decree will not change the fact that each spouse continues to be on the hook for the rent, no matter who lives there. Spouses handle this situation in their property division agreement, compensating the departed tenant with funds from the remaining tenant's share. In sum, a family court judge has the power to order one spouse to leave the shared home, but the judge cannot change the joint and several financial obligation of each spouse to the landlord.

- When violence—or even the threat of it—is involved, the fearful spouse has the right to get a restraining order, as part of either a divorce filing or, in some states, a separate proceeding. For advice, call the police department, your local courthouse, a women's shelter, or an advocacy organization for victims of domestic violence.

- If one tenant changes the locks without your consent to keep the other out, you probably have no legal liability. (If your lease or rental agreement—like the one in this book—prohibits changing the locks without the landlord's permission, you probably have grounds for eviction, though.) But you usually shouldn't participate in acts that will keep one member of a couple out (say, by changing the locks yourself) without a court order that specifically prohibits the subject from coming near the remaining tenant.

- Find out if your state or municipality provides legal rights to unmarried people in long-term relationships (perhaps under common law marriage or domestic partner laws). If so, these couples might have rights similar to those enjoyed by married couples.

- When unmarried couples—whether of the same or opposite sex—separate, the law treats them as roommates. But in many states, a fearful member of an unmarried couple can qualify for a civil restraining order banning the other from the joint home, using a procedure similar to that available to married couples.

- **Antidiscrimination status and eviction protection.** It's illegal in many states to discriminate against someone who is a victim of domestic violence. This means that landlords cannot reject a rental applicant or terminate the lease or rental agreement of an existing tenant solely because the person is a victim of domestic violence. (See Chapter 5 for complete information on discrimination.)

- **Early termination rights.** In several states, a tenant who is a victim of domestic violence can end a lease with 30 days' notice, upon showing the landlord proof (such as a protective order) of status as a domestic violence victim. In a few states, tenant victims who have reported domestic violence, stalking, or sexual assaults (or who have protective orders) may terminate without giving the usual amount of notice. Similarly, some victims of domestic violence may terminate without notice and avoid liability for future rent if the victim shows the landlord a protective order or temporary injunction concerning the victim or any other occupant.

- **Changed locks.** Many states require landlords to change the locks to protect a resident tenant when shown a court order directing a perpetrator to stay away.

- **Limits on rental clauses.** In many states, landlords cannot include clauses providing for termination in the event a tenant calls for police help in a domestic violence situation, nor can landlords make tenants pay for the cost of emergency response.

- **Section 8 tenants.** Under normal circumstances, Section 8 tenants may move without jeopardizing their right to continued public assistance only if they notify their public housing authority ahead of time, terminate their lease according to the lease's provisions, and locate acceptable replacement housing. Domestic violence victims, however, can circumvent these requirements if they have otherwise complied with other Section 8 requirements, have moved in order to protect someone who is or has been a domestic violence victim, and "reasonably believed" that they were imminently threatened by harm from further violence. (Violence Against Women and Department of Justice Reauthorization Act of 2005, 42 U.SC. § 1437f (r)(5).)

If you live in a state that doesn't give victims of domestic violence early termination rights or other domestic violence protections, don't automatically say "No" to an early termination or other related request. Because your policy will usually affect female, not male, tenants, it could be challenged in court as indirectly discriminating on the basis of sex (several lawsuits brought in states without statutory protections have succeeded on this theory). Aside from your vulnerability to being sued, keep in mind that a victim might have to move quickly to avoid danger. Also, consider that your bottom line might benefit from allowing the tenancy to end immediately—what you lose in rent might pale in comparison with what your repair costs could be if your property is damaged, not to speak of the fallout from negative publicity if the situation escalates.

Although your state (and the federal law mentioned above) might give some special protections to domestic violence victims, these laws do not prohibit you from terminating, if necessary, for nonpayment of rent. Unfortunately, when the abuser leaves the property, the victim remains and often struggles to pay rent. You can legally terminate the tenancy of a domestic violence victim who falls behind in the rent, just as you would any tenant who hasn't paid.

When a Cotenant Leaves

When a cotenant leaves and the remaining tenant proposes a substitute cotenant, you want three things to happen:

- The departing tenant should sign a Landlord-Tenant Agreement to Terminate Lease (shown below).
- You should investigate the proposed new tenant, beginning with the application process (like any new tenancy).
- The remaining tenant(s), including the replacement tenant, should sign a new lease or rental agreement.

There are three reasons why you should start a new tenancy: (1) to ensure that you continue to receive the entire rent, (2) to ensure that any new tenant meets your tenant selection criteria, and (3) to avoid the return—or attempted return—of the departed tenant who claims that he or she never *really* intended to leave.

The rent. Even though the remaining tenants (individually and as a group) are on the hook for the rent, they might not be able (or willing) to pay the departing tenant's share. Getting rent from a tenant who has left for parts unknown can be difficult. You are almost always better off signing a lease with an acceptable new tenant than trying to track down an old one to collect rent.

Who is entitled to live in the rental unit. As an added advantage, formally terminating a cotenant's lease or rental agreement and preparing a new one, signed by the remaining tenant(s) and any replacement tenant, will make it clear that the outgoing tenant is no longer entitled to possession of the property. Although you don't want to become entangled in your tenants' personal lives, you also want to avoid being dragged into disputes regarding who is entitled to a key and the use of your rental property.

Leases vs. Rental Agreements

Our discussion of subleasing and assigning assumes that there is an underlying lease for a term of one year or more. If there is a long amount of time remaining on a lease, both landlord and tenant will be very concerned about a number of issues, including a tenant's obligation for remaining rent and the landlord's duty to find a new tenant and limit (mitigate) the landlord's losses.

By contrast, a month-to-month tenancy lasts no more than 30 days. When a tenant wants to leave before the end of the 30 days (to sublet and return, say, on day 28, or to assign the rental agreement and not return at all), the short amount of time (and rent money) remaining on the rental agreement might make a landlord less willing to accept the substitute.

You should not be any less thorough in checking the background of a proposed subtenant or assignee of a rental agreement, however. In theory, the amount of money at stake might be less than that involved in a lease, since the tenancy usually can be terminated with 30 days' notice for any reason. In reality, however, other considerations (such as the health and safety of other tenants, or the possibility of accepting a tenacious bad apple who proves difficult and expensive to evict) suggest the need for the same background checking that is used in evaluating any new tenant.

But what happens if, despite your vigilance, a new person moves in without your permission? Assuming you see no reason to change your mind, you have a right to evict all cotenants under the terms of the clause in your lease or rental agreement that prohibits unauthorized sublets.

Common Terms

Prime Tenant. We use this term to refer to the original tenant—someone you chose from a pool of applicants and who has signed a lease or rental agreement. This is our shortcut term—it has no legal meaning.

Some common terms that do have accepted legal meaning are:

Tenants. Renters who signed a lease or a rental agreement, or who gained the status of tenants because the landlord accepted their presence on the property or accepted rent from them. A tenant has a legal relationship with the landlord that creates various rights and responsibilities for both parties.

Cotenants. Two or more tenants who rent the same property under the same lease or rental agreement. As far as the landlord is concerned, each is 100% responsible for carrying out the agreement (in legal slang, "jointly and severally liable"), including paying all the rent.

Subtenant. Someone who subleases (rents) all or part of the premises from a tenant (not from the landlord).

Assignment. The transfer by a prime tenant of all rights of tenancy to another tenant (the "assignee"). Unlike a subtenant, an assignee rents directly from landlord.

Roommates. Two or more people, usually unrelated, living under the same roof and sharing rent and expenses. A roommate is usually a cotenant, but in some situations might be a subtenant.

What to Do When a Tenant Wants to Sublet or Assign

Despite your best efforts, you will encounter tenants who will want to leave before the expiration of their lease. Sometimes, these tenants simply disappear. More conscientious tenants might want to leave "legally" by proposing a substitute renter for the balance of the term. What should you do if a tenant approaches you with a request to move out, and suggests a potential replacement tenant? Because Clause 10 of our lease and rental agreement forms prohibit sublets or assignments without your written consent, you have some options.

Create a New Tenancy

In most situations, your best bet when confronted with a tenant who wants to sublease or assign is to simply insist that the tenancy terminate and a new one begin—with the proposed "subtenant" or "assignee" whom you have approved as the new prime tenant.

Suppose a tenant wants to sublet the apartment for six months during an overseas trip, or assign the last four months of the lease because of a job transfer. If the proposed new tenant passes your standard screening process, accept the tenant—but require the new tenant to sign a new lease and become a prime tenant. This gives you the most direct legal relationship with the substitute.

It's a two-step process: First, release your original tenant from all obligations under the lease (see the sample Landlord-Tenant Agreement to Terminate Lease, below). Second, begin the new tenancy with the substitute in the same way that you begin any tenancy: Sign a lease, present a move-in letter, and so on.

Comparing Subleases and Assignments		
	Sublease	**Assignment**
Rent	New tenant (subtenant) is liable to the prime tenant, not to the landlord. Prime tenant is liable to landlord.	New tenant (assignee) is liable to the landlord. Old tenant is liable if new tenant doesn't pay.
Damage to premises	Prime tenant is liable for damage caused by new tenant.	Absent an agreement to the contrary, prime tenant is not liable for damage caused by new tenant.
Violations of lease	Landlord can't sue new tenant for money losses caused by violating lease, because new tenant never signed lease. New tenant can't sue landlord for lease violations, either.	New tenant and landlord are bound by all terms in lease except those that were purely personal to the landlord or old tenant.
Eviction	Landlord can sue to evict new tenant for any reason old tenant could have been evicted. But to evict subtenant, landlord must also evict old tenant.	Landlord can sue to evict new tenant for any reason old tenant could have been evicted.

What are the pros and cons of this approach as compared to accepting a subtenancy or assignment? Here are a few:

- **Subtenancy.** If you allow a subtenancy, you have no direct legal relationship with the new tenant. This means that if you should need to sue for damage to the property or failure to pay rent, you must sue the original tenant, not the subtenant.

- **Assignment.** If you allow a tenant to assign the lease, the new tenant (the assignee) steps into the original tenant's legal shoes and (unlike a subtenant) has a complete legal relationship with you. In short, you can take legal action directly against the assignee in any dispute. In addition, you get one significant advantage: If the new tenant fails to pay the rent, the old one is still legally responsible to do so. So why prefer a new tenancy? Simply because insisting on a regular tenancy will do away with any misunderstanding about who is liable if disagreements later arise concerning liability for damages or rent.

The sample Landlord-Tenant Agreement to Terminate Lease below will terminate the original tenancy so that you can rent the property to the new tenant. Then, if and when the first tenant wants to return and the second voluntarily leaves, you can again rent to the first, using a new lease. A copy of the Landlord-Tenant Agreement to Terminate Lease is available on the Nolo website. See Appendix B for the link to the forms in this book.

In most cases, tenants should be happy that you're letting them off the hook. But what if the original tenant really does want to return and is concerned that the second person might not leave? Your answer should normally be a polite version of "That's your problem." Think of it this way: Your tenant is admitting to not completely trusting the proposed tenant to move out. You don't want to be in the middle of this type of situation. Let the original tenant bear the brunt of any problem that might arise.

Sublets

A *subtenant* is someone who rents all or part of the property from a tenant and does not sign a rental agreement or lease with you. A subtenant either:

- rents (sublets) an entire dwelling from a tenant who moves out temporarily— for example, for the summer, or

- rents one or more rooms from the tenant, who continues to live in the unit.

The key to subtenant relationships is that the original tenant retains the primary relationship with you and continues to exercise some control over the rental property, either by occupying part of the unit or by reserving the right to retake possession at a later date. The prime tenant functions as the subtenant's landlord. The subtenant is responsible to the prime tenant for the rent, which is usually whatever figure they have agreed to between themselves. The prime tenant, in turn, is responsible to the landlord for the rent. The written or oral agreement by which a tenant rents to a subtenant is called a sublease, because it is under the primary lease.

Subtenancies are often a pain in the neck for landlords. Besides the obvious hassles of dealing with people coming and going, landlords in some states are limited by law to the kinds of lawsuits they can bring against subtenants—for example, you may be able to sue to correct behavior that is contrary to the lease, but not sue for money damages. This means, for instance, that a subtenant may go to court to force you to maintain habitable housing, but you could not sue that subtenant for money damages if the vacated rental is a mess and the security deposit is insufficient to cover your loss (you would have to sue the original tenant). If you have an excellent long-term tenant who really wants to return after subleasing for a few months, you might want to risk it.

> **CAUTION**
>
> **Don't accept rent from a subtenant.** Repeatedly taking rent from a subtenant, plus taking other actions that indicate that you have basically forgotten about the prime tenant, might turn a subtenancy into a tenancy—and take the prime tenant off the hook for rent.

Landlord-Tenant Agreement to Terminate Lease

___Robert Chin_____ (Landlord)

and ___Carl Mosk_____ (Tenant)

agree that the lease they entered into on _____November 1, 20xx_____ , for premises at

_56 Alpine Terrace, Hamilton, Tennessee_____ ,

will terminate on ___January 5, 20xx_____ .

_Robert Chin_____   _December 28, 20xx_____
Landlord/Manager   Date

_Carl Mosk_____   _December 28, 20xx_____
Tenant   Date

Assignments

From a landlord's point of view, assignments are usually preferable to subleases. With an assignment, you have more control over the tenant, because you have a direct legal relationship with the assignee.

An *assignee* is a person to whom the prime tenant has turned over the entire lease. In most states, this means simply that the prime tenant has moved out permanently. The assignee not only moves into the premises formerly occupied by the prime tenant, but into the prime tenant's legal shoes, as well. Unlike a subtenant, whose legal relationship is with the prime tenant, not you, the assignee rents directly from you. If things go wrong with respect to behavior or money matters under the lease, the assignee can sue or be sued by the landlord.

Allow a Sublet or an Assignment

Although you are almost always better off starting a new, independent tenancy with a proposed stand-in tenant, there are situations in which you might want to agree to a subtenancy or an assignment.

You might, for example, want to accommodate—and keep—an exceptional, long-term tenant who has every intention of returning and whose judgment and integrity you trust. If the proposed stand-in meets your normal tenant criteria, it might be worth the risk of a subtenancy or an assignment in order to keep the prime tenant.

Another good reason is a desire to have a sure source of funds in the background. This could come up if you have a prime tenant who is financially sound and trustworthy, but a proposed stand-in who is less secure but meets your other tenant criteria. By agreeing to a sublet or an assignment, the prime tenant remains in the background and is still responsible for the rent. The risk and hassle of might be worth what you gain in keeping a sure and reliable source of funds on the hook.

> **EXAMPLE:** The Smith family rented a duplex for a term of two years but, after 18 months, the father's employer transferred him to another city. Mr. Smith asked Bob, the landlord, to agree to an assignment of the balance of the lease to Mr. Smith's 19-year-old son, who wanted to finish out his school year at the local college. Knowing that the son was a decent and conscientious young man, Bob agreed, but did not insist that Mr. Smith terminate his tenancy.
>
> Bob realized that keeping Dad in the picture was insurance against the unlikely but possible event that the son would not be able to keep up with the rental payments. Another way Bob could accomplish this same goal would be to end the old lease and create a new one with Mr. Smith's son, but require that Dad be a cosigner.

If you would prefer not to allow a subtenancy or an assignment, but the original tenant presses you, don't reject a proposed subtenant or assignee unless you have a good business reason. In a few states, including California and Florida, you can't unreasonably withhold your consent when asked to allow a sublet or an assignment, no matter what the lease or rental agreement says. In broad terms, this requirement means that you must use the same criteria in evaluating the proposed stand-in that you used when choosing the prime tenant.

If the substitute fails the test that you apply to all potential tenants, you will be legally justified in saying no.

Then, if the prime tenant goes ahead and breaks the lease, leaving you with lost rents and rerental expenses, you can sue. You should be able to show a judge that you fairly considered (but objectively rejected) the proposed new tenant as part of your duty to try to limit (mitigate) your losses. But if the prime tenant convinces the judge that you unreasonably turned down an acceptable substitute tenant, chances are you'll lose.

Only Landlords Can Evict Tenants

A cotenant may not terminate another cotenant's tenancy. Termination and eviction are available only to landlords.

But a tenant with a subtenant has considerably more power. If you allow a subtenancy, realize that your tenant is also a "landlord" (the subtenant's landlord). And as a landlord to a subtenant, your tenant *does* have the right to terminate and evict the subtenant.

Most owners want to control when and if the local police show up on their property to enforce eviction decrees. For this reason alone, you should prohibit "tenancies within tenancies" by insisting that every occupant become a full-fledged cotenant.

How to Assign a Lease

Typically, to accomplish an assignment the landlord and the tenant write "Assigned to John Doe" on the lease at each place where the prime tenant's name appears. The new tenant, John Doe, then signs at each place where the original tenant signed. If this is all that's done, the prime tenant remains liable for the rent, but not for damage to the property.

We suggest that a formal "Consent to Assignment of Lease" document also be used, such as the sample shown above. The Nolo website includes a downloadable copy. See Appendix B for the link to the forms in this book. Using this Consent to Assignment of Lease form protects you in two additional respects:

- It makes it clear that the prime tenant remains liable for the rent if the assignee defaults.
- It obligates the prime tenant to cover damages to the property beyond normal wear and tear if the assignee refuses or is unable to do so.

Cotenants Can Sublet and Assign, Too

The legal principles that apply to tenants who want to sublet or assign also apply to a cotenant who wants to do the same thing. For example, one of several roommates might want to sublet for a period of time, or assign the remainder of the lease. If you followed our advice and insisted that all roommates be official cotenants on the lease, you are well positioned to react to the cotenant's request, just as you would if the request came from a solo tenant.

Assignment doesn't, however, completely sever the legal relationship between you and the original tenant. Oddly enough, the original tenant remains responsible for the rent if the assignee fails to pay. Absent an agreement to the contrary, however, the prime tenant is not liable for damage to the premises caused by the assignee. (The Consent to Assignment of Lease form, discussed above, protects you by incorporating this promise.)

Generally, the landlord and assignee are bound by promises made in the lease signed by the original tenant. For example, the lease provision in which the landlord agreed to return the security deposit in a certain manner is still in effect; it now benefits the assignee. And the assignee must honor the previous tenant's promise to abide by the lease's noise rules and use restrictions. Only in very unusual situations, where a lease provision is purely personal, is it not transferred. For example, a promise by a tenant to do a landlord's housekeeping in exchange for a rent reduction would not automatically pass to an assignee.

Consent to Assignment of Lease

Landlord/Manager: ___Carolyn Friedman___ ("Landlord")

Tenant/Assignor: ___Joel Oliver___ ("Tenant")

Assignee: ___Sam Parker___ ("Assignee")

Landlord, Tenant, and Assignee agree as follows:

1. Tenant has leased the property at ___5 Fulton, Indianapolis, Indiana___ ("Premises") from Landlord.

2. The lease was signed on ___April 1, 20xx___ and will expire on ___March 31, 20xx___.

3. Tenant is assigning the balance of Tenant's lease to Assignee, beginning on ___November 1, 20xx___, and ending on ___March 31, 20xx___.

4. Tenant's financial responsibilities under the terms of the lease are not ended by virtue of this assignment. Specifically, Tenant understands that:

   a. If Assignee defaults and fails to pay the rent as provided in the lease, namely on ___the first of the month___, Tenant will be obligated to pay the rent and any late fees within ___three___ days of being notified by Landlord; and

   b. If Assignee damages the Premises beyond normal wear and tear and fails or refuses to pay for repairs or replacement, Tenant will be obligated to pay.

5. As of the effective date of the assignment, Tenant permanently gives up the right to occupy the Premises.

6. Assignee is bound by every term and condition in the lease that is the subject of this assignment.

Carolyn Friedman   _October 1, 20xx_
Landlord/Manager   Date

Joel Oliver   _October 1, 20xx_
Tenant   Date

Sam Parker   _October 1, 20xx_
Assignee   Date

CAUTION

Liability for injuries remains the same. If a subtenant or an assignee is injured on your property, the question of whether you are liable will be the same as if the injured person were the original tenant.

When a Tenant Brings in a Roommate

Suppose now that love (or poverty) strikes, and your tenant wants to move in a roommate. Assuming you've restricted the number of people who can live in the unit in your lease or rental agreement (as our forms do in Clause 3), the tenant must get your written permission to move in a roommate.

Giving Permission for a New Roommate

Although you might be motivated to accommodate your tenant's request, your decision should be based principally on whether you believe the new person will be a decent tenant. After all, if the original tenant moves out at some later date (maybe even because the new person is so awful), you will remain stuck with this person. So, always have the proposed new tenant complete a rental application and follow your normal screening procedures. If the new person meets your standards, and there is enough space in the unit, you probably want to say yes.

CAUTION

Don't give spouses the third degree. The one exception to the rule of checking new tenants carefully has to do with spouses. If the new tenant is a spouse and there's no problem with overcrowding, you probably shouldn't refuse. Refusal without a good, solid reason could be considered illegal discrimination based on marital status. In short, it's fine to check the person out, but say no only if you discover a real problem.

Preparing a New Rental Agreement or Lease

Ensure that any new roommate becomes a full cotenant by preparing a new lease or rental agreement—possibly with some changed terms, such as the amount of rent—for signature by all tenants. (Chapter 14 discusses how.) Do this before the new person moves in to avoid the possibility of a legally confused situation.

We suggest that you send a letter to the original tenant and the new cotenant as soon as you decide to allow the newcomer to move in. A sample Letter to Original Tenant and New Cotenant is shown below and the Nolo website includes a downloadable copy. See Appendix B for the link to the forms in this book.

Raising the Rent

When you allow an additional tenant, it is both reasonable and legal (in either a lease or a rental agreement situation) to raise the rent (and/or the security deposit), unless you live in an area covered by a rent control law that prohibits you from doing so. More people living in a residence means more wear and tear and higher maintenance costs in the long run. Also, as long as your increase is reasonable, it should not be a big issue with existing occupants, who, after all, will now have someone else to pay part of the total rent.

Just as you might want to take this opportunity to raise the rent, you might also want to increase the amount of the security deposit. Again, however, if the property is subject to rent control, you'll want to check the rent control laws regarding increasing the security deposit (as well as rent).

TIP

Make rent policy clear in advance. To avoid making tenants feel that you invented a rent increase policy at the last minute to unfairly extract extra money, it's a good idea to establish in advance your rent policies for units occupied by more than one person. A move-in letter is a good place to do this. That way, your request for higher rent when an additional roommate moves in will simply be in line with what you charge everyone who occupies a unit of a certain size with a certain number of people.

Letter to Original Tenant and New Cotenant

Date _July 22, 20xx_

Dear _Abby Rivas_ _____ and
     New Cotenant

Phoebe Viorst _____ ,
Original Tenant or Tenants

As the landlord of _239 Maple Street_ _____
_____ [*address*], I am pleased that
Abby _____ [*new cotenant*]
has proved to be an acceptable applicant and will be joining _Phoebe_ _____
_____ [*original tenant or tenants*] as a cotenant. Before
Abby _____ [*new cotenant*]
moves in, everyone must sign a new lease that will cover your rights and responsibilities. Please contact me at the address or phone number below at your earliest convenience so that we can arrange a time for us to meet and sign a new lease. Do not begin the process of moving in until we have signed a lease.

Sincerely yours,

Sam Stone _____
Landlord

1234 Central Avenue _____
Street Address

Sun City, Minnesota _____
City and State

_612-555-4567_ _____
Phone

Amending a Lease or Rental Agreement for COVID-related Reasons

Many landlords are adjusting their rental practices to reflect new arrangements necessitated by coronavirus-related concerns. These changes often involve temporarily amending parts of the lease or rental agreement relating to:

- **Rent:** Landlords are extending rent due dates, accepting rent in installments, reducing rent, and renouncing late fees.
- **Guest policies:** Landlords are being flexible with guest policies, and are amending or adding guest clauses to reflect the temporary presence of an additional person who has had to move due to health problems, job or housing loss, or the need to leave a household with an actively sick roommate.
- **Security deposits:** Landlords are agreeing to use the deposit to cover rent, and allowing it to be replenished over a set period of time.

You might need to address other issues with your tenants. Nolo offers an amendment form ($1.00) to guide you through possible variations. We caution all users to determine whether they are subject to a federal, state, or local eviction; and whether the moratorium imposes restrictions on items such as late fees, rent repayment plans, and security deposit use.

To purchase the amendment form, go to Nolo.com and type "Coronavirus-Related Amendment to Residential Lease" in the search box on the home page.

Guests and New Occupants You Haven't Approved

Our form rental agreement and lease include a clause requiring your written consent for guests to stay for more than a certain amount of time. We recommend that you allow guests to stay up to ten days in any six-month period without your written permission (see Clause 3 of the form lease and rental agreements in Chapter 2). The value of this clause is that a tenant who tries to move someone in for a longer period has clearly violated a defined standard, which gives you grounds for eviction.

When deciding when and whether to enforce a clause restricting guest stays, you'll need to use common sense. For example, the tenant whose boyfriend regularly spends two or three nights a week will quickly use up the ten-day allotment. However, it would be unrealistic to expect the boyfriend (assuming he has his own apartment) to become a cotenant, and you might not object to the arrangement at all. In short, you'll want to turn a blind eye.

At the same time, you probably want to keep your lease or rental agreement clause restricting guests, in the event that an occasional arrangement starts to become too permanent. But don't be surprised if a tenant claims that your prior willingness to disregard the clause limiting guests means you gave up the right to enforce it. The best way to counter this claim is to be as consistent as you can. (Don't let one tenant have a guest five nights a week and balk when another does so for two.) As long as you are reasonably consistent, a court will likely side with you if push comes to shove and you decide to evict a tenant who completely refuses to obey your rules.

Remind tenants that they are responsible for their guests' behavior and that guests must also comply with the lease or rental agreement provisions—for example, pet rules, noise limits, use of parking spaces, and the like. See Clause 24 of the form lease and rental agreements in Chapter 2.

> **CAUTION**
>
> **Avoid discrimination against guests.** In many states and cities, you cannot legally object to a tenant's frequent overnight guests based on your religious or moral views. For example, it is illegal to discriminate against unmarried couples, including gay or lesbian couples, in many states and cities. It is also illegal to discriminate against tenants' guests because of their race or inclusion in another protected category.

If a tenant simply moves a roommate in on the sly, or it appears that a "guest" has moved in clothing and furniture and begun to receive mail at your property, it's best to take decisive action right away. If you think your tenant is reasonable, send a letter telling the tenant that the new roommate or longtime guest must move out immediately. (You can use the Warning Letter for Lease or Rental Agreement Violation in Chapter 16 for this purpose.) But if you feel that the tenant will not respond to an informal notice, use a formal termination notice as explained in Chapter 17. If you allow the situation to continue, there's a high risk that the roommate will be legally a subtenant—one you haven't screened or approved. This can have significant negative consequences: Although subtenants don't have all the rights of a tenant, they are entitled, in an eviction proceeding, to the same legal protections as a tenant. And a subtenant might even turn into a de facto prime tenant if the prime tenant suddenly moves out.

Again, your best choice is to insist that the roommate or guest fill out a formal application.

If you do not want to rent to the guest or roommate, and if that person remains on the premises, make it immediately clear in writing that you will evict all occupants based on breach of the occupancy terms of the lease if the person doesn't leave immediately.

Housesitters Are Subtenants

Many tenants, particularly with pets, have housesitters stay in their rental while they're away for a long vacation or business trip. Even if your tenant doesn't collect rent from a housesitter, that person is still legally a subtenant. Treat a housesitter the way you'd treat any proposed subtenant, and remind the tenant that your written consent is required.

 SEE AN EXPERT

Get help to evict unwanted occupants. If you want to get rid of an unacceptable new occupant, initiate legal proceedings quickly. The longer you wait, the easier it will be for unauthorized occupants to claim that your lack of action means you consented to their presence, giving them the status of a tenant. Technically, these proceedings are not an eviction (only tenants can be evicted), but are instead either a criminal complaint for trespassing or a civil suit aimed at ridding the property of a squatter. If you are faced with this situation, contact the local police and ask for assistance. If they refuse to act (which is common, since they will be worried that the trespasser might have attained the status of a tenant), you will probably need to consult a lawyer for advice.

Short-Term Rentals Like Airbnb

Online businesses such as Airbnb act as clearinghouses for short-term (less than 30-day) vacation rentals. Using residential property as a short-term rental raises concerns not only for landlords, but also for neighbors, other tenants in the building, and city governments. Here's an overview of the key issues.

Landlords' Concerns

Especially in vacation-destination cities, tenants sometimes list their rented apartments and homes on short-term rental sites, essentially subletting their rentals, pocketing the money, and also increasing wear and tear on the premises. Landlords are universally against such use, but the issue is whether their rental agreements or leases clearly prohibit this practice.

This book is intended for landlords who engage in the traditional business of landlording, so we include language in Clause 10 of our lease and rental agreement forms that prohibits vacation and short-term rentals. We do not address the thorny problems faced by landlords whose tenants, with the landlords' permission, rent their homes to short-term occupants.

Cities' Concerns

Many local governments point out that using single-family apartments and homes for short-term rentals effectively turns the residences into hotels. This type of use violates laws regulating hotels, which require permits, inspections, and the payment of taxes. In an effort to govern these pseudo-hotels, many cities, counties, and other municipalities have legal restrictions on short-term home rentals. Local rules vary greatly from place to place. The restrictions in some cities are quite severe and make most short-term rentals illegal.

> ! CAUTION
> **Be sure to check condo or homeowners' association restrictions.** If your rental property is a condominium or cooperative, or is part of a planned development, your use of your property is governed by deed-like restrictions commonly called covenants, conditions, and restrictions (CC&Rs), or by bylaws adopted by the governing board. These might bar short-term rentals entirely, or subject them to restrictions. Unlike zoning laws or local ordinances, CC&Rs and bylaws are enforced by the homeowners' association or coop board, which may impose fines on violators and place liens on the property to collect them.

Residential property owners who decide to forgo traditional long-term renting, and instead use their property for a series of short-term rentals, should not use the forms in this book, and we do not offer any advice on whether this practice would be legal under local laws. Similarly, tenants who want to sublet their rentals to short-term occupants should not use this book or its forms.

How to Find Your Local Laws and Other Legal Restrictions on Short-Term Rentals

Airbnb's website (Airbnb.com) has a summary of the legal requirements of more than 70 cities, with links for more information (look for the "Responsible Hosting" section of the website). If your city isn't listed, the first place to check is your city's municipal or administrative code, which might be available online. To find yours, check out https://statelocal.co or Municode.com, or call your city's zoning board or local housing authority. You might also check out the Short-Term Rental Advocacy Center (www.stradvocacy.org) for information about short-term rental restrictions.

Landlord's Duty to Repair and Maintain the Premises

FORMS IN THIS CHAPTER

Chapter 9 includes instructions for and samples of the following forms:

- Resident's Maintenance/Repair Request
- Time Estimate for Repair
- Semiannual Safety and Maintenance Update
- Agreement Regarding Tenant Alterations to Rental Unit

The purchase of this book includes free downloadable and customizable copies of all of these forms. See Appendix B for the download link and instructions.

Landlords are required by law to provide rental property that meets basic structural, health, and safety standards. If your property falls short, tenants might have the legal right to:

- reduce or withhold rent
- pay for repairs themselves and deduct the cost from the rent
- sue you, or
- move out without notice and without responsibility for future rent.

Some states' laws are more burdensome for landlords than others. Regardless of how tough or lenient the laws are where you live, though, you're better off maintaining your rentals in a manner that goes beyond simply satisfying the law. You'll reap other, long-term benefits, such as:

- **Happy tenants.** Tenants who live in safe and well-maintained rentals are likely to stay longer, resulting in fewer interruptions of your income stream.
- **Better negotiations with tenants.** You can negotiate a reasonable solution with the tenant because you know you are likely to win if the dispute ends up in court.
- **Lower risk of lawsuits.** You're far less likely to be sued by tenants.
- **Cheaper insurance.** A good safety record can result in lower premiums.

RELATED TOPIC
Related topics covered in this book include:

- Writing clear lease and rental agreement provisions for repair and maintenance: Chapter 2
- Setting valid occupancy limits: Chapter 5
- Delegating maintenance and repair responsibilities to a manager: Chapter 6
- Highlighting repair and maintenance procedures in a move-in letter to new tenants and using a Landlord-Tenant Checklist to keep track of the condition of the premises: Chapter 7
- Your liability for injuries caused by defective housing conditions: Chapter 10
- Your responsibility to clean up environmental hazards: Chapter 11

- Your responsibility for crime: Chapter 12
- Your right to enter rental premises for repairs and inspections: Chapter 13
- Inspecting the rental unit before the tenant moves out: Chapter 15
- How to negotiate with tenants over legal disputes such as rent withholding: Chapter 16
- How to research state laws, local ordinances, and court cases on repair and maintenance responsibilities: Chapter 18.

Your Duty to Keep the Premises Livable

You are legally required to keep rental premises livable. This requirement is called the "implied warranty of habitability."

In other words, when you rent out a unit, you give the tenant an unspoken guarantee that it will be habitable for the duration of the tenancy.

Every state recognizes this warranty, and many local health and safety laws (particularly in urban areas) impose their own requirements that supplement state requirements.

The specifics of what constitutes a habitable rental come from either:

- local building codes or state statutes that specify minimum requirements for heat, water, plumbing, and other essential services, or
- widely held notions of what constitutes decent housing, derived from court opinions.

Unfortunately, in many states it's not clear which source is the basis for the implied warranty. Why does it matter? Because the source of the warranty dictates both your responsibilities and the legal consequences of not following the law.

Finally, a quaint-sounding but still very powerful legal rule, the "implied covenant of quiet enjoyment," also contributes to your duty to offer and maintain fit premises. The law creates an unspoken covenant (a promise) between you and your tenants that you will not disturb their right to use the rented space peacefully and reasonably, and conversely, that you'll act in a way that enables peaceful use. Like the implied warranty of habitability, the quiet enjoyment rule is an obligation that landlords and tenants must honor, whether they like it or not, and even when they don't know about it.

Examples of landlord violations of the covenant of quiet enjoyment include:

- tolerating a nuisance, such as allowing garbage to pile up or a major rodent infestation
- failing to provide sufficient working electrical outlets, so that tenants cannot use appliances, and
- entering the rental unannounced or without adequate notice or reason.

The covenant of quiet enjoyment is not as far-reaching as the implied warranty of habitability. However, the remedies available to tenants when landlords breach either of them are substantially the same.

Local or State Housing Laws

In a few states, complying with applicable state or local housing codes is all it takes to satisfy the implied warranty of habitability. Landlords in these states enjoy the luxury of being able to look at the codes to learn their repair and maintenance responsibilities.

These codes regulate structural aspects of buildings and usually set space and occupancy standards, such as the minimum size of sleeping rooms. They also establish minimum requirements for light and ventilation, sanitation and sewage disposal, heating, water supply (such as how hot the water must be), fire protection, and wiring (such as the number of electrical outlets per room). In addition, the codes typically make property owners responsible for keeping common areas (or parts of the premises that the owner controls) clean, sanitary, and safe.

Substantial compliance with the housing codes (rather than literal, 100% compliance) is generally sufficient.

Court Decisions

In many states, the implied warranty of habitability is independent of any housing code. The standard is whether the premises are "fit for human occupation" or "fit and habitable." Usually, however, a substantial housing code violation is also a breach of the warranty of habitability. But even if you comply with housing codes, a court can require more of you.

Who Pays to Fix Habitability Problems?

In most situations, landlords are responsible for remedying habitability issues throughout the tenancy when problems arise as a result of normal wear and tear or the actions of a third party, such as a vandal. But if a tenant's actions make the property unfit—for example, by severing the power supply to the furnace—the financial burden of repairs falls on the tenant. You remain responsible for seeing that the work gets done and the property is returned to a habitable state, but you can bill the tenant for the repair. (Clause 11 of the form lease and rental agreements in Chapter 2 alerts the tenant to this responsibility.)

What "Fit" and "Habitable" Mean

You must always:

- Keep common areas, such as hallways and stairways, safe and clean.
- Maintain electrical, plumbing, sanitary, heating, ventilating, air-conditioning, and other facilities and systems, including elevators.
- Supply water, hot water, and heat in reasonable amounts at reasonable times.
- Provide trash receptacles and arrange for trash removal.

Additional responsibilities can depend on your circumstances. Here are some other factors to consider.

The climate. In climates that experience severe winters, storm windows or shutters might be considered basic equipment. Housing in wet, rainy areas needs to be protected from the damp. In Oregon, for example, courts have specifically made landlords responsible for waterproofing. In areas prone to insect infestations, landlords might be required to provide extermination services. Florida landlords, for example, must exterminate bedbugs, mice, roaches, and ants.

The neighborhood. In a high-crime area, good locks, security personnel, exterior lighting, and secure common areas might be as necessary as water and heat.

The environment. Lead-based paint, mold, asbestos building materials, and other environmental hazards can pose significant health problems and might make buildings unfit for habitation.

How to Meet Your Legal Repair and Maintenance Responsibilities

Conscientious landlords will do the following, even if not legally required.

1. Comply With State and Local Housing Codes

Complying with all state and local housing requirements should adequately protect you from most tenant claims of uninhabitability. State laws generally require you to make all repairs and do whatever is necessary to put and keep the premises in a fit and habitable condition. Local housing codes are often more specific, and you need to know what they call for in the way of structural requirements, facilities, and essential services such

as plumbing and heat. Your local building or housing authority or code enforcement office can provide this information.

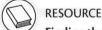

RESOURCE

Finding the laws. Appendix A includes citations for the major state laws affecting landlords. You can find these statutes online, or contact your state consumer protection agency for pamphlets or brochures that describe your repair and maintenance responsibilities in less legalistic terms. For a list of state consumer protection agencies, go to www.usa.gov/state-consumer. To find building codes for your state, search "building code" on your state government website (find yours at www.usa.gov/states-and-territories).

How Housing Codes Are Enforced

Local building, health, or fire department authorities discover code violations through:

- **Routine inspections.** When property changes hands or is used as collateral for a loan, there's usually an inspection.
- **Complaints.** Tenants might also point out code violations if they do not pay the rent, or attempt to pay less, on the grounds that the premises are substandard. If you try to evict a tenant for not paying rent, the tenant might claim housing code violations as justification.

Once a violation is found, you'll get a citation requiring you to remedy it within a certain amount of time. If you don't make the repairs within the time allowed, the city or county might sue you. Moreover, in many cities, ongoing noncompliance is a criminal misdemeanor punishable by fines or even imprisonment. In some cases, local officials might require you to provide tenants with temporary alternative housing until the violation is corrected.

Complying With Changes to Housing Codes

When a housing code changes, it doesn't necessarily mean that all existing buildings are in violation because they are not "up to code." Especially when it comes to items that would involve major structural changes, lawmakers often exempt certain older buildings. They do it by writing a clause into the code that exempts all buildings constructed before a certain date (sometimes that date is the same as when the new code takes effect, but not always). Such exemptions often do not apply to renovations or remodeling undertaken after the code changed, meaning that, over the years, you might eventually have to comply with the new rules.

Many types of code changes—for example, those involving locks, peepholes, and smoke detectors—must be made regardless of the age of the building and whether or not you do any remodeling.

2. Get Rid of Dangers to Children

Local ordinances prohibit "attractive nuisances." These are conditions that tend to attract children, such as abandoned vehicles; wells and shafts; basements; abandoned equipment or appliances; excavations; and unsafe fences, structures, or foliage. If children are hurt while playing in or on an attractive nuisance on your property, you might be held liable.

3. Don't Allow Nuisances, Such as Excessive Noise

Besides "attractive nuisances," local housing codes prohibit nuisances in general, broadly defined as situations dangerous to human life or detrimental to health, as determined by the public health officer. Overcrowding, insufficient ventilation or illumination or inadequate sewage or plumbing facilities, and allowing drug dealing on the premises are all examples of nuisances. A landlord found to have created or allowed ("tolerated") a

nuisance will be subject to the code's enforcement and penalty provisions.

Be especially vigilant when it comes to noise, which can be a major nuisance. Landlords often hear complaints about noisy tenants. If you ignore such complaints, you can get hit with code violations, court-ordered rent reductions, and even punitive damages. For more advice on dealing with noisy tenants, including how to write an effective warning letter, see "When Warning Notices are Appropriate" in Chapter 16.

Clause 13 of our form lease and rental agreements in Chapter 2 prohibits tenants from causing disturbances or creating a nuisance.

4. Consider Smoking Restrictions

It's not unusual for rental owners to adopt no-smoking (and no-vaping) policies in common areas and individual rental units. Many owners have found that advertising a smoke-free environment gives them a distinct marketing advantage.

A smoke-free policy will also apply to marijuana: Even if your state has decriminalized the possession and use of small amounts, smokers do not have a right to light up in violation of their landlords' no-smoking policies.

Several cities have also passed no-smoking laws for multifamily buildings. For more information, the American Nonsmokers' Rights Foundation offers comprehensive resources about smoke-free policies for property owners at www.no-smoke.org.

If you do allow smoking in units, you might face complaints from nonsmoking tenants bothered by fumes.

Frustrated neighbors have advanced creative and successful arguments based on three legal theories:

- **Nuisance.** Tenants have argued that the presence of smoke, like any noxious fume or noise, constitutes a legal nuisance in that it exposes others to a serious health risk. When courts buy this argument, the fact that the smokers did not have a no-smoking clause in their lease or rental agreement is immaterial.

- **Covenant of quiet enjoyment.** Neighbors have also claimed that their ability to use and enjoy their homes has been significantly diminished by the presence of smoke.
- **Warranty of habitability.** Some neighbors have persuaded judges that the smoke is so pervasive and noxious that it renders their rental unfit. In many states, this allows affected neighbors to break their leases.

Also, tenants with certain disabilities are protected from secondhand smoke under the Americans with Disabilities Act and the federal Fair Housing Act, as well as state and local regulations.

You might also want to consider addressing the use of e-cigarettes, which are electronic heating devices that heat and vaporize a solution that typically contains nicotine. Although there's no "secondhand smoke," there *is* "secondhand aerosol" ("vapor"). This by-product is a visible soup that contains nicotine, ultrafine particles, and low levels of toxins that are known to cause cancer. For more information on the effects of secondhand aerosol, search for "Electronic Smoking Devices and Secondhand Aerosol" at www.no-smoke.org.

TIP

Consider letting tenants who complain about smoke break their lease. Because nonsmoking tenants frequently succeed when they take their complaints to court, letting tenants break their lease without penalty is probably a wiser decision than fighting it out in court.

RESOURCE

Current information on nonsmoking policies and e-cigarettes. Check the American Nonsmokers' Rights Foundation website (www. no-smoke.org) for lists of state and local laws restricting smoking (search "Smokefree Lists, Maps, and Data") and e-cigarettes.

Medical Marijuana Smoking

Many states have passed "compassionate use" laws, which decriminalize marijuana use for those using it for medical reasons, but federal law has not followed suit—the cultivation, possession, and use of marijuana is still illegal under federal law. For this reason, landlords are free to disallow marijuana possession, use, or growing on the premises, even where the tenant has state-sanctioned, medical approval to use it. Accordingly, even tenants who have a recognizable disability under federal law cannot expect landlords to vary a no-marijuana policy pursuant to an accommodation under the federal Americans with Disabilities Act (ADA).

In practical terms, marijuana smoke can have the same effect on tenants in a multifamily building as regular tobacco smoke. Fortunately for tenants who have a legitimate need for marijuana and medical permission to use it, many drops, liquids, and solid foods ("edibles") contain the necessary chemical ingredients of marijuana but omit the smoke. Tenants who purchase and responsibly consume such items should not pose a problem for landlords or other tenants.

---

5. Don't Try to Evade Your Legal Responsibilities

Landlords cannot avoid their responsibility to provide habitable rentals.

Some landlords try to have tenants sign a lease containing a clause removing the duty, or they argue that by voluntarily moving into or remaining in substandard housing, tenants have waived their rights to habitable rentals.

Courts have universally rejected these tactics. In almost all states, neither a tenant waiver (at the beginning of the tenancy or during its life) nor a disclaimer in the lease will relieve you of the responsibility to provide fit and habitable housing.

In some situations you can, however, legally delegate some repair and maintenance responsibilities to tenants.

See "Delegating Landlord's Responsibilities to Tenants," below.

⊘ **CAUTION**

Review your lease or rental agreement carefully. Preprinted leases available in office supply stores or online are not usually customized for each state's laws. A generic form might include clauses that are illegal in your state. To be on solid ground, familiarize yourself with your state and local laws, and review every clause in your lease and rental agreement for compliance. By using the lease or rental agreement in this book (also available on Nolo.com), along with the state-specific charts in this book, you can avoid many of the problems posed by generic forms.

6. Enforce Tenants' Maintenance Duties

State and local housing laws require tenants to maintain their units. If a dwelling is rendered uninhabitable due to the tenant's actions, the tenant will have a difficult, if not impossible, time fighting eviction or avoiding responsibility for the repair bill. (If the tenant won't pay up, you can deduct the expense from the security deposit.) Your lease or rental agreement should spell out basic tenant obligations—such as those listed here— regardless of whether they are required by law. See Clause 11 of the form agreements in Chapter 2.

Keep the rental unit as clean and tidy as possible. The age and condition of the unit have an effect on what you should expect from tenants. Be realistic with your expectations, and if you have to do a major cleanup when the tenant moves out, you can deduct reasonable costs from the security deposit.

Keep plumbing fixtures as clean as possible. Again, overall condition is a factor here. For example, makeup stains on the sink could have been prevented by proper cleaning, so the tenant is responsible. On the other hand, if the paint on the bathroom ceiling peels from damp and mildew because there's no fan and the window is painted shut, the bathroom will be hard to dry out despite the tenant's best efforts. As the person with control over the ventilation, you would be responsible for the resulting damage—and possible health risk.

Common Myths About Repairs and Maintenance

Many landlords (and tenants) are under the mistaken impression that every time a rental unit turns over, certain maintenance work is legally required. This simply isn't true.

Paint. No state law requires you to repaint the interior, but local ordinances might (New York City's does). So long as the existing paint isn't creating a habitability problem—for example, paint that's so thick around a window that the window can't be opened—you can skip the new paint. The presence of deteriorating lead-based paint, however, needs special attention. It can create all sorts of health and legal problems—for example, if a child becomes ill from eating lead-based paint chips, a court might find you liable for breaching the warranty of habitability.

Drapes and carpets. So long as drapes and carpets are not a health hazard, you aren't legally required to replace them. For example, you'd want to replace damp or mildewy drapes and carpets with holes that create a tripping hazard.

Windows. A tenant who carelessly breaks a window is responsible for repairing it. If a burglar, vandal, or neighborhood child broke a window, however, you are responsible for fixing it.

Keys. Many tenants think that they're entitled to fresh locks upon move-in. In some states and in some cities, this is true. But even when you're not legally required to rekey, you should do so in order to reduce the chance of unauthorized people entering the unit.

Dispose of garbage, rubbish, and other waste. Although you're responsible for mitigating ongoing pest problems, a rodent or cockroach infestation resulting from the accumulation of trash in the unit is not your responsibility.

Use systems and appliances properly. Electrical, plumbing, sanitary, heating, ventilating, air-conditioning, and other facilities and other systems, including elevators, all serve in some way or another to make our lives easier and safer.

However, misuse (or non-use) of these systems can create health hazards. Tenants are expected to use the facilities in the way they are intended to be used.

Report problems. Some states require tenants to inform the landlord, as soon as practicable, of defective conditions that the tenant believes the landlord doesn't know about and has a duty to repair. This includes items that the tenant has damaged. For example, tenants who carelessly break the heater can't simply decide to live without heat for a while—they must let you know what's happened. You have a duty to repair, but you are free to use the tenants' security deposit to fix habitability problems they caused.

> **CAUTION**
>
> **Be sure your lease or rental agreement makes the tenants financially responsible for the results of negligence or misuse.** (See Clause 11 of the form agreements in Chapter 2.) You want your lease or rental agreement to be clear that when tenants or their guests cause damage, they are responsible for making repairs or reimbursing you for doing so. If tenants refuse to repair or pay, you can use the security deposit to cover the bill, then demand that the tenants bring the deposit up to its original level. If they refuse to replenish the deposit, you might have grounds to terminate the tenancy and sue them for the costs you've incurred.

7. Repair What You Provide or Promise

When you provide amenities beyond what's necessary for basic living—such as drapes, washing machines, swimming pools, saunas, parking places, intercoms, and dishwashers—you're likely legally required to maintain or repair them. The law reasons that by offering or advertising these amenities as part of your rental, you promise to maintain them throughout the tenancy.

Your promise to maintain is either express (laid out in the lease or rental agreement) or implied. You can create an implied promise in many ways— for example, by advertising that a rental includes an amenity, or by establishing a practice of repair that the tenant begins to rely on. Here are some typical examples of implied promises.

> **EXAMPLE 1:** Tina sees Joel's ad for an apartment, which says "heated swimming pool." After Tina moves in, utility costs rise, and Joel stops heating the pool regularly. Joel has violated his implied promise to keep the pool heated. If he wants more flexibility, he shouldn't advertise the pool, and let prospective tenants know that the availability of the pool is subject to change.

> **EXAMPLE 2:** When Joel's rental agent shows Tom around the building, she goes out of her way to show off the laundry room, saying, "Here's the terrific laundry room—it's for the use of all the tenants." Tom rents the apartment. Later, all the washing machines break down, but Joel won't fix them. Joel has violated his implied promise to maintain the laundry room appliances in working order.

> **EXAMPLE 3:** Tina's apartment has a built-in dishwasher. When she rented the apartment, neither the lease nor the landlord said anything about the dishwasher or who was responsible for repairing it. The dishwasher has broken down a few times, and whenever Tina asked Joel to fix it, he did. By doing so, Joel has established a usage or practice that he—not the tenant—is responsible for repairing the dishwasher.

If you violate an express or implied promise relating to the condition of the premises, the tenant can sue you for money damages for breach of contract, and might be able to pursue other legal remedies, discussed below.

8. Set Up a Responsive Maintenance System—And Stick to It

The best way to avoid repair-related legal or financial hassles in the first place is to implement a maintenance program designed to satisfy code requirements and ensure that the building is safe and habitable. In doing so, you should be mindful of a larger goal: to attract and keep reliable tenants who will stay as long as possible.

Avoiding Problems With a Good Maintenance and Repair System

Your best defense against disputes with tenants is to establish and communicate a clear, easy-to-follow procedure for tenants to ask for repairs. In addition, develop a system for documenting and responding quickly to all complaints, and schedule annual safety inspections. If you employ a manager or management company, make sure they follow your guidelines as well.

Recommended Repair and Maintenance System

An ideal process will:

1. Provide tenants with a safe, well-maintained property.
2. Clearly set out the tenant's responsibilities for repair and maintenance (see, for example, the Clauses 11, 12, and 13 of the form agreements in Chapter 2).
3. Utilize the written Landlord-Tenant Checklist form (Chapter 7) to check over the premises and arrange for repairs of any problems before new tenants move in.
4. Make it easy for tenants to use the rental responsibly. Don't assume tenants know how to handle routine maintenance problems such as a clogged toilet or drain. Make it a point to explain the basics when a tenant moves in and include a brief list of maintenance dos and don'ts with your move-in materials. For example, explain:
   - how to avoid overloading circuits
   - proper use of garbage disposal
   - location and use of fire extinguisher, and
   - problems tenant should definitely not try to handle, such as electrical repairs.
5. Encourage tenants to immediately report plumbing, heating, weatherproofing, or other defects or safety or security problems— whether in the tenant's unit or in common areas, such as hallways and parking garages. Use the Resident's Maintenance/Repair Request form discussed below.
6. Document all complaints, including those made orally. The records should include a box to indicate your immediate and any follow-up responses (and subsequent tenant communications), as well as a space to enter the date and brief details of when the problem was fixed. The Resident's Maintenance/Repair Request form, below, can serve this purpose.
7. Maintain a file on each unit. Keep a file for each rental unit with copies of all complaints and repair requests from tenants and your response. As a general rule, you should respond in writing to every tenant repair request (even if you also do so orally or by email). In Chapter 7, "Using Email for Notices and Other Communications to Tenants" explains why it's important to communicate with tenants in writing, rather than just using email.
8. Give yourself the flexibility to handle repairs as soon as possible, but definitely within the time any state law requires. Notify the tenant by phone and follow up in writing if repairs will take more than 48 hours, excluding weekends. Keep the tenant informed—for example, if you have problems scheduling a plumber, let your tenant know with a phone call, note, or email.

9. Provide for regular check-ins with tenants. Twice a year, give your tenants a checklist on which to report any potential safety hazards or maintenance problems that might have been overlooked (see the Semiannual Safety and Maintenance Update, described in "Tenant Updates and Landlord's Regular Safety and Maintenance Inspections," below). Respond promptly and in writing to all requests, keeping copies in your file.

10. Provide for annual inspections. Once a year, inspect all rental units, using the Landlord-Tenant Checklist as a guide as discussed in "Tenant Updates and Landlord's Regular Safety and Maintenance Inspections," below. Keep copies of the filled-in checklist in your file.

11. Make it easy for tenants to contact you. Especially for multiunit projects, place conspicuous notices in several places around the property about your determination to operate a safe, well-maintained building, and list phone numbers and email addresses for tenants to use for maintenance requests.

12. Regularly communicate with tenants. Tenants will be more likely to keep you apprised of maintenance and repair problems if you remind them that you are truly interested. A notice regarding complaint procedures such as the one below will be helpful.

13. Ensure you hire the best contractors. Take care when hiring and supervising contractors for projects involving specialized skills or major repairs. Check individual references and licenses and state rules before hiring any outside workers—whether a handyperson or skilled contractor.

> ### Sample Notice to Tenants Regarding Complaint Procedure
>
> Fair View Apartments wants to maintain all apartment units and common areas in excellent condition so that tenants enjoy safe and comfortable housing. If you have any questions, suggestions, or requests regarding your unit or the building, please direct them to the manager between 9 a.m. and 6 p.m., Monday through Saturday, either by calling 555-9876 or by dropping off a completed Maintenance/Repair Request form at the manager's office. In case of an emergency, please call 555-1234 at any time.

Resident's Maintenance/Repair Request Form

Many tenants will find it easiest (and most practical) to call or email you or your manager with a repair problem or complaint, particularly in urgent cases. You must have voicemail available at all times to accommodate tenant calls. Check your messages frequently.

We also suggest you provide all tenants with a Resident's Maintenance/Repair Request form. Give each tenant five or ten copies when they move in and explain how the form should be used to request specific repairs. (See the sample, below.) Be sure that tenants know to describe the problem in detail and to indicate the best time to make repairs. Email tenants a blank copy of the form.

You (or your manager) should complete the entire Resident's Maintenance/Repair Request form or keep a separate log for every tenant complaint, including those made by phone. (See the discussion below.) Keep a copy of this form or your log in the tenant's file, along with any other written communication. Keep good records of how and when you handled tenant complaints, including

Resident's Maintenance/Repair Request

Date: _____August 29, 20xx_____

Address: _____392 Main St., #402, Houston, Texas 77002_____

Resident's name: _____Mary Griffin_____

Phone (home): _____555-4321_____   Phone (work): _____555-5679_____

Email: _____

Problem (be as specific as possible): _____Garbage disposal doesn't work_____

_____

_____

_____

_____

Best time to make repairs: _____After 6 p.m. or Saturday morning_____

Other comments: _____

_____

_____

_____

I authorize entry into my unit to perform the maintenance or repair requested above, in my absence, unless stated otherwise above.

_____Mary Griffin_____
Resident

. . . .

FOR MANAGEMENT USE

Work done: _____Fixed garbage disposal (removed spoon)_____

Time spent: _____1/2_____ hours

Date completed: _____August 30, 20xx_____   By: _____Paulie_____

Unable to complete on: _____ , because: _____

_____

Notes and comments: _____

_____

_____Hal Ortiz_____   _____August 30, 20xx_____
Landlord/Manager   Date

reasons for any delays and notes on conversations with tenants. For a sample, see the bottom of the Resident's Maintenance/Repair Request form (labeled For Management Use, shown above). You might also jot down any other comments regarding repair or maintenance problems you observed while handling the tenant's complaint. The Resident's Maintenance/Repair Request form can be downloaded from the Nolo website; see Appendix B for the link to the forms in this book.

Tracking Tenant Complaints

When tenants call or email you with a problem or complaint, we suggest you always fill out this form. It's also a good idea to keep a separate chronological log or calendar with similar information on tenant complaints. A faithfully kept log will qualify as a "business record," admissible as evidence in court, that you can use to establish that you normally record tenant communications when they are made. By implication, the *absence* of an entry is evidence that a complaint was *not* made.

This argument can be important if your tenant has reduced or withheld rent or broken the lease on the bogus claim that the tenant's requests for maintenance or repairs went unanswered.

Some cloud-based property management platforms offer portals where tenants can lodge complaints and request repairs online. You can learn more about online property management programs at www.softwareadvice.com/property/rental-property-management-software-comparison.

Responding to Tenant Complaints

You should respond almost immediately to all complaints about defective conditions by talking to the tenant and following up (preferably in writing). Explain when repairs can be made or, if you don't yet know, tell the tenant that you will be back in touch promptly. Use a form such as the Time Estimate for Repair shown below. The Nolo website includes a downloadable copy. See Appendix B for the link to the forms in this book.

This doesn't mean you have to jump through hoops to fix things that don't need fixing or to engage in heroic efforts to make routine repairs. It does mean you should take prompt action under the circumstances—for example, responding immediately to broken door locks or security problems. Similarly, you should treat a lack of heat or hot water (especially in winter in cold areas) and safety hazards such as broken steps or exposed electrical wires as emergencies.

One way to think about how to respond to repair problems is to classify them according to their consequences. Most of the time, the appropriate response will become clear once you've considered the results of inaction:

- **Personal security and safety problems = injured tenants = lawsuits.** Respond and get work done immediately if the potential for harm is very serious, even if this means calling a 24-hour repair service or having to put up a piece of plywood over a broken ground floor window in the middle of the night.
- **Major inconvenience to tenant = seriously unhappy tenant = tenant's self-help remedies (such as rent withholding) and vacancies.** Respond and attempt to get work done as soon as possible, or within 24 hours, if the problem is a major inconvenience to tenant, such as a plumbing or heating problem.
- **Minor problem = slightly annoyed tenant = bad feelings.** Respond in 48 hours (on business days) if not too serious.

Even if you spend a few extra dollars to meet these deadlines, responding quickly to tenants' concerns will serve you well in the long run.

If you're unable to take care of a repair right away, and if it isn't so serious that it requires immediate action, let the tenant know when the repair will be made. It's often best to do this orally (leaving a voicemail is sufficient), and follow up in writing. If there's a delay in handling the problem (maybe the part you need has to be ordered), explain why you won't be able to act immediately.

Time Estimate for Repair

Stately Manor Apartments

August 30, 20xx
Date

Mary Griffin
Tenant

392 Main St., #402
Street Address

Houston, Texas 77002
City and State

Dear Mary Griffin ,
_____
Tenant

Thank you for promptly notifying us of the following problem with your unit: _____

Garbage disposal doesn't work

_____

_____

_____

We expect to have the problem corrected on _____ September 3, 20xx _____ due to the following:

Garbage disposal part is out of stock locally, but has been ordered and will be delivered in

a day or two

_____

_____

_____

We regret any inconvenience this delay might cause. Please do not hesitate to point out any other problems that arise.

Sincerely,

Hal Ortiz
Landlord/Manager

> **CAUTION**
>
> **Respect tenants' privacy.** To gain access to make repairs, the landlord can enter the rental premises only with the tenant's consent, or after having given reasonable notice or the specific amount of notice required by state law, usually 24 hours. See Chapter 13 for rules and procedures for entering a tenant's home to make repairs and how to deal with tenants who make access inconvenient for you or your maintenance personnel.

> **TIP**
>
> **If you can't attend to a repair right away, take steps to make your tenants happy.** Do what you can to keep tenants from withholding rent in response to a repair issue. Some landlords voluntarily offer a "rent rebate" if a problem can't be corrected in a timely fashion, especially if it's serious, such as a major heating or plumbing problem. A rebate builds goodwill and avoids the hassles associated with rent withholding.

If, despite all your efforts to conscientiously find out about and make needed repairs on a timely basis, a tenant threatens to withhold rent, move out, or pursue another legal remedy, you should respond promptly in writing, stating:

- when the repair will be made and the reasons for the delay, or
- why you believe the problem doesn't justify rent withholding or another action—for example, point out that the sound from the toilet might be annoying, but the toilet still flushes and is usable.

At this point, if you feel the tenant is sincere, you might also consider suggesting that you and the tenant mediate the dispute. If you feel the tenant is using a phony complaint to justify not paying the rent, take action to terminate the tenancy as soon as the rent is overdue.

Tenant Updates and Landlord's Regular Safety and Maintenance Inspections

In addition to a thorough and prompt system for responding to problems, you should establish a nonintrusive system of frequent and periodic maintenance inspections. In short, encouraging your tenants to promptly report problems as they occur should not be your sole means of handling your maintenance and repair responsibilities. If tenants are not conscientious, or if they simply don't notice that something needs to be fixed, the best reporting system will not do you much good. Here's how to stay ahead of trouble.

Insist on a Tenant Semiannual Safety and Maintenance Update

You can (nicely) insist that your tenants think about and report needed repairs by giving them a Semiannual Safety and Maintenance Update form to list any problems in the rental unit or on the premises. Asking tenants to return an update form twice a year should also help you in court if you are up against a tenant who is raising a false implied warranty of habitability defense, particularly if the tenant did not note any problems in the most recent update. As with the Resident's Maintenance/Repair Request form, be sure to note how you handled the problem on the bottom of the form. A sample Semiannual Safety and Maintenance Update is shown below and the Nolo website includes a downloadable copy. See Appendix B for the link to the forms in this book.

Perform Your Own Annual Safety Inspection

Sometimes, even a specific request that tenants bring safety and maintenance issues to your attention isn't enough. In the end, you must get into the unit and inspect for yourself.

Semiannual Safety and Maintenance Update

We're asking all tenants to complete the following checklist and note any safety or maintenance problems in your unit or on the premises. Please:

- Describe the specific problems and the rooms or areas involved. Here are some examples of the types of things we want to know about: garage roof leaks, excessive mildew in rear bedroom closet, fuses blow out frequently, door lock sticks, water comes out too hot in shower, exhaust fan above stove doesn't work, smoke alarm malfunctions, peeling paint, and mice in basement.
- Point out any potential safety and security problems in the neighborhood and anything you consider a serious nuisance.
- Indicate the approximate date when you first noticed the problem and list any other recommendations or suggestions for improvement.

Please return this form with this month's rent check. Thank you.

—The Management

Name: _____ Mary Griffin _____

Address: _____ 392 Main St., #402 _____

_____ Houston, Texas _____

Please indicate (and explain below) problems with:

- ☐ Floors and floor coverings _____
- ☐ Walls and ceilings _____
- ☐ Windows, screens, and doors _____
- ☐ Window coverings (drapes, miniblinds, etc.) _____
- ☐ Electrical system and light fixtures _____
- ☑ Plumbing (sinks, bathtub, shower, or toilet) _____ Water pressure low in shower _____
- ☐ Heating or air conditioning system _____
- ☑ Major appliances (stove, oven, dishwasher, refrigerator) _____ Exhaust fan above stove doesn't work _____
- ☐ Basement or attic _____
- ☑ Locks or security system _____ Front door lock sticks _____
- ☐ Smoke detector _____
- ☐ Fireplace _____
- ☐ Cupboards, cabinets, and closets _____
- ☐ Furnishings (table, bed, mirrors, chairs) _____
- ☐ Laundry facilities _____
- ☐ Elevator _____
- ☐ Stairs and handrails _____
- ☐ Hallway, lobby, and common areas _____
- ☐ Garage _____

☑ Patio, terrace, or deck _____ Shrubs near back stairway need pruning _____

☐ Lawn, fences, and grounds _____

☐ Pool and recreational facilities _____

☐ Roof, exterior walls, and other structural elements _____

☐ Driveway and sidewalks _____

☑ Neighborhood _Tenant in #501 often plays music too loud_ _____

☐ Nuisances _____

☐ Other _____

_____

Specifics of problems: _____

_____

_____

_____

_____

_____

Other comments: _____

_____

_____

_____

_____

_____

Mary Griffin _____ _February 1, 20xx_
Tenant   Date

· ·

FOR MANAGEMENT USE

Action/Response: _____ Fixed kitchen exhaust fan and sticking front door lock on February 15, _____ and adjusted water pressure in shower. Pruned shrubs on February 21. Spoke with tenant in _____ #501 about keeping music low on February 2. _____

_____

_____

_____

_____

_____

Hal Ortiz _____ _February 22, 20xx_
Landlord/Manager   Date

You should perform an annual "safety and maintenance inspection" as part of your system for repairing and maintaining the property. For example, you might make sure that items listed on the Semiannual Safety and Maintenance Update—such as smoke detectors, heating and plumbing systems, and major appliances—are in fact safe and in working order. If a problem develops with one of these items, causing injury to a tenant, you might be able to defeat a claim that you were negligent by arguing that your periodic and recent inspection of the item was all that a landlord should reasonably be expected to do.

In many states, you have the right to enter a tenant's home for the purpose of a safety inspection. This does not mean, however, that you can just let yourself in unannounced. All states that allow for inspections require advance notice; some specify 24 hours, others simply state that the landlord must give "reasonable notice." To be on the safe side, check your state's statutes and, if all that is required is "reasonable notice," allow 24 hours at least.

If your state allows landlords to enter for this purpose (and if you have given adequate notice and have not otherwise abused your right of entry by needlessly scheduling repeated inspections), a tenant's refusal to allow an inspection is grounds for eviction.

On the other hand, if your state doesn't allow the landlord to enter and inspect the dwelling against the tenant's will, you have a problem. Even if your own lease or rental agreement provision allows for inspections, the provision might be considered illegal and unenforceable. Also, evicting

---

Make Your Contractors' Insurance Policies Cover You, Too

If you hire a contractor to do extensive work, you should make sure that the contractor has insurance—and that it covers you, too.

Here's the problem you will avoid: Suppose your contractor does a poor job that results in an injury to a tenant or guest. The injured person might sue you, and, unless your own insurance policy covers contractors' negligence, you won't be covered. Even if your policy does provide coverage, you'll be better off if coverage comes from the contractors' policy—the fewer claims made on your policy, the better.

Require contractors to do the following:

- **Add you as an "additional insured" to their commercial general liability policy.** Ideally, have contractors do this before you sign a contract with them, and certainly before they begin work. As an additional insured, you will be covered in case someone makes a claim on the policy based on actions of the contractor at your work site.
- **Provide you with a "certificate of liability insurance,"** proving that the contractor has the insurance and that you were added. Ask for an

"ACORD 25" form, which the insurance company should supply.

- **Send you a copy of their policy.** Make sure that the work you're having done is covered by the policy. The name on the policy should be the same name the contractor is using on the work contract with you.
- Include an insurance clause in the contract. In your written agreement with the contractor, insist on a clause like the following: "Contractor will have a commercial general liability insurance policy of at least [*dollar amount*] per occurrence and [*dollar amount*] aggregate in effect as of the date contractor begins work. Contractor will maintain the policy throughout the duration of the job, and will promptly notify [*owner's name*] of any diminution in coverage or cancellation. In the event of any claim, this policy will apply as primary insurance. Contractor will provide additional insurance for any work that requires additional insurance. Contractor will not begin work until Contractor has given [*owner's name*] a satisfactory certificate of insurance."

a tenant who refused to allow such an inspection might constitute illegal retaliatory eviction.

When faced with uncooperative tenants, point out that you take your responsibility to maintain the property very seriously. Remind them that you'll be checking for plumbing, heating, electrical, and structural problems that they might not notice, which could develop into bigger problems later if you're not allowed to check them out. Most tenants won't object to yearly safety inspections if you give plenty of notice and try to conduct the inspection at a time convenient for the tenant. (You might offer to inspect in the tenants' presence, so they can see for themselves that you aren't just being nosy.)

Tenants' Options When the Premises Are Unfit

If you fail to live up to your legal duty to maintain your property, your tenants might have a variety of legal responses, each one designed to pressure you into compliance. Even the most conscientious landlord might encounter tenants who attempt to avoid paying rent by claiming that the premises are unfit. If you are a victim of a scam like this, you'll need to know how to defend yourself.

Your tenants' options will probably include one or more of what we call the "big sticks" in a tenant's self-help arsenal. These include:

- withholding the rent
- repairing the problem (or having it repaired by a professional) and deducting the cost from the rent
- calling state or local building or health inspectors
- moving out, or
- paying the rent and then suing you for the difference between the rent the tenant paid and the value of the defective premises.

Tenants' Responses to Unfit Premises: Paying Less Rent

In this section, we'll explain the two options that involve paying less rent: rent withholding and "repair and deduct." (We'll explain the others below.)

Tenants cannot use these options unless four conditions are met:

- **The problem is serious.** The issue must imperil the tenant's health or safety. Not every building code violation or annoying defect in a rental home (like the water heater's ability to reach only 107 degrees F, short of the code-specified 110 degrees) justifies use of a "big stick" against the landlord.
- **You ignored the problem.** For example, the tenant told you about the problem and gave you a reasonable opportunity (or the minimum amount of time required by law) to get it fixed, but you didn't. Some states specify response times (ten days to three weeks is common); in others, you must respond within a reasonable time under the circumstances.
- **The problem isn't the tenant's fault.** If a tenant (or a guest) caused the problem, either deliberately or carelessly, the tenant's use of one of the self-help options won't be upheld.
- **It's allowed under state law.** Some states explicitly prohibit tenants from withholding rent or using the repair and deduct remedy. In these states, often a tenant's only remedy is to move out and seek damages from the landlord.

Rent Withholding

If you don't keep your property livable, your tenant might be able to stop paying rent until you repair it. Called rent withholding or rent escrowing, most states have established this tenant remedy by statute or court decision; some cities also have ordinances allowing it. See "State Laws on Rent Withholding and Repair and Deduct Remedies," in Appendix A. Rent withholding is not a legal option unless authorized by law.

The term "withholding" is actually a bit misleading: In many states and cities a tenant can't simply keep the rent money until you fix the problem. Instead, tenants often have to deposit the withheld rent with a court or a neutral third party until the repairs are accomplished.

Some states that allow rent withholding do so in a roundabout way, by giving tenants an "affirmative defense" to an eviction action. In these states, tenants can defend against an eviction by arguing that the landlord's failure to maintain a fit and habitable rental excused them from the duty to pay rent. If the judge or jury sides with the tenant, the tenant won't be evicted.

Tenants can withhold rent only when:

- The lack of maintenance or repair has made the dwelling unlivable.
- The problems were not caused by the tenant or a guest, either deliberately or through neglect.
- You've been told about the problem and haven't fixed it within a reasonable time or the minimum amount required by state law.

In addition, under most rent withholding laws, tenants cannot withhold rent if they are behind in the rent or in violation of an important lease clause. In short, tenants who use this drastic measure need to be squeaky clean.

Typical Rent Withholding Requirements

If rent withholding is allowed in your state or city, check the law to find out:

- what circumstances justify rent withholding (normally, only significant health and safety problems justify the use of the remedy, but statutes vary as to the particulars)
- whether the tenant must give you a certain type of notice and period of time (10 to 30 days is typical) to fix the defect
- whether the tenant must ask a local court for permission to withhold rent, provide compelling reasons why the rental is not livable, and follow specific procedures, and
- whether the tenant must place the unpaid rent in a separate bank account or deposit it with a court or local housing agency, and how this is done.

Illegal Lease Clauses: Don't Limit Your Tenant's Right to Withhold the Rent Under State Law

Some landlords insert clauses in their leases and rental agreements purporting to prohibit a tenant from withholding the rent, even if a property is uninhabitable. Many withholding laws make this practice flatly illegal. But even when a state statute or court decision does not specifically prohibit this side step, courts can still ignore these clauses. Why? Because judges allow tenants to waive the right to withhold rent only when the waiver results from good-faith landlord-tenant negotiations—not just a landlord's unilateral decision.

If you give your tenants a preprinted lease containing a habitability waiver, and tell them to take it or leave it, a judge is likely to decide that the so-called waiver is invalid. In short, your attempt to take away the right to use this option could be worthless.

What Happens to the Rent?

While repairs are being made, the tenant might have to pay the entire rent to the court or housing authority, or might be directed to pay some rent to you and the balance to the court or housing authority. Sometimes, when a court or housing authority is holding the rent, you can ask for a release of some of the withheld rent to pay for repairs. After the court or local housing inspectors certify the rental as being habitable, any money in the account is returned to you, minus court costs and inspection fees (but subject to the tenant's claim for rent abatement; see below).

If your state's withholding law doesn't require the tenant to escrow the rent, and a court hasn't been involved, tenants can make their own arrangements as to what to do with the money.

Careful tenants (who want to prove that they are withholding rent for legitimate reasons) will devise their own escrow system, perhaps by placing the rent in an attorney's trust account or a separate bank account.

Rogue Rent Withholding

Sometimes tenants in states that don't allow rent withholding attempt to reduce the rent anyway. For example, if the water heater is broken and you haven't fixed it despite repeated requests, your tenant might unilaterally decide to deduct a few hundred dollars each month.

Can you terminate and evict a tenant who gives you a short rent check in a state that has not authorized rent withholding? In some states, the answer is yes. In others, however, a tenant's partial withholding might survive an eviction lawsuit, especially if the defects were significant and your failure to fix them flagrant and long-standing. The wise strategy is to not gamble—if you lose the eviction lawsuit, you might get hit with the tenant's court costs and attorneys' fees. Attend to maintenance problems before they escalate into rent wars.

Once you've made the repairs, don't be surprised if your tenants argue that they should be compensated for living in substandard conditions. They might demand a retroactive reduction in rent, known as rent abatement or recoupment, starting from the time that the premises became uninhabitable. (Some states limit tenants to a reduction starting from the time you were notified of the problem.)

Your tenants might seek a retroactive rent abatement through the court or by negotiating with you. The following section describes how a judge will determine how much you should compensate your tenant for the inconvenience of having lived in a substandard rental unit. If a court is not involved, you and the tenant can use this same system in your own negotiations.

Determining the Value of a Defective Rental Unit

Judges determine the worth of a defective, unlivable unit in one of two ways:

By estimating the market value. Some statutes and court cases say that landlords of defective rentals are entitled to only the fair market value of the premises in that condition.

For example, if an apartment with a heater normally rented for $1,200 per month, but the judge determines that the market value of the unit without operable heating is $600, you would be entitled to only $600 a month from the escrowed funds. The difficulty with this approach—as with many things in law—is that it is staggeringly unrealistic. An apartment with no heat in winter has *no* market value, because no tenant would want to live there, and no landlord could legally offer it for rent. Therefore, any determination of market value of an uninhabitable rental is nothing more than a guesstimate.

By percentage reduction. A slightly more sensible approach is to start by asking how much of the unit is affected by the defect. Then, reduce the rent by a percentage proportionate to the percentage of the unit that the defect made uninhabitable. For example, if the roof leaked into the living room of a $1,500-a-month apartment, rendering the room unusable, a tenant might reduce the rent by the percentage of the rent attributable to the living room. If the living room were the main living space and the other rooms were too small to live in comfortably, the percentage of loss would be much greater than it would be in more spacious apartments. This approach is also far from being an exact science.

EXAMPLE: When Henry and Sue moved into their apartment, it was neat and well maintained. Soon after, the building was sold to an out-of-state owner, who hired an off-site manager to handle repairs and maintenance. Gradually, the premises began to deteriorate. At the beginning of May, 15 months into their two-year lease, Henry and Sue could count several violations of the building code, including the landlord's failure to maintain the common areas, remove the garbage promptly, and fix a broken water heater.

Henry and Sue sent numerous repair requests to their landlord over a two-month period, during which they gritted their teeth and put up with the situation. Finally, they checked out their state's rent withholding law. They learned that tenants living in substandard conditions could pay rent into an escrow account set up by their local court instead of making payments to their landlords. Henry and Sue went ahead and deposited their rent into this account.

During the time that they lived in these uninhabitable conditions, Henry and Sue were not required to pay full rent. Using the "market value" approach, the court decided that their defective rental was worth half its stated rent. Accordingly, since the landlord owed them a refund for portions of their rent for May and June, Henry and Sue would be paid this amount from the escrow account.

The balance of the rent in the account would be released to the landlord (less the costs of the escrow and the tenants' attorneys' fees), but only when the building inspector certified to the court that the building was up to code and fit for human habitation.

Henry and Sue could continue to pay 50% of the rent until needed repairs were made and certified by the building inspector.

Repair and Deduct

If you let your rental property fall below the fit and habitable standard, tenants might be able to use a legal procedure called "repair and deduct." It works like this: Under certain conditions, tenants can (without the landlord's permission and without filing a lawsuit) have the defect repaired and subtract the cost of the repairs from the following month's rent. The repair and deduct remedy is available only if state or local law has authorized it.

Like the rent withholding option described above, tenants can only invoke the repair and deduct remedy when they meet specific criteria. Most states require that the defect must be inexpensive, involve an essential service, or both (depending on the wording of the statute). Additionally, the subject of the repair must clearly be the landlord's responsibility. Let's look more closely at these requirements.

Repairs Must Qualify

A few states allow the repair and deduct remedy only for minor repairs, such as a leaky faucet or stopped-up sink. Most states place a limit on the amount that tenants can deduct, usually a dollar amount or a specific percentage of the month's rent. For example, a tenant might only be able to repair and deduct no more than the greater of $300 or one-half the monthly rent.

Also, most states allow tenants to use the repair and deduct remedy only for fixing essential services (such as water and heat) or for remedying conditions that materially affect the habitability of the premises, safety of the tenant, or terms of the lease.

EXAMPLE: On a chilly November evening, the pilot light for Larry's heater failed. He called his building manager, who promised to fix it soon. After calling the manager several more times to no avail and suffering through three frigid days with no heat, Larry called a heater repairperson, who came promptly and replaced the broken mechanism for $200. Since Larry lives in a state that allows the repair and deduct remedy, Larry deducted $200 from his next rent check and gave his manager the repair bill.

Repairs Must Be Your Responsibility

Tenants cannot use the rent deduction method to fix a defect or problem that the tenants or their guests caused. Also, because tenants in most states have a legal duty to keep the dwelling as clean and orderly as the premises permit, they cannot use the remedy if the problem is traceable to their unsanitary or unreasonable use of the property.

You Must Be Notified of the Problem

Before using the repair and deduct remedy, tenants must notify you of the problem. However, they do not have to inform you that they intend to utilize the remedy if you fail to respond. Each state has its own procedures and timeline for notification. Most states require the tenants' notice to be in writing, but some simply require that the tenants give the landlord or manager "reasonable" notice of the problem (this could be orally or in writing).

You Must Have Had an Opportunity to Fix the Problem

Statutes often give landlords a specified amount of time to repair before tenants can legally use the repair and deduct remedy. For nonemergency repairs, landlords typically have ten to 14 days after the notification to repair. Landlords must respond to emergency repair requests (such as a hole in the roof or a defective heater in winter) promptly. However, some states don't impose a time limit; instead, you must make the repairs in a reasonable time.

There's a Limit to How Much Rent the Tenant Can Deduct

In states that allow the repair and deduct remedy, the amount the tenant deducts is always limited to the actual and reasonable amount spent on the repair. In addition, many states impose a limit on tenants' repairs—either a specific dollar amount or a percentage of the monthly rent. In most states, when tenants use the repair and deduct remedy, they must submit an itemized accounting of and receipts for the repairs they had made at the time they pay their reduced rent.

There's a Limit to Use of the Repair and Deduct Remedy

Many states limit how often tenants can use the repair and deduct remedy—for example, no more than once or twice in any 12-month period. Just because tenants have reached their limit on using the remedy does not mean, however, that a landlord who has refused to fix a problem can ignore it. The tenants can still invoke any of the other remedies described in this chapter: rent withholding, filing a lawsuit in small claims court, or moving out.

Negative Consequences of Repair and Deduct

A tenant's use of the repair and deduct remedy can have unpleasant consequences. The tenant has little incentive to hire the best person for the job, and will try to find someone who can complete the repair quickly. This often results in shoddy work at a premium price. Careful adherence to the high-quality maintenance system described below should help you avoid this fate.

> **EXAMPLE:** When Matt opened the cupboard underneath his bathroom sink, he saw that the flexible hose connecting the pipe nipple to the sink was leaking. He turned off the water and called his landlord, Lee, who promised to attend to the problem right away. After three days without a bathroom sink, Matt called a plumber, who replaced the hose for $175. Matt deducted this amount from his next rent check. Lee thought no more about this until he got a frantic call from the tenant in the apartment beneath Matt's. She described her ceiling as looking like a giant, dripping sponge. Lee called his regular plumber to check the problem out. His plumber told Lee that the repair on Matt's sink had been done negligently, resulting in a major leak into the walls. If Lee had called his own plumber, the job would have been done right in the first place, saving Lee lots of money and hassle.

A tenant's use of repair and deduct will also complicate (or frustrate) your accounting records. You should be tracking maintenance costs in order to itemize them on your Schedule E tax return. But when tenants use repair and deduct, you have no receipt (with your name on it), and no direct way to prove the expense (short of arguing that the lowered rent reflects that expense). Keep things straightforward by paying for repairs yourself.

Your Options When a Tenant Withholds Rent

When confronted with a tenant who does not pay all or part of the rent, many landlords almost reflexively turn to a lawyer to bring an eviction lawsuit. But even if you successfully evict the tenant (which won't happen if the judge finds the tenant's rent withholding was justified), it is usually only after considerable cost. Pursuing eviction is appropriate in some circumstances, especially when tenants are clearly wrong and simply throwing legal sand in the air in an effort to obscure the fact that they can't or won't pay rent. But it's important to realize that tenants can fall into at least two other categories:

- tenants whose arguments have validity— that is, the repairs or maintenance should have been done more promptly, and
- tenants who sincerely thought they had the right to withhold or repair and deduct rent, but who overreacted to the problem or just did the wrong thing under the law.

How you react when a tenant reduces, repairs and deducts, or withholds rent should depend on which category the tenant fits into. The following sections look at your options depending on the three categories: obvious troublemakers, mistaken but sincere tenants who are worth salvaging, and tenants who had some justification for using the remedy they chose.

Obvious Troublemakers

If you keep your rental properties in good shape and properly handle repair and maintenance problems, your best bet might be to promptly and legally terminate the tenancy of any tenant who withholds rent.

If you're heading for court, you might need to consult a lawyer or research your state's eviction laws. If you do end up in court, be prepared to prove the following:

- The claimed defect was nonexistent, and nothing justified the tenant's failure to pay the rent.
- The tenant caused the defect in order to avoid paying rent.
- The claimed defect was not really serious or substantial enough to give the tenant the right to pursue a particular remedy.
- Even if the defect was substantial, you were never given adequate notice and a chance to fix it. (At this point you should present your detailed complaint procedure to the court as we recommend above. You should show, if possible, that the tenant didn't follow your procedure.)
- The tenant failed to comply with some other aspect of the rent withholding law. For example, in states that require the tenant to place the withheld rent in escrow with the court, a tenant's failure to do so may defeat any attempt to use the procedure at all. Tenants who repeatedly fail to use the escrow procedure might be candidates for eviction.

CAUTION
If in doubt, hold off on eviction. Sometimes it's hard to know if a tenant is truly a bad apple or just badly confused about their legal rights. Until you are sure the tenant fits into the first category (reduced, withheld, or deducted rent in bad faith), don't try to evict the tenant. Under the law of virtually every state, retaliatory evictions—evictions landlords pursue to get back at tenants for asserting their rights—are severely punished.

Sample Letter Suggesting Compromise on Rent Withholding

May 3, 20xx

Tyrone McNab
Villa Arms, Apt. 4
123 Main Street
Cleveland, Ohio 44130

Dear Mr. McNab:

I am writing you in the hope that we can work out a fair compromise to the problems that led you to withhold rent. You have rented a unit at the Villa Arms for the last three years, and we have never had a problem before. Let's try to resolve it.

To review briefly, on May 1, Marvin, my resident manager at Villa Arms, told me that you were temporarily withholding your rent because of several defective conditions in your apartment. Marvin said you had asked him to correct these problems a week ago, but he hasn't as yet attended to them. Marvin states that you listed these defects as some peeling paint on the interior wall of your bedroom, a leaky kitchen water faucet, a running toilet, a small hole in the living room carpet, and a cracked kitchen window.

I have instructed Marvin to promptly arrange with you for a convenient time to allow him into your apartment to repair all these problems. I am sure these repairs would already have been accomplished by now except for the fact that Hank, our regular repairperson, has been out sick for the last few days.

I understand that these problems are annoying and significant to you, and I acknowledge that they should have been attended to more promptly. However, I do not believe that they justify rent withholding under state law. Rent withholding is allowed only when the defects make the premises unfit for habitation. I do not think, however, that in the long run either one of us would be well served by stubbornly standing on our rights or resorting to a court fight. My first wish is to come to an amicable understanding with you that we can live with and use to avoid problems like this in the future.

Because of the inconvenience you have suffered as a result of the problems in your apartment, I am prepared to offer you a prorated rebate on your rent for ten days, this being the estimated length of time it will have taken Marvin to remedy the problems from the day of your complaint. As your monthly rent is $900, equal to $30 per day, I am agreeable to your paying only $600 rent this month.

If this is not acceptable to you, please call me at 555-1234 during the day. If you would like to discuss any aspect of the situation in more detail, I would be pleased to meet with you at your convenience. I will expect to receive your check for $600, or a call from you, before May 10.

Sincerely,

Sandra Schmidt

Sandra Schmidt
Owner, Villa Arms

Mistaken But Sincere Tenants

Sometimes, tenants withhold rent thinking that doing so is their legal right, and that something about the rental truly justifies their paying a reduced rent—even when they're wrong. If you think the tenants are being sincere and aren't just making up an excuse for not paying rent, your best option usually is to talk with the tenants in a face-to-face meeting.

If, for example, the tenants used the repair and deduct remedy but never gave you notice of the problem, it might make sense to accept the tenant's solution, but make sure they know how to notify you of problems in the future. This sort of compromise might be painful, but it's not nearly as bad as risking an eviction lawsuit where a judge might agree with the tenants' course of action.

The chances for resolving a conflict will be greater if you have a compromise system in place when you need it. When you encounter rent problems with tenants who aren't clear candidates for eviction, consider taking the following steps:

1. Meet with the tenants and negotiate. Make it clear that your goals are to establish a good solution to the current disagreement and avoid problems in the future—not to determine who is "right."
2. If negotiation fails, suggest mediation by a neutral third party. (Try to learn more about mediation options in your area before an issue arises so you can move quickly when you need the service.)
3. Put your solution in writing.
4. If the process indicates a larger problem with tenant dissatisfaction, encourage tenants to meet with you regularly to improve the overall situation.

These steps will lead to a mutually acceptable resolution in the majority of cases. On your end, this might mean you agree to have the necessary work done promptly and to do a better job of maintaining the unit in the future. You might also give the tenant a prorated reduction in rent for the period between the time the tenant notified you of the defect and the time it was corrected. In exchange, the tenants might promise to promptly notify you of problems before resorting to the same tactic in the future.

> **EXAMPLE:** A leaky roof during a rainy month deprives a tenant, Steve, of the use of one of his two bedrooms. If Steve gave his landlord, Joe, notice of the leak, and Joe did not take care of the problem quickly, Steve might be justified in deducting $300 from the $800 rent for that month. However, if Steve didn't tell Joe of the problem until the next month's rent was due, a compromise might be reached where Steve bears part of the responsibility, by agreeing to deduct only $100 from the rent.

The first step in working toward a compromise with tenants is to call them. If you're reluctant to call, you might want to try a letter or email. See the sample letter above suggesting a compromise on rent withholding.

Tenants Who Are Partially Right

Sometimes, despite your best efforts to keep on top of maintenance, a repair job falls through the cracks. It could happen if you're on vacation and your backup falls through, or if you simply need a better manager. When tenants are justified in using rent withholding or repair and deduct, admit it and take steps to rectify the situation.

After you've mended the relationship with your tenants, use what happened as an opportunity to review, revise, and improve your maintenance and repair procedures:

- **Complaint procedure.** Do you have a complaint system that makes it easy for tenants to communicate their concerns? Are complaint forms readily available and easy to use?
- **Tenant education.** Do your tenants know that you intend to respond quickly to repair and maintenance problems? Do you need to remind all tenants, via a tenant notice or newsletter, of your complaint procedure?

- **Management response.** Does management respond reasonably quickly to tenants' requests for repairs?

Use the detailed advice on setting up and implementing a maintenance program provided earlier in this chapter as a guideline when you're evaluating how to avoid similar problems in the future.

Tenants' Responses to Unfit Premises: Calling Inspectors, Filing Lawsuits, and Moving Out

Tenants who are faced with unfit rentals have options besides withholding rent, including calling government inspectors, breaking the lease and moving out, and suing in small claims court.

Reporting Code Violations to Housing Inspectors

Tenants can complain to a local building, health, or fire department about problems such as inoperable plumbing, a leaky roof, or bad wiring. If an inspector comes out and discovers code violations, you will be given an order to correct the problem. Fines and penalties usually follow if you fail to comply within a certain amount of time (often five to 30 business days). If you don't respond to fines or penalties, the city or county might sue you. In many cities, your failure to respond promptly to citations is a misdemeanor (minor crime) punishable by hefty fines or even imprisonment. In rare cases—especially if tenants' health is imperiled—local officials might even require that the building be vacated.

In many areas, getting reported to a building inspector is a very big deal. But there is wide variation in the enforcement of code violations: In some areas, there is a shortage of inspectors, while in others the courts are too busy to follow up on citations. But don't rely on the system's inefficiencies to let you off the hook: Tenants who don't get the response they want from making

a complaint will simply turn to a more effective remedy, such as moving out.

Suing the Landlord

Consumers have the right to expect at least a minimum level of quality when they exchange their hard-earned dollars for a product or service. When their purchase is flawed, they are entitled to compensation. Tenants are consumers of rental properties, and when tenants are forced to live with substandard housing, they are entitled to compensation.

Tenants whose homes are defective may remain in possession of the premises and sue their landlord for the following:

- partial or total refund of rent paid while the housing conditions were substandard
- the value, or repair costs, of property lost or damaged as a result of the defect—for example, furniture ruined by water leaking through the roof
- compensation for personal injuries— including pain and suffering—caused by the defect
- attorneys' fees, and
- any other damage or loss they can reasonably show resulted from the landlord's actions or inactions.

In some states, tenants can also ask a court to order the landlord to repair the defects and reduce rent until the defects have been remedied.

 CAUTION
You may not retaliate against a tenant who files a lawsuit and stays on the property. (See Chapter 16 for a discussion of retaliatory eviction.) You might not understand why a tenant would take the extreme step of suing you and yet still wish to remain on the property. Nevertheless, a tenant who sues and stays is exercising a legal right. Landlord retaliation, such as delivering a rent increase or a termination notice, is illegal and will give the tenant yet another ground on which to sue.

Moving Out

If a dwelling isn't habitable and you haven't fixed it, your tenants have the right to move out—either temporarily or permanently. Moving out is justified only when the rental has truly serious problems, such as the lack of essential services or the total or partial destruction of the premises. Tenants may also use this option if environmental health hazards such as lead paint dust make the unit uninhabitable.

Severe Code Violations Will Close Your Building

If a judge decides that a building's condition substantially endangers the health and safety of its tenants, and repairs are so extensive they can't be made while tenants inhabit the building, the result might be an order to vacate the building. You usually won't have a chance to come to the court hearing to object to this dire consequence—your tenants will simply be told to get out, sometimes within hours.

In some states, you must pay for comparable temporary housing for your ousted tenants. Some statutes also make you cover tenants' moving expenses. When the repairs are completed, most statutes require you to give the original tenants the option of moving back in before you try to fill the building with new tenants.

To find out whether landlords are liable for relocation expenses, check your state statutes (listed in "State Landlord-Tenant Statutes" in Appendix A). Look in the index to your state's codes under "Landlord-Tenant" for subheadings such as "Relocation Assistance" or "Padlock Orders."

Tenants' Right to Move Out When the Unit Is Uninhabitable

Every state's law requires you to provide habitable housing, and allows tenants to move out if you don't do your job. Depending on the circumstances, tenants may move out permanently, by terminating the lease or rental agreement, or temporarily. This remedy is borrowed directly from consumer protection laws. Just as the purchaser of a seriously defective car can sue to undo the contract or return the car for a refund, tenants can consider the housing contract terminated and simply return the rental unit to you if the housing is unlivable.

The law, of course, has a convoluted phrase to describe this simple concept. It's called "constructive eviction," which means that, by supplying unlivable housing, you have for all practical purposes "evicted" the tenant. Tenants who have been constructively evicted (that is, they have a valid reason to move out) have no further responsibility for rent.

Your state might have specific laws about constructive eviction, such as the type of notice tenants must provide before moving out. Your state law might give you anywhere from five to 30 days to fix the problem, depending on the seriousness of the situation. Check your state landlord-tenant statutes for details.

Temporary moves. In many states, if you fail to provide heat or other essential services, tenants may procure reasonable substitute housing during the period of your noncompliance. Often, landlords are on the hook for any reasonable costs the displaced tenants incur as a result of their temporary move.

Permanent moves. Tenants who move out permanently because of habitability problems might also be entitled to compensation for out-of-pocket losses. For example, you might be responsible for tenants' moving expenses and the cost of a hotel while they look for a new place. Also, if the tenants paid full rent despite substandard conditions before their move, they can sue you for the difference between the value of the defective dwelling and the rent paid. In addition, if the tenants can't find comparable housing for the same rent, and they end up paying more rent than they would have under the lease they signed with you, you might be on the hook for the difference.

EXAMPLE: Susan signed a one-year lease for a beachfront apartment. She thought it was a great deal because the monthly rent of $700 was considerably less than similar properties in the neighborhood. Susan's dream apartment began to turn into a nightmare when she discovered, soon after moving in, that the bedroom was full of mildew that interfered with her breathing. After numerous complaints to the landlord, which were ignored, Susan moved out at the end of four months and rented a comparable apartment nearby for $800. She then sued her ex-landlord for the following:

- **Compensation for the months she endured the defective conditions.** Susan asked for the difference between the agreed-upon rent and the true value of the mildew apartment, for each of the four months she paid rent.
- **The benefit of her bargain.** Susan pointed out that the rent for the first apartment was a real bargain, and that she had been unable to find a similar apartment for anything less than $800 per month. She sued for the additional rent she now has to pay at her new place ($100), times eight—the number of months left on her original lease.
- **Moving costs.** Susan sought reimbursement for the $250 she paid a moving company to transport her belongings to her new home.

After hearing Susan's arguments and the landlord's feeble defense, the judge decided that Susan was entitled to:

- **Compensation for past problems.** The mildew problem, which had forced Susan to sleep in the living room, had essentially reduced the one-bedroom apartment to a studio apartment, which would have rented for $400 per month. Accordingly, Susan was entitled to a refund of $300 for each of the four months, a total of $1,200.
- **The benefit of her bargain.** The judge acknowledged that a similar apartment, such as the one she rented when she moved out, cost $100 more per month than the one she had originally rented, and awarded her that amount per month times eight, totalling $800.

- **Moving costs.** The judge ruled that Susan's moving costs of $250 were reasonable, and ordered the landlord to pay them.

Tenants' Right to Move Out When the Rental Is Damaged

Tenants whose home is significantly damaged—either by natural disaster or any other reason beyond their responsibility or control—have the right to consider the lease at an end and to move out. Whether you or your tenants have financial responsibilities when the rental is damaged depends on your lease or rental agreement. Tenants might have the legal right to your assistance with substitute housing or living expenses. Obviously, tenants whose rental unit is destroyed by a natural disaster have less reason to expect resettlement assistance from you than those whose home is destroyed by fire caused by your botching an electrical repair. And the tenants whose home burns down because they left the stove on all night will probably find themselves at the other end of a lawsuit.

Natural or third-party disasters. Your legal responsibility depends on state law and the cause of the damage. If a fire, flood, tornado, earthquake, or other natural disaster renders your rental unlivable, or if a third party causes the destruction (for instance, an arsonist), look to your insurance policy for help repairing or rebuilding the unit (if you have "loss of rents" coverage, you might get compensated for not receiving the tenants' rent). While waiting for the insurance coverage to kick in, give month-to-month tenants a termination notice (typically 30 days' notice is required). In some states, you might have to pay the tenant for substitute housing for 30 days. For tenants who have a lease, you might be obligated to pay for substitute housing for a longer period. To be prudent, raise the issue of tenant assistance with your insurance broker when purchasing a policy, so that you know exactly where you stand if a disaster strikes.

Destruction that is traceable to the landlord. If it can be shown that you or your employees were even partially responsible for the damage, your legal responsibility to tenants is likely to increase.

You might be expected to cover the costs of temporary housing for a longer period. If the substitute housing is more expensive, you might also be stuck paying the difference between the new rent and the old rent.

The facts surrounding the property damage, applicable state law, and the extent and wording of your policy itself will determine if you have insurance coverage. Some policies exclude coverage for natural disasters, but include (as is standard) coverage for the owner's negligent acts.

If tenants move out due to damage or destruction of the premises, for whatever cause, it's important for you and the tenants to sign a written termination of the rental agreement or lease once the tenants have relocated. See the sample Landlord-Tenant Agreement to Terminate Lease in Chapter 8. By terminating all tenancies, you can repair or rebuild without the pressure of tenants waiting to move back in. If you ultimately do want to rerent to the same tenants, you can draw up a new lease or rental agreement when the rental is ready.

Minor Repairs

You are much more likely to face complaints about minor issues than about major problems that make a unit unlivable. Although you are always responsible for handling major problems (such as habitability issues), you are free to delegate responsibility for minor problems to a tenant—particularly one who is especially reliable and handy. "Delegating Landlord's Responsibilities to Tenants," below, shows how to delegate minor repairs and maintenance.

Minor repair and maintenance includes:

- small plumbing jobs, like replacing washers and cleaning drains

- system upkeep, like changing heating filters
- structural upkeep, like replacing excessively worn flooring
- small repair jobs, like fixing broken light fixtures or replacing the grout around bathtub tile, and
- routine repairs to and maintenance of common areas, such as pools, spas, and laundry rooms.

Most often, landlords are responsible for minor repairs. But you aren't required to keep the rental premises looking just like new—ordinary wear and tear does not have to be repaired during a tenancy. (When the tenant moves out, you can deal with ordinary wear and tear, but the costs of repairs cannot come out of the security deposit.)

When tenants or their guests cause a minor repair problem, carelessly or intentionally, the tenants are responsible. If your lease or rental agreement prohibits tenants from making repairs themselves, they must pay for the repair costs.

Whenever a repair problem arises that isn't caused by the tenants, and it's more than just a cosmetic issue, you will likely have to repair it for one of the following reasons:

- A state or local building code requires you to keep the damaged item in good repair.
- A state or local law specifically makes it your responsibility.
- Your lease, rental agreement, or advertising materials describe or list particular items, such as hot tubs, trash compactors, and air conditioners. By implication, you have a responsibility to maintain and repair them throughout the tenancy.
- You made explicit promises when showing the unit—for example, by noting that there's a high-tech security system or central air conditioning.
- By maintaining and fixing a particular feature in the past, you have implied a promise that it will function throughout the tenancy.

Each of these reasons is discussed below. If you're not sure whether a minor repair or maintenance problem is your responsibility, scan the discussion to find out.

Building Codes

Building codes often cover minor details that aren't related to habitability. For example, a code might specify a minimum number of electrical outlets per room; if a broken circuit breaker results in fewer working outlets, you are legally required to fix the problem.

Landlord-Tenant Laws

Many laws require landlords to perform specific minor repairs and maintenance. For example, landlords in many areas must provide garbage receptacles and arrange for garbage pick-up. Some areas might have unique rules. Alaska law, for example, makes landlords responsible for maintaining appliances they've supplied. (Alaska Stat. § 34.03.100.)

If you're a landlord of a single-family residence, your state law might allow you to delegate some of your minor responsibilities—such as disposing of garbage—to your renters. For details, check your state's landlord-tenant codes under "State Landlord-Tenant Statutes," which are listed in Appendix A.

Promises in the Lease or Rental Agreement

When it comes to legal responsibility for repairs, your own lease or rental agreement is often just as important (or more so) than building codes or state laws. If your written agreement describes or lists items such as drapes, washing machines, swimming pools, saunas, parking places, intercoms, or dishwashers, they must be offered and maintained in working order throughout the tenancy.

Promises in Ads

If you describe or list a feature, such as heated bathroom flooring, in your advertising, you must provide it in working order throughout the tenancy—even if it's a luxury, and even if your written rental agreement doesn't mention the amenity

Promises Made Before You Rented the Unit

It's hard to refrain from announcing rosy plans for amenities or services that haven't yet materialized ("We plan to redo this kitchen—you'll love the snappy way that trash compactor will work!"). Whenever you make promises like these, even if they're not in writing, your tenant can legally hold you to them.

Implied Promises

Suppose your rental agreement doesn't mention a garbage disposal, and neither did your advertisements. And you never pointed it out when showing the unit. However, there was a working garbage disposal in the unit when the tenant moved in. Now the garbage disposal is broken—do you have to fix it? Many courts will hold you responsible for maintaining all significant aspects of the rental unit. If you offer a unit that *already has* certain features—light fixtures that work, doors that open and close smoothly, faucets that don't leak, tile that doesn't fall off the wall—many judges reason that you have made an implied contract to keep them in workable order throughout the tenancy.

The flip side of this principle is that when your tenant has paid for a hamburger, the waiter—you—doesn't have to deliver a steak. In other words, if the rental was shabby but livable when the tenants moved in, and you never gave them reason to believe that it would be spruced up, they have no legal right to demand improvements—unless, of course, they can point to health hazards or code violations. As when you offer secondhand goods "as is" for a low price, legally your buyer/tenant is stuck with the deal.

Your conduct can also create an implied contract. If you consistently fix or maintain a particular feature of a rental, such as a dishwasher, you have an implied obligation to continue doing so.

Tenant Options If Landlord Refuses to Make Minor Repairs

If you have determined that the repair problem is minor and falls fairly in your lap, it's wise to attend to it promptly. Although your tenant's health and safety isn't immediately imperiled, don't test your luck: The repair might become major (and expensive), it might potentially cause injury, or it could affect other renters (presenting the unpleasant possibility of a cadre of disgruntled tenants).

When landlords refuse to fix minor problems, tenants have several options. They can:

- fix it themselves
- report you to housing inspectors, if the problem involves a code violation
- attempt to use one of the legal options designed for habitability problems, such as rent withholding or repair and deduct
- break the lease and move out, or
- sue you.

Even though some of these options might not be legitimate, your being in the right can be an illusory victory. Legal disputes—in court or out—are expensive and time-consuming. Unless the tenant is a whining prima donna who demands constant, unnecessary repairs, it's usually wiser to fix the problem and nip the issue in the bud.

Fixing the Problem Themselves

Your exasperated tenants might decide to DIY the problem. If you're lucky, they're handy and use the proper procedures and materials. But there is always the possibility that the tenants will do a slipshod job, either negligently or out of spite.

> **EXAMPLE:** Colin decided to replace a window that was broken by his son's basketball. He removed the shards of glass, fitted a new pane in place and caulked the circumference. Unfortunately, he used the wrong type of caulk; a year later it cracked, allowing rainwater to seep onto the windowsill and down the wall. His landlord Sarina was furious when she realized that she would have to replace the sill and the drywall, simply because Colin's work was amateurish. The cost of these repairs exceeded Colin's security deposit, and Sarina had to sue him in small claims court for the balance, which she had a hard time collecting.

Reporting Code Violations

If the minor repair problem constitutes a code violation, your tenants might report you to the building or housing agency in charge of enforcing the code. Whether the agency responds will depend on the seriousness of the violation, its workload, and its ability to enforce its compliance orders. Because the problem is minor, it's unlikely to get much action, especially if code enforcement officials are already overworked. But your tenants' complaint will remain on file and create a public record that might come back to haunt you.

> **EXAMPLE:** Randall was a successful landlord who owned several properties. A rotten and poorly supported deck at one of his apartment houses collapsed, killing one tenant and injuring several others. Randall was sued by the injured tenants and the family of the deceased for intentionally violating building codes when constructing the deck. Local news coverage made much of the fact that he had been cited numerous times for minor code violations; this publicity made it extremely difficult for him to get a fair trial. The jury found in favor of the plaintiffs and awarded them several million dollars. Because this tragedy was not the result of Randall's negligence, but rather an expected consequence of deliberately ignoring proper building procedures, Randall's insurance company refused to cover the award. Randall was forced to declare bankruptcy.

Using Rent Withholding or Repair and Deduct

Tenants often make the mistake of using these powerful remedies for minor repairs. If your tenants use them improperly, you likely have grounds to terminate and evict for nonpayment of rent. Be sure to read your state's statute or other authority carefully to make sure that there's no way your tenants can justify their actions under your state's withholding or repair and deduct laws.

Breaking the Lease

Disgruntled tenants might decide it's not worth putting up with your unwillingness to handle minor repairs, and simply move out. A truly minor defect does not justify the extreme step of breaking the lease. Unfortunately, being in the right does you little good here—in most states, you'll have to take reasonable steps to rerent and credit the new rent to the departed tenant's responsibility for the balance of the rent. The fact that the tenants left because they didn't like the squeaky closet door does not relieve you of your duty to mitigate your losses.

Suing in Small Claims Court

Be it ever so minor, your tenants are entitled to get what they paid for—and if they don't, one option they have is to sue you. Small claims court is usually the court of choice.

Small claims court judges usually won't order you to perform minor repairs. The judge might, however, order that you compensate the tenants for having to live in a rental unit with repair problems, on the theory that the tenants aren't getting the full benefit of what they agreed to pay rent for, such as a unit with a functioning dishwasher or working air conditioning. You might be ordered to pay the tenants the difference between what they've paid in rent and the value of the unit with repair problems. To calculate this amount, the judge will use one of the methods described above in "Tenant Responses to Unfit Premises."

How much of a threat is a small claims suit? A judge is not going to adjust the rent because a little grout is missing from the bathroom tile. But if the dishwasher is broken, three faucets leak noisily, and the bathroom door won't close, your tenant's chances of winning go way up.

Delegating Landlord's Responsibilities to Tenants

Sometimes, it makes sense to delegate certain repair and maintenance responsibilities to the tenants themselves—perhaps you live at a distance and the tenants are responsible and handy. But is it legal to hand off your responsibilities to the tenants? Courts in each state have faced this question and have come to several different conclusions. While we cannot offer an analysis of every state's position, here are the basics.

Do Not Delegate Responsibility for Major Repairs and Maintenance to the Tenant

By law, rental housing must be habitable, because society has decided that it is unacceptable for landlords to offer substandard dwellings. For this reason, tenants in most states cannot waive the implied warranty of habitability or the covenant of quiet enjoyment. In other words, even when a tenant is willing to live in substandard housing, society has decided that it will not tolerate such an arrangement.

It is a small but logical step to the next question of whether you can delegate to the tenant the responsibility of keeping the premises fit for habitation. Many courts have held that you cannot, fearing that tenants are rarely in the position, either practically or financially, to do the kinds of repairs needed to achieve and maintain habitability.

Even if you do have the legal right, it is always a mistake to delegate to a tenant your responsibility for major maintenance of essential services, such as heat, plumbing, or electricity, or repairs involving the roof or other parts of the building structure. Even inexpensive jobs can have enormous repercussions if done poorly. For instance, replacing an electrical outlet seems simple, but shoddy work can have devastating effects (fire or electrocution).

How to Delegate Minor Repairs and Maintenance to Tenants

The legality and appropriateness of delegating minor repairs is an entirely different discussion. Under the law of some states, and as a matter of sensible practice in all states, you may delegate minor repairs and maintenance responsibilities to tenants. Tasks such as mowing the lawn, trimming the bushes, and sweeping the lobby don't relate to keeping the structure habitable.

Practically speaking, however, you must be willing to check to see if the work is done properly. If you wish to delegate responsibilities to a tenant, be advised that, as far as any *other* tenants are concerned (and probably with respect to the living space of the tenant-repairperson, too), your delegation of certain maintenance and repair duties doesn't relieve you of the ultimate responsibility for meeting state and local health and safety laws.

Always remember that the implied warranty of habitability makes you responsible for maintenance of common areas—for example, cleaning hallways and mowing the lawn. If you transfer this duty to someone who fails to do it, the transfer will not shield you if you are hauled into court for failure to maintain the premises. On the other hand, if you monitor the work, and step in to do it right if the tenant does a poor job, there should be no practical problems.

Repair and maintenance arrangements between landlords and tenants often lead to dissatisfaction—typically, the landlord feels that the tenant has neglected certain tasks, or the tenant feels that there is too much work for the money. When a court is asked to step in, the validity of the arrangement will typically be judged along the following lines:

- **Was it in writing?** Any agreement as to repairs or maintenance should be written and signed, either as part of the lease or rental agreement (see Clause 12 of the form agreements in Chapter 2), or as a separate employment agreement (discussed below).
- **Was it a fair bargain?** You must adequately pay the tenant for the services provided. Often, this payment consists of a reduction in rent. A judge might look askance at a $50 reduction in monthly rent for 20 hours of work, which represents a pay scale well below the minimum wage.
- **Is it fair to other tenants?** Some courts will also inquire as to whether your agreement adversely affects your obligations to other tenants. For example, if your tenant-maintenance person does his job poorly or only now and then, the other tenants will have to live with his spotty performance.
- **Have you treated the delegation separately from your other duties as the landlord?** The agreement you have with your tenant has nothing to do with your other responsibilities. For example, if you and your tenant agree that she will do gardening work in exchange for a reduction in rent, and you feel that she is not doing a proper job, you may not respond by shutting off her water or retaliating in other ways. The proper recourse is to discuss the problem with the tenant and, if it persists, to cancel the arrangement.

> CAUTION
> **Be careful delegating repairs involving hazardous materials.** Even the simplest repair can create an environmental health hazard. For example, preparing a surface for a seemingly innocuous paint job might actually involve the creation of lead-based paint dust, and the quick installation of a smoke alarm could disturb an asbestos-filled ceiling. When you delegate repairs to tenants, you expose yourself to more liability: You might be sued by the tenant for exposure-related injuries, sued by other affected tenants, and cited by the relevant regulating agency for allowing an untrained or uncertified person to work with toxic materials.

Delegating Repair Responsibilities to Tenants in Single-Family Residences

In several states, the landlord and tenant of a single-family dwelling may agree in writing that the tenant is to perform some of the landlord's statutory duties. For example, tenants in single-family homes often arrange for garbage receptacles and garbage disposal, perform minor plumbing repairs, change lightbulbs, and handle yard work, in addition to making other specified repairs. States allowing this type of delegation typically require that the transaction be entered into in good faith—meaning that each side completely understands their rights and responsibilities, and neither pressures the other. In addition, the work usually must not be necessary to cure the landlord's failure to substantially comply with health and safety codes.

Although the possibility for delegation is greater in some single-family rental situations than it is in a multiunit context, we caution owners of single-family rental properties to think carefully before entering into an arrangement of this type. Unless you are very sure about the skill and integrity of your tenant, the potential for shoddy work and disagreements are as great as they are in any rental situation, and the consequences (poor work done to an entire house) might be even greater.

Compensating a Tenant for Repair and Maintenance Work

Paying a tenant to do minor tasks, such as cleaning common areas or maintaining the landscaping, is preferable to giving the tenant a reduction in rent for work performed. Why? Because if the job is not done right, you can simply cancel the employment arrangement. If the arrangement is part of the lease or rental agreement, you'll have to amend the document to reflect the end of the maintenance agreement, as well as the end of any rent reduction. When the maintenance agreement is separate, it can't interfere with or cause confusion about the fact that the tenant is expected to adhere to the lease or rental agreement.

You Might Have to Pay Federal and State Tax on Your Tenant-Repairperson

Paying your handy tenant $300 per month, or reducing the rent by this amount, in exchange for maintenance and repair duties might have important tax consequences for you. That person might be considered your "employee" (as distinguished from an independent contractor). If you "pay" the person more than a certain amount per year, either in cash or in the form of a rent reduction, you might be obliged to pay Social Security and meet other legal obligations as an employer. These obligations are covered in the Chapter 6 discussion of compensating a tenant-manager.

Landlord Liability for Tenant Repair and Maintenance Work

The delegation of basic repair and maintenance work to a tenant might not relieve you of liability if the repair is done poorly and someone is injured or property is damaged as a result.

Of course, you could always try to recoup your losses by suing the tenant-repairperson (called "seeking indemnity" in legalese), but your chances of recovery will be slim unless your tenant has sufficient monetary assets. On the other hand, a third-party maintenance or repair service will generally carry its own insurance (you should confirm this before you engage their services).

The cruelest cut of all could be the ability of the tenant-repairperson to sue you for injuries received while performing repair tasks. The tenant could argue—successfully, in some courts and in front of some juries—that you had no business entrusting a dangerous job to someone whose expertise was not proven.

A carefully written exculpatory clause might shield you from liability in some situations, but you can never be 100% sure that the clause will be upheld in court. Exculpatory clauses are explained in Chapter 10.

EXAMPLE: Clem, the landlord, hired Tom, the teenage son of a longtime tenant, for yard work. Part of Tom's job consisted of mowing the two front lawns, which were separated by a gravel walkway. Tom cut the first lawn and, without turning off the mower, pushed it over the gravel to the second lawn. Pieces of gravel were picked up by the blades and fired to the side, where they struck and partially blinded a child playing in the next yard. Clem was sued and faced an uphill battle with his insurance company as to whether Tom's negligence was covered under Clem's policy.

Tenants' Alterations and Improvements

Your lease or rental agreement probably includes a clause prohibiting tenants from making any alterations or improvements without your express, written consent; see Clause 12 of our lease or rental agreement forms in Chapter 2. For good reason, you'll want to make sure tenants don't change the light fixtures, replace the window coverings, or install a built-in dishwasher unless you agree first.

In spite of your wish that your tenants leave well enough alone, you're bound to encounter the tenant who remodels without your knowledge or consent. On the other hand, you might also hear from an upstanding tenant that she would, indeed, like your consent to her plan to install a bookshelf or closet system. To deal with unauthorized alterations or straightforward requests, you'll need to understand some basic rules.

RELATED TOPIC

Tenants with disabilities have rights to modify their living space that might override your ban against alterations without your consent. See Chapter 5 for details.

Improvements That Become Part of the Property (Fixtures)

Anything your tenant attaches to the ground itself or a building, fence, or deck (lawyers call such items "fixtures") belongs to you, absent an agreement saying it belongs to the tenant. This is an age-old legal principle, and, for good measure, it's wise to spell it out in your lease or rental agreement. This means that you are legally entitled to refuse your tenant's offer to remove the fixture and return the premises to its original state at move-out.

When a landlord and departing tenant haven't decided ahead of time as to who will own the fixture, the dispute often ends up in court. Judges use a variety of legal rules to determine whether an object—an appliance, flooring, shelving, or plumbing—is something that the tenant can remove or is a permanent fixture belonging to you. Here are some of the questions judges ask when separating portable from nonportable additions:

- **Did your tenant get your permission?** If the tenant never asked you for permission to install a closet organizer, or did and got no for an answer, a judge is likely to rule for you—particularly if your lease or rental agreement prohibits alterations or improvements.

- **Did the tenant make any structural changes that affect the use or appearance of the property?** If so, chances are that the item will be deemed yours, because removing it could leave an unsightly area or alter use of part of the property. For example, if a tenant modifies the kitchen counter to accommodate a built-in dishwasher and then takes the dishwasher with her, you will have to install another dishwasher of the same dimensions or rebuild the space. The law doesn't impose this extra work on landlords, nor does it force you to let tenants do the return-to-original work themselves.

- **Is the object firmly attached to the property?** In general, anything that's nailed, screwed, or cemented to the building is likely to be deemed a fixture. For example, anchoring a bookcase to the wall might convert it from being the tenant's personal property to a fixture belonging to you. Similarly, closet rods bolted to the wall become part of the structure and would usually be counted as fixtures. On the other hand, shelving systems that are secured by isometric pressure (spring-loaded rods that press against the ceiling and floor) involve no actual attachment to the wall and, for that reason, are not likely to be classified as fixtures.

- **What did you and the tenant intend?** Courts will evaluate whether your conversations with the tenant created any expectations about the improvements. In some circumstances, courts will infer an agreement from your actions—for instance, if you stopped by and gave permission for your tenant to install what you referred to as a portable air conditioner, or helped lift it into place. By contrast, if the tenant removes light fixtures and, without your knowledge, installs a custom-made fixture that could not be used in any other space, it is unlikely that the judge would find that the tenant reasonably expected to keep it at the end of the tenancy.

Easily-Removed Improvements

The act of plugging in an appliance doesn't make the appliance a part of the premises. The same is true for simple connectors or fittings that join an appliance to an electrical or water source. For example, a refrigerator or freestanding stove remains the property of the tenant. Similarly, portable dishwashers that connect to the kitchen faucet by means of a coupling are easily removed without damage, and are considered personal property.

Responding to Improvement and Alteration Requests

If a tenant approaches you with a request to alter your property or install a new feature, chances are that your impulse will be to say no. Don't be too hasty—as you'll see below, requests for telecommunications access (cable access, satellite dishes, and antennas) are governed by special rules. As for other types of requests, perhaps the question comes from an outstanding tenant whom you would like to accommodate and would hate to lose. Instead of adopting a rigid approach, consider these alternatives.

Option One. Could the improvement or alteration be removed easily? For example, if your tenant has a year's lease and you plan to repaint when she leaves, you can easily fill and paint any small holes left behind when she removes the bookshelf bolted to the wall (and you can bill her for the spackling costs, as explained below). Knocking out a wall to install a wine closet is a more permanent change and not one you're likely to agree to.

Option Two. Would the alteration enhance your property? For example, a wine closet might actually add value to your property. If so, depending on the terms of the agreement you reach with your tenant, you might actually come out ahead.

Before you accommodate your tenant's requests, evaluate these options. For example, you might have no use for an air conditioner attached to the window frame, and your tenant might want to take it with her. You'll need to make sure that she understands that she must restore the window frame to its original condition, and that if her restoration attempts aren't acceptable, you will deduct from her security deposit the amount of money necessary to do the job right. (And if the deposit is insufficient, you can sue her in small claims court for the excess.) On the other hand, a custom-made window insulation system might enhance your property (and justify a higher rent later on) and won't do your tenant any good if she takes it with her. (Be prepared for your tenant to ask you to pay for at least some of it.)

Agreement Regarding Tenant Alterations to Rental Unit

_____Iona Lott_____ ("Landlord")

and _____Doug Diep_____ ("Tenant")

agree as follows:

1. Tenant may make the following alterations to the rental unit at: _____75A Cherry Street, Pleasantville,_____

    _____North Dakota_____

    _____1. Plant three rose bushes along walkway at side of residence._____

    _____2. Install track lighting along west (ten-foot) kitchen wall._____

    _____

    _____

    _____

    _____

    _____ .

2. Tenant will accomplish the work described in Paragraph 1 by using the following materials and procedures:

    _____1. Three bare-root roses, hybrid teas, purchased from Jackson-Perky and_____

    _____planted in march._____

    _____2. The fixture that will be installed is the "Wallbright" track lighting system purchased from_____

    _____Lamps and more (plus necessary attachment hardware). Tenant will hire a qualified,_____

    _____licensed professional to install the fixture, and will obtain any necessary permits._____

    _____

    _____ .

3. Tenant will do only the work outlined in Paragraph 1 using only the materials and procedures outlined in Paragraph 2.

4. The alterations carried out by Tenant:

    ☑ will become Landlord's property and are not to be removed by Tenant during or at the end of the

    tenancy, or

    ☐ will be considered Tenant's personal property, and as such may be removed by Tenant at any time up

    to the end of the tenancy. Tenant promises to return the premises to their original condition upon

    removing the improvement.

5. Landlord will reimburse Tenant only for the costs checked below:

    ☑ the cost of materials listed in Paragraph 2

    ☑ labor costs at the rate of $ __75_____ per hour for work done in a workmanlike manner

    acceptable to Landlord, up to _____10_____ hours.

6. After receiving appropriate documentation of the cost of materials and labor, Landlord shall make any payment called for under Paragraph 5 by:

   ☑ lump sum payment, within _____10_____ days of receiving documentation of costs, or

   ☐ by reducing Tenant's rent by $ _____ per month for the number of months necessary to cover the total amounts under the terms of this agreement.

7. If under Paragraph 4 of this contract the alterations are Tenant's personal property, Tenant must return the premises to their original condition upon removing the alterations. If Tenant fails to do this, Landlord will deduct the cost to restore the premises to their original condition from Tenant's security deposit. If the security deposit is insufficient to cover the costs of restoration, Landlord may take legal action, if necessary, to collect the balance.

8. If Tenant fails to remove an improvement that is Tenant's personal property on or before the end of the tenancy, it will be considered the property of Landlord, who may choose to keep the improvement (with no financial liability to Tenant), or remove it and charge Tenant for the costs of removal and restoration. Landlord may deduct any costs of removal and restoration from Tenant's security deposit. If the security deposit is insufficient to cover the costs of removal and restoration, Landlord may take legal action, if necessary, to collect the balance.

9. If Tenant removes an item that is Landlord's property, Tenant will owe Landlord the fair market value of the item removed plus any costs incurred by Landlord to restore the premises to their original condition.

10. If Landlord and Tenant are involved in any legal proceeding arising out of this agreement, the prevailing party shall recover reasonable attorney fees, court costs, and any costs reasonably necessary to collect a judgment.

_____Iona Lott_____   _____February 10, 20xx____
Landlord   Date

_____Doug Diep_____   _____February 10, 20xx____
Tenant   Date

If you and the tenant reach an understanding, put it in writing. As shown in the sample Agreement Regarding Tenant Alterations to Rental Unit, above (and included as a download on the Nolo website—see Appendix B for the link), you will want to carefully describe the project and materials, including:

- whether the improvement or alteration is permanent or portable
- the terms of reimbursement, if any, and
- how and when you'll pay the tenant, if at all, for labor and materials.

Our agreement makes it clear that the tenant's failure to properly restore the premises, or removal of an alteration that was to be permanent, will result in security deposit deductions or legal action if necessary.

Cable TV Access

If your building is already wired for cable, tenants who want to sign up need only call the cable provider to activate the existing cable line to their unit. But what if you don't have cable access available already? And what if you have a contract with one provider, but the tenant wants another? Congress has decreed that all Americans should have as much access as possible to information that comes through a cable or through wireless transmissions. (Federal Telecommunications Act of 1996, 47 U.S.C. §§ 151 and following.) The act makes it very difficult for state and local governments, zoning commissions, homeowners' associations, or landlords to restrict a person's ability to take advantage of these types of communications.

Previously Unwired Buildings

If your property does not have cable, you may continue to say no to tenants who ask you for access. But don't be surprised if, in response, your tenant mounts a satellite dish on the balcony, wall, or roof. We discuss your ability to regulate these devices below.

Exclusive Contracts With Cable Providers

The FCC has ruled that in every state, exclusive contracts that you might have with cable companies are unenforceable, and exclusive clauses in existing contracts will not be enforced. So any exclusive clauses you now have in your contracts are unenforceable, and you may not enter into any new ones. But this isn't the same as saying that you have to let multiple providers into your building when they ask: You remain free to evaluate each company (though you can't offer exclusive access to only one).

Hosting Competing Cable Companies in Multiunit Buildings

Several cable companies might be competing for your tenants' business. It used to be that adding a cable provider meant letting that company run cable from the street all the way to each rental unit that signed up for the provider's service. The initial section of that cable run, a large cable called the riser, runs from the street to a ground-level utility closet and up to the utility closets on each floor. Adding this cable is not a big deal. But the second leg, called the "home run" portion, consists of wires that run from the riser through hallway ceilings on each floor and toward each individual apartment (the last 12 inches are called "home wires"). Adding a second set of home run wires is expensive and sometimes impossible.

However, you might be able offer the home run part of existing cable to a different cable provider when a tenant asks to switch providers. A federal appellate case covering Colorado, Kansas, New Mexico, Oklahoma, Utah, and Wyoming has held that when a cable company no longer services a customer in a multiunit building, the building owner has the right to ask the provider to share the home run portion of their cable with a competitor, unless the owner's contract with the cable company gives the company the right to maintain unused cable. (*Time Warner Entertainment Co., L.P. v. Everest*, 381 F.3d 1039 (2004).)

!) CAUTION

Don't confuse "forced access" with your rights as a landlord. Forced access refers to the technology that lets consumers choose from among several internet service providers (ISPs) when they subscribe to a cable modem-based broadband service. The argument around forced access is between cable providers and ISPs. Many state laws require cable companies to provide open access to ISPs.

If you have a contract with a cable provider and would like to invite competitors to service tenants who want alternate service, check the contract carefully for language covering maintenance of the cables the provider installed. Look for clauses that give the company the right to maintain and control cables regardless of whether they're currently in use. You might want to review the contract with your attorney. When you negotiate future contracts, keep these points in mind:

- Get rid of language that gives the provider the right to control or maintain inside wiring (including home run wiring) after the contract with you or any individual tenant expires.
- Be sure that you get control of unused home run wiring at the expiration of your contract or when a tenant decides to discontinue service. This will explicitly give you the right to offer it to a competitor. If the cable provider really wants your business, it might agree that unused home run wires will be deemed abandoned. Or, you might have to buy the wires from the provider.

TIP

Require telecom companies to label their cables when they bring them into your building. Under the National Electrical Code and FCC regulations, telecoms must remove, abandon, or sell their cables when their license with you is up. If they refuse to do so—or if they're bankrupt—you'll have to do it. To make sure you can identify the abandoned risers (the large cables that run from the street to utility closets) and don't mistakenly cut current risers, require companies to label them with permanent, weatherproof tags, and to give you an as-built diagram that will be amended if the company does any further work during the license term.

Satellite Dishes and Antennas

Tenants often buy or lease satellite dishes and attach them to roofs, windowsills, balconies, and railings. They run wires from the dishes under doors or through open windows to an individual TV, computer, or router. These devices receive wireless signals transmitting television, Internet, and radio service. Most landlords aren't fans of satellite dishes, citing their unsightly looks, damage to the structure caused by the installation, and the potential for liability should one fall and injure someone below.

Fortunately, the Federal Communications Commission (FCC) has provided considerable guidance on residential use of satellite dishes and antennas ("Over-the-Air Reception Devices Rule," 47 CFR § 1.4000, further explained in the FCC's Fact Sheet, "Over-the-Air Reception Devices Rule"). Basically, the FCC prohibits landlords from imposing restrictions that unreasonably impair your tenants' abilities to install, maintain, or use an antenna or dish that meets the FCC's criteria. For details on permissible restrictions, visit www.fcc.gov/consumers/guides/installing-consumer-owned-antennas-and-satellite-dishes, or call the FCC at 888-225-5322.

Landlord's Liability for Tenant Injuries From Dangerous Conditions

As a landlord, you are responsible for keeping your rental property reasonably safe for tenants and guests. Otherwise, you might be liable for the harm that results from your neglect. Injured tenants can seek financial compensation for medical bills, lost earnings, pain, physical disability, disfigurement, and emotional distress. Tenants can also hold you responsible for property damage that results from faulty or unsafe conditions. Don't underestimate the consequences of a judgment against you: In extreme cases, a single personal injury verdict could result in business and even (in some situations) personal bankruptcy.

If a tenant is injured on your property, contact your insurance company the minute you hear about it—your policy probably requires it. Your agent will tell you what steps to take next, such as writing down the details of the accident and preserving evidence. The majority of claims against landlords are settled without a lawsuit, usually though negotiations handled by your insurance company.

This chapter provides an overview of your liability for tenant injuries. Most important, it offers suggestions on how to avoid injuries and liability in the first place.

 RELATED TOPIC
Related topics covered in this book include:

- Lease and rental agreement provisions covering landlords' and tenants' responsibilities for repairs, damage to premises, and liability-related issues, such as disclosure of hidden defects: Chapter 2
- How to minimize your liability for your property manager's mistakes or illegal acts: Chapter 6
- How to comply with state and local housing laws: Chapter 9
- Maintenance and how to avoid potentially dangerous situations on your rental property: Chapter 9

- Your liability for environmental health hazards: Chapter 11
- Your liability for crime on the premises, including injuries or losses to tenants by strangers or other tenants, and liability for drug dealing on rental property: Chapter 12
- Your liability for nonphysical injuries caused by intentional discrimination (Chapter 5), invasion of privacy (Chapter 13), and retaliatory conduct against the tenant (Chapter 16), and
- How to choose a lawyer and pay for legal services: Chapter 18.

Scenarios Where Landlords Have Been Held Liable for Injuries

Here are just a few examples where a landlord's negligence has resulted in a monetary award:

- Tenant falls down a staircase due to a defective handrail.
- Tenant trips over a hole in the carpet on a common stairway not properly maintained by the landlord.
- Tenant injured and property damaged by fire resulting from an obviously defective heater or wiring.
- Tenant gets sick from pesticide sprayed in common areas and on exterior walls without notice.
- Tenant's child is scalded by water from a water heater with a broken thermostat.
- Tenant slips and falls on a puddle of oil-slicked rainwater in the garage.
- Tenant's guest slips on ultraslick floor wax applied by the landlord's cleaning service.
- Tenant receives electrical burns when attempting to insert a stove's damaged plug into a wall outlet.
- Tenant slips and falls on wet grass cuttings left on a common walkway.

How to Prevent Injuries

Preventing an injury is a lot better than arguing about whose fault it was. In the following sections, we suggest ways to protect yourself from lawsuits and hefty insurance settlements—and make your tenants' lives safer and happier at the same time.

How to eliminate some risks—such as mopping up a spilled bucket of water—is obvious. But not every problem has a straightforward solution.

Don't hesitate to ask for advice from people who are experienced in identifying and dealing with risks. One excellent resource is your insurance company's safety inspector; your insurance agent can tell you whom to contact. Another good approach is to ask your tenants to notify you as soon as possible about all safety risks, no matter how small.

1. Maintain the Property

Our first piece of advice might sound obvious, but is often overlooked.

Create a regular inspection schedule, and stick to it. Look for structural problems, environmental health hazards, and any other conditions that could contribute to an injury. For example, you can head off many trip-and-fall accidents simply by providing good lighting in hallways, parking garages, and other common areas. Keep records on the dates and details of your property inspections and any follow-up repairs done.

If you're routinely at the rental property, keep an eye out for any dangerous conditions while you go about your day-to-day business. Document any problems you encounter and fix them promptly.

You can also ask your tenants, manager, and employees to help you spot problems.

Whenever you become aware of a repair problem with a potential for injury, put it on the top of your to-do list. If a condition poses a high risk of injury or damage, call in a specialist. For example, if large cracks are suddenly appearing in a concrete walkway, call in a structural engineer—not your general handyperson.

2. Comply With Building Codes

Local and state health, safety, and building codes often establish specific mandates for properties. For example, electrical codes specify how large a load you can place on individual circuits; building codes tell you how sturdy your deck piers must be. Once you establish basic compliance with these rules, you can't just forget about them: Stay on top of changes to the codes by reviewing them at least once a year.

3. Warn of Dangers You Can't Fix

You have a duty to warn tenants and others about naturally occurring dangers (such as loose soil) and man-made dangers (like low doorways or steep stairs) that might not be obvious to tenants or their guests, but which you know about (or should have discovered through proper maintenance procedures). Disclose hidden defects such as these in your lease or rental agreement (see Clause 22 of the agreements in Chapter 2), or include a description of the hazards in a move-in letter (Chapter 7). By informing tenants in writing of the hidden defect, no one will be able to successfully claim you didn't provide warning.

Whenever feasible and appropriate, post a visual warning of some sort near the hazard. Visual warnings include red flags, construction cones, yellow caution tape, or a skull-and-crossbones symbol. Document your visual warning by taking a picture and saving it in your files.

4. Solicit and Respond Quickly to Tenants' Safety Complaints

As explained in "Responding to Tenant Complaints" in Chapter 9, tell tenants that you are always receptive to concerns regarding building safety and repairs.

When you receive a complaint, consider the potential risk posed by the condition as well as what it will take to fix it, and respond appropriately. For example, a sticky front door lock that still works might merit having the locksmith come the next day; a completely broken lock poses a more serious safety concern and warrants a call to the 24-hour locksmith.

Back up your policy of soliciting and promptly responding to tenants' concerns with a good record-keeping system. Doing so will help you if you are challenged later. For example, suppose a tenant notifies you of a loose step. As soon as possible, you should post warning tape and signs, ask tenants to use another entrance, and arrange to have it repaired soon. Having a record of the measures you took to remedy the issue, as well as notes about or copies of your response to the tenant, will show that you did all that was reasonably necessary. If tenants disregard your warnings and use the stairs anyway, you'll be able to show that you acted prudently and should not be responsible for injuries that tenants suffered as a result.

5. Install and Maintain Basic Safety Features

Many state and city laws require certain safety features, such as smoke and carbon monoxide detectors. Even when you live in an area without many safety laws, consider taking reasonable safety precautions: If a tenant is injured by something that could have been prevented by a simple act on your part you could still be held liable.

Smoke detectors, carbon monoxide detectors, fire extinguishers, good interior lighting, and ample outside lighting are just a few examples of basic (and inexpensive) safety measures.

Candidly appraise the crime situation around your property, too. If there's a reasonable measure you can take to discourage crime, do it. For example, motion sensor lights, neighborhood watch signs, and video doorbells are all simple precautions that can have a big impact. Chapter 12 discusses liability for criminal acts on the property.

6. Don't Allow Dangerous Pets

In some situations, you could be liable for the injuries caused by a tenant's pet, be it a common household companion or an exotic animal.

An injured person would have to show that you:

1. actually knew (or, under the circumstances, must have known) of the animal's dangerous propensities, and
2. could have prevented the injury (by demanding its removal and evicting, if necessary).

Fear of liability is not a reason to impose a blanket no-pets rule; cases against landlords for injuries inflicted by tenants' pets are actually very rare.

But just as you keep an eye on other dangerous conditions on the property, be aware of the potential for injury from pets. A demonstrably dangerous pet is legally a nuisance, and you have the right to require that the tenant get rid of the animal or face eviction. In Chapter 9, see "Don't Allow Nuisances."

 CAUTION

Don't let tenants keep wild animals.
Legally, keeping wild animals is generally considered an "ultrahazardous activity." As soon as you are aware that a wild animal is being housed on the property, the law presumes that you fully appreciate—and accept liability for—the danger posed by the animal. So, if your tenant keeps a monkey and you know (or must have known) about it, a court will assume that you understood the danger, and might hold you liable if the animal causes injury when you failed to take steps to prevent it.

7. Remove Dangers to Children

If children are drawn onto your property due to an irresistibly interesting (to children) but dangerous feature (known in legal jargon as an "attractive nuisance"), you must exercise special care.

Unlocked sheds, old play equipment, abandoned outbuildings, and unattended construction materials are all examples of the many things that can be attractive nuisances. Most laws don't provide clear legal guidelines about what's considered an attractive nuisance. Rather, if you have seen kids playing in an area they're not supposed to be in, or if you think you might have been curious about a certain feature as a child, it's safe to say you have an attractive nuisance on your hands.

If the danger can be cleaned up or removed (like a pile of junk or an abandoned refrigerator), do so. If not, place physical barriers that will keep children away. Warning signs aren't enough—young children can't read, and many children ignore warnings.

Even if you don't create a dangerous situation yourself, but knowingly allow a tenant to do so, you might be liable for a child's injury. For example, a rickety tree house that your tenant builds in the backyard or a flimsy play structure that parents buy for their own children might attract other neighborhood children. If one of them falls from the tree or structure and is injured, you could be liable because you allowed the attractive nuisance on your property.

EXAMPLE: An apartment building owner took great pride in the fishpond in the courtyard. The yard was accessible to the general public, and neighborhood children frequently came to watch the fish. When one child fell in and nearly drowned, the child's parents sued the landlord. The landlord was found liable for the child's accident on the grounds of negligence—the landlord knew that unattended children were visiting the fishpond, and should have anticipated that a child could fall into the pond. The landlord should have gotten rid of the pond or fenced it off so that small children couldn't enter.

Although people might come to different conclusions when asked whether a certain situation is an attractive nuisance, the phrase isn't completely undefined. Some laws regulate specific activities and conditions that legislators have concluded are attractive and dangerous to children. For example, laws commonly require removing doors from unused refrigerators and fencing off or removing abandoned cars or piles of junk.

Inform tenants of your concerns regarding anything that might be attractive and dangerous to children. For example, if the tenant of your single-family home has placed a trampoline on the property, insist that the tenant erect a sturdy fence around it so that neighborhood kids don't wander in and use it without supervision. If it can't be fenced, insist that it be removed.

8. Take Special Precautions With Swimming Pools

Swimming pools can get landlords in deep trouble: Children love them, and they're extremely dangerous. Many places have laws that require swimming pools to be surrounded by fences that meet strict construction and height requirements.

If a drowning occurs at a pool that violates fencing or other construction and safety laws, it's likely that the landlord will be held liable for the death. Even if you are not subject to pool fence laws, you can still be held liable if a tragedy occurs, because common sense should have told you to fence off the pool.

If your property includes a pool, complying with all applicable safety laws is only the first step in preventing injury and avoiding liability. Post signs that remind adults to supervise children and state that you do not provide a lifeguard.

Using Exculpatory Clauses to Shield Yourself From Liability

Landlords used to be able to protect themselves from most lawsuits brought by tenants by using a lease clause that absolved the landlord of responsibility for injuries suffered by a tenant, even those caused by the landlord's negligence. Known as "exculpatory clauses," these blanket provisions are now rarely enforced by courts.

However, you might want to include a narrowly worded "exculpatory clause" in your lease when you delegate appropriate repair and maintenance duties to a tenant (see Chapter 9 for tips on delegation of repairs). In this situation, you might want to make it clear that tenants are not to look to you if they are injured in the course of their duties. An exculpatory clause, however, will not shield you from liability if your tenant injures a third party.

EXAMPLE: Sadie and Hal live in one half of their duplex and rent out the other. They offer Fred, their tenant, a rent reduction if he agrees to take on the landscaping. As part of the bargain, Fred agrees to absolve Sadie and Hal of any liability if a hazard in the landscaping causes him an injury. Because this agreement is the result of good-faith negotiations on both sides, each party receives a benefit from the deal, and the delegated duties could safely and reasonably be performed by their tenant, the agreement (and the liability waiver) would likely be upheld if either side challenged it later in court.

When Fred trips on a sprinkler and hurts his ankle, he is bound by the exculpatory clause and cannot sue Sadie and Hal for his injury. But when Mac, a delivery person, slips on wet grass cuttings that Fred carelessly leaves on the walkway, Fred, Sadie, and Hal find themselves at the other end of Mac's personal injury claim.

You can't use an exculpatory clause to shield yourself from all liability; if you're negligent, you're almost certainly going to be held responsible for any tenant injuries that result, no matter what your lease says.

9. Supervise Contractors and Other Workers

If construction work is done on your property, insist that the contractor in charge of the work and any workers (including your own) secure the site and remove or lock up dangerous tools or equipment when they leave.

Remember, a pile of sand or a stack of sheet rock might look like work to an adult, but fun to a child. You might consider sending your tenants written notice of the intended project, suggesting that they take care during the construction period.

Liability and Other Property Insurance

A well-designed insurance program can protect your rental property from losses caused by many types of perils, including damage caused by fire, storms, burglary, and vandalism. A comprehensive liability policy will also include liability insurance, covering injuries or losses suffered by others as the result of defective conditions on the property. Equally important, liability insurance covers the cost of settling personal injury claims, including lawyers' bills for defending personal injury lawsuits. The terms of your mortgage or loan probably require you to purchase property and liability insurance.

Buy Commercial General Liability Coverage

Commercial general liability coverage is the broadest type of liability coverage that you can purchase. Liability policies cover you against lawsuit settlements and judgments up to the amount of the policy limit, including both what you pay the injured person and their lawyers' bills. They provide coverage for a host of common perils, such as a tenant falling and getting injured on a defective staircase. Liability policies usually state a dollar limit per occurrence and an aggregate dollar limit for the policy year. For example, your policy might cover up to $300,000 per occurrence for personal injury and up to a total of $1 million in any one policy year.

Depending on the value of your property and the value of the assets you are seeking to protect, buying more coverage in the form of an "umbrella policy" is a very good idea, especially in large metropolitan areas, where personal injury damage awards can be very high. Umbrella policies are not expensive, because they are rarely called upon—so the additional premium is a relatively cheap way to obtain peace of mind.

Buy a policy that covers not only physical injury but also libel, slander, discrimination, unlawful and retaliatory eviction, and invasion of privacy suffered by tenants and guests. This kind of coverage can be very important in discrimination claims. See Chapter 5.

Buy Non-Owned Auto Liability Insurance

Non-owned auto insurance protects you from liability for any accidents and injuries your agents and employees cause while using their own vehicle to perform tasks for you. You should have liability insurance not only on your own vehicles but also on your manager's personal car or truck, if it will be used for business purposes.

What Liability Insurance Doesn't Cover

Punitive damages are extra monetary awards, above the amount needed to compensate an injured person. They are intended to punish willful or malicious behavior.

Terrorism Insurance

The huge losses of September 11, 2001 produced a predictable response from insurance companies: They began writing liability and property policies that specifically excluded coverage for losses due to acts of terrorism. Congress reacted by passing the Terrorism Risk Insurance Act (15 U.S.C. §§ 6701 and following; expires December 31, 2027) to help ensure that property owners have access to adequate, affordable terrorism insurance. The law requires insurance companies to offer coverage for losses due to acts of terrorism, and to void any clauses in existing policies that exclude coverage. If you want coverage under an existing policy, you are entitled to buy it. For more information, see the U.S. Department of the Treasury's website at www.treasury.gov, and type Terrorism Risk Insurance Program into the search box on the home page.

As you might expect, insurers would like to be able to exclude punitive damages from coverage, but the industry has never adopted a standard exclusion clause. (Insurance policies are typically made up of canned, template clauses that virtually every insurance company uses.) If a policy doesn't specifically state whether punitive damages are covered (and most don't), it will be up to the courts of the state where the policyholder lives to decide whether standard policy language covers punitive awards.

Courts in some states have ruled that punitive damages are not covered by standard comprehensive liability policies, while others have reached the opposite conclusion. Your insurance agent should be able to tell you how the courts in your state have ruled.

It's clear, however, that intentional harm or violations of criminal statutes are *not* covered. But it is often a matter of debate as to whether a particular act was intended. While illegal discrimination, physical assaults, harassment, or retaliation (by you or your manager) are often treated by insurers as intentional acts not covered by the policy, most liability insurers will at least pay for the defense of such lawsuits.

CAUTION

Understand exclusions and restrictions. Make sure you know what your policy covers and what's excluded. Does the policy exclude damage from a leaking sprinkler system? From a boiler explosion? From an earthquake? If so, and if these are risks you face, find out whether they can be covered by paying an extra premium. Check out pet restrictions. Find out whether your insurance policy includes restrictions as to species, breeds of dog, or weight and number of pets allowed.

Choosing Property Insurance

When you buy property coverage, consider the following four questions:

1. What Business Property Is Insured?

Be sure your insurance covers all the property you want protected. In addition to your basic property insurance, which insures the entire building, you might need additional policies to cover:

- additions under construction
- outdoor fixtures, such as pole lights
- appliances, such as washing machines and dryers
- items used to maintain the building, such as gardening equipment and tools
- boilers and heavy equipment, or
- personal business property such as computers used in managing your rental business.

TIP

Tell tenants that your insurance does not cover loss or damage (caused by theft or fire) to their personal property. Tenants need to buy their own renters' insurance to cover their personal property. This does not mean, however, that you cannot be sued by tenants (or their insurance company) if your negligence causes a loss. Your commercial general liability policy should cover you in this event.

2. What Perils Are Insured Against?

Your policy will describe the dangers, or "perils," that it covers. Fire damage is covered by even the most basic policies, but damage from mud slides, windstorms, and the weight of snow might be excluded. Earthquake insurance and flood insurance are typically separate. (They are often expensive and have a very high deductible, but are worth considering if your building is susceptible to earthquake or flood damage.) Whatever policy you decide on, read it carefully before you pay for it—not just when you've suffered a loss.

Check out "loss of rents" insurance, which covers you when something such as fire or another calamity causes tenants to have to move. This coverage will kick in even if you can move the tenant to another, vacant unit.

CAUTION

Your insurance might not cover losses due to COVID-19. As of mid-2021, the law surrounding the question of whether landlords can collect from their insurers for losses caused by the pandemic remains unsettled. Ask your insurance broker about coverage you could buy to insure against losses you might incur as a result of the continuing pandemic.

3. How Much Insurance Should You Buy?

Obviously, the greater the amount of coverage, the higher the premiums. You don't want to waste money on insurance, but you do want to carry enough so that your business can survive a lawsuit or natural disaster. Check with your lender, who might require minimum coverage amounts.

At the least, buy enough insurance on the building to rebuild it. There's no need to insure the total value of your real property (land and structures), because land doesn't burn.

If you're not sure how much it would cost you to rebuild, order an appraisal. (Get a rebuilding quote, not a quote on the sales value of the structure.) Because the cost of rebuilding tends to increase over time, it's wise to get a new appraisal every few years. Your insurance agent should be able to help you.

4. Should You Buy Coverage for Replacement Cost?

Basic fire insurance contracts cover the actual cash value of the structure, not its full replacement value. But policies are available with replacement cost coverage. This is the coverage you want.

Plain "cost of replacement" coverage, however, won't be adequate if you need to bring an older building up to code after a fire or other damage. Legal requirements adopted since the building was constructed will probably require a stronger, safer, more fire-resistant building when you rebuild. Upgrades like this can cost far more than simply replacing the old building. Anticipate this possibility by purchasing a policy that will not only replace the building but also pay for all legally required upgrades. This coverage is called "Ordinance of Law Coverage," and it is almost never included in standard policies—you must ask for it.

Working With an Insurance Agent

Finding and working with the right insurance agent is almost as important as securing the right insurance policy. Ideally, your relationship with your insurance agent will be for the long haul: Your insurance needs to grow and adapt to your business needs over time.

Find a knowledgeable agent. The best agents take the time to understand and analyze your business operations with the goal of creating a customized program. Working with an agent who covers other landlords is especially advantageous, because that person is already a fair way along the learning curve when it comes to helping you select affordable and appropriate policies.

Talk to other landlords or people in the real estate industry about their experiences with agents and insurance companies. The most reliable recommendations will come from locals who've been through (and had claims processed as a result of) natural disasters—they will know who comes through and who doesn't.

Steer clear of an agent who whips out a package policy and claims it will solve your problems. While there are some excellent packages available, neither you nor your insurance agent will know for sure until the agent asks you a lot of questions and thoroughly understands your business. If the agent is unable or unwilling to tailor your coverage to your particular business, find someone else.

Be frank with your agent. Reveal all areas of unusual risk. If you fail to disclose all the facts, you might not get the coverage you need. Or, in some circumstances, the insurance company might later take the position that you misrepresented the nature of your operation and, for that reason, deny you coverage.

Insist on a highly rated carrier. Insurance companies are rated according to their financial condition and size. The most recognized rater is the A.M. Best Company, which assigns letter ratings according to financial stability (A++ is the highest) and Roman numeral ratings reflecting the size of a company's surplus (XV is the best). Given that 80% of American companies receive an A rating or higher, you don't want to choose a company rated less than that. As to surplus, you will be on solid ground to require an "X." For details, visit www.ambest.com and search for the guide, *Understanding Best's Credit Ratings* (January 2, 2019).

RELATED TOPIC

If you have a manager or other employees, you might need workers' compensation insurance. See Chapter 6.

CAUTION

Consider insuring the cost of rubble removal and engineering surveys. If your building suffers catastrophic damage, you're going to be left with mess that needs to be completely demolished and disposed of before you can build again. In addition to a demolition crew, you might have to hire an engineer to oversee the whole process. Standard policies don't cover these potentially astronomical costs. For example, if your pile of debris contains asbestos or lead paint, you'll likely have to follow—and pay the high price of—special disposal procedures. You can buy an endorsement for a reasonable sum that will protect you.

Saving Money on Insurance

Few landlords can really afford to adequately insure themselves against every possible risk. The condition and location of your property are two factors you don't have much control over, but they will largely dictate your insurance needs—and costs. You can lessen your financial burden by taking the following steps to evaluate what type and what amount of insurance is essential.

Set Priorities

As a baseline, you'll need to get enough property and liability coverage to protect yourself from common claims. Your agent will be able to advise you on what types of coverage are typical for landlords in your area.

Beyond the basics, you'll need to do a cost-benefit analysis for insuring against serious or unique risks. Ask these questions: What types of property losses would threaten the viability of my business? What kinds of liability lawsuits might wipe me out? By answering these questions, you can work with your agent to tailor your coverage to protect against these potentially disastrous losses.

Select High Deductibles

The difference between the cost of a policy with a $250 deductible (the amount of money you must pay out of pocket before insurance coverage kicks in) and one with a $500, $1,000, or even higher deductible is significant—particularly if you add up the premium savings for five or ten years. Consider using money saved with a higher deductible to buy other types of insurance you really need. For example, the amount you save by having a higher deductible might pay for "loss of rents" coverage.

Take Preventive Measures to Avoid Losses

Good safety and security measures, such as regular property inspections, building upgrades (such as a fire-resistant roof or an interior sprinkler system), or requiring that tenants purchase renters' insurance might eliminate the need for some types of insurance or lead to lower insurance rates. (When tenants have renters' policies, accidents that they cause will be covered by their policies; without them, your policy might end up footing the bill. When the chances of a claim go down, rates should decrease, too.) Ask your insurance agent what you can do to get a better rate.

Comparison Shop

No two companies charge exactly the same rates; you might be able to save a significant amount by shopping around. Check to make sure that you're comparing pricing for policies that have nearly identical coverage—sometimes it helps to create a spreadsheet listing deductible amounts, coverage amounts, and the type of coverage for each quote. Beware of discount insurance or exceptionally low quotes—it's true that you get what you pay for when purchasing insurance. Make sure you know what you're buying, and review your coverage and rates periodically.

RESOURCE
For more information on choosing business insurance, see the Insurance Information Institute's website at www.iii.org.

Your Liability for Tenant Injuries

If a tenant is injured on your property, are you liable? It depends on the situation. You might be liable for injuries resulting from your:

- negligence or unreasonably careless conduct
- violation of a health or safety law
- failure to make certain repairs
- failure to keep the premises habitable, or
- reckless or intentional acts.

And, in rare instances, you might be liable under a state or local law for certain kinds of injuries.

An injured tenant is free to use a combination of these legal arguments in an attempt to hold you liable.

Negligence

Most personal injury cases brought by tenants allege that the landlord acted negligently—in a way that wasn't reasonable under the circumstances—and that the negligence caused the injury.

The success or failure of a negligence claim depends on the unique facts of the case. For example, when your tenant trips on a step she says she couldn't see and is injured, your liability hinges on the conditions of the fall. If she didn't see the step because the stairwell was unlit, you could be liable if a court finds you were negligent in not installing lights. However, if she fell in a well-lit lobby on a highly visible and intact step, it's less likely that a court would find you negligent.

Both courts and insurance adjusters consider the following six questions when evaluating a tenant's negligence claim.

Question 1: Did you control the area where the tenant was hurt or the thing that hurt the tenant?

In most cases, you will be held responsible for an injury if you were legally obligated to maintain and repair the injury-causing factor. For example, if the disrepair of a common-area stairway causes a tenant to fall, you will likely be held liable. Similarly, if a malfunction in the building's utility systems causes injury (like a broken thermostat that sends boiling water into a tenant's sink), you will likely be held responsible. On the other hand, if a tenant is hurt by his own falling bookcase, you won't be held responsible, because you had no control over how the bookcase was built, set up, or maintained.

Question 2: Was an accident foreseeable?

For a tenant to hold you liable, the tenant must demonstrate that an accident was foreseeable. For example, common sense tells anyone that loose handrails or stairs are likely to lead to accidents, but it would be unusual for injuries to result from peeling wallpaper or a thumbtack that's fallen from a bulletin board. If a freak accident happens, chances are you will not be held liable.

Question 3: How difficult or expensive would it have been for you to reduce the risk of injury?

The chances that you will be held responsible for an accident are greater if a reasonably priced preventive measure could have averted it—for example, if something as simple as a warning sign, a bright light, or caution tape could have prevented people from tripping over an uneven step leading to a patio, you should have put it in place.

That being said, if there is a great risk of very serious injury, you will be expected to spend more money to avert it. For example, a high-rise deck with rotten support beams must be repaired or removed, regardless of the cost, because there is a great risk of collapse and dreadful injuries to anyone on the deck. If you knew about the condition of the deck and failed to repair it, you would surely be held liable if an accident did occur.

Question 4: Was a serious injury likely to result from the problem?

If a major injury was likely to arise from a dangerous situation—for example, the pool ladder was broken, making it likely a tenant would fall as he climbed out—you are expected to take the situation seriously and fix it fast.

If your answer to these first four questions is YES, it means that you had a legal duty to address the dangerous condition on your property. In legal terms, this responsibility is called a "duty of due care."

Before going on to the remaining two questions used to establish negligence, consider the following examples.

> **EXAMPLE 1:** Mark broke his leg when he tripped on a loose step on the stairway from the lobby to the first floor. Because the step had been loose for several months, chances are his landlord's insurance company would settle a claim like this. Mark's position is strong because:
> - Landlords are legally responsible for (in control of) the condition of the common stairways.
> - It was highly foreseeable to any reasonable person that someone would slip on a loose step.
> - Securing the step would have been simple and inexpensive.
> - The probable result of leaving the stair loose—falling and injuring oneself on the stairs—is a serious matter.

> **EXAMPLE 2:** Lee slipped on a marble that had been dropped on the public sidewalk outside his apartment by another tenant's child a few minutes earlier. Lee twisted his ankle and lost two weeks' work. Lee will have a tough time establishing that his landlord had a duty to protect him from this injury because:
> - Landlords have little control over the public sidewalk.
> - The likelihood of injury from something a tenant drops is fairly low.

> - The burden on a landlord to eliminate all possible problems at all times by constantly inspecting or sweeping the sidewalk is unreasonable.
> - Finally, the seriousness of any likely injury resulting from not checking constantly is open to debate.

> **EXAMPLE 3:** James suffered a concussion when he hit his head on a dull-colored overhead beam in the apartment garage. When the injury occurred, he was standing on a stool, loading items onto the roof rack of his SUV. Did his landlord have a duty to take precautions in this situation? Probably not, but it's not cut-and-dried:
> - Landlords exercise control over the garage and have a responsibility to reasonably protect tenants from harm there.
> - The likelihood of injury from a beam is fairly slim, because most people don't stand on stools in the garage, and those who do have the opportunity to see the beam and avoid it.
> - As to eliminating the condition that led to the injury, it's highly unlikely anyone would expect a landlord to rebuild the garage. But it's possible that a judge might think it reasonable to paint the beams a bright color and post warning signs, especially if lots of people put trucks and other large vehicles in the garage.
> - Injury from low beams is likely to be to the head, which is a serious matter.
>
> In short, this situation is too close to call, but an insurance adjuster or a jury might decide that James was partially at fault (for not watching out for the beams) and reduce any award accordingly.

If, based on these first four questions, you had a legal duty to deal with a condition on the premises that posed a danger to tenants, keep going. There are two more questions to consider.

Question 5: Did you fail to take reasonable steps to prevent an accident?

The law doesn't expect you to take Herculean measures to shield tenants from a condition that poses some risk. You are required to take only reasonable precautions. For example, if a stair was in a dangerous condition, was your failure to fix it unreasonable under the circumstances? Let's take the broken step that Mark (Example 1, above) tripped over. Obviously, leaving it broken for months is unreasonably careless—that is, negligent—under the circumstances.

But what if the step had torn loose only an hour earlier, when another tenant dragged a heavy footlocker up the staircase? Mark's landlord would probably concede that he had a duty to maintain the stairways, but would argue that the manager's daily sweeping and inspection of the stairs that same morning met that burden. In the absence of being notified of the problem, the landlord would probably claim that his inspection routine met his duty of keeping the stairs safe. If a jury agreed, Mark would not be able to establish that the landlord acted unreasonably under the circumstances.

Question 6: Did your failure to take reasonable steps to keep tenants safe cause an injury?

This question establishes the crucial link between your negligence and a tenant's injury. A tenant has to prove that an injury was the result of your carelessness, and not some other reason. Sometimes this is self-evident: One minute a tenant is fine, and the next minute has slipped on a freshly washed floor and broken an arm. But it's not always so simple. For example, in the case of the loose stair, the landlord might be able to show that the tenant barely lost his balance because of the loose stair and that he had really injured his ankle during a touch football game he'd just played.

Landlord Liability for Injuries to Guests and Trespassers

If you have acted negligently and a tenant's guest or even a trespasser is injured, will you be liable? The answer varies by state. In a few states, you're liable no matter why the injured person was on your property. As a general rule, however, you have a reduced duty of care when it comes to nontenants, especially trespassers. For example, a tenant who is injured by a fall from an unfenced porch will have a fairly strong negligence suit, while a trespasser—even one who innocently visits the wrong address—who falls off the same porch might have a weaker case against you.

Here's a final example, applying all six questions to a tenant's injury.

EXAMPLE: Scotty's apartment complex had a pool bordered by a concrete deck. On his way to the pool, Scotty slipped and fell, breaking his arm. The concrete where he fell was slick because the landlord had spilled cleaning solution on it. Consider these questions:

- Did the landlord control the pool area and the cleaning solution? Absolutely. The pool was part of a common area, and the landlord had done the cleaning.
- Was an accident like Scotty's foreseeable? Certainly. It's likely that a barefoot person heading for the pool would slip on slick cement.
- Could the landlord have eliminated the dangerous condition without much effort or money? Of course. All that was necessary was to hose the deck down.
- How serious was the probable injury? Falling on cement presents a high likelihood of broken bones, a serious injury.

The answers to these four questions establish that the landlord owed Scotty a duty of care.

- Had his landlord also breached this duty? A jury would probably answer yes—and conclude that leaving spilled cleaning solution on the deck was an unreasonable thing to do.
- Did the spilled cleaning solution cause Scotty's fall? This one is easy, because several people saw the accident and others could describe Scotty's robust fitness before the fall. Because Scotty himself hadn't been careless, he has a good case.

Violation of a Health or Safety Law

Many state and local laws require smoke detectors, sprinklers, inside-release security bars on windows, childproof fences around swimming pools, and so on. To put real teeth in these important laws, legislators (and sometimes the courts) have decided that a landlord who doesn't take reasonable steps to comply with certain health or safety statutes is automatically negligent: If that negligence results in an injury, the landlord is liable. A tenant doesn't need to prove that an accident was foreseeable or potentially serious; nor does a tenant have to show that complying with the law would have been relatively inexpensive. The legal term for this rule is "negligence per se."

> **EXAMPLE:** A local housing code specifies that all kitchens must have grounded power plugs. There are no grounded plugs in the kitchen of one of your rental units. As a result, a tenant is injured when using an appliance in an otherwise safe manner. In many states, your violation of the law would mean you were legally negligent. If a tenant can show that the ungrounded plug caused injury, you will be held liable.

Your violation of a health or safety law might also indirectly cause an injury. For example, if you let the furnace deteriorate in violation of local law, and a tenant is injured trying to repair it, you will probably be liable, unless the tenant's repair efforts are extremely careless.

> **EXAMPLE:** The state housing code requires landlords to provide hot water. In the middle of the winter, a tenant's hot water heater has been broken for a week, despite his repeated complaints to the landlord. Finally, to give a sick child a hot bath, a tenant carries pots of steaming water from the stove to the bathtub. Doing this, he spills the hot water and burns himself seriously.
>
> The tenant sues the landlord for failure to provide hot water as required by state law. Many people would probably conclude that the tenant's response to the lack of hot water was a foreseeable one, and, knowing this, the landlord's insurance company would probably be willing to offer a fair settlement.

Failure to Make Certain Repairs

For perfectly sensible reasons, many landlords do not want tenants to undertake even fairly simple tasks like painting, plastering, or unclogging a drain. Many leases and rental agreements (including the ones in this book) prohibit tenants from making any repairs or alterations without the landlord's consent, or limit what a tenant can do. If you do allow tenants to perform maintenance tasks, do so with a clear, written agreement, as explained in Chapter 9.

But in exchange for reserving the right to make all these repairs yourself, the law imposes responsibility. If, after being told about a problem, you don't maintain or repair something you're responsible for—for example, an electrical switch—and the tenant is injured as a result, you could be held liable. The legal reason is that you breached the contract (the lease) by not making the repairs. (You might also be negligent; remember, a tenant can present multiple reasons why you should be held liable.)

> **EXAMPLE:** The sash cords in the living room window in Shanna's apartment break, making it necessary to support the entire weight of the window while raising or lowering it and securing it with a block of wood. Because Shanna's lease includes a clause forbidding repairs of any nature, she reports the problem to Len, the owner. Despite his promises to repair the window, Len never gets around to it. One hot summer evening Shanna attempts to raise the heavy window, but her hands slip and the window crashes down on her arm, breaking it. Shanna threatens to sue Len, claiming that he negligently delayed the repair of the window, and further that the lease clause forbidding any repairs by the tenant contractually obligated Len to attend to the problem in a reasonably prompt manner. Mindful of the strength of Shanna's arguments, and fearful that a jury would side with Shanna and give her a large award, Len's insurance company settles the case for several thousand dollars.

Failure to Keep the Premises Habitable

One of your basic responsibilities is to keep the rental property in a "habitable" condition. If you don't, you might be liable for injuries caused by the substandard conditions. For example, a tenant who is bitten by a rat in a vermin-infested building might argue that your failure to maintain a rat-free building breached your duty to keep the place habitable, which in turn led to the injury. The tenant must show that you knew of the defect and had a reasonable amount of time to fix it.

This theory applies only when the defect is so serious that the rental unit is unfit for human habitation. For example, a large, jagged broken picture window would make the premises unfit for habitation in North Dakota in winter, but a torn screen door in Southern California obviously would not.

EXAMPLE: Jose notified his landlord about the mice that he had seen several times in his kitchen. Despite Jose's repeated complaints, the landlord did nothing to eliminate the problem. When Jose reached into his cupboard for a box of cereal, he was bitten by a mouse. Jose sued his landlord for the medical treatment he required, including extremely painful rabies shots. He alleged that the landlord's failure to eradicate the rodent problem constituted a breach of the implied warranty of habitability, and that this breach was responsible for his injury. The jury agreed and gave Jose a large monetary award.

(Jose might also claim that the landlord was negligent because he didn't get rid of the mice or violated a state or local statute concerning rodent control.)

Reckless or Intentional Acts

"Recklessness" usually means extreme carelessness regarding an obvious defect or problem. A landlord who is aware of a long-existing and obviously dangerous defect but doesn't correct it might be guilty of recklessness, not just ordinary carelessness.

If you or an employee acted recklessly, a tenant's monetary recovery could be significant. This is because a jury has the power to award not only actual damages (which include medical bills, loss of earnings, and pain and suffering) but also "punitive" damages for outrageous or extremely careless behavior. Punitive damages, which are not covered by insurance, are awarded to punish recklessness and to send a message to others who might behave similarly. The size of the punitive award is likewise up to the jury and is often reduced later by a judge or appellate court.

EXAMPLE: The handrail along the stairs in Jack's apartment had been hanging loose for several months. Two or three times, Jack taped the supports to the wall, which did no good. One night when Hilda, one of Jack's tenants, reached for the railing, the entire thing came off in her hand, causing her to fall and break her hip.

Hilda sued Jack for her injuries. In her lawsuit, she pointed to the ridiculously ineffective measures that Jack had taken to deal with a clearly dangerous situation, and charged that he had acted with reckless disregard for the safety of his tenants. (Hilda also argued that Jack was negligent because of his unreasonable behavior and because he had violated a local ordinance regarding maintenance of handrails.) The jury agreed with Hilda and awarded her punitive damages in addition to actual damages.

Intentional Harm

If you or your manager struck and injured a tenant during an argument, you would be liable for imposing intentional harm on the tenant. Less obvious, but no less serious, are emotional or psychological injuries that are inflicted intentionally. Common situations that result in claims of intentional infliction of emotional distress include:

- **Sexual harassment.** Repeated, disturbing attentions of a sexual nature which leave a tenant fearful, humiliated, and upset can form the basis for a claim of intentional harm; or one extremely serious incident.

EXAMPLE: Rita's landlord Mike took every opportunity to make suggestive comments about her looks and social life. When she asked him to stop, he replied that he was "just looking out for her" and stepped up his unwanted attentions. Rita finally had enough, broke the lease, and moved out. When Mike sued her for unpaid rent, she turned around and sued him for the emotional distress caused by his harassment. He was slapped with a multithousand-dollar judgment, including punitive damages.

Limiting Your Personal Liability With a Corporation or Limited Liability Company

You might want to organize your rental property business as a corporation or a limited liability company (LLC). Legally, it's an entity that's separate from the individuals who own or operate it. Even when you're the only owner and the only employee, you and your corporation or LLC are separate legal entities, so long as you treat your business as a separate entity and follow certain organizational and operational procedures. This means that the corporation or LLC, not your personal bank account, is liable for any awards or settlements won by injured tenants. (If you are successfully sued for discrimination committed by one of your employees or managers, however, your status as a corporation or an LLC might not protect you from being personally liable.)

If you don't form an LLC or a corporation, you can protect personal assets to a large degree by purchasing adequate insurance.

RESOURCE

LLC or Corporation? **by Anthony Mancuso (Nolo), helps you decide, based on your circumstances and the laws of your state, whether it's better to form a corporation or an LLC.**

- *Form Your Own Limited Liability Company*, by Anthony Mancuso (Nolo), explains LLCs and shows you how to form one in your state.
- Nolo.com offers an online way to form an LLC that's valid in your state.
- *Incorporate Your Business*, by Anthony Mancuso (Nolo), explains corporations and how to form one in your state.

- **Assault.** Threatening or menacing someone without actually touching them is an assault, which can be enormously frightening and lead to psychological damage.
- **Repeated invasions of privacy.** Deliberately invading a tenant's privacy—by unauthorized entries, for example—might cause extreme worry and distress.

The Law Makes You Liable

In rare circumstances, you might be responsible for a tenant's injury even though you did your best to create and maintain a safe environment and were not negligent. This legal principle is called "strict liability," or liability without fault.

In most states, strict liability is imposed only when a hidden defect poses an unreasonably dangerous risk of harm to a group of persons who can't detect or avoid it. For example, Massachusetts landlords are subject to strict liability if a child under six years old is poisoned by lead-based paint in the rental. (Mass. Gen. Laws ch. 111 § 199 (2021).)

When a Tenant Was at Fault, Too

When the tenant is partially to blame for an injury, your liability for the tenant's losses will be reduced accordingly.

Tenant Carelessness

A tenant's own carelessness might affect how much the tenant can collect, even when a landlord has also been negligent. In some states, a tenant's own behavior might bar any recovery at all—it depends on the law:

- In a number of states, tenants can collect according to the percent of blame attributed to the landlord, no matter how careless the tenant was, too. For example, a tenant can collect 75% of the damages if the landlord was 75% to blame.

- Some states allow tenants to recover a portion of their damages only if their carelessness was equal to or lower than the landlord's. In these states, for example, if the tenant and landlord were equally blameworthy, the tenant could collect half of the damages. A tenant who was 51% at fault couldn't collect at all.

- In other states, tenants can recover a portion of their damages only if their carelessness was less than the landlord's. If the tenant and landlord were equally at fault, the tenant gets nothing; a tenant who was 25% at fault gets 75% of the damages.

- A few states don't allow tenants to collect a dime if they were at all careless, even just 1% at fault.

Tenant Risk-Taking

If a tenant deliberately chose to act in a way that caused or worsened the injury, another doctrine that will reduce the tenant's damages might apply. Called "assumption of risk," it refers to a tenant who knows the danger of a certain action and takes the chance anyway.

EXAMPLE: In a hurry to get to work, a tenant takes a shortcut to the garage by using a walkway that he knows has uneven, broken pavement. The tenant disregards the sign posted by his landlord: "Use Front Walkway Only." If the tenant trips and hurts his knee, he'll have a hard time pinning blame on his landlord, because he deliberately chose a known, dangerous route to the garage.

In some states, tenants who are injured as a result of putting themselves in harm's way cannot recover anything, even if a landlord's negligence contributed to the injury. In other states, a tenant's recovery is diminished according to the extent that the tenant appreciated the danger involved.

How Much Money an Injured Tenant Might Recover

A tenant who was injured on your property and has convinced an insurance adjuster or jury that you are responsible can ask for monetary compensation, called "compensatory damages." Compensatory damages can include:

Medical care and related expenses. This includes doctors' and physical therapists' bills, as well as the anticipated costs of future care.

Missed work time. A tenant who misses work to recover or receive medical treatment can sue for lost wages and income, as well as anticipated lost income due to continuing care.

Pain and other physical suffering. The type of injury the tenant has suffered and its expected duration affect the amount awarded for pain and suffering. Insurance adjusters require impartial corroboration of a tenant's level of discomfort, such as a doctor's prescription of strong pain medication. The longer a tenant's recovery period, the greater the pain and suffering.

Permanent physical disability or disfigurement. Long-lasting or permanent effects—such as scars, back or joint stiffness, or a significant reduction in mobility—increase the amount of damages.

Loss of family, social, career, and educational experiences or opportunities. A tenant who demonstrates that the injury prevented a promotion or better job can ask for compensation for the lost income.

Emotional damages resulting from any of the above. Emotional pain, including stress, embarrassment, depression, and strains on family relationships, may be compensated. Insurance adjusters require proof, such as evaluations from a therapist, physician, or counselor.

Punitive damages. Judges and juries award punitive damages when they decide that the landlord acted outrageously, either intentionally or recklessly. As a general rule, you won't be liable for punitive damages if you refrain from extreme neglect and intentional wrongs against tenants and others.

RESOURCE

For free information on legal issues regarding liability and insurance, see the articles and FAQs at Nolo.com.

How to Win Your Personal Injury Claim, by Joseph Matthews, explains personal injury cases and how to work out a fair settlement without going to court.

Everybody's Guide to Small Claims Court, by Cara O'Neill, provides detailed advice on small claims court, which, in most states, allows lawsuits where between $3,000 to $10,000 is at issue.

Represent Yourself in Court, by Paul Bergman and Sara Berman, will help you prepare and present your case should you end up in court.

Mediate, Don't Litigate: Strategies for Successful Mediation, by Peter Lovenheim and Lisa Guerin, gives detailed information on the mediation process. (eBook version only, available at Nolo.com.)

These Nolo books are available at bookstores and public libraries. You can also order or download them at Nolo.com or by calling 800-728-3555.

Landlord's Liability for Environmental Health Hazards

FORMS IN THIS CHAPTER

Chapter 11 includes samples of the following:

- *Protect Your Family From Lead in Your Home* pamphlet
- *Disclosure of Information on Lead-Based Paint and/or Lead-Based Paint Hazards* form

The purchase of this book includes free downloads of these documents. See Appendix B for the download link.

In 1863, an English judge could write that "Fraud apart, there is no law against letting [leasing] a tumble-down house." But in 21st century America, it's no longer legal to be a slumlord. If you don't make needed repairs and, as a result of defective conditions, a tenant is injured, you might be found liable.

In this chapter, we focus on another landlord responsibility: the duty to divulge and remedy environmental health hazards. You can be held liable for tenant health problems resulting from exposure to environmental hazards, based on many of the legal theories discussed in Chapter 10, such as negligence and negligence per se (negligence that is automatic when a statute is broken).

Read on for an overview of the legal and practical issues involving landlord liability for environmental health hazards, specifically asbestos, lead, radon, carbon monoxide, mold, and bed bugs.

 RELATED TOPIC
Related topics covered in this book include:
- How to make legally required disclosures of environmental hazards to tenants: Chapter 2
- Maintaining habitable property by complying with housing laws and avoiding safety problems: Chapter 9
- Your liability for tenant's injuries from defective housing conditions: Chapter 10.

Asbestos

Exposure to asbestos has long and definitively been linked to an increased risk of cancer.

Houses built before the mid-1970s often contain asbestos insulation around heating systems, in ceilings, and in other areas. Until 1981, asbestos was also widely used in many other building materials, such as vinyl flooring and tiles. Asbestos that begins to break down and enter the air—for example, when it's disturbed during maintenance or renovation work—can become a significant health problem. Asbestos fibers enter the lungs and lodge there, causing disease.

Until the mid-1990s, private owners of residential rental property had no legal obligation to test for the presence of asbestos. Landlords whose tenants developed an asbestos-related disease could successfully defend themselves if they could convince the judge or jury that they did not know of the presence of asbestos on the rental property.

Landlords' protection from liability for asbestos exposure all but evaporated in 1995, when the U.S. Occupational Safety and Health Administration (OSHA) issued a 200-page regulation setting strict workplace standards for the testing, maintenance, and disclosure of asbestos. Because your building will be a "workplace" for anyone who performs renovations or repairs, it will be subject to OSHA's rules if it contains (or might contain) asbestos. Once you comply with workplace regulations and learn of the presence of dangerous asbestos, you're on notice that it could affect your tenants, too.

OSHA Regulations for Landlords

OSHA regulations require rental property owners to install warning labels, train staff, and notify people who work in areas that might contain asbestos. In certain situations, owners must actually test for asbestos.

These regulations apply to large landlords who employ maintenance staff (or managers who do maintenance work) and small-scale landlords who have no employees, but who do hire outside contractors for repair and maintenance jobs. OSHA regulations apply to any building constructed before 1981, even if you don't plan to remodel or otherwise disturb the structure. Unless you rule out the presence of asbestos by having a licensed inspector test the property, it is *presumed* that asbestos is present, and the regulations apply.

OSHA protections vary according to how much asbestos you're disturbing:

- **Custodial work.** Employees and contractors whose work involves direct contact with asbestos or materials that are presumed to include it—for example, certain types of floors and ceilings—or who clean in areas near asbestos are subject to OSHA regulations for "general industry."

  The cleaning service that washes asbestos tiles in the lobby of a pre-1981 building and the handyman who installs smoke alarms in acoustic-tile ceilings made with asbestos both fall within the custodial work category.

  Custodial workers must receive two hours of instruction (including appropriate cleaning techniques) and use special procedures under the supervision of a trained superior.

  The general industry standard does not require testing for asbestos. Of course, if you know that high levels of asbestos are present, even custodial tasks must be performed with appropriate levels of protection, such as special masks and clothing

- **Renovation or repairs.** Stricter procedures are triggered by removal, repair, or renovation of asbestos or asbestos-containing materials. At this level of activity, you must test for the presence of asbestos and assess exposure by monitoring the air. Workers must get 16 hours of training per year, oversight by a specially trained person, and respiratory protection in some situations. In addition, employers must conduct medical surveillance of certain employees and maintain specified records for many years. So, for example, your decision to replace that ugly, stained acoustic-tile ceiling would require, first, that the material be tested for asbestos, followed by worker training and protection measures appropriate for the level of exposure. If you hire a contractor to do the job, the contractor will take care of these requirements, and you'll see the work reflected in the contractor's invoice.

CAUTION

There is no escaping OSHA's asbestos regulations under the theory that what you don't know about can't cause legal problems. You might think that you can escape OSHA's asbestos regulations by personally doing minor repair and maintenance and hiring independent contractors to do the major jobs. This might work for a while, until you hire a law-abiding contractor who acknowledges the independent duty to protect employees and performs asbestos testing. The results of the tests will, of course, become known to you, because you'll see the report and pay the bill.

Key Aspects of OSHA Asbestos Regulations

Which buildings are affected. The regulations apply to pre-1981 structures and newer structures found to contain asbestos.

Where asbestos is likely to be found. The regulations cover two classes of materials: those that definitely contain asbestos and those that the law *presumes* to contain asbestos. The second class is extremely broad, encompassing, among other things, any surfacing material that is "sprayed, troweled on, or otherwise applied." This means virtually every dwelling built before 1981 must be assumed to contain asbestos.

What work is covered. The regulations apply to custodial work and to renovation and repair work.

How to Limit Your Liability for Asbestos

If asbestos is present on your property and you knew about it, and can be shown to be the cause of a tenant's illness, you could be found liable. Some states consider the presence of airborne asbestos to be a breach of the implied warranty of habitability, which (depending on the specifics of a state's law) would give the tenant the right to break the lease and move out without notice, pay less rent, withhold the entire rent, or sue to force you to bring the dwelling up to a habitable level. A more serious consequence is a personal injury lawsuit directed at you, as the person responsible for the tenant's exposure and resulting injury.

Limiting your liability for asbestos-related injuries (to tenants and workers alike) begins with understanding a fundamental point: Unless you perform detailed testing to rule out the presence of asbestos, every pre-1981 structure must be treated as if it does contain asbestos. Take these steps:

- Get a copy of the OSHA regulations or the guidelines that are based on them. (See "Asbestos resources," below.)
- Realize that almost any repair or maintenance work—no matter how small—might involve asbestos materials. Test for the presence of asbestos in advance for the benefit of workers and tenants.
- If you learn of the presence of asbestos, tell your tenants. For example, if there is asbestos in the walls that hasn't begun to break down, point out that it's not likely to pose a danger and that you will monitor the situation.
- If possible, don't disturb asbestos. Unless the asbestos has begun to break down and enter the air, it is usually best to leave it alone and monitor it. This means that it simply might not make economic sense to do certain types of remodeling jobs. Seek an expert's opinion before taking action.
- If you must disturb asbestos, warn all tenants before the work starts, giving them an opportunity to avoid the area. Use written notices and place cones and caution tape around the area. You might even consider temporarily relocating your tenants. The costs of a few days or weeks in alternate housing pales compared to the expense, monetary and human, of responding to an exposed tenant's personal injury lawsuit.
- If you learn that asbestos is airborne (or is about to be), seek an expert's advice on how to remedy the situation. When removal is necessary, hire trained asbestos removal specialists, and make sure the debris is legally disposed of in approved hazardous waste disposal sites.

- Make sure tenants don't disturb any spaces containing asbestos. You might need to prohibit tenants from hanging planters from the ceiling or otherwise making holes in the ceiling. See Clause 12 of the form lease and rental agreement in Chapter 2, which prohibits tenant repairs.
- Require tenants to report any deterioration to you—for example, in sprayed-on acoustical plaster ceilings.
- Monitor asbestos as part of regular safety and maintenance procedures, discussed in Chapter 9.

RESOURCE

Asbestos resources. For information on asbestos rules, inspections, and control, contact the nearest office of OSHA, go to OSHA.gov, or call 800-321-OSHA. At www.osha.gov/asbestos, you'll find the regulations, as well as informative materials that interpret and apply the regulations.

For additional information on asbestos, including negative health effects, see the EPA website at www.epa.gov/asbestos, especially the "Building Owners and Managers" section.

Lead

Exposure to lead-based paint or lead water pipes can result in serious health problems, particularly in children. Brain damage, attention disorders, and hyperactivity have all been associated with lead poisoning.

Landlords who are found responsible for lead poisoning (even if they did not know of the presence of the lead) might face liability for a child's lifelong disability. Jury awards and settlements for lead poisoning are typically enormous, because they cover education and lifelong remedial treatment, and include an award for the estimated loss of earning capacity caused by the injury.

Buildings constructed before 1978 are likely to contain some source of lead, be it lead-based paint, lead pipes, or lead-based solder used on copper pipes. (In 1978, the federal government required the reduction of lead in house paint; lead pipes are generally found only in homes built before 1930. Lead-based solder in home plumbing systems was banned in 1988.) Pre-1950 housing that has been allowed to deteriorate is by far the greatest source of lead-based paint poisoning.

A federal law, the Residential Lead-Based Paint Hazard Reduction Act (commonly referred to as Title X (Ten)) is aimed at evaluating the risk of poisoning in each housing situation and taking appropriate steps to reduce the hazard. Most states have also enacted similar laws.

Is Your Property Exempt From Federal Lead Regulations?

Certain rental properties are exempt from the federal lead paint disclosure and renovation regulations, including:

- Housing for which a construction permit was obtained, or on which construction was started, after January 1, 1978. Older buildings that have been completely renovated since 1978 are not exempt, even if every painted surface was removed or replaced.
- Housing certified as lead-free by a state-accredited lead inspector. Lead-free means the absence of any lead paint, even paint that has been completely painted over and encapsulated.
- Lofts, efficiencies, studios, and other "zero-bedroom" units, including dormitory housing and rentals in sorority and fraternity houses. (University-owned apartments and married student housing are not exempt.)
- Short-term vacation rentals of 100 days or less.
- A single room rented in a residential home.

- Housing designed for persons with disabilities (as explained in HUD's Fair Housing Accessibility Guidelines, 24 CFR, Ch. I, Subchapter A, App. II), unless any child under six years old resides there or is expected to reside there.
- Retirement communities (housing designed for seniors, where one or more tenant is at least 62 years old), unless children under the age of six are present or expected to live there.

State lead laws can apply even if the property is exempt under federal rules.

Must You Have an Inspection?

Inspections are not required by federal or state law, but local law might require them. Landlords must inspect for lead-based paint hazards, defined as peeling paint or deteriorated subsurfaces such as exposed, painted wood beneath a newer coat of paint.

Even though it's not required, you might want to have an inspection done so that you can tell tenants that the property is lead-free and exempt from federal regulations. (See list of exemptions, above.) Also, if you take out a loan or buy insurance, your bank or insurance company might require a lead inspection.

Professional lead inspectors don't always inspect every unit in large, multifamily properties. Instead, they inspect a sample of the units and apply their conclusions to the property as a whole. Giving your tenants the results and conclusions of a building-wide evaluation satisfies the law, even if a particular unit was not tested. If, however, you have specific information regarding a unit that is inconsistent with the building-wide evaluation, you must disclose it to the tenant.

Disclose Lead Paint Hazards to Tenants

To comply with Title X, you must give tenants —before they sign or renew a lease or rental agreement—any information you have on lead paint hazards on the property, including individual rental units, common areas and garages, tool sheds, other outbuildings, signs, fences, and play areas. If you have had your property tested (testing must be done by state-certified inspectors; see "Lead hazard resources," below), you must show a copy of the report, or a summary written by the inspector, to tenants.

With certain exceptions (listed below), every lease and rental agreement must include a disclosure page, even if you have not tested. You can use the EPA's form, "Disclosure of Information on Lead-Based Paint and/or Lead-Based Paint Hazards." See Appendix B for a download link for English and Spanish versions of the form.

As you'll see, the disclosure form has a place for the tenant to initial, indicating that the tenant has reviewed the form. Note the time you received it, too, if you and the tenant are also signing the lease or rental agreement on the same day. If you're ever challenged, you'll be able to prove that the tenant received the disclosure form before signing the rental documents.

Make a copy of the signed form and give it to the tenant; keep the original for at least three years. If a federal or state agency questions whether you're complying with the lead disclosure law (such agencies periodically do random checking), you'll have a cabinet full of signed forms as evidence. And if a tenant claims to have developed symptoms of lead poisoning from living in your rental property, you'll have proof that you disclosed what you knew.

Give Tenants the EPA Booklet on Lead

You must give all tenants the lead hazard information booklet *Protect Your Family From Lead in Your Home,* written by the Environmental Protection Agency (EPA), see "Lead hazard resources," below. A copy of the pamphlet (in English and Spanish) that you can print out and attach to the lease can be downloaded from the Nolo website. (See Appendix B.) The cover of this pamphlet is shown below. The pamphlet is also available in Vietnamese, Russian, Arabic, and Somali. For copies, see www.epa.gov/lead. The graphics in the original pamphlet must be included.

Some state agencies that want to give consumers additional information about lead have their own pamphlets, but you may not use them in place of the EPA version unless the EPA has approved them. To find out if your state has published an approved alternative, go to your state's department or agency in charge of consumer affairs, and use the search function to look for lead disclosure forms.

Enforcement and Penalties

The federal Housing and Urban Development Department (HUD) and the EPA enforce renters' rights to know about the presence of lead-based paint by using "testers," as they do when looking for illegal discrimination. Posing as applicants, testers look to see whether landlords comply with federal law.

Disclosure of Information on Lead-Based Paint and/or Lead-Based Paint Hazards

Lead Warning Statement

Housing built before 1978 may contain lead-based paint. Lead from paint, paint chips, and dust can pose health hazards if not managed properly. Lead exposure is especially harmful to young children and pregnant women. Before renting pre-1978 housing, lessors must disclose the presence of known lead-based paint and/or lead-based paint hazards in the dwelling. Lessees must also receive a federally-approved pamphlet on lead poisoning prevention.

Lessor's Disclosure

(a) Presence of lead-based paint and/or lead-based paint hazards (check (i) or (ii) below):

    (i) _____ Known lead-based paint and/or lead-based paint hazards are present in the housing (explain).

    _____

    _____

    (ii) __✓__ Lessor has no knowledge of lead-based paint and/or lead-based paint hazards in the housing.

(b) Records and reports available to the lessor (check (i) or (ii) below):

    (i) _____ Lessor has provided the lessee with all available records and reports pertaining to lead-based paint and/or lead-based paint hazards in the housing (list documents below).

    _____

    _____

    (ii) _____ Lessor has no reports or records pertaining to lead-based paint and/or lead-based paint hazards in the housing.

Lessee's Acknowledgment (initial)

(c) _____ Lessee has received copies of all information listed above.

(d) __✓__ Lessee has received the pamphlet *Protect Your Family from Lead in Your Home.*

Agent's Acknowledgment (initial)

(e) _____ Agent has informed the lessor of the lessor's obligations under 42 U.S.C. 4852d and is aware of his/her responsibility to ensure compliance.

Certification of Accuracy

The following parties have reviewed the information above and certify, to the best of their knowledge, that the information they have provided is true and accurate.

Bill Perry	*May 9, 20xx*		
Lessor	Date	Lessor	Date
Paula Hart	*Mary 9, 20xx*		
Lessee	Date	Lessee	Date
Agent	Date	Agent	Date

Landlords who fail to distribute the required booklet or who don't give tenants the disclosure statement when the lease or rental agreement is signed can receive one or more of the following penalties:

- a notice of noncompliance—the mildest reprimand—typically, you'll be given a certain number of days in which to notify all tenants.
- a civil penalty, which can include fines of tens of thousands of dollars per violation for willful and continuing noncompliance
- an order to pay an injured tenant up to three times the tenant's actual damages, or
- a criminal fine of many thousands of dollars per violation. (42 U.S.C. § 4852d, 15 U.S.C. § 2615(b).)

Government testers are also on the lookout for property owners who falsely claim that they don't know of lead-based paint hazards on their property. Here's how it often comes up: A tenant who becomes ill with lead poisoning complains to HUD that you said that you knew of no lead-based paint hazards on your premises. If HUD decides to investigate whether you knew about the hazard and failed to tell tenants, its investigators get access to your records. They comb leasing, maintenance, and repair files—virtually all your business records. If HUD finds evidence that you knew or had reason to know of lead paint hazards, such as a contract from a painting firm that includes costs for lead paint removal or a loan document indicating the presence of lead paint, you will be hard-pressed to explain why you checked the box on the disclosure form stating that you had no reports or records regarding the presence of lead-based paint.

RESOURCE

The Residential Lead-Based Paint Hazard Reduction Act, or Title X (Ten) can be found at 42 U.S.C. § 4852d. The Environmental Protection Agency (EPA) has written regulations that explain how landlords should implement lead hazard reduction. (24 Code of Federal Regulations Part 35, and 40 Code of Federal Regulations Part 745.) For more information, see "Lead hazard resources," below.

Give Tenants Information When You Renovate

If you renovate occupied rental units or common areas in buildings built before 1978, you must give current tenants lead hazard information before the work begins. (40 CFR §§ 745.80–88.) Contractors must be certified and follow specific work practices to prevent lead dust contamination.

The obligation to distribute lead information rests with the renovator. If you hire an outside contractor to perform renovation work, the contractor is the renovator. But if you or your property manager, superintendent, or other employees perform the renovation work, you are the renovator and are obliged to give out the information.

The type of information depends on where the renovation is taking place. If an occupied rental unit is being worked on, you must give the tenant a copy of the EPA pamphlet *The Lead-Safe Certified Guide to Renovate Right* (*Renovate Right*). If common areas will be affected, you must distribute the pamphlet to every unit. For advice on distributing this pamphlet to tenants, see the EPA's *Small Entity Compliance Guide to Renovate Right* on the EPA website.

 TIP

Put it in the contract. When you hire a contractor to perform renovations, make sure your renovation contract or work agreement requires the contractor to provide all required lead hazard information to tenants as provided under federal law and regulations and any applicable state law.

What Qualifies as a Renovation?

According to EPA regulations, a renovation is any change to an occupied rental unit or common area that disturbs painted surfaces. Here are some examples:

- removing or modifying a painted door, wall, baseboard, or ceiling
- scraping or sanding paint, or
- removing a large structure like a wall, partition, or window.

Repainting a rental unit in preparation for a new tenant doesn't qualify as a renovation unless it's accompanied by sanding, scraping, or other surface preparation activities that might generate paint dust.

Not every renovation triggers the federal law. There are four big exceptions:

Renovations in lead-free properties. If the rental unit or building in which the renovation takes place has been certified as containing no lead paint, you're not required to give out information.

Emergencies. If a sudden or unexpected event, such as a fire or flood, requires you to make emergency repairs to a rental unit or common area, there's no need to distribute lead hazard information to tenants before work begins.

Minor repairs or maintenance. Minor work that affects less than six square feet of a room's painted surface, or 20 square feet or less on the exterior, is also exempt. This includes routine electrical and plumbing work, so long as no more than two square feet of the wall, ceiling, or other painted surface gets disturbed by the work.

Common area renovations in buildings with three or fewer units.

Give the EPA Pamphlet When Renovating Occupied Units

Before starting a renovation to an occupied rental unit, the renovator must give the EPA pamphlet, *The Lead-Safe Certified Guide to Renovate Right*, to at least one adult occupant of the unit. This requirement applies to all rental properties, including single-family homes and duplexes, unless the property has been certified lead-free by an inspector.

The renovator (whether you or an outside contractor) may mail or hand-deliver the pamphlet to the tenant. If renovators mail it, they must get a "certificate of mailing" from the post office dated at least seven days before the renovation work begins. Make sure the tenant will receive the pamphlet no more than 60 days before work begins—in other words, delivering the pamphlet more than 60 days in advance won't do. The renovator should use the confirmation form at the end of the *Renovate Right* pamphlet to record the delivery method and outcomes.

Give Out Notice When Renovating Common Areas

If your building has four or more units, the renovator—you or your contractor—must notify tenants of all affected units about the renovation and tell them how to get a free copy of the EPA pamphlet *Renovate Right.* (40 CFR § 745.84(b)(2).)

In most cases, common area renovations affect all units, meaning that you must notify all tenants about the renovation. But if you're renovating a "limited use common area" in a large (at least 50 units) apartment building, such as the 16th-floor hallway, you need only notify those units serviced by, or in proximity to, the area.

To comply, the renovator must deliver a notice to every affected unit describing the nature and location of the renovation work, and the dates you expect to begin and finish work. (See a sample "Common Area Renovations Notice," below.) If you can't provide specific dates, you may use terms like "on or about," "early June," or "late July." The notices *must be delivered within 60 days before work begins.* You can slip the notices under apartment doors or give them to any adult occupant of the rental unit. You may not mail them. After the notices are delivered, keep a copy in your file, with a note describing the date and manner in which you delivered the notices.

Penalties

Failing to give tenants the required information about renovation lead hazards can result in harsh penalties. Renovators who knowingly violate the regulations can get hit with a penalty of up to $37,500 per day for each violation, and can even face prison time. (40 CFR § 745.87; 15 U.S.C. § 2615.)

State and Local Laws on Lead

Most states also prohibit the use of lead-based paint in residences and require careful handling of existing lead paint and lead-based building materials. If your state has its own lead hazard reduction law, you'll see that, like its federal cousin, it does not directly require you to test for lead. Does this mean that you need not conduct inspections? Not necessarily. In New York City, for example, landlords must perform annual visual inspections of rental units where a child under age six resides. Landlords must inspect for "lead-based paint hazards," defined as peeling paint or deteriorated subsurfaces. New York City landlords must also visually inspect any apartments that become vacant on or after November 12, 1999 before the unit may be reoccupied.

Common Area Renovations Notice

> March 1, 20xx
>
> Dear Tenant,
>
> Please be advised that we will begin renovating the hallways on or about March 15, 20xx. Specifically, we will be removing and replacing the baseboards, wallpaper, and trim in the 2nd, 3rd, and 4th floor corridors; and sanding and repainting the ceilings. We expect the work to be completed in early May 20xx.
>
> You can obtain a free copy of the Environmental Protection Agency's pamphlet, *The Lead-Safe Certified Guide to Renovate Right*, from Paul Hogan, the building manager. Paul can be reached at 212-555-1212.
>
> We will make every attempt to minimize inconvenience to tenants during the renovation process. If you have questions about the proposed renovation work, feel free to contact Mr. Hogan or me.
>
> Very truly yours,
>
> *Lawrence Levy*
>
> Lawrence Levy, Manager

Check your state's consumer protection agency to find out if state laws contain additional requirements regarding lead.

Leaded Miniblinds

Some vinyl miniblinds imported from China, Taiwan, Indonesia, or Mexico that were manufactured before 1996 are likely to contain lead. Over time, the plastic in these blinds deteriorates from sun and heat, which results in lead dust on the surface of the blinds. There's no easy way to definitively identify the leaded blinds, so if you have old vinyl miniblinds from this time period, consider replacing them to avoid any risk. Even if they're not the leaded type, updating your blinds will give your rental a nice refresh.

Why You Should Test for Lead

If you suspect that there might be lead lurking in your rental property's paint or water, you face a difficult choice. If you have the property tested and learn that lead is present, you'll know that your property has a hidden and dangerous defect. As a result, you must tell tenants and deal with the possibility that they will refuse to live on your property. If they stay, there's the potential of an expensive lead problem or risk of liability for injuries. But if you don't test, you'll live with the nagging fear that your property might be making your tenants sick and damaging the development of their children.

It might be tempting to adopt an ostrich-like approach and hope that all will work out. The odds might be with you for a while, but eventually this will prove to be a short-sighted solution. Here are five reasons why:

- Lead hazard control is much less burdensome than going through a lawsuit, let alone living with the knowledge that a child's health has been damaged.
- Ignorance of the condition might not shield you from liability. At some point, a court is bound to rule that the danger of lead paint in older housing is so well-known that owners of older housing are presumed to know of the danger. If that happens to you, a jury

will have a difficult time believing that you were truly ignorant. Moreover, an injured tenant might be able to show the court that it was likely that you, in fact, knew of the lead problem and chose to ignore it.

- Recognizing that children are the ones most at risk for lead poisoning, you cannot simply refuse to rent to tenants with children—this is illegal discrimination in all states.
- If you include a clause in your lease or rental agreement attempting to shift responsibility for lead-based injuries from yourself to the tenant, you could effectively establish that you were aware of the lead problem. (Why else would you include it?) Many courts won't uphold this type of clause anyway.
- If you refinance or sell the property, the lender will probably require lead testing before approving a loan.

In sum, there is no effective way to hide a lead problem over the long run. Your best bet is to tackle it directly on your own terms, before you are forced to deal with it. The next section explains how to go about getting information on testing and reducing one of the most serious lead hazard risks: lead-based paint.

Your Insurance Policy Might Not Cover Lead-Paint Poisoning Lawsuits

If you are hit with a lead poisoning lawsuit, don't assume that your insurance company will be there to defend you or compensate the victim. Depending on the terms of your policy, your insurer might be able to deny coverage for lead exposure claims—even if the suit is without merit. If you know (or presume) that your property contains lead-based paint, review your liability coverage with your insurance broker.

Because lead liability lawsuits are so expensive, some insurance companies have simply stopped writing general liability insurance on older buildings. Others exclude coverage for lead-based paint liability claims. You can still get coverage, but it might be limited or come at a higher cost.

 **RESOURCE**

Lead hazard resources. The National Lead Information Center has information on the evaluation and control of lead-based paint and other hazards, disclosure forms, copies of the *Protect Your Family From Lead in Your Home* and *Renovate Right* pamphlets, and lists of EPA-certified lead paint professionals. Call 800-424-LEAD or go to www.epa.gov/lead. The EPA also provides pamphlets, documents, forms, and information on all lead paint hazards and federal laws and regulations on its website, and offers useful advice on topics such as finding a contractor licensed to test for and remove lead. (Check out its guide for "small entities," called *Small Entity Compliance Guide to Renovate Right.*) The EPA website (EPA.gov) also includes a map with links to state and local websites.

HUD, specifically its Office of Lead Hazard Control and Healthy Homes (see www.hud.gov/healthyhomes), has many useful resources, including guidelines for evaluating and controlling lead-based paint hazards in housing.

State housing departments have information on state laws and regulations. Start by calling your state consumer protection agency. For a list of state consumer protection agencies, go to www.usa.gov/state-consumer.

If you'd like to check your state and local health departments for information on lead poisoning prevention programs, go to the Centers for Disease Control and Protection website at www.cdc.gov/nceh/lead, and choose the "State & Local Programs" link.

Call In Expert Help to Clean Up Lead-Based Paint

Lead is relatively easy to detect—you can buy home-use kits that contain a swab that turns color when wiped on a lead-based surface.

Knowing how much lead is present, and how to best clean it up, however, are subjects for the experts. An environmental engineer will be able to tell you how much lead is present at floor level and above, which will alert you as to whether your property exceeds the amounts allowable by law.

In most states, you cannot legally perform lead abatement work without a special license from the state. To be on the safe side, hire only certified people.

Why not do it yourself? Because a DIY job, no matter how well-intentioned, might actually make the problem much worse. Widespread paint removal, or sanding and repainting, often releases tremendous amounts of lead dust, the deadliest vector for poisoning. You also need special equipment to do a safe cleanup. Regular household cleaners, even trisodium phosphate (TSP), do not do a very effective job of capturing lead, nor can a standard vacuum cleaner filter out microscopic lead particles.

Theoretically, some lead dust problems might be containable by frequent, lead-specific, and thorough cleaning, rather than repainting, and some cleaning companies specialize in lead dust cleaning. But painting over lead paint, if possible, is a better solution, even if it appears more costly than dust maintenance. It will certainly cost less than a lawsuit.

Radon

Radon is a naturally occurring radioactive gas that is associated with lung cancer. It can enter and contaminate a house built on soil and rock containing uranium deposits, or enter through water from private wells drilled in uranium-rich soil. Radon becomes a lethal health threat when it is trapped in tightly sealed or poorly ventilated homes, when it escapes from building materials that have incorporated uranium-filled rocks and soils (like certain types of composite tiles or bricks), or when it is released into the air from aerated household water that has passed through underground concentrations of uranium. Problems occur most frequently in areas where rocky soil is relatively rich in uranium and in climates where occupants keep their windows tightly shut.

The Environmental Protection Agency estimates that millions of American homes have unacceptably high levels of radon. Fortunately, measuring indoor radon levels is simple and inexpensive, and good ventilation will effectively disperse the gas in most situations. Mitigation measures range from the obvious (open the windows and provide cross-ventilation) to the more complex (sealing cracks in the foundation, or sucking radon out of the soil before it enters the foundation and venting it through a pipe into the air above the door). A typical household radon problem can usually be solved for $1,000 to $2,000.

If you own rental property in an area known to have radon problems but don't test, warn tenants, or take action, you could be sued for harm that tenants suffer as a result.

Whether to test for radon depends on the circumstances of each rental property; you are not legally required to test. Your city planning department or your insurance broker might know about local geology and radon dangers. Certainly, if you know radon levels are dangerously high in your area, you should test rental property. For the most professional results, hire an inspector certified by the EPA. Testing takes at least three days, and sometimes months. Do-it-yourself radon testing kits are also available. If you use one, make sure it says "Meets EPA Requirements." Kansas State University's National Radon Program Services (www.sosradon.org/purchase-kits) is a good source of discounted kits.

If testing indicates high radon levels, warn tenants and correct the problem. Start by giving them the EPA booklet *A Radon Guide for Tenants* (see "Radon resources," below).

RESOURCE

Radon resources. For information on the detection and removal of radon, contact the U.S. Environmental Protection Agency Radon Hotline Line at 800-767-7236, or visit www.epa.gov/radon. The EPA site links to state agencies that regulate radon, gives information on finding a qualified radon reduction provider, and includes a map of radon zones by state. You can also download a copy of the booklet *A Radon Guide for Tenants.*

Carbon Monoxide

Carbon monoxide (CO) is a colorless, odorless, lethal gas that can build up and kill within a matter of hours. Unlike any of the environmental hazards discussed so far, CO cannot be covered up or managed.

When CO is inhaled, it enters the bloodstream and replaces oxygen. Dizziness, nausea, confusion, and tiredness can result; high concentrations bring on unconsciousness, brain damage, and death. It is possible for someone to be poisoned from CO while sleeping, without waking up. Needless to say, a CO problem must be dealt with immediately.

Sources of Carbon Monoxide

Carbon monoxide is a byproduct of fuel combustion; electric appliances cannot produce it. Common home appliances, such as gas dryers, refrigerators, ranges, water heaters or space heaters; oil furnaces; fireplaces; charcoal grills; and wood stoves all produce CO. Cars and gas gardening equipment also produce CO. If appliances or fireplaces are not vented properly, CO can build up within a home and poison the occupants. In tightly sealed apartments, indoor accumulations are especially dangerous.

Preventing Carbon Monoxide Problems

If you have a regular maintenance program, you should be able to spot and fix the common malfunctions that cause CO buildup.

Take these steps to avoid CO problems in your rental:

- Check chimneys and appliance vents for blockages.
- In your rules and regulations, prohibit the indoor use of portable gas grills or charcoal grills.
- Warn tenants never to use a gas range, clothes dryer, or oven as a heat source.

- Prohibit nonelectric space heaters, or specify that they must be inspected annually.
- Check the pilot lights of gas appliances as part of your regular maintenance routine. They should show a clear blue flame; a yellow or orange flame might indicate a problem.

But even the most careful service program can't prevent unexpected problems like the blocking of a chimney by a bird's nest or the sudden failure of a machine part. Defend against these threats by installing CO detectors, explained below.

Carbon Monoxide Detectors

To ensure that residents are alerted immediately to the buildup of CO, install a monitoring device, or detector, which will emit a loud shriek when CO is present. Unlike smoke detectors, which are required in every state, CO detectors are not universally mandated. But that's changing as more and more legislators recognize the need for these safety devices.

Single-family dwellings, which are more likely to have fossil-fuel-burning appliances than multifamily properties, are targeted most frequently, with laws requiring CO detectors in new construction, at renovation, and upon sale or transfer. Over half the states also require detectors in rentals. The National Conference of State Legislatures maintains a list of state laws at NCSL.org (type "carbon monoxide detectors state statutes" into the search box on the home page).

Savvy landlords will skip the research and just install the detectors. Make sure the device is "UL approved." Battery-operated models work fine, but like smoke detectors, their batteries must be changed regularly (look for models with long-lasting lithium ion batteries). Models that are connected to the building's interior wiring or plugged in, with batteries as a back-up, are a better choice.

Responsibility for Carbon Monoxide Buildup

Most CO hazards are caused by a malfunctioning appliance or a clogged vent, flue, or chimney. It follows that the responsibility for preventing a CO buildup depends on who is responsible for the upkeep of the appliance.

Appliances. Appliances that are part of the rental, especially built-in units, are typically your responsibility, although the tenant is responsible for intentional or unreasonably careless damage. For example, if the pilot light on the gas stove that came with the rental is improperly calibrated and emits high amounts of CO, you must fix it. On the other hand, if your tenants bring in a portable oil space heater that malfunctions, that is their responsibility.

Vents. Vents, chimneys, and flues are part of the structure, and their maintenance is typically your job. In single-family houses, however, it is not unusual for landlords and tenants to agree to shift maintenance responsibility to the tenant. As always, write down any maintenance jobs that you have delegated so that it's clear. Chapter 9 discusses the pros and cons of delegating repairs to tenants.

RESOURCE

Carbon monoxide resources. The EPA offers useful instructional material, including downloadable pamphlets, at www.epa.gov/indoor-air-quality-iaq. Local natural gas utility companies often have consumer information brochures available to their customers.

Mold

Across the country, tenants have won multimillion-dollar cases against landlords for significant health problems—such as rashes, chronic fatigue, nausea, cognitive losses, hemorrhaging, and asthma—allegedly caused by exposure to "toxic mold" in their building.

Mold is among the most controversial of environmental hazards. The scientific and medical communities do not agree about which molds, and what situations, pose serious health risks to people in their homes. Nevertheless, courts have increasingly found landlords legally liable for tenant health problems associated with exposure to mold. It is crucial to identify and avoid problems with mold in your rental property before you find yourself in court.

Unsightly as it might be, not all mold is harmful to human health—for example, the mold that grows on shower tiles is not dangerous. It takes an expert to know whether other molds are harmful or just annoying. Your first response to discovering mold shouldn't be to call in the folks with the white suits and ventilators. Most of the time, standard cleaning procedures will remove mold. Better yet, focus on early detection and prevention of mold, as discussed below. This will help limit health problems of tenants as well as physical damage to structural components of your property.

Laws on Mold

No federal law sets permissible exposure limits or building tolerance standards for mold in rental properties, and only a few states have taken steps toward establishing permissible mold standards. This is bound to change as state legislators and federal regulators begin to study mold more closely.

A few cities have enacted ordinances related to mold. For example, San Francisco has added mold to its list of public health nuisances, which means tenants can sue landlords under private and public nuisance laws if they fail to clean up serious outbreaks. (San Francisco Health Code § 581.)

Your Liability for Tenant Exposure to Mold

Because there's little law on mold, you must look to your general responsibility to maintain and repair rental property for guidance. Your legal duty to provide and maintain habitable premises naturally extends to fixing leaking pipes, windows, and roofs—the causes of most mold. If you don't take care of leaks, and mold grows as a result, tenants might successfully sue you over the damage to their personal belongings. And, depending on the severity of the mold problem and your negligence in screening for or fixing it, a tenant could successfully sue you for medical bills and lost wages due to mold-caused health problems.

The picture changes when mold grows as the result of your tenant's behavior, such as keeping the apartment tightly shut, creating high humidity, and failing to keep it reasonably clean. You can't be expected to police your tenant's lifestyle (and in many states, privacy statutes prevent you from unannounced inspections, as explained in Chapter 13). When a tenant's own negligence is the sole cause of injury, you are not liable.

> ⓘ **CAUTION**
> **Using a lease clause stating that you won't be liable for injuries due to mold probably won't do you any good.** Courts are likely to see this ploy as against public policy, and won't enforce it.

Preventing Mold Problems

Your efforts should be directed squarely at preventing the conditions that lead to the growth of mold. This requires maintaining the structural integrity of your property (the roof, plumbing, and windows) and adopting a thorough and prompt system for detecting and handling problems.

Here's how to proceed:

1. **Watch for moisture.** Before new tenants move in, inspect the premises and look for moisture problems (use the Landlord-Tenant Checklist form in Chapter 7). Mold often grows on

water-soaked materials, such as wall paneling, paint, fabric, ceiling tiles, newspapers, or cardboard boxes. Throw in a little warmth and molds grow very quickly, sometimes spreading within 24 hours. Buildings in warm humid climates experience the most mold problems. But mold can grow wherever moisture is present; floods, leaking pipes, windows, or roofs are the leading causes. Poor ventilation makes the problem worse.

2. **Make sure every tenant understands the factors that contribute to the growth of mold.** Use your lease or house rules to educate tenants about sensible practices to reduce the chances of mold—or to fix problems should they arise. Give tenants specific advice, such as how to:
   - ventilate the rental unit
   - avoid creating areas of standing water— for example, by emptying saucers under houseplants, and
   - clean vulnerable areas, such as bathrooms, with cleaning solutions that discourage mold growth.

   The mold section of the EPA website includes lots of practical tips.

3. **Require tenants to immediately report signs of mold,** or conditions that might lead to mold, such as plumbing leaks and weatherproofing problems.

4. **Check for conditions, such as leaky pipes, that could cause mold.** Do this as part of your recommended maintenance inspections (discussed in Chapter 9).

5. **Make all necessary repairs and maintenance to clean up or reduce mold.** For example:
   - Consider installing exhaust fans in rooms with high humidity (bathrooms, kitchens, and service porches), especially if window ventilation is poor.
   - Provide dehumidifiers in chronically damp climates, or rental units with poor ventilation.
   - Reduce window condensation by using storm windows or double-glazed windows.
   - Quickly respond to tenant complaints and clean up mold as discussed below.

EXAMPLE: The shower tray in Jay's bathroom begins to leak, allowing water to penetrate walls, floors, and ceilings below. Sydney, Jay's landlord, has repeatedly stressed the need for ventilation and proper housekeeping, and has encouraged all his tenants, including Jay, to promptly report maintenance problems. Jay ignores Sydney's recommendations, and mold grows in the bathroom. Jay develops a bad rash that he claims is a direct result of his exposure to the bathroom mold. Jay will have a tough time holding Sydney legally responsible for his health problems, simply because he failed to take advantage of Sydney's proven readiness to address the problem, which would have avoided the harm.

Testing for Mold Toxicity

Most of the time it's not necessary to test mold that's discovered at your rental. You're better off directing your efforts to speedy cleanup. Knowing what kind of mold you have will not, in most cases, affect how you clean it up.

Properly testing for mold is costly. Over-the-counter test kits, which cost around $30 to $50, provide questionable results. A professional's basic investigation for a single-family home can cost much more. OSHA offers an online certification course (search for mold inspector certification on the OSHA website), as do a few states. Before hiring an inspector, find out if your state has set standards for certification (search for mold certification and your state's name).

This said, it will be necessary to call in the testers if you are sued. In that event, your insurance company will hire lawyers who will be in charge of arranging for experts.

How to Clean Up Mold

Most mold is harmless, *not a threat to health*, and easily dealt with. More often than not, a weak bleach solution (one cup of bleach per gallon of water) will remove mold from nonporous materials:

- Use gloves and avoid exposing eyes and lungs to airborne mold dust (if you disturb mold and cause it to enter the air, use masks). Allow for frequent work breaks in areas with plenty of fresh air. Test your cleaning method on a small patch and watch to see if workers develop adverse health reactions, such as nausea or headaches. If so, call in a construction professional who is familiar with working with hazardous substances.
- Clean and remove mold from all infested areas.
- Don't try removing mold from fabrics such as towels, linens, drapes, carpets, or clothing—just dispose of them.
- Contain the work space by using plastic sheeting and enclosing debris in plastic bags.

If the mold is extensive, consider hiring an experienced mold remediation company with excellent references, and any state-required licenses or certification. For more information, check out the sites noted in "Mold resources," below.

CAUTION

People with respiratory problems, fragile health, or compromised immune systems should not participate in clean-up activities. If your tenant raises health concerns and asks for clean-up assistance, provide it—it's a lot cheaper than responding to a lawsuit.

Insurance Coverage of Mold Problems

If structural aspects of your property have been ruined by mold and must be replaced (and especially if there's a lawsuit on the horizon brought by ill tenants), contact your insurance broker immediately. Your property insurance might cover the cost of the cleanup and repairs if the damage is from an unexpected and accidental event, such as a burst pipe, wind-driven rain, sewerage backup, or unanticipated roof leak.

Damage due to mold in a chronically damp basement will probably not be covered under your policy, because insurance will not cover the consequences of poor maintenance. If mold grows as a result of a flood, you might also be out of luck—flooding is excluded from most insurance coverage.

Your liability policy might also cover you if you are sued by ill tenants.

However, many carriers try to avoid coverage for mold-related claims by arguing that mold falls within the "pollution exclusion" (most policies do not cover you if you commit or allow pollution—for example, if you deliberately dump solvents on the property). Additionally, many insurers exempt damage due to mold in new or renewed property insurance policies. Read your policy (and ask your broker) to see whether mold-related claims are covered under your policies.

RESOURCE

Mold resources. For information on the detection, removal, and prevention of mold, see www.epa.gov/mold; be sure to check out "Mold Remediation in Schools and Commercial Buildings Guide" (which includes multifamily properties) and "A Brief Guide to Mold, Moisture, and Your Home." Publications written with the homeowner in mind are available from the California Department of Public Health at www.cdph.ca.gov (go to "Mold" in the "A to Z Index"). To check local mold-related rules, see your city's or county's website (find yours at www.statelocalgov.net).

Bed Bugs

They come out at night to gorge on human blood, but can last a year between meals. A single female will lay 500 eggs in her lifetime. You'll find them in sleazy digs with slobby tenants, as well as upscale apartments with fastidious residents. They're expert hitchhikers who can catch a ride on your suitcase, furniture, or clothing. No one really knows how to kill them. What are they? They're 21st-century bed bugs, and if they show up at your rental property, you'll probably conclude that mold, asbestos, or even lead-based paint are benign by comparison. Here's how to protect your tenants and your business from this potentially devastating pest.

How to Deal With an Infestation

The EPA's website contains extensive, up-to-date information about how landlords should deal with a bed bug infestation—visit www.epa.gov/bedbugs/what-landlords-need-know-about-bed-bugs. A key bit of advice is to be proactive: Encourage tenants to promptly report any suspected bed bug problems. The sooner you learn about a bed bug infestation, the better you'll be able to manage it. Follow our advice in Chapter 9 for setting up a system for tenants to report problems in their rental unit.

What Kills Bed Bugs?

Although bed bugs are hard to kill using today's approved materials, exterminators have three ways to go after bed bugs:

- Insecticidal dusts, such as finely ground glass or silica, will scrape off the insects' waxy exterior and dry them out.
- Contact insecticides (such as chlorfenapyr, available only to licensed pest control operators) kill the bugs when they come into contact with it. For more information, search "Chlorfenapyr" at EPA.gov.
- Insect growth regulators (IGR) interfere with the bugs' development and reproduction, and though quite effective, take a long time.

Pest control operators often use IGR in combination with other treatments. Most controllers recommend multiple treatments over a period of weeks, interspersed with near-fanatical vacuuming to capture dead and weakened bugs. Anecdotal reports claim that even with repeated applications of pesticides, it's not possible to fully eradicate heavy infestations. Honest exterminators will not certify that a building is bed bug free.

Proper Cleaning and Housekeeping: Can You Insist on It?

Running a rental business involves striking a delicate balance between insisting that tenants take proper care of your property, and respecting their privacy. You can require that rental units be kept in a sanitary condition, but you can't inspect your tenants' housekeeping efforts every week.

When it comes to effectively eliminating bed bugs, however, extreme housekeeping is needed. Hopefully, your tenants will be so grateful that you're taking steps to deal with the bugs that they will cooperate voluntarily. If necessary, however, you might need to perform the vacuuming yourself (or hire someone to do it). Don't balk over the expense—compared to a widespread infestation and the potential of an empty building, the cost of a cleaning service is minimal.

! **CAUTION**
Talk to a lawyer before deciding to evict a tenant who refuses to participate in your bed bug eradication program, or who reintroduces infested items. You might be within your rights, but you might also be courting a retaliatory eviction lawsuit, especially if the tenant was not the source of the infestation.

Who Pays for All This?

In keeping with your obligation to provide fit and habitable housing, you must pay to exterminate pests that tenants have not introduced. In many states, this duty is explicit. For example, in Florida, bed bugs are one of the many vermin that landlords are required to get rid of in order to maintain a fit and habitable rental. (Fla. Stat. § 83.51.) Arizona also makes landlords responsible for eradication. (Ariz. Rev. Stat. § 33-1319.) Most states do not have explicit laws, but fortunately, as explained below, your insurance might defray some of the costs.

Eradicating infestations caused by the tenant, however, can rightly be put on the tenant's tab. But determining who introduced the bed bugs is often very difficult. Even if you identify the unit where the infestation started (or when the rental is a single-family home), that doesn't mean the tenants caused the problem. If they're new tenants, expect them to argue that the former occupants are responsible.

Unless you discover that the new tenant came from a building that was also infested, you'll have a hard time pinning responsibility on your new resident.

Another potential loss is the cost of replacing belongings that can't be salvaged. In extreme cases, bed bugs infest every nook and cranny of a rental and its contents—books, clothes, furniture, appliances. One New York landlord reported getting a phone call from a tenant who discovered bed bugs and moved out with only the clothes on his back, leaving everything—*everything*—behind. This tenant sued the owner for the cost of replacing his belongings, claiming that the landlord's ineffective eradication methods left him no choice.

Should this claim get before a judge, your liability would probably depend on the judge's view of the reasonableness of your response and the tenant's reaction. The more you can show that you took immediate and effective steps to eliminate the problem, the better you would fare. As for the tenant's response, understand that the psychological effects of living with bugs that bite you while you sleep can be very strong.

Will Your Insurance Step Up?

If you're facing a bed bug problem, you might get at least some help from your insurance policy. Here's the scoop.

Eradication. Property insurance typically does not cover instances of vermin or insect infestation.

Tenants' damaged belongings, medical expenses, and moving and living expenses. Your commercial general liability policy will probably cover you here, up to the limits of the policy.

Loss of rents. If you must leave a rental vacant while you have it treated, and you have loss of rents/business interruption insurance, it might cover you for your loss of rental income during this period.

If your tenants have renters' insurance, it might help. If you can confidently trace the infestation to particular tenants' actions, you could present the bills to these tenants, suggesting that they refer the matter to their insurance company. The liability portion of their renters' policy should cover them.

Disclosure to Future Tenants

The last thing you want to tell prospective tenants is that you had a bed bug problem. Knowing that a bed bug can remain alive and dormant for over a year, and that eradication attempts are often not 100%, many prospects will never consider living in a unit that has experienced a bed bug problem, even when you've done everything possible to deal with the bugs.

Whether to disclose, however, might not be an option for you. Many state and local laws require landlords to disclose a property's bed bug history, as well as tenant and landlord duties when an infestation appears. For example, Maine requires landlords to disclose the property's history. (14 Me. Rev. Stat. § 6021-A.) Maine's law also requires tenants to promptly report problems, and to vacate the premises if necessary. Arizona prohibits landlords from knowingly renting an infested unit (Ariz. Rev. Stat. § 33-1319), and New York City requires landlords to inform tenants of the building's and the rental unit's bed bug history for the past year (N.Y.C. Admin. Code § 27-2018.1).

The majority of tenants, however, will not have the benefit of explicit disclosure laws. But that doesn't mean that you shouldn't be forthright.

First, if a prospect questions you directly about a bed bug problem, especially if it's clear that this issue is of critical importance, you must answer truthfully or risk the consequences:

- **Breaking the lease.** A tenant who learns after the fact that you didn't answer truthfully will have legal grounds for breaking the lease and leaving without responsibility for future rent.
- **Increased chances of damages.** If the bug problem reappears and tenants sue over lost or damaged possessions, costs of moving and increased rent, and the psychological consequences of having lived with the bugs, their chances of recovering will be enhanced by your lack of candor. A lawyer will argue that your failure to disclose a dangerous situation set the tenants up for misery that could have been avoided had you been truthful.

Now, suppose you are not questioned about a rental's bed bug history, you remain silent, and a problem reappears. Will your new tenants have a strong case for breaking the lease without responsibility for future rent, or use your silence as a way to increase their chances of collecting damages from you? The answer will depend on the facts, such as how aggressively and thoroughly you attempted to rid the property of bugs.

RESOURCE

Bed bugs. For more information on the eradication and prevention of bed bugs, check out Techletter.com, maintained by a pest management consulting firm. Read their articles or order the comprehensive *Bed Bug Handbook: The Complete Guide to Bed Bugs and Their Control.*

Landlord's Liability for Criminal Activity

No one expects you to build a moat around your rental property and provide round-the-clock armed security. But in virtually every state, landlords are expected to take reasonable precautions to:

- protect tenants from assailants, thieves, and other criminals
- protect tenants from criminal acts of fellow tenants
- warn tenants about dangerous situations you are aware of but cannot eliminate, and
- protect the neighborhood from illegal and noxious activities, such as drug dealing, by your tenants.

If you fail to take these measures, you could be liable or partially liable for resulting injuries or losses.

This chapter discusses landlords' duties created by building codes, ordinances, statutes, and common law created by court decisions to protect your tenants and the neighborhood. It also discusses special issues regarding terrorism relating to landlords and rental property.

Troubled Property: Is It Time to Cut Your Losses?

If you own property in a high-crime area, you could find it impossible to raise rents enough to cover the costs of providing secure housing and purchasing comprehensive insurance. The truth is that you might be better off selling at a loss than courting an excessive risk that you will be sued for criminal acts on your property. If you do keep high-crime property, consider ways to legally separate it from your other assets—for example, by establishing a corporation or limited liability company.

 RELATED TOPIC

Related topics covered in this book include:

- How to choose the best tenants and avoid legal problems: Chapter 1
- Lease and rental agreement provisions prohibiting tenants' illegal activities and disturbances: Chapter 2
- How to avoid renting to convicted criminals without violating privacy and antidiscrimination laws: Chapter 5
- How to minimize danger to tenants from a manager by checking applicants' backgrounds and references: Chapter 6
- Highlighting security procedures in a move-in letter to new tenants: Chapter 7
- Responsibilities for repair and maintenance under state and local housing law: Chapter 9
- Landlord's liability for a tenant's injuries from defective housing conditions: Chapter 10
- Landlord's right of entry and tenant's privacy: Chapter 13
- Evicting a tenant for drug dealing and other illegal activity: Chapter 17.

Comply With All State and Local Laws on Security

You should learn and comply with all security laws, both state and local, that apply to you. For information on security regulations, contact your state or local housing agency or rental property owners' association. Here's an idea of what to expect.

Specific Rules

In many areas of the country, local building and housing codes have security rules designed to protect tenants. For example, some city ordinances require front-door peepholes, intercom systems, deadbolt locks, and specific types of lighting on rental property.

Only a few states have targeted laws on landlords' responsibilities to provide secure premises. For example:

- Under Florida law, landlords must provide locks and keep common areas in a "safe condition." When an assailant was able to enter a rental because of a broken back door lock, the tenant victim was allowed to argue to a jury that the landlord was partially responsible. (*Paterson v. Deeb*, 472 So.2d 1210 (Fla. Dist. Ct. 1985).)

- All Texas rental units must be equipped with specific security devices, such as window latches on exterior windows, doorknob locks or keyed deadbolts on each exterior door, and sliding door pin locks on exterior sliding glass doors. (Tex. Prop. Code § 92.151-170.)

If you violate a law designed to protect tenants' safety—like a local ordinance requiring deadbolts—your tenants can complain to the agency in charge of enforcing the codes, often a local building or housing authority. The violation might also make you automatically liable for losses that stem from the violation. (The legal term for this is "negligence per se"—see Chapter 10.) If you're sued after a crime occurs, you cannot argue that it was unreasonable to expect you to provide the security measure in question.

General Security Responsibilities

Even if your state and local laws offer little specific direction, you still likely have a duty to keep your premises "clean and safe" or "secure." Some courts interpret tenant safety laws more strictly than others.

> **EXAMPLE 1:** The housing code in Andrew's city sets minimum security standards for apartment houses, including a requirement that all areas of rental property be kept "clean and safe." The garage in Andrew's apartment house is poorly lit and accessible from the street because the automatic door works excruciatingly slowly. Andrew adds a few lights, but the garage is still far from bright. Andrew would be wise to spend the money to do the lighting job right and fix the garage door, because conditions like these could violate the "clean *and safe*" housing code requirement. If someone came in through the substandard garage door and assaulted a tenant, Andrew would likely be sued and found partially liable for the tenant's injuries.

> **EXAMPLE 2:** Martin is a tenant in a state that requires rental housing to be maintained in a "fit and habitable" condition. Courts in his state have interpreted this to mean, among other things, that multifamily dwellings should be reasonably secure from strangers' unwanted intrusions. One evening, Martin is assaulted in the elevator by an intruder who entered through the unlocked lobby door. Martin sues his landlord, Jim, and is able to show that the front door lock had been broken for a long time and that Jim had failed to fix it. The jury decides that Jim's failure to provide a secure front door violated the requirement to keep the place habitable, that he was aware of the problem and had plenty of time to fix it, and that the unsecured front door played a significant role in the assault. The jury awards Martin several thousand dollars for his injuries, lost wages, and pain and suffering.

Keep Your Promises About Security

If you promise tenants certain security features—such as a doorman, security patrols, interior cameras, or an alarm system—you must either provide them or risk liability (at least partially) for any criminal act that they likely would have prevented.

Don't Exaggerate in Ads or Oral Descriptions

Landlords know that the promise of a safe environment is often a powerful marketing tool. In ads or during discussions with interested renters, you will naturally point out security locks, outdoor lighting, and burglar alarms, because these features might be as important to prospective tenants as a fine view or a swimming pool.

Take care, however, not to exaggerate your security measures. Legally, you are obligated to provide and maintain all amenities you describe. A jury could find your failure to do so a contributing factor in any crime committed on the premises, making you liable for a tenant's losses or injuries.

You won't be liable for failing to provide what was promised, however, unless your failure caused or contributed to the crime. For example, burned-out lightbulbs in the parking lot won't make you liable if a burglar gets in through an unlocked trap door on the roof.

> **EXAMPLE:** The manager of Jeff's apartment building gave him a thorough tour of the building before he decided to move in. Jeff was particularly impressed with the security locks on the gates of the high fences at the front and rear of the property. Confident that the interior of the property was accessible only to tenants and their guests, Jeff didn't hesitate to take his kitchen garbage to the dumpsters at the rear of the building late one evening. There he was accosted by an intruder who got in through a rear gate that had a broken lock. Jeff's landlord was held liable, because he had failed to maintain the sophisticated, effective locks that he had promised.

Ads That Invite Lawsuits

Advertisements like the following will come back to haunt you if a crime occurs on your rental property:

- "No one gets past our mega-security systems. A highly-trained guard is on duty at all times."
- "We provide highly safe, highly secure buildings."
- "You can count on us. We maintain the highest apartment security standards in the business."

Be Careful With Your Lease or Rental Agreement

Your lease and its accompanying documents create a contract, and your tenants have a right to expect and rely on any security measures it mentions.

> **EXAMPLE:** The information packet given to Mai when she moved into her apartment stressed the need to keep careful track of door keys: "If you lose your keys, call the management, and the lock will be changed immediately." When Mai lost her keys, she immediately called the management company but couldn't reach anyone, because it was after 5 p.m. on a Saturday and there was no after-hours emergency contact. Sunday evening, Mai was assaulted by someone who got into her apartment by using her lost key. Mai sued the owner and management company. She argued that because they had disregarded their promise to change the locks promptly, they shared partial responsibility with the assailant for her injuries. The jury agreed and awarded Mai a large sum.

> **CAUTION**
>
> **Don't go overboard by specifying in your lease or rental agreement all the security measures you don't provide.** Some landlords think that if they provide no security and say that tenants are completely on their own, they can eliminate liability for the acts of criminals. Although making it clear that you provide little or no security probably can reduce your potential liability for tenant injuries that result from criminal activity, you can't excuse yourself from providing what is required by law. For example, if a local ordinance provides that exterior doors must have locks, you will increase—not decrease—your potential liability by failing to provide a front door lock.

Maintain What You Already Provide

Sometimes your actions can obligate you as much as an oral or written statement. If you provide enhanced security measures, such as security locks or a nighttime guard, you might be bound to maintain these features, even if they were never explicitly promised verbally or in writing. Many landlords react with understandable frustration when their well-meaning (and expensive) efforts to protect tenants result in *increased* risk of liability. But the right response is not to provide minimal security. Instead, be practical and keep your eye on your goal: Over time, using proven security measures will yield contented, long-term tenants and fewer legal hassles.

Prevent Criminal Acts

The best way to avoid crime-related liability is to prevent criminal acts in the first place. The good news is that many successful prevention techniques—proper lighting, sturdy locks, criminal-unfriendly landscaping, and well-trained on-site personnel—are not very expensive. Even if you must take more expensive measures, whatever you spend will pale in comparison to the costs that could result from crime on the premises, such as:

- increased insurance premiums
- jury verdicts in excess of your insurance coverage
- expensive attorneys' fees, and
- lost income due to due to constant tenant turnover.

Don't pinch pennies here.

Evaluate Your Situation

The security steps you need to take depend on context: Is your rental a duplex or a high-rise? Is it in a peaceful neighborhood or high-crime area? Assess your needs and come up with a plan before you dash off to buy a security system you might not need.

Start With Your Own Inspection

Walk around your property and ask yourself two questions:

- Would I, or a member of my family, feel reasonably safe here, at night or alone?
- If I were a thief or an assailant, how difficult would it be to get into the building or an individual rental unit?

Schedule more than one assessment walk, at different times of the day and night. You might see something at 11 p.m. that you wouldn't notice at 11 a.m.

Consider the Neighborhood

Keep up-to-date on crime in the area. If your neighborhood hasn't had any incidents, you have less reason to equip your property with extensive security devices. If there have been criminal incidents in the neighborhood, talk to the neighbors and the police department about what measures have proven to be effective.

Your Crime Prevention Checklist

- Meet or exceed state and local housing code requirements for safety devices.
- Don't hype your security measures.
- Provide and maintain adequate security measures based on an analysis of the vulnerability of your property and neighborhood.
- Implement management practices—such as strict key control—that will increase safety on the premises.
- Educate tenants about crime problems and prevention strategies.
- Make it clear that tenants—not you—are primarily responsible for their own protection.
- Inspect the premises regularly to spot security problems.
- Ask tenants for suggestions about how to make the premises safer.
- Quickly respond to tenants' suggestions and complaints.
- If an important component of your security systems breaks, fix it on an emergency basis and provide appropriate alternative security.
- Be aware of threats to tenants' security from the manager or other tenants and handle safety and security problems pronto, especially those involving drug dealing.
- Buy adequate liability insurance to protect you from lawsuits related to crime on the property.

Get Advice From Experts

Most police departments will work with you to develop a sound security plan and educate tenants. Some will send an officer out to assess the vulnerability of your property and recommend security measures. Many will train tenants in neighborhood watch techniques, such as how to recognize and report suspicious behavior.

Another professional resource that might not immediately come to mind is your own insurance company. Some companies, having figured out that it's cheaper to offer preventive consultation services than to pay out huge awards to injured clients, provide free crime-deterrence consultations. For example, drawing on its experience handling claims generated by security breaches, your insurance company might be able to tell you which equipment has (and has not) proven to be effective in preventing break-ins and assaults.

Another resource for advice is the private security industry. These "security system" firms typically analyze your property and then recommend appropriate equipment—whether it be bars on windows or an internal electronic surveillance system. Even if you do not ultimately engage their services, a professional evaluation might prove quite valuable as you design your own approach. Get several estimates and check references before selecting a security firm.

Security companies have a vested interest in getting you to buy products and services that might not be needed. If you own lots of rental properties, it might be worth your while to hire an independent security consultant for a disinterested evaluation. Visit the International Association of Professional Security Consultants' website (IAPSC.org) for a list of advisors in your area.

Take Basic Security Steps

We recommend at least the following security measures for every rental property:

- **Exterior lighting.** Exterior lighting at entranceways and walkways should be on a timer or activated by motion. Do not rely on managers or tenants to turn on exterior lights. Many security experts regard the absence or failure of exterior lights as the single most common facilitator of break-ins and crime.
- **Interior lighting.** Have bright interior lights in hallways, stairwells, doorways, and parking garages.
- **Locks.** Sturdy dead-bolt door locks on individual rental units and solid window and patio door locks are essential, as are front-door peepholes in each unit (with a wide-angle lens for viewing). Lobby doors should have dead-bolt locks
- **Landscaping.** Keep plants neat and compact. Shrubs should be no higher than three feet, and trees should be cleared to seven feet from the ground. Trees and shrubbery should not obscure entryways or provide easy hiding places near doorways or windows. If yard maintenance is the tenants' responsibility in a single-family house, you might need to supervise the job.
- **Security alarm** connected to a 24-hour security service.
- **Window bars.** Solid metal window bars or grills over ground floor windows are often a good idea in high-crime neighborhoods, but local fire codes might restrict their use. All grills or bars must have a release mechanism that allows occupants to open them from the inside.

Multiunit buildings might require additional measures:

- **Buzzers.** Intercom and buzzer systems that allow tenants to identify visitors and unlock the front door from their apartments help prevent unauthorized entry.

- **Doorman.** In some areas, a 24-hour doorman is essential and might do more to reduce crime outside your building than anything else. Spread over a large number of units, a doorman might cost less than you think. If you hire a firm, insist on references and proof of insurance. You can also hire your own guard, but that gets complicated very quickly, because you will be responsible for training and weapons (if any).

- **Secure common areas.** Driveways, garages, and underground parking need to be well-lit and as secure (inaccessible to unauthorized entrants) as possible. Fences and automatic gates might be necessary in some areas.

- **Elevators.** Limiting access to the elevators by requiring a passkey and installing closed-circuit monitoring can reduce the chances that an assailant will choose this site.

- **Security cameras.** A 24-hour internal security system with cameras and real-time monitoring is an effective crime detector.

Initiate Good Management Practices

Physical safety devices and improvements aren't the only ways to improve security and decrease liability. Your business practices, including personnel policies, are crucial and should include the following:

Keep tenant information locked up. Keep tenant files in a locked cabinet or password-protected computer. As an added precaution, identify residences by your own code, so that no one but you and your manager can find tenants' addresses by reading their file.

Don't Rely on "Courtesy Officers"

Some rental property owners provide on-site security by renting to police officers who, in exchange for a reduced rent, agree to be the resident "courtesy officer." The idea is to provide a professional presence on the property without paying for a regular security service. It's a poor idea, for several reasons:

- Calling the officer/tenant a courtesy officer does not change the fact that your tenants will look to that person to provide consistent security protection. (In fact, because you are paying the officer by the rent reduction, the officer is not working as a courtesy at all.) A court would hold the police officer (and you) to the same standard of conduct expected of professional guard services.

- Because courtesy officers can provide security only when they are home, the protection will be unpredictable. Tenants won't know when they can count on security coverage, and might do things (like coming home late at night) under the mistaken impression that the officer/tenant is on the property.

- The value of your officer/tenant's services will be as good as wakefulness and attention allows. You are essentially asking the officer to assume a second job. Paying a tenant for intermittent security creates an employer-employee relationship, meaning you'll have to pay Social Security taxes and meet other employer obligations. (See Chapter 6 on tax issues and resident managers.) And if a court finds your officer/tenant partially responsible for crime on the premises (by allowing unauthorized access, for example), you will be liable as an employer.

A security service, on the other hand, is an independent contractor and takes care of these bookkeeping details. Independent contractors are generally responsible for their own missteps and should be insured (be sure you check). Of course, you could still be sued, but hiring an independent contractor reduces the chances of your ultimately being held liable.

Signs of a Meth Lab

Residential real estate is well-suited for manufacturing methamphetamine (crystal meth), because production doesn't require a large space. Meth is easily made by cooking common products such as cold remedies, salt, lighter fluid, gas, drain cleaners, and iodine on a stove or hot plate. Explosions and fires are common, and the byproducts of production pose an extreme health hazard.

According to the U.S. Drug Enforcement Administration, the following could signal the presence of a meth operation:

- a large amount of cold tablet containers that list ephedrine or pseudoephedrine as ingredients
- jars containing clear liquid with a white or red colored solid on the bottom
- jars labeled as containing iodine or dark shiny metallic purple crystals inside of jars
- jars labeled as containing red phosphorus or a fine dark-red or purple powder
- coffee filters containing a white pasty substance, a dark-red sludge, or shiny white crystals
- bottles labeled as containing sulfuric, muriatic, or hydrochloric acid
- bottles or jars with rubber tubing attached
- cookware containing a powdery residue
- an unusually large number of cans of camp fuel, paint thinner, acetone, starter fluid, lye, and drain cleaners containing sulfuric acid or bottles containing muriatic acid
- large amounts of lithium batteries, especially ones that have been stripped
- soft silver or gray metallic ribbon (in chunk form) stored in oil or kerosene
- propane tanks with fittings that have turned blue, and
- strong urine-like odor, or unusual chemical smells like ether, ammonia, or acetone.

If you think there's a meth lab in an apartment or house, contact law enforcement immediately.

If you're left with an abandoned meth lab, here's what to do next:

- **Notify the police and fire department.** They will send a hazardous materials team to deal with the initial clean-up.
- **Lock up and stay out.** Turning on lights could cause an explosion, and inhaling the fumes is very dangerous. Leave everything to the experts (see below).
- **Notify your insurance company.** Some policies might cover the cleanup costs.
- **Cleaning.** Nearly everything in the unit will need to be cleaned or replaced. Hire a company that specializes in meth lab cleanups to deal with the carpeting, walls, and fixtures. Hire a licensed company if your state issues such licenses (contact the local health department to find out). Many states (either under the department of health or an environmental protection agency) offer advice and information about cleaning up meth labs.
- **Test the apartment and get the official okay.** Use a company other than the one that cleaned the property to certify that the hazards have been fully mitigated, and comply with any state- or local-mandated clearance requirements.
- **Find out whether you must notify future tenants.** Some states require landlords to tell applicants that the unit was a meth lab. Your state health department or health inspectors can tell you what your disclosure duties are. The federal government website, USA.gov, includes of list of state departments of health (www.usa.gov/state-health). The rental property's address might also appear on the U.S. Drug Enforcement Agency's "National Clandestine Laboratory Register" (www.dea.gov/clan-lab), for an indefinite time.

Insist that employees respect tenants' privacy. Impress upon your employees the need to preserve your tenants' privacy. Tenants who want friends, family, or bill collectors to know where they live will tell them—you shouldn't.

Train employees to avoid dangerous situations and correct worrisome ones. Teach managers and employees to rigorously abide by your safety rules and to report areas of concern. Consider sending employees to management courses on security offered by many landlords' associations.

Protect yourself and your employees when showing a unit. Ask for a photo ID and make a photocopy or take a picture, which you should store in the office in a secure place. At the end of the tour, return the copy to the applicant or destroy it (or delete the photo) in the applicant's presence. Apply this practice to all applicants, not just those you think might pose a problem; selective practices invite discrimination claims (for example, don't ask for ID from only men, or any other protected class).

Don't undermine security measures with poor practices. Once you install security equipment, you must use it intelligently. For example, suppose you install locking gates at the property's entrance, but leave a key for the postal carrier in an unlocked box nearby. If an assailant gains entry by using that key, a jury could determine that you should be held partially responsible for the harm that ensued, because you were careless with the key.

Safeguard keys. Because the security of your rental property depends in large part on the locks on rental unit doors and the keys to those doors, you should:

- Keep all duplicate keys in a locked area, identified by a code that only you and your manager know. Several types of locking key drawers and sophisticated key safes are available. Check ads that cater to the residential rental industry, or contact local locksmiths and security firms.
- Don't label keys with the rental unit number or name and address of the apartment building, and advise your tenants to take the same precaution.
- Allow only yourself and your manager access to master keys.
- Keep track of all keys provided to tenants and, if necessary, to your employees. Be sure all loaned keys are returned.
- Require tenants to return all keys at move-out.
- Rekey every time a new tenant moves in or loses a key.
- Give careful thought to the security problem of the front door lock: If the lock opens by an easy-to-copy key, you can't prevent a tenant from copying the key and giving it to others or using it after moving out. Consider using locks that have hard-to-copy keys, or (with rental houses or small properties) rekey the front door when a tenant moves. Consider using easy-to-alter card or keypad systems that allow you to change front door access on a regular basis or when a tenant moves. Again, locksmiths and security firms can advise you on options available.
- Give keys only to people you know and trust. If you have hired contractors whom you do not know personally, open the unit for them and return to close up when they are done. Keep in mind that often even known and trusted contractors hire others you don't know.

When a Tenant Wants to Supply Additional Security

The form lease and rental agreements (Chapter 2) forbid the tenant from rekeying or adding locks or a burglar alarm without your written consent. But think carefully before you refuse permission to install extra protection. If a crime occurs that would have been foiled had the security item been in place, and you get sued, you will obviously be at a disadvantage before a judge or jury.

If you let a tenant add additional security measures, make sure the tenant gives you duplicate keys or instructions on how to disarm the alarm system and the name and phone number of the alarm company, so that you can enter in case of emergency.

Educate Tenants About Crime Prevention

After you have identified the vulnerabilities of the neighborhood—for example, by talking to the police—don't keep this information to yourself. Share it with your tenants. It's best to do this when you first show the rental unit to prospective tenants. We recommend a two-step process:

- Alert tenants to the specific risks of your neighborhood (for example, "problems are worst Friday and Saturday night between 10 p.m. and 1 a.m.") and what they can do to minimize the chances of assault or theft.
- No matter how secure your building, warn tenants of the limitations of the security measures you have provided.

This twofold approach allows you to cover your legal bases by both disclosing the risks and frankly informing tenants that you cannot ensure their safety in all possible situations. If, despite your best efforts, a crime does occur on your property, your candid disclosures regarding the safety problems of your neighborhood and the limitations of the existing security measures might help shield you from liability.

From the tenants' point of view, such disclosures highlight the need to be vigilant and assume some responsibility for safety. If you do not disclose the limitations of the security you provide (or if you exaggerate) and a crime does occur, one of the first things your tenants will say (to the police, their lawyer, and the jury) is that they were simply relying upon the protection you said would be in place.

Identify Specific Concerns

Give tenants information specific to your rental property. Here are some ideas:

- If there has been crime in the area, especially in your building, inform your tenants but don't disclose the identity of the victim.

- Update your information on the security situation as necessary. For example, let tenants know if there has been an assault in or near the building by sending them a note and post a notice in the lobby, including the physical description of the assailant.
- If you hire a professional security firm to evaluate your rental property, share the results of the investigation with your tenants.
- Encourage tenants to set up a neighborhood watch program. Many local police departments will come out and meet with residents attempting to organize such a program.
- Encourage tenants to report any suspicious activities or security problems to you, such as loitering, large numbers of late-night guests, or broken locks. (Chapter 9 recommends a system for handling tenant complaints.)

For information on preparing tenants for disasters and emergencies, see the federal government's website, Ready.gov.

Explain the Limitations of Your Security Measures

An important component of your disclosures to tenants involves disabusing them of any notion that you are their guardian angel. Let them know where your security efforts end, and where their own good sense (and the local police force) must take over. Specifically:

- Point out each security measure—such as locking exterior gates, key locks on windows, and peepholes in every front door—and explain how each measure works. It's best to do this in writing, either as part of a move-in letter to new tenants or at the time a new security item is installed.
- Note particular aspects of the property that are, despite your efforts, vulnerable to the presence of would-be assailants or thieves. Say, for example, your apartment parking garage has a self-closing door. When you

explain how this door works, you might also point out that it's not instantaneous. For example, a fast-moving person could, in most situations, slip into the garage behind an entering car despite the self-closing door. Pointing this out to your tenants might result in their paying more careful attention to the rearview mirror.

- Place signs in potentially dangerous places that will remind tenants of possible dangers and the need to be vigilant. For example, place a notice in the lobby asking tenants to securely shut and lock the front door behind them.
- Suggest safety measures. For example, tenants arriving home after dark might call ahead and ask a neighbor to be an escort.

Giving your tenants information on how they, too, can take steps to protect themselves will also help if you are sued. If tenants argue that you failed to inform them of a dangerous condition, you will be able to show that you have done all that could be expected of a reasonably conscientious landlord.

Inspect and Maintain Your Property

Landlords are most often found liable for crime on their property when a criminal gained access through broken doors or locks. By contrast, a jury is far less likely to fault a landlord who can show that reasonable security measures were in place and working, but were unable to stop a determined criminal.

Inspect your property frequently, so that you discover and fix problems before an opportunistic criminal comes along. At the top of your list should be fixing burned-out exterior floodlights and broken locks, and cutting back overgrown vegetation that provides a hiding spot for lurking criminals.

The people who actually live in your rental property will generally know first about security hazards. One good approach is to post notices in central locations, such as in an elevator and the lobby, asking tenants to promptly report any security problems. If you rent a duplex or house, periodically meet with your tenants and discuss any changes in the neighborhood or the structure of the building.

Protect Yourself, Too

Landlords and managers need to take precautions for their own safety as well as for that of tenants. Whether or not you live on the rental property:

- Promptly deposit rent checks and money orders. If possible, do not accept cash.
- When you show a vacant apartment, consider bringing someone with you. A would-be assailant might be deterred by the presence of another person. If you must show apartments by yourself, alert a family member or friend to the fact that you are showing a vacant unit, and when you expect to be done.
- Especially if your building is in a high-crime area, carry a small alarm device (such as beeper-sized box that emits a piercing alarm when its pin is removed), and carry a cell phone.
- Work on vacant units during the day and be alert to the fact that, although keeping the front door open (to the building or the unit) might be convenient as you go to and fro for materials and equipment, it is also an invitation to someone to walk right into the building.

Handle Security Complaints Immediately

Take care of complaints about a dangerous situation or a broken security item immediately, even if it's the middle of the night. A broken lock or disabled intercom system is an invitation to crime and needs to be addressed pronto.

If it's impossible to fix a problem immediately, alert tenants and take other measures. For example, you might hire a security officer and close off other entrances for a few days if your front door security system fails and a necessary part is not immediately available. Failing to do this could saddle you with a higher level of legal liability should a tenant be injured by a criminal act while the security system is out of service or a window lock broken. A few examples of quick and appropriate responses:

- The glass panel next to the front door is accidentally broken late one afternoon by a departing workman. Conscious that this creates a major security problem, you call a 24-hour glass replacement service to get it replaced immediately.

- The intercom system fails due to a power surge following an electrical storm. You hire a 24-hour guard for the two days it takes to repair the circuitry.

- Several exterior floodlights are knocked out by vandals throwing rocks at 6 p.m. A tenant, who has been encouraged by management to immediately report problems of this nature, calls you. You alert the police and ask for an extra drive-by during the night, post signs in the lobby and the elevator, close off the darkened entrance, and advise tenants to use an alternate, lighted entryway. The next day, you get the floodlights repaired and equipped with wire mesh protection.

Protect Tenants From Each Other

What if one of your tenants is responsible for criminal activity on the premises, or poses a danger? (Physical disputes between tenants in the same household—domestic violence—are discussed in Chapter 8.) You have a duty to take reasonable steps to protect tenants if another resident threatens harm or property damage. If you don't, and a tenant is injured or robbed by another tenant, you could be sued and pay a hefty judgment. As with your duty to protect tenants from crime at the hands of strangers, your duty to keep the peace among your tenants is limited to what is *reasonably* foreseeable and to what a *reasonable* person in your position would do.

Note that the scenarios and advice that follow assume that you are not dealing with a dangerous tenant who is also legally disabled. In that situation, you might need to work with your tenant if you can reasonably expect that the behavior will stop. See "Do You Need to Accommodate Tenants With Disabilities Who Are Dangerous" in Chapter 5.

TIP

Encourage tenants to report other tenants' suspicious or illegal activity. Establish a system to collect tenants' complaints and concerns about other tenants or the manager, just the way you handle repair complaints. Not only will this let you respond quickly, but it will serve an additional function: If you are sued for something a manager or tenant does, and if your business records show that there were no prior complaints regarding the person's behavior, that will bolster your claim that you acted reasonably under the circumstances (by continuing to rent to or employ the individual), because you had no inkling that trouble was likely.

When to Act

If you learn that a tenant has threatened or committed violence on your property, you might need to take action. Whether to act—by terminating the tenancy—depends on the seriousness of the behavior, and the likelihood that similar acts will occur again on your property. Unless there's a clear history of serious problems with the offending tenant, landlords often win these cases.

EXAMPLE 1: Evelyn decides to rent an apartment to David, although she knows that he was convicted of domestic violence many years earlier. For two years David is a model tenant, until he hits another tenant, Chuck, in the laundry room over a disagreement as to who was next in line for the dryer. Chuck sues Evelyn but is unable to convince a jury that she should bear some responsibility for his injuries, because he cannot show that the incident was foreseeable.

EXAMPLE 2: Mary rents to Carl, who appears to be a nice young man with adequate references. On the rental application, Carl states that he has no criminal convictions. Several months later, Carl is arrested for burglary and assault of another tenant in the building. It turns out that Carl had recently been released from state prison for burglary and rape. Because Mary had no knowledge of his criminal past, she is not held liable for his actions. Mary had no obligation to confirm his representations on his rental application.

On the other hand, tenants sometimes win if they can show that the landlord knew about a resident's tendency toward violence and failed to take reasonable precautions to safeguard the other tenants.

EXAMPLE: Bill receives several complaints from tenants about Carol, a tenant who pushed another resident out of the elevator, slapped a child for making noise, and verbally abused a tenant's guest for parking in Carol's space. Despite these warning signs, Bill doesn't terminate Carol's tenancy or even speak with her about her behavior. When Carol assaults a resident whom she accused of reading her newspaper, Bill is held partly liable on the grounds that he knew of a dangerous situation but failed to address it.

What to Do

When you learn of the potential for danger from a tenant and decide to act, your response should be swift and appropriate.

Law enforcement. In an emergency—for example, a tenant brandishes a gun—call the police. Do the same if drugs are involved.

Eviction. In less dire circumstances, you'll probably want to evict the worrisome tenant, and possibly post a guard and warn other tenants until the tenant is gone. Many states now make it relatively simple for landlords to evict troublemakers. These laws specify that harm or the threat of harm to other persons justifies a quick eviction.

Incentives. If you don't want to go through the hassle of eviction, and you want to get someone out quickly, consider offering a financial incentive to leave. Let the tenant break the lease without a penalty—it's a small price to pay to defuse a dangerous situation.

Negotiation. If the danger seems minor, you can try to talk to the troublemaker and head off future problems. For example, suppose a tenant complains about a neighbor who bangs on the walls and yells every time the tenant practices the violin during the afternoon, and the pounding is getting louder every day. The tenant can reasonably expect you to intervene and attempt to broker a solution—perhaps an adjustment of the violinist's practice schedule or some heavy-duty earplugs for the neighbor.

Protect Tenants From Your Employees

Your property manager occupies a critical position in your business. The manager interacts with every tenant and often has access to their personal files *and* their homes. If your manager commits a crime—especially if you had any warning that it might occur—you are likely to be held liable. The same goes for other employees, such as maintenance personnel. Your liability usually turns on whether you acted reasonably under the circumstances in hiring and supervising your employees. Let's take a closer look at what this means.

RELATED TOPIC
Chapter 6 discusses managers in detail.

Check Your Employees' Backgrounds

It is essential to thoroughly check the background of your potential manager and other on-site workers. If a manager or another worker commits a crime on the property, you are likely to be sued for negligent hiring. You might be found liable if all of the following are true:

- You failed to investigate your employee's background to the full extent allowed by the privacy laws in your state.
- A proper investigation would have revealed a disqualifying past criminal conviction.
- The employee's offense against the tenant is reasonably related to the past conviction.

> **EXAMPLE:** When his longtime manager suddenly leaves, Martin feels pressured to replace her fast. He hires Jack without checking his background or the information provided on the application. Martin takes Jack at his word when he says that he has no felony convictions. Several months later, Jack is arrested for stealing electronic equipment from a tenant's home that he entered using the master key. Martin is successfully sued when the tenant learns that Jack had two prior felony convictions for burglary and grand theft.

Supervise Your Manager

As the manager's employer, you could also be held liable if your manager's negligence makes it possible for another person to commit a crime against a tenant. For example, if your manager's sloppy practices make it possible for a criminal to get a tenant's key, you will be held responsible on the grounds that you failed to properly supervise the manager.

Deal With Drug-Dealing Tenants

If you look the other way while tenants engage in illegal activity on your property—such as dealing drugs, storing stolen property, engaging in prostitution, or participating in gang-related activity—you can end up paying huge fines or even losing your property altogether to government seizure. This discussion focuses on the most common problem, drug dealing, but it applies equally to other illegal activities.

It's your responsibility to know what's going on at your property. In some situations, government agencies can imposes fines or seize property even though the landlord knew almost nothing about the tenants' activities. So, keep yourself well-informed, and if you have the slightest suspicion that illegal drug dealing is taking place on the rental property, act quickly and decisively. If you do nothing—either out of inertia, fear of reprisals from drug dealers, or a mistaken belief that you're unlikely to get in trouble—you will almost surely regret it.

The Cost of Renting to Drug-Dealing Tenants

Increasingly, laws and court decisions hold landlords liable when a tenant engages in a continuing illegal activity such as drug dealing. If you don't quickly evict drug-dealing tenants, you'll run into some big problems:

- Good tenants will be difficult to find and keep, and the value of your property will plummet.
- Good tenants, trying to avoid drug-dealing ones, will be able to legally move out without notice and before a lease runs out. They will argue that the presence of the illegal activity has, for all practical purposes, evicted them, in that the problems associated with drug dealing prevent them from the "quiet enjoyment" of their home or violate the implied warranty of habitability. In many states, the tenants will have a very strong case to break their lease.
- Tenants injured or annoyed by drug dealers, both in the building and neighborhood, will sue you for violating nuisance laws and building codes.

- Local, state, or federal authorities might levy stiff fines against you and might even empty your building for allowing the illegal activity to continue.
- Law enforcement authorities might pursue criminal penalties against both the tenants *and* you for knowingly allowing the activity to continue.
- Your rental property might even be confiscated by the state or federal government.

Nice Properties Are Not Immune

You might think that drug crime is a problem only in seedy neighborhoods. Think again. Drug dealers often prefer smaller apartment complexes with some measure of security over large, unprotected housing units. A drug dealer, like a law-abiding tenant, wants a safe, controlled environment.

Lawsuits Against You for Harboring a Nuisance

In legal terms, a nuisance is a pervasive, continuing, and serious condition—like a pile of stinking garbage or a group of drug dealers—that threatens public health, safety, or morals. In some states, it also includes obnoxious activity that is simply offensive, like excessive noise or open sexual conduct. Property used as a drug house, whose presence injures and interferes with the rights of neighbors to use and enjoy their property, easily qualifies as a legal nuisance.

The government, and sometimes the neighbors, can sue to get a nuisance stopped (abated), often by court order and fines against the landlord. Even though the tenant causes the nuisance, the punishment might be directed at you, as the landlord.

EXAMPLE: Alma owned a duplex in Wisconsin, which defines drug houses as nuisances. (Wisc. Stat. Ann. § 823.113.) Despite repeated complaints from the neighbors that one of her tenants was conducting a drug operation in his home (and in spite of the tenant's two arrests for dealing from that address), Alma did nothing about the problem. Responding to pressure from fed-up neighbors, the local police finally sued Alma to evict the tenant and close the duplex. The property was padlocked.

Using public nuisance abatement laws against crime-tolerant landlords is increasingly common in cities with pervasive drug problems. In extreme cases, where the conduct giving rise to the nuisance complaint is illegal (drug dealing or prostitution, for example), landlords themselves face civil fines or jail time. See "Civil and Criminal Nuisance Laws," below.

Each state has its own standards for determining when landlords can be found responsible under nuisance law. In most states, however, landlords must have had *some* knowledge of the illegal activity before property can be seized. Generally, landlords are given a short time in which to cure the problem before the ax falls and the property is seized.

In reality, because most landlords are acutely aware of their tenants' illegal behavior—having been informed by disgusted neighbors and overwhelmed law enforcement—even in states that require that you have clear actual knowledge of the situation, this knowledge standard is usually met. Put another way, it's a rare situation in which you can credibly claim that you didn't know about drug-dealing tenants.

Know the Law

It is important to know the nuisance laws in your state. At the very least, this will alert you to the standard by which your actions (or inaction) will be judged should there be proceedings brought against you or your property. Chapter 18 gives tips on how to unearth the laws that apply to you.

Tenants and neighbors, not just the government, can sue you for knowing about the activity but failing to take steps to clean up the property. They can seek:

- Monetary compensation for each of them for having put up with the situation. Each neighbor generally sues for the maximum allowed in state small claims court ($5,000 to $10,000 in most states), and the landlord often pays the maximum to *each* one. See the discussion of small claims courts in Chapter 16.
- An order from the judge directing you to evict the troublemakers, install security, and repair the premises. (Such orders are not available in all states.)

Private use of nuisance abatement laws is not as common as governmental use, but the practice will probably grow as people learn of others' successes.

Small (But Sometimes Mighty) Claims Court

The private enforcement of public nuisance laws has been creatively and successfully pursued in small claims courts in California and several other states, where groups of affected neighbors have brought multiple lawsuits targeted at drug houses.

In Berkeley, California, after failing to get the police and city council to close down a crack house, neighbors sought damages stemming from the noxious activities associated with the house. Each of the 18 plaintiffs collected the maximum amount allowed in small claims court ($3,500 at the time), avoided the expense of hiring counsel, and sent the landlord a very clear and expensive message. The problem was solved within a few weeks.

Civil and Criminal Nuisance Laws

	Civil Nuisance Laws	Criminal Nuisance Laws
Activities the laws target	Unhealthy, immoral, or obnoxious behavior which might also be, but is not necessarily, a violation of the criminal law	Criminal behavior
Examples of targeted activities	Excessive noise, piles of garbage and trash, and inordinate amounts of foot or car traffic	Drug dealing, prostitution, gambling, and gang activities
Who can sue	Public agencies such as city health departments, law enforcement agencies, and, in many states, affected neighbors, who can band together and sue for large sums in small claims court	Law enforcement agencies only
How landlord's liability is determined	"Preponderance of evidence" shows landlord intentionally tolerated the illegal activity, or was negligent or reckless in allowing it to occur	Prosecutor must prove guilt "beyond a reasonable doubt" and usually must show landlord had some knowledge of illegal activity.
Possible consequences to the landlord	A court ordering the offending tenant, and sometimes the landlord, to compensate other tenants. If a health, fire, or other enforcement agency brings the nuisance action based on many violations, it can result in a court order closing down the entire building.	Liability for money damages plus fines and imprisonment. Government can also close the property.

Losing Your Property: Forfeiture Laws

Federal or state forfeiture proceedings—where the government *takes your property* because of the illegal activities of one or more tenants—are the most dramatic possible consequence of owning crime-ridden rental property. Forfeitures are rare and not something you are likely to encounter if you follow the suggestions in this book for choosing decent tenants and maintaining safe and secure rental property. But they happen.

Unlike the nuisance abatement laws, which depend upon a pervasive and continuing pattern of illegal activity, forfeitures can result from a single incident. Also, unlike nuisance abatement laws, which temporarily deprive you of the use of your property, the consequence of a forfeiture is the complete and final transfer of title to the government.

Federal laws. The government can seize property that has "facilitated" an illegal drug transaction or that has been bought or maintained with funds, such as rent payments, gained through illegal drug dealing. (Comprehensive Drug Abuse Prevention and Control Act of 1970, 21 U.S.C. § 881.) The government's power under this law must give any landlord pause. To start forfeiture proceedings, the government need show only that it is *reasonably probable* that illegal activities are occurring on the premises, and may rely on circumstantial evidence and hearsay to do so. You must then prove either that the property did not facilitate the crime, or that the tenants' activities were done without your knowledge or consent. Your deliberate blindness will be of no avail. To prevail, you must show that you have done *all* that reasonably could be expected to prevent the illegal use of your property.

You Might Forfeit the Rent Money, Too

If you know, or have reason to know, that a tenant's rent was earned in the course of an illegal act, the rent money is itself forfeitable, no matter where the act was committed. A clever dealer, for example, might live in your nice, respectable building and conduct his trade elsewhere—but if he pays the rent with the money received in drug transactions, the rent money will be forfeited if the government can show that you knew (or had reason to know) of its source.

It is harder for the government to prove that you knew of the source of the rental payments than it is to show that you knew about illegal activity on the premises—but not impossible. To protect yourself, be able to point to a careful background check (regarding the tenant's job, credit, and bank account) that you performed before renting to the tenant. If you can show that there appeared to be a legitimate source of income to cover the rent, it will be harder for the government to argue that it should have been obvious that the rent constituted ill-gotten gain. Your refusal to accept cash rent might also help protect you from an assertion that the money was the fruit of a drug transaction.

State laws. Every state has adopted the Uniform Controlled Substances Act, modifying it to suit their policy aims. The act specifies that land involved in drug transactions is *not* forfeitable. Drug "containers," however, can be seized, and some states have interpreted that term to include property—for example, the rental property where drugs were kept. In many states, the act has been changed to include rental or other property that "facilitated" the illegal act.

In order for forfeiture to occur under the act, the government must show that you had knowledge of the illegal activity, but this requirement is interpreted very differently in different states. In some states, the prosecutor need only show that you had constructive knowledge of drug dealing—that a reasonable person in these circumstances would reach this conclusion. In others, the state must prove that you actually knew of the drug problem. In a few states, landowners are accountable if they were negligent in not knowing of the drug-related activities of their tenants. In any case, it is difficult to successfully prove ignorance.

How to Prevent Drug Lawsuits and Seizures

If you follow these steps, it is unlikely that conditions will deteriorate to the point that neighbors or the government feel it is necessary to step in and take over:

- Carefully screen potential renters.
- Keep the results of your background checks that show that your tenants' rent appeared to come from legitimate sources (jobs and bank accounts).
- Don't accept cash rental payments.
- Include a clause in your lease or rental agreement prohibiting drug dealing and other illegal activity, and promptly evict tenants who violate it.
- Let tenants know you intend to keep drug dealing out of the building.
- Respond to tenant and neighbor complaints about drug dealing on the property.
- Be aware of heavy traffic in and out of the premises.
- Inspect the premises and improve lighting and security.
- Get advice from police and security professionals *immediately* if you learn of a problem.

- Consult security experts to determine whether you have done all that one could reasonably expect to discover and prevent illegal activity on your property.

If You Are Sued

If your efforts at crime prevention fail, and a tenant is injured, will you be responsible? As mentioned, if you violated a specific law requiring a safety measure, and that's what led directly to the injury or loss, you will probably be liable. But you also have a general duty to take reasonable precautions to protect tenants from foreseeable criminal assaults and property crimes. To get an idea of whether or not your precautions were reasonable under the circumstances, take a look at these six key questions. They're also discussed in Chapter 10, because they're used if an insurance adjuster or a court evaluates your negligence and assesses responsibility when a tenant suffers accidental injury. Consider the following:

1. Did you control the area where the crime occurred? You aren't expected to police the entire world. But a lobby, hallway, or other common area is an area of high landlord control, which heightens your responsibility. However, you exert much less control over the sidewalk outside the front door, so it might be more difficult for you to minimize the chances of a crime occurring there.

2. How likely was it that a crime would occur? You are duty-bound to respond to the foreseeable, not the improbable. Have there been prior criminal incidents at a particular spot in the building? Elsewhere in the neighborhood? If you know that an offense is likely (because of a rash of break-ins or prior crime on the property), you have a heightened legal responsibility in most states to take reasonable steps to guard against future crime.

3. How difficult or expensive would it have been to reduce the risk that this crime would occur? If cheap or simple measures would have significantly lowered the risk of the crime that occurred, it is likely that a court would find that you had a duty to undertake them. For instance, suppose the assailant entered via a broken lock on the front door. Replacing a lock is generally quick and inexpensive, so the chances that you'll be liable in this situation go up. However, if the only solution to the problem was costly, such as structural remodeling or hiring a full-time doorman, it is doubtful that a court would expect it of you.

4. How serious an injury was likely to result from the crime? The consequences of a criminal incident (break-in, robbery, rape, or murder) can be very serious.

5. Did you fail to take reasonable steps to prevent a crime? As ever, reasonableness is evaluated in the context of each situation. For example, if you let the bushes near a door grow high and don't replace outdoor lights, it's clear you are not taking reasonable preventive steps. But suppose you cut the bushes back halfway and installed one light. Would that have been enough? It would be up to a jury to decide.

"Reasonable precautions" in a crime-free neighborhood are not the same as those called for when three apartments in your building have been burglarized within a month. The greater the danger, the more you must do.

6. Did your failure to take reasonable steps to keep tenants safe contribute to the crime? A tenant must be able to connect your failure to provide reasonable security with the criminal incident itself. In other words, even if the front door was unsecured, if the assailant entered by breaking a window, the sorry state of the front door will be irrelevant. It is often very difficult for tenants to convince a jury that the landlord's breach caused (or contributed to) the assault or burglary.

If a jury decides that you didn't meet the duty to keep tenants safe, and that this failure facilitated the crime, it will typically split the responsibility for the crime between you and the criminal. For example, jurors might decide that you were 60% at fault and the criminal 40%.

Now let's look at two realistic cases, applying the six questions.

> **EXAMPLE 1:** Elaine was assaulted and robbed by an intruder who entered her apartment through a sliding window that was closed but could not be locked. To determine whether the landlord would be liable, Elaine asked herself the six questions and came up with these answers:
>
> 1. The landlord controlled the window and was responsible for its operation.
> 2. This burglary was foreseeable, because there had been other break-ins at the building.
> 3. Installing a window lock was a minor burden.
> 4. The seriousness of foreseeable injury was high.
> 5. The landlord had done nothing to secure the window or otherwise prevent an intrusion.
> 6. The intruder could not have entered so easily and silently had the window been locked.
>
> Elaine concluded that the landlord owed her the duty to take reasonable steps to fix the problem. She filed a claim with the landlord's insurance company, but it didn't offer a fair settlement, and the case went to trial. The jury decided that the landlord should have installed a window lock and that because the burglar might not have entered at all through a properly secured window, the landlord was partially responsible for Elaine's injuries. The jury fixed the value of her injuries at $500,000 and decided that the landlord was 80% responsible.

EXAMPLE 2: Nick was assaulted in the underground garage of his apartment building by someone who hid in the shadows. The neighborhood had recently experienced several muggings. Nick couldn't identify the assailant, who was never caught. The automatic garage gate was broken and wouldn't close completely, allowing anyone to slip inside.

Nick decided that:

1. The landlord controlled the garage.
2. In view of the recent similar crimes in the neighborhood, an assault was foreseeable.
3. Fixing the broken gate wouldn't have been a great financial burden.
4. The likelihood of injury from an assault was high.

Nick concluded that the landlord owed him a duty of care in this situation. He then considered the last two questions. The garage door was broken, which constituted a breach of the landlord's duty. But the garage was also accessible from the interior of the building, making it possible that the assailant was another tenant or a guest. Nick's case fell apart because the landlord's failure to provide a secure outside door hadn't necessarily contributed to the crime. If the assailant was another tenant or guest, the landlord's failure to fix the gate would have been completely unconnected to the crime. Nick probably would have had a winning case if he could prove that the assailant got in through the broken gate.

Landlord's Right of Entry and Tenants' Privacy

FORMS IN THIS CHAPTER

Chapter 13 includes instructions for and a sample of the following form:

- Notice of Intent to Enter Dwelling Unit

The purchase of this book includes a free downloadable and customizable copy of this form. See Appendix B for the download link and instructions.

Next to disputes over rent or security deposits, one of the most common—and emotion-filled—misunderstandings between landlords and tenants involves conflicts between your right to enter the rental property and a tenant's right to be left alone at home. Fortunately, many of these problems can be avoided if you adopt fair—and, of course, legal— entry policies, and clearly explain these policies to tenants from the first day of your relationship. (If you employ a manager or management company, they must also follow your guidelines.)

RELATED TOPIC
Related topics covered in this book include:

- Recommended lease and rental agreement clause for landlord's access to rental property: Chapter 2
- How to make sure your manager doesn't violate tenants' right of privacy: Chapter 6
- How to highlight access procedures in a move-in letter to new tenants: Chapter 7
- Tenants' right of privacy and landlord's policy on guests: Chapter 8
- Procedures for respecting tenants' right of privacy while handling tenant complaints about safety and maintenance problems and conducting an annual safety inspection: Chapter 9
- How to protect the confidentiality of tenants' credit reports and notify tenants of any security breaches: Chapter 9
- Tenants' right of privacy if drug dealing or terrorist activity is suspected: Chapter 12
- How to handle disputes with tenants through negotiation, mediation, and other means: Chapter 16
- State Laws on Landlord's Access to Rental Property: Appendix A.

General Rules of Entry

You have a legal responsibility to keep fairly close tabs on the condition of the property. For this reason, and because it makes good sense to allow landlords reasonable access to their property, nearly every state has, by judicial decision or statute, recognized landlords' rights to enter rented premises in certain circumstances.

For details on state rules, including allowable reasons for entry and notice requirements, see "State Laws on Landlord's Access to Rental Property" in Appendix A.

How to Respect Tenants' Privacy Rights

Step 1: Know and comply with your state's law on landlord's access to rental property.

Step 2: Include in your lease or rental agreement a clause that complies with the law and gives you reasonable rights of entry.

Step 3: To avoid uncertainty, highlight your policies on entry in a move-in letter to new tenants and in other periodic communications.

Step 4: Notify tenants when you plan to enter their rental unit.

Step 5: Provide as much notice as possible before you enter, or, at a minimum, the amount of time required by state law.

Step 6: Keep written records of your requests to enter rental units.

Step 7: Protect yourself from a tenant's claim that you, your employee, or an independent contractor is a thief—for example, try to arrange repairs only when the tenant is home.

Step 8: Meet—and possibly mediate—with any tenants who object to your access policies to come up with a mutual agreement regarding your entry.

Step 9: Never force entry, short of a true emergency.

Step 10: Consider terminating the tenancy of any tenant who unreasonably restricts your right to enter the rental unit.

Allowable Reasons for Entry

About half the states have access laws specifying the circumstances under which landlords can legally enter rented premises. Most access laws allow landlords to enter rental units to make repairs, inspect the property, and show the property to prospective tenants or buyers.

In all states, even in the absence of a statute, landlords may enter to deal with a true emergency (see "Entry in Case of Emergency," below) and when the tenant has abandoned the property (left for good).

Notice Requirements

State access laws typically specify the amount of notice required for landlord entry—usually 24 hours or two days (unless it is impracticable to do so—for example, in cases of emergency). A few states simply require the landlord to provide "reasonable" notice, often presumed to be 24 hours.

Must Notice Be in Writing?

Not all states require that notice be in writing, but it's a good idea to give written notice. If the tenant later claims that you didn't follow legal procedures regarding right to entry, your copy of a written notice that you mailed, left in the tenant's mailbox, or posted on the door is proof that you gave notice. It's also wise to document all oral or email requests for entry—but written notice is preferable (as explained in "Using Emails for Notices or Other Communications to Tenants" in Chapter 7). A sample letter requesting entry and a formal Notice of Intent to Enter Dwelling Unit form are included below.

Time of Day You May Enter

Most state access laws either don't address the hours when a landlord may enter or simply allow entry at "reasonable" times, without setting specific hours and days. Weekdays between 9 a.m. and 6 p.m., and Saturday mornings between 10 a.m. and 1 p.m., would likely be considered reasonable hours by a court.

The Best Approach

If your state does not set specific rules regarding landlords' entry, this doesn't mean you can—or should—enter a tenant's home at any time for any reason. Once you rent residential property, you must respect it as your tenant's home. We recommend you:

- provide as much notice as possible (in writing)
- try to arrange a mutually convenient time
- enter only for legitimate business reasons, and
- try to give at least 24 hours' notice.

In some circumstances, less notice (say, ten or 15 hours) might be fine—for example, if you find out Thursday evening that an electrician is available Friday morning to put extra outlets in the tenant's apartment. Except for an emergency, less than four hours' notice is not ordinarily considered reasonable. Common sense suggests that you be considerate of your tenants' privacy and do your best to accommodate their schedules. You'll go a long way toward keeping tenants and avoiding disputes and legal problems by doing so.

Entry in Case of Emergency

In all states, you can enter a rental unit without giving notice to respond to a true emergency. A true emergency is an occurrence that threatens life or property if not corrected immediately.

Here are some examples of emergency situations when it would be legal to enter without giving the tenant notice:

- Smoke is pouring out the tenant's window. You call the fire department and use your master key—or even break in if necessary—to try to deal with the fire.

- A ground-floor tenant reports water coursing down one of his interior walls. It's okay to enter the unit above and find the water leak.
- Your on-site manager hears screams coming from the apartment next door. He knocks on the apartment door, but no one answers. After calling the police, he uses his pass key to enter and see what's wrong.

On the other hand, your urge to repair a problem that's important but doesn't threaten life or property—say, a stopped-up drain that isn't causing damage—isn't a true emergency.

If you do have to enter a tenant's apartment in an emergency, leave a note or call the tenant explaining the circumstances and noting the date and time you entered. Here's an example:

Sample Note to Tenant Regarding Entry in Case of Emergency

September 2, 20xx

Dear Tammy,

Due to your oven being left on, I had to enter your apartment this afternoon around 3 o'clock. Apparently, you left your apartment while bread was still in the oven, and didn't return in time to take it out. Joe, your upstairs neighbor, called me and reported smoke and a strong burning smell coming from your kitchen window, which is below his. I entered your apartment and turned the oven off and removed the bread. Please be more careful next time.

Sincerely,

Herb Layton

Herb Layton

To facilitate your right of entry in an emergency, make sure your lease or rental agreement forbids tenants from rekeying, adding additional locks, or installing a security system without your permission. (See Clause 12 of the form agreements in Chapter 2.)

If you grant permission to change or add locks, insist that your tenant give you duplicate keys. If you allow the tenant to install a security system, get the name and phone number of the alarm company and instructions on how to disarm the system.

> ⓘ **CAUTION**
>
> **Don't change locks.** If your tenant installs a lock without your permission, don't change the lock, even if you immediately give the tenant a key. This invites a lawsuit and false claims that you tried to lock the tenant out or stole the tenant's possessions.

Entry With the Permission of the Tenant

You can always enter rental property, even without notice, if the tenant agrees. If your need to enter is only occasional, you can probably rely on a friendly telephone call to the tenant asking for permission.

> **EXAMPLE:** Because of corrosion problems with the pipes leading to water heaters, you want to inspect all apartments in your building. You call your tenants, explain the situation, and arrange a mutually convenient date and time to inspect the pipes.

When a tenant agrees to let you enter the apartment or rental unit but has been difficult and not always reliable in the past, you might want to cover yourself by documenting the tenant's apparent cooperation. Send a confirmatory thank-you note and keep a copy for yourself. If this note is met with unease or outright hostility, you should send the tenant a formal notice of your intent to enter.

If you have a maintenance problem that needs regular attention—for example, a fussy heater or temperamental plumbing—you might want to work out a detailed agreement with the tenant covering entry.

CAUTION

Don't be too insistent on entry. If you pressure a tenant for permission to enter, perhaps implying or even threatening eviction if the tenant doesn't allow immediate or virtually unrestricted access, you might face a lawsuit for invasion of privacy.

Entry to Make Repairs or Inspect the Property

Many states allow you and your repairperson to enter the tenant's home to make necessary or agreed-upon repairs, alterations, or improvements or to inspect the rental property.

Entry to Make Repairs

If you need to make a repair, you generally must enter only at reasonable times and give the amount of notice required by state law (if no state law, reasonable notice). However, if this is impracticable—for example, a repairperson is available on a few hours' notice—you will probably be on solid ground if you explain the situation to your tenant and then give shorter notice. If your tenant agrees to a shorter notice period, you have no problem.

> **EXAMPLE:** Amy told her landlord Tomas that her bathroom sink was stopped up and draining very slowly. Tomas called the plumber, who said that he had several large jobs in progress but would be able to squeeze in Amy's repair at some point within the next few days. The plumber promised to call Tomas before he came over. Tomas relayed this information to Amy, telling her he would give her as much notice as he could of when the plumber expected to be there. Amy said okay.

How to Give Tenants Notice of Entry

In many situations, the notice period will not be a problem, because your tenant will be delighted that you are making needed repairs and will cooperate with your entry. But if the time is inconvenient for the tenant, try to be accommodating and reschedule a more convenient appointment.

As every experienced landlord knows, though, some tenants are uncooperative when it comes to providing reasonable access to make repairs, while at the same time demanding that repairs be made immediately.

Here's how to avoid claims that you're violating tenants' privacy:

- Meet your state notice requirements; or, if there's no specified amount of notice, provide at least 24 hours' notice.
- Provide written notice whenever possible— either a brief letter or a formal Notice of Intent to Enter Dwelling Unit (see samples below). A downloadable copy of the formal notice is on the Nolo website. See Appendix B for the link to the forms in this book.
- Document oral or email notice by keeping a log of your requests for entry.
- If you can't reach the tenant personally or by phone, and if your intended date of entry makes mailing a letter impractical, try sending a text or email (assuming your lease or rental agreement includes these communication methods as permissible notice methods). It's a good idea to also post a note detailing your plan on the tenant's front door. If, despite all of these efforts, your tenant does not receive notice, you are probably on solid ground to enter and do the repair—you've done all that you reasonably could to comply with the notice requirements.
- Keep a copy of all requests for entry (written and oral) in your tenant's file, along with other communications, such as Resident's Maintenance/Repair Request forms (discussed in Chapter 9).

Notice of Intent to Enter Dwelling Unit

To: _Anna Rivera_
Tenant

123 East Avenue, Apt. #4
Street Address

Rochester, New York 14610
City and State

THIS NOTICE is to inform you that on _____ January 7, 20xx _____ ,

at approximately _____ 1:00 _____ A̶M̶/PM, the landlord, or the landlord's agent, will enter the premises

for the following reason: _____

_____

☑ To make or arrange for the following repairs or improvements:

_____ fix garbage disposal _____

_____

_____

_____

_____ .

☐ To show the premises to:

    ☐ a prospective tenant or purchaser.

    ☐ workers or contractors regarding the above repair or improvement.

☐ Other: _____

_____

_____ .

You are, of course, welcome to be present. If you have any questions or if the date or time is inconvenient, please

notify me promptly by ☐ calling ☒ texting ☐ emailing at _____ 716-555-7899 _____ .
                                                                       Phone Number

Marlene Morgan _____   _January 5, 20xx_
Landlord/Manager   Date

TIP

Let the tenant know if your plans change.
A tenant might be understandably annoyed if you or your repairperson show up late or not at all—for example, if you're supposed to come at 2 p.m. and don't show up until 8 a.m. the next morning. If it isn't possible to come on time, call the tenant and explain the problem, and ask permission to enter later on. If the tenant denies permission, you'll have to give a second notice.

Sample Informal Letter Requesting Entry

January 5, 20xx

Anna Rivera
123 East Avenue, Apartment 4
Rochester, New York 14610

Dear Ms. Rivera:

In response to your complaint regarding the garbage disposal in your apartment, I have arranged to have it repaired tomorrow, on Tuesday, January 6, at 2:00 p.m. I attempted to reach you today (at both your home and work phone numbers) and notify you of this repair appointment. Because I was unable to reach you by phone, I am leaving this note on your door.

Sincerely,

Marlene Morgan
Marlene Morgan

Entry to Inspect

It's an excellent idea to inspect your rental properties at least once or twice a year. That way you can find small problems before they become big ones, and tenants can't claim that they didn't have an opportunity to report complaints to you.

The lease and rental agreements in this book (see Clause 17 in Chapter 2) give you the right to enter a tenant's unit—after giving reasonable notice—to make this kind of regular inspection.

If you don't have an access clause in your lease or rental agreement, state law might give you the right, anyway. Most states with privacy statutes grant landlords the right to inspect rental property. Otherwise, you must determine whether the courts in your state have addressed the issue of landlord inspections.

CAUTION

Don't abuse your right to inspect. Don't use your access right to harass or annoy the tenant. Repeated inspections absent a specific reason, even when proper notice is given, are an invitation to a lawsuit.

How to Avoid Tenant Theft Claims

By planning ahead, you can minimize the chances that you or your repairpersons will be accused of theft. Give plenty of notice of your entry—this gives the tenant the chance to hide valuables. Try to arrange repairs or visit the rental unit only when the tenant is home. If that's not possible, you or your manager should be present. Carefully check references of all repairpeople, and allow only people you trust to enter or remain in the rental without you.

Entry During Tenant's Extended Absence

Several states with access statutes give landlords the legal right to enter the rental unit during a tenant's extended absence, often defined as seven days or more. You are allowed entry to maintain the property as necessary and to inspect for damage and needed repairs. For example, if your rental is in an area with sustained freezing temperatures, it makes sense to check on pipes when the tenant is away for winter vacation.

While many states do not address this issue either by way of statute or court decision, you should be on safe legal ground to enter rental property during a tenant's extended absence, as long as there is a genuine need to protect the property from damage. For example, if the tenant leaves the windows wide open just before a driving rainstorm, you would be justified in entering to close them.

TIP

Require tenants to report extended absences. Your lease or rental agreement should require tenants to inform you when they will be gone for an extended time. Alert tenants of your intent to enter the premises during these times if necessary. See Clause 18 of the form agreements in Chapter 2.

Entry to Show Property to Prospective Tenants or Buyers

Most states with access laws allow landlords to enter rented property to show it to prospective tenants and prospective purchasers. Follow the same notice procedures for entry to make repairs, discussed above. As always, be sure your lease or rental agreement authorizes this type of entry. See Clause 17 of the form agreements in Chapter 2.

You can use the same Notice of Intent to Enter Dwelling Unit as the one used for entry to make repairs.

Showing Property to Prospective New Tenants

If you don't plan to renew a tenant's about-to-expire lease, or have given or received a notice terminating a month-to-month tenancy, you may show the premises to prospective new tenants towards the end of the outgoing tenant's stay. It is not a good idea, however, to show property if the current tenants are under the impression that their lease or rental agreement will be renewed, or if a dispute exists over whether the current tenants have a right to stay. If there's a chance the dispute will end up in court as an eviction lawsuit, the current tenants might be able to hang on for several weeks or even months. Showing the property in this situation only causes unnecessary friction, and is of little value—you won't be able to give new tenants a firm move-in date until the issues are resolved.

The form lease and rental agreements in this book include a clause that might limit your liability if, for reasons beyond your control, you must delay a new tenant's move-in date after you've signed a lease or rental agreement. See Clause 17 in Chapter 2.

Showing Property to Prospective Buyers

You may also show your property—whether apartments in a multiple-unit building, a rented single-family house, or a condominium unit— to potential buyers or mortgage companies. Remember to give tenants the required amount of notice. It's also a good idea to give tenants the name and phone number of the realty company handling the property sale and the name of the agent or broker involved.

Problems usually occur when an overeager real estate salesperson shows up on the tenant's doorstep without warning, or asks to be let in to show the place with little or no notice. In this situation, tenants have the right to say, "We're busy right now—try again in a few days after we've set a time convenient for all of us." Naturally, this type of misunderstanding is not conducive to good landlord-tenant relations, not to mention a sale of the property. Insist that the real estate salespeople you deal with abide by the law and respect your tenants' rights to advance notice.

Putting For Sale or For Rent Signs on the Property

Landlords often put "For Sale" or "For Rent" signs in front of an apartment building or a rented single-family house. Even when the sign says "Don't Disturb Occupants" and you are conscientious about giving notice before showing property, prospective buyers or renters might still disturb tenants with unwelcome inquiries.

To head off conflict, avoid putting a "For Sale" sign on the property. With the advent of online multiple-listing services and video house listings, signs aren't always necessary. Indeed, many real estate agents sell houses and other real estate without ever placing a "For Sale" sign on the property, except when an open house is in progress. If you or your real estate agent must put up a sign advertising sale or rental of the property, make sure it clearly warns against disturbing the occupant and includes a telephone number to call—for example, "Shown by Appointment Only" or "Inquire at 555-1357—Do Not Disturb Occupants Under Any Circumstances." If your real estate agent refuses to accommodate you, find a new one who will respect your tenants' privacy and keep you out of a lawsuit.

Getting the Tenant's Cooperation

Showing a house or an apartment occupied by a tenant isn't easy on anyone. You can make things easier, though, by securing the cooperation of the tenant. One good plan is to meet with the tenant in advance and offer a reasonable rent reduction in exchange for cooperation—for example, two open houses a month and showing the unit on two hour's notice, as long as it doesn't occur more than five times a week. Depending on how much the tenant will be inconvenienced, a 10% to 20% rent reduction might be reasonable.

However, you should make it clear to all that a rent reduction is in force only so long as the tenant continues to go along with it. Technically, any written agreement changing the rent is really an amendment to the rental agreement, and rental agreement clauses under which tenants give up their privacy rights are typically void and unenforceable if it comes to a court fight. This might be one of the few situations when an informal understanding that the rent be lowered so long as the tenant agrees to the frequent showings is better than a written agreement.

Entry After the Tenant Has Moved Out

You may enter the premises at any time after the tenant has completely moved out. It doesn't matter whether the tenant left voluntarily or involuntarily.

In addition, if you believe a tenant has abandoned the property—that is, skipped out without giving any notice or returning the key—you have the right to enter.

Entry by Others

This section describes how to handle situations when other people, such as municipal inspectors, want to enter your rental property.

Health, Safety, or Building Inspections

Even if your state has guidelines for your entry to rental property, the rules are different for entry by state or local health, safety, or building inspectors.

Investigation of a Suspected Violation

If inspectors have a valid reason to suspect that a rental unit violates housing codes or local standards—for example, a credible neighbor has complained about noxious smells coming from the property—they will usually knock on the tenant's door and ask permission to enter. Except in the case of genuine emergency, your tenant has the right to say no.

Inspectors have ways to get around tenant refusals. A logical first step (maybe even before they stop by the rental unit) is to ask you to let them in. Because you can usually enter on 24 hours' notice, this is probably the simplest approach. We recommend that you cooperate with all such requests for entry.

If inspectors can't reach you (or you don't cooperate), they will probably get a search warrant. The inspectors must first convince a judge that the source of their information—perhaps a complaining neighbor—is reliable, and that there is a strong likelihood that public health or safety is at risk.

Inspectors who believe that a tenant will refuse entry often bring along police officers who, armed with a search warrant, can use the full force of the law to overcome the tenant's objections.

Routine Inspections

State or local laws sometimes allow fire, health, and other municipal inspectors to inspect apartment buildings even when there's no suspicion of noncompliance. (Most ordinances exempt single-family homes and condominiums.) Your tenant has the right to refuse entry, at which point the inspector will have to secure a warrant.

A warrant will enable the inspector to enter to check for fire or safety violations. Again, if there is any expectation that your tenant will resist, a police officer will usually accompany the inspector.

An inspector who arrives when the tenant isn't home might ask you to open the door on the spot, in violation of your state's privacy laws. If the inspectors come with a warrant, you can give consent—because of the warrant, even the tenant couldn't legally refuse entry. But if the inspector is there without a warrant, you cannot speak for the tenant and say, "Come on in." Again, the inspectors must show you a warrant before you can let them in.

To find out whether your city has a municipal inspection program, call your city manager's or mayor's office.

Inspection Fees

Many cities impose fees for inspections, on a per unit or building basis or on a sliding scale based on the number of your holdings. Some fees are imposed only when violations are found. If your ordinance imposes fees regardless of violations, you can pass the inspection cost on to the tenant in the form of a rent hike. It's not illegal to do this, and, even in rent-controlled states or cities, the cost of an inspection might justify a rent increase.

If your ordinance imposes a fee only when violations are found, you should not pass the cost on to the tenant if the noncompliance is not the tenant's fault. For example, if inspectors find that you failed to install state-mandated smoke alarms, you should pay for the inspection; but if the tenant has allowed garbage to pile up in violation of city health laws, the tenant should pay the inspector's bill.

Police and Law Enforcement

Even the police may not enter a tenant's rental unit unless they can show you or your tenant a recently issued search or arrest warrant, signed by a judge. Put another way, even though you own the property, you don't have the legal right to give police permission to enter your tenant's home unless you've been shown a warrant. (*Chapman v. United States*, 365 U.S. 610 (1961).)

The police do not need a search warrant, how-ever, if they need to enter to prevent a catastrophe such as an explosion or to intervene in an ongoing crime, to retrieve or preserve evidence of a serious crime, or if they are in hot pursuit of a fleeing criminal.

Also, different rules apply if law enforcement suspects your tenant is engaging in terrorist activity. See "Cooperating With Law Enforcement in Terrorism Investigations," just below.

Cooperating With Law Enforcement in Terrorism Investigations

The USA PATRIOT Act (PL 107-56) authorizes the FBI to obtain "tangible things," including books, records, or other documents, for use in terrorism investigations. The FBI must, however, have an order issued by a U.S. magistrate. You cannot be sued if you cooperate in good faith pursuant to this section. However, you may not disclose to anyone else that the FBI has gathered this information.

Landlords have broad immunity against suits by tenants when they cooperate with law enforcement's antiterrorism efforts. You cannot be sued by tenants if you "[furnish] any information, facilities, or technical assistance in accordance with a court order or request for emergency assistance under this Act." (USA PATRIOT Act, Title II, § 225.) You should ask for a subpoena or warrant before you turn over tenant records or otherwise make your rental property or tenant belongings available to law enforcement.

For more information on terrorism and rental properties, contact the local office of the FBI; a list is at FBI.gov.

Your Right to Let Others In

Unless one of the situations described above applies, you should not give others permission to enter a tenant's home.

Occasionally, you or your resident manager will be faced with a very convincing stranger who will tell a heart-rending story:

- "I'm Nancy's boyfriend, and I need to get my clothes out of her closet now because I'm traveling for work."
- "If I don't get my heart medicine that I left in this apartment, I'll have a medical emergency."
- "I'm John's father, and I just got in from the East coast, my wallet has been stolen, and I have no place to stay."

The problem arises when you can't contact the tenant at work or elsewhere to ask whether it's okay to let the desperate individual in. This is one reason why you should always know how to reach your tenants during the day.

The story the desperate person tells you might be the truth, and maybe your tenant would have no problem with your letting the person in. But you can't know this, and it doesn't make sense to expose yourself to potential liability resulting from having let a clever con artist into your tenant's home. There is always the chance that the person is really a smooth talker whom your tenant has a dozen good reasons to keep out. If you do let a stranger in without your tenant's permission, your tenant could sue you for invasion of privacy and for any losses your tenant suffers as a result.

In short, never let a stranger into your tenant's home without your tenant's permission. If you have been authorized to allow a certain person to enter, you should ask for identification. Although this no-entry-without-authorization policy might be difficult to adhere to in the face of a convincing story, stick to it. You have much more to lose in admitting the wrong person to the tenant's home than you would have to gain from letting in someone who "looks okay."

Other Types of Invasions of Privacy

Unauthorized entry into your tenant's unit is just one form of invasion of privacy. Here are a few other common situations, with advice on how to handle them.

Giving Information About the Tenant to Strangers

As a landlord, you might be asked by strangers, including creditors, banks, employers, and prospective landlords, to provide information about your tenants. Did they pay the rent on time?

Did they maintain the rental property? Cause any problems?

Basically, you have a legal right to give out truthful, normal business information about your tenant to people and businesses who ask and have a legitimate reason to know—for example, a bank processing a tenant's loan application or a prospective landlord who wants a reference. First, get assurance that the caller is legit (you can always check first with the tenant). Give only relevant information, in response to the caller's appropriate questions. Resist your natural urge to be helpful, unless the tenant has given you written permission to release information. (We discuss release forms in Chapter 1.) You have nothing to gain, and possibly a lot to lose, if you give out information that your tenant feels constitutes a serious violation of privacy.

And if you give out incorrect information—even if you believe it to be accurate—you can get in a legal mess if the person to whom you disclose it relies on it to take some action that negatively affects your tenant. For example, if you tell others that a tenant has filed for bankruptcy (and this isn't true), the tenant has grounds to sue you for defamation (libel or slander) if he is damaged as a result—for example, if he doesn't get a job.

Some landlords feel that they should communicate information to prospective landlords, especially if the tenant failed to pay rent or maintain the premises or created other serious problems. If you give out this information, be absolutely factual and don't provide more information than requested. If you go out of your way to give out negative information— for example, you try to blackball the tenant with other landlords in your area—you definitely risk legal liability for defamation.

Posting Information About Tenants Online

Online sites such as Yelp enable consumers to post reviews of everything from restaurants to car repair shops to doctors. Naturally, reviews of residential rentals are right up there in popularity, and many landlords squirm when encountering reviews of their buildings and management practices. It wasn't long before landlords created their own online outlets, using public and free sites designed to warn other property owners about problem tenants.

We urge you to think twice before posting information to one of these sites. A California court ruled that such Internet postings are not immune from libel suits, and that if the posting contains demonstrably false statements, the poster could end up liable for damages. (*Bently Reserve L.P. v. Papaliolios*, 218 Cal.App. 4th 418 (2013).) The same reasoning would apply to negative remarks about a tenant posted by a landlord. While you might ultimately prevail in a suit brought by a tenant you've reviewed, the battle is a headache you don't need.

CAUTION

Beware of gossipy managers. On-site managers who gossip about tenants can create serious problems. Gossip about tenants—such as casual remarks about who pays rent late, has overnight visitors, or stumbles home drunk—might seem innocent but can be an invasion of privacy. As the landlord, you are liable for your manager's actions. Impress on your managers their duty to be professional and not discuss tenants' personal matters— no matter how trivial the topic.

Calling or Visiting Tenants at Work

Should you need to call your tenants at work (say, to schedule a time to make repairs), try to be sensitive to whether they can receive personal calls. While some people have bosses who don't get upset about occasional personal calls, others have jobs that are greatly disrupted by any phone call.

Under no circumstances should you continue to call a tenant at work who asks you not to do so. This is especially true when calling about late rent payments or other problems.

Never leave specific messages with your tenant's employer, especially those that put the tenant in a negative light. A landlord who leaves a message like "Tell your employee I'll evict her if she doesn't pay the rent" can expect at least a lot of bad feeling on the part of the tenant and, at worst, a lawsuit, especially if your conduct results in the tenant's losing a job or a promotion.

No matter what you think of your tenant, you should respect the sensitive nature of the tenant's employment relationship. Don't visit your tenant at work—say, to collect late rent—unless you're invited or there's a very compelling reason to do so. Such a reason might be an emergency or you haven't been able to reach the tenant at home after repeated attempts (perhaps to serve eviction papers or notice of a rent increase).

Undue Restrictions on Guests

A few landlords, overly concerned about tenants moving new occupants into the property, go overboard in keeping tabs on the tenants' legitimate guests who stay overnight or for a few days. Often their leases, rental agreements, or rules and regulations require a tenant to "register" any overnight guest.

Clause 3 of the form agreements (Chapter 2) limits guests' visits to no more than ten days in any six-month period, to avoid having a guest turn into an illegal subtenant. While you should be concerned about guests becoming permanent unauthorized residents, it is overkill to require a tenant to inform you of a short-term guest. Keep in mind that although you manage your tenant's home, you don't have the right to restrict the tenant's social life or pass judgment on the propriety of overnight guests.

You could be held liable if you or your manager attempt to inappropriately control or regulate your tenants' lives.

> ### Send Only Business-Related Emails, Texts, and Faxes to Residents
>
> Many state and federal laws prohibit the sending of unsolicited emails, texts, and faxes. For the most part, if you have an established business relationship with someone (such as a landlord-tenant relationship), you may email, text, or fax them with relevant information. For example, you may send current, prospective, and prior tenants information that relates to some aspect of the tenancy. You may also contact vendors and suppliers to address contracts or business dealings. However, many laws require you to include a way for the recipient to opt out of communications, as well as a clear description of how the recipient can contact you.
>
> The legal "dos and don'ts" of communications can be confusing. To avoid headaches, it's probably best play it safe: Don't send emails, texts, or faxes that are unrelated to your business. For example, resist the temptation to invite residents by fax to participate in your son's baseball team fundraiser. Also, don't send commercial or advertising materials to anyone unless they've specifically opted in to your communications.
>
> If electronic marketing is an essential part of your business plan, consider consulting with an attorney to discuss how to make sure you're complying with anti-spam and antisolicitation laws.

Spying on a Tenant

As a result of worrying too much about a tenant's visitors, a few landlords have attempted to interrogate tenants' visitors, knock on tenants' doors to see who answers, or even peek through windows. This sort of conduct (aside from being creepy) can result in a court's assessing you punitive damages in an invasion of privacy lawsuit. As far as talking to tenants' guests is concerned, keep your conversations to pleasant hellos or nonthreatening small talk.

Watch Out for Drug Dealing on Your Property

It's crucial that you keep a careful eye on your tenants if you suspect they're engaging in drug dealing or other illegal behavior. Landlords have a responsibility to keep their properties safe—that includes keeping dealers out by carefully screening prospective tenants (see Chapter 1) and kicking them out pronto when they are discovered. Landlords who allow drug dealing on their properties might find themselves as defendants in costly lawsuits brought by neighbors or even government agencies. Chapter 12 discusses your liability for drug-dealing tenants and gives tips on how to balance your duty to maintain safe premises with your tenants' legitimate expectations of privacy.

"Self-Help" Evictions

It is illegal for you to come on the rental property and do such things as remove windows and doors, turn off the utilities, or change the locks. For details, see "Illegal 'Self-Help' Evictions" in Chapter 17.

What to Do When Tenants Unreasonably Deny Entry

Even when you give a generous amount of notice and have a legitimate reason, tenants sometimes just won't let you in. If a tenant repeatedly and unreasonably refuses to allow you or your employees to enter, you can probably legally enter anyway, provided you do so in a peaceful manner.

Never push or force your way in—being confrontational increases the chance that something will go wrong, and expose you or your employees to legal liability or even bodily harm. For practical reasons, don't enter alone. If you really need entry and the tenant isn't home, bring someone along who can act as a witness in case the tenants later claim property is missing or damaged.

Another problem landlords face is that some tenants change their locks without permission. In most situations, doing so is against state law, because it restricts your right of access in a true emergency or when you have given proper notice. Your lease or rental agreement should require tenants to obtain your written permission to change locks, and provide you with a working copy of the key to the new locks. You'll also want to require tenants to obtain your written permission to install any burglar alarms or security systems, and give you detailed instructions on how to operate and disarm them. See Clause 12, Chapter 2.

If you have a serious conflict over access with an otherwise satisfactory tenant, a sensible first step is to meet with the tenant to see if the problem can be resolved. If you come to an understanding, follow up with a note to confirm your agreement. Here's an example:

Sample Note Confirming Agreement Regarding Entry

January 5, 20xx

Dear Anna,

This will confirm our conversation of January 5, 20xx regarding access to your apartment at 123 East Avenue, Apt. 4, for the purpose of making repairs. The management will give you 24 hours' advance written notice, and will enter only during business hours or weekdays. The person inspecting will knock first, then enter with a pass key if no one answers.

Thank you,

Marlene Morgan

If this doesn't work, consider mediation by a neutral third party. It's an especially good way to resolve disputes when you want the tenant to stay.

If attempts at compromise fail, you can terminate the tenancy. Unless your tenant has a long-term lease, you can give the tenant the notice required by law and terminate the tenancy, rather than put up with a problem tenant.

And, in every state, you can usually evict the tenant, including those with long-term leases, for violating a term of the lease or rental agreement. To do this, you must comply with your state law as to reasons for entry and notice periods. And your lease or rental agreement must contain an appropriate right-of-entry provision. The cause justifying eviction is the tenant's breach of that provision (see Clause 17 in the form lease and rental agreements, Chapter 2). Keep copies of any correspondence and notes of your conversations with the tenant.

If a lawsuit seems inevitable, you might need to consult a lawyer or do some legal research on your state's eviction laws. If you end up in court, be prepared to prove your attempts at entry were legal—as to purpose and amount of notice required. A good record-keeping system is crucial.

Tenants' Remedies If a Landlord Acts Illegally

Conscientious landlords should be receptive to tenants' complaints that their privacy is being violated, and attempt to work out an acceptable solution. If you violate a tenant's right to privacy and you can't work out a compromise, the tenant might bring a lawsuit and ask for money damages. You could be held liable for your property manager's disrespect of the tenant's right of privacy, even if you never knew about the manager's conduct. A tenant who can show a repeated pattern of illegal activity, or even one clear example of outrageous conduct, might be able to get a substantial recovery.

In most states, it's easy for tenants to pursue lawsuits in small claims court without a lawyer. For details on small claims court procedures and the maximum amount for which someone can sue, see Chapter 16.

Depending on the circumstances, tenants might be able sue you for:

- **Trespass:** entry without consent or proper authority
- **Invasion of privacy:** interfering with their right to be left alone
- **Breach of the implied covenant of quiet enjoyment:** interfering with their right to undisturbed use of the rental, or
- **Infliction of emotional distress:** acts that you intend to cause serious emotional consequences to the tenant.

These types of lawsuits are beyond the scope of this book and require expert legal advice.

Finally, repeated abuses by a landlord of tenants' right of privacy might legally entitle the tenants to break a lease by moving out, without liability for further rent.

Ending a Tenancy

 FORMS IN THIS CHAPTER
Chapter 14 includes instructions for and samples of the following forms:
• Amendment to Lease or Rental Agreement
• Tenant's Notice of Intent to Move Out
• Indemnification of Landlord
The purchase of this book includes free downloadable and customizable copies of all of these forms. See Appendix B for the download link and instructions.

Most tenancies end because the tenant leaves voluntarily. Some tenants give proper legal notice and leave at the end of a lease term; others aren't so thoughtful and give inadequate notice, break the lease for a trumped-up reason, or just move out in the middle of the night. And, of course, some tenants fail to live up to their obligations for reasons they can't control—for example, when a tenant dies during the tenancy.

As a landlord, you should understand the important legal issues that arise at the end of a tenancy, including:

- the type of notice a landlord or tenant must provide to end a month-to-month tenancy
- your legal options if a tenant doesn't leave after receiving (or giving) a termination notice or after the lease has expired
- what happens when a tenant leaves without giving required notice, and
- the effect of a condominium conversion on a tenant's lease.

This chapter starts with a brief discussion of a related topic—how to legally change a lease or rental agreement during a tenancy.

 RELATED TOPIC
Related topics covered in this book include:
- How to advertise and rent property before a current tenant leaves: Chapter 1
- Writing clear lease and rental agreement provisions on notice required to end a tenancy: Chapter 2
- Raising the rent: Chapter 3
- Highlighting notice requirements in a move-in letter to the tenant: Chapter 7
- Handling tenant requests to sublet or assign the lease, and what to do when one cotenant leaves: Chapter 8
- Tenant's right to move out if the rental unit is damaged or destroyed: Chapter 9
- Preparing a move-out letter and returning security deposits when a tenant leaves, and how to deal with any abandoned property: Chapter 15
- How and when to prepare a warning letter before terminating a tenancy: Chapter 16

- Terminating a tenancy when a tenant fails to leave after receiving a 30-day notice or violates the lease or rental agreement—for example, by not paying rent: Chapter 17
- State Rules on Notice Required to Change or End a Tenancy: Appendix A.

Changing Lease or Rental Agreement Terms

Once you sign a lease or rental agreement, you've created a legal contract between you and your tenant.

If you use a lease, you cannot unilaterally change the terms of the tenancy for the length of the lease. For example, you can't raise the rent unless the lease allows it or the tenant agrees.

If the tenant agrees to changes, however, you can make the changes in the same manner described below for changes to month-to-month agreements. All changes should be in writing and signed by each of you.

Amending a Month-to-Month Rental Agreement

You don't need a tenant's consent to change something in a month-to-month rental agreement. Legally, you need only send the tenant a notice of the change. The most common reason landlords amend a rental agreement is to increase the rent.

To change a month-to-month tenancy, most states require 30 days' notice, subject to any local rent control ordinances (see "State Rules on Notice Required to Change or Terminate a Month-to-Month Tenancy" in Appendix A for a list of each state's notice requirements). You'll need to consult your state statutes for the specific requirements for delivering the notice to the tenant. Most states allow you to deliver the notice by first-class mail.

TIP

Contact the tenant and explain the changes. It makes good personal and business sense for you or your manager to notify tenants personally about a rent increase or other changes before you send them a written notice. That way, you'll be able to give a bit of explanation for the changes and address any concerns.

You usually don't need to redo the entire rental agreement in order to make a change or two. It's just as legal and effective to attach a copy of the notice making the change to the rental agreement. However, in some situations you might want the change to appear on the written rental agreement itself.

If the change is small and simply alters part of an existing clause—such as increasing the rent or making the rent payable every 14 days instead of every 30 days—you can cross out the old language in the rental agreement, write in the new, and sign in the margin next to the new words. Make sure the tenant also signs next to the change. Add the date, in case there is a dispute later as to when the change became effective.

> **EXAMPLE:** On February 1, Sam gave his tenant notice that the rent will increase to $2,000 as of May 1. Sam gave the correct amount of notice, which was 30 days. Next to the rent clause in the original rental agreement, Sam wrote "As of May 1, 20XX, the rent will be $2,000." Sam and the tenant sign in the margin of the original agreement on March 3, and add the date they signed.

If the changes are lengthy, you can either add an amendment page to the original document or prepare a new rental agreement, as discussed below. If you use an amendment, it should refer clearly to the agreement it's changing and be signed by the same people who signed the original agreement. A sample Amendment to Lease or Rental Agreement form is shown below and the Nolo website includes a downloadable copy. See Appendix B for the download link.

Preparing a New Rental Agreement

If you want to add a new clause or make several changes to your rental agreement, it's best to substitute a whole new agreement for the old one. This is simple if you use the lease or rental agreement shown in this book (Chapter 2) and included on this book's companion page on Nolo's website. If you prepare an entirely new agreement, be sure that you write "Canceled by mutual consent, effective _(date)_" on the old one, and each of you should sign it. All tenants (and any cosigner or guarantors) should sign the new agreement.

The new agreement should take effect on the date that you cancel the old one.

To avoid problems, be sure there is no time overlap between the old and new agreements, and do not allow a gap between the cancellation date of the old agreement and the effective date of the new one.

TIP

A new tenant should mean a new agreement. Even when a new tenant is filling out the rest of a former tenant's lease term under the same conditions, you'll need to prepare a new agreement in the new tenant's name. See Chapter 8 for details on signing a new agreement when a new tenant moves in.

How Month-to-Month Tenancies End

This section discusses how you or the tenant can end a month-to-month tenancy.

Giving Notice to the Tenant

You can end a month-to-month tenancy simply by giving the proper amount of notice. No reasons are required in most states. Cities and states with rent control (such as Oregon, California, New Hampshire, and New Jersey) are exceptions, because landlords in these cities and states must

Amendment to Lease or Rental Agreement

This is an Amendment to the lease or rental agreement dated _____March 1, 20xx_____ ("Agreement")

between _____Olivia Matthew_____ ("Landlord")

and _____Steve Phillips_____ ("Tenant")

regarding property located at _____1578 Maple St., Seattle, WA_____ ("Premises").

Landlord and Tenant agree to the following changes and/or additions to the Agreement:

1. Beginning on June 1, 20xx, Tenant shall rent a one-car garage, adjacent to the Premises, from Landlord for the sum of $75 per month.

2. Tenant may keep one German shepherd dog on the Premises. The dog shall be kept in the backyard and not in the side yard. Tenant shall clean up all animal waste from the yard on a daily basis. Tenant agrees to repair any damages to the yard or Premises caused by his dog, at Tenant's expense.

_Olivia Matthew_____   _May 20, 20xx_____

Landlord/Manager   Date

_Steve Phillips_____   _May 20, 20xx_____

Tenant   Date

_____   _____

Tenant   Date

_____   _____

Tenant   Date

have a just or legally recognized reason to end a tenancy. All you need to do is give the tenant a written notice, allowing the tenant the minimum number of days required by state law (typically 30) to move, and stating the date on which the tenancy will end (see "State Rules on Notice Required to Change or Terminate a Month-to-Month Tenancy" in Appendix A). After that date, the tenant no longer has the legal right to occupy the premises.

In most states, a landlord who wants to terminate a month-to-month tenancy must provide the same amount of notice as a tenant—typically 30 days. But this is not true everywhere. For example, in Georgia, landlords must give 60 days' notice to terminate a month-to-month tenancy, while tenants need only give 30 days' notice. (Ga. Code Ann. § 44-7-7.)

State and local rent control laws can also impose notice requirements on landlords. Things are different if you want tenants to move because they have violated a term of the rental agreement—for example, by failing to pay rent. If so, notice requirements are commonly greatly shortened, sometimes to as little as three days.

All states (and even some cities) have their own rules and procedures for preparing and serving termination notices. For example, some states specify that the notice be printed in a certain size or style of typeface. If you don't follow these procedures, the notice terminating the tenancy might be invalid. It is impossible for this book to provide specific forms and instructions for every rental situation. Consult a landlords' association or local rent control board and your state statutes for more information and sample forms (Chapter 18 shows how to do your own legal research). Your state consumer protection agency might also have useful advice. Once you understand how much notice you must give, how the notice must be delivered, and any other requirements, you'll be in good shape to handle this work yourself—usually with no lawyer needed.

RESOURCE

California resource for terminating tenancies. If you are a California landlord, see *The California Landlord's Law Book: Evictions*, by Nils Rosenquest. It covers rules and procedures and contains forms for serving termination notices in California. This book is available at bookstores and public libraries. You can also order it directly from Nolo's website (Nolo.com), or by phone (800-728-3555).

Must Tenants Give Notice on the First of the Month?

In most states, tenants can give notice at any time—in other words, they don't have to give notice so that the tenancy will end on the last day of the month or the rental cycle. For example, a tenant who pays rent on the first of the month, but gives notice on the tenth, will be obliged to pay for ten days' rent for the next month, even if the tenant moves out earlier.

Some landlords insist that tenants give notice only on the day rent is due, possibly to avoid having to prorate the rent as described above. But a rule like this might violate your state's law on the proper use of security deposits. Here's how: Suppose a tenant pays rent on the first, but gives you his 30-day notice on the tenth, because he intends to move out on the tenth day of the following month. If you stick to your rule, you'll expect him to pay for an additional 20 days (the balance of the next month), and if he doesn't, you'll probably use the security deposit to cover that debt. But that might not be a proper use of the deposit in your state, especially if your statute does not allow you or the tenant to modify the conditions under which the landlord can retain the deposit. If the rule applies to tenants only (that is, *you* remain free to deliver a 30-day notice at any time, and the 30 days begins as of the day of delivery), the chances that your rule will hold up will be even slimmer.

As convenient as it might be to deal with tenant turnover on the day rent is due and avoid having to prorate rent (and though the prospect of requiring that rent be paid over an extended period is attractive), we urge you to accept notice at any time during the rent term.

How Much Notice the Tenant Must Give You

In most states, tenants who wish to move out must give you at least 30 days' notice. Some states allow less than 30 days' notice in certain situations—for example, when a tenant must leave early because of military orders. And, in some states, tenants who pay rent more frequently than once a month can give notice to terminate that matches their rent payment interval—for example, tenants who pay rent every two weeks would have to give 14 days' notice. If your tenant joins the military and wants to terminate a rental agreement, federal law specifies the maximum amount of notice you may require (but if state law requires less notice, you must follow state rules). See "Special Rules for Tenants Who Enter Military Service," below.

To educate your tenants about what to expect, your rental agreement should include your state's notice requirements for ending a tenancy (see Clause 4 of the form agreements in Chapter 2). It is also wise to list termination notice requirements in the move-in letter you send to new tenants.

Restrictions on Ending Tenancies

The general rules for terminating a tenancy described in this chapter don't apply in all situations:

- **Rent control ordinances.** Many rent control cities and states require "just cause" (a good reason) to end a tenancy, such as moving in a close relative. You will likely have to state your reason in the termination notice you give the tenant.
- **Discrimination.** It is illegal to end a tenancy because of a tenant's race, religion, or other reason constituting illegal discrimination.
- **Retaliation.** You cannot legally terminate a tenancy to retaliate against a tenant for exercising any right under the law, such as the tenant's right to complain to governmental authorities about defective housing conditions.

For details on your state's rules, see "State Rules on Notice Required to Change or Terminate a Month-to-Month Tenancy" in Appendix A.

Insist on a Tenant's Written Notice of Intent to Move

In many states, a tenant's notice must be in writing and give the exact date the tenant plans to move out. Even when it's not required by law, you should insist that the tenant give you notice in writing (as does Clause 4 of the form agreements in Chapter 2).

Insisting on written notice will prove useful should the tenant not move as planned after you have signed a lease or rental agreement with a new tenant. The new tenant might sue you to recover the costs of temporary housing or storage fees because you could not deliver possession. In turn, you will want to sue the old (holdover) tenant for causing the problem by failing to move out. You will have a much stronger case against the holdover tenant if you can produce a written promise to move on a specific date instead of your version of a conversation (which will undoubtedly be disputed by the tenant).

A sample Tenant's Notice of Intent to Move Out form is shown below and the Nolo website includes a downloadable copy (see Appendix B for the download link). Give a copy of this form to all tenants who tell you they plan to move, and tell them that the termination date will be the one they enter on the form, not necessarily the date they told you of in a conversation.

Accepting Rent After a 30-Day Notice

If you accept rent for any period beyond the date the tenants told you they are moving out, this cancels the termination notice and creates a new month-to-month tenancy. To start the termination process again, you must give the tenant another 30-day notice.

Tenant's Notice of Intent to Move Out

April 3, 20xx
Date

Anne Sakamoto
Landlord

888 Mill Avenue
Street Address

Nashville, Tennessee 37126
City and State

Dear ___Ms. Sakamoto___,
               Landlord

This is to notify you that the undersigned tenants, ___Patti and Joe Ellis___

_____ , will be moving from

___999 Brook Lane, Apartment Number 11, Nashville, Tenn.___ ,

on ___May 3, 20xx___ , ___30 days___ from today.

This provides at least ___30 days'___ written notice as required in our rental agreement.

Sincerely,

Patti Ellis
Tenant

Joe Ellis
Tenant

_____
Tenant

EXAMPLE: On April 15, George sends his landlord Yuri a 30-day notice of his intent to move out. A few weeks later, however, George changes his mind and decides to stay. He simply pays the usual $800 monthly rent on May 1. Without thinking, Yuri cashes the $800 check. Even though she's already rerented to a new tenant who plans to move in on May 16th, Yuri is powerless to evict George unless she first gives him a legal (usually 30-day) notice to move. Unless the lease Yuri signed with the new tenant limits her liability, she will be liable to the new tenant for failing to put her in possession of the property as promised.

Sample Letter Extending Tenant's Move-Out Date

Hannah Lewis
777 Broadway Terrace, Apartment #3
Richmond, Virginia 23233

Dear Hannah:

On June 1, you gave me a 30-day notice of your intent to move out on July 1. You have since requested to extend your move-out to July 18 because of last-minute problems with closing escrow on your new house. This letter is to verify our understanding that you will move out on July 18, instead of July 1, and that you will pay prorated rent for 18 days (July 1 through July 18). Prorated rent for 18 days, based on your monthly rent of $900 or $30 per day, is $540.

Please sign below to indicate your agreement to these terms.

Sincerely,

Fran Moore

Fran Moore, Landlord

Agreed to by Hannah Lewis, Tenant:
Signature *Hannah Lewis*
Date *June 20, 20xx*

CAUTION

If you collected "last month's rent" when the tenant moved in, do not accept rent for the last month of the tenancy. You are legally obligated to use this money for the last month's rent. Accepting an additional month's rent might extend the tenancy.

If the tenants ask for more time, but you don't want to continue the tenancy as before, you might want to give the tenants a few days or weeks more, and prorate the rent. Prepare a written agreement to that effect and have the tenants sign it. See the sample letter extending the tenant's move-out date.

When the Tenant Doesn't Give the Required Notice

All too often, tenants will send or give you a "too short" notice of intent to move. And it's not unheard of for tenants to move out with no notice or with a wave as they hand you the keys.

Tenants who leave without giving enough notice have lost the right to occupy the premises, but are still obligated to pay rent through the end of the required notice period. For example, if the notice period is 30 days, but a tenant moves out after telling you 20 days ago that he intended to move, he still owes you for the remaining ten days.

In most states, you have a legal duty to try to rerent the property before you can charge the tenants for giving you too little notice, but few courts expect a landlord to accomplish this in less than a month. This rule, called the landlord's duty to mitigate damages, is discussed in "If the Tenant Breaks the Lease," below.

When You or Your Tenant Violates the Rental Agreement

If you seriously violate the rental agreement and fail to fulfill your legal responsibilities—for example, by not correcting serious health or safety

Special Rules for Tenants Who Enter Military Service

Tenants who enter active military service after signing a lease or rental agreement have a federally legislated right to get out of their rental obligations. (War and National Defense Servicemembers Civil Relief Act, 50 U.S.C. §§ 3901 and following.) The Servicemembers Act protects tenants who are part of the "uniformed services," which includes the armed forces, commissioned corps of the National Oceanic and Atmospheric Administration (NOAA), commissioned corps of the Public Health Service, and the activated National Guard.

Tenants must mail written notice of their intent to terminate their tenancy for military reasons to the landlord or manager. The notice terminates the tenancy of the servicemember and any dependents listed on the lease or rental agreement.

The term "dependent" is defined more broadly than under the U.S. tax code (as explained in Table 5, "Overview of the Rules for Claiming an Exemption for a Dependent," in IRS Publication 501, *Exemptions, Standard Deduction, and Filing Information*). A dependent for purposes of the Servicemembers Act includes a child, spouse, or anyone whom the servicemember has supported within the preceding 180 days, by paying for more than half that person's living expenses. (50 U.S.C.A. § 3911(4).)

Rental agreements. Once the notice is mailed or delivered, the tenancy will terminate 30 days after the next rent due date. For example, if rent is due on the first of June and the tenant mails a notice on May 28, the tenancy will terminate on July 1. This rule takes precedence over any longer notice periods that might be specified in your rental agreement or by state law. If state law or your agreement provides for shorter notice periods, however, the shorter notice will control. Recently, many states have passed laws that offer the same or greater protections to members of the state militia or National Guard.

Leases. A tenant who enters military service after signing a lease may terminate the lease by following the procedure for rental agreements, above. For example, suppose a tenant signs a one-year lease in April, agreeing to pay rent on the first of the month. The tenant enlists October 10 and mails you a termination notice on October 11. In this case, you must terminate the tenancy on December 1, 30 days after the first time that rent is due (November 1) following the mailing of the notice. This tenant will have no continuing obligation for rent past December 1, even though this is several months before the lease expires.

problems—tenants might be able to legally move out with no written notice or by giving less notice than is otherwise required. Called a "constructive eviction," this doctrine typically applies only when living conditions are intolerable—for example, when a tenant has had no heat for an extended period in the winter, or when a tenant's use and enjoyment of the property has been substantially impaired because of drug dealing in the building.

What exactly constitutes a constructive eviction varies slightly under the laws of different states.

Generally, if a rental unit has serious habitability problems for anything but a very short time, tenants might be entitled to move out without giving notice.

Along the same lines, landlords may terminate on short notice (and evict the tenants, if necessary) when tenants violate a lease or rental agreement—for example, by failing to pay rent or seriously damaging the property. Chapter 17 explains the situations in which landlords can quickly terminate for tenant misbehavior, and gives an overview of evictions.

How Leases End

As a general rule, neither you nor the tenant may unilaterally terminate a lease, unless the other party has violated the terms of the lease.

If you and the tenant both live up to your promises, the lease simply ends of its own accord at the end of the lease term. At this point, the tenant must either:

- move
- sign a new lease (with the same or different terms), or
- stay on as a month-to-month tenant with your approval.

As every landlord knows, however, life is not always so simple. Sooner or later, a tenant will stay beyond the end of the term or leave before it without any legal right to do so.

Giving Notice to the Tenant

Even though a lease clearly states when it will expire, it's a good practice to remind tenants about an approaching expiration date. And some states or cities (especially those with rent control) actually require reasonable notice before the lease expiration date if you want the tenant to leave.

Giving tenants at least 60 days' written notice before the lease expires has several advantages:

- **Getting the tenants out on time.** Two months' notice allows plenty of time for tenants to look for another place if they don't—or you don't—want to renew the lease.
- **Giving you time to renegotiate the lease.** If you would like to continue renting to your present tenants, but also want to change some lease terms or increase the rent, your notice reminds the tenants that the terms of the old lease will not automatically continue. Encourage the tenants to stay, but mention that you need to make some changes to the lease.
- **Getting new tenants in quickly.** If you know tenants are planning to move out at the end of the lease term, you can show the unit to prospective tenants ahead of time and minimize the time the space is vacant.

RENT CONTROL

Your options might be limited in a rent control area. If your property is subject to rent control, you might be required to renew a tenant's lease unless there is a legally approved reason (just cause) not to. Reasons such as your tenant's failure to pay rent or your desire to move in a close relative commonly justify nonrenewal. If you do not have a reason for nonrenewal that qualifies as just cause, you might be stuck with a perpetual month-to-month tenant. Check your state's or city's rent control rules carefully.

When the Tenant Continues to Pay Rent After the Lease Expires

It's fairly common for landlords and tenants to forget (or ignore) that a lease has expired. The tenants keep paying the rent, and the landlord keeps cashing the checks. By accepting rent, you've either created a month-to-month tenancy or automatically renewed the lease.

A new month-to-month tenancy. In most states, by accepting rent after the expiration, you create a new, oral, month-to-month tenancy on the terms that appeared in the old lease. In other words, you'll be bound by the terms and rent in the old lease for at least the first 30 days. If you want to change the terms or sign a new lease, you must abide by the law regarding giving notice for a month-to-month tenancy.

EXAMPLE 1: Zev had a one-year lease and paid rent on the first of every month. When the lease expired, Zev stayed on and his landlord, Maria, accepted another month's rent check from him. Under the laws of their state, this made Zev a month-to-month tenant, subject to the terms and conditions in his now-expired lease.

Maria wanted to institute a "no pets" rule and to raise the rent. But since Zev was now a month-to-month tenant, she had to give him 30 days' notice (as required by her state's law) to change the terms of the tenancy. She lost a full month of the higher rent while she complied with the 30-day requirement.

EXAMPLE 2: Learning from her experience with Zev, Maria gave her tenant Alice a 60-day notice before Alice's lease expired. In that notice, Maria also told Alice about the new "no pets" rule and the rent increase. Alice, who wanted to get a cat, decided to move when the lease expired. Meanwhile, Maria was able to show Alice's apartment to prospective tenants and chose one who moved in—and started paying the higher rent—shortly after Alice's lease expired.

If you present the tenants with a new lease and they decide not to sign it, they can stay on as month-to-month tenants. The terms of the old lease will apply until you give them proper written notice to move on.

Automatic lease renewal. In a few states, when the lease expires and you continue to accept rent, the law states that you and the tenant have entered into a new lease for the same length and with the same terms as the old lease. In other words, you have automatically renewed the lease.

Retaliation and Other Illegal Tenancy Terminations

Just as you can't engage in illegal discrimination when you rent a unit, you can't unlawfully discriminate when it comes to terminating a month-to-month tenancy or deciding not to renew a lease—for example, by deciding not to continue to rent to persons of a certain ethnicity because of your political beliefs.

The second major landlord "no-no" when it comes to tenancy nonrenewals is retaliation. In most states, you may not end a tenancy in retaliation for engaging in legally protected actions, such as complaining to a building inspector that a rental unit is uninhabitable. If you do, and try to evict the tenants when they don't leave, the tenants can defend themselves by proving retaliation. Chapter 16 discusses laws prohibiting retaliation.

To avoid problems of tenants staying longer than you want, remind tenants in advance about their approaching lease expiration date, and don't accept rent after this date. If a tenant just wants to stay a few days after a lease expires, and you agree, it is wise to put your arrangement in a letter. See the sample letter extending the tenant's move-out date above.

When a Lease Ends and You Want the Tenant Out

Once the lease expires, you don't have to keep renting to the tenants (unless rent control laws state otherwise). If the tenants remain after the lease ends, and offer rent that you *do not accept*, they become "holdover" tenants. In some states, you must still give notice, telling the tenants to leave within a few days; if the tenants don't leave at the end of this period, you can start an eviction lawsuit. A few states allow landlords to file for eviction immediately, as soon as the lease expires.

CAUTION

Avoid lease and rental agreement clauses that make holdover tenants pay a higher rent. Some landlords attempt to discourage tenants from staying past the end of their tenancy by making the tenants agree, in advance, to pay as much as three times the rent if they do. Clauses like this might not be legal—they are a form of "liquidated damages" (damages that are set in advance, without regard to the actual harm suffered by the landlord), which are illegal in residential rentals in many states. (However, they have been upheld in Texas.) The clause would probably not hold up in an area subject to rent control, nor would it survive a challenge if the clause describes the rent hike as a "penalty."

Evicting Tenants in Properties Purchased Following Foreclosure

The federal "Protecting Tenants at Foreclosure Act of 2009" (PTFA) provides that when a "federally related" mortgage loan (almost every loan) is foreclosed upon and the bank or mortgage holder buys at the sale and takes over as owner, most residential leases will survive—meaning the tenants can stay until the end of the lease. Under the PTFA, month-to-month tenants (with some important qualifications) are also entitled to 90 days' notice before having to move out. State and local laws might offer greater tenant protections.

For details about PTFA, as well as information on state and local protections for tenants in property purchased at foreclosure, check the website of the National Housing Law Project (NHLP.org).

When the Tenant Breaks the Lease

Tenants who leave before a lease expires and who refuse to pay the remainder of the rent due under the lease are said to have "broken the lease."

Once the tenants leave for good, you have the legal right to retake possession of the premises and rerent to another tenant. A key question that arises, though, is how much do tenants owe if they leave before the lease is up?

The general rule is that tenants who sign a lease agree at the outset to pay a fixed amount of rent: the monthly rent multiplied by the number of months of the lease. The tenants pay this amount in monthly installments over the term of the lease. In short, when they sign a lease, tenants agree to pay all rent for the entire lease term. The fact that the tenants pay rent monthly doesn't change their responsibility to pay rent for the entire lease term (but see the exceptions explained below in "When Breaking a Lease Is Justified).

Depending on the situation, you can use the tenants' security deposit to cover part of the shortfall, or sue the tenants for the rent owed.

Is the Tenant Really Gone?

Sometimes, it's hard to tell whether a tenant has left permanently. People sometimes disappear for weeks at a time, for a vacation or family emergency. And, even tenants who don't intend to come back might leave behind enough discarded clothing or furniture to make their intent unclear.

Often, your first hint that a tenant has abandoned the premises will be the fact that you haven't received the rent. Or you might simply walk by a window and notice the lack of furniture, or learn from neighbors that the tenant hasn't been seen for a long time. Ordinarily, the mere appearance that the rental unit is no longer occupied doesn't give you the legal right to immediately retake possession. It does, however, often give you legal justification to inspect the place for signs of abandonment.

Here are some tips for inspecting property you suspect has been abandoned:

- Is the refrigerator empty, or is most of the food spoiled?
- Have electricity and internet services been canceled?
- Are closets and kitchen cupboards empty?

If you conclude, under your state's rules, that the property is abandoned, you have the right to retake possession. Each state has its own definition of abandonment and its own rules for regaining possession of rental property. See the Chapter 15 discussion of abandoned property.

Rather than trying to figure out if the situation satisfies your state's legal rules for abandonment, it might be easier to find the tenants and ask them if they plan to come back. If they indicate that they're gone for good, get it in writing. You can write up a simple statement for each tenant along these lines: "I, Terri Tenant, have permanently

Consider a Buyout Agreement With a Tenant Who Wants to Leave Early

A tenant who wants to get out of a lease early might offer to pay to be released without further responsibility. In the world of big business, this is known as a "buyout." For example, a tenant who wants to leave three months early might offer to pay half a month's extra rent and promise to be extra accommodating when you want to show the unit to prospective tenants. A sample Buyout Agreement is shown below.

Sample Buyout Agreement Between Landlord and Tenant

This Agreement is entered into on January 3, 20xx between Colin Crest, Tenant, who leases the premises at 123 Shady Lane, Capitol City, California, and Marie Peterson, Landlord.

1. Under the attached lease, Tenant agreed to pay Landlord monthly rent of $1,000. Tenant has paid rent for the month of January 20xx.

2. Tenant's lease expires on June 30, 20xx, but Tenant needs to break the lease and move out on January 15, 20xx.

3. Landlord agrees to release Tenant on January 15, 20xx from any further obligation to pay rent in exchange for Tenant's promise to pay January's rent plus one and one-half months' rent ($1,500) by January 15, 20xx.

4. Tenant agrees to allow Landlord to show his apartment to prospective new tenants on four hours' notice, seven days a week. If Tenant cannot be reached after Landlord has made a good-faith effort to do so, Landlord may enter and show the apartment.

5. If Tenant does not fulfill his promises as described in Paragraphs 3 and 4 above, the attached lease, entered into on January 3, 20xx, will remain in effect.

Colin Crest   _January 3, 20xx_
Colin Crest, Tenant   Date

Marie Peterson   _January 3, 20xx_
Marie Peterson, Landlord   Date

moved out of my rental unit at [address] and have no intention of resuming my tenancy"—and ask the tenant to sign and date it. Or, use our Tenant's Notice of Intent to Move Out form (shown above), modified as needed. The Nolo website includes a downloadable copy of the form. See Appendix B for the link to the forms in this book.

If you aren't able to reach the tenants using the contact information they provided, phone each personal and business reference on the tenants' rental application. If that doesn't work, ask neighbors and, finally, check with the police.

Another way to find tenants who have left a forwarding address with the Post Office but not with you is to send the tenants a "return receipt requested" letter, and check the box on the form that asks the postal service to note the address where the letter was delivered. You'll get the tenants' new address when you receive the return receipt.

> **TIP**
>
> **Require tenants to notify you of extended absences.** Clause 18 of the form lease and rental agreements (Chapter 2) requires tenants to inform you when they will be gone for an extended time, such as two or more weeks.
>
> By requiring tenants to notify you of long absences, you'll know whether property has been abandoned or the tenant is simply on vacation. In addition, if you have such a clause and, under its authority, enter an apparently abandoned unit only to be confronted later by an indignant tenant, you can defend yourself by pointing out that the tenant violated the lease.

Why bother trying hard to get hold of the missing tenants? It's for your own protection: If you rerent the unit after trying unsuccessfully to contact the original tenants, and the original tenants reappear claiming they still live there, evidence of your efforts will help you defend yourself against a lawsuit.

When Breaking a Lease Is Justified

There are some important exceptions to the blanket rule that tenants who break a lease owe the rent for the entire lease term. Tenants might be able to legally move out without providing proper notice in the following situations:

- **You violated an important lease provision.** If you don't live up to your important obligations under the lease—for example, if you fail to maintain the unit in accordance with health and safety codes—a court will conclude that you have "constructively evicted" the tenant. That releases the tenant from further obligations under the lease. But the violation must be significant—failure to produce a promised second parking spot, for example, probably won't justify lease breaking.
- **State law allows the tenant to leave early.** A few states' laws allow tenants to break a lease in certain situations:
  - **Job relocation or need to move because of health or age.** In Delaware, tenants need only give 30 days' notice to end a long-term lease if they need to move because a present employer relocates or because health problems of a tenant or a family member require a permanent move. In New Jersey, tenants who have suffered a disabling illness or accident can break a lease and leave after 40 days' notice upon presenting proper proof of disability. In Rhode Island, tenants who are 65 years of age or older (or who will turn 65 during the term of a rental agreement) can terminate the rental agreement in order to enter a residential care and assisted living facility, a nursing facility, or a unit in a private or public housing complex designated by the federal government as housing for the elderly.

- **Domestic violence.** Many states provide special protections for victims of domestic violence. For a list of states that give domestic violence victims early termination rights, see "State Laws in Domestic Violence Situations," in Appendix A.
- **Military Service.** In all states, tenants who enter active military duty after signing a lease must be released after delivering proper notice. (See "Special Rules for Tenants Who Enter Military Service," above.)

When your tenants claim to have a good reason for a sudden move, you might want to research your state's law to see whether they are still on the hook for rent:

- **The rental unit is damaged or destroyed.** If the rental is significantly damaged—either by natural disaster or any other reason beyond the tenants' control—the tenants can consider the lease terminated and move out.
- **You seriously interfere with the tenant's ability to enjoy the tenancy**—for example, by sexually harassing a tenant or violating a tenant's privacy rights.

Your Duty to Mitigate Your Loss When the Tenant Leaves Early

When tenants break the lease and move out without legal justification, you usually can't just sit back and wait until the lease expires, and then sue the departed tenants for the total lost rent. In most states, you must try to rerent within a reasonable time to keep your losses to a minimum—in legalese, you must "mitigate damages." Each state's mitigation rule is listed in "Landlord's Duty to Rerent" in Appendix A.

Even if this isn't the law in your state, trying to rerent is a sound business strategy. It's much better to have rent coming in every month than to wait, leaving a rental unit vacant for months, and then try to sue (and collect from) tenants who are probably long gone.

If your state requires you to mitigate damages but you don't make an attempt to rerent (or make an inadequate one), and instead sue the former tenants for the whole rent, you will collect only the equivalent of the rent you would've collected during a reasonable amount of time it took you to find replacement tenants. This amount can depend on how easy it is to rerent in your area. Usually, it's about one to three months' rent.

> **CAUTION**
> **No double-dipping is allowed.** Even if your state doesn't strictly enforce the mitigation-of-damages rules, if you rerent the property, you cannot also collect from the former tenant. Courts do not allow you to unjustly enrich yourself this way.

How to Mitigate Your Damages

When you're sure that tenants have left permanently, you can turn your attention to rerenting the unit.

You do not need to lower your standards just to fill the vacancy—for example, you are entitled to reject applicants with poor credit or rental histories. Also, you need not give the suddenly available property priority over other rental units that you were planning to focus on first.

You are not required to rent the premises at a rate below its fair market value. Keep in mind, however, that refusing to rent at less than the original rate might be foolish. If you are ultimately unable to collect from the former tenants, you will get *no* income from the property.

Keep Good Records

If you end up suing a former tenant, you will want to be able to show the judge that you acted reasonably in your attempts to rerent the property. Don't rely on your memory and powers of persuasion to convince the judge. Keep detailed records, including:

- the original lease
- receipts for cleaning and painting, with photos of the unit showing the need for repairs, if any
- your expenses for storing or properly disposing of any belongings the tenant left
- receipts for advertising the property and bills from credit reporting agencies investigating potential renters
- a log of the time you spent showing the property, and a value for that time
- a log of any people who offered to rent and, if you rejected them, documentation as to why, and
- if the current rent is less than the original tenant paid, a copy of the new lease.

EXAMPLE: When the mail began to pile up and the rent went unpaid, Jack suspected that Lorna, his tenant, had broken the lease and moved out. When his suspicions were confirmed, he added her apartment to the list of vacant units that needed his attention. In the same way that he prepared every unit, Jack cleaned the apartment and advertised it. Three months after Lorna left, Jack succeeded in rerenting the apartment.

Jack sued Lorna in small claims court and won a judgment that included the costs of advertising and cleaning and the three months' rent that he lost before he rerented the unit.

The Tenant's Right to Find a Replacement Tenant

Tenants who wish to leave before the lease expires sometimes offer to find a suitable new tenant. Unless you have a new tenant waiting, you have nothing to lose by cooperating. Refusing to cooperate could even hurt you: If you refuse an acceptable new tenant and then withhold the lease-breaking tenants' deposit or sue for unpaid rent, you might wind up losing in court, because you turned down the chance to reduce your losses (mitigate your damages).

Of course, if the rental market is really tight in your area, you might be able to lease the unit easily at a higher rent, or you might already have an even better prospective tenant on your waiting list. In that case, you won't care if tenants break the lease, and you might not be interested in any new tenant they suggest.

If you and the outgoing tenants agree on replacement tenants, you and the new tenants should sign a new lease, and the outgoing tenants should sign a termination of lease form (discussed in Chapter 8). Because this is a new lease—not a sublease or an assignment of the existing lease—you can raise the rent (unless local rent control ordinances prohibit it).

When You Can Sue

When tenants break their lease, you can use their security deposit to cover the rerental costs and the difference between the original and the replacement rent. But if the security deposit isn't enough to make you whole, you might need to sue.

Deciding *where* to sue is usually easy: Small claims court (discussed in Chapter 16) is usually the court of choice because it doesn't require a lawyer and is fast and affordable. If you're seeking an amount that's substantially above your state's small claims court limit, you can file in regular court (but if the excess is small, you can forgo the excess and stay in small claims). If your lease contains an attorneys' fees clause (as does the form agreement in Chapter 2), you might be able to recover your attorneys' fees.

EXAMPLE: Cree has a year's lease at $800 per month. She moves out with six months ($4,800 of rent) left on the lease. Cree's landlord, Robin, cannot find a new tenant for six weeks, and when she finally does, the new tenant will pay only $600 per month.

Unless Cree can show Robin acted unreasonably, Cree would be liable for the $200 per month difference between what she paid and what the new tenant pays, multiplied by the number of months left in the lease at the time she moved out. Cree would also be responsible for $1,200 for the time the unit was vacant, plus Robin's costs to find a new tenant. Cree would thus owe Robin $2,400 plus advertising and applicant screening costs. If Robin sues Cree for this money and uses a lawyer, and if there is an attorneys' fees clause in her lease, Cree will also owe Robin these costs, which can be upwards of a few thousand dollars.

Knowing *when* to sue is trickier. If you start legal proceedings as soon as the original tenant leaves, you won't know the extent of your losses, because you might find another tenant who will make up part of the lost rent. Must you wait until the end of the original tenant's lease? Or can you bring suit when you rerent the property?

The standard approach, and one that all states allow, is to go to court after you rerent the property. At this point, your losses—your expenses and the rent differential, if any—are known and final. The disadvantage is that you have had no income from that property since the original tenants left, and the original tenants might be long gone and not worth chasing down.

CAUTION

Give accurate and updated information to credit bureaus about former tenants. The Fair Debt Collection Practices Act (FDCPA) (15 U.S.C. §§ 1692 and following) also applies when you give information to a credit reporting agency about a current or former tenant. The act makes it illegal to give false information, and, if the tenant disputes the debt, you must mention the fact that the sum is disputed when you report it. You must notify the credit bureau if the tenant pays all or part of the debt.

The FDCPA even makes it illegal to give falsely *positive* information which you know to be untrue. When a credit bureau calls to ask about your least-favorite tenant who's applied for a home loan, don't describe him in falsely glowing terms, no matter how much you'd like to see him leave!

Termination Fees

A termination fee is a preset fee that landlords impose when tenants break a lease. They're often called cancellation fees, reletting fees, rerenting fees, or decorating fees. They're intended to compensate the landlord for the inconvenience and extra work caused by a broken lease. Landlords who have to mitigate damages often add this fee to whatever rent loss the landlord suffered before rerenting the unit. Landlords who do not have to mitigate damages might use the fee to cover both the inconvenience of the broken lease plus any lost rents.

The problem with termination fees is that they are preset damage amounts and, as such, are liquidated damages—prohibited in many states. Even in states that don't ban liquidated damages, they are ripe for attack under consumer protection statutes, which offer other ways to go after liquidated damages. The advice given to landlords by their attorneys and trade associations is uniform: Don't use them.

If you're determined to use a preset termination fee, understand that it must accurately reflect the financial losses you suffer when a tenant takes off unexpectedly, such as staff time spent securing the apartment or trying to locate the departed tenant.

To accurately and fairly charge lease-breaking tenants for the cost of rerenting, do a "time and motion" analysis of your actual costs to rerent, and add in your advertising costs, too. Because you'll be spending that money earlier than you'd planned, thanks to the tenant's early departure, figure out how much interest you'll be losing when you remove that money from your interest-bearing bank account. For example, if you typically spend

$1,500 every time you rerent, and your tenant left six months early, your damages would be six months' of interest on $1,500.

> **! CAUTION**
>
> **Don't ask for the return of "rent concessions."** If you've offered a free month's rent as a concession for new tenants, demanding its return when that tenant breaks a lease is risky. A court is likely to see your concession as simply a roundabout way to charge a lower, market rent spread over the period of the lease, and will not allow you to recoup it.

A Tenant's Death: Consequences for Cotenants and the Landlord's Duties

When a tenant dies, landlords, family members, subtenants, and cotenants will naturally be concerned about what happens to the lease or rental agreement. As the landlord, you're likely to encounter some of the issues addressed below.

Death of a Tenant With No Cotenants: Requests for the Tenant's Property

You are legally required to take reasonable precautions to preserve a deceased tenant's property. When a tenant who lives alone passes away, your first response should be to secure the premises after the body has been removed. The best way to do this is to change the locks, so that anyone else who might have had a key cannot get in.

It's very common for friends or relatives of a recently deceased tenant to ask for items such as the tenant's address book (to notify friends and family of the death), or clothing needed for the funeral. These are reasonable requests, but when landlords allow a visitor to enter the rental, they run the risk that the person will take valuable items, and that the executor or administrator of the tenant's estate or next of kin will sue the landlord for allowing it to happen.

On the other hand, most landlords won't want to supervise a grieving family member's visit to the rental. In practice, landlords and would-be visitors work it out, ideally when the visitor has a provable, close relationship to the tenant and lives locally. (For some protection, you might want to ask the visitor to sign an indemnification agreement, explained below.)

Family members or others might also want access to the rental in the weeks after the tenant's death. At this point, careful landlords will not allow access unless the visitor can prove that they have a legal right to have it. The proof that visitors can bring with them when approaching you depends on how the estate will be settled. Here are the possibilities.

Estates That Are in Probate

If the deceased tenant's estate has begun the probate process in court (a proceeding that divvies up the assets and pays bills), the judge will have appointed a personal representative of the estate. This person is called the executor if the deceased person named one in a will; if there was no will, the court appoints an administrator. The personal representative is not necessarily a relative of the deceased.

The personal representative is the only person who has the right to take possession of the deceased tenant's property. The personal representative's authority comes from documents called Letters Testamentary (for executors) or Letters of Administration (for administrators), which are issued by the court (states use these or similar-sounding names for these documents). These papers look official and have a court seal, and any personal representative should have a set of originals. The representative seeking access should make an appointment to see you and bring the originals plus a copy to leave with you.

Small Estates That Will Avoid Formal Probate

Estates that are worth less than a certain amount (for example, $166,250 in California, excluding certain assets) will not go through probate, nor will probate be involved if the tenant used a probate-avoiding living trust (see below). Because there's no court proceeding for a small estate, the visitor won't have any official letters to show you.

If the deceased had a will, the named executor will distribute the assets according to the will's terms. If the deceased died without a will, the person or persons who are entitled to the property, as determined by the laws of intestate succession of the state in which the deceased resided, are entitled to the property. In either situation, the claimants must fill out and have notarized an affidavit that attests to their right to obtain the property. The claimants show this affidavit to banks, storage unit owners, and so on—and to landlords. Importantly, claimants must typically wait a period of time after the person dies before claiming the personal property.

As explained, the most official-looking document that a small estate claimant has will be a self-sworn statement that he or she is entitled to the property. The claimant-visitor should show you an original affidavit and leave you with a copy. But because the affidavit was prepared without court oversight, you might worry that you have no way of verifying that the visitor is entitled to the property inside the tenant's unit.

You can address that worry to some extent by asking the claimant to sign an agreement, promising to reimburse you for any monetary losses you might suffer as a result of the claimant's actions. For example, if the tenant's estate later claimed that the visitor removed cash and jewelry, and a court held you partially responsible because you allowed the visitor to enter, the visitor would be legally bound to pay any damages that you were ordered to pay to the estate.

The indemnification agreement shown below accomplishes this task. The indemnification agreement asks the visitor to state why he or she is entitled to access. You should ask for identification, and to see a copy of the tenant's will if the visitor claims to be the executor. The form you present to the visitor will hopefully have a deterring effect on anyone who thinks they can enter and take what they see. Below, you'll see a filled-out sample of the Indemnification of Landlord form.

CAUTION

The indemnification agreement isn't a total shield. Keep in mind that the tenant's estate is not bound by the claimant-visitor's agreement with you, which means that the estate can still look to you to make good on any losses caused by the visitor's removal of property. In theory, you can then look to the visitor for reimbursement, relying on the agreement the claimant signed and suing if necessary. But the indemnification agreement is only as good as the visitor's ability to pay off any judgment you obtain. So if someone takes valuables and disappears, or has few assets (is "judgment proof," in legalese), you will have a hard time collecting. Understanding this, you might not find the indemnification agreement very comforting.

FORM

You'll find a downloadable copy of the Indemnification of Landlord form on the Nolo website. See Appendix B for the link to the forms in this book.

Estates That Avoid Probate Through the Use of Living Trusts

A living trust is a probate-avoiding tool that allows a deceased's property to be distributed without going to probate court. The trust names a "successor trustee," who assumes control of the deceased's property when the deceased dies. The successor trustee gathers all of the property, both tangible and intangible, and distributes it to the beneficiaries as specified in the trust.

Although successor trustees don't have to go to court and obtain official letters, they will have the next best thing: a copy of the trust document itself, which was prepared by the deceased and usually signed in the presence of a notary. The trustee should bring this to the property and show it to you, directing your attention to the clause that names the successor trustee. Alternatively, trustees might show you a copy of the "Certification of Trust," a short document that accompanies a trust (it might also be called an "abstract of trust" or a "memorandum of trust").

Indemnification of Landlord

This indemnification agreement is between ___Walter Lee_____, ("Landlord")
Landlord/Manager of the rental property at ___75 B St. Oakhurst, CA_____ ("Rental Premises")
and _____Sophie Jones_____ ("Visitor"). This agreement concerns Visitor's access to the
Rental Premises rented by ____Barbara Jones_____ ("Deceased Tenant").

No executor or administrator has been appointed to represent the estate of Deceased Tenant. Visitor is Deceased
Tenant's ____daughter_____ (for example, daughter, friend), and is taking responsibility,
in the absence of a court-appointed personal representative, to gather and dispose of Deceased Tenant's property
according to all applicable laws.

[*Check if applicable*]

☑ Visitor is Deceased Tenant's executor.

Visitor accepts responsibility for any liability to Deceased Tenant's estate or third parties resulting from Visitor's
removal of property from the Rental Premises.

In the event of any third-party claim, demand, suit, action, or proceeding (collectively referred to as "Claim") against
Landlord based upon Visitor's removal or use of property, Landlord will have the right to select counsel to defend itself.
If the Claim results in an enforceable judgment or is settled, Visitor will indemnify and hold harmless Landlord and any
successors or assigns. Visitor will cooperate fully in the defense of any such Claim. Landlord may settle any such Claim
against it or waive any appeal of any judgment of a trial court or arbitrator against it.

___Sophie Jones_____   ___April 10, 20xx_____
Visitor's signature   Date
Sophie Jones
_____
Print name

___Walter Lee_____   ___April 10, 20xx_____
Landlord or Manager's signature   Date
Walter Lee
_____
Print name

Visitor's contact information: Home

___1707 20th Avenue_____   _____San Rafael, CA 91234_____
Street   City, state, zip
___∅_____   _____415-123-4567_____
Phone   Cell

Visitor's contact information: Work

___505 Folsom Street_____   _____San Francisco, CA 94102_____
Street   City, state, zip
___415-987-6543_____   _____415-123-4567_____
Phone   Cell

Other ID (such as a driver's license): ___Calif. Driver's License #R0261345_____

It establishes the existence of the trust without revealing any of the details about who gets what, and it's the document that the trustee shows to banks and so on. For added assurance, you might require the indemnification agreement, described above.

Keep in mind that even if the named beneficiary for a particular item under the terms of the trust shows up and asks for that item, you do not have the right to turn it over—that task belongs solely to the successor trustee, who should distribute it to the beneficiary as directed by the terms of the trust.

CAUTION

Do not use the indemnification agreement for people who want to take property that they claim belongs *to them*. It's one thing for an executor, trustee, or personal representative to ask to remove the tenant's property; it's another matter altogether when people ask to take property that they claim belongs to them. Your state law might provide a method that such persons can use, but it's typically not available until some weeks after the tenant's death, and the claimant must show up with a signed affidavit (sworn statement) attesting, among other things, to the claimant's right to the property. So, if your deceased tenant's friend wants the return of his tools that he loaned to your tenant, he'll have to wait and do a bit of paperwork.

Death of a Tenant With Cotenants or Subtenants: Requests for the Tenant's Property

The deceased tenant might have had a cotenant (each signed the same lease or rental agreement), or a resident subtenant (who rented directly from the tenant). In either case, these residents are now living among the deceased's tenant's belongings, and might face the same requests from family or kin that you would encounter if the tenant had lived alone. Understandably, those residents might look to you for guidance.

Begin by understanding that relatives and friends of the deceased roommate have no immediate right to the deceased's belongings. And, the remaining residents do not have to admit anyone to their home unless they want to (law enforcement situations excepted, of course).

Although remaining tenants have no specific responsibility for preserving the tenant's belongings, they could face civil liability to the estate if they let someone in who wrongfully removes the deceased's property. But remaining tenants should use common sense: If the deceased's brother asks for clothing for the funeral, and they feel comfortable monitoring his activity while in the rental, they're unlikely to encounter problems.

If the people approaching the remaining tenants are, instead, the executor, administrator, successor trustee, or beneficiary in a small estate situation, remaining cotenants and subtenants should ask for the documents explained in sections above.

CAUTION

Remaining residents should protect themselves from claims that they have taken the deceased's property. The last thing they want is a claim by the estate that the roommates helped themselves to your deceased tenant's valuables. If remaining roommates are concerned about this eventuality, consider offering to do an inventory of the deceased tenant's belongings as soon as possible.

What Happens to the Lease or Rental Agreement?

The landlord and the tenant's estate (or next of kin), and possibly any cotenants or subtenants, will need to confront the question of what happens to the tenant's rental agreement or lease now that the tenant is dead—and in particular, whether you are entitled to rent past the date of the tenant's death; and in a cotenancy situation, whether remaining cotenants can demand rent from the estate (if so, for how long). Occasionally, relatives or friends want to take over the tenant's unit. Do they have the right to do so? The answers depend on whether the tenant lived alone or with cotenants, and rented under a rental agreement or a lease.

Single Tenants With Month-to-Month Rental Agreements

State laws determine when a month-to-month, deceased tenant's responsibility for rent ends. For example, California courts have ruled that the obligation ends 30 days after the date the rent was last paid. So, if rent was last paid on October 1 for the period October 1 to 31, the tenancy expires on October 31st. It does not matter whether the tenant died on the 2nd of the month or the 30th of the month—as of 12:01 am on November 1, the rental agreement is over and so is any obligation to pay rent. Not all states follow this method; you'll need to learn the procedure in your state. (See "Doing Your Own Legal Research," in Chapter 18.)

This rule will not prevent the landlord, however, from being compensated by the estate if the tenant's belongings remain on the property after the rent obligation ends. This often happens while the legalities of who is entitled to what are being sorted out. When the tenant's belongings remain in the unit, the landlord is dealing with a "holdover tenant" situation, and is entitled to rent for those days. Landlords can deduct this amount from the security deposit, or (when the deposit is insufficient) make a claim to the estate for prorated rent through the date the property remained on the premises (this is how the landlord would ask for unpaid back rent, too).

If the security deposit cannot cover the holdover rent and there's a probate proceeding, you can file a creditor's claim form (available from the court clerk) with the probate clerk of the court. You will have a specified amount of time in which to file the claim, usually beginning when the court officially appoints the estate's executor. If the estate doesn't go through probate (many small estates do not), you can bill the next of kin.

In practice, landlords will avoid keeping a deceased tenant's belongings in a rental. Instead, they will want to get the rental on the market as soon as possible, and that means emptying the unit of the tenant's property. But you can't just throw the property away or sell it. You must follow the procedures required under your state's statute regarding dealing with a deceased tenant's property; or if there isn't one, follow the statute regarding tenants' abandoned property. Any proceeds and claims should be directed to the estate. (State laws on handling abandoned property are covered in Appendix A.)

Because the tenancy will legally end as of the date specified by state law, you are not obliged to accept a substitute tenant proposed by the deceased tenant's family or friends. If someone would like to move in, you should treat that person just as you would any other applicant, by evaluating the applicant's creditworthiness and rental history with the same care you use with any applicant.

Cotenants and Subtenants With Month-to-Month Rental Agreements

When a cotenant dies, the remaining tenants retain their monthly rental agreement—it is generally not automatically terminated by law, as it is when a sole tenant dies. But the remaining cotenants must come up with the full rent as soon as the deceased's obligations end (see above), and in practice, this means quickly finding a new roommate whom you will accept as a new tenant.

Until a new cotenant joins the tenancy as a cotenant, the remaining cotenants must cover the entire rent. Because the deceased's obligation to pay rent will have ended on a certain date, the remaining tenants cannot look to the estate to pay the deceased's share after that date while they look for a new roommate.

If there is a subtenant who paid rent to the deceased (as opposed to the landlord), the subtenant's rights will end at the same time as the deceased tenant's monthly agreement ends. Unless the subtenant makes a new arrangement with you, or you accept rent from the subtenant, the subtenant will have to move at the end of the period for which rent was paid. An exception might exist if a rent control ordinance addresses the situation.

Single Tenants With Leases

Unlike the result described above for month-to-month tenants, when a tenant with a lease dies, the lease might not be terminated, depending on state law. Instead, you might be able to treat the situation as you would if the tenant had broken the lease by moving away midterm, without a legal justification.

In other words, the tenant (now, the estate or next of kin) remains responsible for the rent through the end of the lease term, but the landlord must use reasonable efforts to find a replacement tenant. When the landlord begins receiving rent from the next tenant (or when the landlord could have received rent, had the landlord used reasonable efforts to find a replacement), the estate's responsibility for rent ends. Not all states handle the situation this way; again, you'll need to learn the rule in your state.

Cotenants With Leases

Finally, when one member of a cotenancy dies, the remaining tenants are not treated as if they have moved out mid-lease. Instead, as happens when a cotenant moves out without dying, those who remain must shoulder the entire rent themselves if they hope to avoid termination for nonpayment of rent. Typically, they find a replacement whom they present to the landlord.

Once you accept the replacement, by adding the new person to the lease or otherwise treating the newcomer as a tenant (by accepting rent from the new resident, for example), the new assortment of cotenants can work out among themselves how they will divide up responsibility for the rent.

What Happens to the Deceased Tenant's Security Deposit?

Security deposits can involve hefty sums. In these days of high rents, many thousands of dollars might be sitting in the landlord's bank account. What happens to the deceased tenant's deposit depends on whether the tenant was renting solo, or was in a cotenancy situation.

Solo Tenants With Rental Agreements or Leases

As explained above, state law determines when the tenancy will terminate—for deceased tenants who rented month to month or for lease-holding tenants. Landlords must handle the deposit as they would under normal circumstances, deducting for damage and unpaid rent, and sending the balance, if any, to the estate.

If the deposit is inadequate to cover deductions for unpaid rent and damage, you can make a claim to the estate for any unpaid rent through the date the deceased's property remained on the premises. If the estate is in probate, you will need to submit a filled-out creditor's claim form (available from the court clerk) to the probate clerk of the court. You'll have a specified amount of time in which to file the claim, beginning when the court officially appoints the estate's executor. If the estate doesn't go through probate (many small estates do not), you can bill the next of kin.

Cotenants With Rental Agreements or Leases

By contrast to the result just above, the fate of the deposit of a deceased cotenant is quite murky. The estate, of course, would like the landlord to return the deceased tenant's share of the deposit as of the date the rental agreement terminated or when responsibility for the rent under a lease ended. The remaining cotenants, on the other hand, might want the deposit to stay put, ready to cover any damage you assess when the last of them move out (particularly if they believe that existing damage was caused by their deceased roommate).

Your preference probably would be to do nothing—your interest is in keeping the deposit topped-off and firmly in your bank account, returning it to whatever tenants are on the scene when the entire tenancy ends. Remember, you generally don't care how cotenants divided up the deposit (or how they allocated the rent). As long as the sums are paid in full, you're happy and it's up to the roommates to share the responsibilities in a way that they can agree upon.

Despite all of this, although it involves considerable work on your behalf, the fairest and safest course for both the remaining tenants and the estate (and any new roommate) would be for you to conduct an inspection when the estate's obligation for rent ends, as if the entire tenancy were ending. But understand that you are under no legal obligation to do so—that's because the tenancy is not ending, and final inspections are required only when, in fact, the tenancy is about to end. So if you are asked to perform an interim inspection, it's your call as to whether to do so.

With an interim inspection held soon after the deceased tenant's death, you can assess any damage, deduct from the deposit as needed, "return" the balance to the remaining cotenants, and demand that the entire deposit be immediately topped-off again. The remaining cotenants can sort out among themselves who was responsible for the deductions. In theory, the estate would be entitled to the deceased tenant's full share of the deposit if the deceased didn't contribute to the deductions, and the remaining cotenants should forward that amount. But if you deduct only for damage caused by the deceased tenant, for example, that amount would be subtracted from the deceased tenant's share and the remaining tenants would return only the balance to the estate.

> **EXAMPLE:** Tom, Dick, and Harry were cotenants who each contributed $1,000 toward the $3,000 security deposit. Tom died suddenly and Dick and Harry decided to remain in the rental. They asked their landlord, Len, to conduct a "final inspection," as if they were vacating. Len decided to deduct for repairing holes in the wall of Tom's bedroom, which would require $500 worth of work. Len sent a check for $2,500 to Dick (who had written the original check, having collected shares from Tom and Harry), who sent $500 to Tom's estate.
>
> Because they were remaining, Dick and Harry had to immediately pay the $3,000 deposit themselves (essentially, they and Len simply traded checks). When they found Rex, a new roommate whom the landlord accepted as a tenant, Rex contributed his $1,000 to the $3,000 deposit, by writing $500 checks to Dick and Harry.

The advantage of this process to the remaining residents is that when the deceased tenant's share of the deposit is insufficient to cover that tenant's damage, the other cotenants can protect their shares by making a claim on the estate right away. For example, suppose the damage caused by Tom required $1,500 worth of repairs. You're entitled to deduct that amount, without regard to whether it exceeds Tom's portion of the deposit. With proper documentation, Dick and Harry could make a claim on Tom's estate for the $500 not covered by Tom's share. This system is also fair for any new roommate—Rex, who took over Tom's bedroom, will not end up being charged with damage that occurred before he moved in.

Condominium Conversions

Converting a rental property into condominiums usually means the end of a tenant's tenancy. But condo conversions are not always simple.

Many states regulate the conversion of rental property into condominiums. Here are some of the basic issues that your state's condo conversion law might address:

- **Government approval.** Converting rental property to condos usually requires plan approval (often called a "subdivision map approval") from a local planning agency. If the property is subject to rent control, there are probably additional requirements.

- **Public input.** In most situations, the public—including current tenants—can speak out at hearings regarding the proposed condominium conversion and its impact on the rental housing market. Landlords usually must give tenants notice of the time and place of these hearings.

- **Tenants' right of first refusal.** Most condominium conversion laws demand that landlords offer the units for sale first to the existing tenants, at prices that are the same as or lower than the intended public offering. To keep tenant opposition to a minimum, you could decide to voluntarily offer existing tenants a chance to buy at a significantly lower price.

- **Tenancy terminations.** Month-to-month tenants who don't buy their units should receive notice to move at some point during the sales process. Tenants with leases usually have a right to remain through the end of the lease. The entire condo conversion approval process typically takes many months—time enough for current leases to expire before the final okay has been given.

- **Renting after the conversion has been approved.** If you offer a lease or rental agreement *after* the condo conversion has been approved, many states require you to give the tenant plenty of clear written warnings (in large, bold-faced type) that the unit might be sold and the tenancy terminated on short notice. But, if you continue to rent units after you've gotten subdivision approval, you'll usually do so on a month-to-month basis, so the short notice really won't be any different from what any month-to-month tenant would receive.

- **Relocation assistance and special protections.** Some statutes require owners to pay current tenants a flat fee to help with relocation. Some also require owners to provide more notice or additional relocation assistance for elderly tenants or those with small children.

RELATED TOPIC

For advice on researching your state's statutes and court cases on condominium conversions, see the discussion of legal research in Chapter 18.

Returning Security Deposits and Other Move-Out Issues

FORMS IN THIS CHAPTER

Chapter 15 includes instructions for and samples of the following forms:

- Move-Out Letter
- Letter for Returning Entire Security Deposit
- Security Deposit Itemization (Deductions for Repairs and Cleaning)
- Security Deposit Itemization (Deductions for Repairs, Cleaning, and Unpaid Rent)

The purchase of this book includes free downloadable and customizable copies of all of these forms. See Appendix B for the download link and instructions.

Fights over security deposits account for a large percentage of landlord-tenant disputes. Failure to return security deposits as legally required can result in substantial financial penalties if a tenant files suit. This chapter will walk you through some simple steps to minimize the possibility that you'll spend hours in court.

We cover key aspects of state security deposit laws in this chapter and in Chapter 4. Check local ordinances in all areas where you own property. Many cities—particularly those with rent control—add their own rules on security deposits.

RELATED TOPIC
Related topics covered in this book include:

- How to avoid deposit disputes by using clear lease and rental agreement provisions: Chapter 2
- Deposit limits; requirements for keeping deposits in a separate account or paying interest; last month's rent and deposits: Chapter 4
- Highlighting security deposit rules in a move-in letter to new tenants; taking photographs and using a Landlord-Tenant Checklist to keep track of the condition of the premises before and after the tenant moves in: Chapter 7
- Notice requirements for terminating a tenancy: Chapter 14
- State Security Deposit Rules: Appendix A.

Preparing a Move-Out Letter

Chapter 7 explains how a move-in letter can help get a tenancy off to a good start. Similarly, a move-out letter can help reduce the possibility of disputes over the return of security deposits.

Your move-out letter should tell tenants how you expect the unit to be left, explain your inspection procedures, list the kinds of deposit deductions you can legally make, and tell tenants when and how you will send any refund that is due.

A sample Move-Out Letter is shown below and the Nolo website includes a downloadable copy. See Appendix B for the link to the forms in this book. You might want to add or delete items depending on your own needs and how specific you wish to be.

Here are a few points to consider including in a move-out letter:

- specific cleaning requirements, such as what to do about dirty walls, or how to fix holes left from picture hooks
- instructions regarding recycling and disposing of paint and household hazardous wastes
- a reminder that fixtures (items that tenants attach more or less permanently to the wall, such as built-in bookshelves) must be left in place (see the discussion of fixtures in Chapter 9 and Clause 12 of the form agreements in Chapter 2)
- details about how and when the final inspection will be conducted
- a request for a forwarding address where you can mail the deposit
- information about state laws (if any) that allow a landlord to keep a security deposit when the tenant doesn't supply a forwarding address within a certain amount of time ("Mailing the Security Deposit Itemization," below), and
- information on state laws regarding abandoned property (discussed at the end of this chapter).

Inspecting the Unit When a Tenant Leaves

After tenants leave, you will need to inspect the unit for needed cleaning and damage repair. At the final inspection, check each item addressed in the Landlord-Tenant Checklist you and the tenants (hopefully) signed at move-in. (An excerpt is shown below. See Chapter 7 for a complete checklist.) Note any item that needs cleaning, repair, or replacement in the right column, *Move-Out Condition*.

Move-Out Letter

July 5, 20xx
_____
Date

Jane Wasserman
_____
Tenant

123 North Street, Apartment #23
_____
Street Address

Atlanta, Georgia 30360
_____
City and State

Dear ___Jane_____,
                Tenant

We hope you have enjoyed living here. In order that we can mutually end our relationship on a positive note, this move-out letter describes how we expect your unit to be left and what our procedures are for returning your security deposit.

Basically, we expect you to leave your rental unit in the same condition it was when you moved in, except for normal wear and tear. To refresh your memory on the condition of the unit when you moved in, I've attached a copy of the Landlord-Tenant Checklist you signed at the beginning of your tenancy. I'll be using this same form to inspect the unit when you leave.

Specifically, here's a list of items you should thoroughly clean before vacating:

- ✔ Floors
  - ✔ sweep wood floors
  - ✔ vacuum carpets and rugs (shampoo if necessary)
  - ✔ mop kitchen and bathroom floors
- ✔ Walls, baseboards, ceilings, and built-in shelves
- ✔ Kitchen cabinets, countertops and sink, stove and oven—inside and out
- ✔ Refrigerator—clean inside and out, empty it of food, and turn it off, with the door left open
- ✔ Bathtubs, showers, toilets, and plumbing fixtures
- ✔ Doors, windows, and window coverings
- ✔ Other

microwave oven—clean inside and out
_____
_____
_____
_____

_____

_____

_____

_____

_____

_____

_____

If you have any questions as to the type of cleaning we expect, please let me know.

Please don't leave anything behind—that includes bags of garbage, clothes, food, newspapers, furniture, appliances, dishes, plants, cleaning supplies, or other items that belong to you.

Please be sure you have disconnected phone and utility services, changed your address for regular deliveries and subscriptions, and sent the post office a change of address form.

Once you have cleaned your unit and removed all your belongings, please call me at _____555-1234_____ to arrange for a walk-through inspection and to return all keys. Please be prepared to give me your forwarding address where we should mail your security deposit.

It's our policy to return all deposits either in person or at an address you provide within ____one month____ _____ after you move out. If any deductions are made—for past-due rent or because the unit is damaged or not sufficiently clean—they will be explained in writing.

If you have any questions, please contact me at _____555-1234_____.

Sincerely,

Denise Parsons
Landlord/Manager

Many landlords do a final inspection on their own and simply send tenants an itemized statement with any remaining balance of the deposit. If at all possible, we recommend that you perform the inspection with the tenants, rather than by yourself. A few states actually require this. Doing the final inspection with the tenants present (in a conciliatory, nonthreatening way) will eliminate any uncertainty about what deductions (if any) you propose to make from the deposit. It also gives tenants a chance to present their point of view. But, best of all, this approach reduces the risk that tenants who feel unpleasantly surprised by the amount you withhold from the deposit will promptly take the matter to small claims court.

If you have any reason to believe a tenant will take you to court over your security deposit deductions, have the unit examined by another, more neutral person. This person should be available to testify in court on your behalf, if necessary, should you end up in small claims court.

> **TIP**
>
> **Photograph "before" and "after."** In Chapter 7, we recommend that you take photos or videos of the unit before tenants move in. You should do the same when tenants leave, so that you can make comparisons and have visual proof in case you are challenged later in court.

To be on the safe side, keep your inspection notes, photos, videos, and related records for at least two years. Technically speaking, in most states tenants have up to four years to sue you over security deposit agreements, but the chances of former tenants suing after a year or so has passed are slim.

Landlord-Tenant Checklist

Property Address: _____ 572 Fourth St., Apt. 11, Washington, D.C. _____

General Condition of Rental Unit and Premises

	Move-In Condition Date of Walk-Through: May 1, 20xx	Move-Out Condition Date of Walk-Through:
Living Room		
Flooring	OK, slight wearing from normal use	
Walls & Ceilings	OK	
Light Fixtures	OK	
Windows & Screens	miniblinds on both windows discolored	
Doors & handles/locks	OK	
Fireplace	OK	
...tector & CO detector		

Should You Let the Tenant Clean or Fix the Damage?

Many tenants, faced with losing a large chunk of their security deposit, will ask for the chance to do some more cleaning or repair any damage you've identified in the final inspection. A few states require you to offer tenants a second chance at cleaning before you deduct cleaning charges from the security deposit. Even if your state doesn't require it, you might wish to offer a second chance if the tenant seems sincere and capable of doing the work. This could help avoid arguments and maybe even a small claims action. But, if you need to get the apartment ready quickly for a new tenant or doubt the tenant's ability to do the work, just say no. And think twice if repairs are required, not just cleaning. If a tenant does a repair poorly, you might end up having to do it over.

Applying the Security Deposit to the Last Month's Rent

When giving notice, a tenant might ask you to apply the security deposit toward the last month's rent. Unless a portion of the tenant's deposit was designated to pay the last month's rent, though, you're not legally obliged to apply it in this way.

Think twice before agreeing to apply a deposit you are already holding towards the last month's rent. The problem is that you don't know what the property will look like when the tenant leaves. If the tenant leaves the property a mess, but the whole security deposit has gone to pay the last month's rent, you'll have nothing left to use to repair or clean the property. You will have to absorb the loss or sue the tenant.

If, despite the above advice, you're inclined to allow the deposit to serve as last month's rent, tell the tenant that you'll need to make a quick inspection first. If you perform the inspection and think that the tenant will leave the property clean and undamaged, you can agree to the request. Send the tenant a written statement describing how you applied the deposit to the last month's rent.

Some tenants will not pay the last month's rent in spite of your refusal to go along with the request, in hopes that you'll use the deposit anyway. You can instead treat the tenant's nonpayment (or partial payment) of the last month's rent as an ordinary case of rent nonpayment. This means preparing and serving the notice necessary to terminate the tenancy, and, if the tenant doesn't pay, following up with an eviction lawsuit. But because it typically takes at least several weeks to evict a tenant, this probably won't get the tenant out much sooner than planned. However, it will provide you with a court judgment for the unpaid last month's rent. Having a judgment means that you can use the security deposit to pay for cleaning and repair costs, and apply any remainder to the judgment for nonpayment of rent. If there's still rent money owed, you can attempt to enforce the judgment, as discussed below ("When the Deposit Doesn't Cover Damage and Unpaid Rent").

Basic Rules for Returning Deposits

The general rule is that you're entitled to deduct from a tenant's security deposit whatever amount you need to fix damaged or dirty property (outside of "ordinary wear and tear") or to make up unpaid rent (see "Purpose and Use of Security Deposits" in Chapter 4). But you must follow your state's procedures for returning security deposits.

The amount of time you have to itemize and return deposits varies by state, but most states require you to return a tenant's deposit at some point between 14 and 30 days after the tenant moves out. See the entry "Deadline for Landlord to Itemize and Return Deposit" in the "State Security Deposit Rules" chart in Appendix A. A few states require landlords to give tenants advance notice of intended deductions; see "Advance notice of deduction" in the same chart.

State security deposit statutes typically require you to mail, within the time limit, the following to the tenant's last known address (or forwarding address if you have one):

- the tenant's entire deposit, with interest if required, or
- a written, itemized accounting of how the deposit has been applied, along with payment for any deposit balance, including interest (if required).

Even if there is no specific time limit in your state law requiring itemization, promptly presenting the tenant with a written itemization of all deductions and a clear reason why each was made is an essential part of a savvy landlord's overall plan to avoid disputes. In general, we recommend 30 days as a reasonable time to return deposits.

💡 **TIP**

Send an itemization even if you don't send money. Quite a few landlords mistakenly believe that they don't have to account for the deposit to a tenant who's been evicted by court order or who breaks the lease. But a tenant's misconduct does not entitle a landlord to pocket the entire deposit without further formality. In general, even if the tenant leaves owing several months' rent—more than the amount of the deposit—you still must notify the tenant in writing, within the time limit, as to how the deposit has been applied toward cleaning or repair charges and unpaid rent. You might then need to sue the tenant if the deposit doesn't cover damage and unpaid rent.

Deductions for Cleaning and Damage

Most disputes over security deposits revolve around whether it was reasonable for the landlord to deduct the cost of cleaning or repairing the premises after the tenant moved. Unfortunately, standards in this area are often vague. Typically, you may charge for any cleaning or repairs necessary to restore the rental unit to its condition at the beginning the tenancy, but not the cost of repairing the results of ordinary wear and tear.

Reasonable Deductions

A few examples of items that often justify security deposit deductions include stained or ripped carpets or curtains (particularly smoke-contaminated ones), damaged furniture, dirty appliances, and broken fixtures. You might also need to take care of such things as flea infestations left behind by the tenant's dog or mildew in the bathroom caused by the tenant's failure to clean properly.

That said, the details of every move-out differ, and you won't find any hard and fast rules on what damages should be considered your tenant's responsibility. But here are some basic guidelines:

- Don't charge the tenant for grime, filth, or damage that was present when the tenant moved in.
- Don't charge the tenant for replacing an item when a repair would be sufficient. For example, a tenant who damaged the kitchen counter by placing a hot pan on it shouldn't be charged for replacing the entire counter if an expertly done patch will do the job. You can take into account the overall condition of the unit, though—if it's a pristine luxury property, you don't need to make do with a patch.
- Do account for the length of the tenancy. The longer a tenant has lived in a place, the more wear and tear can be expected. In practical terms, this means that you can't always charge a tenant for cleaning carpets, drapes, or walls, or repainting.

- Don't charge an additional amount at move-out for cleaning if the tenant paid a nonrefundable cleaning fee. (Landlords in some states are allowed to charge a cleaning fee, which is separate from the security deposit and is specifically labeled as nonrefundable.)
- Do charge a fair price for repairs and replacements.

You can deduct a reasonable hourly charge if you or your employees do any necessary cleaning. If you have cleaning done by an outside service, keep your canceled checks or credit card receipts, and have the service itemize the work.

It's wise to patronize only those cleaning services whose employees are willing to testify for you, or at least send a letter describing what they did in detail, if the tenant sues you in small claims court contesting your deposit deductions. See "If a Tenant Sues You," below.

TIP

Don't overdo deductions from security deposits. When you make deductions for cleaning or damage, it's often a mistake to be too aggressive. Tenants who believe they've been wronged (even if it isn't true) are likely to go to small claims court. Even if you prevail, the value of the time you'll spend defending the case will be considerable. In the long run, it might be wiser to withhold a smaller portion of the deposit in the first place.

See "Wear and Tear vs. Tenant Damage?" below, for examples of what courts have treated as ordinary wear and tear, versus damage that the tenant must pay for.

Common Disagreements

Landlords and tenants frequently disagree on who's responsible for damage to paint, carpets, and fixtures.

Wear and Tear vs. Tenant Damage	
Ordinary Wear and Tear: Landlord's Responsibility	**Damage or Excessive Filth: Tenant's Responsibility**
Curtains faded by the sun	Cigarette burns in curtains or carpets
Cracks in or flaking of old grout causing loose tiles	Smashed or broken tiles
Minor marks on or nicks in wall	Large marks on or holes in wall
Dents in the wall where a door handle bumped it	Door off its hinges
Moderate dirt or spotting on carpet	Rips in carpet or pet urine stains
A few small tack or nail holes in wall	Lots of picture holes or gouges in walls that require patching as well as repainting
A rug worn thin by normal use	Stains in rug caused by leaking fish tank
Worn gaskets on refrigerator doors	Broken refrigerator shelf
Faded paint on bedroom wall	Water damage on wall from hanging plants
Dark patches of ingrained soil on hardwood floors that have lost their finish and have been worn down to bare wood	Water stains on wood floors and windowsills caused by windows being left open during rainstorms
Loose cabinet doors that won't close	Sticky cabinets and interiors
Stains on old porcelain fixtures that have lost their protective coating	Grime- or soap scum-coated bathtub or toilet
Moderately dirty miniblinds	Missing or bent miniblinds
Bathroom mirror beginning to "de-silver" (black spots)	Mirrors caked with lipstick and makeup
Toilet flushes inadequately because mineral deposits have clogged the jets	Toilet won't flush properly because it's stopped up with a diaper

Painting

Although most state and local laws (with the exception of New York City) provide no firm guidelines as to who is responsible for repainting when a rental unit needs it, courts usually rule that if a tenant has lived in your unit for many years, repainting should be done at your expense, not the tenant's. On the other hand, when tenants have lived in a unit for less than a year, and the walls were freshly painted when they moved in but are now a mess, you are entitled to charge the tenants for all costs of cleaning the walls. If repainting badly smudged walls is cheaper and more effective than cleaning, you can charge for repainting.

When to Charge Tenants for Repainting

One landlord we know uses the following approach when tenants move out and repainting is necessary:

- If the tenants occupied the premises for six months or less, and the walls are dirty, the full cost of repainting (labor and materials) is subtracted from the deposit.
- If the tenants lived in the unit between six months and a year, and the walls are dirty, two-thirds of the painting cost is subtracted from the deposit.
- Tenants who occupy a unit for between one and two years and leave dirty walls are charged one-third of the repainting cost.
- No one who stays for two years or more is ever charged a painting fee. No matter how dirty the walls become, the landlord always repaints when it's been more than two years since the previous painting.

Obviously, these general rules should be modified to fit particular circumstances.

Rugs and Carpets

If the living room rug was already threadbare when the tenant moved in a few months ago and looks even worse now, it's pretty obvious that the tenant's footsteps have simply contributed to the inevitable, and that this wear and tear is not the tenant's responsibility. On the other hand, a brand-new, good quality rug that becomes stained and full of bare spots within months has probably been subjected to the type of abuse the tenant will have to pay for. In between, it's anyone's guess. But the longer a tenant has lived in a unit, and the cheaper or older the carpet was when the tenant moved in, the less likely the tenant is to be held responsible for its deterioration.

> **EXAMPLE:** A tenant has ruined an eight-year-old rug that had a life expectancy of ten years. If a replacement rug would cost $1,000, you would charge the tenant $200 for the two years of life that would have remained in the rug had their dog not ruined it.

Fixtures

The law generally considers pieces of furniture or equipment that are physically attached to the rental property, such as bolted-on bookshelves, to be your property, even if the tenant (not you) paid for them. Disputes often arise when tenants, unaware of this rule, install a fixture and then attempt to remove it and take it with them when they leave. To avoid this kind of dispute, the lease and rental agreements in this book forbid tenants from altering the premises without your consent. That includes the installation of fixtures. See Clause 12 of the form agreements in Chapter 2.

If the tenant leaves behind built-in bookshelves, you can remove the shelves, restore the property to the same condition as before they were installed, and subtract the cost from the tenant's security deposit. Unless your lease or rental agreement says otherwise, you do not have to return the bookshelves to the tenant. Legally, you've only removed something that has become part of the premises and, hence, your property. Chapter 9 offers suggestions on how to avoid disputes with tenants over fixtures.

Deductions for Unpaid Rent

You can deduct unpaid rent from a tenant's security deposit, including any unpaid utility charges or other financial obligations required under your lease or rental agreement.

> ! **CAUTION**
> **Even when the debt far exceeds the amount of the security deposit, do not ignore your statutory duties to itemize and notify the former tenant of your use of the security deposit.** Itemization might seem pointless when you're owed more than the deposit, but some courts will penalize you for ignoring the statute, even if you later obtain a judgment that puts the stamp of approval on your use of the funds.

Month-to-Month Tenancies

Ideally, month-to-month tenants will give the right amount of notice and pay for the last month's rent. Usually, the required notice period is the same as the rental period: 30 days. Then, when the tenant leaves as planned, the only issue with respect to the security deposit is whether the tenant has caused any damage or left the place dirty. But there are three common variations on this ideal scenario, and they all allow you to use the security deposit for unpaid rent:

- The tenant leaves as announced, but with unpaid rent.

- The tenant leaves later than planned, and hasn't paid for the extra days.
- The tenant leaves as announced, but hasn't given you the right amount of notice.

Let's look at each situation.

The Tenant Leaves Owing Rent

If the tenant is behind on the rent, you're entitled to deduct—either during the tenancy or when the tenant leaves—what's owed from the security deposit. If you deduct during the tenancy, you must still follow your state's law on itemization at the end of the tenancy.

The Tenant Stays After the Announced Departure Date

A tenant who fails to leave when planned (or when requested, if you have terminated the rental agreement) isn't entitled to stay on rent free. When the tenant eventually leaves, you can calculate the exact amount owed by prorating the monthly rent for the number of days the tenant failed to pay.

> **EXAMPLE:** Your tenant Erin gives notice on March 1 of her intent to move out on April 1. She pays you the rent of $1,200 for March. But because she can't get into her new place on time, Erin stays until April 5 without paying anything more for the extra five days. You are entitled to deduct 5/30 (one-sixth) of the total month's rent, or $200, from Erin's security deposit.

The Tenant Gives Inadequate Notice

A tenant who gives notice is required to pay rent for the entire notice period required by law—even when the tenant leaves before the full period has expired. If the tenant gave less than the legally required amount of notice and moved out, you are entitled to rent for the balance of the notice period unless the place is rerented within the 30 days.

EXAMPLE 1: Your tenant Tom moves out on the fifth day of the month, without giving you any notice or paying any rent for the month. The rental market is flooded, and you are unable to rerent the property for two months. You are entitled to deduct an entire month's rent (for the missing 30 days' notice) plus one-sixth of one month (for the five holdover days for which Tom failed to pay rent).

EXAMPLE 2: Sheila pays her $900 monthly rent on October 1. State law requires 30 days' notice to terminate a tenancy. On October 15, Sheila informs you that she's leaving on the 25th. This gives you only ten days' notice, when you're entitled to 30. You're entitled to rent through the 30th day, counting from October 15, or November 14, unless you find a new tenant in the meantime. Because the rent is paid through October 31, Sheila owes you the prorated rent for 14 days in November. At $900 per month or $30 a day, this works out to $420, which you can deduct from Sheila's security deposit.

Fixed-Term Leases

When a tenant leaves before a fixed-term lease expires, you're usually entitled to the balance of the rent due under the lease, minus any rent you receive from new tenants or could have received from diligent efforts to rerent the property.

When a tenant leaves less than a month before the lease is scheduled to end, you can be almost positive that, if the case goes to court, a judge will conclude that the tenant owes rent for the entire lease term. It would be unreasonable to expect you to find a new tenant immediately. But if the tenant leaves more than 30 days before the end of a lease, your duty to look for a new tenant will be taken more seriously by the courts.

See Chapter 14 for more on your duty to try to rerent the property promptly.

EXAMPLE: On January 1, Anthony rents a house from Will for $1,200 a month and signs a one-year lease. Anthony moves out on June 30, even though six months remain on the lease, making him responsible for a total rent of $7,200. Will rerents the property on July 10, this time for $1,250 a month (the new tenants pay $833 for the last 20 days in July), which means that he'll receive a total rent of $7,083 through December 31. That's $117 less than the $7,200 he would have received from Anthony had he lived up to the lease, so Will may deduct $117 from Anthony's deposit. In addition, if Will has spent a reasonable amount of money to find new tenants (for newspaper ads, rental agency commissions, and credit checks), he may also deduct this sum from the deposit.

Deducting Rent After You've Evicted a Tenant

If you successfully sue to evict a holdover tenant, you will obtain a court order telling the tenant to leave (which you give to a law enforcement agency to enforce) and a money judgment ordering the tenant to pay you rent through the date of the judgment. Armed with these court orders, you can subtract from the security deposit:

- the amount of the judgment, and
- prorated rent for the period between the date of the judgment and the date the tenant actually leaves.

EXAMPLE: Marilyn sues to evict a tenant who fails to pay May's rent of $900. She gets an eviction judgment from the court on June 10 for rent prorated through that date. The tenant doesn't leave until the 17th, when the sheriff comes and puts him out. Marilyn can deduct the following items from the deposit:

- costs of necessary cleaning and repair, as allowed by state law
- the amount of the judgment (for rent through June 10), and
- rent for the week between judgment and eviction (seven days at $30/day, or $210).

Before you subtract the amount of a court judgment for unpaid rent from a deposit, deduct any cleaning and repair costs and any unpaid rent not included in the judgment. The reason is simple: A judgment can be collected in all sorts of ways—for example, you can go after the former tenant's wages or bank account—if the security deposit is not large enough to cover everything owed you.

However, it's much harder to collect money the tenant owes you for damage and cleaning when you don't have a judgment for the amount. If you don't subtract these items from the deposit, you'll have to file suit in small claims court as discussed below. But if you subtract the amount for cleaning, damage, and any unpaid rent not covered in the judgment first, you will still have the judgment if the deposit isn't large enough to cover everything.

EXAMPLE 1: Amelia collected a security deposit of $1,200 from Timothy, whom she ultimately had to sue to evict for failure to pay rent. Amelia got a judgment for $160 court costs plus $1,000 unpaid rent through the date of the judgment. Timothy didn't leave until the sheriff came, about five days later, thus running up an additional prorated rent of $100. Timothy also left dirt and damage that cost $1,000 to clean and repair.

Amelia (who hadn't read this book) first applied the $1,200 security deposit to the $1,160 judgment, leaving only $40 to apply toward the rent of $100 which was not reflected in the judgment, as well as the cleaning and repair charges, all of which totaled $1,100. Amelia must now sue Timothy for the $1,060 that wasn't covered by the judgment.

EXAMPLE 2: Now, assume that Monique was Timothy's landlord in the same situation. But Monique applied Timothy's $1,200 deposit first to the cleaning and damage charges of $1,000, and then to the $100 rent not reflected in the judgment. This left $100 to apply to the $1,160 judgment, the balance of which she can collect by garnishing Timothy's wages or bank account.

Preparing an Itemized Statement of Deductions

Once you've inspected the premises and decided what you need to deduct, you're ready to prepare a statement for the tenant. The statement should list each deduction and briefly explain what it's for.

This section includes samples of security deposit itemization forms that address three different situations. Copies of all three forms can be downloaded from the Nolo website.

(See Appendix B for the link to the forms in this book.) Whatever form you use, be sure to keep a copy in your tenant records and receipts for repairs or cleaning in case the tenant ends up suing you. See "If a Tenant Sues You," below.

CAUTION
If your city or state requires you to pay interest on a tenant's entire deposit, you must also refund this amount. For details, see Chapter 4.

Sample 1: Returning the Entire Deposit

If you are returning a tenant's entire security deposit (including interest, if required), simply send a brief letter like the one below.

Sample 2: Itemizing Deductions for Repairs, Cleaning, and Related Losses

If you're making deductions from the tenant's security deposit only for cleaning and repair, use the Security Deposit Itemization (Deductions for Repairs and Cleaning). A sample is shown above.

For each deduction, list the item and the dollar amount. If you've already had the work done, attach receipts to the itemization. If your receipts aren't very detailed, add more information on labor and supplies, for example:

- "Carpet cleaning by ABC Carpet Cleaners, $160, required because of several large grease stains and candle wax embedded in living room rug."
- "Plaster repair, $400, of several fist-sized holes in bedroom wall."
- "$250 to replace curtains in living room, damaged by cigarette smoke and holes."

If you can't get necessary repairs made or cleaning done within the time required to return the security deposit, make a reasonable estimate of the cost. But keep in mind that if the tenant subsequently sues you, you will need to produce receipts for at least as much as the amount you deducted.

Letter for Returning Entire Security Deposit

October 11, 20xx
_____
Date

Gerry Fraser
_____
Tenant

976 Park Place
_____
Street Address

Sacramento, CA 95840
_____
City and State

Dear Gerry _____ ,
                    Tenant

Here is an itemization of your $ _____$1,500_____ security deposit on the property at _976 Park Place_

_____ ,

which you rented from me on a _____ month-to-month _____ basis on

march 1, 20xx and vacated on _September 30, 20xx_ .

You left the rental property in satisfactory condition, so I am returning the entire amount of the security

deposit of _$1,500, plus $150 in interest, for a total of $1,650_ .

Sincerely,

Tom Stein

Landlord/Manager

Security Deposit Itemization
(Deductions for Repairs and Cleaning)

Date _____November 8, 20xx_____

From: _____Rachel Tolan_____

_____123 Larchmont Lane_____

_____St. Louis, Missouri 63119_____

To: _____Lena Coleman_____

_____456 Penny Lane, #101_____

_____St. Louis, Missouri 63119_____

Property Address: _____789 Cora Court, St. Louis, Missouri_____

Rental Period: _____January 1, 20xx to October 31, 20xx_____

1. Security Deposit Received: $ _____1,000_____

2. Interest on Deposit (if required by lease or law): $ _____N/A_____

3. Total Credit (sum of lines 1 and 2): $ _____1,000_____

4. Itemized Repairs and Related Losses:

    _____Repainting of living room walls, required_____

    _____by crayon and chalk marks_____

    _____ $ _____300_____

5. Necessary Cleaning:

    _____Sum paid to resident manager for 5 hours_____

    _____cleaning at $20/hour: debris-filled_____

    _____garage, dirty stove, and refrigerator_____ $ _____100_____

6. Total Cleaning & Repair (sum of lines 4 and 5): $ _____400_____

7. Amount Owed (line 3 minus line 6):

    ☐ Total Amount Tenant Owes Landlord: $ _____

    ☑ Total Amount Landlord Owes Tenant: $ _____600_____

Comments: _____A check for $600 is enclosed._____

When you're trying to put a dollar amount on damages, the basic approach is to ask yourself if the tenant has damaged or substantially shortened the useful life of an item that would wear out regardless. If the answer is yes, you can charge the tenant the prorated cost of the item, based on the age of the item, how long it might have lasted otherwise, and the cost of replacement.

Sample 3: Itemizing Deductions for Repairs, Cleaning, and Unpaid Rent

If you have to deduct for unpaid rent as well as cleaning and repairs, use the form Security Deposit Itemization (Deductions for Repairs, Cleaning, and Unpaid Rent). A sample is shown below.

Handling Deposits When a Tenant Files for Bankruptcy

Landlords often see a tenant's bankruptcy filing as the ultimate monkey wrench in what might already be a less-than-perfect landlord-tenant relationship. Indeed, unless you've completed your eviction case and have received a judgment for possession before the tenant files for bankruptcy, you'll have to go to the bankruptcy court and ask for permission to begin (or continue) your eviction case. (How to handle evictions and bankruptcy is explained in Chapter 17.) Fortunately, the effect of the bankruptcy on your use of the security deposit is not so drastic.

Your course of action depends on when the tenant filed the bankruptcy petition, and when you used the deposit to cover unpaid rent or damage. Here are three common scenarios and the rules for each:

- **You use the security deposit, then tenant files for bankruptcy.** In this situation, the tenant hasn't paid the rent, or has caused damage, or both. You assess your total losses and deduct from (or use up) the deposit, and then the tenant files for bankruptcy. No problem here, because you used the money before the

tenant filed. You're also on solid ground if you've gone to court and obtained a money judgment that can be satisfied fully, or at least partially, by the security deposit. The key is to use the funds, or get the judgment, before the tenant files.

> **TIP**
> **Take care of business quickly.** You probably won't know about your tenant's plans to file for bankruptcy. It's wise to assess your losses soon after the tenant vacates and to leave a paper trail that will establish that you used the deposit before the filing date. If you keep deposits in a separate bank account and move these funds to another account as you use them, you'll have good proof.

- **You receive notice of tenant's bankruptcy before you use the security deposit.** Here, the tenant causes damage, or fails to pay the rent, or both. Before you have the chance to use the security deposit to pay for the damage or rent, you receive a notice from the bankruptcy court stating that the tenant has filed. Once you receive this notice, federal law prohibits you from taking any action against the tenant, including using the security deposit, without first getting permission from the court (this is called a "Relief from Stay").

  Instead of going to court to get the relief, you can just sit tight and wait until the bankruptcy proceeding is over. Then, if the trustee doesn't make a claim to the deposit money, you can use it to cover the tenant's debt. In most cases, any rent due will be discharged at the end of the bankruptcy case.

  However, sometimes money is available to creditors to compensate for losses. If so, and if the court asks you to file a bankruptcy claim, things can get complicated. If this is your situation, we recommend consulting with a bankruptcy lawyer.

Security Deposit Itemization
(Deductions for Repairs, Cleaning, and Unpaid Rent)

Date _____December 19, 20xx_____

From: _____Timothy Gottman_____

_____8910 Pine Avenue_____

_____Philadelphia, Pennsylvania 19106_____

To: _____Monique Todd_____

_____999 Laurel Drive_____

_____Philadelphia, Pennsylvania 19106_____

Property Address: _____456 Pine Avenue #7, Philadelphia, Pennsylvania 19106_____

Rental Period: _____January 1, 20xx to October 31, 20xx_____

1. Security Deposit Received: $ _____1,200_____

2. Interest on Deposit (if required by lease or law): $ _____N/A_____

3. Total Credit (sum of lines 1 and 2): $ _____1,200_____

4. Itemized Repairs and Related Losses:

   _____Carpet repair $160, curtain cleaning $140, plaster_____

   _____repair $200, painting of living room $300_____

   _____(receipts attached)_____ $ _____800_____

5. Necessary Cleaning:

   _____Sum paid to resident manager for 10 hours_____

   _____cleaning at $20/hour: debris-filled garage,_____

   _____dirty stove and refrigerator_____ $ _____200_____

6. Defaults in Rent Not Covered by Any Court Judgment
   (list dates and rates):

   _____5 days at $20/day from November 6 to_____

   _____November 11 (date of court judgment or_____

   _____date of physical eviction)_____ $ _____100_____

7. Amount of Court Judgment for Rent, Costs, Attorneys' Fees: $ _____1,160_____

8. Other Deductions:

Specify: _____

_____

_____ $ _____

9. Total Amount Owed Landlord (sum of lines 4 through 8): $ _____ 2,260 _____

10. Amount Owed (line 3 minus line 9):

☑ Total Amount Tenant Owes Landlord: $ _____ 1,060 _____

☐ Total Amount Landlord Owes Tenant: $ _____

Comments: _The security deposit has been applied as follows: $1,000 for damage and cleaning_
charges, $100 for defaults in rent (not covered by any court judgment),
and the remaining $100 toward payment of the $1,160 court judgment. This leaves
$1,060 still owed on the judgment. Please send that amount to me at once or I shall
take appropriate legal action to collect it.

It's also a good idea to consult with a bankruptcy lawyer when a large sum is at stake or if you have any questions about how to handle the security deposit.

- **Tenant files for bankruptcy, then causes damage that would normally be covered by the security deposit.** Follow the same advice given for the second example.

Mailing the Security Deposit Itemization

Some tenants will want to personally pick up any deposit as soon as possible. If that isn't feasible, mail your security deposit itemization to the tenant's last known address or forwarding address as soon as is reasonably possible, along with payment for any balance you owe. Send the itemization as soon as you have all the necessary information—waiting until the end of the legally specified period almost guarantees that anxious former tenants will contact you. And, if you miss the deadline, you might be liable for hefty financial penalties, as discussed in "If a Tenant Sues You," below. Some states require landlords to use certified mail; check your state's statutes for any special mailing requirements. If the tenant didn't leave a forwarding address, mail the itemization and any balance to the address of the rental property itself. That, after all, is the tenant's last address known to you. If your former tenant has left a forwarding address with the Post Office, it will forward the mail.

It will be useful for you to know the tenant's new address if the tenant's deposit doesn't cover all proper deductions and you want to sue in small claims court. (See the discussion below.) It will also help you collect any judgment you have against the tenant.

You can learn the new address in two ways:

- **Set up an account with the Postal Service.** You can pay the Postal Service in advance to tell you whenever one of your letters is forwarded. Because of the cost involved, this procedure makes sense for landlords with multiple rental units.

- **Use "Return Receipt Requested."** For smaller landlords or people who rarely face this situation, it might not be worth your while to use the option above. Instead, you can send the letter "Return Receipt Requested" and, on the Postal Service form, check the box that tells the carrier to note the address where the letter was delivered. This address will be on the receipt that is sent back to you.

If the tenant didn't give the Postal Service a forwarding address, the letter will come back to you. The postmarked envelope is your proof of your good-faith attempt to notify the tenant, in case the tenant ever accuses you of not returning the money properly. Some states allow landlords to retain the deposit if they cannot locate a former tenant after a reasonable effort or the passage of a certain amount of time, such as 60 or 90 days. If your state laws don't specify what happens to the deposit when you can't locate the tenant, you'll need to seek legal advice on how to handle the funds.

Security Deposits From Cotenants

When you rent to two or more cotenants (tenants who all signed the same written lease or rental agreement), you usually don't have to return or account for any of the security deposit until they all leave. In other words, you're entitled to the benefit of the whole deposit until the entire tenancy ends. Legally, any question as to whether a departing cotenant is owed any share of the deposit should be worked out among the cotenants.

From a practical point of view, however, you might want to work out an agreement with a departing cotenant who wants part of the deposit back. For instance, you might be willing to refund a share of the deposit if the new cotenant gives you a check for the same amount. The drawback of this approach is that the new cotenant will not want to get stuck paying for damage that was caused by the departing tenant. To minimize the chances of that happening, you might be asked to do an inspection in the middle of the lease term, before the departing tenant leaves. (An inspection in the midst of the lease term could present an opportunity to discover and correct problems before they grow.)

> **EXAMPLE:** Bill and Mark were cotenants who had each contributed $500 toward the $1,000 security deposit. Bill needed to move before the lease was up and asked Len, their landlord, if he would accept Tom as a new cotenant. Len agreed.
>
> Bill wanted his $500 back, and, although Tom was willing to contribute his share of the deposit, he did not want to end up paying for damage that had been caused before he moved in. To take care of this, Len agreed to inspect if Tom would first give him a check for $500. When he got the check, Len inspected and found $200 worth of damage. He deducted this amount from Bill's share of the deposit and wrote Bill a check for $300. Len left it up to Bill and Mark to fairly apportion the responsibility for the damage. With Tom's $500 check, the security deposit was once again topped off.

If a Tenant Sues You

No matter how meticulous you are about properly accounting to your tenants for their deposits, you might be sued by a tenant who disagrees with your assessment of the cost of cleaning or repairs. Tenants might also sue if you fail to follow state or local laws regarding how and when to return the security deposit.

Tenants often sue in small claims court, where it's cheap to file, lawyers aren't necessary, and disputes are usually decided within 30 to 60 days, without formal rules of evidence. (We use the term small claims court here, but the exact name varies. Small claims court equivalents are called "Justice of the Peace," "Conciliation," "District," "Justice," "City," or "County" court in different places.)

The maximum amount for which someone can sue in small claims court depends on state law. State limits range from about $5,000 to $10,000. For details, see "State Small Claims Court Limits" in Appendix A.

CAUTION

Penalties for violating security deposit statutes can turn a minor squabble into an expensive affair. While it is rarely worth your while to go to court over a matter of $50 or even a couple of hundred dollars, the same is not true for the tenant. Why? Because many statutes allow a victorious tenant to collect not only actual damages (the amount improperly deducted from the deposit), but penalties as well.

This section suggests several strategies for dealing with small claims suits over security deposits, including how to prepare and present a case in small claims court.

RESOURCE

For more information on small claims court procedures, see *Everybody's Guide to Small Claims Court*, by Cara O'Neill (Nolo).

How Long Tenants Have to File Suit

Before going to court, the tenant will most likely express dissatisfaction by way of a letter or phone call demanding that you refund more than you did or fix some other problem involving the deposit. In some states, this sort of demand must be made before the tenant can begin a small claims suit.

Tenants who are going to sue will probably do it fairly promptly, but state law might allow them a few years after the tenancy ends to file. Don't throw out cleaning bills, receipts for repairs, or photographs showing dirt and damages after only a few months, lest you be caught defenseless.

Who Goes to Small Claims Court?

If your business is incorporated, you can send an employee such as a property manager, as long as the person is authorized to represent you in legal proceedings. If you are not incorporated, you'll probably have to go yourself, but a few states allow managers to go in your place. In some states you can be represented by a lawyer, but it's rarely worth the cost. Small claims court procedures are straightforward and understandable to nonlawyers.

Settling a Potential Lawsuit

If you receive a demand letter or phone call from a tenant, your best bet is almost always to try to work out a reasonable compromise. Be open to the idea of returning more of the deposit than you'd like, even if you believe your original assessment of the cost of repairs and cleaning was justified. For practical reasons, it usually doesn't make sense for you or an employee to prepare for a small claims trial and spend time in court to argue over $50, $100, or even $200. This is especially true because, fair or not, some judges are prone to simply resolving the dispute by splitting the difference between the landlord's and the tenant's claims.

If you and the tenant can't reach a reasonable compromise, you might consider getting help from a local landlord-tenant mediation service.

If you arrive at a compromise with your former tenant, insist that your payment be accepted as full and final satisfaction of your obligation to return the deposit. The best way to do this is to prepare and have the tenant sign a brief settlement agreement, like the sample shown below.

Sample Settlement Agreement Regarding Return of Security Deposit

Lionel Washington, "Landlord," and LaToya Jones, "Tenant," agree as follows:

1. Landlord rented the premises at 1234 State Avenue, Apartment 5, Santa Fe, New Mexico, to Tenant on July 1, 20xx, pursuant to a written rental agreement for a tenancy from month to month.

2. Under the Agreement, Tenant paid Landlord $1,000 as a security deposit.

3. On October 31, 20xx Tenant vacated the premises.

4. Within 30 days (the time required by New Mexico law) after Tenant vacated the premises, Landlord itemized various deductions from the security deposit totaling $380 and refunded the balance of $620 to Tenant.

5. Tenant asserts that she is entitled to the additional sum of $300, only $80 of the deductions being proper. Landlord asserts that all the deductions were proper and that he owes Tenant nothing.

6. To settle the parties' entire dispute, and to compromise on Tenant's claim for return of her security deposit, Landlord pays to Tenant the sum of $150, receipt of which is hereby acknowledged by Tenant as full satisfaction of her claim.

Lionel Washington	*12/1/xx*
Lionel Washington, Landlord	Date
LaToya Jones	*12/1/xx*
LaToya Jones, Tenant	Date

Splitting the Difference With Tenants

One landlord we know with thousands of units experiences about 250 move-outs each month. In about one-third, he receives a complaint from a tenant who claims too much of the deposit was withheld.

This landlord's general policy is to offer to settle for 70% of the disputed amount. Because the average amount withheld is $175, this means the landlord is usually willing to reduce his claim by $52.50. If a tenant refuses to accept this compromise, the landlord will often make a second offer of a 50% reduction.

He does this not because he thinks his original assessment was wrong, but because he finds that settling with tenants costs a lot less than fighting in court. However, if the settlement offer isn't accepted promptly by the tenant, he fights to win—and almost always does.

One downside of this practice is that it signals to other tenants (assuming they speak to each other) that they can always bargain down the amount deducted from their deposits. However, if the rate of disputes does not increase over time, you can conclude that word has not spread.

Preparing for a Small Claims Court Hearing

If compromise is not possible and the tenant sues you, the court will officially notify you of the date, time, and place of the small claims court hearing.

It's still not too late at this stage to try to work out a settlement. However, if you compromise at this stage, insist that the tenant formally dismisses the small claims courts suit, and get your settlement in writing.

Before your court hearing, gather tangible evidence supporting your claim, such as photos showing the premises needed cleaning or were damaged when the tenant left. It's essential to take to court as many of the following items of evidence as you can, even if they are not directly related to the dispute:

- Copies of the lease or rental agreement, signed by you and the tenant.
- Copies of move-in and move-out letters clarifying rules and policies on cleaning, damage repair, and security deposits.
- A copy of the Landlord-Tenant Checklist that you should have filled out at move-in and move-out, signed by both you and the tenant. This is particularly important if the tenant admitted, on the checklist, to damaged or dirty conditions at move-out.
- Photos or a video of the premises before the tenant moved in that show that the place was clean and undamaged.
- Photos or a video after the tenant left, which show the mess or damage.
- An itemization of hours spent by you or your repair or cleaning people, with the hourly costs for the work, plus copies of receipts for cleaning materials; or credit card itemizations or canceled checks.
- Damaged items small enough to bring into the courtroom (for example, a curtain with a cigarette hole).
- Receipts (or canceled checks showing payment) for professional cleaning and repair.
- One, or preferably two, witnesses who were familiar with the property, who saw it just after the tenant left, and who will testify that the place was a mess or that certain items were damaged. People who helped in the cleaning or repair are particularly effective witnesses. There is no rule that says you can't have a close friend or relative testify for you, but, given a choice, it's better to have a witness who's neither a friend nor kin.
- If it's difficult for a witness to come to court, a written statement (a signed letter) or a declaration under penalty of perjury (an affidavit) will be accepted in most states. Documents, however, usually aren't as effective as live testimony. If you present a written statement from a witness, the

statement should include the date of the event, exactly what the witness saw in terms of damage, any credentials that make the person qualified to testify on the subject, and any other facts that relate to the dispute

Sample Declaration of Cleaning Service

I, Paul Stallone, declare:

1. I am employed at A & B Maintenance Company, a contract cleaning and maintenance service located at 123 Abrego Street, Central City, Iowa. Gina Cabarga, the owner of an apartment complex at 456 Seventh Street, Central City, Iowa, is one of our accounts.

2. On May 1, 20xx I was requested to go to the premises at 456 Seventh Street, Apartment 8, Central City, Iowa, to shampoo the carpets. When I entered the premises, I noticed a strong odor, part of what seemed like stale cigarette smoke. An odor also seemed to come from the carpet.

3. When I began using a steam carpet cleaner on the living room carpet, I noticed a strong smell of urine. I stopped the steam cleaner, moved to a dry corner of the carpet and pulled it from the floor. I then saw a yellow color on the normally white foam-rubber pad beneath the carpet, as well as smelled a strong urine odor, apparently caused by a pet (probably a cat) having urinated on the carpet. On further examination of the parts of the carpet, I noticed similar stains and odors throughout the carpet and pad.

4. In my opinion, the living room carpet and foam-rubber pad underneath need to be removed and replaced, and the floor should be sanded and sealed.

I declare under penalty of perjury under the laws of the State of Iowa that the foregoing is true and correct.

Paul Stallone   6/15/xx

Paul Stallone, Cleaner   Date

Small Claims Suits Don't Affect Other Lawsuits

Nothing that happens in small claims court affects the validity of any judgment you already have against the tenant—for example, from an earlier eviction suit. So, if you got a judgment against a tenant for $1,200 for unpaid rent as part of an eviction action, this judgment is still good, even though a tenant wins $200 against you in small claims court based on your failure to return the deposit.

Penalties for Violating Security Deposit Laws

When you don't follow state or local security deposit laws to the letter, you might pay a heavy price if a tenant sues you and wins. In addition to whatever amount you wrongfully withheld, you might have to pay the tenant extra or punitive damages (penalties imposed when the judge feels that the defendant has acted especially outrageously) and court costs. In many states, if you "willfully" (deliberately and not through inadvertence) violate the security deposit statute, you might forfeit your right to retain any part of the deposit and be liable for two or three times the amount wrongfully withheld, plus attorneys' fees and costs.

When the Deposit Doesn't Cover Damage and Unpaid Rent

Tenants aren't the only ones who can use small claims court. If the security deposit doesn't cover what a tenant owes you for back rent, cleaning, or repairs, it might make sense to file a small claims lawsuit against the former tenant.

Be sure your claim doesn't exceed your state's small claims court limit or, if it does, consider capping the amount you demand to no more than the court's limit. Given the costs of going to formal court, reducing your demand often makes financial sense.

The Demand Letter

If you decide that it's worthwhile to go after your tenant for money owed, your first step is to write a letter asking for the amount of your claim. Although this might seem like an exercise in futility, the law in many states requires that you make a formal demand for the amount sued for before filing in small claims court. But, even if there isn't a requirement, it's almost essential that you send some sort of demand letter. It's not only useful in trying to settle your dispute, it's also an excellent opportunity to carefully organize the case you will present in court.

Your demand can consist of a brief cover letter along with a copy of your earlier written itemization of how you applied the tenant's security deposit to the charges (in which you also requested payment of the balance). The tone of your cover letter should be polite, yet firm. Ask for exactly what you want, and be sure to set a deadline. Conclude by stating that you will promptly file a lawsuit in small claims court if you don't reach an understanding by the deadline.

Should You Sue?

If your demand letter doesn't produce results, think carefully before you rush off to your local small claims court. Ask yourself three questions:

- Do I have a strong case?
- Can I locate the former tenant?
- Can I collect a judgment if I win?

If the answer to any of these questions is no, filing a lawsuit is probably not worth your trouble.

Do You Have a Strong Case?

Review the items of evidence listed above in "Preparing an Itemized Statement of Deductions." If you lack a substantial number of these pieces of evidence, you might end up losing, even if you're in the right.

Can You Locate the Former Tenant?

To begin your small claims court case, legal papers must be sent to the tenant. So, you'll need an address where the tenant lives or works. If the tenant left a forwarding address, this shouldn't be an issue. But if you don't have a home or work address for the tenant, you'll need to do a little detective work if you want to sue.

Start by sending a postcard or letter to the tenant at the last known address (it might be your rental) with the words, "Return Service Requested," on the front. If the tenant asked the Post Office to forward mail to a new address, the letter will be returned to you with a sticker noting the new address.

You can also use the Internet to your advantage. For better or worse, you can learn a lot about people simply by searching their full name and last-known city of residence. Search results will often yield a new address. Although many "people finder" websites charge you for the information, you often can find what you need for free. Or, if your search comes up with nothing, do some sleuthing on social media. For example, look for your former tenants on Facebook—many people update their location information and leave it public for all to see. Even if you don't get a full address this way, you might get some clues as to where to look further.

Finally, you could use a commercial service, known as a judgment recovery agency, to find your ex-tenant. Typically, these outfits not only find the tenant, but collect any judgment that the landlord has against the tenant. If you don't yet have a judgment, you'll simply pay for the service, which might not be cost-efficient if the amount of money at stake is modest.

Can You Collect a Judgment If You Win?

Winning a small claims court case won't do you any good if you can't collect the judgment. Suing a person you know to be bankrupt, insolvent, or just plain broke might not be worth the effort, because you'll have little chance of transforming your court judgment into cash. When you evaluate the solvency of the tenant, keep in mind that small claims judgments are good for ten years in many states. So, if you have a spat with a student or someone who might get a job soon, it could be worthwhile to get a judgment with the hope of collecting later.

Using Collection Agencies

If you don't want to sue in small claims court, consider hiring a licensed local collection agency to try to collect from the tenant. The agency will probably want to keep as its fee one-third to one-half of what it collects for you. (The older the debt or the more difficult it is to locate the tenant, the more the agency will charge.)

If the agency can't collect, you can authorize it to hire a lawyer to sue the ex-tenant, usually in a formal (non-small-claims) court. Many collection agencies pay all court costs, hoping to recover them if and when they collect the resulting judgment. In exchange for taking the risk of paying costs and losing the case, however, collection agency commissions often rise an additional 15%–20% when they hire a lawyer to sue.

Of course, turning a matter over to a collection agency doesn't necessarily mean you wash your hands of the matter. The collection agency still takes direction from you. If the tenant defends against a lawsuit filed by a collection agency's lawyer, you must be involved in the litigation. The only way to walk away from it completely is to sell the debt to the collection agency, which might pay you only a fraction of the amount owed.

Pay particular attention to the issue of how you will collect a judgment. The best way to collect any judgment is to garnish wages, so if your ex-tenant is working, there is an excellent chance of collecting if payment is not made voluntarily.

You can't, however, garnish a welfare, Social Security, unemployment, pension, or disability check. So, if the person sued gets income from one of these sources, you're wasting your time unless you can identify some other asset that you can efficiently get your hands on.

Bank accounts, motor vehicles, and real estate are other common collection sources. But people who run out on their debts don't always have much in a bank account (or they might have moved the account to make it difficult to locate), and much of their personal property might be exempt under state debt protection laws.

> ![caution] **CAUTION**
> **Take care of your reputation.** If you are a landlord with many rental units and regularly use a local small claims court, it's especially important that every case you bring is a good one. You don't want to lose your credibility with the court by ever appearing to be unfair or poorly prepared.

Ex-Tenants Who Have Moved Out of State

If the ex-tenant whom you plan to sue in small claims court has moved to another state, going to court to collect unpaid rent or other sums due might prove challenging. That's because the rules on suing out of state defendants vary from state to state. You'll need to clear two legal hurdles, as well as deal with the practicalities of collecting.

Can the Small Claims Court Hear Your Case?

The first legal challenge is easy to meet: Is this the kind of case that the small claims court can hear? Yes—small claims courts handle cases in which the plaintiff (you) sues someone (the defendant) to obtain a money judgment for an amount the plaintiff claims the defendant owes. Is the amount you want to recover within the court's dollar limits? Most likely so, unless your tenants owe you many, many thousands of dollars (you can check the small claims court limits in Appendix A).

Can You File Your Case in Your Local Court?

Your next hurdle—choosing the proper court location (called "venue")—could be a sticking point. In many small claims courts, you must file where the defendant resides or does business. For instance, if you wanted to file in the Magistrate Court in Fulton County, Georgia, you'd have to prove that the defendant lives or does business in Fulton County—something you can't do if the defendant is living out of state and not doing any business in Fulton County. If your state has equally stringent venue requirements (for small claims and for formal trial courts), you'll be out of luck. Your only option will be filing in whatever far off state your ex-tenant has relocated to—which likely wouldn't be worth the effort (see below).

But fortunately, venue rules vary from state to state (and can vary even amongst the various court levels within a state) so there's a still chance you might be able to file closer to home. Finding out will require researching your state's venue requirements. Many court websites provide that information. Or you can check your state's statutes and rules of court online on your state's legislative website.

Here are examples of typical venue rules you might find helpful:

- Many states have venue rules for contract cases that allow filing where the parties entered into the contract, where it was to be performed, where it was broken, where the contractual payments were made, or where the defendant lived or worked when the contract was signed.
- Some states allow landlords and tenants to file rental-related claims where the property is located.
- Check your contract—most courts allow claimants to file in the venue the parties agreed to in the contract. Your contract might contain a helpful venue clause—and if it doesn't, consider including one in the future.

If your state's venue rules preclude you from filing in small claims court, don't give up. Check the venue rules of a higher trial court. Formal trial courts might have more forgiving rules, allowing you to sue an out of state defendant. Litigating your case in a formal court shouldn't require too much additional effort if it's a winner.

If the ex-tenant doesn't show up, you'll win by default.

If, after diligent research, you find that your state doesn't have a favorable venue rule, and you don't want to (or can't) file in formal trial court, you'll likely have to file in a small claims court in the state where your ex-tenant now resides. This option might not be as bad as it seems. You can appear by telephone or written affidavit in some small claims courts, so you might be able to litigate your claim without leaving home. As a last resort, check whether the ex-tenant's current state allows attorney representation in small claims court—many do. Depending on the size of your money claim and the likelihood of actually collecting a judgment, hiring a lawyer might be the way to go.

Finding and Serving Your Ex-tenant

So much for the legal hurdles. Now, you'll need to determine how to notify the defendant of the lawsuit and its hearing or trial date (known as "serving" the paperwork). If you're lucky enough to file on your home turf, you'll follow your state's out-of-state service guidelines. It's often as simple as using certified or registered mail. But even if you must personally serve the defendant, you should be able to go online and find a process server who works in the area where your ex-tenant currently resides. Often, you can hire the local sheriff's office to personally serve the defendant for a reasonable fee. Call the local sheriff and ask if the office serves civil process papers, or visit the office's website— you'll likely find the relevant information in a "civil" or "civil process" section.

Collecting If You Win

The last practical issue is often the most challenging. If you win, you still could have a problem collecting your money judgment if the defendant doesn't pay voluntarily. If your ex-tenant has no property in your state, you'll need to focus your efforts on where the tenant now lives.

While states must honor each other's judgments, the defendant's state of residence can impose worky procedural requirements. For instance, you might have to file a certified judgment in the defendant's local court, where you will ask the judge to issue a writ of execution or similar official order. The local sheriff or marshal will need the order to levy on the defendant's bank account or garnish wages.

Do all of these hoops sound maddening? It is—although collecting the money judgment should be a matter of doggedly following the out-of-state court's particular procedures, researching and abiding by another state's rules can be time-consuming and costly. When you consider the amount you'd recover, you might reasonably conclude that this out-of-state tenant is not worth pursuing.

What to Do With Property Abandoned by a Tenant

Whether a tenant moves out voluntarily or with the aid of a sheriff or marshal after you win an eviction lawsuit, you might find yourself not only cleaning up and repairing damage, but also dealing with personal property left behind. Usually, it's just stuff that the tenant obviously doesn't want, such as leftover food, half-filled cleaning supplies, and garbage. When it's clear that you're dealing with garbage, you're perfectly within your rights to dispose of it.

Getting rid of things with some value—such as bicycles, jewelry, clothes, or furniture—is another story. In some states, you can face serious liability for disposing of the tenant's personal property (other than obvious trash) unless you follow specific state rules. Typically, the more valuable the property left behind, the more formalities you must follow. Not surprisingly, states that heavily regulate other aspects of landlords' dealings with tenants also impose complicated requirements on how you handle abandoned property. States with fewer laws governing the landlord-tenant relationship tend to pay scant attention to the subject.

This section provides an overview of how to handle abandoned property. It covers the general legal issues that should be understood by all landlords.

Because state laws vary so much, we can't give you detailed state-by-state instructions on how to comply. For this reason, it's critical that you read your own state statute for details on issues such as how to notify tenants and how much time you must give them to reclaim property before you can dispose of or sell it. In addition, you would be wise to check with your local landlords' association or state consumer protection agency to make sure that the process set out in your statute is all you need to know. In some states, courts have modified the procedures in the statutes, often imposing additional requirements—and, unfortunately, legislatures don't always revisit their statutes to bring them into line with court-ordered changes. "State Laws on Handling Abandoned Property" in Appendix A gives you citations to your state's statutes.

SEE AN EXPERT

If you're dealing with property of obviously significant value or have good reason to suspect that a tenant will cause problems later, consult a lawyer before you dispose of, donate, or sell the tenant's possessions. Protect yourself against departing tenants' claims that you have destroyed or stolen their property. In legal jargon, mishandling former tenants' property is known as "unlawful conversion"—taking someone else's property and converting it to your own use or benefit, either by selling it, disposing of it, or using it yourself.

Why Has the Tenant Left?

In many states, your options when dealing with tenants' abandoned property differ depending on the circumstances of the tenant's departure. Here are typical scenarios, covered at length below:

- **Planned moves.** The tenant decides to move at the end of a lease or after giving you a termination notice. In this situation, many states give you maximum flexibility to dispose of leftover belongings.
- **Post-termination moves.** The tenant decides to move after receiving a termination notice from you (even one for cause, such as nonpayment of rent). Many states give you maximum flexibility to dispose of leftover belongings in this situation.
- **Evicted tenants.** The tenants are physically evicted, along with their personal belongings that might be dumped on the street or sidewalk by the sheriff. Some states require landlords to take significant care with the property of former tenants who were evicted—though some require less effort.
- **Unannounced departures.** The tenant simply disappears. In a few states, property belonging to tenants who simply move out unexpectedly must be treated differently from property that's left after a clearly deliberate move.

When you read your state's law, be on the lookout for different rules based on the reason for the tenant's departure.

Planned Moves and Post-Termination Moves

Often, when tenants leave voluntarily but inconsiderately leave you with a pile of stuff, you will have more latitude when it comes to discarding abandoned property than if you had evicted the tenants. The reasoning here is that tenants who decide upon and plan their own departure—even the ones who leave after receiving a three-day notice—have time to pack or dispose of their belongings themselves. Tenants who fail to take care of their own property are in no position to demand that you, the landlord, handle their property with kid gloves—and many state laws don't require that you do so.

Evicted Tenants

Law enforcement officials who physically evict tenants will also remove property from the rental unit. In these situations, tenants arguably have less opportunity to arrange for proper packing, storing, or moving than they would if they were moving voluntarily (even though most states give tenants a few days' warning of the sheriff's impending visit). For this reason, landlords in some states must make an effort to preserve the property, locate the tenant, and wait before disposing of or selling items left behind. Typically, law enforcement officials are permitted to place the tenant's possessions on the sidewalk or street; then the landlord might be required to step in and store the possessions.

Paradoxically, some states take the opposite approach, reasoning that tenants who have lost an eviction lawsuit aren't entitled to special treatment when it comes to reclaiming items left in the rental unit.

Unannounced Departures

Odd as it seems, it's not unusual for tenants to simply disappear with no notice, leaving considerable belongings behind. Sometimes, the tenants are behind on the rent and figure that abandoning their possessions will be cheaper, in the long run, than paying the rent. Here again, your state might impose detailed procedures, requiring you to store the property for a significant time or make extra efforts to locate the tenants. One reason for this consideration is to protect tenants who have *not* abandoned the tenancy or their possessions, but have gone on a trip or vacation and simply didn't bother to tell you. The idea is that by taking special pains to determine the tenants' intent, and by giving them ample time to claim their things, landlords can avoid problems caused by misunderstanding the tenants' intentions.

By following the rules requiring landlords to store property and attempt to locate tenants, you will reduce tenants' ability to sue you for prematurely disposing of property. "If the Tenant Breaks the Lease" in Chapter 14 discusses how to tell whether tenants have really abandoned the premises, and how to attempt to locate them.

Distress and Distraint: What Are They?

A few states still have statutes on the books that provide for "distress" or "distraint." These were medieval procedures that allowed landlords who were owed money, after or even during the tenancy, to simply grab their tenants' possessions. In the words of one judge, it "allowed a man to be his own avenger." In America, the practice of requiring security deposits was developed in states that did not allow landlords to use distress and distraint.

This crude, quick, and drastic remedy was the ultimate in self-help. It won't surprise you to learn that in states that still have laws providing for distress or distraint, courts have stepped in and ruled it unconstitutional, or have added so many safeguards (notice, a hearing, and so on) that the original process is unrecognizable. If you encounter an enticing distress or distraint statute when reading your state's laws, resist the temptation to follow it and instead follow modern laws on collecting overdue rent.

When the Tenant Owes You Money

It's annoying enough to have to deal with a tenant's abandoned belongings—but it's even worse when that tenant also owes you money. When a tenant who has moved voluntarily, been evicted, or simply disappeared also owes you back rent or money for damages, you might be tempted to first take or sell whatever property of value that's left behind, and worry about finding the tenant later. Doing so is risky in many states, though—even if you have a court judgment for money damages.

Some states do allow you to keep or sell abandoned property if the tenant owes you money, even without a court judgment directing the tenant to pay. In legal parlance, you have an "automatic lien" on your tenants' belongings. This differs from the normal lien process—which involves formally recording your claim (your lien) against the tenant's property, then "getting in line" in case others have filed ahead of you.

If your state statute gives you a lien on your tenant's property, we advise you to use it very carefully. In particular:

- **Use restraint when seizing consumer or other goods that might not be fully paid for.** If your tenants financed their TV, sofa, or computer and are making installment payments, the merchant has a lien that's ahead of yours. This is called a "superior" lien—meaning that the merchant, not you, has first claim to the item when the tenants stop paying. (Not surprisingly, tenants typically stop payments after abandoning the item.) You cannot simply seize and sell an abandoned item, such as a computer, that is not paid off. Instead, you will have to turn the item over if the merchant comes to collect it. If you have already sold the item, you might have to pay the merchant the balance due or the value of the item. You can try to avoid owing the merchant by publicizing your intent to seize and sell the item, as explained below.

- **Follow your state's rules for publicizing your lien.** Many states require landlords to post notices in newspapers announcing their intent to sell an item abandoned by tenants. This is to make sure that others—like the merchants mentioned above—who have superior liens on tenants' property don't lose out when you jump ahead of them and take or sell the item. Merchants are presumed to read the legal notices; failure to do so might result in the merchants' losing their right to assert the superiority of their lien. It's a good idea to publicize the sale of tenants' valuable abandoned property even if your statute doesn't require it.

- **Don't seize items that are necessary for basic living.** Many states that give landlords an automatic lien exempt certain items, such as season-appropriate clothing, blankets, tools, and things needed for a minor child's education, from your grasp. If you're not sure whether an item is a tool of your ex-tenant's trade or simply supports a hobby, don't take it.

> ⓘ CAUTION
> **Check out court cases—don't rely on statutes alone.** In most states with lien statutes on the books, courts have stepped in with additional requirements, such as giving notice and an opportunity for the tenants (and other creditors) to be heard. Read any cases that have interpreted your lien law (see Chapter 18 for help in doing legal research), or ask your landlords' association or lawyer for assistance.

Having read about the hassles and risks of seizing tenants' property to satisfy unpaid rent or debts, you might be wondering whether it's ever worth it. The answer is no, hardly ever, unless the tenant has left an item of sizeable value and owes you a large debt. In that situation, precisely because the item's valuable exposes you to some risk, consult with an attorney before proceeding.

Legal Notice Requirements

Many states require landlords to provide tenants written notice that they are dealing with abandoned property. A few states even provide a form, which you'll see printed right in the statute. The notice must typically give tenants a set amount of time to reclaim the property, after which landlords can take steps to deal with it. Some state rules require added information in the notice, such as:

- **A detailed description of the property left behind.** It's a good idea to have an objective person (such as another tenant in the building or a neighbor) witness your inventory of the abandoned property, to protect yourself against charges that you have taken or destroyed the tenant's property. Don't open locked trunks or suitcases; just list the unopened containers. You might consider photographing or videotaping the property.
- **The estimated value of the abandoned property.** Here, you estimate what you could get for it at a well-attended flea market or garage sale.
- **Where the property can be claimed.** Many states require you to provide the address of the rental premises or an outside storage place.
- **The deadline for tenants to reclaim property, such as seven or ten days.** This is usually set by state law.
- **What will happen if property is not reclaimed.** How to legally rid yourself of the abandoned property might also be directed by state law.

Even if your state law doesn't explicitly require you to send tenants this kind of detailed notice and allow a reasonable amount of time for tenants to pick up their belongings, it's a good practice to protect yourself. Mail your notice "return receipt requested" so that you will have proof that the tenants received it—this will be useful should an ex-tenant show up months later looking for belongings left behind.

How to Handle Abandoned Property When Tenants Don't Respond

If the ex-tenant doesn't contact you within the time specified in the notice, follow your state rules regarding what to do with property. In some states, landlords are pretty much free to do what they want—that is, you can throw the property out, sell it, or donate it. In some states, as explained above, landlords can use the property to satisfy unpaid rent or damages, or might be allowed to keep it even when there's no debt. Other states require you to give the property to the state. If your state has legislated the issue, you might encounter laws about:

- **Procedures based on the value of the property.** Several states allow landlords to keep or dispose of property only if the expense of storing or selling it exceeds a specified figure (such as a few hundred dollars) or the property's value.
- **Sale of abandoned property.** Some states require landlords to inventory, store, and sell tenants' property. A few require landlords to sell the property at a public sale (supervised by a licensed and bonded public auctioneer) after first publishing a notice in the newspaper.
- **Proceeds of sale of property.** States that require you to store and sell the property on behalf of the tenant also allow you to use any money you make from the sale to cover the costs of advertising and holding the sale and storing the property. For example, you might be able to charge the tenant the prorated daily rental value for keeping the property on your premises or any out-of-pocket costs you incur, such as renting storage space and moving the property into storage. As explained above, some states allow you to use the proceeds to cover any money owed to you by the tenant for things such as unpaid rent or damage to the premises. In many states, the excess proceeds of selling the tenant's property belong to the tenant, or you might be required to pay the balance to a government agency, such as the state treasurer. State rules are often very specific on this issue, so don't just keep sale proceeds without a clear understanding of your state law.

TIP

Don't hassle tenants over small sums of money. Most of the time, tenants aren't going to leave anything of great value. You're probably better off giving the tenants their belongings and not charging for storage, particularly if you didn't incur any out-of-pocket expenses. It's just not worth it to get into fights over $100 worth of old dishes, books, and clothes.

Exceptions to State Rules on Abandoned Property

Your state's rules on abandoned property don't apply to obvious garbage—nor do they apply in the following situations.

Fixtures. When tenants attach something more or less permanently to the property, such as built-in bookshelves, it is called a "fixture." As described in "Tenants' Alterations and Improvements" in Chapter 9, absent a written agreement such as a lease provision, fixtures installed by tenants become the landlord's property and don't have to be returned to tenants.

Motor vehicles. Tenants sometimes leave an inoperable or "junker" automobile in your parking lot or garage. State rules on abandoned property often don't apply to motor vehicles . If a tenant leaves a car or another vehicle, call the local police, giving the vehicle's license plate number, make, and model, and indicate where it's parked. The police will probably ticket it, and ultimately arrange to have it towed after determining that it's abandoned.

Landlord Liability for Damage to Tenants' Property

Most courts won't hold landlords liable for damage to tenants' abandoned property, unless the damage results from the landlords' willful destruction or negligence. However, to be safe, use reasonable care in moving and storing tenants' belongings until you're legally able to sell or dispose of them.

Problems With Tenants: How to Resolve Disputes Without a Lawyer

 FORMS IN THIS CHAPTER

Chapter 16 includes instructions for and a sample of the following form:

• Warning Letter for Lease or Rental Agreement Violation

The purchase of this book includes a free downloadable and customizable copy of this form. See Appendix B for the download link and instructions.

Legal disputes—actual and potential—come in all shapes and sizes when you're a landlord. Here are some of the more common ones:

- **Rent.** You and your tenant disagree about the validity, timing, or procedure of a rent increase.
- **Habitability.** Tenants threaten to withhold rent because they claim something has made the rental unusable.
- **Access to the premises.** Tenants won't let you show their apartment to prospective new tenants or enter for some other legal reason.
- **Security deposits.** You and a departing tenant disagree about how much security deposit you owe the tenant.
- **Lease or rental agreement violations.** Your tenant (or former tenant) violated a term in your lease or rental agreement.

How you handle such disputes can have a profound effect on your bottom line, not to mention your mental health. Rarely should lawyers and litigation be your first choice. Instead, you will usually want to consider alternatives that can give you better control over your time, energy, and money. In some cases, such as a tenant's nonpayment of rent, your only option might be to terminate the tenancy.

This chapter discusses four commonly available options to resolve a legal dispute without a lawyer:

- negotiation
- mediation
- arbitration, and
- small claims court.

While we focus here on disputes with tenants, much of this advice is useful for resolving all types of business disputes—for example, with your manager, insurance company, or repairperson.

This chapter also explains how to avoid charges of retaliation in your dealings with tenants.

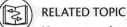

RELATED TOPIC

How to terminate a tenancy based on nonpayment of rent and illegal acts is discussed in Chapter 17.

Put It in Writing

To help avoid legal problems in the first place, and minimize those that can't be avoided, try to adopt efficient, easy-to-follow systems to document important facts of your relationship with your tenants. Throughout this book, we recommend many forms and record-keeping systems that will help you do this, including move-in and move-out letters, a landlord-tenant checklist, and a maintenance/repair request form. The goal is to establish a good paper trail for each tenancy, beginning with the rental application and lease or rental agreement through a termination notice and security deposit itemization. Such documentation will be extremely valuable if attempts at resolving your dispute fail and you end up evicting or suing a tenant, or being sued by a tenant. Also, keep copies of any correspondence and notes of your conversations with tenants. Chapter 7 recommends a system for organizing tenant information, including records of repair requests.

Negotiating a Settlement: Start by Talking

If you have a conflict with your tenant, a sensible first step is to meet with the tenant—even one you consider to be a hopeless troublemaker—to attempt to resolve the problem. Unless you have the legal grounds (and the determination) to evict a tenant, it's almost always better to try to negotiate a settlement rather than let the dispute escalate into a court fight.

Try to evaluate the legal and financial realities of your dispute objectively. Your goal should be to achieve the best result at the lowest cost. If instead you act on the conviction that your rights are being trampled by the other side (whether you're right or wrong makes no difference), chances are you'll end up spending far too much time and money fighting over the principle involved. Over time, a landlord who is controlled by this sort of emotional reaction is almost sure to be emotionally and financially poorer than one who focuses on the overall objective: to make a good living and enjoy doing it.

Your first step in working toward a compromise is to contact the tenant and arrange a time to meet in person.

Dropping over unannounced to talk might work in some circumstances but is generally a bad idea—your tenant might feel threatened and become defensive. You could call the tenant, or write a text, a letter, or an email offering to meet with the tenant to work something out. (See, for example, the sample letter in Chapter 9 in which the landlord suggests a compromise with a tenant who withholds rent because of claimed defective conditions in his apartment.)

Here are some helpful pointers for negotiating with tenants:

- **Solicit the tenant's point of view.** Once the tenant starts talking, listen closely and don't interrupt. Show you're listening—even if you disagree. Sometimes it's even a good idea to repeat the tenant's concerns to show you're listening.

- **Avoid personal attacks.** This only raises the level of hostility and makes settlement more difficult. Equally important, don't react impulsively or emotionally to the tenant's remarks.

- **Be courteous, but don't be weak.** If you have a good case, let the tenant know you have the resources and evidence to fight and win if you can't reach a reasonable settlement.

- **Before the negotiation goes too far, determine whether the tenant is a truly an unbearable jerk whom you really want to be rid of or just another slightly annoying person.** If a tenant falls into the first category, your strategy should be to terminate the tenancy as soon as legally and practically possible.

- **If possible, structure the negotiation as a mutual attempt to solve a problem.** For example, if a tenant's guests have been disturbing the neighbors, jointly seek solutions that recognize the interests of both parties.

- **Try to figure out the tenant's priorities.** Maybe dollars are less important than pride, in which case a formula for future relations that meets the needs of a thin-skinned tenant to be treated with respect might solve the problem.

- **Put yourself in the tenant's shoes.** What resolution would you want? Your answer might be something like "a sense that I've won." That's a perfectly reasonable desire—the best settlements are often those in which both sides feel they've won (or at least not given up anything fundamental). So, your goal is to let the tenant have at least a partial sense of victory on one or more of the issues in dispute.

- **When you propose a specific settlement, make it clear that you're attempting to compromise.** Offers of settlement (clearly labeled as such) can't be introduced against you if you end up in court.

- **Money is a powerful incentive to settlement.** If you are going to have to pay something eventually, or spend a lot of time and money on a costly eviction lawsuit or preparing a small claims case, it makes financial sense to come to the negotiating table willing to pay. You might offer to lower the rent for a short period of time, reduce money owed for damages to the premises, or pay an outright cash settlement for the tenant to leave (with payment made only when the tenant leaves and hands you the keys). Savvy landlords know that many financially strapped tenants settle at a surprisingly low figure if they can walk away from the bargaining table with money in hand. If this saves the costs and delays inherent in a long eviction battle, and allows you to rerent the unit to a paying tenant, it can be well worth it.

- **If you reach an understanding with your tenant, promptly write it down and have all parties sign it.** You or your lawyer should volunteer to prepare the first draft. If you're paying the tenant some money as part of your agreement, make sure the tenant acknowledges in writing that your payment fully satisfies all claims. Chapter 15 includes an example of a settlement agreement for a security deposit dispute that you can use as a model for settling disputes.

- **If the negotiation process indicates a larger problem with tenant dissatisfaction, brainstorm how to avoid similar disputes in the future**—for example, you might need to revise your systems for handling repair complaints or returning security deposits.

 RESOURCE

Recommended reading on negotiation.
Getting to Yes: Negotiating Agreement Without Giving In, by Roger Fisher, William Ury, and Bruce M. Patton (Penguin Books). This classic offers a strategy for coming to mutually acceptable agreements in all kinds of situations, including landlord-tenant disputes.

The Power of a Positive No: Save the Deal, Save the Relationship and Still Say No, by William Ury (Bantam Books). This sequel to *Getting to Yes* discusses techniques for negotiating with obnoxious, stubborn, and otherwise difficult people.

When Warning Notices Are Appropriate

In some situations, it's appropriate to give a written notice to cease the problem or disruptive activity, particularly if you think the tenant will actually pay attention. You might also want to send a written warning notice if your oral warning or attempts to negotiate have been unsuccessful.

A sample Warning Letter for Lease or Rental Agreement Violation is shown below, and the Nolo website includes a customizable copy (see Appendix B for the download link).

Be sure your letter includes the following information:

- Details of the problem behavior, including dates and times of the occurrence.
- What exactly you want the tenant to do (or not do).
- The specific lease or rental agreement provision that addresses the behavior, such as a clause on tenants' rights to quiet enjoyment (Clause 13 of our form lease and rental agreements in Chapter 2), a clause requiring tenants to repair damaged property (Clause 11 of our form agreements), or a lease restriction on guests (Clause 3 of our form agreements).
- The consequences of failing to comply (such as termination or eviction proceedings).

CAUTION

Don't waste your time sending a warning letter to someone unlikely to respond—for example, a tenant who is always late in paying rent or whose behavior (such as drug dealing or violence) justifies immediate action. Instead, start termination proceedings right away.

What happens if the tenant doesn't reform, despite your reminder? If the misbehavior warrants terminating the tenancy, you'll have to give the tenant a formal termination notice that meets your state's requirements. (Termination notices are explained in Chapter 17.)

Warning Letter for Lease or Rental Agreement Violation

November 4, 20xx
Date

Jerry Brooks
Tenant

179 Lynwood Drive
Street Address

Tampa, Florida 33611
City and State

Dear Jerry ,
Tenant

This is a reminder that your lease prohibits annoying, disturbing, or interfering with the quiet enjoyment and peace and quiet of any other tenant or nearby resident (Clause 13) [violation]. It has come to my attention that, starting on November 2, 20xx , [date of violation] and continuing to the present, you have broken this condition of your tenancy by holding several noisy parties that lasted until 2 a.m., disturbing other tenants .

It is our desire that you and all other tenants enjoy living in your rental unit. To make sure this occurs, we enforce all terms and conditions of our leases. So please immediately keep noise within reasonable limits and no loud parties after midnight on weekends or 10 p.m. on weekdays .

If it proves impossible to promptly resolve this matter, we will exercise our legal right to begin eviction proceedings.

Please contact me if you would like to discuss this matter further and clear up any possible misunderstandings.

Yours truly,

Clark Johnson
Landlord/Manager

Belle Epoque, 387 Golf Road
Street Address

Tampa, Florida 33611
City and State

813-555-1234
Phone

> ! **CAUTION**
> **Your warning note will not qualify as a termination notice.** For example, if your tenants have a dog in violation of the lease, and they keep the pet despite your polite note asking them to remove the dog, in most states you'll have to give the tenants a formal notice telling them to get rid of the dog within a certain number of days or move. (If they do neither, you can file for eviction.)

Understanding Mediation

If you're unsuccessful negotiating a settlement, but still want to work something out, you could try mediation with a neutral third party, a process that is often available at little or no cost from a publicly funded program. (See "How to Find a Mediation Group," below.)

Mediation is usually preferable to other ways of settling your dispute, especially if any of the following are true:

- You're dealing with someone who has been a good tenant in the past and you think the tenant is worth dealing with in the future.
- The tenant agrees to split the cost (if any) of mediation.
- The tenant is receptive to attempting to avoid the expense and delay of litigation, or the possibility of being evicted.
- The tenant is up to date on rent (or the rent money is put in some type of escrow account).
- You want to avoid the risk of one influential tenant poisoning your relationship with others.

If mediation doesn't make sense, make clear your intention (and legal right) to sue or evict the tenant.

Many people confuse mediation with arbitration. While both are nonjudicial ways to resolve disputes, there's a huge difference: Arbitration results in a binding decision, while mediation doesn't. Mediators have no power to make orders, but can help the parties work out a mutually acceptable solution to their dispute.

Mediation in landlord-tenant disputes is usually fairly informal. Most likely, the mediator will have everyone sit down together at the beginning and allow both parties to express all their issues—even emotional ones. This often cools people off considerably and frequently results in a fairly quick compromise. If the dispute is not resolved easily, however, the mediator might suggest ways to resolve the problem, or might even keep everyone talking long enough to realize that the real problem goes deeper than the one being mediated. Typically this is done through a caucus process—each side is in a private room.

The mediator talks to each party separately to determine their bottom line. Then, shuttling back and forth, the mediator helps the parties structure an acceptable solution. At some point, everyone signs off on the resolution.

For example, if a tenant has threatened rent withholding because of a defect in the premises, the mediator might discover that the tenant's real grievance is that your manager is slow to make repairs. This might lead to the further finding that the manager is angry with the tenant for letting her kids trample his garden. So, the final solution might fall into place only when the tenant agrees to provide better supervision for the kids in exchange for the manager getting the repairs done pronto.

Does mediation really work? Surprisingly, yes, when you consider the fact that no one orders a certain outcome. One reason for success is the basic cooperative spirit that goes into mediation. By agreeing to mediate a dispute in the first place, you and the tenant set the stage for cooperating to solve your dispute. Also, the fact that no judge or arbitrator has the power to impose what might be an unacceptable solution reduces the fear factor on both sides. This, in turn, often means both landlord and tenant take less extreme—and more conciliatory—positions.

How to Deal With Noisy Tenants

Tenants often cite noise as one of their biggest complaints about apartment living. Many types of noise, including street traffic, garbage trucks, or rowdy bars, are out of the landlord's control. If tenants complain about noises outside the building, your best bet is to steer them to the city manager or mayor's office for help. Most cities have local ordinances that prohibit excessive, unnecessary, and unreasonable noise, and police enforce these laws. If the problem is a neighbor's barking dog, the local animal control agency is responsible. Most local noise ordinances designate certain "quiet hours"—for example, from 10 p.m. to 7 a.m. on weekdays. Some universally disturbing noises, such as honking car horns, are commonly banned or restricted. Many communities also prohibit sustained noise that exceeds a certain decibel level (set according to the time of day and the neighborhood zoning).

Noise caused by other tenants, however, is your responsibility. Anyone who lives in an apartment building should expect to hear some sounds of their neighbors' daily lives. But when the occasional annoying sound turns into an ongoing din—whether a blasting stereo, loud TV, or barking dog—expect to hear complaints from other residents. You should take these complaints seriously. As discussed in Chapter 9, tenants are entitled to quiet enjoyment of the premises—the right to occupy their apartments in peace, free of excessive noise. You could face legal problems if you fail to stop regular and ongoing disturbances.

Landlords who tolerate excessive and unreasonable noise despite repeated complaints might get hit with code violations or a small claims lawsuit or court-ordered rent reductions. Good tenants might move out.

Here are some tips to avoid problems with noisy tenants:

- Include a clause in your lease or rental agreement prohibiting tenants from causing disturbances or creating a nuisance that interferes with other tenants' peace and quiet and prevents neighbors from enjoying the use of their own homes. (See Clause 13 of the form agreements in Chapter 2.)

- Include noise guidelines in your tenant rules and regulations, such as the hours that loud music and dance parties will not be tolerated. Look at your local noise ordinance for guidance and remind tenants of noise laws that apply in your community, such as prohibitions against honking car alarms, firecrackers, or disorderly conduct. You might make the same points in a move-in letter to new tenants.

- Consider requiring rugs or carpets on wood floors to muffle the noise heard by tenants downstairs.

- Check out inexpensive ideas to soundproof paper-thin walls.

- Respond quickly to noise complaints. Start with an oral request to keep the noise down. If you don't see results, move on to a warning letter (such as the sample shown above). Terminate the tenancy if necessary.

- Keep records of all tenant complaints about a neighbor's noise (with details on the date, time, and location of the noise), so that you have solid documentation to back up a termination or eviction case. If the noise is really bad, make a tape recording as additional evidence.

- If violence is involved, such as a domestic disturbance, call the police immediately.

RESOURCE

The Noise Pollution Clearinghouse (www.nonoise.org) is an excellent source of information on state and local noise laws. If you can't find your local ordinance there, do some online legal research (Chapter 18 explains how).

For a general overview of noise involving neighbors, see *Neighbor Law*, by Emily Doskow and Lina Guillen, published by Nolo and available at Nolo.com or by phone at 800-728-3555.

RESOURCE
Recommended reading on mediation. *Mediate, Don't Litigate*, by Peter Lovenheim and Lisa Guerin (Nolo), available as a downloadable electronic book at Nolo.com. This book explains the mediation process from start to finish, including how to prepare for mediation and draft a legally enforceable agreement.

How to Find a Mediation Program

For information on local mediation programs, call your mayor's or city manager's office, and ask for the staff member who handles "landlord-tenant mediation matters" or "housing disputes." That person should refer you to the public office or business or community group that attempts to informally—and at little or no cost—resolve landlord-tenant disputes before they reach the court stage. Most local courts also provide referrals to community mediation services. For lists of professional mediators and extensive information on mediation, see Mediate.com.

Using Arbitration

Many organizations that offer mediation also conduct arbitration if the parties can't reach an agreement. Almost any dispute with a tenant or other party that can be litigated can be arbitrated. With arbitration, you get a relatively quick, relatively inexpensive solution to a dispute without going to court. Like a judge, the arbitrator—a neutral third party—has power to hear the dispute and make a final, binding decision. Where does this power come from? From you and the other party. In binding arbitration, you agree in advance in writing to submit to arbitration and to be bound by the arbitrator's decision.

In some states, you can include a clause in your lease or rental agreement that requires that arbitration be used for any contractual dispute.

In California, arbitration clauses in residential leases are unenforceable, though landlords and tenants can later agree to use an arbitrator if they wish. (*Jaramillo v. JH Real Estate Partners, Inc.* 111 Cal. App. 4th 394 (2003).) But, arbitration is usually better suited for resolving disputes over longer-term leases of expensive properties. Otherwise, you and the tenant can also decide to use arbitration after a dispute arises. If you and the tenant agree to binding arbitration, an informal hearing is held. Everyone tells their side of the story, and an arbitrator reaches a decision, which is enforceable in court.

If the losing party doesn't pay the money required by an arbitration award, the winner can convert the award to a court judgment, enforceable like any other court order. Unlike a judgment based on litigation, however, you generally can't take an appeal from an arbitration-based judgment. (An exception is when there was some element of fraud in the procedures leading to the arbitration award.)

How to Find an Arbitrator

To find an arbitrator or learn more about arbitration, contact the American Arbitration Association, the oldest and largest organization of its kind, with offices throughout the country. For more information, visit www.adr.org.

Keep in mind that you are not required to use an organization for arbitration. You and the other party are free to choose your own arbitrator or arbitration panel and to set your own procedural rules. Just remember that for arbitration to be binding and legally enforceable, you need to follow the simple guidelines set down in your state's arbitration statute. You can usually find the statute by looking in the statutory index under "Arbitration" or checking the table of contents for the civil procedure sections. See Chapter 18 for advice on doing this kind of legal research.

Representing Yourself in Small Claims Court

If your attempts at settling a dispute involving money fail, you might end up in a lawsuit. Fortunately, in many instances you can competently and cost-efficiently represent yourself in court. This is almost always true when your case is at the small claims level.

Small claims courts go by various names in different states. No matter their name, they serve the same purpose: to provide a speedy, inexpensive resolution of disputes that involve relatively small amounts of money (generally less than $10,000). "State Small Claims Court Limits," in Appendix A, lists each state's small claims court limit.

Most people who go to small claims court handle their own cases. In fact, in some states, lawyers aren't allowed to represent clients in small claims court. In any event, representing yourself is almost always the best choice—after all, the main reason to use the small claims court is because the size of the case doesn't justify the cost of hiring a lawyer.

A landlord can use small claims court for many purposes—for example, to collect unpaid rent or to seek money for property damage after a tenant moves out and her deposit is exhausted. Small claims court offers a great opportunity to collect money that would otherwise be lost because it would be too expensive to sue in regular court. And, in a few states, eviction suits can be filed in small claims court.

Landlords can also be sued in small claims court—for example, by a tenant who claims that you failed to return a security deposit. Chapter 15 discusses small claims suits over security deposits.

TIP

Don't waste your time suing deadbeats. As a general rule, if you suspect you cannot collect the money—from a paycheck, a bank account, or another financial resource—don't waste your time in small claims court. A judgment you can't collect is worthless.

RESOURCE

Recommended reading on small claims court. *Everybody's Guide to Small Claims Court*, by Cara O'Neill (Nolo), provides detailed advice on bringing or defending a small claims court case, preparing evidence and witnesses for court, and collecting your money judgment when you win. *Everybody's Guide to Small Claims Court* will also be useful in defending yourself against a tenant who sues you in small claims court. Your state's small claims court website (listed in the chart in Appendix A) will also have useful information on local rules and procedures.

Learning the Rules

Small claims court procedures are relatively simple and easy to master. Basically, you pay a small fee, file your lawsuit with the court clerk, see to it that the papers are served on your opponent, show up on the appointed day, tell the judge your story, and present any witnesses and other evidence. The key to winning is usually to present evidence to back up your story. For example, a photograph of a dirty or damaged apartment and the convincing testimony of someone who helped you clean up are usually all you need to prevail if you are trying to recover money over and above the tenant's deposit or defending against a tenant's suit for the return of a deposit.

Procedural rules—the rules that tell you about what you need to do and when you need to do it—are usually published on small claims court websites. In addition, small claims court clerks are expected to explain procedures to you. In some states, clerks might even help you fill out the applicable forms. Be persistent: If you ask enough questions, you'll get the answers you need to handle your own case comfortably. Also, in some states, you can consult a small claims court adviser for free.

Meeting the Jurisdictional Limits

The maximum amount you can sue for in small claims court varies from state to state. Generally, the limit is $5,000 to $10,000. But, more recently, recognizing that formal courts have become prohibitively expensive for all but large disputes, many states have begun to increase the monetary size of the cases their small claims courts can consider. Check your state's small claims court limit on the chart in Appendix A, but also ask the court clerk for the most current limit; state legislatures regularly increase these limits. (Your state might have waived the jurisdictional limit altogether when the landlord is suing over unpaid rent during the coronavirus pandemic, for example.)

TIP
You can scale your case down to fit small claims court limits. Don't assume that your case can't be brought in small claims court if your claim is for more than the limit. Rather than hiring a lawyer or trying to go it alone in formal court, your most cost-effective option might be to stay in small claims, sue for the maximum, and forget the rest.

How to Avoid Charges of Retaliation

As we've discussed throughout this book, residential tenants have a number of legal rights and remedies. While the specifics vary by state, tenants typically have:

- the right to complain to governmental authorities about health or safety problems, and, in many states, the right to withhold rent from, or even to file a lawsuit against, a landlord who fails to keep the premises in proper repair
- the right to be free from discriminatory conduct based on factors such as race, religion, children, sex, and disability; and to complain about violations to administrative agencies or courts
- privacy rights limiting landlord access, and

- the right to engage in political activity; for example, a tenant who actively campaigns for local candidates whom you find obnoxious, organizes a tenant union, or campaigns for a rent control ordinance, has an absolute right to do so without fear of intimidation.

In most states, the law forbids landlords from retaliating against tenants who assert their legal rights.

For example, the right of a tenant to complain to the local fire department about a defective heater would be worth little if you, angry about the complaint, could retaliate against her with an immediate termination notice or rent increase. The general idea is that tenants should not be punished by landlords just because they are invoking their legal rights or remedies.

Unfortunately, tenants sometimes unfairly accuse landlords of retaliatory misconduct—for example, a tenant who can't or won't pay a legitimate rent increase might claim you are guilty of retaliation. The same sort of abuse of tenant protection laws can occur when you seek to terminate the tenancy for a perfectly legitimate reason and the tenant doesn't want to move. How do you cope with this sort of cynical misuse of the law? As with most things legal, it depends on the circumstances.

When faced with a tenant who attempts to defeat your legitimate rent increase or tenancy termination with phony retaliation claims, don't discredit your skills and knowledge—they work in your favor in these sorts of disputes. As a businessperson, you are always observing your market and strategizing how to survive and thrive. You can use these same skills to anticipate possible tenant tactics, and develop a rough plan for dealing with them. (If you're unsure about how to proceed, it can't hurt to schedule a one- or two-hour consult with a local landlord attorney to learn more.)

Most tenants, on the other hand, probably won't be acting strategically, and might even be running on pure emotion. Additionally, many tenants have little to no understanding of the law. That said, in rent control situations where the stakes are particularly high, you might find yourself up against a very well-educated opponent.

Here are some tips on how to anticipate what tenants might do.

Establish a communication system—and use it. Create written systems and procedures for how you communicate with tenants and address their needs and concerns. For example, set up clear, easy-to-follow procedures for tenants to ask for repairs, and respond quickly when complaints are made. Perform annual safety inspections. (We show you how in Chapter 9.) Use your forms without changing them—and don't vary them for each tenant. Having strict procedures (and consistently following them) will go a long way toward demonstrating that a complaint is phony.

Be prepared to demonstrate that you have a good reason to end a tenancy. Even if the law in your area doesn't require landlords to have a reason for terminating a tenancy, you should always document and keep records of bad tenant behavior. For example, a tenant might claim that you terminated the tenancy for retaliatory reasons. You need to be prepared to prove that your reasons were valid and not retaliatory.

This burden isn't as onerous as it might first appear. From a business point of view, few landlords will ever want to evict an excellent tenant. And, assuming there is a good reason why you want the tenant out—for example, the tenant repeatedly pays rent late in violation of the rental agreement—all you need to do is document the late payments.

Have legitimate business reasons for any rent increase or other change in the conditions of the tenancy, and make the changes reasonable. The best answer to a charge of retaliation is proof that your actions were the result of legitimate business reasons, and were not a response to tenants exercising their rights.

Before you take major action towards a tenant, consider the current situation. Be sensitive to the state of your relationship with tenants. For example, if a tenant makes an arguably legitimate complaint at about the timing of a rent increase or the way you served a month-to-month termination notice, wait. Address the complaint first. Next, let some time pass. Then, do what you planned to do anyway (assuming you can document a legitimate reason for your action). Be sure to check "State Laws Prohibiting Landlord Retaliation" in Appendix A to see whether your state has laws as to the time period when retaliation is presumed.

Holding off might cost you a few bucks, result in some inconvenience, or even cause you to lose some sleep. But suffering some short-term discomfort is preferable to being involved in litigation over whether your conduct was in retaliation for the tenant's complaint.

> **EXAMPLE:** A tenant, Fanny, makes a legitimate complaint to the health department about a defective heater in an apartment she rents from Abe. Even though Fanny does so without the courtesy of telling Abe first, Fanny is still within her legal rights to make the complaint. About the same time Fanny files the complaint, neighboring tenants complain to Abe, not for the first time, about Fanny's loud parties that last into the wee hours of the morning. Other tenants threaten to move out if Fanny doesn't leave. In response to the neighboring tenants' complaints, Abe gives Fanny a 30-day notice. She refuses to move, and Abe must file an eviction lawsuit. Fanny responds that the eviction was in retaliation for her complaint to the health department. A contested trial results. Perhaps Abe will win in court, but the timing the termination has made proving his case more difficult.

If you were faced with the situation in the example above, here's a better way to handle it:

Step 1. Fix the heater.

Step 2. Write to the tenant, reminding her of your established complaint procedures. Tell her very politely that you consider this sort of repair a routine matter which, in the future, can be handled more quickly and easily by telling you instead of the public agency. A sample letter is shown below.

**Sample Letter Reminding Tenant
of Complaint Procedure**

February 1, 20xx

Fanny Hayes
Sunny Dell Apartments
123 State Street, Apt. 15
Newark, NJ 07114

Dear Ms. Hayes:

As you know, Ms. Sharon Donovan, my resident manager at Sunny Dell Apartments, repaired the heater in your unit yesterday, on January 31.

Ms. Donovan informs me that you never complained about the heater or requested its repair. In fact, she learned about the problem for the first time when she received a telephone call to that effect from Cal Mifune of the County Health Department. Apparently, you notified the Health Department of the problem without first attempting to resolve it with Ms. Donovan.

While you certainly do have a legal right to complain to a governmental agency about any problem, you should be aware that the management of Sunny Dell Apartments takes pride in its quick and efficient response to residents' complaints and requests for repairs.

In the future, we hope that you'll follow our complaint procedure and contact the manager if you have a problem with any aspect of your apartment.

Sincerely,

Abe Horowitz

Abe Horowitz, Owner

Step 3. Carefully document the noise complaints of the neighbors. If possible, get them in writing. Ask the neighbors whether they would testify in court if necessary. Also, consider whether an informal meeting among all affected parties, or a formal procedure, such as mediation, might solve the problem.

Step 4. Write the tenant about the neighbors' complaints. The first letter should be conciliatory. Offer to meet with the tenant to resolve the problem, but also remind the tenant of the rental agreement (or lease) provision prohibiting nuisances (such as excessive noise) that disturb the quiet enjoyment of other tenants. If the first letter doesn't work, follow up with another letter, even if you don't think it will do any good. These letters will help you greatly should a court fight develop later.

Step 5. If possible, wait a few months. In the meantime, carefully document any more complaints before giving the tenant a 30-day notice. As a general rule, the longer you can reasonably delay court action, the less likely a claim of retaliation by the tenant will stick.

Your careful documentation, polite but firm contacts, and repeated "second chances" might make the tenant realize that trying to claim retaliation won't work. However, even if the tenant persists and you end up in court, you should win easily.

Defending yourself in an eviction case against charges of retaliation is beyond the scope of this book. We strongly advise you to hire a lawyer. Also, take a look at your liability insurance—it might cover your tenant's claim. If so, you can turn your legal defense over to the insurance company.

Late Rent, Terminations, and Evictions

Sometimes even the most sincere and professional attempts at conscientious landlording fail, and you need to get rid of a troublesome tenant.

Termination is the first step toward an eventual eviction. You'll need to send the tenants a notice announcing that the tenancy is over, and that, if they don't leave, you'll file an eviction lawsuit. Or, you might send the tenants a notice giving them a few days to clean up their act (pay the rent, find a new home for the dog). If the tenants leave (or reform) as directed, no one moves or goes to court.

Eviction itself—that is, physically removing tenants and their possessions from your property—can't be done until you prove to a court that the tenants did something that justifies ending the tenancy. If you win the eviction lawsuit, you can't just move the tenants and their things out onto the sidewalk—in most states, you must hire the sheriff or marshal to perform that task.

This chapter explains when and how you can terminate a tenancy based on nonpayment of rent and other acts. It also provides an overview of what you can legally do—and not do—following a termination notice.

RELATED TOPIC
Related topics covered in this book include:
- Rent control laws that require a legally recognized reason, or "just cause," to evict: Chapter 3
- Evicting a resident manager: Chapter 6
- Substantially failing to maintain rental property so that tenants cannot use it (constructive eviction): Chapter 9
- Ending a month-to-month tenancy with a 30-day notice: Chapter 14
- How to end a tenancy at a property that you have purchased at foreclosure: Chapter 14
- Using a security deposit to cover unpaid rent after you've evicted a tenant: Chapter 15
- How to use a warning letter, negotiation, or mediation to resolve a dispute with a tenant: Chapter 16
- How to get legal help for an eviction lawsuit: Chapter 18.

CAUTION
Watch out for charges of retaliation. Landlords in most states may not end a tenancy in response to a tenant's legitimate exercise of a legal right, such as rent withholding, or in response to a complaint to a housing inspector or after a tenant has organized other tenants. What if your tenant has exercised a legal right (such as using a repair and deduct option) but is also late with the rent? Naturally, the tenant will claim that the real motive behind your eviction is retaliation.

In some states, the burden will be on you to prove that your motive is legitimate if you evict within a certain time (typically six months) of a tenant's use of a legal remedy or right. In others, it's up to the tenant to prove your motive. Chapter 16 includes advice on how to avoid charges of retaliation, and Appendix A gives details on state laws prohibiting landlord retaliation.

RESOURCE
California landlords should consult *The California Landlord's Law Book: Evictions*, by Nils Rosenquest (Nolo). It contains eviction information and court forms.

The Landlord's Role in Evictions

The key to an eviction lawsuit (sometimes called an unlawful detainer, or UD, lawsuit) is properly terminating the tenancy before you go to court. You can't proceed with your lawsuit, let alone get a judgment for possession of your property or for unpaid rent, without terminating the tenancy first.

Proper termination usually means giving your tenant written notice in a form and manner specified by law. If the tenant doesn't move (or otherwise comply with the notice), you can file a lawsuit to evict.

State laws set out very detailed requirements for landlords who want to end a tenancy. Each state has its own procedures as to how termination notices and eviction papers must be written and delivered ("served"). The type of notice required often depends on the situation. You must follow state rules and procedures exactly.

Otherwise, you will experience delays in evicting tenants—and maybe even lose your lawsuit— no matter how many checks your tenants have bounced.

Because an eviction judgment means the tenants won't have a roof over their heads, eviction laws are usually very demanding of landlords. In addition, rent control laws tend to offer even greater eviction protection to tenants, by requiring landlords to have a legally recognized reason—known as "just cause"—to evict.

Alternatives to Eviction

Before you proceed with an eviction lawsuit, consider whether it might be cheaper in the long run to pay the tenants a few hundred dollars to leave right away. A potentially lengthy lawsuit—during which you can't accept rent (and might not ever be able to collect even if you win)—can be more expensive and frustrating than buying out the tenants and quickly replacing them with better ones. Especially if there's a possibility that your tenants might win the lawsuit (as well as a judgment against you for court costs and attorneys' fees), you could be better off compromising—perhaps letting the tenant stay a few more weeks at reduced or no rent.

Chapter 16 provides tips on avoiding an eviction lawsuit by negotiating a settlement with problem tenants.

Even if you follow all procedures and bring an eviction lawsuit for a valid reason, you are not assured of winning if the tenant decides to mount a defense. You always run the risk of encountering a judge who, despite the merits of your position, will hold you to every technicality and bend over backwards to sustain the tenant's position. The way that you have conducted business with the tenant might also affect the outcome: A tenant might allege behavior on your part, such as retaliation, that will shift attention away from the tenant's wrongdoing and sour your chances of victory.

Simply put, unless you thoroughly know your legal rights and duties as a landlord before you go to court, and unless you dot every "i" and cross every "t," you might end up losing. Our advice, especially if your action is contested, is to be meticulous in your business practices and lawsuit preparation.

It is beyond the scope of this book to provide all the step-by-step instructions and forms necessary to terminate a tenancy or evict a tenant. This chapter will get you started, and Chapter 18 shows how to research termination and eviction rules and procedures in your state. Many are clearly set out in state statutes. Other useful resources for eviction procedures and forms include:

- the website of the court that handles evictions in your area—many have detailed DIY instructions
- your state consumer protection or attorney general's office (find yours at www.usa.gov/state-consumer)
- your state bar association (the American Bar Association has a bar directory on its website, www.americanbar.org, and
- your state or local apartment association.

California landlords should use the Nolo book described in the "Resource" section above.

Termination Notices

You can terminate a month-to-month tenancy simply by giving the proper amount of notice (30 days in most states). You do not normally need to provide a reason for the termination. Leases, on the other hand, expire on their own at the end of their term, and you generally aren't required to renew them. (In most rent control situations, however, you'll need a just cause for refusing to renew a lease on substantially similar terms.)

When tenants do something wrong, you usually won't want to wait until the lease is up. State laws allow you to end tenancies early by serving tenants with one of three types of termination notices. Which one you should use depends on the reason why you want the tenants to leave.

Although terminology varies somewhat from state to state, the substance of the three types of notices is similar:

- **Pay rent or quit** notices are typically used when tenants have not paid the rent. The notice gives the tenants a few days (three to five in most states) to pay or move out ("quit").
- **Cure or quit notices** are typically given after tenants violate a term or condition of the lease or rental agreement. Typically, tenants are given an amount of time in which to correct, or "cure," the violation. Tenants who fail to cure must move or face an eviction lawsuit.
- **Unconditional quit notices** are the harshest of all. They order tenants to vacate the premises with no chance to pay the rent or correct the lease or rental agreement violation. In most states, unconditional quit notices are allowed only when tenants have repeatedly:
  - violated a lease or rental agreement clause
  - paid rent late
  - seriously damaged the premises, or
  - engaged in illegal activity.

Many states have all three types of notices on the books. But, in some states, the unconditional quit notice is the *only* notice recognized by statute. Landlords in these states are free to give tenants an opportunity to cure, but no law requires them to do so.

You might have a choice among these three notices, depending on the situation. For example, a Wisconsin landlord may give month-to-month tenants an unconditional quit or a pay rent or quit notice for late payment of rent. The tenants cannot insist on the more lenient notice.

Many states have standards for the content and look of a termination notice, requiring certain language and specifying size and appearance of type (consult your state's statute, as noted in Appendix A, before writing your notice). When you're sure that the notice complies with state law, resist any temptation to add threatening graphics or language. The Fair Debt Collection Practices Act

(discussed below) and its state counterparts forbid you from threatening unlawful actions or implying that you are affiliated with the government. Threats (or implications) that you will resort to a self-help eviction (covered below), or even using a picture of a policeman, might constitute a deceptive collection practice.

For the details about and citations to your state's termination notice statutes, see the following charts in Appendix A:

- "State Rules on Notice Required to Change or Terminate a Month-to-Month Tenancy"
- "State Laws on Termination for Nonpayment of Rent"
- "State Laws on Termination for Violation of Lease," and
- "State Laws on Unconditional Quit Terminations."

Late Rent

Not surprisingly, the number one reason landlords terminate a tenancy is nonpayment of rent. When tenants are late with the rent, in most states you must send a pay or quit termination notice, giving the tenants a few days in which to pay up. The exact number of days varies from state to state. But not every state requires you to give a second chance to pay the rent; in a few states, if the tenants fail to pay rent on time, you can simply demand that they leave by sending an unconditional quit notice.

Legal Late Periods

In most states, you can send a pay rent or quit notice as soon as the tenant is even one day late with the rent. A handful of states will not let you send a termination notice until the rent is a certain number of days late. In these states, tenants enjoy a statutory "grace period," plus the time specified in the pay rent or quit notice, in which to come up with the rent. See "State Rent Rules," in Appendix A, for states that impose a grace period.

Involving Your Lawyer Might Trigger the Fair Debt Collection Practices Act

The Fair Debt Collection Practices Act (15 U.S.C. §§ 1692 and following) governs debt collectors and requires, among other things, that debtors be given 30 days in which to respond to a demand for payment (even if your pay or quit notice specifies fewer days). If you prepare and send your own pay or quit notices, you aren't a "debt collector," and you won't have to comply with this act. However, if your lawyer sends the notice, the act might apply in the following situations.

When your lawyer regularly sends notices for you and is genuinely involved in each case. A lawyer who regularly handles rent demand notices on behalf of landlord-clients is considered a "debt collector" in some states. Consequently, the tenant must have 30 days to pay or quit, no matter what your statute says. However, if your lawyer does not regularly engage in debt collection, it's likely that the lawyer will not be considered a regular debt collector. (*Goldstein v. Hutton*, 374 F.3d 56 (2004).)

A pay-or-quit notice that's signed or sent by a manager in these states, however, won't violate federal law, so long as it was the manager's job to collect rent before the tenant defaulted in the payment of rent. (*Franceschi v. Mautner-Glick Corp.*, 22 F.Supp.2d 250 (S.D. N.Y. 1998).)

When your lawyer rubber-stamps your notices. Under the Fair Debt Collection Practices Act, it's illegal to use someone else's name for its intimidation value. (15 U.S.C. § 1692j(a).) If your attorney simply sends out termination notices at your bidding (or lends you stationery or a signature stamp), and if the lawyer does not consider the facts of each case, you might be violating this law. The consequence is that *you* will be held to the letter of the act—and your pay-or-quit notice will, among other things, become a 30-day notice. (*Nielsen v. Dickerson*, 307 F.3d 623 (7th Cir. 2002).)

The lesson to be learned here is to handle your notices yourself!

EXAMPLE: Lara, a Maine tenant, couldn't pay her rent on time. State law required her landlord, Luke, to wait until the rent was seven days late before sending a termination notice. Luke sent the notice eight days after the rent due date, informing Lara that she must pay or move within seven days. In all, Lara had fourteen days in which to pay the rent before Luke could file for eviction.

TIP
Late rent fees are unaffected by pay rent or quit time periods or legal late periods. If your lease or rental agreement specifies late fees, they'll kick in as soon as your lease or rental agreement (or in some states, state law) says they can. The number of days specified in your pay rent or quit notice will not affect them, nor will a legally required grace period.

Accepting Rent After You Deliver a Termination Notice

If the tenant is late with the rent and you deliver a termination notice—whether or not it gives the tenant a few days to pay the rent—you can expect a phone call, an email, or a visit from your tenant, hoping to work something out. Chapter 16 offers some pointers on negotiating and dealing with these requests. Here are the legal rules.

When the Tenant Pays the Whole Rent

When you send a pay rent or quit notice but then accept rent for the entire rental term, you have canceled the termination notice for that period. In most states, it's as if the tenant had paid on time in the first place.

EXAMPLE: Zoe's rent was due on the first of the month. She didn't pay on time, and her landlord sent her a three-day pay rent or quit notice. Zoe borrowed money from her parents and paid on the third day, saving her tenancy and avoiding an eviction lawsuit.

When the Tenant Is Chronically Late Paying Rent

In several states, you don't have to give tenants a second chance to pay the rent if they are habitually late. In these states, you're legally required to give the tenant a chance to pay and stay only once or twice within a certain timeframe. If your state gives you a "no second chances" option for repeated late rent episodes, you'll see the rule reflected on the chart, "State Laws on Unconditional Quit Terminations" in Appendix A.

Some states insist that you give the tenant a *written* pay rent or quit notice for the first late payment, so that there is proof that rent was late. Other states allow you to use the unconditional quit notice merely for "repeated lateness." In that case, you need not have given the tenant a notice to pay or quit for the first tardiness, but it's good business practice to do so, anyway. If your tenant claims to have always paid the rent on time, you'll have prior pay rent or quit notices to show otherwise.

TIP

You can always use a 30-day notice for month-to-month tenants who are chronically late. You need not worry about the complexities of your state's unconditional quit procedure for month-to-month tenants who repeatedly pay late. Simply terminate the tenancy with a 30-day notice. This way you avoid a potential challenge to your use of the unconditional quit notice. Even if you live in a rent-controlled area that requires landlords to have good reason to evict, repeatedly paying late is usually ample legal reason to end a tenancy.

Special Rules for Tenants in Military Service

If your tenant is in the military or the activated reserves, your ability to evict for nonpayment of rent is subject to the War and National Defense Servicemembers Civil Relief Act, 50 U.S.C. § 3951. The act does not prevent you from serving a termination notice for nonpayment of rent. Instead, it requires the court to stay (postpone) an eviction for up to three months unless the judge decides that military service does not materially affect the tenant's ability to pay the rent.

The act applies only to evictions for nonpayment of rent. It does not apply to evictions for other reasons, such as keeping pets in violation of the lease or failing to move when a lease is up. Nor does it apply if you've terminated a rental agreement with a 30-day notice.

- **Tenants affected.** The act applies to the tenant and when your tenant's spouse, children, or other dependents occupy the rental unit. Courts give a broader meaning to the term "dependent" than the one used by the IRS.
- **Rental amount.** The act's protections apply when the rent is $2,400 per month or less (adjusted annually for inflation). To learn the current rent ceiling, type "housing price inflation adjustment" in the query box of your browser, then choose the link that goes to the Federal Register. At press time, the figure was $4,089.62 as of 2021.
- **The effect on an eviction lawsuit.** Once you have filed your lawsuit, you must tell the court that the tenant is an active serviceperson. The judge will decide whether the serviceperson's status in the military affects his or her ability to pay the rent. If the judge decides that it does, the case can be stayed for up to three months.
- **Requisitioned pay.** The Secretary of Defense or the Secretary of Transportation may order that part of the serviceperson's pay be allotted to pay the rent. Ask the judge in your case to write a letter to the service branch, asking that a reasonable amount be sent to you to pay the rent. Be advised, however, that current Defense Finance and Accounting Service regulations make no provision for such allotments.

When You Accept a Partial Rent Payment

By accepting even part of the rent a tenant owes—whether for past months or even just the current month—you will, in most states, cancel the effect of a pay rent or quit notice. But you can still go ahead with your attempts to get the tenant out—just pocket your tenant's partial payment with one hand and simultaneously present a new termination notice with the other.

> **EXAMPLE:** Danny's rent of $900 was due on the first of the month. Danny didn't pay January's rent and didn't have enough for February, either. On February 2, Danny's landlord, Ali, sent him a three-day notice to pay $1,800 or leave. Danny paid $900 on February 3 and thought that he'd saved his tenancy. He was amazed when, later that day, Ali handed him a new notice to pay $900 or leave. Ali properly filed for eviction on February 7 when Danny failed to pay.

> CAUTION
> **Both you and the tenant are bound by any written agreement you make to set up a payment schedule for delayed or partial rent.** If the tenant does not end up honoring this agreement, you can take steps to terminate the tenancy.

Other Tenant Violations of the Lease or Rental Agreement

In addition to nonpayment of rent, you may terminate a tenancy if a tenant violates other terms of the lease or rental agreement, such as:

- keeping a pet in violation of a no-pets rule
- bringing in an unauthorized roommate
- subleasing or assigning without your permission
- repeatedly violating "house rules" that are part of the lease or rental agreement, such as using common areas improperly, making too much noise, having unruly guests, or abusing recreation facilities, and

- giving false information concerning an important matter on the rental application or lease.

Giving Tenants Another Chance

The laws in most states insist that you give tenants a few days (anywhere from three to 30 days, depending on the state) to correct, or "cure," the violation before the tenancy can end. However, there are two important "but ifs" that allow you to use an unconditional quit notice instead of the more generous cure or quit notice:

- **Repeated violations.** If the tenants have violated the same lease clause two or more times within a certain period of time, they might lose the right to a second chance. Under some laws, you can give them an unconditional quit notice instead.
- **The violation cannot be corrected.** Some lease violations cannot be corrected because the effect of the violation is permanent. For instance, suppose your lease prohibits tenant alterations or improvements without your consent (see Clause 12 of the form agreements in Chapter 2). If, without asking, your tenant removes and discards the living room wallpaper, you can hardly demand that the tenant cease violating the lease clause, because it is simply too late to save the wallpaper. If a lease violation cannot be cured, you can use an unconditional quit notice.

Criminal Convictions

You are generally free to reject prospective tenants with criminal records for offenses that reasonably make them poor risks as tenants (convictions for past drug use excepted; see Chapter 5). Sometimes, however, you don't discover the convictions until you've already accepted a person as a tenant. Maybe you never checked the applicant's background, or you didn't have access to reliable information.

Regardless of why you didn't know beforehand, if you learn that a tenant has a record—and particularly if it includes a sex offense—your first impulse will probably be to look for a way to remove the tenant from your building. Here's what to do:

- **Month-to-month tenants.** In most states, you may terminate any month-to-month tenancy with a 30-day notice, and you need not give a reason, as long as you do not have discriminatory or retaliatory motives. Note, however, that tenants in rent control cities with "just cause" eviction protection might be protected from termination on this basis. The same is true for all tenants in New Hampshire, New Jersey, and Oregon (where statewide just cause protections apply), and for some tenants in California (where statewide protections might cover tenants not otherwise protected by local ordinances).
- **Tenants with leases.** You will not be able to terminate otherwise law- and rule-abiding tenants purely because you discover a criminal past, no matter how unsavory or alarming. However, if your lease or rental agreement states that false and material information on the rental application will be grounds for termination (as does the one in this book), you can terminate and evict on this basis. In some states, your right to do so is established by state law, even if your rental agreement or lease is silent on the matter.

Violations of a Tenant's Legal Responsibilities

Virtually every state allows you to terminate the tenancy of a tenant who has violated basic responsibilities imposed by law, including:

- grossly deficient housekeeping practices that cause a health hazard, such as allowing garbage to pile up

- seriously misusing appliances, like damaging the freezer while attempting to defrost it with an icepick
- repeatedly interfering with other tenants' ability to peacefully enjoy their homes by hosting late parties, playing incessant loud music, or running a noisy small business, for example
- substantially damaging the property—for instance, knocking holes in the walls or doors, and
- allowing or participating in illegal activities on or near the premises, such as drug dealing or gambling.

Many landlords incorporate these obligations into their leases or rental agreements. But, even if these obligations are not mentioned in your rental documents, tenants are still legally bound to observe them.

Tips on Dealing With a Tenant During an Eviction

- Avoid all unnecessary personal contact with the tenant during the eviction process unless it occurs in a structured setting—for example, at a neighborhood dispute resolution center or in the presence of a neutral third party.
- Keep your written communications to the point and as neutral as you can, even if you are boiling inside.
- Don't limit the tenant's access during the eviction process—the tenant has the right to stay on the property until the day the sheriff or marshal shows up to evict.

If a tenant or guest substantially damages the premises, you'll be within your rights to use an unconditional quit notice. The law does not require you to give tenants accused of serious misbehavior a second chance. Tenants who have earned this type of termination notice generally get only five to ten days to move out.

Tenant's Illegal Activity on the Premises

Many states have simplified procedures for evicting drug-dealing tenants. Indeed, in some states you risk having authorities close down or even confiscate your property if you fail to evict known drug dealers.

You usually don't have to wait until the tenant is convicted of a crime or even arrested. In some states, for example, a judge will order a tenant's eviction if the landlord has a "reasonable suspicion" that criminal activity has taken place and that the tenant or tenant's guests are involved. ("Reasonable suspicion" is easier to establish than "beyond a reasonable doubt.") By contrast, in other states, you may not begin an eviction for illegal activity unless there's been a criminal conviction for criminal acts on the rented premises.

Evictions based on criminal activity are often called "expedited evictions," because they take less time than a normal eviction. Expedited evictions are preceded by an unconditional quit notice that tells the tenant to move out (and do it quickly). If the tenant stays, you can go to court and file for eviction. The court hearing on the eviction is typically held within a few days, and, if you win, the tenant is given very little time to move.

How Eviction Lawsuits Work

When the deadline in the termination notice passes, your tenant will not be automatically evicted. In almost every state, when tenants refuse to leave after receiving a termination notice, you must file—and win—an eviction lawsuit before law enforcement can physically evict the tenants. The whole process can take weeks—or even longer when tenants fight the eviction in court.

What Court Hears Evictions?

Depending on the law where you live, eviction lawsuits are filed in a formal trial court (called "municipal," "county," or "justice") or in small claims court. A few states, including Illinois, Massachusetts, and New York, have separate landlord-tenant courts to hear eviction suits in larger cities. Some states give landlords a choice of courts to file in, while others require eviction lawsuits to be in a specific court. An Internet search for your town's name and "eviction court" should help you determine where to file your eviction case, or you can call the clerk at your local small claims court for assistance.

If you have a choice between regular trial court and small claims court, you'll want to consider the:

- **Amount of unpaid rent.** If you're also suing for unpaid rent that exceeds the small claims court's jurisdictional limit, you must use a higher court (unless you trim your demand to not exceed the limit). States' small claims court limits are listed on the chart in Appendix A.

- **Attorneys' fees clause.** If your lease or rental agreement contains an attorneys' fees clause, and you have a strong case and a reasonable chance of collecting from your tenant, you might want to hire an attorney and go to formal court, figuring that the fee will come from the tenant's pocket when you win. On the other hand, if the tenant has little or no funds, filing in small claims court might be a financially wiser choice, given the fact that your chances of actually collecting are low.

Regular trial courts differ from small claims (or landlord-tenant) courts in several respects:

- In small claims court, the regular rules of evidence are greatly relaxed. You can show or tell the court your side of the story without adhering to the "foundation" requirements that apply in higher courts. ("Laying a foundation" is explained in "Rules of Evidence in Formal Court," below.)

- In some regular courts, you and the tenant might engage in a pretrial process called "discovery," in which you must produce to each other all the evidence that relates to the dispute. Information gathered during discovery can be used at trial. Aside from making mandatory disclosures to each other, the parties have the option of deposing (questioning under oath) witnesses, serving interrogatories on one another (sets of preprinted questions intended to reveal information normally involved in a landlord-tenant dispute), and sending each other "requests for admissions" (statements of fact that the other side is asked, under oath, to admit or deny). The discovery process is normally available in formal court, but not in small claims or landlord-tenant courts.

- In regular court, you and the tenant may each attempt to wash the case out of court quickly by filing pretrial requests to the court to dismiss or limit the case. In small claims and landlord-tenant court, the idea is to decide the entire case after one efficient court hearing, without using motions or other pleadings.

RESOURCE

Everybody's Guide to Small Claims Court, **by Cara O'Neill (Nolo),** describes the workings of your small claims court in detail.

Represent Yourself in Court: Prepare & Try a Winning Civil Case, by Paul Bergman and Sara J. Berman (Nolo), explains how to present evidence and arguments in formal court.

First Steps: The Complaint and Summons

You start an eviction lawsuit by filing a legal document—often called a Complaint—with the court. In the Complaint, you list the facts that you think justify evicting your tenant, and ask the court to order the tenant to leave the rental, pay back rent, and reimburse you for damages, court costs, and (sometimes) attorneys' fees.

Fortunately, your Complaint need not be lengthy or complicated. Some courts will provide a preprinted Complaint form that allows you to simply check the appropriate boxes that describe your situation and arguments. Many courts put official forms online; typically, you can download the PDF file and complete it by hand, or complete it online and then print it (but not save it). If your court offers downloadable forms, you can most likely find them in a "Forms" link on the court's homepage.

In states that don't provide standardized forms, you can still create your own documents for filing by using legal form books (available at law libraries). These books contain "canned" forms that fit many different situations. When you sign your Complaint, be sure to note under your typed name that you are appearing "Pro per" or "Pro se" if you have not hired a lawyer.

Normally, you cannot sue a tenant for anything but back rent and damages. Because an eviction procedure is so quick, most states do not allow you to add other claims to an eviction Complaint. For example, if you claim that the tenants have damaged the sofa, and their security deposit won't cover the cost of replacement, you must sue the tenants in small claims court in a separate lawsuit. Similarly, some states will not allow you to include in your request for damages an unpaid late fee, even when your lease or rental agreement has optimistically deemed the fee "additional rent." (And, if the property is subject to rent control and the rent is already at the maximum allowed, adding the fee to the monthly rent will result in an illegal rent amount.)

When you file a Complaint, the clerk will assign a date for the court to hear your case. That date is entered on the Summons, a document notifying the tenant about the lawsuit. The Summons states

Rules of Evidence in Formal Court

It's important to back up your eviction lawsuit with as much hard evidence as possible. For example, if the basis of the termination is that the tenant has violated the no-pets policy agreed to in the lease, be sure that you have a copy of the lease signed by the tenant.

In small claims court, you can present practically any evidence you want to the judge. But, if you are in a formal court, the judge will not consider evidence until you have established that it is likely to be trustworthy. Presenting the legal background of evidence is called "laying a foundation." Here are a few hints on how to prepare evidence:

- **Photographs.** If your termination notice is based on your tenant knocking a hole in the kitchen wall, show the judge a photograph of the gaping hole. To get the picture into evidence, someone will have to testify that the picture is an accurate depiction of how the wall looked. Ask a neutral witness to look at the wall and come to court ready to testify that the photo is an accurate portrayal. Your witness need not have taken the photo.

- **Letters.** You might have sent a termination notice for nonpayment of rent because your tenant

improperly used the repair and deduct remedy by failing to give you a reasonable amount of time to fix the problem. You'll want to show the judge a copy of the letter you sent to the tenant promising to fix the defect within the week (the tenant didn't wait). In court, this means you'll need to introduce your letter into evidence. To do this, you can simply testify that the letter is a true copy, that the signature is your own, and that you mailed or handed it to your tenant.

- **Government documents.** If your tenant has withheld rent because of what the tenant claims are uninhabitable conditions, you might decide to evict for nonpayment of rent. If the tenant filed a complaint with a local health department, and it issued a report giving your property a clean bill of health, you'll want the report considered by the court (admitted into evidence). Ask the health department inspector to testify to having written the report as part of the normal duties of investigating possible health violations. To get the inspector to court, you'll need to ask the judge for an order, called a "subpoena," that you can serve on the inspector.

that the tenant must answer the Complaint in writing and appear in court on the designated day, or lose the lawsuit. You must then arrange for the tenant to be given the Complaint and the Summons. In legal jargon, this is called "service of process."

State laws are quite detailed as to the proper way to deliver, or "serve," court papers. Most importantly, neither you (including anyone who has an ownership interest in your business) nor your employees can serve these papers. (In some states, any adult not involved in the lawsuit can serve papers.) The method of delivery is specified, as well: Typically, the preferred way is "personal" service, which means that a law enforcement officer or professional process server personally hands the tenant the papers.

If, despite repeated attempts, the process server cannot locate the tenant, most states allow something called "substituted service." This means the process server leaves a copy of the papers with a competent adult at the tenant's home, or mails the papers first-class and also leaves a copy in a place where the tenant will likely see it, such as posted on the front door.

Failure to properly serve the tenant is one of the most common errors landlords make, and can result in the court's dismissing your lawsuit before you get to trial. Even a minor mistake—such as forgetting to check a box, checking one you shouldn't, or filling in contradictory information—increases the chance that your tenant will win the lawsuit or that the court will dismiss the suit on its own. It is vital that you pay close attention to your state's and court's eviction rules and procedures.

Attorneys and Eviction Services

Depending on your location, your situation, and the availability of self-help eviction guides, you might be able to handle all, or most of, an eviction lawsuit yourself. Many landlords hire "legal typing services" or "independent paralegals" (discussed in Chapter 18) to help with evictions. But, in the following situations, you should strongly consider consulting an attorney who specializes in landlord-tenant law:

- Your tenant is represented by a lawyer.
- Your property is subject to rent control rules governing eviction.
- The tenant you are evicting is an ex-manager whom you have fired.
- Your tenant contests the eviction in court.
- Your tenant files for bankruptcy.
- Your case goes to trial.
- The property you own is too far from where you live. Because you must file an eviction lawsuit where the property is located, the time and travel involved in representing yourself might be significant.

The Tenant's Answer to the Complaint

The next step in a typical eviction lawsuit is for the tenant to respond to your claims.

In some states, tenants who have been served with an eviction lawsuit can just show up at the hearing and present their defenses in person. In other states, tenants must file a document called an Answer on or before the date printed on the Summons. Like your Complaint, it need not be a complex document, and might be on a standardized form provided by the court.

In general, Answers can contain two kinds of responses:

- **Denials.** The tenant might dispute your reasons for eviction. For example, if you are evicting for nonpayment of rent, your tenant might deny that the rent is unpaid and claim that he paid his rent to the manager. Or, if you've filed an eviction lawsuit because the tenant has a dog, the tenant might deny this by checking the "denials" box on the answer form, and claim that the animal belongs to the tenants in the next unit. If the court doesn't provide an Answer form (which means defendants have to draft their own), you'll see a typed paragraph that looks something like this: "Defendant denies the allegations in Paragraph X of Plaintiff's Complaint." (You are the plaintiff in the lawsuit; the tenant is the defendant.)

- **Affirmative defenses.** In the Answer, the tenant can provide "affirmative defenses"—good legal reasons (such as claims of discrimination or retaliation) that they hope will excuse what would otherwise be grounds for eviction. For example, tenants who are being evicted for not paying the rent might claim a habitability defense, and argue that they followed your state's repair-and-deduct law, using some of the rent money to pay for repairing a serious problem you ignored.

When Tenants Ignore the Summons and Complaint

If you properly terminate a tenancy and the tenants don't respond to the Summons and Complaint by filing an Answer or showing up in court, you will usually automatically win the lawsuit. The court will grant what's called a "default judgment" against the tenants, ordering them to pay unpaid rent and (possibly) your attorneys' fees and court costs. You will still have to hire local law enforcement to carry out the actual eviction, and you'll have to look to your security deposit to cover the monetary judgment. If the deposit is insufficient, you can always sue for the balance in small claims court.

Complete Your Lawsuit, Even If You Think You've Won Already

It's very common for tenants to move out after receiving a Summons and Complaint. When this happens, you might be tempted to forget about the lawsuit—especially if the security deposit will cover your losses, or you know that attempting to collect any excess won't be worth your time and trouble.

Never walk away from a lawsuit without formally ending it. In most courts, this means you will need to file a document asking the court to dismiss the case (a Motion to Dismiss). Most likely, your court has a standardized form for this. Sometimes, you'll need to appear in person before the judge and request dismissal.

Officially ending the case in this manner preserves your reputation as someone who uses the courts with respect—if you are simply a no-show for your court date, expect a chilly reception the next time you appear in court. In addition, if you don't appear for trial but the tenant does, the court might find in favor of the tenant, and order you to allow the tenant to move back in and pay the tenant's court costs and attorneys' fees.

If you and the tenant have reached a settlement that involves the tenant paying you money, but the tenant hasn't paid yet, it's a good idea to take the written settlement agreement with you to court. Ask the judge to dismiss the case, but make the settlement agreement—and its performance—part of the ruling. Depending on the rules in your state, you will then have a court order (sometimes called a "stipulated settlement") that you can immediately use if the tenant fails to pay. (You can take it to a collection agency or use it to garnish wages.) Otherwise, you'll have to take the written agreement to small claims court to get a judgment.

Finally, don't overlook the possibility that the tenant might not have actually moved out (or might move back in). You'll be on safe ground if you get a formal dismissal before you retake possession of the rental unit.

The Trial

Most eviction cases never end up in trial—often because the tenant moves out or negotiates a settlement with the landlord. But each case that does go to trial will have its own unpredictable twists and turns that can greatly affect trial preparation and tactics. For this reason, you will probably need to hire a lawyer, if you haven't done so already, to help you prepare for and conduct the trial.

At trial, you will need to prove the claims you raised in your Complaint and present evidence disputing the tenant's Answer. In a suit based on nonpayment of rent, for example, the evidence you present will differ depending on how the tenant responds to your Complaint. If the tenant claims you failed to keep the premises habitable, you would have to demonstrate that the tenant's argument is false—perhaps by producing a copy of your maintenance records or photos and video of the unit's condition. On the other hand, if the tenant denies receiving a termination notice, you wouldn't have to show evidence of the unit's condition—rather, you'd need to produce proof of the notice's delivery.

All contested evictions are similar, however, in that you have to establish the basic elements of your case through solid evidence that supports your case (and refutes your tenant's defense). In formal court, you'll have to abide by your state's and court's rules of evidence. But in an informal court, you might be able to introduce letters and secondhand testimony ("I heard her say that … "). Also, you can introduce evidence without elaborate "foundations." (See "Rules of Evidence in Formal Court," above.)

The Judgment

The judge will close the eviction hearing or trial after listening to the witness testimony, reviewing the evidence, and consulting any relevant statutes, ordinances, and higher court opinions. Usually, the judge will decide the matter on the spot or very soon thereafter.

If You Win

If you win the eviction case, you get an order from the judge declaring that you are entitled to possession of the property (you might also get a money judgment for back rent, court costs, and attorneys' fees). You'll need to take the order, called a judgment, to the local law enforcement official who will carry out the eviction.

Unfortunately, having a judgment for the payment of money is not the same as having the money itself. Your tenant might be unable (or unwilling) to pay you—despite the fact that you have converted your legal right to be paid into a court order. If the tenant doesn't pay, you will have to collect the debt—for example, by using the tenant's security deposit, garnishing wages, attaching a bank account, or hiring a collection agency to do these things on your behalf.

If You Lose

If you lose the eviction case, your tenant can stay, and you'll likely end up paying for your tenant's court costs and fees. You might also be hit with money damages if the judge decides you acted illegally, as in the case of discrimination or retaliation.

If your tenant wins by asserting a habitability defense, the court might keep the case open even after the trial is over. That's because the court doesn't want to simply return the tenant to an unfit dwelling. In some states, a judge can order you to make repairs while the rent is paid into a court account; then, when an inspector certifies that the dwelling is habitable, the judge will release the funds.

How Tenants Can Stop or Postpone an Eviction

If you win the eviction lawsuit, you'll want to move quickly to have the tenant physically removed from the property. In rare instances, tenants might be able to get the trial judge to stop the eviction, but only if they can convince the court of two things:

- Eviction would cause a severe hardship for the tenants or their family. For example, the tenants might be able to persuade the judge that alternate housing is unavailable, or that their employment will be in jeopardy if they are forced to move.
- The tenants are willing and able to pay any back rent owed, future rent, and your costs of bringing the lawsuit, as well.

It's very unusual for a judge to stop an eviction, for the simple reason that if the tenants' sympathetic predicament (and sufficient monetary reserves) weren't persuasive enough to win the case in the first place, it's unlikely that these arguments can prevail after the trial.

The tenants could, however, ask for a postponement of the eviction. Typically, evictions are postponed in three situations:

- **Pending an appeal.** If the tenants file an appeal, they might ask the trial judge to postpone ("stay") the eviction until a higher court decides the case. In a few states, tenants who have lost their eviction suit in small claims court might receive an automatic postponement during the appeal. (This is one reason to research your state's small claims court rules when deciding where to file an eviction suit.)
- **Until the tenants' circumstances improve.** Tenants might be able to persuade a judge to give them a little more time to find a new home.
- **Until the weather improves.** Contrary to popular belief, judges in many cold-climate states (including Alaska, Minnesota, and North Dakota) are not required to postpone an eviction on frigid days. But there's nothing to

stop tenants from asking the judge, anyway. In the District of Columbia, however, a landlord may not evict on a day when the National Weather Service predicts at 8:00 a.m. that the temperature at the National Airport will fall below freezing, or when precipitation is falling at the location of the rental unit. (D.C. Code § 42-3505.01(k).)

- **During the pandemic or another emergency.** Many states forbade evictions during the early months of the COVID-19 pandemic. When this book went to press, only a few states had bans on evictions due to the pandemic. However, many cities and towns still have bans and tenant protections in place. Aside from bans, many places, such as Washington, D.C., enacted legislation stating that no evictions can take place during a declared public health emergency. This means that for as long as the pandemic persists, and whenever any sort of public health emergency is declared, landlords will want to check the current status of state and local eviction bans and tenant protections before filing an eviction suit.

Eviction

In most states, you cannot move tenants' belongings out on the street yourself, even after winning an eviction lawsuit. You must give the judgment to a local law enforcement officer, along with a fee that the tenants have been charged as part of your costs. The sheriff or marshal gives the tenants a notice telling them that law enforcement will be back, sometimes within just a few days, for the physical eviction if the tenants haven't left yet.

Illegal "Self-Help" Evictions

As any experienced landlord will attest, there are occasional tenants who do things so outrageous that the landlord is tempted to bypass normal legal protections and take direct and immediate action to protect the rental property. For example, a landlord who is responsible for paying the utility charges might be tempted to simply not pay the bill in the hopes that the resulting lack of water, gas, or electricity will hasten a particularly outrageous tenant's departure. When you realize how long a legal eviction can sometimes take, these actions can almost seem sensible.

If you are tempted to take the law into your own hands, heed the following advice: *Don't do it!* Virtually every state forbids "self-help" evictions, and their statutes warn landlords that their eviction procedures are the *only* legal way to retake possession of rental property. In many states, the penalties for violating these laws are steep—not to mention that you could find yourself on the wrong end of a lawsuit for trespass, assault, battery, slander and libel, intentional infliction of emotional distress, and wrongful eviction.

If you are sued by a tenant whom you forcibly evicted or tried to evict, the fact that the tenant didn't pay rent, left your property a mess, verbally abused you, or otherwise acted outrageously will not be a valid defense. You will very likely lose the lawsuit, and it will cost you far more than evicting the tenant using normal court procedures.

You might be responsible for paying for the tenant's monetary losses (such as the cost of temporary housing, the value of food that spoiled when the refrigerator stopped running, or the expense of an electric heater when the gas was shut off), as well as other penalties. In some states, tenants can collect monetary damages and retain the right to remain in the premises; in others, they are entitled to only monetary compensation. See "Consequences of Self-Help Evictions" in Appendix A.

Even if your state has not legislated against self-help evictions, throwing your tenants out on your own is highly risky and likely to land you in more legal entanglements than had you simply pursued an eviction lawsuit in the first place.

Also, self-help evictions lend themselves to nastiness and even violence. The last thing you want is a patrol car at the curb while you and your tenants wrestle over the sofa on the lawn. And you can almost count on a lawsuit over the "disappearance" of your tenants' valuable possessions, which they'll claim were lost or taken when you removed their belongings.

Using a neutral law enforcement officer to enforce a judge's eviction order avoids your having to personally participate in any of the unpleasantries that might arise.

> ⊘ **CAUTION**
>
> **Don't seize tenants' property under the guise of handling "abandoned" property.** A few states allow you to freely dispose of tenants' leftover property after they've moved out. Do so only if it is clear that the tenants have left permanently with the intent to turn the place over to you. Seizing property under a bogus claim that the tenants had abandoned it exposes you to significant monetary penalties.

Stopping Eviction by Filing for Bankruptcy

It's not unusual for tenants with significant financial burdens to declare bankruptcy. There are several kinds of bankruptcy; the most common are Chapter 7, in which most debts are wiped out after as many creditors as possible have been paid; and Chapter 13, in which some debts—but not necessarily all—are paid off over time according to a court-approved plan.

If your tenants have filed for either Chapter 7 or 13 bankruptcy and are behind in the rent, become unable to pay the rent, or violate another term of the tenancy (such as keeping a pet in violation of

a no-pets clause), you can't deliver a termination notice or proceed with an eviction as you would under "normal" circumstances. This prohibition is known as an "automatic stay," and it means that you need to go to the federal bankruptcy court and ask the judge to "lift," or remove the stay. (11 U.S.C. § 365(e).)

In most cases, the bankruptcy court will lift the stay within a matter of days, and you can proceed with your termination and eviction. (A shortened process is available if your tenant is using illegal drugs or endangering the property, as explained below in "Bankrupt Tenants, Drugs, and Damage.")

The automatic stay does not apply, however, if you completed your eviction proceeding and got a judgment for possession *before* the tenants filed for bankruptcy. Landlords can proceed with the eviction without having to go to court and ask for the stay to be lifted.

The Lease After Bankruptcy

You might find yourself with new tenants if your existing tenants file for Chapter 7 bankruptcy. How could this happen? If the current tenant can't cure back rent or wants to move out, the bankruptcy trustee appointed to the case can take over a valuable lease and rent the space to new tenants at a profit (as long as the lease doesn't contain a clause prohibiting subletting). The upside? Because the trustee steps into the tenants' shoes, the trustee must pay any past-due rent and abide by the lease terms. By contrast, in a Chapter 13 case, a trustee won't take over a lease, and tenants who are behind on the rent but would like to stay must propose a plan to bring the rent current within a reasonable period. (11 U.S.C. §§ 365(b)(1)(A), (B), & (C).)

In very narrow circumstances, and only for evictions based on rent nonpayment, the bankruptcy court might not allow the eviction even if you got a judgment before the tenants filed for bankruptcy. Here are the specifics:

- Along with their bankruptcy petition, the tenants must go to court and file a paper certifying that state law allows them to avoid eviction by paying the unpaid rent, even after the landlord has won a judgment for possession. Very few states extend this option to tenants. The certification must be served on the landlord.
- At the same time, the tenants must deposit with the clerk of the bankruptcy court any rent that would be due 30 days from the date the petition was filed.
- The tenants then have 30 days after filing the petition to actually pay the back rent. They must file another certification with the bankruptcy court (and serve it on the landlord), stating that they have paid the amount due.

At any point during these 30 days, you can file an objection to the tenants' certification, and you'll get a hearing in the bankruptcy court within ten days. If you convince the judge that the tenants' certifications are not true, the court will lift the stay and you can proceed to recover possession of the property.

Bankrupt Tenants, Drugs, and Damage

You might find yourself needing to evict tenants who are using illegal drugs on the property or endangering your property. If the tenants file for bankruptcy before you win a judgment for possession, you'll be able to proceed with the eviction without asking the bankruptcy judge to lift the stay. Here are the steps to take:

- **When you've begun an eviction case but don't have a judgment.** Prepare a certification, or sworn statement, that you have begun an unlawful detainer case based on the tenants' endangerment of the property or use of illegal drugs on the property (or such use by the tenants' guests).
- **When you haven't yet filed your eviction lawsuit.** Prepare a certification, or sworn statement, that the activity described above has happened within the past 30 days.
- **File the certification with the bankruptcy court and serve the tenants as you would serve any legal notice.**

Tenants who object must file with the court, and serve on you, a certification challenging the truth of your certification. The bankruptcy court will likely hold a hearing within ten days, at which the tenants must convince the court that the situation you describe did not exist or has been remedied. If the court rules for you, you may proceed with the eviction without asking that the stay be lifted; but if the tenants win, you may not proceed.

Lawyers and Legal Research

Landlords should be prepared to deal with most routine legal questions and problems without a lawyer. However, sometimes good advice from a specialist in landlord-tenant law will be helpful, if not essential. Throughout this book, we point out instances when an attorney's advice or services would be useful. For example, nearly all landlords should get professional legal advice when tackling:

- housing discrimination lawsuits
- personal injury claims, and
- complicated evictions.

This chapter recommends a strategy for efficiently and effectively using legal services and keeping up to date on landlord-tenant law.

In reality, it doesn't make sense to run your business without ever consulting a lawyer. When faced with potentially serious and expensive legal issues, it makes sense to get expert help.

How Lawyers Can Help Landlords

Lawyers do a lot more than handle lawsuits. You can always ask your lawyer to:

- prepare (or review your drafts of) key documents
- confirm that you have a good claim or defense in a potential lawsuit with a tenant
- write a letter to or call the tenant to get a problem resolved quickly
- summarize and point you to the law that applies in a given situation
- provide assistance with evictions, including preparing notices and forms
- answer questions along the way if you're representing yourself in court or in a mediation proceeding, and
- handle legal problems that are—or are threatening to become—serious, such as a tenant's personal injury lawsuit or discrimination charge.

In other words, your challenge isn't to avoid lawyers altogether, but rather to use them cost-effectively. Ideally, this means finding a lawyer who's willing to serve as a kind of law coach, to help you educate yourself. With some knowledge and experience under your belt, you'll be able to do routine or preliminary legal work on your own, turning to your lawyer only occasionally for advice and fine-tuning.

Finding a Lawyer

How frequently you'll need a lawyer's help depends on many factors, including the type, number, and location of your rental units; the kinds of problems you run into with tenants; the number of property managers and other employees you hire; and your willingness to do some of the legal work yourself.

While looking for a lawyer you can work with, and during your subsequent relationship with that person, always remember one key thing: You're the boss. Just because your lawyer has specialized training, knowledge, skills, and experience in dealing with legal matters is no reason for you to abdicate control over decisions or the amount of attention you give to any single matter. You have an intimate knowledge of your business and are in the best position to call the shots—don't let an overeager attorney try to run your business while overcharging you for the privilege. Instead, find a lawyer who's willing and able to provide the amount and type of legal services you need.

Compile a List of Prospects

Finding a good, reasonably priced lawyer expert in landlord-tenant legal issues is not always easy. A random name picked from a legal directory or an attorney you've used for other legal needs, such as a divorce, likely won't result in someone who knows enough about landlord-tenant law to provide the assistance you need.

As a general rule, deep experience in landlord-tenant law is most important. As with so many other areas of the law, the information needed to practice effectively in this field is specialized—so much so that a general practitioner simply won't do.

The best way to find a suitable attorney is by referral from a trusted friend or acquaintance who has actually worked with a landlord-tenant attorney. Other landlords and rental property owners in your area are also good referral sources. By asking your professional circle for some names, you'll probably come up with a solid list of lawyers experienced in landlord-tenant law.

RESOURCE

Looking for a lawyer? Aside from seeking personal referrals, you can search for landlord-tenant specialists on many online lawyer directories, such as Nolo.com, Lawyers.com, and Martindale.com. Most lawyer directories allow you to search for attorneys based on location as well as the areas of law they practice. Some listings also include reviews from clients and peers.

Keep in mind that these online resources are simply modern versions of the yellow pages: Many of the listed lawyers have paid to have their names show up on the relevant pages.

Shop Around

Once you have a list of prospects, meet with each attorney and make your own evaluation—many lawyers will speak to you for a half-hour or so for free or at a reduced rate. Briefly explain your business and legal needs and how much work you plan to do yourself.

Look for experience, personal rapport, and accessibility. Some of these traits will be apparent almost immediately; others might take longer to discover. Ask the lawyer to provide references you can talk to—preferably other local landlords.

A good lawyer will be:

- **Transparent.** Is the lawyer upfront about fees? Willing to answer your questions? Stay away from lawyers who make you feel uncomfortable asking questions. Pay particular attention to the rapport between you and your lawyer. No matter how experienced and well-recommended a lawyer is, if you feel uncomfortable with that person, you won't achieve an ideal lawyer-client relationship. Trust your instincts and seek a lawyer whose personality is compatible with your own. Be sure you understand how the lawyer charges for services.

- **Cooperative.** If you plan to be actively involved in dealing with your legal business, look for a lawyer who doesn't resent your participation and control. By reading this book all the way through and consulting other resources, such as those available online or at a nearby law library, you can answer many of your questions on your own. For example, you might do the initial legal work in evictions and similar procedures yourself, but hand off any hotly contested or complicated cases to your lawyer.

  Unfortunately, some lawyers are uncomfortable with the idea of helping clients help themselves. They see themselves as experts and expect their clients to accept and follow their advice. Obviously, this is not the type of lawyer a self-helper wants.

- **Flexible.** Is the lawyer willing to assist you on an hourly basis when you handle your own legal work and have questions? Ask if the lawyer is willing to answer your questions over the phone and charge only for the brief amount of time the conversation lasted. If the lawyer is willing to provide advice only during more time-consuming (and profitable) office appointments, keep looking. Plenty of lawyers will gladly bill you hourly to help you help yourself. By providing helpful consultations on problems that are routine or involve small dollar amounts, a lawyer can generate referrals for full-service representation on bigger, more complex matters that you (or your friends or family) face in the future. And if the lawyer later tries to dissuade you from representing yourself or won't give advice over the phone despite your invitation to bill you for it, find someone else.

- **Thorough.** Will the lawyer clearly lay out all your options for handling a particular legal problem, including alternate dispute resolution methods such as mediation?

- **Accessible.** Will the lawyer be accessible when you need legal services? Unfortunately, the complaint logs of all legal regulatory groups indicate that many lawyers are not reasonably available to their clients in times of need. If there's a delay of several days before you can talk to your lawyer, you'll lose precious time, not to mention sleep. And almost nothing is more aggravating than to leave a legal question or project in a lawyer's hands and then have weeks or even months go by without anything happening. Ask potential lawyers to commit to returning your phone calls promptly, working hard on your behalf, and following through on all assignments.

- **Knowledgeable.** Find a lawyer who makes a genuine effort to stay informed and gain experience. Ask the lawyer how they stay up-to-date with changes in laws and procedures. For example, if your property is subject to rent control, does the lawyer know the ins and outs of the rent control laws? Has the attorney taken specialized courses in landlord-tenant law? How does the attorney stay informed about recent changes in the law?

- **Specialized.** Does the lawyer represent mostly landlords, mostly tenants, or a mix of both? Leaning more heavily towards one has its

pros and cons: Chances are that a lawyer who represents both landlords and tenants can advise you well on how to avoid many legal pitfalls of being a landlord. On the other hand, you'll want to steer clear of lawyers who represent mostly tenants, because their sympathies (world view) are likely to be different from yours.

Types of Fee Arrangements With Lawyers

How you pay your lawyer depends on the type of legal services you need and the amount of legal work you have. Once an agreement is reached, it's a good idea (and legally required in most states) to ask for a fee agreement—a written explanation of how the fees and costs will be billed and paid. As part of this, negotiate an overall cap on what you can be billed absent your specific agreement.

If a lawyer will be delegating some of the work on your case to a less-experienced associate, paralegal, or secretary, that work should be billed at a lower hourly rate. The rates of all professionals you'll work with should be recorded in your initial written fee agreement.

Lawyers charge for their services in a variety of ways. Most lawyers tailor their billing methods to meet the needs of each client, and you might find that a lawyer will use a combination of two or more of these billing methods, depending on the type of work. For example, a lawyer might charge a flat fee to review your contract and an hourly rate to answer follow up questions.

Hourly fees. In most parts of the United States, you can get competent services for your rental business for $150 to $350 an hour, with most lawyers billing in 6-, 10-, or 15-minute increments. Comparison shopping among lawyers will help you avoid overpaying. But the cheapest hourly rate isn't necessarily the best—more experienced attorneys will take less time to get up to speed with and advise you on your situation.

Flat fees. Sometimes, a lawyer will quote you a flat fee for a specific job. For example, a lawyer might offer to represent you in court for routine eviction cases (such as for nonpayment of rent) that are straightforward matters, even when they are contested by the tenant (which is actually fairly rare). In a flat-fee agreement, you pay the same amount regardless of how much time the lawyer spends on a particular job. If you own many rental units and anticipate sending the lawyer a lot of business over the years, you have a golden opportunity to negotiate flat fees that are substantially below the lawyer's normal hourly rate.

Retainers. Lawyers often require clients to pay a retainer fee or deposit. There are two types of retainers: a "true" retainer, and an advance payment (or deposit) retainer. The fact that lawyers use the term "retainer" to refer to both can be confusing, so make sure you're perfectly clear about the type of retainer your lawyer is collecting.

True retainer. A true retainer is a nonrefundable, flat, monthly or annual fee you pay to have access to the lawyer. Usually, a retainer fee pays for the lawyer's work on routine matters only—you'll be charged extra for complicated matters and court costs and fees. The key to making a true retainer fee arrangement work is to have a written agreement clearly defining what sort of work the lawyer will perform without charging additional fees (and what the rate for additional work will be).

True retainer fee arrangements are rare and suited only for larger landlords (a dozen or more rental units) with regular legal needs. Also, retainer fee agreements are usually best negotiated after you and your lawyer have worked together long enough to have established a pattern—you know and trust each other well enough to work out a mutually beneficial arrangement.

Retainer deposit. You are more likely to encounter a retainer deposit, where the lawyer requires you to pay a certain sum up front. The deposit is held in the lawyer's trust account until the attorney has earned the fees by performing work. Many lawyers collect retainer deposits regardless of whether they're charging you a flat fee or billing you hourly.

The retainer deposit can also be used to pay for court filing fees and other costs, such as service of process or unusually large photocopying jobs. Find out from the lawyer how frequently you'll receive a statement of work performed, and whether the lawyer requires you to refresh the deposit to maintain a minimum. You are entitled to a refund of any deposit the lawyer doesn't actually earn.

Some landlords who anticipate using the lawyer's service on an ongoing basis allow their retainer to remain in the attorney's trust account, to be applied towards the next legal matter that arises. The amount lawyers collect as a retainer deposit varies, but you can expect it to be a minimum of $1,500.

Prepaid legal fees. In many ways, prepaid legal plans are the "poor-person's" traditional retainer fee agreement. For a low monthly cost, many plans offer a certain number of phone consultations with a lawyer, as well as the opportunity to have a lawyer review documents you've prepared. You do not receive a refund of your fee if you don't use the service. For sophisticated landlords, having access to a second opinion before making a legal decision can be helpful. For most landlords, though, developing a relationship with a local attorney is a better plan—you'll pay for assistance only when you need it, and someone local will likely be able to offer you advice you didn't even know you needed. Also, with many prepaid services, you aren't able to get quick assistance with court matters, such as evictions and security deposit-related suits. Because the quality of assistance you receive under these plans varies, do your homework before signing up: Look at online reviews, check out the lawyers who work for the service in your area, and make sure that the service is able to assist you in landlord-tenant matters specifically.

Contingency fees. Under a contingency fee arrangement, you pay no fees for the lawyer's work until and unless the lawyer negotiates a successful monetary settlement or wins a monetary judgment at trial. The lawyer is entitled to whatever percentage of the award you agreed to in your fee agreement. There's no "typical" contingency percentage—often, the riskier the case, the higher the percentage. Although you won't pay for the lawyer's time under a contingency fee agreement, you are usually responsible for paying the (comparatively much smaller) amounts due for court costs, filing fees, and administrative costs. Contingency fees are common in personal injury cases, but relatively unusual for the kinds of legal advice and representation landlords need.

Saving on Legal Fees

Because you'll likely be charged by the hour, you'll want to use your time with your lawyer as efficiently as possible.

Be organized. Before your appointment, gather all documents you think the lawyer might want to see. Organize them in chronological order or label them with sticky notes so you can find them quickly. Consider writing out a chronology of events with bullet points. If your lawyer needs a copy of a document, hold onto the original and ask the lawyer to scan or copy it. Alternatively, you can provide your lawyer with a flash drive containing your documents, offer to email copies, or ask the lawyer if they use any cloud-based document sharing services.

Prepare. Before you call or visit your lawyer, put your questions in writing and give them to your lawyer. That way, the lawyer can research answers in advance and let you know if you need to provide any more information. Early preparation also helps focus the meeting, so there is less of a chance of digressing into (and having to pay to discuss) unrelated topics.

Educate yourself. Read trade journals, attend landlord association meetings, and take classes. Because laws change frequently, you need to keep up with legal developments affecting your business. Send pertinent articles to your lawyer—and encourage your lawyer to do the same for you. This can dramatically reduce legal research time. You can learn many of the basic rules relevant to landlords by reading books such as this and researching on the internet.

Be a good client. Mutual respect is key in an attorney-client relationship. The single most important way to show your lawyer how much you value the relationship is to pay your bills on time. Beyond that, let your lawyer know about plans for expansion and your business's possible future legal needs. And drop your lawyer a line when you've recommended them to your landlord colleagues.

Bundle your legal matters. You'll save money if you consult with your lawyer on several matters at one time. For example, in a one-hour conference, you might be able to review several items—such as a new lease or rental agreement clause, anti-age-discrimination policy, or advertisement for your apartment complex.

Significant savings are possible, because lawyers commonly divide their billable hours into parts of an hour. For example, if your lawyer bills in 15-minute intervals and you only talk for five minutes, you are likely to be charged for the whole 15. So it usually pays to gather your questions and ask them all at once, rather than calling every time you have a question.

 TIP

Carefully review lawyer bills. Always read your bill. Like everyone else, lawyers make mistakes, and your charges might be wrong. For example, a "0.1" of an hour (six minutes) might be transposed into a "1.0" (one hour) when the data are entered into the billing system. That's $200 instead of $20 if your lawyer charges $200 per hour. If you have any questions about your bill, feel free to ask your lawyer. You have the right to a clear explanation of your bill.

Use nonlawyer professionals for evictions. In some states, nonlawyer professionals can assist with evictions and might be called "unlawful detainer assistants," "legal typing services," or "independent paralegals." For a flat fee that is usually much lower than what lawyers charge, and often at a faster pace, nonlawyer eviction services take the basic information from you, provide the appropriate eviction forms, and fill them out according to your instructions.

This normally involves typing your eviction papers so they'll be accepted by the court, arranging for filing, and then serving the papers on the tenant.

Unlawful detainer assistants, paralegals, and typing services usually handle only routine cases. They can't give legal advice about the requirements of your case and can't represent you in court if the tenant contests the eviction suit. You must decide how to proceed with your case, and it's up to you to supply the correct and necessary information for filling out forms.

To find a nonlawyer eviction service, check with a landlords' association, or search online for "eviction services," "paralegals," or "unlawful detainer assistant." Be sure the eviction service or typing service is reputable and experienced, as well as reasonably priced. Typically they charge by the page or by the document. Ask for references and check them. As a general matter, the longer a nonlawyer eviction service has been in business, the better.

RESOURCE
Recommended reading on lawsuits. California landlords can handle eviction lawsuits themselves by using *The California Landlord's Law Book: Evictions*, by Nils Rosenquest (Nolo). Contact your state or local apartment association for information on any step-by-step guides to evictions in your state.

Represent Yourself in Court: Prepare & Try a Winning Case, by Paul Bergman and Sara Berman (Nolo), offers more general advice on handling any civil lawsuit on your own or with a lawyer-coach's help.

Costs Can Add Up

In addition to the fees they charge for their time, lawyers often bill for some costs as well—and these costs can add up quickly. When you receive a lawyer's bill, you might be surprised at both the amount of the costs and the variety of the services for which the lawyer expects reimbursement. Expect to see charges for:

- overnight mail
- messenger service
- expert witness fees
- court filing fees
- process servers
- work by investigators
- work by legal assistants or paralegals
- deposition transcripts
- online legal research, and
- travel.

Many lawyers absorb the cost of photocopying, faxes, phone calls, and the like as normal office overhead—part of the cost of doing business—but that's not always the case. So in working out the fee arrangements, discuss the costs you'll be expected to pay. If a lawyer is intent on nickel-and-diming you, look elsewhere. On the other hand, it is reasonable for a lawyer to pass along costs of things like court costs, process server fees, and any work by investigators.

TIP
Lawyer fees are a tax-deductible business expense. If you visit your lawyer on a personal legal matter (such as reviewing a contract for the purchase of a house) and you also discuss a business problem (such as a new policy for hiring managers), ask your lawyer to allocate the time spent and send you separate bills. At tax time, you can easily list the business portion as a tax-deductible business expense.

Resolving Problems With Your Lawyer

If you see a problem emerging with your lawyer, nip it in the bud. Don't just sit back and fume; call or write your lawyer. Have an honest discussion about your feelings. Maybe you're upset because your lawyer hasn't kept you informed about what's going on in your lawsuit, or maybe your lawyer missed a promised deadline for reviewing your new system for handling maintenance and repair problems. Or maybe last month's bill was shockingly high or you'd like a more detailed explanation of how your lawyer's time was spent.

Your Rights as a Client

As a client, you are entitled to:

- courteous treatment by your lawyer and staff members
- an itemized statement of services rendered and a full advance explanation of billing practices
- charges for agreed-upon fees and no more
- prompt responses to phone calls, emails, and letters
- confidential legal conferences, free from unwarranted interruptions
- up-to-date information on the status of your case
- diligent and competent legal representation, and
- clear answers to all questions.

Here's one way to test whether a lawyer-client relationship is a good one: Ask yourself if you feel able to talk freely with your lawyer about your degree of participation in any legal matter and your control over how the lawyer carries out a legal assignment. If you can't frankly discuss these sometimes-sensitive matters with your lawyer, fire that lawyer and hire another one. If you don't, you'll surely waste money on unnecessary legal fees and risk having legal matters turn out badly.

Remember that you're always free to change lawyers. If you do, be sure to fire your old lawyer—in writing—before you hire a new one. Otherwise, you could find yourself being billed by both lawyers at the same time. Also, get all important legal documents back from a lawyer you no longer employ. Tell your new lawyer what your old one has done to date and pass on the file.

In the following situations, firing your lawyer might not be enough:

- If you have a dispute over fees, the local bar association might be able to mediate it for you.
- When a lawyer violates legal ethics rules—for example, by representing you despite a conflict of interest, overbilling you, or not representing you zealously—the state agency that licenses lawyers can discipline or even disbar the lawyer. Although lawyer oversight groups might be biased in favor of the legal profession, they often take action when a lawyer has done something seriously wrong.
- When a lawyer has made a major mistake—for example, missing the deadline for filing a case—you can sue for malpractice. Most lawyers carry malpractice insurance, and your dispute might be settled out of court.

Attorneys' Fees in a Lawsuit

If your lease or written rental agreement has an attorneys' fees provision (see Clause 21 of the form agreements in Chapter 2), you are entitled to recover your attorneys' fees if you win a lawsuit concerning the meaning and implementation of that agreement. There's no guarantee, however, that a judge will award attorneys' fees equal to your attorney's actual bill, or that you will ultimately be able to collect the money from the tenant or former tenant. Also, as discussed in Chapter 2, an attorneys' fees clause in your lease or rental agreement usually works both ways. That is, even when the clause doesn't say so, you're liable for the tenant's attorneys' fees if you lose. (Landlord's insurance does not cover such liability where the lawsuit is unrelated to items covered by the policy, such as eviction lawsuits by the landlord and security deposit refund suits by the tenant.)

If you're involved in a dispute where you might be entitled to attorneys' fees, discuss the matter with your lawyer right from the beginning. Sometimes lawyers will take steps to put more detail in your billing statements so as to create a record that can be easily submitted to and understood by the court.

Doing Your Own Legal Research

Using this book is a good way to educate yourself about the laws that affect your business—but one book is not enough by itself. Some landlord associations publish legal updates in their newsletters and on their websites to keep members abreast of new laws and regulations.

While we recommend that you stay up to date on state, local, and federal laws that affect your landlording business (see the section just below), at some point you'll probably need to do further research. For example, you might want to read a court case or research a question about landlord-tenant law.

You can learn a lot on your own. Every state has placed its statutes online—do a search for your state's name and "statutes and laws." Rules put out by federal and state regulatory agencies are often available online, too. In addition to the internet, law libraries are full of valuable resources, such as updated copies of statutes and books summarizing landlord-tenant law and the landlord-tenant relationship. Your first step is to find a law library that's open to the public. Your county courthouse or state capitol building might have a public library. Publicly funded law schools generally permit the public to use their libraries, and some private law schools grant access to their libraries—sometimes for a modest fee.

Don't overlook the reference department of the public library. Many large public libraries have a fairly decent legal research collection, and even small public libraries can often access online legal research and other resources. Your lawyer might be able to provide you with some research material, too.

RESOURCE
Recommended reading on legal research.
We don't have space here to teach you how to do your own legal research. To get started, though, see Nolo's Laws and Legal Research page at www.nolo.com/legal-research. Here you can learn about researching and understanding statutes, and get advice on finding local ordinances and court cases. To go further, we recommend *Legal Research: How to Find & Understand the Law*, by the Editors of Nolo (Nolo). This nontechnical book gives easy-to-use, step-by-step instructions on how find legal information.

Where to Find State, Local, and Federal Laws

Every landlord is governed by state, local, and federal law. Sometimes, these various laws overlap—when they do, the stricter laws apply. In practical terms, this usually means that the laws that give tenants the most protection (rights and remedies) will prevail over less-protective laws.

State Laws

Most landlords are primarily concerned with state law. State statutes regulate many aspects of the landlord-tenant relationship, including deposits, landlord's right of entry, discrimination, housing standards, rent rules, repair and maintenance responsibilities, and eviction procedures.

The website of your state consumer protection agency or attorney general's office might provide a guide to state laws that affect landlords, and copies of the state statutes themselves. Also, representatives of state agencies can often help explain how the landlord-tenant laws they administer are interpreted. For a list of state consumer protection agencies, go to www.usa.gov/state-consumer.

We refer to many of the state laws affecting landlords throughout this book and include citations so that you can do additional research. State laws or codes are collected in volumes and are available online (discussed below) and in many public and law libraries. Depending on the state, statutes might be organized by subject matter or by title number ("chapter"), with each title covering a particular subject matter, or simply numbered sequentially, without regard to subject matter.

"Annotated codes" contain not only all the text of the laws (as do the regular codes), but also a brief summary of some of the court decisions (discussed below) interpreting each law and often references to treatises and articles that discuss the law. Annotated codes have comprehensive indexes by topic, and are kept up to date with paperback supplements ("pocket parts") stuck in a pocket inside the back cover of each volume.

Most states have made their statutes available online. You can find these on the website maintained by the Cornell Legal Information Institute (www.law.cornell.edu).

If you know the statute's number or citation (such as those in the charts in Appendix A of this book), you can go directly to the statute. If you don't know the statute number, you can enter a keyword that is likely to be in it, such as "deposit" or "security deposit." If you just want to browse through the statutes, you can search the table of contents for your state's laws. With a little trial and error, you should have no trouble finding a particular landlord-tenant statute.

RESOURCE

For a complete discussion of landlord-tenant laws in California, see *The California Landlord's Law Book: Rights & Responsibilities*, by Nils Rosenquest and Janet Portman, and *The California Landlord's Law Book: Evictions*, by Nils Rosenquest. These books are published by Nolo and are available at bookstores and public libraries. They can also be ordered directly from Nolo's website at Nolo.com or by calling 800-728-3555.

CAUTION

Rental Property in Tennessee. In 2021, Tennessee enacted a law that replaces ("preempts") all local landlord-tenant laws with state law. It forbids localities from passing any legislation in the area of landlord-tenant law, even when the subject of the proposed legislation isn't covered by state law. The preemption law applies in all counties with populations of more than 75,000 as measured by the 2010 federal census. If you own rental property in a county where this law applies, any landlord-tenant laws passed by your town, city, or county might now be unenforceable. For more information, contact your town, city, or county government or a local landlord-tenant attorney.

Local Ordinances

Local ordinances, such as rent control rules, health and safety standards, and requirements that you pay interest on tenants' security deposits, will also affect your business. Many municipalities have websites—just search for the name of a particular city. Sometimes the site is nothing more than a not-so-slick public relations page, but sometimes it includes a large body of information, including local ordinances available for searching and downloading. Check out State & Local Government on the Net (www.statelocalgov.net) and Municode.com's Code Library—both are good sources for finding local governments and laws online.

Finally, your local public library or office of the city attorney, mayor, or city manager can provide information on local ordinances that affect landlords. If you own rental property in a city with rent control, be sure to get a copy of the ordinance, as well as all rules issued by the rent board covering rent increases and hearings.

Federal Statutes and Regulations

Congress has enacted laws, and federal agencies such as the U.S. Department of Housing and Urban Development (HUD) have adopted regulations, covering discrimination, wage and hour laws affecting employment of managers, and landlord responsibilities to disclose environmental health hazards. We refer to relevant federal agencies throughout this book and suggest you contact them for publications that explain federal laws affecting landlords, or copies of the federal statutes and regulations themselves.

We include citations for many of the federal laws affecting landlords throughout this book. The U.S. Code (U.S.C.) is the starting place for most federal statutory research. It consists of 54 separately numbered titles. Each title covers a specific subject.

Most federal regulations are published in the Code of Federal Regulations (CFR), organized by subject into 50 separate titles.

To access the U.S. Code online, visit the Cornell Legal Information Institute (www.law.cornell.edu). This site provides the entire U.S. Code as well as the Code of Federal Regulations. Finally, check USA.gov, the official U.S. website for government information.

How to Research Court Decisions

Sometimes the answer to a legal question cannot be found in a statute. This happens when:

- Court cases and opinions have greatly expanded or explained the statute, taking it beyond its obvious or literal meaning.
- The law that applies to your question has been made by judges, not legislators.

Court Decisions That Explain Statutes

Statutes and ordinances do not explain themselves. For example, a state law might require you to offer housing that is weatherproofed, but it might not tell you whether you must provide both storm windows and window screens. However, a court might have addressed your question in the context of a lawsuit. If a judge interpreted the statute and wrote an opinion on the matter, that written opinion, once published, will become "the law" as much as the statute itself. If a higher court

(an appellate court) has also examined the question, then its opinion will rule.

To find out if there are written court decisions that interpret a particular statute or ordinance, look in an "annotated code" (discussed in "Where to Find State, Local, and Federal Laws," above). If you find a case that seems to answer your question, it's crucial to make sure that the decision you're reading is still "good law"—that a more recent opinion from a higher court has not reached a different conclusion. You must make sure that you are relying on the latest and highest judicial pronouncement. *Legal Research: How to Find & Understand the Law*, by the Editors of Nolo (Nolo), has a good, easy-to-follow explanation of how to expand and update your research.

Court Decisions That Make Law

Many laws that govern the way you must conduct your business don't have an initial starting point in a statute or ordinance. These laws are entirely court made, and are known as "common" law. For example, many states don't have a statute on the implied warranty of habitability—instead, the law was created by a court decision.

Researching common law is more difficult than statutory law, because you don't have the launching pad of a statute or ordinance. With a little perseverance, however, you can find your way to the cases that have developed and explained the legal concept you wish to understand.

A good beginning is to ask the librarian for any "practice guides" written in the field of landlord-tenant law. These are outlines of the law, written for lawyers, that are kept up to date and are designed to get you quickly to key information. Because they are so popular and easy to use, they are usually kept behind the reference counter and can't be checked out. More sophisticated research techniques, such as using a set of books called "Words and Phrases" (which sends you to cases based on keywords), are explained in the book *Legal Research*, mentioned above.

How to Read a Case Citation

If a case you have found in an annotated code (or through a practice guide or keyword search) looks important, you might want to read the opinion. You'll need the title of the case and its "citation," which is like an address for the set of books, volume, and page where the case can be found. Ask the law librarian for help.

Although it might look about as decipherable as hieroglyphics, a case citation gives lots of useful information in a small space. It tells you the names of the people or companies involved, the volume of the reporter (series of books) in which the case is published, the page number on which it begins, and the year in which the case was decided.

EXAMPLE: *Smith Realty Co. v. Jones,* 123 N.Y.S.2d 456 (1994). Smith and Jones are the names of the parties having the legal dispute. The case is reported in Volume 123 of the New York Supplement, Second Series, beginning on page 456. The court issued the decision in 1994.

Most states publish their own official state reports. All published state court decisions are also included in seven regional reporters (Atlantic, North Eastern, North Western, Pacific, South Eastern, Southern, and South Western). There are also special reports for U.S. Supreme Court and other federal court decisions.

State Landlord-Tenant Law Charts

How to Use the State Landlord-Tenant Law Charts

The State Landlord-Tenant Law Charts are comprehensive, 50-state charts that give you two kinds of information:

- citations for key statutes and cases, which you can use if you want to read the law yourself or look for more information (see the legal research discussion in Chapter 18), and
- the state rules themselves, such as notice periods and deposit limits—in other words, what the statutes and cases say.

When you're looking for information for your state, simply find your state along the left-hand list on the chart, and read to the right—you'll see the statute or case, and the rule.

COVID-19-Related Emergency Laws and
Orders Might Affect These Statutes

Federal, state and local governments have all passed emergency laws and orders in response to the COVID-19 pandemic. Many of these laws affect the landlord-tenant relationship by addressing issues such as evictions, late rent fees, and tenant screening.

Emergency laws passed by the federal government (such as the CARES Act and the now-overturned Centers for Disease Control and Prevention's eviction moratorium) apply to landlords and tenants in all states. Along with federal laws, landlords and tenants must also follow the laws, orders, and regulations that apply in the state (and city or county) where their rental is located. Each state is handling the situation differently. In some states, governors are issuing emergency orders, while in others the state court or the state legislature (or a combination of any of these branches of government) are creating emergency rules.

As this book went to press, these COVID-inspired laws, regulations, and orders were changing daily. Printing in these charts what we know today would be misleading to you when you refer to the chart tomorrow. That's because even when you have a starting point (the first instance of the law or order), it can be very difficult to pin down the most recent version. For example, a governor might have issued an emergency order on April 1, 2020 that laid out details about when landlords can and cannot charge late fees for unpaid rent. However, that April 1, 2020 order might have been amended in October 2021. Most of the time, when you look at the April 1, 2020 order online, there is no indication that it has been amended or repealed.

Because of the rapidly changing nature of these COVID-19-related laws, there's no way we can accurately and fully address how they affect

the charts we provide here in Appendix A. However, we can provide you with some tips and hints about how to find COVID-19-related emergency laws that might apply to your situation:

- **Start by going to Nolo's article,** *Emergency Bans on Evictions and Other Protections Related to Coronavirus*, for state-by-state information on state responses, particularly in regards to evictions (type the article's name into the search box on the home page, or go directly to www.nolo.com/evictions-ban).

- **Go to your state's designated COVID-19 website.** Every state has one, and you can find it by searching the internet for your state's name and "official COVID-19 website." From this page, you might be able to access quite a few official COVID-19-related emergency rules and regulations.

- **Read your state's emergency declaration.** Nearly every state has declared a state of emergency due to the pandemic. As of press time, many—but not all—states have ended their state of emergency, so you'll need to check your state's current status. Even if a declaration doesn't address landlord-tenant matters, it can provide a launching point for additional research. Most states' emergency declarations can be found on the state's official COVID-19 website or on the governor's official website.

- **Visit your state governor's official website.** Governors' executive orders are the most likely source of regulations that will apply to the landlord-tenant relationship. Look for "emergency orders" or "executive orders." If your state governor's website has a separate category for COVID-19-related orders, look there first for applicable orders. Regardless, to find relevant orders you should also use the website's search function to search for terms such as "rent," "landlord," "tenant," "evict," and "renter." Be creative with the terms you search for; not all states use the same terminology.

- Be warned: Many titles of executive orders consist of only a number or date when they were issued—the titles usually do not contain other information about the topic or substance of the order. Also, many executive orders are amended, extended, or repealed by subsequent orders that refer to the original order by nothing more than the original order's number or date—which means that a search of a keyword such as "rent" might not help in finding all the relevant orders. You might have to read through many orders to find any that apply to your situation.

- It's helpful to find the very first order that addresses your situation, then read subsequent ones to learn the current status of the original order. If you're still having difficulty, try searching the Internet for your governor's name and the topic you're interested in—many times, this will reveal a press release or news report that will indicate the date when your governor issued the relevant order (and might give you a link to the order itself).

- **Visit your state judicial branch's website.** If the state's highest court has issued orders relating to COVID-19, the information will likely be linked from the judicial branch's home page. Often, a state's judicial branch will step in with landlord-tenant COVID-19 orders after being directed to do so by the governor. For example, at one point during the pandemic, Virginia's governor encouraged the state's highest court to extend the eviction moratorium, and the court issued an order doing so.

- **Visit your state legislature's website.** If your state's legislature has passed emergency COVID-19-related laws, you will most likely find them linked from the legislature's homepage. At press time, only a few states' legislatures have passed COVID-19 laws. However, the longer the pandemic drags on, the more likely it is that state legislatures will step in and pass more long-term COVID-19-related statutes.

- **Search the Internet for news on the issue.** Try searching for your exact question. Most search engines will recognize plain-language queries, and will display relevant results with dates. For example, if you're wondering whether landlords in your state can charge late fees during the pandemic, you could search for "Can landlords charge a late fee in [your state] during COVID-19?" Look for the most recent posts. Attorney blogs, legal aid websites, news outlet articles, landlord organizations' websites, and tenant rights' groups' websites often have the most accurate and up-to-date information. As with any Internet research project, be sure to evaluate whether the source of the information is a reputable one, and try to find a second or third source to confirm the content.

CAUTION

Rental property in Tennessee. In 2021, Tennessee enacted a law that replaces ("preempts") all local landlord-tenant laws with state law. It forbids localities from passing any legislation in the area of landlord-tenant law, even when the subject of the proposed legislation isn't covered by state law. The preemption law applies in all counties with populations of more than 75,000 as measured by the 2010 federal census. If you own rental property in a county where this law applies, any landlord-tenant laws passed by your town, city, or county might now be unenforceable. For more information, contact your town, city, or county government or a local landlord-tenant attorney.

State Landlord-Tenant Statutes

Here are some of the key statutes pertaining to landlord-tenant law in each state. In some states, important legal principles are contained in court opinions, not codes or statutes. Court-made law and rent stabilization—rent control—laws and regulations are not reflected in this chart. Note that because some states exempt certain occupancies from their general landlord-tenant statutes, such as rentals of mobile homes and short-term rentals, it's a good idea to confirm that these statutes apply to your rental situation. You'll find the details about each state's exemption statutes, if any, in the following chart titled "State Landlord-Tenant Law Exemption Statutes."

State	Statute	State	Statute
Alabama	Ala. Code §§ 35-9-1 to 35-9-100; 35-9A-101 to 35-9A-603	Louisiana	La. Rev. Stat. Ann. §§ 9:3251 to 9:3261.2; La. Civ. Code Ann. art. 2002; 2668 to 2729
Alaska	Alaska Stat. §§ 34.03.010 to 34.03.380	Maine	Me. Rev. Stat. Ann. tit. 14, §§ 6000 to 6046
Arizona	Ariz. Rev. Stat. Ann. §§ 12-1171 to 12-1183; 33-301 to 33-381; 33-1301 to 33-1381; 36-1637	Maryland	Md. Code Ann. [Real Prop.] §§ 8-101 to 8-604; 8-901 to 8-911
Arkansas	Ark. Code Ann. §§ 18-16-101 to 18-16-306; 18-16-501 to 18-16-509; 18-17-101 to 18-17-913	Massachusetts	Mass. Gen. Laws Ann. ch. 111, § 127L; ch. 186, §§ 1A to 30; ch. 186a, §§ 1 to 6; ch. 239, § 8A
California	Cal. Civ. Code §§ 789.3; 790 to 793; 827; 1925 to 1934; 1940 to 1954.05; 1954.50 to 1954.605; 1961 to 1995.340; 2079.10a; Cal. Health & Safety Code §§ 25400.28; 26147 to 26148; Cal. Bus. & Prof. Code § 8538; Cal. Govt Code § 8589.45	Michigan	Mich. Comp. Laws §§ 125.530; 554.131 to 554.201; 554.601 to 554.641; 600.2918
		Minnesota	Minn. Stat. Ann. §§ 504B.001 to 504B.471
		Mississippi	Miss. Code Ann. §§ 89-7-1 to 89-8-29
Colorado	Colo. Rev. Stat. §§ 13-40-101 to 13-40-123; 13-40.1-101 to 13-40.1-102; 38-12-101 to 38-12-105; 38-12-301 to 38-12-1007; 38-12-1201 to 38-12-1205	Missouri	Mo. Rev. Stat. §§ 441.005 to 441.920; 442.055; 535.010 to 535.300
Connecticut	Conn. Gen. Stat. Ann. §§ 47a-1 to 47a-74	Montana	Mont. Code Ann. §§ 70-24-101 to 70-27-117; 75-10-1305
Delaware	Del. Code Ann. tit. 25, §§ 5101 to 5907	Nebraska	Neb. Rev. Stat. §§ 69-2302 to 69-2314; 76-1401 to 76-1449
Dist. of Columbia	D.C. Code Ann. §§ 42-3201 to 42-3651.08; D.C. Mun. Regs., tit. 14, §§ 300 to 399	Nevada	Nev. Rev. Stat. Ann. §§ 40.215 to 40.425; 118A.010 to 118A.530
Florida	Fla. Stat. Ann. §§ 83.40 to 83.683; 404.056; 715.10 to 715.111	New Hampshire	N.H. Rev. Stat. Ann. §§ 477:4-g; 540:1 to 540:29; 540-A:1 to 540-A:8; 540-B:1 to 540-B:10
Georgia	Ga. Code Ann. §§ 44-1-16; 44-7-1 to 44-7-81	New Jersey	N.J. Stat. Ann. §§ 2A:18-51 to 2A:18-61.67; 2A:18-72 to 2A:18-84; 2A:42-1 to 2A:42-96; 46:8-1 to 46:8-64; 55:13A-7.14; 55:13A-7.18; 55:13A-7.19; N.J.A.C. §§ 5:10-5.1, 5:10-27.1
Hawaii	Haw. Rev. Stat. §§ 521-1 to 521-83	
Idaho	Idaho Code §§ 6-301 to 6-324; 55-208 to 55-308	
Illinois	425 Ill. Comp. Stat. § 60/3; 430 Ill. Comp. Stat. § 135/10; 735 Ill. Comp. Stat. §§ 5/9-201 to 5/9-321; 765 Ill. Comp. Stat. §§ 705/0.01 to 742/30; 750/1 to 750/35; 755/1 to 755/999	New Mexico	N.M. Stat. Ann. §§ 47-8-1 to 47-8-51; N.M. Admin. Code § 20.4.5.13
		New York	N.Y. Real Prop. Law §§ 220 to 238; Real Prop. Acts §§ 701 to 853; Mult. Dwell. Law (all); Mult. Res. Law (all); Gen. Oblig. Law §§ 7-101 to 7-109; N.Y. Envtl. Conserv. Law § 27-2405; N.Y. Exec. Law § 170-d; N.Y. Penal Law §§ 241.00 to 241.05; N.Y. Unconsol. Law §§ 8581 to 8597 (Emergency Housing Rent Control Law); 8601 to 8617 (Local Emergency Housing Rent Control Act); 8621 to 8634 (Emergency Tenant Protection Act)
Indiana	Ind. Code Ann. §§ 8-1-2-1.2; 32-31-1-1 to 32-31-9-15; 36-1-24.2-1 to 36-1-24.2-4		
Iowa	Iowa Code Ann. §§ 562A.1 to 562A.37		
Kansas	Kan. Stat. Ann. §§ 58-2501 to 58-2573; 58-25,127; 58-25,137		
Kentucky	Ky. Rev. Stat. Ann. §§ 224.1-410; 383.010 to 383.715; 902 Ky. Admin. Regs. 47:200		

State Landlord-Tenant Statutes (continued)

North Carolina	N.C. Gen. Stat. §§ 42-1 to 42-14.2; 42-25.6 to 42-76	**Tennessee**	Tenn. Code Ann. §§ 66-7-101 to 66-7-102; 66-7-104; 66-7-106 to 66-7-107; 66-7-109 to 66-7-112; 66-28-101 to 66-28-522
North Dakota	N.D. Cent. Code §§ 23-13-15; 47-06-04; 47-16-01 to 47-16-41; 47-17-01 to 47-17-05	**Texas**	Tex. Prop. Code Ann. §§ 91.001 to 92.355
Ohio	Ohio Rev. Code Ann. §§ 5321.01 to 5321.19	**Utah**	Utah Code Ann. §§ 57-17-1 to 57-17-5; 57-22-1 to 57-22-7; 57-27-201; 78B-6-801 to 78B-6-816
Oklahoma	Okla. Stat. Ann. tit. 41, §§ 101 to 136; 201; tit. 74, § 324.11a	**Vermont**	Vt. Stat. Ann. tit. 9, §§ 4451 to 4469a; 4471 to 4475
Oregon	Or. Rev. Stat. §§ 90.100 to 90.228; 90.243 to 90.265; 90.295 to 90.493; 105.005 to 105.168; 105.190; 479.270 to 479.280	**Virginia**	Va. Code Ann. §§ 54.1-2108.1; 55.1-1200 to 55.1-1259
		Washington	Wash. Rev. Code Ann. §§ 59.04.010 to 59.18.912
Pennsylvania	68 Pa. Cons. Stat. Ann. §§ 250.101 to 399.18	**West Virginia**	W.Va. Code §§ 37-6-1 to 37-6A-6; W. Va. Code St. R. § 64-92-6
Rhode Island	R.I. Gen. Laws §§ 34-18-1 to 34-18-57	**Wisconsin**	Wis. Stat. Ann. §§ 704.01 to 704.95; Wis. Admin. Code ATCP §§ 134.01 to 134.10
South Carolina	S.C. Code Ann. §§ 5-25-1330; 27-40-10 to 27-40-940	**Wyoming**	Wyo. Stat. §§ 1-21-1001 to 1-21-1016; 1-21-1201 to 1-21-1211; 1-21-1301 to 1-21-1304; 34-2-128 to 34-2-129
South Dakota	S.D. Codified Laws Ann. §§ 43-32-1 to 43-32-36		

State Landlord-Tenant Exemption Statutes

Your state's general landlord-tenant statutes (listed in the "State Landlord-Tenant Statutes" chart above) might not apply to all types of rentals and landlord-tenant relationships: Most states define what a rental is for purposes of the statutes. Other states might not define what a rental is, but instead exempt certain types of occupancies from the general landlord-tenant statutes. Some states do both. To check whether your state's general landlord-tenant statutes apply to your situation, review the statutes listed in the "State Landlord-Tenant Statutes" chart for any definition of what your state considers a rental. Next, you'll need to find out whether your situation falls within any exemptions from the general landlord-tenant statutes. This chart provides information about the exemptions that are most relevant to readers of this book. If your state does not have an exemption statute, you'll see "No statute" written in the Exemptions column.

State	Exemption Statute	Exemptions
Alabama	Ala. Code §§ 35-9A-122, 35-9A-601	1. Occupancy under a contract of sale of a dwelling unit or the property of which it is a part, if the occupant is the purchaser or a person who succeeds to the interest of the purchaser 2. occupancy by a member of a social organization in the portion of a structure operated for the benefit of the organization 3. transient occupancy in a hotel, motel, or lodgings 4. occupancy by an employee of a landlord whose right to occupancy is conditional upon employment at the premises 5. occupancy under a rental agreement covering premises rented by the occupant primarily for agricultural purposes 6. continuation of occupancy by the seller or a member of the seller's family for a period of not more than 36 months after the sale of a dwelling unit or the property of which it is a part, and 7. rental agreements most recently entered into, extended, or renewed before January 1, 2007.
Alaska	Alaska Stat. §§ 34.03.330, 34.03.370	1. Occupancy under a contract of sale of a dwelling unit or the property of which it is a part if the occupant is the purchaser or a person who succeeds to the interest of a purchaser 2. occupancy by a member of a social organization in the portion of a structure operated for the benefit of the organization 3. transient occupancy in a hotel, motel, lodgings, or other transient facility 4. occupancy by an employee of a landlord whose right to occupancy is conditioned upon employment substantially for services, maintenance, or repair to the premises 5. occupancy under a rental agreement covering premises used by the occupant primarily for agricultural purposes 6. occupancy under a rental agreement covering premises used as part of a transitional or supportive housing program that is sponsored or operated by a public corporation or by a nonprofit corporation and that provides shelter and related support services, and 7. any rental agreement, lease, or tenancy most recently entered into, extended, or renewed before March 19, 1974.
Arizona	Ariz. Rev. Stat. Ann. § 33-1308	1. Occupancy under a contract of sale of a dwelling unit or the property of which it is a part, if the occupant is the purchaser or a person who succeeds to the purchaser's interest 2. occupancy by a member of a social organization in the portion of a structure operated for the benefit of the organization 3. transient occupancy in a hotel, motel or recreational lodging 4. occupancy by an employee of a landlord as a manager or custodian whose right to occupancy is conditional upon employment at the premises, and 5. occupancy in or operation of public housing as authorized, provided or conducted under or pursuant to any federal law or regulation.

State Landlord-Tenant Exemption Statutes (continued)

State	Exemption Statute	Exemptions
Arkansas	Ark. Code Ann. § 18-17-202	1. Occupancy under a contract of sale of a dwelling unit or the property of which it is a part, if the occupant is the purchaser or a person who succeeds to the purchaser's interest 2. occupancy by a member of a social organization in the portion of a structure operated for the benefit of the organization 3. transient occupancy in a hotel, motel, or other accommodations subject to any sales tax on lodging 4. occupancy by an employee of a landlord whose right to occupancy is conditional upon employment in and about the premises 5. occupancy under a rental agreement covering the premises used by the occupant primarily for agricultural purposes, and 6. residence, whether temporary or not, at a public or private charitable or emergency protective shelter.
California	Cal. Civ. Code § 1940	1. Transient occupancy in a hotel, motel, residence club, or other facility, and 2. occupancy at a hotel or motel where the innkeeper retains a right of access to and control of the dwelling unit and the hotel or motel provides or offers certain services.
Colorado	Colo. Rev. Stat. Ann. § 38-12-511	1. Occupancy under a contract of sale of a dwelling unit or the property of which it is a part, if the occupant is the purchaser, seller, or a person who succeeds to the purchaser's or seller's interest 2. occupancy by a member of a social organization in the portion of a structure operated for the benefit of the organization 3. transient occupancy in a hotel or motel that lasts less than 30 days 4. occupancy by an employee or independent contractor whose right to occupancy is conditional upon performance of services for an employer or contractor 5. occupancy in a structure that is located within an unincorporated area of a county, does not receive water, heat, and sewer services from a public entity, and is rented for recreational purposes, such as a hunting cabin, yurt, hut, or other similar structure 6. occupancy under rental agreement covering a residential premises used by the occupant primarily for agricultural purposes, and 7. any relationship between the owner of a mobile home park and the owner of a mobile home situated in the park.
Connecticut	Conn. Gen. Stat. Ann. § 47a-2	1. Occupancy under a contract of sale of a dwelling unit or the property of which such unit is a part, if the occupant is the purchaser or a person who succeeds to the purchaser's interest 2. occupancy by a member of a social organization in the portion of a structure operated for the benefit of such organization 3. transient occupancy in a hotel, motel, or similar lodging, and 4. occupancy by a personal care assistant or other person who is employed by a person with a disability to assist and support such disabled person with daily living activities or housekeeping chores and is provided dwelling space in the personal residence of such disabled person as a benefit or condition of such employment.

State Landlord-Tenant Exemption Statutes (continued)

State	Exemption Statute	Exemptions
Delaware	Del. Code Ann. tit. 25, §§ 5101, 5102	1. Residence at an institution where such residence is merely incidental to detention or to the provision of medical, geriatric, educational, counseling, religious, or similar services 2. residence by a member of a fraternal organization in a structure operated for the benefit of the organization 3. residence in a hotel, motel, cubicle hotel or other similar lodgings 4. nonrenewable rental agreements of 120 days or less for any calendar year for a dwelling located within the boundaries of Broadkill Hundred, Lewes-Rehoboth Hundred, Indian River Hundred, Baltimore Hundred and Cedar Creek Hundred, and 5. rental agreements for ground upon which improvements were constructed or installed by the tenant and used as a dwelling, where the tenant retains ownership or title thereto, or obtains title to existing improvement on the property.

District of Columbia	D.C. Code Ann. § 42-3502.05	1. Rental units operated by a foreign government as a residence for diplomatic personnel
		2. rental units in an establishment which has as its primary purpose providing diagnostic care and treatment of diseases; and
		3. dormitories.
		Also: Following a determination by the Rent Administrator, any rental intended for use as long-term temporary housing by families with 1 or more members that satisfies each of the following requirements:
		  A. The rental is occupied by families that, at the time of their initial occupancy, have had incomes at or below 50% of the District median income for families of the size in question for the immediately preceding 12 months
		  B. the provider of the rental is a nonprofit charitable organization that operates the rental on a strictly not-for-profit basis, and
		  C. the housing provider offers a comprehensive social services program to resident families.

Florida	Fla. Stat. Ann. § 83.42	1. Occupancy under a contract of sale of a dwelling unit or the property of which it is a part in which the buyer has paid at least 12 months' rent or in which the buyer has paid at least 1 month's rent and a deposit of at least 5 percent of the purchase price of the property, and 2. transient occupancy in a hotel, condominium, motel, roominghouse, or similar public lodging, or transient occupancy in a mobile home park.
Georgia	No statute	

Hawaii	Haw. Rev. Stat. § 521-7	1. Residence in a structure directly controlled and managed by:
		  A. the University of Hawaii or any other university or college in the State for housing its own students or faculty or residence in a structure erected on land leased from the university or college by a nonprofit corporation for the exclusive purpose of housing students or faculty of the college or university, or
		  B. a private dorm management company that offers a minimum of 50 beds to students of any college, university, or other institution of higher education in the State
		2. occupancy under a bona fide contract of sale of the dwelling unit or the property of which it is a part where the tenant is, or succeeds to the interest of, the purchaser
		3. residence by a member of a fraternal organization in a structure operated without profit for the benefit of the organization

State Landlord-Tenant Exemption Statutes (continued)

State	Exemption Statute	Exemptions
Hawaii (continued)		4. transient occupancy on a day-to-day basis in a hotel or motel
		5. occupancy by an employee of the owner or landlord whose right to occupancy is conditional upon that employment for a period of up to four years, pursuant to a plan for the transfer of the dwelling unit or the property of which it is a part to the occupant
		6. a lease of improved residential land for a term of 15 years or more
		7. occupancy by the prospective purchaser after an accepted offer to purchase and prior to the actual transfer of the owner's rights, and
		8. occupancy by the seller of residential real property after the transfer of the seller's ownership rights.
Idaho	No statute	
Illinois	No statute	
Indiana	Ind. Code Ann. § 32-31-2.9-4	1. Occupancy under a contract of sale of a rental unit or the property of which the rental unit is a part if the occupant is the purchaser or a person who succeeds to the purchaser's interest
		2. occupancy by a member of a social organization in the part of a structure operated for the benefit of the organization
		3. transient occupancy in a hotel, motel, or other lodging
		4. occupancy by an employee of a landlord whose right to occupancy is conditional upon employment at the premises, and
		5. rental agreements covering property used by the occupant primarily for agricultural purposes.
Iowa	Iowa Code Ann. §§ 562A.5, 562A.37	1. Occupancy under a contract of sale of a dwelling unit or the property of which it is a part, if the occupant is the purchaser or a person who succeeds to the purchaser's interest
		2. occupancy by a member of a social organization in the portion of a structure operated for the benefit of the organization
		3. transient occupancy in a hotel, motel, or other similar lodgings
		4. occupancy by an employee of a landlord whose right to occupancy is conditional upon employment at the premises
		5. rental agreements covering premises used by the occupant primarily for agricultural purposes, and
		6. rental agreements most recently entered into, extended, or renewed on or before January 1, 1979.
Kansas	Kan. Stat. Ann. §§ 58-2541, 58-2573	1. Occupancy under a contract of sale of a dwelling unit or the property of which it is a part, if the occupant is the purchaser or a person who succeeds to the purchaser's interest
		2. occupancy by a member of a social organization in the portion of a structure operated for the benefit of the organization
		3. transient occupancy in a hotel, motel, or rooming house
		4. occupancy by an employee of a landlord whose right to occupancy is conditional upon employment at the premises
		5. occupancy under a rental agreement covering premises used by the occupant primarily for agricultural purposes, and
		6. any rental agreement most recently entered into, extended, or modified before July 1, 1975.

State Landlord-Tenant Exemption Statutes (continued)

State	Exemption Statute	Exemptions
Kentucky	Ky. Rev. Stat. Ann. § 383.535	1. Occupancy under a contract of sale of a dwelling unit or the property of which it is a part, if the occupant is the purchaser or a person who succeeds to the purchaser's interest 2. occupancy by a member of a social organization in the portion of a structure operated for the benefit of the organization 3. transient occupancy in a hotel, or motel, or lodgings subject to state transient lodgings or room occupancy excise tax act 4. occupancy by an employee of a landlord whose right to occupancy is conditional upon employment at the premises, and 5. occupancy of a dwelling located on land devoted to the production of livestock, livestock products, poultry, poultry products, or the growing of tobacco or other crops.
Louisiana	No statute	
Maine	No statute	
Maryland	Md. Code Ann. [Real Prop.] § 8-201	Tenancies arising after the sale of owner-occupied residential property where the seller and purchaser agree that the seller may remain in possession of the property for a period of not more than 60 days after the settlement.
Massachusetts	No statute	
Michigan	Mich. Comp. Laws § 554.601 Mich. Comp. Laws § 554.632	1. Occupancy in a motel, motor home, or other tourist accommodation, when used as a temporary accommodation for guests or tourists, and 2. premises used as the principal place of residence of the owner and rented occasionally during temporary absences.
Minnesota	No statute	
Mississippi	Miss. Code Ann. § 89-8-3	1. Occupancy under a contract of sale of a dwelling unit or the property of which it is a part, if the occupant is the purchaser or a person who succeeds to the purchaser's interest 2. occupancy by a member of a social organization in the portion of a structure operated for the benefit of the organization 3. transient occupancy in a hotel, motel, or lodgings 4. occupancy under a rental agreement covering premises used by the occupant primarily for agricultural purposes 5. occupancy when the occupant is performing agricultural labor for the owner and such premises are rented for less than fair rental value, and 6. any rental agreement entered into before July 1, 1991.
Missouri	No statute	

		State Landlord-Tenant Exemption Statutes (continued)
State	**Exemption Statute**	**Exemptions**
Montana	Mont. Code Ann. § 70-24-104	1. Occupancy under a contract of sale of a dwelling unit or the property of which it is a part if the occupant is the purchaser or a person who succeeds to the purchaser's interest 2. occupancy by a member of a social organization in the portion of a structure operated for the benefit of the organization 3. transient occupancy in a hotel or motel 4. occupancy under a rental agreement covering premises used by the occupant primarily for commercial or agricultural purposes 5. occupancy by an employee of a landlord whose right to occupancy is conditional upon employment at the premises, and 6. occupancy outside a municipality under a rental agreement that includes hunting, fishing, or agricultural privileges, along with the use of the dwelling unit.
Nebraska	Neb. Rev. Stat. §§ 76-1408, 76-1448	1. Occupancy under a contract of sale of a dwelling unit or the property of which it is a part, if the occupant is the purchaser or a person who succeeds to the purchaser's interest 2. occupancy by a member of a social organization in the portion of a structure operated for the benefit of the organization 3. transient occupancy in a hotel or motel 4. occupancy by an employee of a landlord whose right to occupancy is conditional upon employment at the premises 5. occupancy under a rental agreement covering premises used by the occupant primarily for agricultural purposes 6. a lease of improved or unimproved residential land for a term of five years or more, and 7. rental agreements most recently entered into, extended, or renewed on or before July 1, 1975.
Nevada	Nev. Rev. Stat. Ann. §§ 118A.180, 118A.530	1. Rental agreements for manufactured homes 2. occupancy under a contract of sale of a dwelling unit or the property of which it is a part, if the occupant is the purchaser or successor to the purchaser's interest 3. occupancy by a member of a social organization in the portion of a structure operated for the benefit of the organization 4. occupancy in a hotel or motel for less than 30 consecutive days unless the occupant clearly manifests an intent to remain for a longer continuous period 5. occupancy by an employee of a landlord whose right to occupancy is solely conditional upon employment at the premises 6. occupancy under a rental agreement covering premises used by the occupant primarily for agricultural purposes 7. occupancy by a person who is guilty of a forcible entry or forcible detainer, and 8. rental agreements most recently entered into, extended, or renewed before July 1, 1977.

State Landlord-Tenant Exemption Statutes (continued)

State	Exemption Statute	Exemptions
New Hampshire	N.H. Rev. Stat. Ann. § 540:1-a	1. Rooms in rooming or boarding houses which are rented to transient guests for fewer than 90 consecutive days 2. rooms in hotels, motels, inns, tourist homes, and other dwellings rented for recreational or vacation use 3. single-family homes in which the occupant has no lease, which is the primary and usual residence of the owner 4. shared residential facilities (properties with separate sleeping areas for each occupant and in which each occupant has access to and shares with the owner one or more areas of the property) 5. vacation or recreational rentals 6. residential units leased by a member of a social organization that provides student housing for a postsecondary institution in a structure owned and operated by the social organization, and 7. occupancies in which the occupant is hired to provide care or assistance for a person with disabilities.
New Jersey	N.J. Stat. Ann. § 46:8-9.12 N.J. Stat. Ann. § 46:8-44	1. Seasonal rentals (does not include use or rental of living quarters for seasonal, temporary or migrant farm workers in connection with any work or place where work is being performed) 2. dwelling units in rentals containing not more than two such units 3. owner-occupied premises of not more than three dwelling units, and 4. hotels, motels, or other guest houses serving transient or seasonal guests.
New Mexico	N.M. Stat. Ann. §§ 47-8-9, 47-8-51	1. Occupancy under a contract of sale of a dwelling unit or the property of which it is part, if the occupant is the purchaser or a person who succeeds to the purchaser's interest 2. occupancy by a member of a social organization in the portion of a structure operated for the benefit of the organization 3. transient occupancy in a hotel or motel 4. occupancy by an employee of an owner pursuant to a written rental or employment agreement that specifies the employee's right to occupancy is conditional upon employment at the premises 5. occupancy under a rental agreement covering premises used by the occupant primarily for agricultural purposes, and 6. rental agreements most recently entered into, extended, or renewed on or before July 1, 1975.
New York	N.Y. Mult. Dwell. Law §§ 3, 4, 8, 9, 13, 14	1. Rentals in cities with a population of less than 325,000, and 2. rentals occupied by fewer than three families living independently of each other.
	N.Y. Mult. Resid. Law §§ 3, 4, 9	1. Rentals in cities with a population equal to or greater than 325,000, and 2. rentals occupied by fewer than three families living independently of each other.
North Carolina	N.C. Gen. Stat. Ann. § 42-39	1. Transient occupancy in a hotel, motel, or similar lodging 2. vacation rentals, and 3. dwellings provided without charge or rent.
North Dakota	No statute	

State Landlord-Tenant Exemption Statutes (continued)

State	Exemption Statute	Exemptions
Ohio	Ohio Rev. Code Ann. § 5321.01	1. Tourist homes, hotels, motels, recreational vehicle parks, recreation camps, combined park-camps, temporary park-camps, and other similar facilities where circumstances indicate a transient occupancy 2. farm residences furnished in connection with the rental of land of a minimum of two acres for production of agricultural products by one or more of the occupants 3. manufactured home parks, marinas, and agricultural labor camps, and 4. occupancy in hotels and single room occupancy facilities.
Oklahoma	Okla. Stat. Ann. tit. 41, § 104	1. Occupancy under a contract of sale or contract for deed of a dwelling unit or of the property of which it is a part, if the occupant is the purchaser or a person who succeeds to the purchaser's interest 2. occupancy by a member of a social organization in a structure operated for the benefit of the organization 3. transient occupancy in a hotel, motel, or other similar lodging, and 4. occupancy under a rental agreement covering premises used by the occupant primarily for agricultural purposes.
Oregon	Or. Rev. Stat. §§ 90.110, 90.113, 90.120	1. Occupancy of a dwelling unit for no more than 90 days by a purchaser prior to the scheduled closing of a real estate sale or by a seller following the closing of a sale, in either case as permitted under the terms of an agreement for sale of the property 2. occupancy by a member of a social organization in the portion of a structure operated for the benefit of the organization 3. transient occupancy in a hotel or motel 4. occupancy by a squatter 5. vacation occupancy 6. occupancy by an employee of a landlord whose right to occupancy is conditional upon employment at the premises, and 7. occupancy under a rental agreement covering premises used by the occupant primarily for agricultural purposes. Note that different rules might apply to occupancy of manufactured dwellings, floating homes, and recreational vehicles.
Pennsylvania	No statute	
Rhode Island	R.I. Gen. Laws § 34-18-8	Unless the parties expressly agree to be governed by them, the following occupancies are exempted from the residential landlord-tenant statutes: 1. Occupancy under a contract of sale of a dwelling unit or the property of which it is a part, if the occupant is the purchaser or a person who succeeds to the purchaser's interest 2. occupancy by a member of a social organization in the portion of a structure operated for the benefit of the organization 3. transient occupancy in a hotel, motel, or other lodging 4. occupancy by a paid employee of a landlord, whose right to occupancy is conditional upon employment substantially for services, maintenance, or repair of premises containing more than eleven 11 units, and 5. residence at a transitional housing facility.

State Landlord-Tenant Exemption Statutes (continued)

State	Exemption Statute	Exemptions
South Carolina	S.C. Code Ann. § 27-40-120	1. Occupancy under a contract of sale of a dwelling unit or the property of which it is a part, if the occupant is the purchaser or a person who succeeds to the purchaser's interest 2. occupancy by a member of a social organization in the portion of a structure operated for the benefit of the organization 3. transient occupancy in a hotel, motel, or other accommodations subject to the sales tax on accommodations 4. occupancy by an employee of a landlord whose right to occupancy is conditional upon employment at the premises 5. occupancy under a rental agreement covering the premises used by the occupant primarily for agricultural purposes, and 6. occupancy under a rental agreement for a vacation time share.
South Dakota	No statute	
Tennessee	Tenn. Code Ann. § 66-28-102	1. Rentals in counties with a population of less than 75,000, according to the 2010 federal census 2. rental agreements most recently entered into, extended, or renewed before July 1, 1975 3. occupancy under a contract of sale of a dwelling unit or the property of which it is a part, if the occupant is the purchaser or a person who succeeds to the purchaser's interest 4. transient occupancy in a hotel, motel, or lodgings subject to city, state, or transient lodgings laws, and 5. occupancy under a rental agreement covering premises used by the occupant primarily for agricultural purposes.
Texas	No statute	
Utah	Utah Code Ann. § 57-22-2	1. Boarding houses or similar facilities 2. mobile home lots, and 3. recreational properties rented on an occasional basis.
Vermont	Vt. Stat. Ann. tit. 9, § 4452	1. Occupancy under a contract of sale of a dwelling unit or the property of which it is a part, if the occupant is the purchaser or a person who succeeds to the purchaser's interest 2. occupancy by a member of a social or religious organization in the portion of a building operated for the benefit of the organization 3. transient occupancy in a hotel or motel 4. rental of a mobile home lot 5. transient residence in seasonal or short-term vacation or recreational properties, and 6. occupancy of a dwelling unit without right or permission by a person who is not a tenant.
Virginia	Va. Code Ann. § 55.1-1201	1. Occupancy by a member of a social organization in the portion of a structure operated for the benefit of the organization 2. occupancy in a campground 3. occupancy by a tenant who pays no rent pursuant to a rental agreement 4. occupancy by an employee of a landlord whose right to occupancy in a multifamily dwelling unit is conditioned upon employment at the premises or a former employee whose occupancy continues less than 60 days 5. occupancy under a contract of sale of a dwelling unit or the property of which it is a part, if the occupant is the purchaser or a person who succeeds to the purchaser's interest, and 6. occupancy in a hotel, motel, extended stay facility, vacation residential facility, timeshare, boardinghouse, or similar transient lodging when the occupancy is not the resident's primary residence, or when the resident uses it as a primary residence for less than 90 days.

State Landlord-Tenant Exemption Statutes (continued)

State	Exemption Statute	Exemptions
Washington	Wash. Rev. Code Ann. §§ 59.18.040, 59.18.415, 59.18.430, 59.18.435	1. Occupancy under a bona fide earnest money agreement to purchase or contract of sale of the dwelling unit or the property of which it is a part, where the tenant is, or stands in the place of, the purchaser 2. residence in a hotel, motel, or other transient lodging 3. rental agreements for the use of any single-family residence which are incidental to leases or rentals entered into in connection with a lease of land to be used primarily for agricultural purposes 4. rental agreements providing housing for seasonal agricultural employees while provided in conjunction with such employment 5. rental agreements with the state of Washington, department of natural resources, on public lands 6. occupancy by an employee of a landlord whose right to occupy is conditioned upon employment at the premises 7. leases of single-family dwellings for a period of a year or more or leases of a single-family dwelling containing a bona fide option to purchase by the tenant (but an attorney for the tenant must approve on the face of the agreement any lease exempted from these laws), and 8. leases entered into before July 16, 1973.
West Virginia	No statute	
Wisconsin	Wis. Admin. Code ATCP 134.01	1) Occupancy by a member of a fraternal or social organization which operates that dwelling unit 2) occupancy under a contract of sale, by the purchaser of the dwelling unit or the purchaser's successor in interest 3) occupancy by tourist or transient occupants 4) occupancy that the landlord provides free of charge to any person, or that the landlord provides as consideration to a person whom the landlord currently employs to operate or maintain the premises, and 5) occupancy by a tenant who is engaged in commercial agricultural operations on the premises.
Wyoming	No statute	

State Rent Rules

Here are citations for statutes that set out rent rules in each state. When a state has no statute, the space is left blank. See the "State Rules on Notice Required to Change or Terminate a Month-to-Month Tenancy" chart in this appendix for citations to statutes addressing rent increases.

State	When Rent Is Due	Grace Period	Where Rent Is Due	Late Fees
Alabama	Ala. Code § 35-9A-161 (c)		Ala. Code § 35-9A-161 (c)	
Alaska	Alaska Stat. § 34.03.020(c)		Alaska Stat. § 34.03.020(c)	
Arizona	Ariz. Rev. Stat. Ann. §§ 33-1314(C), 33-1368(B)		Ariz. Rev. Stat. Ann. § 33-1314(C)	Ariz. Rev. Stat. Ann. § 33-1368(B) [1]
Arkansas	Ark. Code Ann. § 18-17-401	Ark. Code Ann. §§ 18-17-701, 18-17-901	Ark. Code Ann. § 18-17-401	
California	Cal. Civ. Code § 1947		Cal. Civ. Code § 1962	Orozco v. Casimiro, 121 Cal. App.4th Supp. 7 (2004) [2]
Colorado		Colo. Rev. Stat. Ann. § 38-12-105(1)(a)		Colo. Rev. Stat. Ann. § 38-12-105(1)(b) [3]
Connecticut	Conn. Gen. Stat. Ann. § 47a-3a	Conn. Gen. Stat. Ann. § 47a-15a	Conn. Gen. Stat. Ann. § 47a-3a	Conn. Gen. Stat. Ann. §§ 47a-4(a)(8), 47a-15a [4]
Delaware	Del. Code Ann. tit. 25, § 5501(b)		Del. Code Ann. title 25, § 5501(b)	Del. Code Ann. tit. 25, § 5501(d) [5]
D.C.		D.C. Code Ann. § 42-3505.31		D.C. Code Ann. § 42-3505.31 [6]
Florida	Fla. Stat. Ann. § 83.46(1)			
Georgia [7]				
Hawaii	Haw. Rev. Stat. § 521-21(b)		Haw. Rev. Stat. § 521-21(b)	Haw. Rev. Stat. § 521-21(f) [8]
Idaho				
Illinois	735 Ill. Comp. Stat. Ann. § 5/9-218		735 Ill. Comp. Stat. Ann. § 5/9-218	
Indiana	Watson v. Penn, 108 Ind. 21 (1886), 8 N.E. 636 (1886)			
Iowa	Iowa Code Ann. § 562A.9(3)		Iowa Code Ann. § 562A.9(3)	Iowa Code Ann. § 562A.93(4) [9]
Kansas	Kan. Stat. Ann. § 58-2545(c)		Kan. Stat. Ann. § 58-2545(c)	
Kentucky	Ky. Rev. Stat. Ann. § 383.565(2)		Ky. Rev. Stat. Ann. § 383.565(2)	
Louisiana	La. Civ. Code Ann. art. 2703		La. Civ. Code Ann. art. 2703	
Maine		Me. Rev. Stat. Ann. tit. 14, § 6028		Me. Rev. Stat. Ann. tit. 14, § 6028 [10]
Maryland				Md. Code Ann. [Real Prop.] § 8-208(d)(3) [11]

[1] Late fees must be set forth in a written rental agreement and be reasonable. (Arizona)

[2] Late fees must reflect landlord's actual damages; courts likely won't enforce a preset fee (liquidated damages clause). (California)

[3] Landlord can't charge tenant a late fee unless the rent payment is late by at least 7 calendar days. Late fee can't exceed the greater of $50 or 5% of the amount past due, and landlords must disclose late fees in lease or rental agreement. (Colorado)

[4] Landlords may not charge a late fee until 9 days after rent is due. (Connecticut)

[5] To charge a late fee, landlord must maintain an office in the county where the rental unit is located at which tenants can pay rent. If a landlord doesn't have a local office for this purpose, tenant has 3 extra days (beyond the due date) to pay rent before the landlord can charge a late fee. Late fee cannot exceed 5% of rent and cannot be imposed until the rent is more than 5 days late. (Delaware)

[6] Fee policy (including a statement of the maximum amount of late fees that may be charged) must be stated in the lease, and cannot exceed 5% of rent due or be imposed until rent is five days late (or later, if lease so provides). Landlord cannot evict for failure to pay late fee (may deduct unpaid fees from security deposit at end of tenancy). During a declared public emergency, landlords may not impose a late fee. (District of Columbia)

[7] Although there is no specific statute regarding late fees, Georgia law states that all contracts for rent bear interest from the time rent is due. (Georgia)

[8] Late charge cannot exceed 8% of the amount of rent due. (Hawaii)

[9] When rent is $700 per month or less, late fees cannot exceed $12 per day, or a total amount of $60 per month; when rent is more than $700 per month, fees cannot exceed $20 per day or a total amount of $100 per month. (Iowa)

[10] Late fees cannot exceed 4% of the amount due for 30 days. Landlord must notify tenants, in writing, of any late fee at the start of the tenancy, and cannot impose it until rent is 15 days late. (Maine)

[11] Late fees cannot exceed 5% of the rent due. (Maryland)

State Rent Rules (continued)

State	When Rent Is Due	Grace Period	Where Rent Is Due	Late Fees
Massachusetts		Mass. Gen. Laws Ann. ch. 186, § 15B(1)(c); ch. 239, § 8A		Mass. Gen. Laws Ann. ch. 186, § 15B(1)(c) [12]
Michigan	*Hilsendegen v. Scheich,* 21 N.W. 894 (1885)			
Minnesota				Minn. Stat. Ann. § 504B.177 [13]
Mississippi				
Missouri	Mo. Rev. Stat. § 535.060			
Montana	Mont. Code Ann. § 70-24-201(2)(c)		Mont. Code Ann. § 70-24-201(2)(b)	
Nebraska	Neb. Rev. Stat. § 76-1414(3)		Neb. Rev. Stat. § 76-1414(3)	
Nevada	Nev. Rev. Stat. Ann. § 118A.210		Nev. Rev. Stat. Ann. § 118A.200	Nev. Rev. Stat. Ann. §§ 118A.200, 118A.210(4) [14]
New Hampshire				N.H. Rev. Stat. § 540:8 [15]
New Jersey		N.J. Stat. Ann. § 2A:42-6.1	N.J. Stat. Ann. § 2A:42-6.1	N.J. Stat. Ann. § 2A:42-6.1 [16]
New Mexico	N.M. Stat. Ann. § 47-8-15(B)		N.M. Stat. Ann. § 47-8-15(B)	N.M. Stat. Ann. § 47-8-15(D) [17]
New York		N.Y. Real Prop. Law § 238-a		N.Y. Real Prop. Law 238-a [18]
North Carolina		N.C. Gen Stat. § 42-46		N.C. Gen. Stat. § 42-46 [19]
North Dakota	N.D. Cent. Code § 47-16-20			
Ohio				*Campus Village Toledo Univ. Park, LLC v. Mowrer,* 68 N.E.3d 219 (Ohio App. 2016); Ohio Rev. Code § 5321.14 [20]
Oklahoma	Okla. Stat. Ann. tit. 41, § 109	Okla. Stat. Ann. tit. 41, § 132(B)	Okla. Stat. Ann. tit. 41, § 109	*Sun Ridge Investors, Ltd. v. Parker,* 956 P.2d 876 (1998) [21]
Oregon	Or. Rev. Stat. § 90.220	Or. Rev. Stat. § 90.260	Or. Rev. Stat. § 90.220	Or. Rev. Stat. § 90.260 [22]
Pennsylvania				
Rhode Island	R.I. Gen. Laws § 34-18-15(c)	R.I. Gen. Laws § 34-18-35	R.I. Gen. Laws § 34-18-15(c)	
South Carolina	S.C. Code Ann. § 27-40-310(c)		S.C. Code Ann. § 27-40-310(c)	
South Dakota	S.D. Codified Laws Ann. § 43-32-12			

[12] Late fees, including interest on late rent, may not be imposed until the rent is 30 days late. (Massachusetts)

[13] Late fee policy must be agreed to in writing, and may not exceed 8% of the overdue rent payment. The "due date" for late fee purposes does not include a date earlier than the usual rent due date, by which date a tenant earns a discount. (Minnesota)

[14] A court will presume that there's no late fee provision unless it's included in a written rental agreement, but the landlord can offer evidence to overcome that presumption. Landlord may charge a reasonable late fee as set forth in the rental agreement, but it cannot exceed 5% of the amount of the periodic rent, and the maximum amount of the late fee must not be increased based upon a late fee that was previously imposed. For tenancies that are longer than week-to-week, landlords can't charge a late fee until at least three calendar days after the rent due date. (Nevada)

[15] Landlord cannot demand an amount greater than the the whole rent in arrears when rent is late. (New Hampshire)

[16] Landlord must wait 5 business days before charging a late fee, but only when the premises are rented or leased by senior citizens receiving Social Security Old Age Pensions, Railroad Retirement Pensions, or other governmental pensions in lieu of Social Security Old Age Pensions; or when rented by recipients of Social Security Disability Benefits, Supplemental Security Income, or benefits under Work First New Jersey. (New Jersey)

[17] Late fee policy must be in the lease or rental agreement and may not exceed 10% of the rent specified per rental period. Landlord must notify the tenant of the landlord's intent to impose the charge no later than the last day of the next rental period immediately following the period in which the default occurred. (New Mexico)

[18] Landlord must wait five days after the rent due date before imposing a late fee. A late fee may not be more than $50 or 5% of the rent, whichever is less. (New York)

[19] Late fee when rent is due monthly cannot be higher than $15 or 5% of the rental payment, whichever is greater (when rent is due weekly, may not be higher than $4.00 or 5% of the rent, whichever is greater); and may not be imposed until the rent is 5 days late. A late fee may be imposed only one time for each late rental payment. A late fee for a specific late rental payment may not be deducted from a subsequent rental payment so as to cause the subsequent rental payment to be in default. (North Carolina)

[20] Late fees won't be enforced if a court finds that they are an "unconscionable penalty." (Ohio)

[21] Reasonable late fees are allowed, but "per-day" or similar charges intended as penalties—rather than actual expenses—are invalid. (Oklahoma)

[22] Landlord must wait 4 days after the rent due date before imposing a late fee, and must disclose the late fee policy in the rental agreement. A flat fee must be "reasonable." A daily late fee may not be more than 6% of a reasonable flat fee, and cannot add up to more than 5% of the monthly rent. (Oregon)

State Rent Rules (continued)

State	When Rent Is Due	Grace Period	Where Rent Is Due	Late Fees
Tennessee	Tenn. Code Ann. § 66-28-201(c)	Tenn. Code Ann. § 66-28-201(d)	Tenn. Code Ann. § 66-28-201(c)	Tenn. Code Ann. § 66-28-201(d) [23]
Texas		Tex. Prop. Code Ann. § 92.019		Tex. Prop. Code Ann. §§ 92.019, 92.0191 [24]
Utah				Utah Code Ann. § 57-22-4(5) [25]
Vermont	Vt. Stat. Ann. tit. 9, § 4455			
Virginia	Va. Code Ann. § 55.1-1204	Va. Code Ann. § 55.1-1204	Va. Code Ann. § 55.1-1204	Va. Code Ann. § 55.1-1204 [26]
Washington		Wash. Rev. Code Ann. § 59.18.170		Wash. Rev. Code Ann. § 59.18.285 [27]
West Virginia				
Wisconsin				Wis. Adm. Code § ATCP 134.09(8) [28]
Wyoming				

[23] Landlord can't charge a late fee until the rent is 5 days late (the day rent is due is counted as the first day). If day five is a Sunday or legal holiday, landlord cannot impose a fee if the rent is paid on the next business day. Fee can't exceed 10% of the amount past due. (Tennessee)

[24] Late fee provision must be included in a written lease and cannot be imposed until the rent remains unpaid two full days after the date it is due. The fee must be reasonable: For properties that have four or fewer units, it cannot be more than 12% of the rent; for properties that have more than four units, it cannot be more than 10% of the rent; OR it must be related to the late payment of rent (such as expenses, costs, and overhead associated with the collection of late payment). Landlord may charge an initial fee and a daily fee for each day the rent is late—the combined fees are considered a single late fee. Tenants can ask landlords to provide statement of whether they owe late fees. (Texas)

[25] Late fees can't exceed the greater of 10% of the rent agreed to in the lease or rental agreement, or $75. The fee must be disclosed in the lease or rental agreement unless the lease or rental agreement is month-to-month and the landlord provides the renter a 15-day notice of the charge. (Utah)

[26] Landlords cannot charge a tenant a late fee unless it is provided for in a written rental agreement or lease. No late charge shall exceed the lesser of 10% of the periodic rent or 10% of the remaining balance due and owed by the tenant. (Virginia)

[27] Nonrefundable fees must be described in lease or rental agreement; otherwise, they will be considered to be deposits. Landlords may not impose late fees until the rent is more than five days late. The fee may commence as of the first day the rent is overdue, and landlords may serve a notice to pay rent or quit as soon as the rent is overdue. If tenants can demonstrate in writing that their primary source of income is a regular, monthly source of governmental assistance that is not received until after the date rent is due in the rental agreement, landlords must adjust rental due date (to no more than five days after the date specified in the rental agreement). (Washington)

[28] Late fee policy must be in the rental agreement, landlord must first apply any prepaid rent (such as last month's rent) to the unpaid rent, and landlord may not charge a fee or impose a penalty for failure to pay the late rent fee. (Wisconsin)

State Rent Control Laws

Rent control (also known as "rent stabilization") limits the amount of rent landlords can charge. Rent control laws vary by state. A few states have statewide rent control, noted with a "Yes" in the "Is There Statewide Rent Control?" column. Most rent control laws, though, are local—passed and enforced by county or city governments. While some states specifically allow local rent control laws—noted with "Yes" in the "Is Local Rent Control Permitted?" column—most states specifically prohibit them; these states have a "No" in the "Is Local Rent Control Permitted?" column. When a state has neither specifically allowed nor prohibited local rent control, you'll see "No statute or case law" in the "Is Local Rent Control Permitted?" column.

Some states require landlords to have "just cause"—good reason—for terminating a tenancy. In other words, a landlord cannot require a tenant to leave or refuse to renew a lease without having a reason specified by state statute. States with just cause statutes are noted with a "Yes" in the "Just Cause Required for Termination" column.

We've noted the applicable statutes or cases for both rent control laws and just cause laws—if any—in the "Legal Authority" column.

State	Is There Statewide Rent Control?	Is Local Rent Control Permitted?	Just Cause Required for Termination?	Legal Authority
Alabama	No	No	No	Ala. Code § 11-80-8.1
Alaska	No	No statute or case law	No	N/A
Arizona	No	No	No	Ariz. Rev. Stat. Ann. § 33-1329
Arkansas	No	No	No	Ark. Code Ann. §§ 14-16-601, 14-54-1409
California	Yes	Yes	Yes	Cal. Civ. Code §§ 1946.2; 1947.12 to 1947.13
Colorado	No	No	No	Colo. Rev. Stat. Ann. §§ 38-12-301 to 38-12-302
Connecticut	No	No. But cities may enact some control over local rents.	No	Conn. Gen. Stat. Ann. § 7-148b
Delaware	No	No statute or case law	No	N/A
District of Columbia	Yes (District wide)	N/A	Yes	D.C. Code Ann. §§ 42-3502.01 to 42.3509.11 (D.C. Code Ann. § 42-3505.01 is just cause statute)
Florida	No	No	No	Fla. Stat. Ann. § 125.0103
Georgia	No	No	No	Ga. Code Ann. § 44-7-19
Hawaii	No	No statute or case law	No	N/A
Idaho	No	No	No	Idaho Code Ann. § 55-307
Illinois	No	No	No	50 Ill. Comp. Stat. Ann. 825/1 to 825/99
Indiana	No	No, unless authorized by an act of the general assembly.	No	Ind. Code Ann. § 32-31-1-20
Iowa	No	No	No	Iowa Code Ann. §§ 331.304, 364.3
Kansas	No	No	No	Kan. Stat. Ann. § 12-16,120
Kentucky	No	No	No	Ky. Rev. Stat. Ann. § 65.875
Louisiana	No	No	No	La. Stat. Ann. § 9:3258; *Javers v. Council of City of New Orleans*, 351 So. 2d 247 (La. Ct. App. 1977), writ denied, 354 So. 2d 200 (La. 1978)
Maine	No	No statute or case law	No	N/A
Maryland	No	Yes	No	*Heubeck v. City of Baltimore*, 205 Md. 203, 107 A.2d 99 (1954); *Westchester West No. 2 Ltd. Partnership v. Montgomery County*, 276 Md. 448, 348 A.2d 856 (1975); *Hardy v. Housing Management Co.*, 293 Md. 394, 444 A.2d 457 (1982)
Massachusetts	No	No	No	Mass. Gen. Laws Ann. ch. 40P, §§ 1 to 5
Michigan	No	No	No	Mich. Comp. Laws Ann. § 123.411
Minnesota	No	No, unless approved in a general election.	No	Minn. Stat. Ann. § 471.9996
Mississippi	No	No	No	Miss. Code. Ann. § 21-17-5
Missouri	No	No	No	Mo. Ann. Stat. § 441.043

	Is There Statewide	Is Local Rent Control	Just Cause Required for	
State	Rent Control?	Permitted?	Termination?	Legal Authority
Montana	No	No statute or case law	No	N/A
Nebraska	No	No statute or case law	No	N/A
Nevada	No	No statute or case law	No	N/A
New Hampshire	No	No	Yes (if the rental is a "restricted property")	N.H. Rev. Stat. Ann. §§ 540:1-a, 540:2; *Girard v. Town of Allenstown*, 121 N.H. 268, 428 A.2d 488 (1981)
New Jersey	No	Yes	Yes	N.J. Stat. Ann. § 2A:18-61.1; *Inganamort v. Borough of Fort Lee*, 62 N.J. 521, 303 A.2d 298 (1973)
New Mexico	No	No	No	N.M. Stat. Ann. § 47-8A-1
New York	Yes	Yes	Yes	N.Y. Unconsol. Law §§ 26-401 to 26-530 (NYC only); N.Y. Unconsol. Law §§ 8581 to 8634 (NY state only, excludes NYC); N.Y. Real Prop. Law § 226-c
North Carolina	No	No	No	N.C. Gen. Stat. Ann. § 42-14.1
North Dakota	No	No	No	N.D. Cent. Code Ann. § 47-16-02.1
Ohio	No	No statute or case law	No	N/A
Oklahoma	No	No	No	Okla. Stat. Ann. tit. 11, § 14-101.1
Oregon	Yes	No	Yes	Or. Rev. Stat. Ann. §§ 90.100, 90.220, 90.323, 90.324, 90.427, 91.225
Pennsylvania	No	No statute or case law	No	N/A
Rhode Island	No	No statute or case law	No	N/A
South Carolina	No	No	No	S.C. Code Ann. § 27-39-60
South Dakota	No	No	No	S.D. Codified Laws § 6-1-13
Tennessee	No	No	No	Tenn. Code Ann. § 66-35-102
Texas	No	No. But municipalities may enact local rent control following a housing emergency caused by a natural or man-made disaster, such as fire, flood, epidemic, air contamination, and extreme heat, among others. The governor must approve the legislation, and the rent control can last only as long as the housing emergency lasts.	No	Tex. Loc. Gov't Code Ann. § 214.902
Utah	No	No	No	Utah Code Ann. § 57-20-1
Vermont	No	No statute or case law	No	N/A
Virginia	No	No statute or case law	No	N/A
Washington	No	No	No	Wash. Rev. Code Ann. § 35.21.830
West Virginia	No	No statute or case law	No	N/A
Wisconsin	No	No	No	Wis. Stat. Ann. § 66.1015
Wyoming	No	No statute or case law	No	N/A

State Rent Control Laws (continued)

State Laws on Attorneys' Fees and Court Costs Clauses

Many leases and rental agreements contain clauses that require tenants to pay the landlord's attorneys' fees and court costs if the parties end up in a court dispute. Some clauses require the "prevailing party" (the party who wins in court) to pay the other party's attorneys' fees and court costs. Landlords should always check their state laws before including these clauses in their leases or rental agreements, though—many states restrict or prohibit the use of these clauses.

State	Rule	Statute
Alabama	Leases and rental agreements cannot require the tenant to pay the landlord's attorneys' fees or costs of collection.	Ala. Code § 35-9A-163(a)(3)
Alaska	Leases and rental agreements cannot require the tenant (or the landlord) to pay the landlord's attorneys' fees.	Alaska Stat. Ann. § 34.03.040(a)(4)
Arizona	Rental document may not provide that tenant pays landlord's attorneys' fees, except that it may provide that the prevailing party in a court action can be awarded attorneys' fees. Also, the prevailing party in an eviction action can be awarded attorneys' fees even if the rental document doesn't mention it.	Ariz. Rev. Stat. § 33-1315
Arkansas	None	
California	None	
Colorado	Leases and rental agreements cannot contain a clause that awards attorneys' fees and court costs to only one party. Any fees or costs clause must award attorneys' fees to the prevailing party in a court dispute concerning the rental agreement or the rental premises.	Colo. Rev. Stat. § 38-12-801
Connecticut	A lease or rental agreement cannot require the tenant to pay attorneys' fees that amount to more than 15% of any judgment against the tenant in any action where money damages are awarded.	Conn. Gen. Stat. Ann. § 47a-4
Delaware	Leases and rental agreements cannot contain a clause providing for the recovery of attorneys' fees in any action relating to the tenancy.	Del. Code Ann. tit. 25, § 5111
District of Columbia	The Rent Administrator, Rental Housing Commission, or a court of competent jurisdiction may award reasonable attorneys' fees to the prevailing party, except in eviction actions authorized under D.C. Code Ann. § 42-3505.01.	D.C. Code Ann. § 42-3509.02
Florida	No ban on attorneys' fees and costs clause. Both landlords and tenants are entitled to recover reasonable attorneys' fees and court costs from the nonprevailing party in a lawsuit brought to enforce the lease or rental agreement, and this right to attorneys' fees and costs cannot be waived in a lease or rental agreement.	Fla. Stat. Ann. § 83.48
Georgia	A clause that provides for the tenant to pay the landlord's attorneys' fees and costs will be void unless it also provides for the landlord to pay the winning tenant's attorneys' fees and costs.	Ga. Code Ann. § 44-7-2
Hawaii	Leases and rental agreements can require the tenant to pay the costs of a suit, unpaid rent, and reasonable attorneys' fees not exceeding 25% of the unpaid rent when a landlord sues for unpaid rent. Leases and rental agreements can also require that reasonable attorneys' fees and costs may be awarded to the prevailing party in any other landlord-tenant dispute.	Haw. Rev. Stat. Ann. § 521-35
Idaho	None	
Illinois	None	
Indiana	None	
Iowa	Neither landlord nor tenant may agree to pay the other's attorneys' fees in a lease or rental agreement.	Iowa Code Ann. § 562A.11
Kansas	Neither landlord nor tenant may agree to pay the other's attorneys' fees in a lease or rental agreement.	Kan. Stat. Ann. § 58-2547
Kentucky	Neither landlord nor tenant may agree to pay the other's attorneys' fees in a lease or rental agreement.	Ky. Rev. Stat. Ann. § 383.570

	State Laws on Attorneys' Fees and Court Costs Clauses (continued)	
State	**Rule**	**Statute**
Louisiana	None	
Maine	Leases and rental agreements cannot require tenant to pay landlord's legal fees in enforcing the lease or rental agreement. However, a lease or rental agreement can provide for the award of attorneys' fees to the prevailing party after a contested hearing to enforce the lease or rental agreement in cases of "wanton disregard" of the terms of the lease or rental agreement.	Me. Rev. Stat. Ann. § 6030
Maryland	None	
Massachusetts	Leases and rental agreements can require parties to pay attorneys' fees and court costs. If a lease or rental agreement provides that only the landlord can recover attorneys' fees and costs, the court will infer a provision that the tenant can also recover attorneys' fees and costs.	Mass. Gen. Laws Ann. ch 186 § 20
Michigan	Leases and rental agreements cannot require a landlord or a tenant to pay the other's legal costs or attorneys' fees in a dispute arising under the lease or rental agreement.	Mich. Comp. Laws § 554.633(1)(g)
Minnesota	If a lease provides for recovery of attorneys' fees by the landlord, the tenant is also entitled to attorneys' fees if the tenant prevails in the same type of action. (Effective for leases entered into on or after August 1, 2011, and for leases renewed on or after August 1, 2012.)	Minn. Stat. Ann. § 504B.172
Mississippi	None	
Missouri	None	
Montana	None	
Nebraska	No lease or rental agreement can require the tenant to pay the landlord's or tenant's attorneys' fees.	Neb. Rev. Stat. Ann. § 76-1415
Nevada	A lease or rental agreement may not provide that the tenant agrees to pay the landlord's attorneys' fees, but it can provide that reasonable attorneys' fees may be awarded to the prevailing party in a court action.	Nev. Rev. Stat. Ann. § 118A.220
New Hampshire	None	
New Jersey	Leases and rental agreements can require parties to pay attorney's fees and court fees. If a lease or rental agreement provides that only the landlord can recover attorney's fees and costs, the court will infer a provision that the tenant can also recover attorney's fees and costs.	N.J. Stat. Ann. § 2A:18-61.66
New Mexico	None	
New York	When a lease includes an attorneys' fees clause in case of a successful action based on tenant's failure to pay rent or perform covenants, the clause will also automatically apply to the landlord if the tenant is successful in the action.	N.Y. Real Prop. Law § 234
North Carolina	Landlords can require tenants to pay attorneys' fees (in an amount no greater than 15% of the amount owed by the tenant or 15% of the monthly rent if it's for an eviction not related to nonpayment of rent) and court costs (filing fees and costs for service of process) if the amounts are disclosed in writing in the lease or rental agreement. Landlords can also file the following administrative fees (which must be written into the lease): Complaint-filing fee: Landlord can charge a complaint-filing fee of no more than the greater of $15 or 5% of the monthly rent. Court appearance fee: Landlord can charge a court appearance fee of 10% of the monthly rent, and only if the landlord's complaint is successful. Second-trial fee: Landlord can charge a fee for an appeal. The fee can't be more than 12% of the monthly rent, and landlord must prevail. Landlords can't waive these limits.	N.C. Gen. Stat. § 42-46

State Laws on Attorneys' Fees and Court Costs Clauses (continued)

State	Rule	Statute
North Dakota	None	
Ohio	Leases and rental agreements cannot require either the landlord or tenant to pay attorneys' fees.	Oh. Rev. Code Ann. § 5321.13(C)
Oklahoma	Leases and rental agreements cannot require either party to pay the other's attorneys' fees.	Okla. St. Ann. tit. 41, § 113
Oregon	If a lease or rental agreement states that one party is entitled to attorneys' fees and costs if the party prevails in a claim based on the lease or rental agreement, the other party is also entitled to the same. The parties cannot waive this rule and agree that only one will get attorneys' fees and costs.	Or. Rev. Stat. Ann. §§ 20.096, 90.255
Pennsylvania	None	
Rhode Island	Leases and rental agreements cannot require the tenant to pay the landlord's attorneys' fees under circumstances not allowed in the landlord-tenant act.	R.I. Gen. Laws § 34-18-17(a)(3)
South Carolina	None	No
South Dakota	None	No
Tennessee	None	No
Texas	If a written lease entitles the landlord to obtain attorneys' fees in an eviction lawsuit, or if the landlord's termination notice advises the tenant that the landlord will be entitled to fees if the tenant does not vacate before the eleventh day after the day of receipt, a prevailing tenant will also be entitled to obtain attorneys' fees.	Tex. Prop. Code Ann. § 24.006
Utah	None	
Vermont	None	
Virginia	A lease or rental agreement can't require the tenant to pay the landlord's attorneys' fees unless specifically allowed under the Virginia Residential Landlord and Tenant Act.	Va. Code Ann. § 55.1-1208
Washington	When a lease or rental agreement provides that attorneys' fees and costs will be provided to one of the parties if that party prevails in a lawsuit, the other party will also be entitled to attorneys' fees and costs in the same situation. The parties cannot waive this reciprocity.	Wash. Rev. Code Ann. § 4.84.330
West Virginia	None	No statute or case law
Wisconsin	Lease or rental agreement cannot require tenant to pay landlord's attorneys' fees or costs incurred in any legal action or dispute arising under the agreement. This does not prevent the recovery of costs or attorneys' fees by a landlord or tenant pursuant to a court order in a small claims or other type of civil lawsuit.	Wis. Admin. Code § ATCP 134.08(4)
Wyoming	None	

State Rules on Notice Required to Change or Terminate a Month-to-Month Tenancy

Except where noted, the amount of notice a landlord must give to increase rent or change another term of the rental agreement in a month-to-month tenancy is the same as that required to end a month-to-month tenancy. Be sure to check state and local rent control laws, which might have different notice requirements.

State	Tenant	Landlord	Statute	Comments
Alabama	30 days	30 days	Ala. Code § 35-9A-441	No state statute on the amount of notice required to change rent or other terms.
Alaska	30 days	30 days	Alaska Stat. § 34.03.290(b)	No state statute on the amount of notice required to change rent or other terms.
Arizona	30 days	30 days	Ariz. Rev. Stat. Ann. §§ 33-1342, 33-1375	Landlords may adopt new rules and regulations that don't substantially modify the rental agreement after giving the tenant 30 days' notice.
Arkansas	30 days	30 days	Ark. Code Ann. § 18-17-704	No state statute on the amount of notice required to change rent or other terms.
California	30 days	30 days to terminate; 30-60+ days to change terms or increase rent, depending on size of increase	Cal. Civ. Code §§ 827, 1946	At least 30 days' notice to change rental terms, but if the change is a proposed rent increase of more than 10% of the rental amount charged to that tenant at any time during the 12 months prior to the effective date of the increase, either in and of itself or when combined with any other rent increases for the 12 months prior to the effective date of the increase, then an additional 30 days' notice is required.
Colorado	21 days	21 days	Colo. Rev. Stat. § 13-40-107	No state statute on the amount of notice required to change rent or other terms, unless there is no written agreement, in which case the landlord must give 60 days' notice.
Connecticut		3 days	Conn. Gen. Stat. Ann. §§ 47a-9, 47a-23	Landlord must provide 3 days' notice to terminate tenancy. Landlord is not required to give a particular amount of notice of a proposed rent increase unless prior notice was previously agreed upon. If landlord makes a new rule or regulation resulting in a substantial modification of the rental agreement, it is not valid unless tenant agrees to it in writing.
Delaware	60 days	60 days	Del. Code Ann. tit. 25, §§ 5106, 5107	For termination, the 60-day notice period begins on the first day of the month following the day of actual notice. For change of terms, upon receiving notice of landlord's proposed change of terms tenant has 15 days to notify landlord of rejection of those terms and intent to terminate the lease. Otherwise, changes will take effect as announced.
District of Columbia	30 days	30-120 days, depending on reason for terminating the tenancy	D.C. Code Ann. §§ 42-3202, 42-3505.01, 42-3509.04(b)	No rent increases shall be effective until the first day on which rent is normally paid occurring more than 30 days after notice of the increase is given to the tenant. Landlords must have good reason (just cause) to terminate a month-to-month tenancy so long as the tenant is still paying rent.

State Rules on Notice Required to Change or Terminate a Month-to-Month Tenancy (continued)

State	Tenant	Landlord	Statute	Comments
Florida	15 days	15 days	Fla. Stat. Ann. § 83.57	No state statute on the amount of notice required to change rent or other terms.
Georgia	30 days	60 days	Ga. Code Ann. §§ 44-7-6, 44-7-7	No state statute on the amount of notice required to change rent or other terms.
Hawaii	28 days	45 days	Haw. Rev. Stat. §§ 521-71, 521-21(d)	Landlord shall not increase rent without written notice given 45 consecutive days prior to the effective date of the increase. The landlord may terminate the rental agreement by notifying the tenant, in writing, at least 45 days in advance of the anticipated termination. The tenant may terminate the rental agreement by notifying the landlord, in writing, at least 28 days in advance of the anticipated termination.
Idaho	One month	15 or 30 days	Idaho Code §§ 55-208, 55-307	A "month" means a calendar month. For landlords: 30 days' notice to increase rent or end tenancy; 15 days' notice to change terms of lease other than rent.
Illinois	30 days	30 days	735 Ill. Comp. Stat. § 5/9-207	No state statute on the amount of notice required to change rent or other terms.
Indiana	One month	One month	Ind. Code Ann. §§ 32-31-1-1, 32-31-5-4	Unless agreement states otherwise, landlord must give 30 days' written notice to modify written rental agreement.
Iowa	30 days	30 days	Iowa Code Ann. §§ 562A.34, 562A.13(5)	To end or change a month-to-month agreement, landlord must give written notice at least 30 days before the next time rent is due (not including any grace period). Each tenant shall be notified, in writing, of any rent increase at least 30 days before the effective date. Such effective date shall not be sooner than the expiration date of original rental agreement or any renewal or extension thereof.
Kansas	30 days	30 days	Kan. Stat. Ann. §§ 58-2556, 58-2570	After the tenant enters into the rental agreement, if a rule or regulation that effects a substantial modification of the rental agreement is adopted, such rule or regulation isn't enforceable against the tenant unless the tenant consents to it in writing.
Kentucky	30 days	30 days	Ky. Rev. Stat. Ann. §§ 383.610, 383.695	If a rule or regulation is adopted after the tenant enters into the rental agreement that works a substantial modification of the bargain, it is not valid unless the tenant consents to it in writing.
Louisiana	10 days	10 days	La. Civ. Code Art. 2728	No state statute on the amount of notice required to change rent or other terms.
Maine	30 days	30 days	Me. Rev. Stat. Ann. tit. 14 §§ 6002, 6015	Landlord must provide 45 days' notice to increase rent.
Maryland	One month	90 days	Md. Code Ann. [Real Prop.] § 8-402(b)(3), (b)(4)	60 days' notice required in Montgomery County (single-family rentals excepted) and Baltimore City.

State Rules on Notice Required to Change or Terminate a Month-to-Month Tenancy (continued)

State	Tenant	Landlord	Statute	Comments
Massachusetts	See comments	See comments	Mass. Gen. Laws Ann. ch. 186, § 12	Interval between days of payment or 30 days, whichever is longer.
Michigan	One month	One month	Mich. Comp. Laws § 554.134	No state statute on the amount of notice required to change rent or other terms.
Minnesota	See comments	See comments	Minn. Stat. Ann. § 504B.135	For terminations, interval between time rent is due or three months, whichever is less; no state statute on the amount of notice required to change rent or other terms.
Mississippi	30 days	30 days	Miss. Code Ann. § 89-8-19	No state statute on the amount of notice required to change rent or other terms.
Missouri	One month	One month	Mo. Rev. Stat. § 441.060	No state statute on the amount of notice required to change rent or other terms.
Montana	30 days	30 days	Mont. Code Ann. §§ 70-24-441, 70-26-109	Landlord may change terms of tenancy with 15 days' notice.
Nebraska	30 days	30 days	Neb. Rev. Stat. §§ 76-1422, 76-1437	A rule or regulation adopted after the tenant enters into the rental agreement is enforceable if the landlord gives reasonable notice to tenant of its adoption and if it doesn't substantially modify the rental agreement.
Nevada	30 days	30 days	Nev. Rev. Stat. Ann. §§ 40.251, 118A.300	Landlords must provide 60 days' notice to increase rent. Tenants 60 years old or older, or physically or mentally disabled, may request an additional 30 days' possession, but only if they have complied with basic tenant obligations as set forth in Nev. Rev. Stat. Chapter 118A (termination notices must include this information).
New Hampshire	30 days	30 days	N.H. Rev. Stat. Ann. §§ 540:2, 540:3, 540:11	Landlord may terminate only for just cause. Tenant's termination: If the date of termination given in the notice does not coincide with the rent due date, tenant is responsible for the rent for the entire month in which the notice expires, up to the next rent due date, unless the terms of the rental agreement provide otherwise.
New Jersey	One month	One month	N.J. Stat. Ann. §§ 2A:18-56, 2A:18-61.1	Landlord may terminate only for just cause. The landlord may increase the rent only at the beginning of the term of the agreement. The landlord cannot increase the rent while an agreement exists. The landlord must offer the tenant the option of entering into a new agreement, at the increased rental rate, after the old agreement expires. If the tenant doesn't sign the new agreement and doesn't move at the expiration of the old agreement, and has been given a valid notice to quit and notice of rent increase, a new tenancy is automatically created at the increased rental rate. New Jersey landlords should check local ordinances, as they might have different rules regarding rent increase notice.

State Rules on Notice Required to Change or Terminate a Month-to-Month Tenancy (continued)

State	Tenant	Landlord	Statute	Comments
New Mexico	30 days	30 days	N.M. Stat. Ann. §§ 47-8-37, 47-8-15(F)	Landlord must deliver rent increase notice at least 30 days before rent due date.
New York	One month, within NYC and statewide	Within NYC and statewide, 30 to 90 days for terminations and rent increases of 5% or more	N.Y. Real Prop. Law §§ 226-c, 232-b	Terminations and rent increases of 5% over existing rent: Tenants occupying for a year or having a lease of at least one year: 30 days' notice. Tenants occupying from one to two years and lease holders of one- to two-year leases: 60 days' notice. Tenants occupying more than two years or having leases of two years or more: 90 days' notice.
North Carolina	7 days	7 days	N.C. Gen. Stat. § 42-14	No state statute on the amount of notice required to change rent or other terms.
North Dakota	One calendar month	One calendar month	N.D. Cent. Code §§ 47-16-07, 47-16-15	Landlord may change the terms of the lease to take effect at the expiration of the month upon giving notice in writing at least 30 days before the expiration of the month. Tenant may terminate with 25 days' notice if landlord has changed the terms of the agreement.
Ohio	30 days	30 days	Ohio Rev. Code Ann. § 5321.17	No state statute on the amount of notice required to change rent or other terms.
Oklahoma	30 days	30 days	Okla. Stat. Ann. tit. 41, § 111	No state statute on the amount of notice required to change rent or other terms.
Oregon	30 days, or 72 hours (lack of bedroom exit only)	Termination: 30 days within the first year (except Portland and Milwaukie, which require a 90-day notice); 90 days after that, only for cause. A landlord with five or more residential dwelling units must also pay tenants the equivalent of one month's rent. Rent increase: See comments	Or. Rev. Stat. §§ 90.275, 90.323, 90.427, 90.460, 91.070	When the rental is in the same building or on the same property as the landlord's residence, and the property has no more than two dwelling units, unique termination periods and notice requirements apply. Temporary occupants are not entitled to notice. Rent cannot be increased during the first year of the tenancy. After that, the rent cannot be increased more than 7% plus the consumer price index (CPI) above the existing rent during any 12-month period. A landlord is exempt from the 7%+CPI increase limit if either: The unit's first certificate of occupancy was issued less than 15 years from the date of the rent increase notice, or the landlord accepts reduced rent as part of a federal, state, or local program or subsidy.

State Rules on Notice Required to Change or Terminate a Month-to-Month Tenancy (continued)

State	Tenant	Landlord	Statute	Comments
Pennsylvania		15 days	68 Pa. Stat. Ann. § 250.501	At the end of the term or due to a breach of the lease landlord must give 15 days' notice to terminate. If notice to terminate is due to tenant's failure to pay rent, notice required is 10 days.
Rhode Island	30 days	30 days	R.I. Gen. Laws §§ 34-18-16.1, 34-18-37	Landlord must provide 30 days' notice to increase rent if tenant is age 62 or younger; if tenant is over 62 years old, landlord must provide 60 days' notice.
South Carolina	30 days	30 days	S.C. Code Ann. §§ 27-40-520, 27-40-770	Rules or regulations adopted after a tenant enters into a rental agreement do not apply to a tenant if the rules or regulations substantially modify the tenant's agreement with landlord and, after receiving notice upon adoption of the right to object, the tenant objects in writing to the landlord within 30 days after the rules are made.
South Dakota	One month	One month	S.D. Codified Laws Ann. §§ 43-8-8, 43-32-13	If tenant (or spouse or minor child) is in active duty in the military, landlord must give two months' notice (unless there is tenant misconduct, a sale of the property, or the property has passed into the landlord's estate). Landlord must give at least 30 days' notice to modify lease (including rent amount). Tenant may terminate lease within 15 days of receipt of the notice of modification.
Tennessee	30 days	30 days	Tenn. Code Ann. §§ 66-28-402, 66-28-512	A rule or regulation adopted after the tenant enters into the rental agreement is enforceable against the tenant if reasonable notice of its adoption is given to the tenant and it does not work a substantial modification of the rental agreement.
Texas	One month	One month	Tex. Prop. Code Ann. §§ 91.001, 92.013	Landlord and tenant may agree in writing to different notice periods, or none at all. No state statute on the amount of notice required to change rent or other terms. A landlord shall give prior written notice to a tenant regarding a landlord rule or policy change that is not included in the lease agreement and that will affect any personal property owned by the tenant that is located outside the tenant's dwelling.
Utah		15 days	Utah Code Ann. § 78B-6-802	No state statute on the amount of notice required to change rent or other terms.
Vermont	One rental period, unless written lease says otherwise	30 days	Vt. Code Ann. tit. 9, §§ 4456(d), 4467	If there is no written rental agreement, for tenants who have continuously resided in the unit for two years or less, 60 days' notice to terminate; for those who have resided longer than two years, 90 days. If there is a written rental agreement, for tenants who have lived continuously in the unit for two years or less, 30 days; for those who have lived there longer than two years, 60 days.

State Rules on Notice Required to Change or Terminate a Month-to-Month Tenancy (continued)

State	Tenant	Landlord	Statute	Comments
Virginia	30 days	30 days	Va. Code Ann. §§ 55.1-1204, 55.1-1253	Rental agreement may provide for a different notice period. By operation of law, month-to-month tenant who does not have a written agreement has a 12-month lease, whose terms and conditions cannot be changed except by agreement of the parties.
Washington	20 days before the end of the "rental period" (the rental period ends the day before rent is due); tenants who are members of the armed forces (as well as their spouses and dependents) may give less than 20 days' notice if they receive permanent change of station or deployment orders that don't allow a 20-day written notice.	Landlord must have a just cause, as enumerated in state law, to terminate a month-to-month tenancy, including one that has resulted from a lease-holding tenant remaining with the consent of the landlord (as a month-to-month tenant). Tenants whose leases are for 6 to 12 months may be terminated upon 60 days' notice in advance of the tenancy end date.	Wash. Rev. Code Ann. §§ 59.18.140, 59.18.200	Landlord must give 60 days' notice to change rent, and any increase in rent may not become effective before the end of the term of the rental agreement, but if the rental is a subsidized tenancy, landlord can give 30 days' notice. If the landlord plans to change rental agreement to exclude children, the landlord shall give tenant at least 90 days' notice. All other changes require 30 days' written notice.
West Virginia	One month	One month	W.Va. Code § 37-6-5	No state statute on the amount of notice required to change rent or other terms.
Wisconsin	28 days	28 days	Wis. Stat. Ann. § 704.19	No state statute on the amount of notice required to change rent or other terms.
Wyoming			No statute	

State Security Deposit Rules

Here are the statutes and rules that govern a landlord's collection and retention of security deposits. Many states require landlords to disclose, at or near the time they collect the deposit, information about how deposits may be used, as noted in the Disclosure or Requirement section. (Required disclosures of other issues, such as a property's history of flooding, are in the chart, "Required Landlord Disclosures.")

Alabama

Ala. Code § 35-9A-201

Limit: One month's rent, except for pet deposits, deposits to cover undoing tenant's alterations, and deposits to cover tenant activities that pose increased liability risks.

Deadline for Landlord to Itemize and Return Deposit: 60 days after termination of tenancy and delivery of possession.

Alaska

Alaska Stat. § 34.03.070

Limit: Two months' rent, unless rent exceeds $2,000 per month. Landlord may ask for an additional month's rent as deposit for a pet that is not a service animal, but may use it only to remedy pet damage.

Disclosure or Requirement: Orally or in writing, landlord must disclose the conditions under which landlord may withhold all or part of the deposit.

Separate Account: Required (but may commingle prepaid rent with security deposits).

Advance notice of deduction: Not required.

Deadline for Landlord to Itemize and Return Deposit: 14 days if the tenant gives proper notice to terminate tenancy; 30 days if the tenant does not give proper notice or if landlord has deducted amounts needed to remedy damage caused by tenant's failure to maintain the property (Alaska Stat. § 34.03.120).

Arizona

Ariz. Rev. Stat. Ann. § 33-1321

Limit: One and one-half months' rent.

Disclosure or Requirement: If landlord collects a nonrefundable fee, its purpose must be stated in writing. All fees not designated as nonrefundable are refundable.

Advance notice of deduction: Not required.

Deadline for Landlord to Itemize and Return Deposit: 14 days (excluding Saturdays, Sundays, and legal holidays); tenant has the right to be present at final inspection.

Arkansas

Ark. Code Ann. §§ 18-16-301 to 18-16-305

Exemption: Security deposit rules do not apply to landlords who own five or fewer units unless the management of the rental (including rent collection) is performed by a third party for a fee.

Limit: Two months' rent, but this limit does not apply to landlords who own 5 or fewer properties, unless the landlord has hired a third party to manage the property.

Advance notice of deduction: Not required.

Deadline for Landlord to Itemize and Return Deposit: 60 days.

California

Cal. Civ. Code §§ 1940.5(g), 1950.5

Limit: Two months' rent (unfurnished); 3 months' rent (furnished). If the tenant is an active service member, no more than one month's rent (unfurnished) or two months' rent (furnished). Add extra one-half month's rent for waterbed.

Advance notice of deduction: Required.

Deadline for Landlord to Itemize and Return Deposit: 21 days.

Colorado

Colo. Rev. Stat. §§ 38-12-102 to 38-12-104

Limit: No statutory limit.

Advance notice of deduction: Not required.

Deadline for Landlord to Itemize and Return Deposit: One month, unless lease agreement specifies longer period of time (which may be no more than 60 days); 72 hours (not counting weekends or holidays) if a hazardous condition involving gas equipment requires tenant to vacate.

Connecticut

Conn. Gen. Stat. Ann. § 47a-21

Limit: Two months' rent (tenant under 62 years of age); one month's rent (tenant 62 years of age or older). Tenants who paid a deposit in excess of one month's rent, who

State Security Deposit Rules (continued)

then turn 62 years old, are entitled, upon request, to a refund of the amount that exceeds one month's rent.

Separate Account: Required.

Interest Payment: Required. Interest payments must be made annually (or credited toward rent, at the landlord's option) and no later than 30 days after termination of tenancy. The interest rate must be equal to the average rate paid on savings deposits by insured commercial banks, rounded to the nearest 0.1%, as published by the Federal Reserve Board Bulletin.

Advance notice of deduction: Not required.

Deadline for Landlord to Itemize and Return Deposit: 30 days, or within 15 days of receiving tenant's forwarding address, whichever is later.

Delaware

Del. Code Ann. tit. 25, §§ 5514, 5311

Limit: One month's rent on leases for one year or more. For month-to-month tenancies, no limit for the first year, but after that, the limit is one month's rent (at the expiration of one year, landlord must give tenant a credit for any deposit held by the landlord that is in excess of one month's rent). No limit for furnished units. Tenant may offer to supply a surety bond in lieu of or in conjunction with a deposit, which landlord may elect to receive.

Separate Account: Required. Orally or in writing, the landlord must disclose to the tenant the location of the security deposit account.

Advance notice of deduction: Not required.

Deadline for Landlord to Itemize and Return Deposit: 20 days.

District of Columbia

D.C. Code Ann § 42-3502.17; D.C. Mun. Regs. tit. 14, §§ 308 to 310

Exemption: Landlords cannot demand or receive a security deposit from a tenant in a rental unit occupied by the tenant as of July 17, 1985, when no security deposit had been required prior to that date.

Limit: One month's rent.

Disclosure or Requirement: In the lease, rental agreement, or receipt, landlord must state the terms and conditions under which the security deposit was collected (to secure tenant's obligations under the lease or rental agreement).

Separate Account: Required.

Interest Payment: Interest payments at the prevailing statement savings rate must be made at termination of tenancy.

Advance notice of deduction: Not required.

Deadline for Landlord to Itemize and Return Deposit: 45 days.

Florida

Fla. Stat. Ann. §§ 83.43(12), 83.49

Limit: No statutory limit.

Disclosure or Requirement: Within 30 days of receiving the security deposit, the landlord must disclose in writing whether it will be held in an interest- or non-interest-bearing account; the name of the account depository; and the rate and time of interest payments. Landlord who collects a deposit must include in the lease the disclosure statement contained in Florida Statutes § 83.49.

Separate Account: Landlord may post a security bond securing all tenants' deposits instead.

Interest Payment: Interest payments, if any (account need not be interest bearing) must be made annually and at termination of tenancy. However, no interest is due a tenant who wrongfully terminates the tenancy before the end of the rental term.

Advance notice of deduction: Required.

Deadline for Landlord to Itemize and Return Deposit: 15 to 60 days depending on whether tenant disputes deductions.

Georgia

Ga. Code Ann. §§ 44-7-30 to 44-7-37

Exemption: Landlord who owns ten or fewer rental units, unless these units are managed by an outside party, need not supply written list of preexisting damage, nor place deposit in an escrow account. Rules for returning the deposit still apply.

Limit: No statutory limit.

Disclosure or Requirement: Landlord must give tenant a written list of preexisting damage to the rental before collecting a security deposit.

Separate Account: Required. Landlord must place the deposit in an escrow account in a state- or federally

State Security Deposit Rules (continued)

regulated depository, and must inform the tenant of the location of this account. Landlord may post a security bond securing all tenants' deposits instead.

Advance notice of deduction: Required.

Deadline for Landlord to Itemize and Return Deposit: 30 days.

Hawaii

Haw. Rev. Stat. § 521-44

Limit: One month's rent. Landlord may require an additional one month's rent as security deposit for tenants who keep a pet.

Advance notice of deduction: Not required.

Deadline for Landlord to Itemize and Return Deposit: 14 days.

Idaho

Idaho Code § 6-321

Limit: No statutory limit.

Separate Account: Required. Security deposits for rentals that are managed by a third-party property manager must be held in a separate account at a federally insured financial institution. The account must be separate from the operating account. (These rules don't apply to managers who are owners, who have a real estate license, or who are nonprofit entities.)

Advance notice of deduction: Not required.

Deadline for Landlord to Itemize and Return Deposit: 21 days, or up to 30 days if landlord and tenant agree.

Illinois

765 Ill. Comp. Stat. 710/1; 715/1 to 715/3

Limit: No statutory limit.

Disclosure or Requirement: If a lease specifies the cost for repair, cleaning, or replacement of any part of the leased premises; or the cleaning or repair of any component of the building or common area that will not be replaced, the landlord may withhold the dollar amount specified in the lease. Landlord's itemized statement must reference the specified dollar amount(s) and include a copy of the lease clause.

Interest Payment: Landlords who rent 25 or more units in either a single building or a complex located on contiguous properties must pay interest on deposits held for more than six months. The interest rate is the rate paid for minimum deposit savings accounts by the largest commercial bank in the state, as of December 31 of the calendar year immediately preceding the start of the tenancy. Within 30 days after the end of each 12-month rental period, landlord must pay any interest that has accumulated to an amount of $5 or more, by cash or credit applied to rent due, except when the tenant is in default under the terms of the lease. Landlord must pay all interest that has accumulated and remains unpaid, regardless of the amount, upon termination of the tenancy.

Advance notice of deduction: Not required.

Deadline for Landlord to Itemize and Return Deposit: For properties with 5 or more units, 30 to 45 days, depending on whether tenant disputes deductions or if statement and receipts are furnished.

Indiana

Ind. Code Ann. §§ 32-31-3-1.1 to 32-31-3-19

Exemption: Does not apply to rental agreements entered into before July 1, 1989.

Limit: No statutory limit.

Advance notice of deduction: Not required.

Deadline for Landlord to Itemize and Return Deposit: 45 days.

Iowa

Iowa Code Ann. § 562A.12

Limit: Two months' rent.

Separate Account: Required.

Interest Payment: Interest payment, if any (account need not be interest bearing) must be made at termination of tenancy. Interest earned during first five years of tenancy belongs to landlord.

Advance notice of deduction: Not required.

Deadline for Landlord to Itemize and Return Deposit: 30 days.

State Security Deposit Rules (continued)

Kansas

Kan. Stat. Ann. §§ 58-2548, 58-2550

Limit: One month's rent (unfurnished); one and one-half months' rent (furnished); for pets, add extra one-half month's rent.

Advance notice of deduction: Not required.

Deadline for Landlord to Itemize and Return Deposit: 30 days.

Kentucky

Ky. Rev. Stat. Ann. § 383.580

Limit: No statutory limit.

Disclosure or Requirement: Orally or in writing, landlord must disclose where the security deposit is being held and the account number.

Before accepting a security deposit, landlords must give tenants a list of pre-existing damage that would justify a charge against the deposit, including the amount of the charge. Tenants have the right to inspect before taking possession. Both parties must sign the list, and if tenants disagree with its accuracy, they must state in writing the basis for their disagreement and sign the statement of dissent. A mutually signed listing is conclusive proof of the listed defects, but not as to latent (unobservable) defects.

Separate Account: Required.

Advance notice of deduction: Required.

Deadline for Landlord to Itemize and Return Deposit: 30 to 60 days depending on whether tenant disputes deductions.

Louisiana

La. Rev. Stat. Ann. § 9:3251

Limit: No statutory limit.

Advance notice of deduction: Not required.

Deadline for Landlord to Itemize and Return Deposit: One month.

Maine

Me. Rev. Stat. Ann. tit. 14, §§ 6031 to 6038

Exemption: Entire security deposit law does not apply to rental unit that is part of structure with five or fewer units, one of which is occupied by landlord.

Limit: Two months' rent.

Disclosure or Requirement: Upon request by the tenant, landlord must disclose orally or in writing the account number and the name of the institution where the security deposit is being held.

Separate Account: Required.

Advance notice of deduction: Not required.

Deadline for Landlord to Itemize and Return Deposit: 30 days (if written rental agreement) or 21 days (if tenancy at will).

Maryland

Md. Code Ann. [Real Prop.] §§ 8-203, 8-203.1, 8-208

Exemption: Security deposit statutes do not apply to a tenancy arising after the sale of owner-occupied residential property where the seller and purchaser agree that the seller may remain in possession of the property for not more than 60 days after the settlement.

Limit: Two months' rent.

Disclosure or Requirement: Landlord must provide a receipt that describes tenant's rights to move-in and move-out inspections (and to be present at each), and right to receive itemization of deposit deductions and balance, if any; and penalties for landlord's failure to comply. Landlord must include this information in the lease.

Separate Account: Required. Landlord may hold all tenants' deposits in secured certificates of deposit, or in securities issued by the federal government or the State of Maryland.

Interest Payment: For security deposits of $50 or more, when landlord has held the deposit for at least six months: Within 45 days of termination of tenancy, interest must be paid at the daily U.S. Treasury yield curve rate for 1 year, as of the first business day of each year, or 1.5% a year, whichever is greater, less any damages rightfully withheld. Interest accrues monthly but is not compounded, and no interest is due for any period less than one month. (See the Department of Housing and Community Development website for a calculator.) Deposit must be held in a Maryland banking institution.

Advance notice of deduction: Required.

Deadline for Landlord to Itemize and Return Deposit: 45 days.

State Security Deposit Rules (continued)

Massachusetts

Mass. Gen. Laws Ann. ch. 186, § 15B

Exemption: Security deposit rules do not apply to any lease, rental, occupancy, or tenancy of 100 days or less in duration which lease or rental is for a vacation or recreational purpose.

Limit: One month's rent.

Disclosure or Requirement: At the time of receiving a security deposit, landlord must furnish a receipt indicating the amount of the deposit; the name of the person receiving it, and, if received by a property manager, the name of the lessor for whom the security deposit is received; the date on which it is received; and a description of the premises leased or rented. The receipt must be signed by the person receiving the security deposit.

Separate Account: Required. Within 30 days of receiving security deposit, landlord must disclose the name and location of the bank in which the security deposit has been deposited, and the amount and account number of the deposit.

Interest Payment: Landlord must pay tenant 5% interest per year or the amount received from the bank (which must be in Massachusetts) that holds the deposit. Interest should be paid yearly, and within 30 days of termination date. Interest will not accrue for the last month for which rent was paid in advance.

Advance notice of deduction: Not required.

Deadline for Landlord to Itemize and Return Deposit: 30 days.

Michigan

Mich. Comp. Laws §§ 554.602 to 554.616

Limit: One and one-half months' rent.

Disclosure or Requirement: Within 14 days of tenant's taking possession of the rental, landlord must furnish in writing the landlord's name and address for receipt of communications, the name and address of the financial institution or surety where the deposit will be held, and the tenant's obligation to provide in writing a forwarding mailing address to the landlord within 4 days after termination of occupancy. The notice shall include the following statement in 12-point boldface type that is at least 4 points larger than the body of the notice or lease agreement: "You must notify your landlord in writing within 4 days after you move of a forwarding address where you can be reached and where you will receive mail; otherwise your landlord shall be relieved of sending you an itemized list of damages and the penalties adherent to that failure."

Separate Account: Required. Landlord must place deposits in a regulated financial institution, and may use the deposits as long as the landlord deposits with the secretary of state a cash or surety bond.

Advance notice of deduction: Required. Not a typical advance notice provision: Tenants must dispute the landlord's stated deductions within 7 days of receiving the itemized list and balance, if any, or give up any right to dispute them.

Deadline for Landlord to Itemize and Return Deposit: 30 days.

Minnesota

Minn. Stat. Ann. §§ 504B.151, 504B.175, 504B.178, 504B.195

Limit: No statutory limit. If landlord collects a "prelease deposit" and subsequently rents to tenant, landlord must apply the prelease deposit to the security deposit.

Disclosure or Requirement: Before collecting rent or a security deposit, landlord must provide a copy of all outstanding inspection orders for which a citation has been issued, pertaining to a rental unit or common area, specifying code violations that threaten the health or safety of the tenant, and all outstanding condemnation orders and declarations that the premises are unfit for human habitation. Citations for violations that do not involve threats to tenant health or safety must be summarized and posted in an obvious place. With some exceptions, landlord who has received notice of a contract for deed cancellation or notice of a mortgage foreclosure sale must so disclose before entering a lease, accepting rent, or accepting a security deposit; and must furnish the date on which the contract cancellation period or the mortgagor's redemption period ends.

Interest Payment: Landlord must pay 1% simple, noncompounded interest per year. (Deposits collected before 8/1/03 earn interest at 3%, up to 8/1/03, then

State Security Deposit Rules (continued)

begin earning at 1%.) Any interest amount less than $1 is excluded.

Advance notice of deduction: Not required.

Deadline for Landlord to Itemize and Return Deposit: Three weeks after tenant leaves and landlord receives forwarding address; five days if tenant must leave due to building condemnation.

Mississippi

Miss. Code Ann. § 89-8-21

Limit: No statutory limit.

Advance notice of deduction: Not required.

Deadline for Landlord to Itemize and Return Deposit: 45 days.

Missouri

Mo. Ann. Stat. § 535.300

Limit: Two months' rent.

Advance notice of deduction: Not required.

Deadline for Landlord to Itemize and Return Deposit: 30 days.

Montana

Mont. Code Ann. §§ 70-25-101 to 70-25-206

Limit: No statutory limit.

Disclosure or Requirement: Before signing a lease, landlords must give tenants a signed statement of the physical condition of the premises, including a statement (if applicable) that the premises have never been leased. Upon request, landlords must furnish a separate written statement of the damage and cleaning charges of the departing tenants. Landlords who fail to comply may not deduct any sums for damage or cleaning unless the landlord can establish by "clear and convincing evidence" that the tenant, tenant's family, licensees, or invitees were responsible.

Advance notice of deduction: Required. Tenant is entitled to advance notice of cleaning charges, but only if such cleaning is required as a result of tenant's negligence and is not part of the landlord's cyclical cleaning program.

Deadline for Landlord to Itemize and Return Deposit: 30 days; 10 days if no deductions.

Nebraska

Neb. Rev. Stat. § 76-1416

Limit: One month's rent (no pets); one and one-quarter months' rent (pets).

Advance notice of deduction: Not required.

Deadline for Landlord to Itemize and Return Deposit: 14 days.

Nevada

Nev. Rev. Stat. Ann. §§ 118A.240 to 118A.250

Exemption: Security deposit rules do not apply to the following, among others: (1) Occupancy under a contract of sale of a dwelling unit or the property of which it is a part, if the occupant is the purchaser or a person who succeeds to the purchaser's interest; (2) Occupancy by an employee of a landlord whose right to occupancy is conditional upon employment in and about the premises; (3) Occupancy by a person who is guilty of a forcible entry or forcible detainer.

Limit: Three months' rent; if both landlord and tenant agree, tenant may use a surety bond for all or part of the deposit.

Disclosure or Requirement: Lease or rental agreement must explain the conditions under which the landlord will refund the deposit.

Advance notice of deduction: Not required.

Deadline for Landlord to Itemize and Return Deposit: 30 days.

New Hampshire

N.H. Rev. Stat. Ann. §§ 540-A:5 to 540-A:8; 540-B:10

Exemption: Entire security deposit law does not apply to landlord who leases a single-family residence and owns no other rental property, or landlord who leases rental units in an owner-occupied building of five units or fewer (exemption does not apply to any individual unit in owner-occupied building that is occupied by a person 60 years of age or older).

Limit: One month's rent or $100, whichever is greater; when landlord and tenant share facilities, no statutory limit.

Disclosure or Requirement: Unless tenant has paid the deposit by personal or bank check, or by a check issued by a government agency, landlord must provide a receipt

State Security Deposit Rules (continued)

stating the amount of the deposit and the institution where it will be held. Regardless of whether a receipt is required, landlord must inform tenant that if tenant finds any conditions in the rental in need of repair, tenant may note them on the receipt or other written instrument, and return either within five days.

Separate Account: Required. Upon request, landlord must disclose the account number, the amount on deposit, and the interest rate. Landlord may post a bond covering all deposits instead of putting deposits in a separate account.

Interest Payment: Landlord who holds a security deposit for a year or longer must pay interest at a rate equal to the rate paid on regular savings accounts in the New Hampshire bank, savings & loan, or credit union where it's deposited. If a landlord mingles security deposits in a single account, the landlord must pay the actual interest earned proportionately to each tenant. A tenant may request the interest accrued every three years, 30 days before that year's tenancy expires. The landlord must comply with the request within 15 days of the expiration of that year's tenancy.

Advance notice of deduction: Not required.

Deadline for Landlord to Itemize and Return Deposit: 30 days; for shared facilities, if the deposit is more than 30 days' rent, landlord must provide written agreement acknowledging receipt and specifying when deposit will be returned—if no written agreement, 20 days after tenant vacates.

New Jersey

N.J. Stat. Ann. §§ 46:8-19 to 46:8-26

Exemption: Security deposit law does not apply to owner-occupied buildings with not more than two rental units where the tenant has failed to provide 30 days' written notice to the landlord invoking the law.

Limit: One and one-half months' rent. Any additional security deposit, collected annually, may be no greater than 10% of the current security deposit.

Separate Account: Required. Within 30 days of receiving the deposit and every time the landlord pays the tenant interest, landlord must disclose the name and address of the banking organization where the deposit is being held, the type of account, current rate of interest, and the amount of the deposit.

Interest Payment: Landlord with 10 or more units must invest deposits as specified by statute or place deposit in an insured money market fund account, or in another account that pays quarterly interest at a rate comparable to the money market fund. Landlords with fewer than 10 units may place deposit in an interest-bearing account in any New Jersey financial institution insured by the FDIC. All landlords may pay tenants interest earned on account annually or credit toward payment of rent due.

Advance notice of deduction: Not required.

Deadline for Landlord to Itemize and Return Deposit: 30 days; five days in case of fire, flood, condemnation, or evacuation.

New Mexico

N.M. Stat. Ann. § 47-8-18

Exemption: Security deposit rules do not apply to the following, among others: (1) Occupancy under a contract of sale of a dwelling unit or the property of which it is a part, if the occupant is the purchaser or a person who succeeds to the purchaser's interest; (2) Occupancy by an employee of an owner pursuant to a written rental or employment agreement that specifies the employee's right to occupancy is conditional upon employment in and about the premises.

Limit: One month's rent (for rental agreement of less than one year); no limit for leases of one year or more.

Interest Payment: Landlord who collects a deposit larger than one month's rent on a year's lease must pay interest, on an annual basis, equal to the passbook interest.

Advance notice of deduction: Not required.

Deadline for Landlord to Itemize and Return Deposit: 30 days.

New York

N.Y. Gen. Oblig. Law §§ 7-103 to 7-108

Limit: One month's limit for units other than those subject to the City Rent and Rehabilitation Law or the Emergency Housing Rent Control Law.

Disclosure or Requirement: If deposit is placed in a bank, landlord must disclose the name and address of the banking organization where the deposit is being held, and the amount of such deposit.

State Security Deposit Rules (continued)

Separate Account: Statute requires that deposits not be commingled with landlord's personal assets, but does not explicitly require placement in a banking institution (however, deposits collected in buildings of six or more units must be placed in New York bank accounts).

Interest Payment: Landlord who rents out nonregulated units in buildings with five or fewer units need not pay interest. Interest must be paid at the "prevailing rate" on deposits received from tenants who rent units in buildings containing six or more units. The landlord in every rental situation may retain an administrative fee of 1% per year on the sum deposited. Interest can be subtracted from the rent, paid at the end of the year, or paid at the end of the tenancy according to the tenant's choice.

Advance notice of deduction: Required.

Deadline for Landlord to Itemize and Return Deposit: 14 days.

North Carolina

N.C. Gen. Stat. §§ 42-50 to 42-56

Exemption: Not applicable to rentals of single rooms.

Limit: One and one-half months' rent for month-to-month rental agreements; two months' rent if term is longer than two months; may also charge a reasonable, nonrefundable pet deposit.

Disclosure or Requirement: Within 30 days of the beginning of the lease term, landlord must disclose the name and address of the banking institution where the deposit is located or the name of the insurance company providing the bond.

Separate Account: Required. The landlord may choose to furnish a bond from an insurance company licensed to do business in N.C. rather than deposit the security deposit in a trust account.

Advance notice of deduction: Not required.

Deadline for Landlord to Itemize and Return Deposit: 30 days; if landlord's claim against the deposit cannot be finalized within that time, landlord may send an interim accounting and a final accounting within 60 days of the tenancy's termination.

North Dakota

N.D. Cent. Code § 47-16-07.1

Limit: One month's rent. If tenant has a pet, an additional pet deposit of up to $2,500 or two months' rent, whichever is greater. To encourage renting to persons with records of felony convictions, landlords may charge these applicants up to two months' rent as security. Applicants who have had court judgments entered against them "for violating the terms of a previous rental agreement" can also be charged up to two months' rent (this appears to refer to prior evictions and might not apply to evictions based on conduct not prohibited by the rental agreement).

Separate Account: Required.

Interest Payment: Landlord must pay interest if the period of occupancy is at least nine months. Money must be held in a federally insured interest-bearing savings or checking account for benefit of the tenant. Interest must be paid upon termination of the lease.

Advance notice of deduction: Not required.

Deadline for Landlord to Itemize and Return Deposit: 30 days.

Ohio

Ohio Rev. Code Ann. § 5321.16

Limit: No statutory limit.

Interest Payment: Any deposit in excess of $50 or one month's rent, whichever is greater, must bear interest on the excess at the rate of 5% per annum if the tenant stays for six months or more. Interest must be paid annually and upon termination of tenancy.

Advance notice of deduction: Not required.

Deadline for Landlord to Itemize and Return Deposit: 30 days.

Oklahoma

Okla. Stat. Ann. tit. 41, § 115

Limit: No statutory limit.

Separate Account: Required.

Advance notice of deduction: Not required.

Deadline for Landlord to Itemize and Return Deposit: 45 days.

State Security Deposit Rules (continued)

Oregon

Or. Rev. Stat. § 90.300

Exemption: Security deposit rules do not apply to the following, among others: (1) Occupancy of a unit for no more than 90 days by a purchaser prior to the scheduled closing of a real estate sale or by a seller following the closing of a sale, in either case as permitted under the terms of an agreement for sale of a dwelling unit or the property of which it is a part (a tenant who holds but has not exercised an option to purchase the unit does not qualify for this exemption); (2) Vacation occupancy; (3) Occupancy by an employee of a landlord whose right to occupancy is conditional upon employment in and about the premises.

Limit: No statutory limit. Landlord may not impose or increase deposit within the first year unless parties agree to modify the rental agreement to allow for a pet or other cause, and the imposition or increase relates to that modification.

Disclosure or Requirement: Landlord must provide a receipt for any security deposit the tenant pays.

Advance notice of deduction: Not required.

Deadline for Landlord to Itemize and Return Deposit: 31 days.

Pennsylvania

68 Pa. Cons. Stat. Ann. §§ 250.511a to 250.512

Limit: Two months' rent for first year of renting; one month's rent during second and subsequent years of renting.

Disclosure or Requirement: For deposits over $100, landlord must deposit them in a federally or state-regulated institution, and give tenant the name and address of the banking institution and the amount of the deposit.

Separate Account: Required. Instead of placing deposits in a separate account, landlord may purchase a bond issued by a bonding company authorized to do business in the state.

Interest Payment: Tenant who occupies rental unit for two or more years is entitled to interest beginning with the 25th month of occupancy. Landlord must pay tenant interest (minus 1% fee) at the end of the third and subsequent years of the tenancy.

Advance notice of deduction: Not required.

Deadline for Landlord to Itemize and Return Deposit: 30 days.

Rhode Island

R.I. Gen. Laws § 34-18-19

Exemption: Security deposit rules do not apply to the following, among others: (1) Occupancy under a contract of sale of a dwelling unit or the property of which it is a part, if the occupant is the purchaser or a person who succeeds to the purchaser's interest; (2) Occupancy by a paid employee of a landlord, whose right to occupancy is conditional upon employment substantially for services, maintenance, or repair of premises containing more than 11 units.

Limit: One month's rent (unfurnished); if furnished, separate furniture security deposit up to one month's rent if furnishings' replacement value at the start of the tenancy is $5,000 or more.

Advance notice of deduction: Not required.

Deadline for Landlord to Itemize and Return Deposit: 20 days.

South Carolina

S.C. Code Ann. § 27-40-410

Exemption: Security deposit rules do not apply to the following, among others: (1) Occupancy under a contract of sale of a dwelling unit or the property of which it is a part, if the occupant is the purchaser or a person who succeeds to the purchaser's interest; (2) Occupancy by an employee of a landlord whose right to occupancy is conditional upon employment in and about the premises; (3) Certain vacation rentals.

Limit: No statutory limit.

Advance notice of deduction: Not required.

Deadline for Landlord to Itemize and Return Deposit: 30 days.

South Dakota

S.D. Codified Laws Ann. §§ 43.32-6.1, 43-32-24

Limit: One month's rent (higher deposit may be charged if special conditions pose a danger to maintenance of the premises).

Advance notice of deduction: Not required.

State Security Deposit Rules (continued)

Deadline for Landlord to Itemize and Return Deposit: Two weeks and must supply reasons if withholding any portion; 45 days for a written, itemized accounting, if tenant requests it.

Tennessee

Tenn. Code Ann. § 66-28-301

Limit: No statutory limit.

Separate Account: Required. Orally or in writing, landlord must disclose the location of the separate account (but not the account number) used by landlord for the deposit.

Advance notice of deduction: Required.

Deadline for Landlord to Itemize and Return Deposit: No statutory deadline

Texas

Tex. Prop. Code Ann. §§ 92.101 to 92.111

Limit: No statutory limit. Landlord may choose to offer the tenant the option to pay a nonrefundable fee in lieu of a security deposit. See Tex. Prop. Code Ann.§ 92.111.

Disclosure or Requirement: If a security deposit isn't required by the lease or rental agreement, but the tenant is liable for damage or rent when they leave, the landlord must notify the tenant in writing about the claim before reporting the claim. Landlords who don't provide notice forfeit the right to collect damages and charges from the tenant.

Advance notice of deduction: Not required.

Deadline for Landlord to Itemize and Return Deposit: 30 days. If landlord wants to condition the refund of the security deposit on the tenant's giving advance notice of surrender, landlord must put this condition in the lease, and it must be either underlined or printed in conspicuous bold print.

Utah

Utah Code Ann. §§ 57-17-1 to 57-17-5

Limit: No statutory limit.

Disclosure or Requirement: For written leases or rental agreements only, if part of the deposit is nonrefundable, landlord must disclose this feature.

Advance notice of deduction: Not required.

Deadline for Landlord to Itemize and Return Deposit: 30 days.

Vermont

Vt. Stat. Ann. tit. 9, § 4461

Exemption: Security deposit rules do not apply to the following, among others: (1) Occupancy under a contract of sale of a dwelling unit or the property of which it is a part, if the occupant is the purchaser or a person who succeeds to the purchaser's interest; (2) Occupancy of a dwelling unit without right or permission by a person who is not a tenant.

Limit: No statutory limit.

Advance notice of deduction: Not required.

Deadline for Landlord to Itemize and Return Deposit: 14 days; 60 days if the rental is seasonal and not intended as the tenant's primary residence.

Virginia

Va. Code Ann. §§ 55.1-1204, 55.1-1206, 55.1-1208, 55.1-1226

Limit: Two months' rent. Alternatively, landlord may permit a tenant to provide damage insurance coverage in an amount not more than two months' rent in lieu of the payment of a security deposit. The damage insurance coverage must meet the requirements listed in Virginia Code Annotated sections 55.1-1226(I)-(K).

Advance notice of deduction: Not required.

Deadline for Landlord to Itemize and Return Deposit: 45 days after termination date or the date the tenant vacates, whichever occurs last; 30 days to itemize any deductions to be made during the course of the tenancy (45 days if the deductions exceed the amount of the security deposit). Lease can provide for expedited processing at the end of the tenancy and specify an administrative fee for such processing, which will apply only if tenant requests it with a separate written document. Landlord must give tenant written notice of tenant's right to be present at a final inspection.

Washington

Wash. Rev. Code Ann. §§ 59.18.260 to 59.18.285; 59.18.610

Limit: Landlords must allow tenants to pay the deposit and fees in installments (does not apply if the deposit and any nonrefundable fees are less than 25% of the monthly rent, or the landlord has not demanded the last month's rent). Tenants with tenancies of three months or more may pay in three equal and consecutive

State Security Deposit Rules (continued)

installments, beginning at the start of the tenancy; two installments for shorter tenancies. Installment schedules must be written and signed. Does not apply to holding deposits (which may not be more than 25% of the first month's rent).

Disclosure or Requirement: In the lease, landlord must disclose the circumstances under which all or part of the deposit may be withheld. No deposit may be collected unless the rental agreement is in writing and a written checklist or statement specifically describing the condition and cleanliness of or existing damages to the premises and furnishings is provided to the tenant at the start of the tenancy.

The landlord must provide tenant with a written receipt for the deposit and provide the name, address, and location of where the deposit will be kept; if location changes, landlord must notify tenant.

Nonrefundable fees must be identified as such in a written rental agreement. If landlords fail to provide a written agreement, tenants are entitled to the return of the fee. If the written agreement does not specify that the fee is refundable, it must be treated as a refundable deposit.

Separate Account: Required.

Advance notice of deduction: Not required.

Deadline for Landlord to Itemize and Return Deposit: 21 days.

West Virginia

W. Va. Code §§ 37-6A-1 to 37-6A-6

Exemption: Agreements for the payment of security deposits entered into before June 10, 2011.

Limit: No statutory limit.

Deadline for Landlord to Itemize and Return Deposit: 60 days from the date the tenancy has terminated, or within 45 days of the occupancy of a subsequent tenant, whichever is shorter. If the damage exceeds the amount of the security deposit and the landlord has to hire a contractor to fix it, the notice period is extended 15 days.

Wisconsin

Wis. Admin. Code ATCP 134.04, 134.06; Wis. Stat. § 704.28

Exemption: Security deposit rules do not apply to the following, among others: (1) A dwelling unit occupied, under a contract of sale, by the purchaser of the dwelling unit or the purchaser's successor in interest; (2) A dwelling unit which the landlord provides free of charge to any person; (3) A dwelling unit which the landlord provides as consideration to a person whom the landlord currently employs to operate or maintain the premises.

Limit: No statutory limit.

Disclosure or Requirement: Before accepting the deposit, landlord must inform tenant of tenant's inspection rights, disclose all habitability defects, and show tenant any outstanding building and housing code violations, inform tenant of the means by which shared utilities will be billed, and inform tenant if utilities are not paid for by landlord.

Advance notice of deduction: Not required.

Deadline for Landlord to Itemize and Return Deposit: 21 days.

Wyoming

Wyo. Stat. §§ 1-21-1207, 1-21-1208

Limit: No statutory limit.

Disclosure or Requirement: Lease or rental agreement must state whether any portion of a deposit is non-refundable, and landlord must give tenant written notice of this fact when collecting the deposit.

Advance notice of deduction: Not required.

Deadline for Landlord to Itemize and Return Deposit: 30 days, when applying it to unpaid rent (or within 15 days of receiving tenant's forwarding address, whichever is later); additional 30 days allowed for deductions due to damage.

Required Landlord Disclosures

Many states require landlords to inform tenants of important state laws or individual landlord policies, either in the lease or rental agreement or in another writing. Commonly required disclosures include a landlord's imposition of nonrefundable fees (where permitted), tenants' rights to move-in checklists, and the identity of the landlord or landlord's agent or manager. Disclosures concerning the security deposit are in the chart, "State Security Deposit Rules." Also, keep in mind that landlords in *all* states must disclose information about lead-based paint to tenants if the building they are renting was built before 1978.

Alabama

Owner or agent identity: Landlord must disclose to the tenant in writing at or before the commencement of the tenancy the name and address of the person authorized to manage the premises, and an owner of the premises or a person authorized to act for and on behalf of the owner for the purpose of service of process and for the purpose of receiving notices and demands. (Exception: does not apply to resident purchaser under a contract of sale (but does apply to a resident who has an option to buy), nor to the continuation of occupancy by the seller or a member of the seller's family for a period of not more than 36 months after the sale of a dwelling unit or the property of which it is a part.) (Ala. Code § 35-9A-202)

Alaska

Owner or agent identity: Landlord must disclose to the tenant in writing at or before the commencement of the tenancy the name and address of the person authorized to manage the premises, and an owner of the premises or a person authorized to act for and on behalf of the owner for the purpose of service of process and for the purpose of receiving notices and demands. (Alaska Stat. § 34.03.080)

Extended absence: The rental agreement must require that the tenant notify the landlord of an anticipated extended absence from the premises in excess of seven days; however, the notice may be given as soon as reasonably possible after the tenant knows the absence will exceed seven days. (Alaska Stat. § 34.03.150)

Arizona

Nonrefundable fees permitted? Yes. The purpose of all nonrefundable fees or deposits must be stated in writing. Any fee or deposit not designated as nonrefundable is refundable. (Ariz. Rev. Stat. § 33-1321)

Move-in checklist required? Yes. Tenants also have the right to be present at a move-out inspection. (Ariz. Rev. Stat. § 33-1321)

Separate utility charges: If landlord charges separately for gas, water, wastewater, solid waste removal, or electricity by installing a submetering system, landlord may recover the charges imposed on the landlord by the utility provider, plus an administrative fee for the landlord for actual administrative costs only, and must disclose separate billing and fee in the rental agreement. If landlord uses a ratio utility billing system, the rental agreement must contain a specific description of the ratio utility billing method used to allocate utility costs. (Ariz. Rev. Stat. Ann. § 33-1314.01)

Owner or agent identity: Landlord must disclose to the tenant in writing at or before the commencement of the tenancy the name and address of the person authorized to manage the premises, and an owner of the premises or a person authorized to act for and on behalf of the owner for the purpose of service of process and for the purpose of receiving notices and demands. (Ariz. Rev. Stat. Ann. § 33-1322)

Business tax pass-through: If the landlord pays a local tax based on rent and that tax increases, landlord may pass through the increase by increasing the rent upon 30 days' notice (but not before the new tax is effective), but only if the landlord's right to adjust the rent is disclosed in the rental agreement. (Ariz. Rev. Stat. Ann. § 33-1314)

Availability of Landlord and Tenant Act: Landlord must inform tenant in writing that the Residential Landlord and Tenant Act is available on the Arizona Department of Housing's website. (Ariz. Rev. Stat. Ann. § 33-1322)

Bed bug information: Landlords must provide existing and new tenants with educational materials on bed bugs, including information and physical descriptions, prevention and control measures, behavioral attraction

Required Landlord Disclosures (continued)

risk factors, information from federal, state, and local centers for disease control and prevention, health or housing agencies, nonprofit housing organizations, or information developed by the landlord. (Ariz. Rev. Stat. Ann. § 33-1319)

Smoke detectors: Landlords must install smoke detectors and give tenant written notification of tenant's responsibilities (tenant must maintain it unless tenant gives written notification to the landlord of its malfunction, at which point landlord must maintain it). (Ariz. Rev. Stat. Ann. § 36-1637)

Arkansas

Move-in checklist required? Yes

Must checklist rights be stated in the lease: No

Checklists, other details: To show compliance with the law of implied warranty of habitability, landlord must provide tenant with a written form in which the tenant can note any habitability-related defects. The landlord is deemed to be in compliance if the tenant signs and returns the form without noting any defects or fails to return the form within two business days. Applies to leases and rental agreements entered into or renewed after November 1, 2021. (Ark. Code Ann. § 18-17-502)

California

Nonrefundable fees permitted? No. (Cal. Civ. Code § 1950.5(m))

Move-in checklist required? No

Must fee policy be stated in the rental agreement? N/A

Registered sexual offender database: Landlords must include this notice in every lease or rental agreement: "Notice: Pursuant to Section 290.46 of the Penal Code, information about specified registered sex offenders is made available to the public via an Internet Web site maintained by the Department of Justice at www.meganslaw.ca.gov. Depending on an offender's criminal history, this information will include either the address at which the offender resides or the community of residence and ZIP Code in which the offender resides." (Cal. Civ. Code § 2079.10a)

Tenant paying for others' utilities: Prior to signing a rental agreement, landlord must disclose whether gas or electric service to tenant's unit also serves other areas,

and must disclose the manner by which costs will be fairly allocated. (Cal. Civ. Code § 1940.9)

Ordnance locations: Prior to signing a lease, landlord must disclose known locations of former federal or state ordnance in the neighborhood (within one mile of rental). (Cal. Civ. Code § 1940.7)

Mold: Prior to signing a rental agreement, landlord must provide written disclosure when landlord knows, or has reason to know, that mold exceeds permissible exposure limits or poses a health threat. Landlords must distribute a consumer handbook, developed by the State Department of Health Services, describing the potential health risks from mold. (Cal. Health & Safety Code §§ 26147, 26148)

Pest control service: When the rental agreement is signed, landlord must provide tenant with any pest control company disclosure landlord has received, which describes the pest to be controlled, pesticides used and their active ingredients, a warning that pesticides are toxic, and the frequency of treatment under any contract for periodic service. (Cal. Civ. Code § 1940.8; Cal. Bus. & Prof. Code § 8538)

Intention to demolish rental unit: Landlords or their agents who have applied for a permit to demolish a rental unit must give written notice of this fact to prospective tenants, before accepting any deposits or screening fees. (Cal. Civ. Code § 1940.6)

No-smoking policy: For leases and rental agreements signed after January 1, 2012: If the landlord prohibits or limits the smoking of tobacco products on the rental property, the lease or rental agreement must include a clause describing the areas where smoking is limited or prohibited (does not apply if the tenant has previously occupied the dwelling unit). For leases and rental agreements signed before January 1, 2012: A newly adopted policy limiting or prohibiting smoking is a change in the terms of the tenancy (will not apply to lease-holding tenants until they renew their leases; tenants renting month-to-month must be given 30 days' written notice). Does not preempt any local ordinances prohibiting smoking in effect on January 1, 2012. (Cal. Civ. Code § 1947.5)

Required Landlord Disclosures (continued)

Flooding: In leases or rental agreements signed after July 1, 2018, landlord must disclose, in at least eight-point type, that the property is in a special flood hazard area or an area of potential flooding if the landlord has actual knowledge of this fact. Actual knowledge includes receipt from a public agency so identifying the property; the fact that the owner carries flood insurance; or that the property is in an area in which the owner's mortgage holder requires the owner to carry flood insurance. Disclosure must advise tenant that additional information can be had at the Office of Emergency Services' website, and must include the Internet address for the MYHazards tool maintained by the Office. Disclosure must advise tenant that owner's insurance will not cover loss to tenant's property, and must recommend that tenant consider purchasing renter's insurance that will cover loss due to fire, flood, or other risk of loss. Disclosure must note that the owner is not required to provide additional information. (Cal. Govt. Code § 8589.45)

Bed bug information: efore signing a lease or rental agreement, landlord must give potential tenants information about bed bugs, including information about their behavior and biology, the importance of cooperation for prevention and treatment, and the importance of prompt written reporting of suspected infestations to the landlord. (Cal. Civ. Code § 1954.603)

Methamphetamine or fentanyl: If a property has been contaminated and is subject to a remediation order, landlord must provide written notice of and a copy of the order to all prospective tenants who have submitted an application. The tenant has to acknowledge receipt of the notice in writing before signing a rental agreement, and the landlord must attach the notice to the rental agreement. If a landlord fails to provide this notice, the prospective tenant can void the rental agreement.

For the rental of mobile homes and manufactured homes, the landlord must notify prospective tenants, in writing, of all methamphetamine or fentanyl laboratory activities that have taken place in the mobile home or manufactured home, and any remediation of the home or vehicle, and the property can't be rented until the prospective tenant is provided with a copy of the order. If there is already a tenant, the landlord must attach the

notice and order to the rental agreement. (Cal. Health & Safety Code § 25400.28)

Death on the premises within the past three years: If an occupant died on the property within three years of the landlord's offer to rent, the landlord must disclose this fact. Landlords are not required to disclose that an occupant of that property was living with human immunodeficiency virus (HIV) or died from AIDS-related complications. (Cal. Civ. Code § 1710.2)

Single-family tenancies not subject to the Tenant Protection Act of 2019: Landlords of single-family rentals that are not subject to the Tenant Protection Act of 2019 must put the following notice in the lease or rental agreement: "This property is not subject to the rent limits imposed by Section 1947.12 of the Civil Code and is not subject to the just cause requirements of Section 1946.2 of the Civil Code. This property meets the requirements of Sections 1947.12 (d)(5) and 1946.2 (e)(8) of the Civil Code and the owner is not any of the following: (1) a real estate investment trust, as defined by Section 856 of the Internal Revenue Code; (2) a corporation; or (3) a limited liability company in which at least one member is a corporation." (Cal. Civ. Code §§ 1946.2(e)(8), 1947.12)

Single-family tenancies subject to the Tenant Protection Act of 2019, owner move-in: For tenancies subject to the Tenant Protection Act, landlord may terminate the lease in order to move in the owner or the owners spouse, domestic partner, children, grandchildren, parents, or grandparents. If the lease was entered into on or after July 1, 2020, though, the landlord can terminate the lease for this reason only when the tenant agrees in writing OR when the lease specifies that the owner can terminate the lease for this reason. (Cal. Civ. Code § 1946.2(b)(2)(A))

Tenancies subject to the Tenant Protection Act of 2019: Owners of rentals subject to the Tenant Protection Act of 2019 must provide the following as a written notice to tenants or include it in the written lease or rental agreement: "California law limits the amount your rent can be increased. See Section 1947.12 of the Civil Code for more information. California law also provides that after all of the tenants have continuously and lawfully occupied the property for 12 months or more or at least one of the tenants has continuously and lawfully occupied

Required Landlord Disclosures (continued)

the property for 24 months or more, a landlord must provide a statement of cause in any notice to terminate a tenancy. See Section 1946.2 of the Civil Code for more information." The notice must be in at least 12-point type. (Cal. Civ. Code § 1946.2(f))

Colorado

Disclosure of landlord: Written rental agreements and leases must include a statement of the name and address of the person who is the landlord or the landlord's authorized agent. If this person's identity changes, the tenants must be notified of the new contact person within one business day after the change, and the landlord must post the identity of the new landlord or authorized agent in a conspicuous location on the rental premises. (Colo. Rev. Stat. Ann. § 38-12-801)

Bed bugs: Upon request from prospective tenants, landlords must disclose whether the unit for rent contained bed bugs within the previous eight months. If requested, landlords must also disclose the last date (if any) the unit being rented was inspected for, and found to be free of, bed bugs. (Colo. Rev. Stat. Ann. § 38-12-1005)

Rental application fee: Landlords who collect a rental application fee must disclose the anticipated expenses for which the fee will be used or itemize the actual expenses incurred. When landlords charge application fees based on the average cost of processing rental applications, they must explain how they determined the average rental application fee. (Colo. Rev. Stat. Ann. § 38-12-903)

Rental application denial: Landlords who deny rental applications must give rejected applicants a written notice of the denial that states the reasons for the denial. If a landlord cannot site the specific screening criteria because of the use of a proprietary screening system, the landlord must instead provide the rejected applicant with a copy of the report from the screening company. Landlords can provide electronic versions of the denial notice, but must provide a paper denial notice upon request. Landlords must make a good-faith effort to provide the notice within 20 calendar days of the denial. (Colo. Rev. Stat. Ann. § 38-12-904)

Connecticut

Common interest community: When rental is in a common interest community, landlord must give tenant written notice before signing a lease. (Conn. Gen. Stat. Ann. § 47a-3e)

Owner or agent identity: Before the beginning of the tenancy, landlord must disclose the name and address of the person authorized to manage the premises and the person who is authorized to receive all notices, demands, and service of process. (Conn. Gen. Stat. Ann. § 47a-6)

Bed bug information: Landlords may not advertise a unit that the landlord knows or reasonably suspects is infested with bed bugs. Before signing a lease, landlords must tell prospective tenants whether the unit (or any contiguous unit owned or subleased by the landlord) is infested. If asked by tenants or prospective tenants, landlords must disclose the last date on which the rental unit was inspected for bed bugs and found to be free of any infestation. (Conn. Stat. Ann. § 47a-7a)

Fire system information: When renting a dwelling unit in a building required to be equipped with a fire sprinkler system pursuant to any statute or regulation, the landlord of such dwelling unit must include notice in the rental agreement as to the existence or nonexistence of an operative fire sprinkler system in such building, and such notice shall be printed in not less than twelve-point boldface type of uniform font. If there is an operative fire sprinkler system in the building, the rental agreement will also state the last date of maintenance and inspection, in not less than twelve-point boldface type of uniform font. (Conn. Stat. Ann. § 47a-3f)

Delaware

Nonrefundable fees permitted? No, except for an optional service fee for actual services rendered, such as a pool fee or tennis court fee. Tenant may elect, subject to the landlord's acceptance, to purchase an optional surety bond instead of or in combination with a security deposit. (*Stoltz Management Co. v. Phillip*, 593 A.2d 583 (1990); Del. Code Ann. tit. 25, § 5311)

Owner or agent identity: On each written rental agreement, the landlord must prominently disclose the names and usual business addresses of all persons who

Required Landlord Disclosures (continued)

are owners of the rental unit or the property of which the rental unit is a part, or the names and business addresses of their appointed resident agents. (25 Del. Code Ann. § 5105)

Summary of Landlord-Tenant Law: A summary of the Landlord-Tenant Code, as prepared by the Consumer Protection Unit of the Attorney General's Office or its successor agency, must be given to the new tenant at the beginning of the rental term. If the landlord fails to provide the summary, the tenant may plead ignorance of the law as a defense. (25 Del. Code Ann. § 5118)

Separate utility metering: Landlords may install meters for the purposes of separately charging individual units for utility services, but can only bill tenants according to these measurements if the rental agreement discloses the existence and use of meters. (25 Del. Code Ann. § 5312)

District of Columbia

Nonrefundable fees permitted? Yes. Must be stated in the rental agreement. (D.C. Code Ann. § 42-3502.22)

Must fee policy be stated in the rental agreement? Yes

General disclosures: Upon receiving a rental application, landlords must provide on a disclosure form published by the Rent Administrator (or in another suitable format until a form is published) along with supporting documents each of the following : (a) the units rental rate; (b) any pending petitions filed that could affect the rental unit, including petitions for rent increases during the following 12 months; (c) any surcharges on the rent (including capital improvement surcharges) and the date they expire; (d) the frequency of possible rent increases; (e) the rent-controlled or exempt status of the rental, its business license, and a copy of the registration or claim of exemption (and any recent related filings); (f) all copies of code violation reports for the rental within the last 12 months, or previously issued reports for violations which have not been abated; (g) the Rent Administrators pamphlet that explains rent increases and petitions that can be filed; (h) the amount of any nonrefundable application fee; (i) the amount of the security deposit, the interest rate on the security deposit, and how the security deposit will be returned when the tenant vacates the unit; (j) ownership information; (k) information about the presence of mold

in the rental unit or common areas in the previous three years, unless the mold has been remediated by certified and licensed indoor mold remediation professional; (l) the voter registration packet developed by the D.C. Board of Elections (this packet should be part of the Rent Administrators disclosure form, but if it has not been included in the form, the landlord should provide the packet if one exists); and (m) a copy of the current Tenant Bill of Rights published by the Office of the Tenant Advocate.

Landlords must give written notice to each tenant, on a form published by the Rent Administrator (or in another suitable format until a form is published), that the disclosure forms and documents for the tenants rental unit are available for inspection. The written notice must include the location of the disclosure forms and a table of contents laying out the categories of information included in the disclosure forms.

Upon a tenant's written request not more than once per calendar year, the landlord, within 10 business days of the request, must also disclose the amount of, and the basis for, each rent increase for the prior three years. If applicable, the disclosure must identify any substantially identical rental unit on which a vacancy increase was based. (D.C. Code Ann. § 42-3502.22)

Rental regulations: At the start of every new tenancy, landlord must give tenant a copy of the District of Columbia Municipal Regulations, CDCR Title 14, Housing, Chapter 3, Landlord and Tenant; and a copy of Title 14, Housing, Chapter 1, § 101 (Civil Enforcement Policy) and Chapter 1, § 106 (Notification of Tenants Concerning Violations). (14 D.C. Mun. Regs. § 300)

Late fees: Landlords can charge late rent fees only if the maximum amount of the late fee that may be charged is disclosed in the written lease or rental agreement. (D.C. Code Ann. § 42-3505.31)

Fire alarms: In buildings with four or more rental, rooming, or sleeping units (including condominium or cooperative units), owners must conspicuously post (and give to each tenant) written information on the following: How to operate manual alarm boxes, how to respond when smoke detectors activate (including abandoning the dwelling unit, closing its door, and

Required Landlord Disclosures (continued)

activating the nearest alarm box), information on whether the building is monitored by a supervising station, and instructions on calling 911. (12 D.C. Mun. Regs. § PM-704G)

Florida

Nonrefundable fees permitted? Yes. No statute directly on point, but by custom, nonrefundable fees are allowed.

Landlord identity: The landlord, or a person authorized to enter into a rental agreement on the landlord's behalf, must disclose in writing to the tenant, at or before the commencement of the tenancy, the name and address of the landlord or a person authorized to receive notices and demands on the landlord's behalf. (Fla. Stat. Ann. § 83.50)

Radon: In all leases, landlord must include this warning: "RADON GAS: Radon is a naturally occurring radioactive gas that, when it has accumulated in a building in sufficient quantities, may present health risks to persons who are exposed to it over time. Levels of radon that exceed federal and state guidelines have been found in buildings in Florida. Additional information regarding radon and radon testing may be obtained from your county health department." (Fla. Stat. Ann. § 404.056)

Georgia

Nonrefundable fees permitted? Yes. (Ga. Code Ann. § 44-7-30)

Other fees: Landlord and tenant may agree that certain prepaid sums, covering future rent or services or utilities supplied to the tenant, will not be returned to the tenant at the end of the tenancy.

Move-in checklist required? Landlords cannot collect a security deposit unless they have given tenants a list of preexisting damages. Landlord must provide tenant with a comprehensive list of any existing damage to the premises before the tenant gives landlord a security deposit. (Ga. Code Ann. § 44-7-33)

Flooding: Before signing a lease, if the living space or attachments have been damaged by flooding three or more times within the past five years, landlord must so disclose in writing. (Ga. Code Ann. § 44-7-20)

Owner or agent identity: When or before a tenancy begins, landlord must disclose in writing the names and addresses of the owner of record (or a person authorized to act for the owner) for purposes of service of process and receiving and receipting demands and notices; and the person authorized to manage the premises. If such information changes during the tenancy, landlord must advise tenant within 30 days in writing or by posting a notice in a conspicuous place. (Ga. Code Ann. § 44-7-3)

Former residents, crimes: Unless asked by a prospective tenant, landlord does not have to disclose whether the rental was the site of a homicide or other felony, or a suicide or a death by accidental or natural causes; or whether it was occupied by a person who was infected with a virus or any other disease that has been determined by medical evidence as being highly unlikely to be transmitted through the occupancy of a dwelling place presently or previously occupied by such an infected person. However, if a prospective tenant asks about any of these things, landlord must answer truthfully to the best of the landlord's individual knowledge. (Ga. Code Ann. § 44-1-16)

Hawaii

Nonrefundable fees permitted? No.

Other fees: The landlord may not require or receive from or on behalf of a tenant at the beginning of a rental agreement any money other than the money for the first month's rent and a security deposit as provided in this section.

Owner or agent identity: Landlord must disclose name of owner or agent; if owner lives in another state or on another island, landlord must disclose name of agent on the island. (Haw. Rev. Stat. § 521-43)

Move-in checklist required? Yes. (Haw. Rev. Stat. § 541-42)

Tax excise number: Landlord must furnish its tax excise number so that tenant can file for a low-income tax credit. (Haw. Rev. Stat. § 521-43)

Idaho

No disclosure statutes.

Illinois

Utilities: Where tenant pays a portion of a master metered utility, landlord must give tenant a copy in writing either as part of the lease or another written agreement of the formula used by the landlord for

Required Landlord Disclosures (continued)

allocating the public utility payments among the tenants. (765 Ill. Comp. Stat. § 740/5)

Rent concessions: Any rent concessions must be described in the lease, in letters not less than one-half inch in height consisting of the words "Concession Granted," including a memorandum on the margin or across the face of the lease stating the amount or extent and nature of each such concession. Failure to comply is a misdemeanor. (765 Ill. Comp. Stat. §§ 730/0.01 to 730/6)

Radon: Landlords are not required to test for radon, but if the landlord tests and learns that a radon hazard is present in the dwelling unit, landlord must disclose this information to current and prospective tenants. If a tenant notifies a landlord that a radon test indicates the existence of a radon hazard in the rental unit, landlord must disclose that risk to any prospective tenant of that unit, unless a subsequent test by the landlord shows that a radon hazard does not exist. Requirements do not apply if the dwelling unit is on the third or higher story above ground level, or when the landlord has undertaken mitigation work and a subsequent test shows that a radon hazard does not exist. (420 Ill. Comp. Stat. §§ 46/15, 46/25)

Smoke detectors: Landlord must give one tenant per dwelling written information about smoke detector testing and maintenance. (425 Ill. Comp. Stat. § 60/3(d))

Carbon monoxide alarms: Landlord must give one tenant per dwelling written information regarding CO alarm testing and maintenance. (430 Ill. Comp. Stat. § 135/10(c))

Indiana

Agent identity: Landlord's agent must disclose in writing the name and address of a person living in Indiana who is authorized to manage the property and to act as the owner's agent. (Ind. Code Ann. § 32-31-3-18)

Smoke detectors: Landlord must require the tenant to acknowledge in writing that the rental unit is equipped with a functional smoke detector. (Ind. Code Ann. § 32-31-5-7)

Floodplain disclosure: If the lowest floor of a rental structure (including a basement) is at or below the 100-year frequency flood elevation, the landlord must disclose in the lease that the structure is located in a floodplain. (Ind. Code Ann. § 32-31-1-21)

Water or sewage disposal services: A landlord who pays for water, sewage disposal, or both, and who passes the costs on to tenants must describe the following in the lease, the tenants' first bill, or in a writing before signing the lease: A description of the water or sewage disposal services to be provided, and an itemized statement of the fees that will be charged. The disclosure must be printed using a font that is at least as large as the largest font used in the document in which the disclosure is included. The disclosure must include a description of the water or sewage disposal services to be provided, an itemized statement of the fees that will be charged, and this statement: "If you believe you are being charged in violation of this disclosure or if you believe you are being billed in excess of the utility services provided to you as described in this disclosure, you have a right under Indiana law to file a complaint with the Indiana Utility Regulatory Commission. You may contact the Commission at (insert phone number for the tenant to contact the Commission)." (Ind. Code Ann. § 8-1-2-1.2)

Iowa

Owner or agent identity: Landlord must disclose to the tenant in writing at or before the commencement of the tenancy the name and address of the person authorized to manage the premises, and an owner of the premises or a person authorized to act for and on behalf of the owner for the purpose of service of process and for the purpose of receiving notices and demands. (Iowa Code § 562A.13)

Utilities: For shared utilities, landlord must fully explain utility rates, charges, and services to the prospective tenant before the rental agreement is signed. (Iowa Code § 562A.13)

Contamination: The landlord or a person authorized to enter into a rental agreement on behalf of the landlord must disclose to each tenant, in writing before the commencement of the tenancy, whether the property is listed in the comprehensive environmental response compensation and liability information system maintained by the federal Environmental Protection Agency. (Iowa Code § 562A.13)

Required Landlord Disclosures (continued)

Kansas

Move-in checklist required? Yes. Within 5 days of move-in, landlord and tenant must jointly inventory the rental. (Kan. Stat. Ann. § 58-2548)

Owner or agent identity: Landlord must disclose to the tenant in writing at or before the commencement of the tenancy the name and address of the person authorized to manage the premises, and an owner of the premises or a person authorized to act for and on behalf of the owner for the purpose of service of process and for the purpose of receiving notices and demands. (Kan. Stat. Ann. § 58-2551)

Kentucky

Move-in checklist required? Yes. Landlord and tenant must complete a checklist before landlord can collect a security deposit. (Ky. Rev. Stat. Ann. § 383.580)

Owner or agent identity: Landlord must disclose to the tenant in writing at or before the commencement of the tenancy the name and address of the person authorized to manage the premises, and an owner of the premises or a person authorized to act for and on behalf of the owner for the purpose of service of process and for the purpose of receiving notices and demands. (Ky. Rev. Stat. Ann. § 383.585)

Methamphetamine contamination disclosure: An owner of contaminated property who rents a property where the local health department has posted a methamphetamine contamination notice must disclose in writing to potential tenants that the property is contaminated and has not been decontaminated pursuant to the state's requirements. The disclosure must contain the physical address of the property, the location within the posted property that was used in the production of methamphetamine, and a copy of the Notice of Methamphetamine Contamination. If a prospective tenant asks, the owner must provide a copy of any documents related to the methamphetamine contamination provided to the owner by law enforcement, the Energy and Environment Cabinet, the Department for Public Health, or the local health department. (Ky. Rev. Stat. Ann. § 224.1-410; 902 Ky. Admin. Regs. 47:200)

Louisiana

Application fee: Landlords can't charge an application fee unless they give applicants a written notice of (1) the amount of the fee (2) whether the landlord will consider credit scores, employment history, criminal history, or eviction records in deciding whether to rent to the applicant; and (3) permission for the applicant to provide a statement of 200 words or less explaining that the applicant has experienced financial hardship resulting from a state or federally declared disaster or emergency and how that hardship impacted the applicant's credit, employment, or rental history (the landlord must reference COVID-19 and hurricanes). (La. Rev. Stat. Ann. § 9:3258.1)

Foreclosure: Before entering into a lease or rental agreement, landlord must disclose to potential tenants their right to receive notification of any future foreclosure action. If the premises are currently subject to a foreclosure action, landlord must also disclose this in writing. (La. Rev. Stat. Ann. § 9:3260.1)

Maine

Utilities: No landlord may lease or offer to lease a dwelling unit in a multiunit residential building where the expense of furnishing electricity to the common areas or other area not within the unit is the sole responsibility of the tenant in that unit, unless both parties to the lease have agreed in writing that the tenant will pay for such costs in return for a stated reduction in rent or other specified fair consideration that approximates the actual cost of electricity to the common areas. (Me. Rev. Stat. Ann. tit. 14, § 6024)

Energy efficiency: Landlord must provide to potential tenants who will pay for energy costs (or upon request from others) a residential energy efficiency disclosure statement in accordance with Title 35-A, section 10006, subsection 1 that includes, but is not limited to, information about the energy efficiency of the property. Before a tenant enters into a contract or pays a deposit to rent or lease a property, the landlord must provide the statement to the tenant, obtain the tenant's signature on the statement, and sign the statement. The landlord must retain the signed statement for at least

Required Landlord Disclosures (continued)

3 years. Alternatively, the landlord may include in the application for the residential property the name of each supplier of energy that previously supplied the unit, if known, and the following statement: "You have the right to obtain a 12-month history of energy consumption and the cost of that consumption from the energy supplier." (Me. Rev. Stat. Ann. tit. 14, § 6030-C)

Radon: Unless a mitigation system has been installed, starting in 2014 and every 10 years after when requested by a tenant, the landlord shall test for radon in the rental. If the building was constructed after March 1, 2014, the landlord shall test for radon within 12 months of the occupancy of the building by a tenant. Within 30 days of receiving test results, the landlord shall provide written notice to existing tenants that includes the date of the test, the results, whether mitigation has been performed, the risk associated with radon, and notice that the tenant has the right to conduct a test. The same written notice must also be given to any new tenants before they sign a lease or pay a deposit to rent. The notice must include an acknowledgment that the tenant has received the disclosure. (Me. Rev. Stat. Ann. tit. 14, § 6030-D)

Bed bugs: Before renting a dwelling unit, landlord must disclose to a prospective tenant if an adjacent unit or units are currently infested with or are being treated for bed bugs. Upon request from a tenant or prospective tenant, landlord must disclose the last date that the dwelling unit the landlord seeks to rent or an adjacent unit or units were inspected for a bed bug infestation and found to be free of a bed bug infestation. (Me. Rev. Stat. Ann. tit. 14, § 6021-A)

Smoking policy: Landlord must give tenant written disclosure stating whether smoking is prohibited on the premises, allowed on the entire premises, or allowed in limited areas of the premises. If the landlord allows smoking in limited areas on the premises, the notice must identify the areas on the premises where smoking is allowed. Disclosure must be in the lease or separate written notice, landlord must disclose before tenant signs a lease or pays a deposit, and must obtain a written acknowledgment of notification from the tenant. (Me. Rev. Stat. Ann. tit. 14, § 6030-E)

Maryland

Move-in checklist required? Yes. Before collecting a deposit, landlord must supply a receipt with details on move-in and move-out inspections, and the receipt must be part of the lease. (Md. Code Ann. [Real Prop.] § 8-203.1)

Habitation: A lease must include a statement that the premises will be made available in a condition permitting habitation, with reasonable safety, if that is the agreement, or if that is not the agreement, a statement of the agreement concerning the condition of the premises; and the landlord's and the tenant's specific obligations as to heat, gas, electricity, water, and repair of the premises. (Md. Code Ann. [Real Prop.], § 8-208)

Owner or agent identity: The landlord must include in a lease or post the name and address of the landlord; or the person, if any, authorized to accept notice or service of process on behalf of the landlord. (Md. Code Ann. [Real Prop.], § 8-210)

Montgomery County: Before a prospective tenant signs a lease for 125 days or more, the landlord of a rental within a condominium or development must provide to the prospective tenant, if applicable, a copy of the rules, declaration, and recorded covenants and restrictions that limit or affect the use and occupancy of the property or common areas and to which the owner of the rental is obligated. The written lease must, if applicable, include a statement that the obligations of the owner that limit or affect the use and occupancy of the property are enforceable against the tenant. (Md. Code Ann. [Real Prop.], § 8-210)

Reusable tenant screening reports: Landlords must notify prospective tenants about whether the landlord accepts reusable tenant screening reports (reports generated by a consumer reporting agency within the previous 30 days that the tenant provides to the landlord and for which the landlord doesn't charge an additional fee). Notice must be made in writing or by posting in a conspicuous manner. (Md. Code Ann. [Real Prop.], § 8-218)

Required Landlord Disclosures (continued)

Massachusetts

Move-in checklist required? Yes, if landlord collects a security deposit. (Mass. Gen. Laws ch. 186, § 15B(2)(c))

Insurance: Upon tenant's request and within 15 days, landlord must furnish the name of the company insuring the property against loss or damage by fire and the amount of insurance provided by each such company and the name of any person who would receive payment for a loss covered by such insurance. (Mass. Gen. Laws ch. 186, § 21)

Tax Escalation: If real estate taxes increase, landlord may pass on a proportionate share of the increase to the tenant only if the lease discloses that in the event of an increase, the tenant will be required to pay only the proportion of the increase as the tenant's leased unit bears to the property being taxed (that proportion must be disclosed in the lease). In addition, the lease must state that if the landlord receives a tax abatement, landlord will refund a proportionate share of the abatement, minus reasonable attorneys' fees. (Mass. Gen. Laws ch. 186, § 15C)

Utilities: Landlord may not charge for water unless the lease specifies the charge and the details of the water submetering and billing arrangement. (Mass. Gen. Laws ch. 186, § 22(f))

Michigan

Move-in checklist required? Yes. However, the requirement does not need to be stated in the lease. (Mich. Comp. Laws § 554.608)

May landlord charge nonrefundable fees? Yes. (*Stutelberg v. Practical Management Co.*, 245 N.W.2d 737 (1976))

Owner or agent identity: A rental agreement must include the name and address at which notice can be given to the landlord. (Mich. Comp. Laws § 554.634)

Truth in Renting Act: A rental agreement must also state in a prominent place in type not smaller than the size of 12-point type, or in legible print with letters not smaller than 1/8 inch, a notice in substantially the following form: NOTICE: Michigan law establishes rights and obligations for parties to rental agreements. This agreement is required to comply with the Truth in Renting Act. If you have a question about the interpretation or legality of a provision of this agreement, you may want to seek assistance from a lawyer or other qualified person." (Mich. Comp. Laws § 554.634)

Rights of domestic violence victims: A rental agreement or lease may contain a provision stating, "A tenant who has a reasonable apprehension of present danger to him or her or his or her child from domestic violence, sexual assault, or stalking may have special statutory rights to seek a release of rental obligation under MCL 554.601b." If the rental agreement or lease does not contain such a provision, the landlord must post an identical written notice visible to a reasonable person in the landlord's property management office, or deliver written notice to the tenant when the lease or rental agreement is signed. (Mich. Comp. Laws § 554.601b)

Minnesota

Owner or agent identity: Landlord must disclose to the tenant in writing at or before the commencement of the tenancy the name and address of the person authorized to manage the premises, and an owner of the premises or a person authorized to act for and on behalf of the owner for the purpose of service of process and for the purpose of receiving notices and demands. (Minn. Stat. Ann. § 504B.181)

Outstanding inspection orders, condemnation orders, or declarations that the property is unfit: The landlord must disclose the existence of any such orders or declarations before the tenant signs a lease or pays a security deposit. (Minn. Stat. Ann. § 504B.195)

Buildings in financial distress: Once a landlord has received notice of a deed cancellation or notice of foreclosure, landlord may not enter into a periodic tenancy where the tenancy term is more than two months, or a lease where the lease extends beyond the redemption period (other restrictions may apply). (Minn. Stat. Ann. § 504B.151)

Landlord and tenant mutual promises: This mutual promise must appear in every lease or rental agreement: "Landlord and tenant promise that neither will unlawfully allow within the premises, common areas, or curtilage of the premises (property boundaries): controlled substances, prostitution or prostitution-related activity; stolen property or property obtained

Required Landlord Disclosures (continued)

by robbery; or an act of domestic abuse, criminal sexual conduct, or harassment, as defined by MN Statute Section 504B.206(1)(a), against a tenant, licensee, or any authorized occupant. They further promise that the aforementioned areas will not be used by themselves or anyone acting under their control to manufacture, sell, give away, barter, deliver, exchange, distribute, purchase, or possess a controlled substance in violation of any criminal provision of chapter 152." (Minn. Stat. Ann. § 504B.171)

Screening fee: Before accepting an applicant's screening fee, landlords must disclose in writing: The name, address, and phone number of the tenant screening service (if landlord uses such a service), and the landlord's acceptance criteria. Landlords must notify rejected applicants within 14 days, identifying the criteria the applicant did not meet. (Minn. Stat. Ann. § 504B.173)

Mississippi

No disclosure statutes.

Missouri

Methamphetamine: Landlord who knows that the premises were used to produce methamphetamine must disclose this fact to prospective tenants, regardless of whether the people involved in the production were convicted for such production. (Mo. Rev. Stat. § 441.236)

Owner or Agent Identity: Landlord must disclose to the tenant in writing at or before the commencement of the tenancy the name and address of the person authorized to manage the premises, and an owner of the premises or a person authorized to act for and on behalf of the owner for the purpose of service of process and for the purpose of receiving notices and demands. (Mo. Rev. Stat. § 535.185)

Radioactive or hazardous material: Landlords who know that the rental property is or was contaminated with radioactive or other hazardous material must disclose this fact to prospective tenants. Landlords have knowledge when they've received a report stating that the property is or was contaminated. Failure to disclose when required is a Class A misdemeanor. (Mo. Rev. Stat. § 442.055)

Montana

Nonrefundable fees permitted? No. A fee or charge for cleaning and damages, no matter how designated, is presumed to be a security deposit. (Not a clear statement that such a fee isn't nonrefundable, but by implication it must be.) (Mont. Code Ann. § 70-25-101(4))

Move-in checklists required? Yes, checklists are required when landlords collect a security deposit. (Mont. Code Ann. § 70-25-206)

Owner or agent identity: Landlords or people authorized to enter into a rental agreement on their behalf shall disclose to the tenant in writing at or before the commencement of the tenancy the name and address of the person authorized to manage the premises; and the owner of the premises or a person authorized to act for the owner for the purpose of service of process and receiving notices and demands. (Mont. Code Ann. § 70-24-301)

Mold: Before signing a lease, if a landlord has knowledge that mold is present in the rental, the landlord must disclose its presence; and if the landlord knows that the building has been tested for mold, the landlord must advise the tenant that testing has occurred and provide a copy of the results (if available), as well as any evidence of subsequent treatment. Landlords can avoid liability for damages resulting from mold if they comply with these rules, provide tenants with a mold disclosure statement in the form prescribed by statute, and obtain the tenants' written acknowledgment of receipt of the statement. (Mont. Code Ann. § 70-16-703)

Methamphetamine contamination: Before signing a lease or rental agreement, a landlord who knows that the property has been contaminated from smoke from the use of meth or was used as a meth lab must disclose this history to a potential tenant. Disclosure is not required if the property has been remediated to the states standards by a contractor who is certified by the state. Landlords who themselves did not cause the contamination, and who have obtained documentation of decontamination that they have provided to tenants, will not be liable in a tenant's lawsuit for damages. (Mont. Code Ann. § 75-10-1305)

Required Landlord Disclosures (continued)

Nebraska

Owner or agent identity: The landlord or any person authorized to enter into a rental agreement on his or her behalf shall disclose to the tenant in writing at or before the commencement of the tenancy the name and address of the person authorized to manage the premises; and an owner of the premises or a person authorized to act for and on behalf of the owner for the purpose of service of process receiving notices and demands. (Neb. Rev. Stat. § 76-1417)

Nevada

Nonrefundable fees permitted? Yes. Lease must explain fees that are required and the purposes for which they are required. (Nev. Rev. Stat. Ann. § 118A.200)

Move-in checklist required? Yes. Lease must include tenants' rights to a checklist and a signed record of the inventory and condition of the premises under the exclusive custody and control of the tenant. (Nev. Rev. Stat. Ann. § 118A.200)

Nuisance and flying the flag: Lease must include a summary of the provisions of NRS 202.470 (penalties for permitting or maintaining a nuisance); information regarding the procedure a tenant may use to report to the appropriate authorities a nuisance, a violation of a building, safety, or health code or regulation; and information regarding the right of the tenant to engage in the display of the flag of the United States, as set forth in NRS 118A.325. (Nev. Rev. Stat. Ann. § 118A.200)

Foreclosure proceedings: Landlord must disclose to any prospective tenant, in writing, whether the premises to be rented is the subject of a foreclosure proceeding (disclosure need not be in the lease). (Nev. Rev. Stat. Ann. § 118A.275)

Lease signed by an agent of the landlord who does not hold a property management permit: In single-family rentals only, unless the lease is signed by an authorized agent of the landlord who holds a current property management permit, the top of the first page of the lease must state, in font that is at least twice the size of any other size in the agreement, that the tenant might not have valid occupancy unless the lease is notarized or signed by an authorized agent of the owner who holds a management permit. The notice must give the current address and phone number of the landlord. In

addition, it must state that even if the foregoing has not been provided, the agreement is enforceable against the landlord. (Nev. Rev. Stat. Ann. § 118A.200)

New Hampshire

Move-in checklist required? Yes. Landlord must inform tenant that if tenant finds any conditions in the rental in need of repair, tenant may note them on the security deposit receipt or other writing (not a true checklist). (N.H. Rev. Stat. Ann. § 540-A:6)

Methamphetamine: If methamphetamine was produced on a property and the department of environmental sciences has not determined that the property meets remediation cleanup standards, the landlord must disclose in writing to the tenant that methamphetamine production has occurred. (N.H. Rev. Stat. § 477:4-g)

New Jersey

Flood zone: Prior to move-in, landlord must inform tenant if rental is in a flood zone or area (does not apply to properties containing two or fewer dwelling units, or to owner-occupied properties of three or fewer units). (N.J. Stat. Ann. § 46:8-50.)

Truth in Renting Act: Except in buildings of two or fewer units, and owner-occupied premises of three or fewer units, landlord must distribute to new tenants at or prior to move-in the Department of Community Affairs' statement of legal rights and responsibilities of tenants and landlords of rental dwelling units (Spanish also). (N.J. Stat. Ann. §§ 46:8-44, 46:8-45, 46:8-46.)

Child protection window guards: Landlords of multi-family properties must include information in the lease about tenants' rights to request window guards. The Legislature's Model Lease and Notice clause reads as follows: "The owner (landlord) is required by law to provide, install and maintain window guards in the apartment if a child or children 10 years of age or younger is, or will be, living in the apartment or is, or will be, regularly present there for a substantial period of time if the tenant gives the owner (landlord) a written request that the window guards be installed. The owner (landlord) is also required, upon the written request of the tenant, to provide, install and maintain window guards in the hallways to which persons in the tenant's unit have access without having to go out of the

Required Landlord Disclosures (continued)

building. If the building is a condominium, cooperative or mutual housing building, the owner (landlord) of the apartment is responsible for installing and maintaining window guards in the apartment and the association is responsible for installing and maintaining window guards in hallway windows. Window guards are only required to be provided in first floor windows where the window sill is more than six feet above grade or there are other hazardous conditions that make installation of window guards necessary to protect the safety of children." The notice must be conspicuous and in boldface type. (N.J. Stat. Ann. § 55:13A-7.14; N.J. Admin. Code §§ 5:10-27.1, 5:10-27 App. 27A)

Water quality: Owners of multifamily properties who must prepare a Consumer Confidence Report, or who receive such a report from a public community water system, must post the report in every routinely used common area (if the property has no such area, owners must give copies to each rental unit). Owners of multifamily properties who supply water, who are not required to prepare a Consumer Confidence Report, but who must test its water, must post a chart containing the results of the tests. Charts must be posted in every routinely used common area (if the property has no such area, owners must give copies to each rental unit). (N.J. Stat. Ann. § 55:13A-7.18)

Application fee: Landlords cannot collect application fees without first disclosing in writing to the applicant whether the landlord will review and consider criminal history and a statement that the applicant may provide evidence demonstrating inaccuracies within the applicant's criminal record or evidence of rehabilitation or other mitigating factors. (N.J. Stat. Ann. § 46:8-55)

Postings in multiple dwellings: Landlords of tenant-occupied multiple dwellings must post in a conspicuous area where likely to be seen by tenants the following information in both English and Spanish: (1) emergency contact info for the owner or managing agent (2) instructions on how to access and use the comprehensive social services information toll-free telephone hotline. The information must also be posted on the website of any management company that manages a tenant-occupied multiple dwelling. (N.J. Stat. Ann. § 55:13A-7.19(1)(a))

Multiple dwelling lease disclosure: Every lease offered to a tenant in a multiple dwelling must include in both English and Spanish: (1) the website address of the management company and (2) instructions on how to access and use the comprehensive social services information toll-free telephone hotline. (N.J. Stat. Ann. § 55:13A-7.19(1)(b))

New Mexico

Owner or agent identity: Landlord must disclose to the tenant in writing at or before the commencement of the tenancy the name and address of the person authorized to manage the premises, and an owner of the premises or a person authorized to act for and on behalf of the owner for the purpose of service of process and for the purpose of receiving notices and demands. (N.M. Stat. Ann. § 47-8-19)

Illegal drug lab on premises: Landlord cannot rent a property where controlled substances were manufactured or located unless landlord provides written notice to tenant of these facts. The tenant must acknowledge receipt of the notice in writing, and the landlord must provide a copy of the notice and acknowledgement to the New Mexico environment department. (N.M. Admin. Code § 20.4.5.13)

New York

Nonrefundable fees permitted? No. (N.Y. Gen. Oblig. Laws § 7-108)

Move-in checklist required? Yes. Tenants are entitled to a pre-move out inspection unless tenant terminates with less than two weeks' notice. (N.Y. Gen. Oblig. Laws § 7-108).

Must fee policy be stated in the rental agreement? No. (N.Y. Gen. Oblig. Laws § 7-108)

Air Contamination: Landlord who receives a government report showing that air in the building has, or may have, concentrations of volatile organic compounds (VOCs) that exceed governmental guidelines must give written notice to prospective and current tenants. The notice must appear in at least 12-point bold face type on the first page of the lease or rental agreement. It must read as follows: "NOTIFICATION OF TEST RESULTS The property has been tested, for contamination of indoor air: test results and additional information are available upon request." (N.Y. Envtl. Conserv. Law § 27-2405)

Required Landlord Disclosures (continued)

Certificate of occupancy: In structures with three or fewer dwelling units, where a certificate of occupancy is required by law, landlords must provide prospective tenants proof of a current certificate prior to signing a lease or rental agreement. Landlords may provide prospective tenants with a copy of the actual certificate, or provide notice of said certificate in bold face type. Waivers of this requirement are void. (N.Y. Real Prop. Law § 235-bb)

Smoke detectors: In multifamily buildings of three or more units, condominiums, and cooperatives located in towns, villages, and cities with populations less than 325,000, landlord must notify tenants in writing, individually or by posting a notice in a common area, of owners' and tenants' duties regarding smoke detectors. (N.Y. Mult. Res. Law §§ 4, 15)

Reasonable accommodation: Landlords must give all tenants and prospective tenants a written notice of their right to request reasonable modifications and accommodations for their disability. The notice must be posted in all vacant available rentals and given to all current tenants within 30 days of the beginning of their tenancy. The notice must contain information about where to file complaints and any other information the Division of Human Rights requires. (N.Y. Exec. Law § 170-d)

North Carolina

Going to court fees: Yes, Landlord may collect only one of the following, when specific conditions are met: Complaint filing fee, court appearance fee, and second trial fee. Failure to pay the fees cannot support a termination notice. (N.C. Gen. Stat. § 42-46)

Eviction fees: If landlords wish to collect fees relating to eviction, they must specify certain types of fees in a written lease. Landlords must disclose their right to collect reasonable attorneys' fees, which cannot exceed 15% of the amount owed by the tenant, or 15% of the monthly rent stated in the lease if the eviction is based on a default other than the nonpayment of rent. Landlords must also disclose the fees they will charge for filing a complaint, to appear in court, and for their second trial (landlord can charge and retain only one of these fees). (N.C. Gen. Stat. Ann. § 42-46)

Attorneys' fees and costs: Landlords cannot charge tenants for attorneys' fees and costs without making certain disclosures. See State Laws on Attorneys' Fees and Court Costs Clauses chart in this appendix. (N.C. Gen. Stat. Ann. § 42-46)

North Dakota

Move-in checklist required? Yes. Landlord must give tenant a statement describing the condition of the premises when tenant signs the rental agreement. Both parties must sign the statement. (N.D. Cent. Code § 47-16-07.2)

Ohio

Owner or agent identity: Every written rental agreement must contain the name and address of the owner and the name and address of the owner's agent, if any. If the owner or the owner's agent is a corporation, partnership, limited partnership, association, trust, or other entity, the address must be the principal place of business in the county in which the residential property is situated. If there is no place of business in such county, then its principal place of business in this state must be disclosed, including the name of the person in charge thereof. (Ohio Rev. Code Ann. § 5321.18)

Oklahoma

Flooding: If the premises to be rented has been flooded within the past five (5) years and such fact is known to the landlord, the landlord shall include such information prominently and in writing as part of any written rental agreements. (Okla. Stat. Ann. tit. 41, § 113a)

Owner information: As a part of any rental agreement the lessor shall prominently and in writing identify what person at what address is entitled to accept service or notice under this act. Landlord must disclose to the tenant in writing at or before the commencement of the tenancy the name and address of the person authorized to manage the premises, and an owner of the premises or a person authorized to act for and on behalf of the owner for the purpose of service of process and receiving notices and demands. (Okla. Stat. Ann. tit. 41, § 116)

Smoke detectors: Landlord must explain to tenant how to test the smoke detector to ensure that it is in working order. (Okla. Stat. Ann. tit. 74, § 324.11a)

Required Landlord Disclosures (continued)

Methamphetamine: Before signing a rental agreement, if the landlord knows or has reason to know that the unit or any part of the premises was used in the manufacture of methamphetamine, the landlord must disclose this information to a prospective tenant. Does not apply when the landlord has tested the unit or premises and the results show that the level of contamination is less than 0.1 mcg per 100cm2 of surface materials in the affected part. (Okla. Stat. Ann. tit. 41, § 118)

Tenant repairs, maintenance, alterations, or remodeling: When landlord and tenant agree that the tenant will perform specified repairs, maintenance tasks, alterations, or remodeling, they must put this agreement in writing, independent of the rental agreement, and presented in a manner that will make it hard to overlook (using ample font size, for example). (Okla. Stat. Ann. tit. 41, § 118)

Oregon

Nonrefundable fees permitted? No. (Or. Rev. Stat. § 90.302)

Must fee policy be stated in the rental agreement? Yes

Other fees? Landlords' written rules may not provide for tenant fees, except for specified events as they arise, including a late rent payment; tenant's late payment of a utility or service charge; a dishonored check, pursuant to Or. Rev. Stat. Ann. § 30.701(5); failure to clean up pet waste in areas other than tenant's unit; failure to clean up garbage and rubbish (outside tenant's dwelling unit); failure to clean pet waste of a service or companion animal from areas other than the dwelling unit; parking violations and improper use of vehicles within the premises; smoking in a designated nonsmoking area; keeping an unauthorized pet capable of inflicting damage on persons or property; and tampering or disabling a smoke detector.

Owner or agent identity: Landlord must disclose to the tenant in writing at or before the commencement of the tenancy the name and address of the person authorized to manage the premises, and an owner of the premises or a person authorized to act for and on behalf of the owner for the purpose of service of process and for the purpose of receiving notices and demands. (Or. Rev. Stat. Ann. § 90.305)

Legal proceedings: If at the time of the execution of a rental agreement for a dwelling unit in premises containing no more than four dwelling units the premises are subject to any of the following circumstances, the landlord must disclose that circumstance to the tenant in writing before the execution of the rental agreement:

a. Any outstanding notice of default under a trust deed, mortgage, or contract of sale, or notice of trustee's sale under a trust deed;

b. Any pending suit to foreclose a mortgage, trust deed, or vendor's lien under a contract of sale;

c. Any pending declaration of forfeiture or suit for specific performance of a contract of sale; or

d. Any pending proceeding to foreclose a tax lien.

(Or. Rev. Stat. § 90.310)

Utilities: The landlord must disclose to the tenant in writing at or before the commencement of the tenancy any utility or service that the tenant pays directly to a utility or service provider that directly benefits the landlord or other tenants. A tenant's payment for a given utility or service benefits the landlord or other tenants if the utility or service is delivered to any area other than the tenant's dwelling unit.

A landlord may require a tenant to pay to the landlord a utility or service charge that has been billed by a utility or service provider to the landlord for utility or service provided directly to the tenant's dwelling unit or to a common area available to the tenant as part of the tenancy. A utility or service charge that shall be assessed to a tenant for a common area must be described in the written rental agreement separately and distinctly from such a charge for the tenant's dwelling unit. Unless the method of allocating the charges to the tenant is described in the tenant's written rental agreement, the tenant may require that the landlord give the tenant a copy of the provider's bill as a condition of paying the charges. (Or. Rev. Stat. Ann. § 90.315)

Recycling: In a city or the county within the urban growth boundary of a city that has implemented multifamily recycling service, a landlord who has five or more residential dwelling units on a single premises must notify new tenants at the time of entering into a rental agreement of the opportunity to recycle. (Or. Rev. Stat. Ann. § 90.318)

Required Landlord Disclosures (continued)

Smoking policy: Landlord must disclose the smoking policy for the premises, by stating whether smoking is prohibited on the premises, allowed on the entire premises, or allowed in limited areas. If landlord allows smoking in limited areas, the disclosure must identify those areas. (Or. Rev. Stat. Ann. § 90.220)

Carbon monoxide alarm instructions: If rental contains a CO source (a heater, fireplace, appliance, or cooking source that uses coal, kerosene, petroleum products, wood, or other fuels that emit carbon monoxide as a by product of combustion; or an attached garage with an opening that communicates directly with a living space), landlord must install one or more CO monitors and give tenant written instructions for testing the alarm(s), before tenant takes possession. (Or. Rev. Stat. Ann. §§ 90.316, 90.317)

Smoke alarm or smoke detector: When tenant moves in, landlord must give tenant written instructions for testing smoke alarms and smoke detectors. (Or. Rev. Stat. Ann. § 479.270)

Flood zone: If a dwelling unit is located in a 100-year flood plain, the landlord must provide notice in the dwelling unit rental agreement that the dwelling unit is located within the flood plain. If a landlord fails to provide a notice as required under this section, and the tenant of the dwelling unit suffers an uninsured loss due to flooding, the tenant may recover from the landlord the lesser of the actual damages for the uninsured loss or two months' rent. (Or. Rev. Stat. Ann. § 90.228)

Renters' insurance: Landlord may require tenants to maintain liability insurance (certain low-income and subsidized tenancies excepted), but only if the landlord obtains and maintains comparable liability insurance and provides documentation to any tenant who requests the documentation, orally or in writing. The landlord may provide documentation to a tenant in person, by mail, or by posting in a common area or office. The documentation may consist of a current certificate of coverage. Any landlord who requires tenants to obtain renters' insurance must disclose the requirement and amount in writing prior to entering into a new tenancy, and may require the tenant to provide documentation before the tenancy begins. (Or. Rev. Stat. Ann. § 90.222)

Homeowner Assessments: If landlord wants to pass on homeowners' association assessments that are imposed on anyone moving into or out of the unit, the written rental agreement must include this requirement. Landlord must give tenants a copy of each assessment before charging the tenant. (Or. Rev. Stat. Ann. § 90.302)

Applicant screening fees: Before accepting application fees, landlords must, among other things, disclose in writing to the applicant (1) the amount of the screening charge (2) the landlord's criteria for selection (3) the screening process and considerations (4) the applicant's right to dispute information in a screening report (5) required nondiscrimination policies (6) the amount of rent and deposits, and (7) whether the landlord requires renters' insurance (and how much). (Or. Rev. Stat. Ann. § 90.295)

Pennsylvania

No disclosure statutes.

Rhode Island

Owner disclosure: Landlord must disclose to the tenant in writing at or before the commencement of the tenancy the name and address of the person authorized to manage the premises, and an owner of the premises or a person authorized to act for and on behalf of the owner for the purpose of service of process and for the purpose of receiving notices and demands. (R.I. Gen. Laws § 34-18-20)

Code violations: Before entering into any residential rental agreement, landlord must inform a prospective tenant of any outstanding minimum housing code violations that exist on the building that is the subject of the rental agreement. (R.I. Gen. Laws § 34-18-22.1)

Notice of Foreclosure: A landlord who becomes delinquent on a mortgage securing real estate upon which the rental is located for a period of 120 days must notify the tenant that the property may be subject to foreclosure; and until the foreclosure occurs, the tenant must continue to pay rent to the landlord as provided under the rental agreement. (R.I. Gen. Laws § 34-18-20)

General liability insurance policy: Landlords must provide a copy of the declaration page from the landlord's general liability policy with the lease, and must provide tenants with a new copy each time the policy is renewed. (R.I. Gen. Laws § 34-18-22)

Required Landlord Disclosures (continued)

South Carolina

Owner or agent identity: Landlord must disclose to the tenant in writing at or before the commencement of the tenancy the name and address of the person authorized to manage the premises, and an owner of the premises or a person authorized to act for and on behalf of the owner for the purpose of service of process and for the purpose of receiving notices and demands. (S.C. Code Ann. § 27-40-420)

Unequal security deposits: If landlord rents five or more adjoining units on the premises, and imposes different standards for calculating deposits required of tenants, landlord must, before a tenancy begins, post in a conspicuous place a statement explaining the standards by which the various deposits are calculated (or, landlord may give the tenant the written statement). (S.C. Code Ann. § 27-40-410)

Smoke detectors: When tenant moves in, owner must give tenant written or verbal instructions, or both, for testing the detectors and replacing batteries in battery-powered detectors. (S.C. Code Ann. § 5-25-1330)

South Dakota

Methamphetamine contamination: Landlord who has actual knowledge of the existence of any prior manufacturing of methamphetamines on the premises must disclose that information to any lessee or any person who may become a lessee. If the residential premises consists of two or more housing units, the disclosure requirements apply only to the unit where there is knowledge of the existence of any prior manufacturing of methamphetamines. (S.D. Codified Laws Ann. § 43-32-30)

Tennessee

Owner or agent identity: The landlord or any person authorized to enter into a rental agreement on the landlord's behalf must disclose to the tenant in writing at or before the commencement of the tenancy the name and address of the agent authorized to manage the premises, and an owner of the premises or a person or agent authorized to act for and on behalf of the owner for the acceptance of service of process and for receipt of notices and demands. (Tenn. Code Ann. § 66-28-302)

Showing rental to prospective tenants: Landlord may enter to show the premises to prospective renters during the final 30 days of a tenancy (with 24 hours' notice), but only if this right of access is set forth in the rental agreement or lease. (Tenn. Code Ann. § 66-28-403)

Texas

Nonrefundable fees permitted? Yes. Landlords cannot collect late fees unless notice of the fee is included in a written lease. (Tex. Prop. Code Ann. § 92.019) (*Holmes v. Canlen Management Corp.*, 542 S.W.2d 199 (1976))

Owner or agent identity: In the lease, other writing, or posted on the property, landlord must disclose the name and address of the property's owner and, if an entity located off-site from the dwelling is primarily responsible for managing the dwelling, the name and street address of the management company. (Tex. Prop. Code Ann. § 92.201)

Emergency contact information: Landlords must provide tenants with an emergency phone number to call when there is a condition affecting physical health or safety of tenant. (Tex. Prop. Code Ann. § 92.020)

Security device requests: If landlord wants tenant requests concerning security devices to be in writing, this requirement must be in the lease in boldface type or underlined. (Tex. Prop. Code Ann. § 92.159)

Return of security deposit: A requirement that a tenant give advance notice of moving out as a condition for refunding the security deposit is effective only if the requirement is in the lease, underlined or printed in conspicuous bold print. (Tex. Prop. Code Ann. § 92.103)

Domestic violence victims' rights: Victims of sexual abuse or assault on the premises may break a lease, after complying with specified procedures, without responsibility for future rent. Tenants will be responsible for any unpaid back rent, but only if the lease includes the following statement, or one substantially like it: "Tenants may have special statutory rights to terminate the lease early in certain situations involving family violence or a military deployment or transfer." (Tex. Prop. Code Ann. § 92.016)

Required Landlord Disclosures (continued)

Tenant's rights when landlord fails to repair: A lease must contain language in underlined or bold print that informs the tenant of the remedies available when the landlord fails to repair a problem that materially affects the physical health or safety of an ordinary tenant. These rights include the right to: repair and deduct; terminate the lease; and obtain a judicial order that the landlord make the repair, reduce the rent, pay the tenant damages (including a civil penalty), and pay the tenant's court and attorneys' fees. (Tex. Prop. Code Ann. § 92.056)

Landlord's towing or parking rules and policies: For tenants in multiunit properties, if the landlord has vehicle towing or parking rules or policies that apply to the tenant, the landlord must give the tenant a copy of the rules or policies before the lease agreement is signed. The copy must be signed by the tenant, included in the lease or rental agreement, or be made an attachment to either. If included, the clause must be titled "Parking" or "Parking Rules" and be capitalized, underlined, or printed in bold print.) (Tex. Prop. Code Ann. § 92.0131.)

Electric service interruption: Landlord who submeters electric service, or who allocates master metered electricity according to a prorated system, may interrupt tenant's electricity service if tenant fails to pay the bill, but only after specific notice and according to a complex procedure. Exceptions for ill tenants and during extreme weather. (Tex. Prop. Code Ann. § 92.008(h))

Selection criteria for applicants: At the time landlords provide prospective tenants with applications, they must also provide printed notice of their tenant selection criteria, including reasons why applications may be denied. The notice must contain certain acknowledgement language that the applicant must sign. (Tex. Prop. Code Ann. § 92.3515)

Fee in lieu of security deposit: If a landlord offers a tenant the option of paying a fee in lieu of a security deposit, the landlord must notify the tenant in writing that (1) the tenant has the option to pay a fee instead of a deposit (2) that the tenant can terminate the agreement to pay a fee in lieu of a deposit at any time and pay a security deposit instead, and (3) the charges for the options. All agreements to pay a fee instead of a security deposit must be in writing. (Tex. Prop. Code Ann. § 92.111)

Floodplain disclosure: Landlords must provide tenants with written notice stating the substantial equivalent of: "Landlord ( ) is or ( ) is not aware that the dwelling you are renting is located in a 100-year floodplain. If neither box is checked, you should assume the dwelling is in a 100-year floodplain. Even if the dwelling is not in a 100-year floodplain, the dwelling may still be susceptible to flooding. The Federal Emergency Management Agency (FEMA) maintains a flood map on its Internet website that is searchable by address, at no cost, to determine if a dwelling is located in a flood hazard area. Most tenant insurance policies do not cover damages or loss incurred in a flood. You should seek insurance coverage that would cover losses caused by a flood." If the landlord knows that flooding has damaged any portion of a dwelling at least once during the five-year period immediately preceding the effective date of the lease, the landlord shall provide a written notice to tenant that's substantially equivalent to: "Landlord ( ) is or ( ) is not aware that the dwelling you are renting has flooded at least once within the last five years." These notices must be given to the tenant in a separate written document at or before the execution of the lease. (Tex. Prop. Code Ann. § 92.0135)

Utah

Nonrefundable fees permitted? Yes. All fees, fines, assessments, interest, or other costs must be included in the lease or rental agreement, unless the rental agreement is on a month-to-month basis and the landlord provides the renter a 15-day notice of the charge. (Utah Code Ann. § 57-22-4)

If there's a written agreement and if any part of the deposit is to be made non-refundable, the landlord must put this in writing at the time the deposit is collected. (Utah Code Ann. § 57-17-2)

Move-in checklists required? Yes. Landlords must give prospective renters a written inventory of the condition of the residential rental unit, excluding ordinary wear and tear; give the renter a form to document the condition of the residential rental and allow the resident a reasonable time after the renter's occupancy of the unit to complete and return the form; or provide the prospective renter an opportunity to conduct a walkthrough inspection of the rental. (Utah Code. Ann. § 57-17-4)

Required Landlord Disclosures (continued)

Applicant Disclosures: Before accepting an application or collecting an application fee, landlord must disclose whether the rental unit is expected to be available, and the criteria landlord will use in evaluating potential renter's application. Failure to comply will not invalidate the lease or provide tenant with a legal cause of action. (Utah Code Ann. § 57-22-4)

Disclosure of management: Before the tenancy begins, the landlord must disclose in writing the owner's name, address, and telephone number or the name, address, and telephone number of any person authorized to manage the rental or act on behalf of the owner and re-ceive notices. (Utah Code Ann. § 57-22-4)

Disclosure of rules: Before the tenancy begins, the land-lord must provide the renter with a copy of any rules and regulations applicable to the rental. The landlord must also provide a signed copy of the written lease or rental agreement. (Utah Code Ann. § 57-22-4)

Methamphetamine contamination: If landlord has actual knowledge that the property is currently con-taminated from the use, storage, or manufacture of methamphetamine, the landlord must disclose that the property is contaminated in the lease. (Utah Code Ann. § 57-27-201)

Vermont

No disclosure statutes.

Virginia

Move-in checklist required? Within five days of move-in, landlord or tenant or both together must prepare a written report detailing the condition of the premises. Landlord must disclose within this report the known presence of mold. (Va. Code Ann. § 55.1-1214)

Tenant rights and responsibilities: Landlords shall offer prospective tenants a written lease or rental agreement that contains the terms of the tenancy and provide with it the statement of tenant rights and responsibilities developed by the Department of Housing and Community Development. (Va. Code Ann. § 55.1-1204)

Renters' insurance: If the lease or rental agreement doesn't require the tenant to obtain renters' insurance, the landlord must provide a written notice to the tenant before signing the lease or rental agreement stating that (1) the landlord isn't responsible for the tenant's personal property (2) the landlord's insurance doesn't cover the tenant's personal property (3) if the tenant wishes to protect personal property, the tenant should purchase renter's insurance; and (4) that any renter's insurance obtained by tenant won't cover flood damage and the renter should find out whether the property is in a special flood hazard area. (Va. Code Ann. § 55.1-1206)

Owner or agent identity: Landlord must disclose to the tenant in writing at or before the commencement of the tenancy the name and address of the person authorized to manage the premises, and an owner of the premises or a person authorized to act for and on behalf of the owner for the purpose of service of process and for the purpose of receiving notices and demands. (Va. Code Ann. § 55.1-1216)

Sale plans: In the event of the sale of the premises, the landlord must notify tenants of the sale and disclose to tenants the name and address of the purchaser and a telephone number for contacting the purchaser. (Va. Code Ann. § 55.1-1216)

Military zone: The landlord of property in any locality in which a military air installation is located, or any person authorized to enter into a rental agreement on landlord's behalf, must provide to a prospective tenant a written disclosure that the property is located in a noise zone or accident potential zone, or both, as designated by the locality on its official zoning map. (Va. Code Ann. § 55.1-1217)

Mold: Move-in inspection report must include whether there is any visible evidence of mold (deemed correct unless tenant objects within five days); if evidence is present, tenant may terminate or not move in. If tenant stays, landlord must remediate the mold condition within five business days, reinspect, and issue a new report indicating that there is no evidence of mold. (Va. Code Ann. § 55.1-1215)

Ratio utility billing: Landlords who use a ratio utility billing service or who intend to collect monthly billing and other administrative and late fees, must disclose these fees in a written rental agreement. (Va. Code Ann. § 55.1-1212)

Required Landlord Disclosures (continued)

Condominium plans: If an application for registration as a condominium or cooperative has been filed with the Real Estate Board, or if there is within six months an existing plan for tenant displacement resulting from demolition or substantial rehabilitation of the property, or conversion of the rental property to office, hotel, or motel use or planned unit development, the landlord or any person authorized to enter into a rental agreement on his behalf must disclose that information in writing to any prospective tenant. (Va. Code Ann. § 55.1-1216)

Defective drywall: Landlords who know of the presence of unrepaired defective drywall in the rental must disclose this before the tenant signs a lease or rental agreement. (Va. Code Ann. § 55.1-1218)

Methamphetamine: When the landlord knows that the unit was used to manufacture methamphetamine, landlord must give the tenant a written disclosure of this use before the tenant signs a lease, if the unit hasn't been mitigated as required by law. (Va. Code Ann. § 55.1-1219)

Insecticide/pesticide application: A. Landlords must give tenants written notice no less than 48 hours prior to applying an insecticide or pesticide in the tenant's dwelling unit unless the tenant agrees to a shorter notification period. If a tenant requests the application of the insecticide or pesticide, the 48-hour notice is not required. Tenants who have concerns about specific insecticides or pesticides must notify the landlord in writing no less than 24 hours before the scheduled insecticide or pesticide application. The tenant shall prepare the dwelling unit for the application of insecticides or pesticides in accordance with any written instructions of the landlord and, if insects or pests are found to be present, follow any written instructions of the landlord to eliminate the insects or pests following the application of insecticides or pesticides. In addition, landlords must post notice of all insecticide or pesticide applications in areas of the rental other than the dwelling units. Such notice shall consist of conspicuous signs placed in or upon the rental where the insecticide or pesticide will be applied at least 48 hours prior to the application. (Va. Code Ann. § 55.1-1223)

Washington

Move-in checklists required? Yes. Checklists are required when landlords collect a security deposit. If landlord fails to provide checklist, landlord is liable to the tenant for the amount of the deposit. (Wash. Rev. Code Ann. § 59.18.260)

Nonrefundable fees permitted? Yes. If landlord collects a nonrefundable fee, the rental document must clearly specify that it is nonrefundable. Landlords cannot collect fees to put a prospective tenant on a waitlist for a rental. (Wash. Rev. Code Ann. § 59.18.285)

Fire protection: At the time the lease is signed, landlord must provide fire protection and safety information, including whether the building has a smoking policy, an emergency notification plan, or an evacuation plan. (Wash. Rev. Code Ann. § 59.18.060)

Owner or agent identity: In the rental document or posted conspicuously on the premises, landlord must designate to the tenant the name and address of the person who is the landlord by a statement on the rental agreement or by a notice conspicuously posted on the premises. If the person designated does not reside in Washington, landlord must also designate a person who resides in the county to act as an agent for the purposes of service of notices and process. (Wash. Rev. Code Ann. § 59.18.060)

Mold: At the time the lease is signed, landlord must provide tenant with information provided or approved by the department of health about the health hazards associated with exposure to indoor mold. (Wash. Rev. Code Ann. § 59.18.060)

Screening criteria: Before obtaining any information about an applicant, landlord must provide (in writing or by posting) the type of information to be accessed, criteria to be used to evaluate the application, and (for consumer reports) the name and address of the consumer reporting agency to be used, including the applicant's rights to obtain a free copy of the report and dispute its accuracy. Landlord must advise tenants whether landlord will accept a comprehensive reusable

Required Landlord Disclosures (continued)

tenant screening report done by a consumer reporting agency (in which case the landlord may not charge the tenant a fee for a screening report). If landlord maintains a website that advertises residential rentals, the home page must include this information. (Wash. Rev. Code Ann. § 59.18.257)

Tenant screening fee: Landlords who do their own screening may charge a fee for time and costs to obtain background information, but only if they provide the information explained in "Screening Criteria," above. (Wash. Rev. Code Ann. § 59.18.257.)

Holding deposits: Fees or deposits to hold a rental cannot exceed 25% of the first months rent. Upon receipt of the fee or deposit, landlords must issue a receipt and a written statement of the conditions, if any, under which the fee or deposit may be retained. (Wash. Rev. Code Ann. § 59.18.253)

West Virginia

Nonrefundable fees permitted? Yes. Nonrefundable fee must be expressly agreed to in writing. (W.Va. Code § 37-6A-1(14))

Carbon monoxide (CO): Anyone who installs a CO detector in a rental unit must inform either the owner, landlord, or resident of the dangers of CO poisoning, and must supply instructions on how to operate the detector. When landlords work on fuel-burning heating or cooking equipment or a units venting system, they must inform tenants of the dangers of CO poisoning and recommend the purchase of a CO detector.

Any landlord who performs repair or maintenance work on a fuel-burning heating or cooking source or a venting system in a rental unit must inform the tenant of the dangers of carbon monoxide poisoning and recommend the installation of a carbon monoxide detector. (W.Va. Code § 15A-10-12)

Methamphetamine: Landlord who has successfully cleaned up a meth lab must give potential tenants the certificate of remediation that was issued by the West Virginia Department of Health and Human Resources. (W.Va. Code § 64-92-6)

Wisconsin

Move-in checklist required? Yes. Tenant has a right to inspect the rental and give landlord a list of defects, and to receive a list of damages charged to the prior tenant. Tenant has 7 days after start of the tenancy to return the list to the landlord. (Wis. Admin. Code § 134.06; Wis. Stat. Ann. § 704.08)

Owner or agent identity: Landlord must disclose to the tenant in writing, at or before the time a rental agreement is signed, the name and address of: the person or persons authorized to collect or receive rent and manage and maintain the premises, and who can readily be contacted by the tenant; and the owner of the premises or other person authorized to accept service of legal process and other notices and demands on behalf of the owner. The address must be an address within the state at which service of process can be made in person. (Wis. Admin. Code § 134.04)

Nonstandard rental provisions: If landlord wants to enter premises for reasons not specified by law, landlord must disclose the provision in a separate written document entitled "NONSTANDARD RENTAL PROVISIONS" before the rental agreement is signed. (Wis. Admin. Code § 134.09)

Uncorrected code violations: Before signing a rental contract or accepting a security deposit, the landlord must disclose to the tenant any uncorrected code violation of which the landlord is actually aware, that affects the dwelling unit or a common area and poses a significant threat to the tenant's health or safety. "Disclosure" consists of showing prospective tenants the portions of the building affected, as well as the notices themselves. (Wis. Stat. Ann. § 704.07(2)(bm); Wis. Admin. Code § 134.04)

Habitability deficiencies: Landlord must disclose serious problems that affect the rental unit's habitability. (Wis. Admin. Code § 134.04)

Utility charges: If charges for water, heat, or electricity are not included in the rent, the landlord must disclose this fact to the tenant before entering into a rental agreement or accepting any earnest money or security

Required Landlord Disclosures (continued)

deposit from the prospective tenant. If individual dwelling units and common areas are not separately metered, and if the charges are not included in the rent, the landlord must disclose the basis on which charges for utility services will be allocated among individual dwelling units. (Wis. Admin. Code § 134.04)

Disposing of abandoned property: If landlord intends to immediately dispose of any tenant property left behind after move-out, landlord must notify tenant at the time lease is signed. (But landlord must hold prescription medications and medical equipment for seven days, and must give notice before disposing of vehicles or manufactured homes to owner and any known secured party.) (Wis. Stat. Ann. § 704.05 (5))

Notice of domestic abuse protections: Landlords must include the following notice in the rental agreement or in an addendum to the agreement: "NOTICE OF DOMESTIC ABUSE PROTECTIONS

(1) As provided in section 106.50(5m)(dm) of the Wisconsin statutes, a tenant has a defense to an eviction action if the tenant can prove that the landlord knew, or should have known, the tenant is a victim of domestic abuse, sexual assault, or stalking and that the eviction action is based on conduct related to domestic abuse, sexual assault, or stalking committed by either of the following:

(a) A person who was not the tenant's invited guest.

(b) A person who was the tenant's invited guest, but the tenant has done either of the following:

  1. Sought an injunction barring the person from the premises.

  2. Provided a written statement to the landlord stating that the person will no longer be an invited guest of the tenant and the tenant has not subsequently invited the person to be the tenant's guest.

(2) A tenant who is a victim of domestic abuse, sexual assault, or stalking may have the right to terminate the rental agreement in certain limited situations, as provided in section 704.16 of the Wisconsin statutes. If the tenant has safety concerns, the tenant should contact a local victim service provider or law enforcement agency.

(3) A tenant is advised that this notice is only a summary of the tenant's rights and the specific language of the statutes governs in all instances." (Wis. Stat. Ann. § 704.14)

Wyoming

Nonrefundable fees permitted? Yes. If any portion of the deposit is not refundable, rental agreement must include this information and tenant must be told before paying a deposit. (Wyo. Stat. § 1-21-1207)

State Laws in Domestic Violence Situations

Many states extend special protections to tenants who are victims of domestic violence, governing what the landlord can and cannot do in response to the situation. Most states also have procedures whereby tenants can obtain restraining orders against perpetrators; often the effect of these orders is to ban the perpetrator-tenant from the rental property (these laws are not cited in this chart). For information on obtaining restraining orders, contact local law enforcement..

Alabama

No statute

Alaska

No statute

Arizona

Ariz. Rev. Stat. Ann. §§ 33-1315, 33-1318, 33-1414

- Lease cannot include a waiver of some or all DV rights
- Landlord entitled to proof of DV status
- Early termination right for DV victim
- Lease cannot prohibit calling the police in a DV situation or otherwise penalize DV victim
- DV victim has the right to have the locks changed
- Penalty for falsely reporting domestic violence (including obtaining early termination)
- Perpetrator of DV liable to landlord for resulting damages

Miscellaneous provisions: Enumerated rights apply to victims of domestic violence and victims of a sexual assault in the tenant's residence.

Arkansas

Ark. Code Ann. § 18-16-112

- Landlord entitled to proof of DV status
- Landlord cannot refuse to rent to victim of DV
- Landlord cannot terminate a victim of DV
- Lease cannot prohibit calling the police in a DV situation or otherwise penalize DV victim
- DV victim has the right to have the locks changed
- Perpetrator of DV liable to landlord for resulting damages
- Landlord or court may bifurcate the lease

California

Cal. Civ. Code §§ 1941.5, 1941.6, 1946.7; Cal. Code Civ. Proc. §§ 1161, 1161.3

- Landlord entitled to proof of DV status
- Landlord cannot refuse to rent to victim of DV
- Landlord cannot terminate a victim of DV
- Early termination right for DV victim
- DV is an affirmative defense to an eviction lawsuit
- DV victim has the right to have the locks changed
- Landlord or court may bifurcate the lease
- Landlord has limited right to evict the DV victim

Miscellaneous provisions: Protection against termination includes elder or dependent adults, and extends to crimes that caused injury or death. Documentation need only show with reasonable certainty that the qualifying act occurred. With additional documentation, tenant may move when the victim was not in the tenant's household or the act did not occur within 1,000 feet of the dwelling, when moving is necessary to increase the safety of the tenant or a member of the tenant's immediate family.

Colorado

Colo. Rev. Stat. §§ 13-40-104 (4), 13-40-107.5 (5), 38-12-401, 38-12-402, 38-12-503

- Lease cannot include a waiver of some or all DV rights
- Landlord entitled to proof of DV status
- Landlord cannot terminate a victim of DV
- Early termination right for DV victim
- Lease cannot prohibit calling the police in a DV situation or otherwise penalize DV victim

Miscellaneous provisions: Legal protections extend to victims of unlawful sexual behavior and stalking, as well as domestic violence. Landlords may not disclose that tenants were victims of such acts, except with permission or as required by law. If tenant terminates lease because of these acts, and the tenant provides the landlord with a new address, the landlord may not disclose the new address to any person except with permission or as required by law.

Connecticut

Conn. Gen. Stat. Ann. § 47a-11e

- Landlord entitled to proof of DV status
- Early termination right for DV victim

State Laws in Domestic Violence Situations (continued)

Delaware

Del. Code Ann. tit. 25, §§ 5141(7), 5314(b), 5316

- Landlord entitled to proof of DV status
- Landlord cannot terminate a victim of DV
- Early termination right for DV victim

District of Columbia

D.C. Code Ann. §§ 2-1402.21, 42-3505.07, 42-3505.08

- Lease cannot include a waiver of some or all DV rights
- Landlord entitled to proof of DV status
- Landlord cannot refuse to rent to victim of DV
- Early termination right for DV victim
- DV is an affirmative defense to an eviction lawsuit
- Lease cannot prohibit calling the police in a DV situation or otherwise penalize DV victim
- DV victim has the right to have the locks changed
- Landlord or court may bifurcate the lease

Miscellaneous provisions: Landlord must make reasonable accommodation in restoring or improving security and safety measures that are beyond the landlord's duty of ordinary care and diligence, when such accommodation is necessary to ensure the tenant's security and safety (tenant may be billed for the cost).

Florida

No statute

Georgia

Ga. Code Ann. § 44-7-23

- Lease cannot include a waiver of some or all DV rights
- Landlord entitled to proof of DV status
- Early termination right for DV victim

Miscellaneous provisions: Tenant can terminate without penalty with 30 days' written notice. The notice shall include a copy of the civil family violence order or criminal family violence order, as well a a police report if the order was an ex parte temporary protective order.

Hawaii

Haw. Rev. Stat. §§ 521-80 to 521-82

- Landlord entitled to proof of DV status
- Early termination right for DV victim
- DV victim has the right to have the locks changed

- Penalty for falsely reporting domestic violence (including obtaining early termination)
- Landlord or court may bifurcate the lease

Miscellaneous provisions: Landlord may not disclose information gathered with respect to tenant's exercise of rights under these laws, unless the tenant consents in writing, the information is required or relevant in a lawsuit, or the disclosure is required by law.

Idaho

No statute

Illinois

735 Ill. Comp. Stat. 5/9-106.2; 765 Ill. Comp. Stat. 750/1 through 750/35

- Landlord entitled to proof of DV status
- Early termination right for DV victim
- DV is an affirmative defense to an eviction lawsuit
- DV victim has the right to have the locks changed
- Landlord or court may bifurcate the lease

Miscellaneous provisions: Landlord may not disclose to others that a tenant has exercised a right under the law; violations expose landlord to damages that result up to $2,000, as well as the tenant's attorneys' fees and costs.

Indiana

Ind. Code Ann. §§ 32-31-9-1 through 32-31-9-15

- Landlord entitled to proof of DV status
- Landlord cannot refuse to rent to victim of DV
- Landlord cannot terminate a victim of DV
- Early termination right for DV victim
- Lease cannot prohibit calling the police in a DV situation or otherwise penalize DV victim
- DV victim has the right to have the locks changed

Iowa

Iowa Code §§ 562A.27A, 562A.27B, 562B.25A(3)

- Lease cannot include a waiver of some or all DV rights
- Landlord entitled to proof of DV status
- Landlord cannot terminate a victim of DV
- Lease cannot prohibit calling the police in a DV situation or otherwise penalize DV victim
- Landlord has limited right to evict the DV victim

State Laws in Domestic Violence Situations (continued)

Miscellaneous provisions: Landlord can recover from the tenant the cost to repair damage caused by emergency responders called by tenant. Cities cannot impose penalties against residents or landlords, including fines, permit or license revocations, and evictions, when they had a reasonable belief that emergency assistance was necessary, and it was in fact needed.

Kansas

Kan. Stat. Ann. § 58-25,137

- Lease cannot include a waiver of some or all DV rights
- Landlord entitled to proof of DV status
- Landlord cannot refuse to rent to victim of DV
- Landlord cannot terminate a victim of DV
- Early termination right for DV victim
- DV is an affirmative defense to an eviction lawsuit
- Penalty for falsely reporting domestic violence (including obtaining early termination)
- Landlord or court may bifurcate the lease

Miscellaneous provisions: Protections extend to victims (within the past twelve months) of domestic violence, sexual assault, human trafficking, and stalking. Landlord may impose a reasonable termination fee for victims who seek early termination, but only if this provision is included in the terms of the rental agreement or lease. Court may impose statutory damages of $1,000 and reasonable attorneys' fees and costs on landlords who violate the statute.

Kentucky

Ky. Rev. Stat. Ann. §§ 383.300, 383.302

- Lease cannot include a waiver of some or all DV rights
- Landlord entitled to proof of DV status
- Landlord cannot refuse to rent to victim of DV
- Landlord cannot terminate a victim of DV
- Early termination right for DV victim
- DV is an affirmative defense to an eviction lawsuit
- DV victim has the right to have the locks changed
- Perpetrator of DV liable to landlord for resulting damages
- Landlord or court may bifurcate the lease

Louisiana

La. Rev. Stat. Ann. § 9:3261.1

- Lease cannot include a waiver of some or all DV rights
- Landlord entitled to proof of DV status
- Landlord cannot refuse to rent to victim of DV
- Landlord cannot terminate a victim of DV
- Early termination right for DV victim
- Lease cannot prohibit calling the police in a DV situation or otherwise penalize DV victim

Miscellaneous provisions: Statute applies only to multifamily housing of six or more units; does not apply if building has ten or fewer units and one is occupied by the owner.

Maine

Me. Rev. Stat. Ann. tit. 14, §§ 6000, 6001, 6002, 6025

- Landlord entitled to proof of DV status
- Landlord cannot terminate a victim of DV
- Early termination right for DV victim
- DV victim has the right to have the locks changed
- Perpetrator of DV liable to landlord for resulting damages
- Landlord or court may bifurcate the lease

Miscellaneous provisions: Landlord may terminate and/or bifurcate the lease with 7 days' notice when a tenant perpetrates domestic violence, sexual assault, or stalking (against another tenant, a tenant's guest, or the landlord or landlord's employee or agent), and the victim is also a tenant.

Maryland

Md. Code Ann. [Real Prop.] §§ 8-5A-01 through 8-5A-06

- Landlord entitled to proof of DV status
- Early termination right for DV victim
- DV is an affirmative defense to an eviction lawsuit

Massachusetts

Mass Gen. Laws ch. 186, §§ 24, 25, 26, and 28; ch. 239, § 2A

- Lease cannot include a waiver of some or all DV rights
- Landlord entitled to proof of DV status
- Landlord cannot refuse to rent to victim of DV
- Early termination right for DV victim

State Laws in Domestic Violence Situations (continued)

- DV is an affirmative defense to an eviction lawsuit
- DV victim has the right to have the locks changed

Michigan

Mich. Comp. Laws § 554.601b

- Landlord entitled to proof of DV status
- Early termination right for DV victim
- Landlord or court may bifurcate the lease

Minnesota

Minn. Stat. Ann. §§ 504B.205, 206

- Lease cannot include a waiver of some or all DV rights
- Landlord entitled to proof of DV status
- Landlord cannot terminate a victim of DV
- Early termination right for DV victim
- DV is an affirmative defense to an eviction lawsuit
- Lease cannot prohibit calling the police in a DV situation or otherwise penalize DV victim

Miscellaneous provisions: Landlord must keep information about the domestic violence confidential. In a multitenant situation, termination by one tenant terminates the lease of all, though other tenants may reapply to enter into a new lease. All security deposit is forfeited.

Mississippi

No statute

Missouri

Mo. Rev. Stat. § 441.920

- Landlord entitled to proof of DV status
- Landlord cannot refuse to rent to victim of DV
- Landlord cannot terminate a victim of DV
- Early termination right for DV victim
- DV is an affirmative defense to an eviction lawsuit
- Penalty for falsely reporting domestic violence (including obtaining early termination)

Miscellaneous provisions: Landlord may impose a reasonable termination fee on a tenant who desires to terminate a lease before the expiration of the date of the lease due to status as a DV victim.

Montana

No statute

Nebraska

Neb. Rev. Stat. § 76-1431

- Landlord has limited right to evict the DV victim

Miscellaneous provisions: Landlord's right to unconditionally terminate the lease following on-site criminal acts, sale of illegal substances, or any act that threatens health and safety does not apply if tenant has sought a protective order against the perpetrator or has asked for police help in an effort to bring charges against the perpetrator.

Nevada

Nev. Rev. Stat. Ann. §§ 118A.345, 118A.347, 118A.510

- Lease cannot include a waiver of some or all DV rights
- Landlord entitled to proof of DV status
- Landlord cannot terminate a victim of DV
- Early termination right for DV victim
- DV victim has the right to have the locks changed
- Perpetrator of DV liable to landlord for resulting damages

Miscellaneous provisions: Protections extend to victims of harassment, sexual assault, and stalking, as well as domestic violence. Landlord may not disclose the fact of a tenant's early termination to a prospective landlord; nor may a prospective landlord require an applicant to disclose any prior early terminations.

Antiretaliation protection extended to tenants who are domestic violence victims or who have terminated a rental agreement pursuant to law.

New Hampshire

N.H. Rev. Stat. Ann. § 540:2.VII

- Landlord entitled to proof of DV status
- Landlord cannot terminate a victim of DV
- DV victim has the right to have the locks changed
- Landlord or court may bifurcate the lease

New Jersey

N.J. Stat. Ann. §§ 46:8-9.5 through 46:8-9.12

- Lease cannot include a waiver of some or all DV rights
- Landlord entitled to proof of DV status
- Early termination right for DV victim

State Laws in Domestic Violence Situations (continued)

Miscellaneous provisions: Landlord may not disclose information provided by a tenant that documents domestic violence.

New Mexico

N.M. Stat. Ann. § 47-8-33(J)

- DV is an affirmative defense to an eviction lawsuit
- Landlord or court may bifurcate the lease

New York

N.Y. Real Prop. Law §§ 227-c(2) and 227–d; N.Y. Real Prop. Acts. Law § 744; N.Y. Crim. Proc. Law § 530.13(1); N.Y. Dom. Rel. Law § 240(3)

- Landlord entitled to proof of DV status
- Landlord cannot refuse to rent to victim of DV
- Landlord cannot terminate a victim of DV.
- Early termination right for DV victim
- DV is an affirmative defense to an eviction lawsuit
- Penalty for falsely reporting domestic violence (including obtaining early termination)

Miscellaneous provisions: Victim must follow statutory requirements in order to take advantage of right of early termination. Anti-discrimination protection and eviction protection do not apply to owner-occupied buildings with two or fewer units.

North Carolina

N.C. Gen. Stat. §§ 42-40, 42-42.2, 42-42.3, 42-45.1

- Landlord entitled to proof of DV status
- Landlord cannot refuse to rent to victim of DV
- Early termination right for DV victim
- DV victim has the right to have the locks changed

North Dakota

N.D. Cent. Code §§ 42-45.1, 47-16-17.1

- Landlord entitled to proof of DV status
- Landlord cannot refuse to rent to victim of DV
- Landlord cannot terminate a victim of DV
- Early termination right for DV victim

Miscellaneous provisions: Landlord may not disclose information provided by a tenant that documents domestic violence. Landlords who violate the provisions providing early termination are subject to damages

including actual damages, $1,000, reasonable attorneys' fees, costs, and disbursements.

Perpetrators who have been excluded from the dwelling by court order, as well as any remaining tenants, remain jointly and severally liable for rent and damages.

Ohio

No statute

Oklahoma

Okla. Stat. tit. 41, § 113.3

- Landlord entitled to proof of DV status
- Landlord cannot refuse to rent to victim of DV
- Landlord cannot terminate a victim of DV
- Early termination right for DV victim
- Landlord has limited right to evict the DV victim

Miscellaneous provisions: Victim of DV, sexual violence, or stalking may terminate a lease without liability for future rent, upon written notice accompanied by a protective order (must have been issued within 30 days of the incident). Landlord may not reject an applicant, refuse to renew a tenancy, or terminate a tenancy because the applicant, tenant (or member the household) is a victim (or alleged victim) of DV, sexual violence, or stalking (current protective order not required). Landlord may not reject an applicant or retaliate against a tenant on the grounds that the applicant or tenant has previously terminated a rental agreement because the applicant or tenant is a victim of DV, sexual violence, or stalking.

Oregon

Or. Rev. Stat. §§ 90.449, 90.453, 90.456, 90.459

- Landlord entitled to proof of DV status
- Landlord cannot refuse to rent to victim of DV
- Landlord cannot terminate a victim of DV
- Early termination right for DV victim
- DV is an affirmative defense to an eviction lawsuit
- Lease cannot prohibit calling the police in a DV situation or otherwise penalize DV victim
- DV victim has the right to have the locks changed
- Landlord or court may bifurcate the lease
- Landlord has limited right to evict the DV victim

State Laws in Domestic Violence Situations (continued)

Pennsylvania

53 Pa.C.S.A. § 304; Pa.R.C.P.M.D.J. No. 514.1

- Landlord has limited right to evict the DV victim

Miscellaneous provisions: The state law (53 Pa. C.S.A. § 304) shields residents, tenants, and landlords from penalties that could otherwise be levied under a local ordinance or regulation when police or emergency services respond to a residence or tenancy to assist a victim of abuse or crime. It does not give domestic violence victims direct protection, nor does it impose duties or restrictions on landlords. However, the City of Philadelphia Fair Housing Ordinance offers some protections for Philadelphia residents: www.phillytenant. org/documents/FairHousingOrdinance2016.pdf. In addition, victims of domestic violence whose tenancy has been terminated by court order (evicted) may file an affidavit with the court, asking for a stay (postponement) of the order of possession. The stay expires when the tenant files an appeal, or 30 days after the entry of judgment, whichever is earlier. (Pa.R.C.P.M.D.J. No. 514.1).)

Rhode Island

R.I. Gen. Laws §§ 34-37-1 through 34-37-4

- Landlord cannot refuse to rent to victim of DV
- Landlord cannot terminate a victim of DV
- Landlord or court may bifurcate the lease

South Carolina

No statute

South Dakota

S.D. Codified Laws §§ 43-32-18.1, 43-32-19.1

- Lease cannot include a waiver of some or all DV rights
- Landlord entitled to proof of DV status
- Early termination right for DV victim

Miscellaneous provisions: When tenants exercise early termination rights and provide the landlord with a forwarding address or other contact information, the landlord may not disclose the new address or information to any person unless the tenant gives permission or as required by law.

Tennessee

Tenn. Code Ann. §§ 66-7-109(e), 66-28-517(g)

- Landlord entitled to proof of DV status
- Landlord cannot terminate a victim of DV
- Landlord or court may bifurcate the lease
- Landlord has limited right to evict the DV victim

Miscellaneous provisions: The rights granted under this law do not apply when the perpetrator is a child or dependent of any tenant. Landlord may evict a victim who allows an ousted perpetrator to return to the premises.

Texas

Tex. Prop. Code Ann. §§ 92.015, 92.016, 92.0161

- Lease cannot include a waiver of some or all DV rights
- Landlord entitled to proof of DV status
- Early termination right for DV victim
- Lease cannot prohibit calling the police in a DV situation or otherwise penalize DV victim

Miscellaneous provisions: Tenant who exercises termination rights will be released from any delinquent rent unless the lease includes a clause that specifically describes tenants' rights in domestic violence situations. Landlord may not prohibit or limit a tenant's right to call police or other emergency assistance, based on the tenant's reasonable belief that such help is necessary.

Utah

Utah Code Ann. § 57-22-5.1

- Landlord entitled to proof of DV status
- Early termination right for DV victim
- Lease cannot prohibit calling the police in a DV situation or otherwise penalize DV victim
- DV victim has the right to have the locks changed

Miscellaneous provisions: When the landlord has rekeyed, a perpetrator who does not receive a key and who is a cotenant but not barred from the rental may ask a court for access and a key or, in the alternative, to be relieved from any further liability under the lease (relief from liability is not available to perpetrators who are found by a court to have committed the underlying act of violence).

State Laws in Domestic Violence Situations (continued)

Vermont

15 Vt. Stat. Ann. § 1103(c)(2)(B); 9 Vt. Stat. Ann. §§ 4471-- 4475

- Landlord entitled to proof of DV status
- Early termination right for DV victim
- DV victim has the right to have the locks changed
- Landlord or court may bifurcate the lease

Miscellaneous provisions: Protected tenants include victims as well as parents, foster parents, legal guardians, and caretakers with at least partial physical custody of a victim of abuse, sexual assault, or stalking. Landlords with documentation or knowledge of a tenant's status as a domestic violence victim must, with exceptions, keep the information confidential (must not divulge to subsequent landlords) unless authorized by the tenant.

Virginia

Va. Code Ann. §§ 55.1-1203, 55.1-1208, 55.1-1230, 55.1-1236

- Lease cannot include a waiver of some or all DV rights
- Landlord entitled to proof of DV status
- Landlord cannot terminate a victim of DV
- Early termination right for DV victim
- DV victim has the right to have the locks changed
- Perpetrator of DV liable to landlord for resulting damages
- Landlord or court may bifurcate the lease

Miscellaneous provisions: Right to change locks extends to "authorized occupants" (persons who occupy with landlord's consent but have not signed a rental agreement and are not responsible for rent). Victim with a restraining order loses the right to continued occupation if the perpetrator reappears and victim fails to notify landlord. (Va. Code Ann. § 55.1-1230.)

A landlord must consider evidence of a rental applicant's status as a victim of family abuse to mitigate any adverse affect of an otherwise qualified applicant's low credit score. Statute provides direction on how applicant can show status as a victim. (Va. Code Ann. § 55.1-1203.)

If an otherwise qualified applicant's status as a domestic violence victim negatively affected the applicants credit score, landlord must disregard the negative effect

(tenant must provide documentation of domestic violence status).

Washington

Wash. Rev. Code Ann. §§ 59.18.130(8)(b)(ii), 59.18.352, 59.18.570, 59.18.575, 59.18.580, 59.18.585

- Landlord entitled to proof of DV status
- Landlord cannot refuse to rent to victim of DV
- Landlord cannot terminate a victim of DV
- Early termination right for DV victim
- DV is an affirmative defense to an eviction lawsuit
- DV victim has the right to have the locks changed

Miscellaneous provisions: Victim tenants can terminate early, but the request to terminate must occur within 90 days of the reported act of violence that gave rise to a protective order or report to a qualified third party. The law also recognizes the possibility that the landlord might be the perpetrator of violence, and provides special protections for victims of landlord violence and stalking. (Wash. Rev. Code Ann. § 59.28.575(b).)

West Virginia

No statute

Wisconsin

Wis. Stat. §§ 106.50, 704.14, 704.16

- Landlord entitled to proof of DV status
- Landlord cannot refuse to rent to victim of DV
- Landlord cannot terminate a victim of DV
- Early termination right for DV victim
- DV is an affirmative defense to an eviction lawsuit
- DV victim has the right to have the locks changed
- Landlord has limited right to evict the DV victim

Wyoming

Wy. Stat. Ann. §§ 1-21-1301 through 1-21-1304

- Lease cannot include a waiver of some or all DV rights
- Landlord entitled to proof of DV status
- Landlord cannot terminate a victim of DV
- Early termination right for DV victim
- DV is an affirmative defense to an eviction lawsuit

State Laws on Rent Withholding and Repair and Deduct Remedies		
State	**Statute or case on rent withholding**	**Statute or case on repair and deduct**
Alabama	Ala. Code § 35-9A-164	Ala. Code § 35-9A-164
Alaska	Alaska Stat. §§ 34.03.100, 34.03.180(a)(3), 34.03.190	Alaska Stat. §§ 34.03.100, 34.03.180
Arizona	Ariz. Rev. Stat. Ann. § 33-1364 and 33-1365	Ariz. Rev. Stat. Ann. §§ 33-1363 and 33-1364
Arkansas	Ark. Code § 18-17-502. Statute prohibits tenants from withholding or offsetting rent for alleged violations of state habitability law.	No statute
California	Cal. Civ. Pro. Code § 1174.2; *Green v. Superior Court*, 10 Cal. 3d 616 (1974)	Cal. Civ. Code § 1942
Colorado	Colo. Rev. Stat. § 38-12-507	Colo. Rev. Stat. § 38-12-507
Connecticut	Conn. Gen. Stat. Ann. §§ 47a-13 to -14h	Conn. Gen. Stat. Ann. § 47a-13
Delaware	Del. Code Ann. tit. 25, § 5308	Del. Code Ann. tit. 25, §§ 5307, 5308
District of Columbia	D.C. Mun. Regs. § 14-4303; *Javins v. First Nat'l Realty Corp.*, 428 F.2d 1071 (D.C. Cir. 1970)	No statute
Florida	Fla. Stat. Ann. § 83.60	Fla. Stat. Ann. § 83.60
Georgia	No statute	Not addressed by statute, but Georgia courts recognize a tenant's right to this remedy. See Georgia Landlord Tenant Handbook, 2020, Georgia Department of Community Affairs; and see *Abrams v. Joel*, 108 Ga. App. 662, 134 S.E.2d 480 (1963)
Hawaii	Haw. Rev. Stat. § 521-78	Haw. Rev. Stat. § 521-64
Idaho	No statute	No statute on repair and deduct generally, but if a landlord won't make repairs, tenant must provide landlord with a written notice with a list of violations. Landlord then has three days to fix; failure to repair allows the tenant to sue the landlord to force compliance. (Idaho Code § 6-320.) Repair and deduct is available specifically (and only) for failure to install and/or maintain smoke detectors. (Idaho Code § 6-320(a)(6).)
Illinois	765 Ill. Comp. Stat. §§ 735/2, 735/2.2 (applies only when a court has appointed a receiver to collect rents, following landlord's failure to pay for utilities)	765 Ill. Comp. Stat. § 742/5
Indiana	No statute	No statute on repair and deduct, but once tenant gives landlord notice of landlord's need to repair, landlord has reasonable amount of time to remedy. If landlord doesn't remedy, tenant can sue for enforcement and might obtain actual and consequential damages, as well as attorneys' fees and court costs. (Ind. Code Ann. § 32-31-8-6.)
Iowa	Iowa Code Ann. § 562A.24	Iowa Code Ann. § 562A.23

State Laws on Rent Withholding and Repair and Deduct Remedies (continued)		
State	**Statute or case on rent withholding**	**Statute or case on repair and deduct**
Kansas	Kan. Stat. Ann. § 58-2561	No statute
Kentucky	Ky. Rev. Stat. Ann. § 383.645	Ky. Rev. Stat. Ann. §§ 383.635, 383.640
Louisiana	No statute	La. Civ. Code Ann. art. 2694
Maine	Me. Rev. Stat. Ann. tit. 14, § 6021	Me. Rev. Stat. Ann. tit. 14, § 6026
Maryland	Md. Code Ann. [Real Prop.] §§ 8-211, 8-211.1	No statute
Massachusetts	Mass. Gen. Laws Ann. ch. 239, § 8A	Mass. Gen. Laws Ann. ch. 111, § 127L
Michigan	Mich. Comp. Laws § 125.530	*Rome v. Walker,* 198 N.W.2d 850 (1972); Mich. Comp. Laws § 554.139
Minnesota	Minn. Stat. Ann. §§ 504B.215(3)(d), 504B.385	Minn. Stat. Ann. § 504B.425
Mississippi	No statute	Miss. Code Ann. § 89-8-15
Missouri	Mo. Ann. Stat. §§ 441.570, 441.580; *Kohner Properties, Inc. v. Johnson,* 553 S.W.3d 280 (Mo. Sup. Ct. 2018)	Mo. Ann. Stat. § 441.234
Montana	Mont. Code Ann. § 70-24-421	Mont. Code Ann. §§ 70-24-406 to -408
Nebraska	Neb. Rev. Stat. § 76-1428	Neb. Rev. Stat. § 76-1427
Nevada	Nev. Rev. Stat. Ann. § 118A.490	Nev. Rev. Stat. Ann. §§ 118A.360, 118A.380
New Hampshire	N.H. Rev. Stat. Ann. § 540:13-d	No statute
New Jersey	*Berzito v. Gambino,* 63 N.J. 460 (1973)	*Marini v. Ireland,* 265 A.2d 526 (1970)
New Mexico	N.M. Stat. Ann. § 47-8-27.2	No statute
New York	N.Y. Real Prop. Law § 235-b, *Semans Family Ltd. Partnership v. Kennedy,* 675 N.Y.S.2d 489 (N.Y. City Civ. Ct.,1998)	For emergency repairs (such as broken door lock) only: N.Y. Real Prop. Law § 235-b; *Jangla Realty Co. v. Gravagna,* 447 N.Y.S. 2d 338 (Civ. Ct., Queens County, 1981)
North Carolina	No statute, but tenants can sue in small claims court, asking a judge to order repairs, to reduce rent while repairs are being made, and for a retroactive rent abatement for the time during which repairs were not made. See, "Landlords Maintenance and Repair Duties: Your Rights as a Residential Tenant in North Carolina," North Carolina Attorney General publication.	No statute, but tenants can repair the problem and sue in small claims court for reimbursement. See, "Landlords Maintenance and Repair Duties: Your Rights as a Residential Tenant in North Carolina," North Carolina Attorney General publication.
North Dakota	No statute	N.D. Cent. Code §§ 47-16-13, 47-16-13.1
Ohio	Ohio Rev. Code Ann. § 5321.07 (does not apply to student tenants; or when landlord owns three or fewer rental units, as long as landlord has given written notice to tenant)	No statute
Oklahoma	Okla. Stat. Ann. tit. 41, § 121	Okla. Stat. Ann. tit. 41, § 121

State Laws on Rent Withholding and Repair and Deduct Remedies (continued)

State	Statute or case on rent withholding	Statute or case on repair and deduct
Oregon	Or. Rev. Stat. § 90.365	Or. Rev. Stat. § 90.365
Pennsylvania	68 Pa. Cons. Stat. Ann. § 250.206; 35 Pa. Cons. Stat. Ann. § 1700-1	*Pugh v. Holmes*, 405 A.2d 897 (1979)
Rhode Island	R.I. Gen. Laws § 34-18-32	R.I. Gen. Laws §§ 34-18-30 to -31
South Carolina	S.C. Code Ann. § 27-40-640	S.C. Code Ann. § 27-40-630
South Dakota	S.D. Codified Laws Ann. § 43-32-9	S.D. Codified Laws Ann. § 43-32-9
Tennessee	Tenn. Code Ann. § 68-111-104	Tenn. Code Ann. § 66-28-502
Texas	No statute	Tex. Prop. Code Ann. §§ 92.056, 92.0561
Utah	No statute	Utah Code Ann. § 57-22-6
Vermont	Vt. Stat. Ann. tit. 9, § 4458	Vt. Stat. Ann. tit. 9, § 4459
Virginia	Va. Code Ann. § 55.1-1244	Va. Code Ann. § 55.1-1244.1
Washington	Wash. Rev. Code Ann. §§ 59.18.110, 59.18.115	Wash. Rev. Code Ann. §§ 59.18.100, 59.18.110
West Virginia	*Teller v. McCoy*, 253 S.E.2d 114 (W.Va. 1978)	*Teller v. McCoy*, 253 S.E.2d 114 (W.Va. 1978)
Wisconsin	Wis. Stat. Ann. § 704.07(4)	No statute
Wyoming	Wyo. Stat. § 1-21-1206	No statute

State Laws on Landlord's Access to Rental Property

In all states, even in the absence of a statute, landlords may enter to deal with a true **emergency** (an imminent and serious threat to health, safety, or property); and when the tenant has **abandoned** the property (left for good). Most states specify nonemergency circumstances that justify entry, and some explicitly include abandonment and "extended absence" (temporary but prolonged absence, which allows a landlord to enter when necessary to protect the property). But even when the statute doesn't mention "extended absence," landlords may enter when it's necessary to avert serious property damage (an emergency situation).

State	State Law Citation	Amount of Notice Required in Nonemergency Situations	Form of Notice	Reasons Landlord May Enter					
				To Deal With an Emergency	To Inspect the Premises	To Make Repairs, Alterations, or Improvements	To Show Property to Prospective Tenants or Purchasers	During Tenant's Extended Absence	When Tenant Has Abandoned the Property
Alabama	Ala. Code §§ 35-9A-303, 35-9A-423	Two days	Not specified	✓	✓	✓	✓	✓	✓
Alaska	Alaska Stat. §§ 34.03.140, 34.03.230	24 hours	Not specified	✓	✓	✓	✓	✓	✓
Arizona	Ariz. Rev. Stat. § 33-1343	Two days; notice period does not apply, and tenant's consent is assumed, if entry is pursuant to tenant's request for maintenance as prescribed in Ariz. Rev. Stat. § 33-1341, paragraph 8	Not specified	✓	✓	✓	✓		✓
Arkansas	Ark. Code Ann. § 18-17-602	No notice specified	Not specified		✓	✓	✓		
California	Cal. Civ. Code §§ 1950.5, 1954	Reasonable notice; 24 hours is presumed reasonable (48 hours for initial move-out inspection)	Written notice required, but oral notice is sufficient if the entry is to show the property to prospective or actual purchasers, but only if the landlord has given written notice within the previous 120 days, telling the tenant that the property is for sale and such oral notice might be given (24 hours' notice is presumed reasonable; landlord must leave a note when leaving).	✓	✓	✓	✓		✓

State Laws on Landlord's Access to Rental Property (continued)

State	State Law Citation	Amount of Notice Required in Nonemergency Situations	Form of Notice	Reasons Landlord May Enter					
				To Deal With an Emergency	To Inspect the Premises	To Make Repairs, Alterations, or Improvements	To Show Property to Prospective Tenants or Purchasers	During Tenant's Extended Absence	When Tenant Has Abandoned the Property
Colorado	Colo. Rev. Stat. Ann. § 38-12-1004	Notice statute relates only to access for inspecting for or treating a bed bug infestation. 48 hours' notice required unless lease says otherwise.	Not specified, unless the access is related to a possible or actual bed bug infestation, in which case notice must be electronic or written.						
Connecticut	Conn. Gen. Stat. Ann. §§ 47a-16 to 47a-16a	Reasonable notice	Written or oral	✓	✓	✓	✓	✓	✓
Delaware	Del. Code Ann. tit. 25, §§ 5113, 5507, 5509, 5510	48 hours	Written, by giving a copy to an adult who resides at the rental unit or at the tenant's usual residence (if it's not the rental) or by mailing via registered or certified mail or first class mail as evidenced by a certificate of mailing postage-prepaid, addressed to the tenant at the rental. The notice can also be posted at the rental unit when it's combined with a return receipt of a certificate of mailing.	✓	✓	✓	✓	✓	
District of Columbia	D.C. Code Ann. § 42-3505.51	48 hours	Written and electronic (including email and mobile text messaging), but if the tenant doesn't provide an acknowledgment of the electronic notice in writing, the landlord must provide a paper notice.	✓	✓	✓	✓		

State Laws on Landlord's Access to Rental Property (continued)

State	State Law Citation	Amount of Notice Required in Nonemergency Situations	Form of Notice	Reasons Landlord May Enter					
				To Deal With an Emergency	To Inspect the Premises	To Make Repairs, Alterations, or Improvements	To Show Property to Prospective Tenants or Purchasers	During Tenant's Extended Absence	When Tenant Has Abandoned the Property
Florida	Fla. Stat. Ann. § 83.53	12 hours for repairs; landlord may enter "when necessary" in an emergency, when a tenant unreasonably withholds consent, or when the tenant is gone (without notifying the landlord) for a period of time equal to one-half the time for periodic rental payments.	Not specified	✓	✓	✓	✓	✓	
Georgia	No statute								
Hawaii	Haw. Rev. Stat. §§ 521-53, 521-70(b)	Two days	Not specified	✓	✓	✓	✓	✓	✓
Idaho	No statute								
Illinois	No statute								
Indiana	Ind. Code Ann. § 32-31-5-6	Reasonable notice	Written or oral	✓	✓	✓	✓		✓
Iowa	Iowa Code Ann. §§ 562A.19, 562A.28, 562A.29	24 hours	Not specified	✓	✓	✓	✓	✓	✓
Kansas	Kan. Stat. Ann. §§ 58-2557, 58-2565	Reasonable notice	Not specified	✓	✓	✓	✓	✓	✓
Kentucky	Ky. Rev. Stat. Ann. §§ 383.615, 383.670	Two days	Not specified	✓	✓	✓	✓	✓	✓
Louisiana	La. Civ. Code art. 2693	No notice specified	Not specified		✓				
Maine	Me. Rev. Stat. Ann. tit. 14, § 6025	24 hours	Not specified	✓	✓	✓	✓		
Maryland	No statute								
Massachusetts	Mass. Gen. Laws Ann. ch. 186, § 15B(1)(a)	No notice specified	Not specified		✓	✓	✓		✓
Michigan	No statute								
Minnesota	Minn. Stat. Ann. § 504B.211	Reasonable notice	Not specified	✓	✓	✓	✓		

State Laws on Landlord's Access to Rental Property (continued)

State	State Law Citation	Amount of Notice Required in Nonemergency Situations	Form of Notice	Reasons Landlord May Enter					
				To Deal With an Emergency	To Inspect the Premises	To Make Repairs, Alterations, or Improvements	To Show Property to Prospective Tenants or Purchasers	During Tenant's Extended Absence	When Tenant Has Abandoned the Property
Mississippi	Miss. Code Ann. § 89-7-49	When a landlord believes tenant has abandoned property, and the tenant owes rent, the landlord may request the constable of the county to go onto the premises to ascertain abandonment and leave a notice.	Written notice						✓
Missouri	No statute								
Montana	Mont. Code Ann. §§ 70-24-108, 70-24-312, 70-24-426	24 hours	Email (if email is provided in the lease or rental agreement), hand delivery, mail with a certificate of mailing or by certified mail, or a post on the main entry door of the dwelling unit.	✓	✓	✓	✓	✓	✓
Nebraska	Neb. Rev. Stat. §§ 76-1423, 76-1432	24 hours	Not specified	✓	✓	✓	✓	✓	✓
Nevada	Nev. Rev. Stat. Ann. § 118A.330	24 hours	Not specified	✓	✓	✓	✓		✓
New Hampshire	N.H. Rev. Stat. Ann. § 540-A:3	Notice that is adequate under the circumstances; however, 48 hours' notice when entering after receiving notice of a bed bug infestation in an adjacent unit	Not specified, but 48 hours when entering to evaluate a possible or actual bed bug infestation.	✓	✓	✓	✓		

State Laws on Landlord's Access to Rental Property (continued)

State	State Law Citation	Amount of Notice Required in Nonemergency Situations	Form of Notice	Reasons Landlord May Enter					
				To Deal With an Emergency	To Inspect the Premises	To Make Repairs, Alterations, or Improvements	To Show Property to Prospective Tenants or Purchasers	During Tenant's Extended Absence	When Tenant Has Abandoned the Property
New Jersey	N.J. Stat. Ann. § 2A:39-1; N.J.A.C. 5:10-5.1 (for buildings with more than one unit)	In buildings with fewer than three units: Landlords can enter only when they have the tenant's permission or a court order. In buildings with three or more units: Landlords have a right to access the unit to inspect it, make repairs or perform mainte-nance, and deal with emergencies, but must give reasonable notice (one day under ordinary circumstances) before entering.	Not specified						
New Mexico	N.M. Stat. Ann. §§ 47-8-24, 47-8-34	24 hours	Written notice	✓	✓	✓	✓	✓	✓
New York	No statute								
North Carolina	No statute								
North Dakota	N.D. Cent. Code § 47-16-07.3	Reasonable notice	Not specified	✓	✓	✓	✓		✓
Ohio	Ohio Rev. Code Ann. §§ 5321.04(A)(8), 5321.05(B)	24 hours	Not specified	✓	✓	✓	✓		
Oklahoma	Okla. Stat. Ann. tit. 41, § 128	One day	Not specified	✓	✓	✓	✓		✓
Oregon	Or. Rev. Stat. §§ 90.322, 90.410	24 hours	Not specified	✓	✓	✓	✓	✓	✓
Pennsylvania	No statute								
Rhode Island	R.I. Gen. Laws § 34-18-26	Two days	Not specified	✓	✓	✓	✓	✓	✓
South Carolina	S.C. Code Ann. §§ 27-40-530, 27-40-730	24 hours	Not specified	✓	✓	✓	✓		✓
South Dakota	No statute								

State Laws on Landlord's Access to Rental Property (continued)

State	State Law Citation	Amount of Notice Required in Nonemergency Situations	Form of Notice	To Deal With an Emergency	To Inspect the Premises	To Make Repairs, Alterations, or Improvements	To Show Property to Prospective Tenants or Purchasers	During Tenant's Extended Absence	When Tenant Has Abandoned the Property
				Reasons Landlord May Enter					
Tennessee	Tenn. Code Ann. §§ 66-28-403, 66-28-507	24 hours (applies only within the final 30 days of the rental agreement term, when landlord intends to show the premises to prospective renters and this right of access is set forth in the rental agreement)	Not specified	✓	✓	✓	✓	✓	✓
Texas	No statute								
Utah	Utah Code Ann. §§ 57-22-4, 57-22-5(2)(c)	24 hours, unless rental agreement specifies otherwise	Not specified			✓			
Vermont	Vt. Stat. Ann. tit. 9, § 4460	48 hours	Not specified	✓	✓	✓	✓		
Virginia	Va. Code Ann. §§ 55.1-1229, 55.1-1249	For routine maintenance only: 24 hours, but no notice needed if entry follows tenant's request for maintenance.	Not specified	✓	✓	✓	✓	✓	✓
Washington	Wash. Rev. Code Ann. § 59.18.150	Two days; one day to show property to actual or prospective tenants or buyers	Written notice, unless it is impracticable to do so.	✓	✓	✓	✓		✓
West Virginia	No statute								
Wisconsin	Wis. Stat. Ann. § 704.05(2); Wis. Adm. Code § ATCP 134.09(2)	With 12 hours' advance notice, landlords may enter at reasonable times. Landlords and tenants may sign a separate "Nonstandard Rental Provision" agreement, in which they provide for entry for reasons not enumerated in this chart.	Not specified	✓	✓	✓	✓	✓	✓
Wyoming	No statute								

State Laws on Handling Abandoned Property

Most states regulate the way landlords must handle property left behind by departed tenants. Many set notice requirements as to how landlords must contact tenants regarding abandoned property. States might also regulate how landlords must store abandoned property and dispose of it when tenants don't claim their belongings. For details, check your state statute, listed in this chart. Keep in mind that court cases not mentioned here might also describe proper procedures in your state.

State	Statute	State	Statute
Alabama	Ala. Code 1975 § 35-9A-423	Missouri	Mo. Rev. Stat. § 441.065
Alaska	Alaska Stat. § 34.03.260	Montana	Mont. Code Ann. § 70-24-430
Arizona	Ariz. Rev. Stat. Ann. § 33-1370	Nebraska	Neb. Rev. Stat. §§ 69-2302 to 69-2314
Arkansas	Ark. Code Ann. § 18-16-108	Nevada	Nev. Rev. Stat. Ann. §§ 118A.450, 118A.460
California	Cal. Civ. Code §§ 1965, 1980 to 1991	New Hampshire	N.H. Rev. Stat. Ann. § 540-A:3(VII)
Colorado	Colo. Rev. Stat. §§ 38-20-116, 13-40-122	New Jersey	N.J. Stat. Ann. §§ 2A:18-72 to 2A:18-84
Connecticut	Conn. Gen. Stat. Ann. §§ 47a-11b, 47a-42	New Mexico	N.M. Stat. Ann. § 47-8-34.1
Delaware	Del. Code Ann. tit. 25, §§ 5507, 5715	New York	No statute
D.C.	D.C. Code §§ 42-32101.01, 42-3505.01a	North Carolina	N.C. Gen. Stat. §§ 42-25.9, 42-36.2
Florida	Fla. Stat. Ann. §§ 83.67; 715.10 to 715.111	North Dakota	N.D. Cent. Code § 47-16-30.1
Georgia	Ga. Code Ann. § 44-7-55	Ohio	*Ringler v. Sias*, 428 N.E.2d 869 (Ohio Ct. App. 1980)
Hawaii	Haw. Rev. Stat. § 521-56	Oklahoma	Okla. Stat. Ann. tit. 41, § 130
Idaho	Idaho Code § 6-316	Oregon	Or. Rev. Stat. §§ 90.425, 105.165
Illinois	735 Ill. Comp. Stat. § 5/9-318	Pennsylvania	68 P.S. § 250.505a
Indiana	Ind. Code. Ann. §§ 32-31-4-1 to 32-31-4-5, 32-31-5-5	Rhode Island	R.I. Gen. Laws § 34-18-50
Iowa	*Khan v. Heritage Prop. Mgmt.*, 584 N.W.2d 725, 730 (Iowa Ct. App. 1998)	South Carolina	S.C. Code Ann. §§ 27-40-710(D), 27-40-730
		South Dakota	S.D. Codified Laws Ann. §§ 43-32-25, 43-32-26
Kansas	Kan. Stat. Ann. § 58-2565	Tennessee	Tenn. Code Ann. § 66-28-405
Kentucky	No statute	Texas	Tex. Prop. Code § 92.014
Louisiana	La. Civ. Code § 2707, La. Civ. Proc. § 4705	Utah	Utah Code Ann. § 78B-6-816
Maine	Me. Rev. Stat. Ann. tit. 14, §§ 6005, 6013	Vermont	Vt. Stat. Ann. tit. 9, § 4462; Vt. Stat. Ann. tit. 12, § 4854a
Maryland	Md. Code, Real Property, § 8-208		
Massachusetts	Mass. Gen. Laws Ann. ch. 239 § 4	Virginia	Va. Code Ann. §§ 55.1-1249, 55.1-1254 to 55.1-1256
Michigan	No statute	Washington	Wash. Rev. Code Ann. § 59.18.310
Minnesota	Minn. Stat. Ann. § 504B.271	West Virginia	W.Va. Code §§ 37-6-6, 55-3A-3
Mississippi	Miss. Code Ann. §§ 89-7-31, 89-7-35, 89-7-41, 89-8-13	Wisconsin	Wis. Stat. Ann. § 704.05(5)
		Wyoming	Wyo. Stat. § 1-21-1210

State Laws Prohibiting Landlord Retaliation

State	Statute	Tenant's Complaint to Landlord or Government Agency	Tenant's Involvement in Tenants' Organization	Tenant's Exercise of Legal Right	Retaliation Is Presumed If Negative Reaction by Landlord Within Specified Time of Tenant's Act
Alabama	Ala. Code § 35-9A-501	✓	✓		
Alaska	Alaska Stat. § 34.03.310	✓	✓	✓	
Arizona	Ariz. Rev. Stat. Ann. § 33-1381	✓	✓		6 months
Arkansas [1]	Ark. Code Ann. § 20-27-608	✓			
California [2]	Cal. Civ. Code §§ 1940.35, 1942.5	✓	✓	✓	180 days
Colorado [3]	Colo. Rev. Stat. §§ 38-12-509, 38-12-1203, 38-12-1205	✓	✓		
Connecticut	Conn. Gen. Stat. §§ 47a-20, 47a-33	✓	✓	✓	6 months
Delaware	Del. Code Ann. tit. 25, § 5516	✓	✓	✓	90 days
District of Columbia	D.C. Code Ann. §§ 42-3505.02, 42-3505.06	✓	✓	✓	6 months
Florida [4]	Fla. Stat. Ann. § 83.64	✓	✓	✓	
Georgia	Ga. Code Ann. § 44-7-24	✓	✓	✓	3 months
Hawaii	Haw. Rev. Stat. § 521-74	✓		✓	
Idaho [5]	No statute				
Illinois	765 Ill. Comp. Stat. § 720/1	✓			
Indiana	Ind. Code Ann. §§ 32-31-8.5-0.5 through 32-31-8.5-6	✓	✓	✓	
Iowa	Iowa Code Ann. § 562A.36	✓	✓		1 year
Kansas	Kan. Stat. Ann. § 58-2572	✓	✓		
Kentucky	Ky. Rev. Stat. Ann. § 383.705	✓	✓		1 year
Louisiana	No statute				

[1] Only prohibits retaliation by landlord who has received notice of lead hazards. (Arkansas)

[2] Applies when a retaliatory eviction follows a court case or administrative hearing concerning the tenant's underlying complaint, membership in a tenant organization, or exercise of a legal right. In this situation, a tenant may claim the benefit of the antiretaliation presumption only if the eviction falls within six months of the final determination of the court case or administrative hearing. (California and Massachusetts) Landlord cannot disclose or threaten to disclose to any government authority information regarding tenants' or occupants' immigration or citizenship status for the purpose of retaliating. Statute also provides for actual damages, punitive damages and attorneys' fees to the prevailing party upon their request. (California)

[3] Statute prohibits landlord from retaliating by increasing rent, decreasing services, or threatening eviction. When a landlord illegally retaliates, tenants may terminate rental agreement and recover either three months' rent or three times their actual damages, whichever is greater, plus attorneys' fees and costs. Also specifies that if a landlord replaces an appliance with a substantially similar one (presumably in response to a complaint), there is no presumption of retaliation. Landlords cannot retaliate against tenants for exercising their rights under or opposing any conduct prohibited under the Immigrant Tenant Protection Act. If a landlord does retaliate, the tenant may bring a civil lawsuit seeking compensatory damages, a civil penalty, attorneys' fees and costs, and other equitable relief the court finds appropriate. (Colorado)

[4] Statute lists retaliatory acts as illustrative, not exhaustive, and includes retaliation after the tenant has paid rent to a condominium, cooperative, or homeowners' association after demand from the association in order to pay the landlord's obligation to the association; when the tenant is a service-member who legally terminates the tenancy; and when the tenant has exercised his or her rights under state, local, or federal fair housing laws. (Florida)

[5] No statute, but Idaho courts have recognized retaliation as a defense to evictions. *Wright v. Brady*, 889 P.2d 105 (Idaho App. 1995). (Idaho)

State Laws Prohibiting Landlord Retaliation (continued)

State	Statute	Tenant's Complaint to Landlord or Government Agency	Tenant's Involvement in Tenants' Organization	Tenant's Exercise of Legal Right	Retaliation Is Presumed If Negative Reaction by Landlord Within Specified Time of Tenant's Act
Maine [6]	Me. Rev. Stat. Ann. tit. 14, §§ 6001(3)(4), 6021-A	✓	✓	✓	6 months
Maryland [7]	Md. Code Ann. [Real Prop.] §§ 8-208.1, 8-208.2	✓	✓		6 months
Massachusetts [2]	Mass. Ann. Laws ch. 239, § 2A; ch. 186, § 18	✓	✓	✓	6 months
Michigan [8]	Mich. Comp. Laws § 600.5720	✓	✓	✓	90 days
Minnesota	Minn. Stat. Ann. §§ 504B.285, 504B.441	✓		✓	90 days
Mississippi [9]	Miss. Code Ann. §§ 89-8-9, 89-8-17			✓	
Missouri	No statute				
Montana	Mont. Code Ann. § 70-24-431	✓	✓		6 months
Nebraska	Neb. Rev. Stat. § 76-1439	✓	✓		
Nevada [10]	Nev. Rev. Stat. Ann. § 118A.510	✓	✓	✓	
New Hampshire	N.H. Rev. Stat. Ann. §§ 540:13-a, 540:13-b	✓	✓	✓	6 months
New Jersey [11]	N.J. Stat. Ann. §§ 2A:42-10.10, 2A:42-10.12	✓	✓	✓	
New Mexico	N.M. Stat. Ann. § 47-8-39	✓	✓	✓	6 months
New York [12]	N.Y. Real Prop. Law § 223-b	✓	✓	✓	One year
North Carolina	N.C. Gen. Stat. § 42-37.1	✓	✓	✓	12 months
North Dakota	No statute				
Ohio	Ohio Rev. Code Ann. § 5321.02	✓	✓		

[6] Also presumption of retaliation when tenant has complained to a fair housing agency, has informed landlord that the tenant or tenant's child is a victim, or has communicated to the landlord about or has filed a complaint about the landlord's or landlord's agent's act of sexual harassment. Retaliation is also presumed if tenant is served with an eviction notice within 6 months of tenant's exercise of rights regarding bed bug infestations (does not apply to eviction for nonpayment or for causing substantial damage). (Maine)

[7] Landlords may not retaliate against tenants who provide information to the landlord regarding the state's lead hazard reduction program. (Maryland)

[8] If landlord tries to increase tenant's obligations under the lease as a penalty for asserting rights, and the tenant doesn't perform these additional obligations, the tenant can use the retaliation as a defense against eviction for failure to perform under the lease. (Michigan)

[9] Mississippi law specifically requires that landlords exercise good faith when they terminate or don't renew a lease. This could expand the categories of behavior that are considered prohibited retaliation. (Mississippi)

[10] Statute protects tenants or tenants' guests who reasonably request emergency assistance. Local government cannot deem the request itself to be a "nuisance." Landlord may, however, take appropriate adverse actions based on information supplied by emergency responders, as can local governments with regard to declaring a nuisance. (Nevada)

[11] If a tenant fails to request a renewal of a lease or tenancy within 90 days of the tenancy's expiration (or by the renewal date specified in the lease if longer than 90 days), a landlord may terminate or not renew without a presumption of retaliation. (New Jersey)

[12] Landlord also cannot retaliate for tenant's attempt to enforce the warranty of habitability, nor evict when tenant objects to a new lease with an "unreasonable" rent increase. Presumption of retaliation applies to nonpayment evictions as well as holdovers. (New York)

State	Statute	Tenant's Complaint to Landlord or Government Agency	Tenant's Involvement in Tenants' Organization	Tenant's Exercise of Legal Right	Retaliation Is Presumed If Negative Reaction by Landlord Within Specified Time of Tenant's Act
Oklahoma [13]	No statute				
Oregon	Or. Rev. Stat. § 90.385	✓	✓	✓	
Pennsylvania	68 Pa. Cons. Stat. Ann. §§ 250.205, 250.504-A, and 399.11		✓	✓	6 months (for exercise of legal rights connected with utility service)
Rhode Island	R.I. Gen. Laws Ann. §§ 34-18-46, 34-20-10, and 34-20-11	✓	✓		6 months
South Carolina	S.C. Code Ann. § 27-40-910	✓			
South Dakota	S.D. Code Laws Ann. §§ 43-32-27, 43-32-28	✓	✓		180 days
Tennessee	Tenn. Code Ann. §§ 66-28-514, 68-111-105	✓		✓	
Texas	Tex. Prop. Code § 92.331	✓	✓	✓	6 months
Utah	*Building Monitoring Sys. v. Paxton,* 905 P.2d 1215 (Utah 1995)	✓			
Vermont [14]	Vt. Stat. Ann. tit. 9, § 4465	✓	✓		90 days
Virginia [15]	Va. Code Ann. §§ 55.1-1258, 55.1-1259	✓	✓	✓	
Washington	Wash. Rev. Code §§ 59.18.240, 59.18.250	✓		✓	90 days
West Virginia	*Imperial Colliery Co. v. Fout,* 373 S.E.2d 489 (1988); *Murphy v. Smallridge,* 468 S.E.2d 167 (W. Va. 1996)	✓		✓	
Wisconsin	Wis. Stat. § 704.45; Wis. Adm. Code § ATCP 134.09(5)	✓	✓	✓	
Wyoming	No statute				

[13] Oklahoma law specifically requires that landlords exercise good faith in their performance under the Oklahoma Residential Landlord and Tenant Act. An argument could perhaps be made that terminating a tenancy or otherwise retaliating against a tenant for taking certain legal measures could be in bad faith. (Oklahoma)

[14] Retaliation presumed only when landlord terminates for reasons other than rent nonpayment, after tenant has filed complaint with a governmental entity alleging noncompliance with health or safety regulations. (Vermont)

[15] Tenants can sue for damages and injunction. (Virginia)

State Laws on Termination for Nonpayment of Rent

In most states, when tenants are late with rent, landlords cannot immediately file for eviction. Instead, landlords must give tenants written notice that they have a specified number of days in which to pay up or move out. If the tenants do neither, the landlord can file for eviction. In some states, landlords must wait a few days after the rent is due before giving tenants notice; other states allow landlords to file for eviction immediately. Note that the following rules might be tempered in domestic violence situations, depending on state law (see the "State Laws in Domestic Violence Situations" chart in this appendix).

State	Statute	Time Tenant Has to Pay Rent or Move Before Landlord Can File for Eviction	Legal Late Period: How Long Landlord Must Wait Before Giving Notice to Pay or Quit
Alabama	Ala. Code § 35-9A-421	7 business days	
Alaska	Alaska Stat. §§ 09.45.090, 34.03.220	7 days	
Arizona	Ariz. Rev. Stat. Ann. § 33-1368	5 days	
Arkansas [1]	Ark. Code Ann. §§ 18-16-701, 18-17-101, 18-60-304	3 days if landlord is filing a civil eviction ("unlawful detainer"); 10 days if landlord is filing a criminal eviction ("failure to vacate") under Ark. Code Ann. § 18-16-101.	5 days
California	Cal. Civ. Proc. Code § 1161(2)	3 days, excluding Saturdays, Sundays, and other judicial holidays	
Colorado [2]	Colo. Rev. Stat. §§ 13-40-104(1)(d), (5)(b)	10 days, 5 for single-family houses being rented under an "exempt residential agreement."	
Connecticut	Conn. Gen. Stat. Ann. §§ 47a-23, 47a-15a	9 days	Unconditional quit notice cannot be delivered until the rent is 9 days late.
Delaware	Del. Code Ann. tit. 25, §§ 5501(d), 5502	5 days	If rental agreement provides for a late charge, but landlord does not maintain an office in the county in which the rental unit is located, due date for the rent is extended 3 days; thereafter, landlord can serve a 5-day notice.
District of Columbia [3]	D.C. Code Ann. § 42-3505.01	Landlords can evict for nonpayment of rent only when the past due rent is equal to more than $600 and any of the following applies: (a) the tenant fails to submit an emergency rental assistance application within 60 days of receiving a notice of past due rent (b) the tenant's application for emergency rental assistance was denied, or the application was approved with a balance of equal to or greater than $600 remaining unpaid, and the landlord and tenant haven't established a rent payment plan within 14 days of the denial; or (c) the tenant has a rent payment plan and is at least $600 or 2 months behind on the terms of the payment plan, whichever is greater.	

[1] Arkansas uses unconditional quit notices (tenant does not have the opportunity to pay rent owed). Tenants who are evicted under the criminal failure to vacate statute are guilty of a misdemeanor and can be fined no more than $25 for each day the tenant remains in the rental after the notice has expired. (Arkansas)

[2] Landlords who own five or fewer single-family rental homes may state in the lease or rental agreement for a single-family home that only five days' notice to pay rent or quit is required. (Colorado)

[3] Before filing a complaint for nonpayment of rent, landlord must send the tenant a notice of past due rent that contains language specified by D.C. Code Ann. § 42-3505.01(b-1)(2). (District of Columbia)

			Legal Late Period: How Long
		Time Tenant Has to Pay Rent or Move Before	**Landlord Must Wait Before**
State	**Statute**	**Landlord Can File for Eviction**	**Giving Notice to Pay or Quit**
Florida	Fla. Stat. Ann. § 83.56(3)	3 days, excluding Saturdays, Sundays, and legal holidays	
Georgia	Ga. Code Ann. §§ 44-7-50, 44-7-52	Landlord can demand the rent as soon as it is due and, if not paid, can file for eviction. Tenant then has 7 days to pay to avoid eviction.	
Hawaii [4]	Haw. Rev. Stat. § 521-68	5 days	
Idaho	Idaho Code § 6-303(2)	3 days	
Illinois	735 Ill. Comp. Stat. § 5/9-209	5 days	
Indiana	Ind. Code Ann. § 32-31-1-6	10 days	
Iowa	Iowa Code § 562A.27(2)	3 days	
Kansas	Kan. Stat. Ann. § 58-2564(b)	3 days (if notice is delivered by mailing, add two days from date of mailing)	
Kentucky	Ky. Rev. Stat. Ann. § 383.660(2)	7 days	
Louisiana	La. Civ. Proc. Code Ann. art. 4701	Landlord can terminate with an unconditional quit notice.	
Maine	Me. Rev. Stat. Ann. tit. 14, § 6002	7 days	Notice cannot be delivered until the rent is 7 days late, and landlord must tell tenant that tenant can contest the termination in court (failure to so advise prohibits entry of a default judgment).
Maryland	Md. Code Ann. [Real Prop.], § 8-401	10 days	
Massachusetts [5]	Mass. Gen. Laws ch. 186, §§ 11, 11A, 12	Tenants with rental agreements or leases: Whatever amount of time is specified in agreement or lease, but if not addressed in the agreement, 14 days' notice in writing (but tenant can avoid by paying rent and costs on or before day the answer is due). Holdover tenants (tenants at sufferance): No specific time for notice to quit, but landlord must give them a reasonable period of time to remove themselves and property from the premises.	
Michigan	Mich. Comp. Laws § 554.134(2)	Landlord may terminate immediately with 7-day notice.	
Minnesota	Minn. Stat. Ann. §§ 504B.135, 504B.291	14 days' notice required if tenancy at will (no lease); 30 days' or more notice for a lease with a term of more than 20 years.	
Mississippi	Miss. Code Ann. §§ 89-7-27, 89-7-45	3 days. Tenant may stay if rent and costs are paid prior to removal.	

[4] Through December 31, 2022, landlords must give 15 days' notice and contain specific language relating to available COVID-19 relief. They must also provide the notice to a mediation center that offers free mediation for residential landlord-tenant matters. See Haw. Rev. Stat. Ann. § 521-68 for details and to check current status of law. (Hawaii)

[5] For tenants at will who have not received notices in the preceding 12 months, 10 days to pay, 4 more to quit (unless notice is insufficient, then 14 days to pay). (Massachusetts)

State Laws on Termination for Nonpayment of Rent (continued)

State	Statute	Time Tenant Has to Pay Rent or Move Before Landlord Can File for Eviction	Legal Late Period: How Long Landlord Must Wait Before Giving Notice to Pay or Quit
Missouri	Mo. Rev. Stat. § 535.010	Landlord can terminate with an unconditional quit notice.	
Montana	Mont. Code Ann. § 70-24-422(2)	3 days	
Nebraska	Neb. Rev. Stat. § 76-1431(2)	7 days	
Nevada [6]	Nev. Rev. Stat. Ann. §§ 40.2512, 40.253	7 days	
New Hampshire [7]	N.H. Rev. Stat. Ann. §§ 540:2, 540:3, 540:9	7 days.	
New Jersey [8]	N.J. Stat. Ann. §§ 2A:18-53, 2A:18-61.1, 2A:18-61.2, 2A:42-9	Landlord can terminate with an unconditional quit notice.	
New Mexico	N.M. Stat. Ann. § 47-8-33(D)	3 days	
New York [9]	N.Y. Real Prop. Law § 235-e(d) N.Y. Real Prop. Acts. Law § 711(2)	14 days	Landlords must send written notice (via certified mail) to tenants who are five days late paying rent. Failure to provide this written notice of nonpayment of rent can be used by tenant as a defense to an eviction suit.
North Carolina	N.C. Gen. Stat. § 42-3	10 days	
North Dakota	N.D. Cent. Code § 47-32-01	Landlord can file for eviction when rent is 3 days overdue and can terminate with an unconditional quit notice.	
Ohio	Ohio Rev. Code Ann. § 1923.02(A)(9)	Landlord can terminate with an unconditional quit notice.	
Oklahoma	Okla. Stat. Ann. tit. 41, § 131	5 days	
Oregon [10]	Or. Rev. Stat. Ann. §§ 90.394(2)(a), 90.394(2)(b)	72 hours (3 days) 144 hours (6 days)	8 days or 5 days. See footnote for details.
Pennsylvania	68 Pa. Cons. Stat. Ann. § 250.501(b)	10 days	
Rhode Island	R.I. Gen. Laws § 34-18-35	5 days. Tenants can stay if they pay rent prior to commencement of suit. If tenants haven't received a pay or quit notice for nonpayment of rent within past 6 months, they can stay if they pay rent and costs prior to eviction hearing.	15 days.

[6] Under Nevada's "summary eviction" procedures, after a landlord serves the tenant with a notice to pay rent or quit, the tenant must go to court within seven days of notice to contest the notice. If the tenant doesn't, the landlord can file a complaint for eviction in court and get an order for law enforcement to remove the tenant within 24-36 hours of the order. (Nevada)

[7] If the tenant pays all rent due, all other lawful charges contained in the lease, $15 liquidated damages, and any filing fee and service charges the landlord incurs, the court will dismiss the eviction action if the landlord files a receipt of the payments to the court before the scheduled hearing date. If the tenant pays but the landlord doesn't submit a receipt, the hearing on the action will happen, but if the tenant proves payment in full the court will dismiss the case. A tenant can have the eviction dismissed in this manner no more than three times in a 12-month period. (New Hampshire)

[8] When tenants fail to pay rent or pay a valid rent increase, landlords can immediately file for eviction. Following the posting of a warrant for removal or a lockout, tenants have three days to pay all rent due, which will result in the court dismissing the case. If, after four or more days, tenants pay all rent plus the landlord's costs, the court will also dismiss the case. In limited situations, landlords may evict tenants who are "habitually late" with the rent with one months notice, with no opportunity for tenants to cure the default. (New Jersey)

[9] If tenant offers landlord full amount of past due rent at any time before the eviction hearing, landlord must accept it and the eviction proceeding will not take place. (New York)

[10] Landlord has a choice: Serve pay or quit notice after rent is 8 days late (tenant has 72 hours to pay or quit), or serve the notice earlier, after rent is overdue 5 days (tenant has longer, 144 hours, to pay or quit). (Oregon)

State Laws on Termination for Nonpayment of Rent (continued)

State	Statute	Time Tenant Has to Pay Rent or Move Before Landlord Can File for Eviction	Legal Late Period: How Long Landlord Must Wait Before Giving Notice to Pay or Quit
South Carolina	S.C. Code Ann. §§ 27-37-10(B), 27-40-710(B)	5 days. If there is a written lease or rental agreement that specifies in bold, conspicuous type that landlord may file for eviction as soon as tenant is 5 days late (or if there is a month-to-month tenancy following such an agreement), landlord may do so without further notice to tenant. If there is no such written agreement, landlord must give tenant 5 days' written notice before filing for eviction.	
South Dakota	S.D. Codified Laws §§ 21-16-1(4), 21-16-2	Landlord must give a 3-day notice to quit (unconditional quit notice) before filing for eviction.	3 days
Tennessee	Tenn. Code Ann. § 66-28-505 (in counties with a population of more than 75,000 according to the 2010 census); Tenn. Code Ann. § 66-7-109 (in counties with a population with fewer than 75,000)	14 days	
Texas	Tex. Prop. Code Ann. § 24.005	3 days' notice to move (lease may specify a shorter or longer time).	
Utah	Utah Code Ann. § 78B-6-802	3 business days	
Vermont	Vt. Stat. Ann. tit. 9, § 4467(a)	14 days	
Virginia [11]	Va. Code Ann. §§ 55.1-1245, 55.1-1250	5 days. After landlord has filed and before the date tenant must answer, tenant who offers to pay rent, costs, interest, and reasonable attorneys' fees has 10 days to do so, after which the lawsuit will be dismissed (if tenant doesn't make the payment, the landlord gets a judgment for possession and all amounts due). Post-judgment, the case will be dismissed if tenant pays all amounts due, including late fees, civil recoveries, and sheriff fees within two days of the scheduled eviction.	
Washington [12]	Wash. Rev. Code Ann. §§ 59.12.030(3), 59.18.057, 59.18.650	14 days.	

[11] A state of emergency declared by the Governor related to the COVID-19 pandemic might affect both landlords and tenants rights. See Va. Code § 55.1-1245. (Virginia)

[12] The notice must conform with the requirements in Wash. Rev. Code Ann. § 59.18.057, and the landlord must provide a copy to the dispute resolution center located within or serving the county where the rental is located. (Washington)

	State Laws on Termination for Nonpayment of Rent (continued)		
State	**Statute**	**Time Tenant Has to Pay Rent or Move Before Landlord Can File for Eviction**	**Legal Late Period: How Long Landlord Must Wait Before Giving Notice to Pay or Quit**
West Virginia	W.Va. Code § 55-3A-1	Landlord can file for eviction immediately, no notice required, no opportunity to cure.	
Wisconsin	Wis. Stat. Ann. § 704.17	Month-to-month tenants: 5 days; landlord can use an unconditional quit notice with 14 days' notice. Tenants with a lease less than one year, and year-to-year tenants: 5 days (cannot use unconditional quit notice). Tenants with a lease longer than one year: 30 days (cannot use unconditional quit notice).	
Wyoming	Wyo. Stat. Ann. §§ 1-21-1002 to 1-21-1003	Landlord must give a 3-day notice to quit (unconditional quit notice) before filing for eviction.	3 days

State Laws on Termination for Violation of Lease

As a prerequisite to filing to evict, many states require landlords to give tenants a specified amount of time to either fix ("cure") or cease the lease or rental agreement violation, or move out ("quit"). In some states, if tenants haven't ceased or cured the violation at the end of that period, the tenants have additional time to move out; in others, tenants must move as soon as the cure period expires. A few states take a harsh approach, and don't require landlords to give tenants a second chance—in these states, landlords can terminate with an unconditional quit notice. Note that the following rules might be tempered in domestic violence situations, depending on state law (see the "State Laws in Domestic Violence Situations" chart in this appendix).

State	Statute	Time Tenant Has to Cure the Violation or Move Before Landlord Can File for Eviction
Alabama	Ala. Code § 35-9A-421	7 business days
Alaska	Alaska Stat. §§ 09.45.090, 34.03.220	10 days for violators of agreement materially affecting health and safety; 3 days to cure for failing to pay utility bills, resulting in shut-off, additional 2 to vacate.
Arizona	Ariz. Rev. Stat. § 33-1368	5 days for violations materially affecting health and safety; 10 days for other violations of the lease terms.
Arkansas	Ark. Stat. §§ 18-17-701, 18-17-702	Tenant has 14 days to cure a remediable violation. If violation materially affects tenant's health and safety, tenant must remedy as promptly as conditions require in case of emergency (or within 14 days after written notice by the landlord if it is not an emergency); failure entitles landlord to terminate the tenancy.
California	Cal. Civ. Proc. Code § 1161(3)	3 days, excluding Saturdays, Sundays, and other judicial holidays
Colorado	Colo. Rev. Stat. §§ 13-40-104(1)(d.5)-(e), (5)(b); 13-40-107.5	10 days to cure a (non-substantial) lease violation, unless the property is leased under an "exempt residential agreement" (in which case it's 5 days to cure). (Colo. Rev. Stat. §§ 13-40-104(1)(e), (5)(b).) No opportunity to cure substantial lease violations, landlords must give three days' notice to move. (Colo. Rev. Stat. §§ 13-40-104(1)(d.5), 13-40-107.5.)
Connecticut	Conn. Gen. Stat. Ann. § 47a-15	15 days; no right to cure for nonpayment of rent or serious nuisance.
Delaware	Del. Code Ann. tit. 25, § 5513(a)	7 days
District of Columbia	D.C. Code § 42-3505.01	30 days
Florida	Fla. Stat. Ann. § 83.56(2)	7 days (no cure for certain substantial violations).
Georgia	Ga. Code Ann. § 44-7-50	Although statute doesn't specifically mention lease violations as grounds for eviction, Georgia courts allow lease violation as a ground for an unconditional quit notice under the statute.
Hawaii	Haw. Rev. Stat. §§ 521-72, 666-3	10 days notice to cure: if it has not ceased, must wait another 30 to file for eviction; 24 hours to cease a nuisance: if it has not ceased in 24 hours, 5 days to cure before filing for eviction.
Idaho	Idaho Code § 6-303	3 days
Illinois	735 Ill. Comp. Stat. 5/9-210	10 days
Indiana	No statute	Landlord can terminate with an unconditional quit notice.
Iowa	Iowa Code § 562A.27(1)	7 days
Kansas	Kan. Stat. Ann. § 58-2564(a)	14 days to cure and an additional 16 to vacate.
Kentucky	Ky. Rev. Stat. Ann. § 383.660(1)	15 days

State Laws on Termination for Violation of Lease (continued)

State	Statute	Time Tenant Has to Cure the Violation or Move Before Landlord Can File for Eviction
Louisiana	La. Civ. Proc. art. 4701	5 days
Maine	Me. Rev. Stat. Ann. tit. 14 § 6002	7 days
Maryland	Md. Real Prop. Code Ann. § 8-402.1	30 days unless breach poses clear and imminent danger, then 14 days (no cure).
Massachusetts	No statute	Landlord can terminate with an unconditional quit notice.
Michigan	Mich. Comp. Laws § 600.5714	For causing serious, continuous health hazards or damage to the premises: 7 days after receiving notice to restore or repair or quit (domestic violence victims excepted).
Minnesota	Minn. Stat. Ann. § 504B.285 (Subd.4)	Landlord can immediately file for eviction.
Mississippi	Miss. Code Ann. § 89-8-13	14 days
Missouri	No statute	Landlord can terminate with an unconditional quit notice.
Montana	Mont. Code Ann. § 70-24-422	14 days; 3 days if unauthorized pet or person on premises, or if the noncompliance is from verbal abuse of the landlord by a tenant.
Nebraska	Neb. Rev. Stat. § 76-1431	14 days to cure, 16 additional days to vacate if not cured within 14 days. If substantially the same violation recurs within six months, the landlord can terminate without opportunity to cure with 14 days' notice.
Nevada	Nev. Rev. Stat. Ann. § 40.2516	5 days to cure
New Hampshire	N.H. Rev. Stat. Ann. § 540:3	30 days
New Jersey	N.J. Stat. Ann. §§ 2A:18-53(c), 2A:18-61.1(e)(1)	3 days; lease must specify which violations will result in eviction. (Some courts have ruled that the tenant be given an opportunity to cure the violation or condition any time up to the entry of judgment in favor of the landlord.)
New Mexico	N.M. Stat. Ann. § 47-8-33(A)	7 days
New York	N.Y. Real Prop. Acts Law §§ 711, 753(4)[NYC]	Regulated units: 10 days or as set by applicable rent regulation. Nonregulated units: No statute. Lease sets applicable cure and/or termination notice periods. Statewide: When eviction is based on violation of lease, court must grant a 30-day stay of the eviction warrant to give tenant an opportunity to cure the breach.
North Carolina	No statute	Landlord can terminate with an unconditional quit notice if lease specifies termination for violation.
North Dakota	No statute	
Ohio	Ohio Revised Code §§ 1923.02(A)(9) and 1923.04	3 days
Oklahoma	Okla. Stat. Ann. tit. 41, § 132(A), (B)	10 days to cure, additional 5 days to vacate.
Oregon	Or. Rev. Stat. §§ 90.392, 90.405	14 days to cure, additional 16 days to vacate; 10 days to remove an illegal pet.
Pennsylvania	No statute	Landlord can terminate with an unconditional quit notice.
Rhode Island	R.I. Gen. Laws § 34-18-36	20 days for material noncompliance.
South Carolina	S.C. Code Ann. § 27-40-710(A)	14 days

State Laws on Termination for Violation of Lease (continued)		
State	**Statute**	**Time Tenant Has to Cure the Violation or Move Before Landlord Can File for Eviction**
South Dakota	S.D. Codified Laws Ann. §§ 21-16-1(7), 21-16-2	Landlord must give tenant 3 days' notice to quit (no opportunity to cure) before filing for eviction, in specified situations. Other situations require no notice.
Tennessee	Tenn. Code Ann. § 66-28-505(a)(3)	14 days
Texas	Tex. Prop. Code § 24.005	3 days
Utah	Utah Code Ann. § 78B-6-802	3 days
Vermont	Vt. Stat. Ann. tit.9 § 4467(b)(1)	30 days
Virginia	Va. Code. Ann. § 55.1-1245	21 days to cure, additional 9 to quit. A state of emergency declared by the Governor related to the COVID-19 pandemic might affect both landlords' and tenants' rights. See Va. Code § 55.1-1245.
Washington	Wash. Rev. Code Ann. §§ 59.12.030(4), 59.18.650	10 days
West Virginia	W.Va. Code § 55-3A-1	Landlord can immediately file for eviction; no notice is required.
Wisconsin	Wis. Stat. Ann. § 704.17	5 days, no opportunity to cure for public housing tenants who have committed drug-related violations.
Wyoming	Wyo. Stat. §§1-21-1002, 1-21-1003	3 days

State Laws on Unconditional Quit Terminations

The following rules might be tempered in domestic violence situations, depending on state law (see the "State Laws in Domestic Violence Situations" chart in this appendix). Some states have enacted temporary COVID-related statutes that typically provide for longer notice periods and expire when the state of emergency has been removed; these statutes are not listed here.

State	Statute	Time to Move Out Before Landlord Can File For Eviction	When Unconditional Quit Notice Can Be Used
Alabama	Ala. Code § 35-9A-421	7 business days	Intentional misrepresentation of a material fact in a rental application or rental agreement; possession or use of illegal drugs in the rental or common areas; illegal use, possession, discharge of a firearm on the premises (some exceptions); criminal assault of a tenant or guest on the premises (some exceptions); any breach for substantially the same acts or omissions for which a notice to terminate has previously been provided for by the landlord and cured by the tenant within the past six months.
Alaska	Alaska Stat. § 34.03.220(a)(1)(2)	5 days	Tenant repeats a violation of the lease or other violation of law within 6 months.
	Alaska Stat. §§ 09.45.090(a)(2)(G), 34.03.310(c)(3)	5 days	Tenant is committing waste or nuisance, is using the rental for an illegal purpose, or is using the rental for purposes other than living or dwelling (in violation of the lease or rental agreement).
	Alaska Stat. §§ 09.45.090(a)(2)(G), 34.03.120(b), 34.03.220(a)(1), and 34.03.310(c)(3)	24 hours to 5 days	Tenant or guest intentionally inflicts "substantial damage" (damage greater than $400) to the premises; or engages in prostitution, an illegal activity involving a place of prostitution, an illegal activity involving alcoholic beverages, an illegal activity involving gambling or promoting gambling, an illegal activity involving a controlled substance, or an illegal activity involving an imitation controlled substance, or knowingly permitting others in the premises to engage in one or more of those activities at the rental premises.
	Alaska Stat. § 34.03.220(e)	3 days	Failure to pay utility bills that resulted in service termination twice within six months.
	Alaska Stat. § 34.03.300(a)	10 days	Refusal to allow the landlord to enter.
Arizona	Ariz. Rev. Stat. Ann. § 33-1368	10 days	Material misrepresentation of criminal record, current criminal activity, or prior eviction record; additional act of noncompliance of same or similar nature after a previous remedy of noncompliance.
		Immediately	Discharging a weapon; homicide, prostitution, criminal street gang activity; use or sale of illegal drugs, assaults, acts constituting a nuisance or breach of the rental agreement that threaten harm to others.
Arkansas	Ark. Stat. Ann. §§ 18-17-701, 18-16-101	5 days	Noncompliance by the tenant with the rental agreement when the violation is not remediable; using (or allowing another person to use) the premises in a way constituting a common nuisance, or permitting/conducting specified criminal offenses; rent unpaid within five days of rent due date. If rent is unpaid within ten days of due date, tenant may be charged with a misdemeanor (fine only).

State Laws on Unconditional Quit Terminations (continued)			
State	Statute	Time to Move Out Before Landlord Can File For Eviction	When Unconditional Quit Notice Can Be Used
California	Cal. Civ. Proc. Code § 1161(4)	3 days	Assigning or subletting without permission, committing waste or a nuisance, illegal activity on the premises.
Colorado	Colo. Rev. Stat. §§ 13-40-104(1)(d.5), (1)(e.5), (5)(b); 13-40-107.5	3 days for substantial violations. (Colo. Rev. Stat. § 13-40-107.5.)	When tenant has substantially violated lease clause (Colo. Rev. Stat. §§ 13-40-104 (1)(d.5), 13-40-107.5.)
		10 days for repeated violation of lease clause, except that landlords who own five or fewer single family rental homes may provide in their lease or rental agreement for a single-family home (an "exempt residential agreement") that only five days' notice is required. (Colo. Rev. Stat. §§ 13-40-104 (1)(e.5), (5)(b).)	Any repeated violation of a lease clause. (Colo. Rev. Stat. § 13-40-104(1)(e.5).)
Connecticut	Conn. Gen. Stat. Ann. §§ 47a-23, 47a-23b, 47a-15	3 days (or 10 days if the tenant is not a resident of the state)	Nonpayment of rent, serious nuisance, violation of the rental agreement, same violation within 6 months relating to health and safety or materially affecting physical premises, rental agreement has terminated (by lapse of time, stipulation, violation of lease, nonpayment of rent after grace period, serious nuisance, occupancy by someone who never had the right to occupy), when summary eviction is justified (refusal to a fair and equitable increase, intent of the landlord to use as a principal residence, removal of the unit from the housing market), domestic or farm worker who does not vacate upon cessation of employment and tenancy.
	Conn. Gen. Stat. Ann. § 47a-31	Immediately	Conviction for prostitution or gambling that occurred at the rental
Delaware	Del. Code Ann. tit. 25, § 5513	7 days	Violation of a lease provision that also constitutes violation of municipal, county, or state code or statute; or a violation of a material lease provision repeated within 12 months of a substantially similar previous violation.
		Immediately	Violation of law or breach of the rental agreement that causes or threatens to cause irreparable harm to the landlord's property or to other tenants.
District of Columbia	D.C. Code § 42-3505.01(c)	30 days	Court determination that an illegal act was performed within the rental unit

State Laws on Unconditional Quit Terminations (continued)

State	Statute	Time to Move Out Before Landlord Can File For Eviction	When Unconditional Quit Notice Can Be Used
Florida	Fla. Stat. Ann. § 83.56(2)(a)	7 days	Intentional destruction of the rental property or other tenants' property or unreasonable disturbances; for destruction, damage, or misuse of the landlord's or other tenants' property by intentional act or a subsequent or continued unreasonable disturbance (after written warning within previous 12 months); a subsequent or continuing noncompliance within 12 months of a written warning by the landlord of a similar violation
Georgia	Ga. Code Ann. §§ 44-7-50, 44-7-52	Immediately	Nonpayment of rent more than once within 12 months; holding over
Hawaii	Haw. Rev. Stat. §§ 521-69, 521-71, 521-72	Immediately	Tenant fails to use the property according to law and the failure causes or threatens to cause damage to any person, certain property, or constitutes a violation of certain codes; tenant fails to maintain unit according to law, and the failure causes or threatens to cause irremediable damage to any person or property. When tenant continues in possession after the agreed date of termination without the landlord's consent, the landlord can give unconditional notice to quit immediately within the first 60 days of holdover.
	Haw. Rev. Stat. § 666-3	5 days	Second failure to abate a nuisance within 24 hours of receiving notice.
Idaho	Idaho Code § 6-303	Immediately	Using, delivering, or producing a controlled substance on the property at any time during the lease term.
		3 days	Assigning or subletting without the consent of the landlord or causing serious damage to the property.
Illinois	735 Ill. Comp. Stat. § 5/9-210	10 days	Failure to abide by any term of the lease
	740 Ill. Comp. Stat. § 40/11	5 days	Unlawful use or sale of any controlled substance
Indiana	Ind. Code Ann. § 32-31-1-8	Immediately	Tenants with lease: holding over. Tenants without lease: committing waste
Iowa	Iowa Code Ann. § 562A.27	7 days	Repeating same violation of lease within 6 months that affects health and safety
	Iowa Code Ann. § 562A.27A	3 days	Creating a clear and present danger to the health or safety of the landlord, tenants, or neighbors within 1,000 feet of the property boundaries
Kansas	Kan. Stat. Ann. § 58-2564(a)	30 days	Second similar material violation of the lease after first violation was corrected
Kentucky	Ky. Rev. Stat. Ann. § 383.660(1)	14 days	Repeating the same material violation of the lease within 6 months of being given a first cure or quit notice

State Laws on Unconditional Quit Terminations (continued)

State	Statute	Time to Move Out Before Landlord Can File For Eviction	When Unconditional Quit Notice Can Be Used
Louisiana	La. Civ. Code art. 2686; La. Code Civ. Proc. art. 4701	5 days	Failure to pay rent, using dwelling for purpose other than the intended purpose (lease may specify shorter or longer notice, or eliminate requirement of notice) or upon termination of the lease for any reason.
Maine	Me. Rev. Stat. Ann. tit. 14, §§ 6001, 6002, 6025	7 days	Holdover tenants if notice is served within 7 days of the end of the original term; substantial and unrepaired damage to the premises; causing, permitting, or maintaining a nuisance; tenant is a perpetrator of domestic violence, sexual assault, or stalking and the victim is also a tenant; tenant or tenants guest is a perpetrator of violence, a threat of violence, or sexual assault against certain others; the person occupying the premises is not an authorized occupant of the premises. Landlord can also terminate when a tenant changes the lock and refuses to provide landlord with a duplicate key.
Maryland	Md. Code Ann. [Real Prop.] § 8-402.1(a)	14 days	Breaching lease by behaving in a manner that presents a clear and imminent danger to the tenant themself, other tenants, guests, the landlord, or the landlord's property, lease provides for termination for violation of lease clause, and landlord has given 14 days' notice.
	Md. Code Ann. [Real Prop.] § 8-401	10 days	When tenant hasn't paid rent and has had 3 judgments of possession entered for rent due and unpaid in the 12 months prior.
Massachusetts	Mass. Ann. Laws ch. 186, § 12	14 days	Tenant at will receiving second notice to pay rent or quit within 12 months
Michigan	Mich. Comp. Laws § 600.5714(d) and (e)	7 days	Failure to pay rent, causing or threatening physical injury to an individual (landlord must have filed a police report)
	Mich. Comp. Laws § 554.134	24 hours	Manufacture, dealing, or possession of illegal drugs on leased premises (landlord must first file a police report)
Minnesota	Minn. Stat. Ann. § 504B.135	14 days	Tenant at will who fails to pay rent when due
Mississippi	Miss. Code Ann. § 89-8-13	14 days	Repeating the same act—which constituted a lease violation and for which notice was given—within 6 months; nonremediable violation of lease or obligations imposed by statute.
Missouri	Mo. Ann. Stat. §§ 441.020, 441.030, 441.040	10 days	Using the premises for gambling, prostitution, or possession, sale, or distribution of controlled substances; assigning or subletting without consent; seriously damaging the premises or violating the lease.
Montana	Mont. Code Ann. § 70-24-422(1)(e)	5 days	Repeating the same act (that constituted a lease violation and for which notice was given) within 6 months
	Mont. Code Ann. § 70-24-422	3 days	Unauthorized pet or person living on premises; destroying or removing any part of the premises; creating a reasonable potential that the premises might be damaged or destroyed, or that neighboring tenants might be injured, due to tenant's drug, or gang-related, or other illegal activity.
	Mont. Code Ann. § 70-24-422(1)(d)	14 days	Any other noncompliance with rental agreement that can't be remedied or repaired.

State Laws on Unconditional Quit Terminations (continued)

State	Statute	Time to Move Out Before Landlord Can File For Eviction	When Unconditional Quit Notice Can Be Used
Nebraska	Neb. Rev. Stat. § 76-1431(1)	14 days	Repeating the same act (that constituted a lease violation and for which notice was given) within 6 months.
	Neb. Rev. Stat. § 76-1431(4)	5 days	When tenant or guest engages in violent criminal activity or sells a controlled substance on the premises, or acts in a way that threatens the health or safety of other tenants, landlord, landlord's employees or agents.
Nevada	Nev. Rev. Stat. Ann. § 40.2514	3 days	Assigning or subletting in violation of the lease; substantial damage to the property; conducting an unlawful business; permitting or creating a nuisance; causing injury and damage to other tenants or occupants of the property or adjacent buildings or structures; unlawful possession for sale, manufacture, or distribution of illegal drugs.
	§ 40.2516	Immediately	Violation of lease term that can't be cured
New Hampshire	N.H. Rev. Stat. Ann. § 540:1-a		Different rules apply depending on whether the property is "restricted" (most residential property) or "nonrestricted" (single-family houses, if the owner of such a house does not own more than 3 single-family houses at any one time; rental units in an owner-occupied building containing a total of 4 dwelling units or fewer; and single-family houses acquired by banks or other mortgagees through foreclosure).
	§ 540:2, 540:3	7 days	Restricted property: Neglect or refusal to pay rent due and in arrears, upon demand; fourth instance within a 12-month period in which the rent has been in arrears; substantial damage to the premises; failure to comply with a material term of the lease; behavior of the tenant or members of his family that adversely affects the health or safety of the other tenants or the landlord or landlord's representatives; failure of the tenant to accept suitable temporary relocation required by lead-based paint hazard abatement; other good cause. Nonrestricted: Neglect or refusal to pay rent due and in arrears, upon demand; substantial damage to the premises; behavior of the tenant or members of tenant's family that adversely affects the health or safety of the other tenants or the landlord or landlord's representatives; failure of the tenant to accept suitable temporary relocation required by lead-based paint hazard abatement; failure to prepare unit for insect (including bedbug) remediation
		30 days	Nonrestricted only: For any legal reason other than those specified just above (for which 7 days' notice is required).

State Laws on Unconditional Quit Terminations (continued)

State	Statute	Time to Move Out Before Landlord Can File For Eviction	When Unconditional Quit Notice Can Be Used
New Jersey	N.J. Stat. Ann. §§ 2A:18-53(c), 2A:19-61.1, 2A:18-61.2(a)	3 days	Disorderly conduct; willful or grossly negligent destruction of landlord's property; assaults upon or threats against the landlord; termination of tenant's employment as a building manager, janitor, or other employee of the landlord; conviction for use, possession, or manufacture of an illegal drug either on the property or adjacent to it within the last two years, unless the tenant has entered a rehabilitation program (includes harboring anyone so convicted); conviction or civil liability for assault or terroristic threats against the landlord, landlord's family, or landlord's employee within the last two years (includes harboring); liability in a civil action for theft from landlord, landlord's family, landlord's employee, or another tenant; committing or harboring human trafficking.
	N.J. Stat. Ann. §§ 2A:18-61.2(b), 2A:18-61.1	One month	Habitual failure to pay rent after written notice; continued violations, despite repeated warnings, of the landlord's reasonable rules and regulations; at the termination of a lease, refusal to accept reasonable changes of substance in the terms and conditions of the lease, including specifically any change in the term thereof.
New Mexico	N.M. Stat. Ann. § 47-8-33(I)	3 days	Substantial violation of the lease
	N.M. Stat. Ann. § 47-8-33(B) & (C)	7 days	Repeated violation of a term of the rental agreement within 6 months
New York	N.Y. Real Prop. Acts. § 711	Immediately	When there is a landlord-tenant relationship, the landlord can begin a special proceeding to remove the tenant when tenant: Holds over after the lease has expired; has a lease for a term of three years or less and has (during the tenancy) taken the benefit of an insolvency statute or been declared bankrupt; or uses the rental as a "bawdy-house," for prostitution, or other illegal business. Other rules will apply to properties subject to statewide rent control/rent stabilization laws or NYC rent control/rent stabilization laws. Contact a local attorney or rent control organization for more information.
North Carolina	N.C. Gen. Stat. § 42-26(a)	Immediately	Violation of a lease term that specifies that eviction will result from noncompliance or holdover of tenancy
North Dakota	N.D. Cent. Code § 47-32-01	No notice required	Entering by force, intimidation, fraud, or stealth; committing acts of force, threats, or menacing conduct; retaining possession by menacing and threats of violence; unreasonably disturbing other tenants' peaceful enjoyment of the premises.
	N.D. Cent. Code §§ 47-32-02 and 47-32-01	3 days	Holding over after the lease has expired; failing to pay rent for three days after it's due; holding over after a sale or any judicial process ending the tenancy; violating a material term of the lease.
	N.D. Cent. Code § 47-16-07.6	No notice required	Making a false claim of a legal disability, in an attempt to obtain an accommodation (waiver of landlord's no pets rule); or knowingly providing fraudulent documentation in connection with such a claim. Each violation is an infraction and entitles the landlord to evict and demand a damage fee of up to $1,000.

State	Statute	Time to Move Out Before Landlord Can File For Eviction	When Unconditional Quit Notice Can Be Used
State Laws on Unconditional Quit Terminations (continued)			
Ohio	Ohio Rev. Code Ann. §§ 1923.02 to 1923.04, 5321.17	3 days	Nonpayment of rent; violation of a written lease or rental agreement; when the landlord has "reasonable cause to believe" that the tenant has used, sold, or manufactured an illegal drug on the premises (conviction or arrest not required).
Oklahoma	Okla. Stat. Ann. tit. 41, § 132	Immediately	Criminal or drug-related activity or repeated violation of the lease
Oregon	Ore. Rev. Stat. §§ 90.396, 90.398, 90.403	24 hours	Violence or threats of violence by tenant or a guest; intentionally causing substantial property damage; giving false information on an application within the past year regarding a criminal conviction (landlord must terminate within 30 days of discovering the falsity); committing any act "outrageous in the extreme" (see statute); intentionally or recklessly injuring someone (or placing them in fear of imminent danger) because of the tenant's perception of the person's race, color, religion, national origin, or sexual orientation; second failure to remove a pet that has caused substantial damage; a repeat within six months of a prior drug or alcohol violation of which notice was given.
Pennsylvania	68 Pa. Cons. Stat. Ann., § 250.501(b) and (d)	10 days	Nonpayment of rent
		15 days (lease 1 year or less or lease of unspecified time)	Violations of the terms of the lease
		30 days (lease more than 1 year)	Violations of the terms of the lease
	68 Pa. Cons. Stat. Ann., § 250.505-A	10 days (any tenancy)	First conviction for illegal sale, manufacture, or distribution of an illegal drug; repeated use of an illegal drug; seizure by law enforcement of an illegal drug within the leased premises
Rhode Island	R.I. Gen. Laws § 34-18-36(e)	20 days	Repeating an act which violates the lease or rental agreement or affects health or safety twice within 6 months (notice must have been given for the first violation).
	R.I. Gen. Laws §§ 34-18-24, 34-18-36(f)	Immediately	Any tenant who possesses, uses, or sells illegal drugs or who commits or attempts to commit any crime of violence on the premises or in any public space adjacent; "Seasonal tenant" whose lease runs between May 1 to October 15 or from September 1 to June 1 of the next year, with no right of extension or renewal, who has been charged with violating a local occupancy ordinance, making excessive noise, or disturbing the peace.
South Carolina	S.C. Code Ann. § 27-40-710	Immediately	Nonpayment of rent after receiving one notification during the tenancy or allowing illegal activities on the property
South Dakota	S.D. Cod. Laws §§ 21-16-1, 21-16-2	3 days	Nonpayment of rent, substantial damage to the property, or holdover

		Time to Move Out Before Landlord Can File For Eviction	When Unconditional Quit Notice Can Be Used
State	**Statute**		
Tennessee	Tenn. Code Ann. §§ 66-7-109, 66-7-111, 66-28-406, 66-28-505, 66-28-517	3 days	In counties with more than 75,000 people: 3 days when tenant or guest willfully or intentionally commits a violent act, threatens health, safety, or welfare or life or property of others on premises, or is an unauthorized subtenant or occupant who refuses to leave. (Tenn. Code Ann. § 66-28-517)
		14 days	14 days when tenant materially violates the lease or rental agreement or engages in acts that materially affect health and safety, and the action is not remediable. (Tenn. Code Ann. § 66-28-505(a)(3))
		7 days	7 days when tenant repeats within six months a violation of being late with rent or damaging property. (Tenn. Code Ann. § 66-28-505(a)(2)(B))
		Immediately (applies only in counties having a population of more than seventy-five thousand (75,000), as measured in the 2010 federal census)	Immediately when tenant misrepresents a disability or disability-related need for the use of a service or support animal or provides false documentation stating that an animal is a service or support animal. (Tenn. Code Ann. §§ 66-28-505(f) and 66-28-406(f))
		14 days	In counties with fewer than 75,000 people: 14 days when tenant willfully or intentionally commits a violent act or threatens health, safety, or welfare of property or people; but if the tenant is in a housing authority or is not mentally or physically disabled, the landlord can give only 3 days' notice. (Tenn. Code Ann. § 66-7-109(a)(1) and (d))
		14 days	14 days if repeats within six months a violation of being late with rent or damaging property. (Tenn. Code Ann. § 66-7-109(a)(2))
		30 days	30 days when tenant violates lease agreement in another way. (Tenn. Code Ann. § 66-7-109(b))
		3 days	3 days when tenant engages in any drug-related criminal activity. (Tenn. Code Ann. § 66-7-109(d)(2))
		3 days	3 days when the landlord seeks to remove an unauthorized subtenant or occupant. (Tenn. Code Ann. § 66-7-109(f))
		Immediately (applies only in counties of fewer than 75,000 residents, as measured in the 2010 federal census)	Immediately when tenant misrepresents a disability or disability-related need for the use of a service or support animal or provides false documentation stating that an animal is a service or support animal. (Tenn. Code Ann. § 66-7-111)

State Laws on Unconditional Quit Terminations (continued)

State Laws on Unconditional Quit Terminations (continued)

State	Statute	Time to Move Out Before Landlord Can File For Eviction	When Unconditional Quit Notice Can Be Used
Texas	Tex. Prop. Code § 24.005	3 days (lease may specify a shorter or longer time)	Nonpayment of rent or holdover
Utah	Utah Code Ann. § 78B-6-802	3 days	Holdover, assigning or subletting without permission, substantial damage to the property, carrying on an unlawful business on the premises, maintaining a nuisance, committing a criminal act on the premises.
Vermont	Vt. Stat. Ann. tit. 9, § 4467	30 days (for material breach of lease or rental agreement)	Violation of a material term of the lease; failure to comply with state's landlord-tenant law.
		14 days (for criminal activity, illegal drug activity, or acts of violence)	14 days' notice applies for termination based on criminal activity, illegal drug activity, or acts of violence which threaten the health or safety of other residents.
Virginia	Va. Stat. Ann. § 55.1-1245	30 days	30 day unconditional quit notice used when: (a) tenant commits an unremediable breach; or (b) tenant repeats a violation of lease (after earlier violation was cured and tenant intentionally commits another breach similar to the first).
		Immediately	Immediate unconditional quit notice used when tenant breaches the lease or rental agreement by committing a willful or criminal act that is a threat to the health or safety of others.
Washington	Wash. Rev. Code Ann. §§ 59.12.030, 59.18.650	3 days	Holdover, serious damage to the property, carrying on an unlawful business, maintaining a nuisance, trespasser, or gang-related activity.
West Virginia	W.Va. Code § 55-3A-1	Immediately	Failure to pay rent, violation of any lease provision, or damage to the property
Wisconsin	Wis. Stat. Ann. § 704.17	14 days (month-to-month tenants)	Failing to pay rent, violating the rental agreement, or causing substantial damage to the property.
		14 days (tenants with a lease of less than one year, or year-to-year tenants)	Failing to pay the rent on time, causing substantial property damage, or violating any lease provision more than once within one year (must have received proper notice for the first violation).
		5 days (all tenants)	Causing a nuisance on the property (landlord must have written notice from a law enforcement agency regarding the nuisance).
Wyoming	Wyo. Stat. §§ 1-21-1002, 1003	3 days	Nonpayment of rent, holdover, damage to premises, interference with another's enjoyment, denying access to landlord, or violating duties defined by statute (such as maintaining unit, complying with lease, disposing of garbage, etc.).

Small Claims Court Limits

State	Statutes	Dollar Limit	Can Hear Eviction Suits?	Court Website
Alabama	Ala. Code §§ 6-3-2; 6-3-7; 12-12-31; 12-12-70; 12-12-71	$6,000	No	http://judicial.alabama.gov/ library/SmallClaimsRules
Alaska	Alaska Stat. §§ 22.15.040; 22.15.050	$10,000	No	https://public.courts.alaska.gov/ web/forms/docs/sc-100.pdf
Arizona [1]	Ariz. Rev. Stat. Ann. §§ 22-501 to 22-524	$3,500	No	www.azcourts.gov/selfservice center/Small-Claims
Arkansas	Ark. Const. amend. 80, § 7; Ark. Code Ann. § 16-17-706	$5,000	No	www.arkansasag.gov/consumer-protection/resources/column-one/legal-resources/guide-to-small-claims-court
California	Cal. Civ. Proc. Code §§ 116.110 to 116.950	$10,000 for individuals, except that a plaintiff may not file a claim over $2,500 more than twice a year. Limit for local public entity or for businesses is $5,000. $6,500 is the limit in suits by an individual against a guarantor that charges for its guarantor or surety services. Until February 1, 2025, court may hear claims for COVID-related rental debt of any amount (limit of two filings per year does not apply to such actions).	No	www.courts.ca.gov/selfhelp-smallclaims.htm
Colorado	Colo. Rev. Stat. §§ 13-6-401 to 13-6-417	$7,500	No	www.courts.state.co.us/Self_ Help/smallclaims
Connecticut	Conn. Gen. Stat. Ann. §§ 47a-34 to 47a-42; 51-15; 51-345; 52-259	$5,000 (except you might be able to get more in landlord-tenant security deposit claims)	No	www.jud.ct.gov/SmallClaims.htm
Delaware	Del. Code Ann. tit. 10, §§ 9301 to 9640	$25,000	Yes	https://courts.delaware.gov/ jpcourt
District of Columbia	D.C. Code Ann. §§ 11-1301 to 11-1323; 16-3901 to 16-3910; 17-301 to 17-307	$10,000	No	www.dccourts.gov/services/ civil-matters/requesting-10k-or-less
Florida	Fla. Sm. Cl. Rule 7.010-7.230; Fla. Sm. Cl. Form 7.300-7.350	$8,000	Yes	https://help.flcourts.org/Other-Resources/Small-Claims
Georgia	Ga. Code Ann. §§ 15-10-1; 15-10-2; 15-10-40 to 15-10-54; 15-10-80; 15-10-87	$15,000 (no limit in eviction cases)	Yes	http://consumer.georgia.gov/ consumer-topics/magistrate-court
Hawaii	Haw. Rev. Stat. §§ 604-5; 633-27 to 633-36.	$5,000; no limit in landlord-tenant residential security deposit cases. For return of leased or rented personal property, the property must not be worth more than $5,000.	No	www.courts.state.hi.us/ self-help/small_claims/ small_claims

[1] Justice Courts, similar to small claims court but with more procedures, have a limit of $10,000. Rules can be found at Ariz. Rev. Stat. Ann. §§ 22-201 to 22-284. (Arizona)

	Small Claims Court Limits (continued)			
State	**Statutes**	**Dollar Limit**	**Can Hear Eviction Suits?**	**Court Website**
Idaho	Idaho Code §§ 1-2301 to 1-2315	$5,000	No	https://courtselfhelp.idaho.gov/Forms/claims
Illinois [2]	735 Ill. Comp. Stat. §§ 5/2-101 to 5/2-208; 705 Ill. Comp. Stat. § 205/11	$10,000	Yes	www.ag.state.il.us/consumers/smlclaims.html
Indiana [3]	Ind. Code Ann. §§ 33-28-3-2 to 33-28-3-10 (circuit court); 33-29-2-1 to 33-29-2-10 (superior court); 33-34-3-1 to 33-34-3-15 (Marion County Small Claims Court)	$10,000 (limit might be different in Marion County)	Yes, if total rent due does not exceed $10,000.	www.in.gov/courts/files/small-claims-manual.pdf
Iowa	Iowa Code §§ 631.1 to 631.17	$6,500	Yes	www.iowacourts.gov/for-the-public/representing-yourself/small-claims
Kansas	Kan. Stat. Ann. §§ 61-2701 to 61-2714	$4,000	No	www.kscourts.org/Public/Small-Claims
Kentucky [4]	Ky. Rev. Stat. Ann. §§ 24A.200 to 24A.360	$2,500	Yes	www.kycourts.gov/Legal-Help/Documents/P6SmallClaimsHandbookweb.pdf
Louisiana	La. Rev. Stat. Ann. §§ 13:5200 to 13:5211 (city court); La. Code Civ. Proc., Art. 4831, 4832, 4845, 4901 to 4925, and Art. 42 (Justice of the Peace Courts).	$5,000 (city court); $5,000 (justice of the peace, but no limit in eviction cases)	Available in Justice of the Peace courts only.	https://lasc.libguides.com/c.php?g=463399&p=3167530
Maine	Me. Rev. Stat. Ann. tit. 14, §§ 7481 to 7487	$6,000	No	www.courts.maine.gov/help/small-claims/index.html
Maryland	Md. Code Ann. [Cts. & Jud. Proc.] §§ 4-405; 6-403	$5,000	Yes, as long as the rent claimed does not exceed $5,000.	www.mdcourts.gov/legalhelp/smallclaims
Massachusetts [5]	Mass. Gen. Laws ch. 218, §§ 21 to 25; ch. 223, § 6; ch. 93A, § 9 (consumer complaints)	$7,000	No	www.mass.gov/small-claims
Michigan	Mich. Comp. Laws §§ 600.8401 to 600.8427	$6,500	No	www.courts.michigan.gov/SCAO-forms/small-claims

[2] An alternative procedure exists for claims of $1,500 or less in Cook County's Pro Se Court. Plaintiffs represent themselves, and lawyers are allowed for defendants. (Illinois)

[3] Tenants who are the object of a self-help eviction or its attempt, who suffer or are at risk of suffering serious harm, may ask the small claims court for an order directing the landlord to stop and return possession of the rental if needed. When a tenant commits or threatens to commit waste to the rental unit, landlords may ask the small claims court for an emergency order directing the tenant to return possession of the rental to the landlord, refrain from committing waste, or both. (Indiana)

[4] Professional moneylenders and collection agents cannot sue in small claims court. (Kentucky)

[5] Triple damages available. (Massachusetts)

Small Claims Court Limits (continued)

State	Statutes	Dollar Limit	Can Hear Eviction Suits?	Court Website
Minnesota [6]	Minn. Stat. Ann. §§ 491A.01 to 491A.03	$15,000	No	www.mncourts.gov/Help-Topics/Conciliation-Court.aspx
Mississippi	Miss. Code Ann. §§ 9-11-9 to 9-11-33; 11-9-101 to 11-9-147; 11-25-1; 11-51-85	$3,500	Yes	www.courts.ms.gov/trialcourts/justicecourt/justicecourt.php
Missouri	Mo. Rev. Stat. §§ 482.300 to 482.365	$5,000	No	www.mo.gov/government/judicial-branch
Montana	Mont. Code Ann. §§ 3-10-1001 to 3-10-1004	$7,000	No	https://dojmt.gov/consumer/guide-to-small-claims-court
Nebraska [7]	Neb. Rev. Stat. §§ 25-505.1; 25-2801 to 25-2807	$3,900 from July 1, 2020, through June 30, 2025 (adjusted every five years based on the Consumer Price Index).	No	https://supremecourt.nebraska.gov/self-help/small-claims
Nevada	Nev. Rev. Stat. Ann. §§ 73.010 to 73.060	$10,000	No	www.civillawselfhelpcenter.org/self-help/small-claims
New Hampshire	N.H. Rev. Stat. Ann. §§ 503:1 to 503:11	$10,000	No	www.courts.nh.gov/small-claims
New Jersey [8]	NJ R LAW DIV CIV PT Rule 6:1-2	$3,000 ($5,000 for claims relating to security deposits); certain landlord-tenant suits cannot be brought.	No	www.njcourts.gov/selfhelp/small_claims.html
New Mexico	N.M. Stat. Ann. §§ 34-8A-1 to 34-8A-10 (metropolitan court); 35-3-3, 35-3-5, 35-8-1 and 35-8-2 (magistrate court); 35-11-2, 35-13-1 to 35-13-3 (appeals)	$10,000	Yes	https://metro.nmcourts.gov/self-help-center.aspx
New York [9]	N.Y. Uniform City Ct. Act §§ 1801 to 1815, 1801-A to 1814-A	$10,000 in New York City; $5,000 in Nassau County, or Western Suffolk County; $3,000 in Eastern Suffolk County, or Town and Village Courts.	No	www.nycourts.gov/courthelp/SmallClaims/index.shtml http://ww2.nycourts.gov/lawlibraries/nycodesstatutes.shtml (state statutes) www.courts.state.ny.us/courthelp/pdfs/SmallClaimsHandbook.pdf www.nycourts.gov/COURTS/nyc/smallclaims/pdfs/smallclaims.pdf www.nycourts.gov/COURTS/nyc/SSI/pdfs/smallclaims.pdf

[6] Consumer complaint small claims: (1) Plaintiff must make written demand for relief at least 30 days before filing suit; (2) attorneys' fees are available. (Minnesota)

[7] Check this website for any changes to jurisdictional limit after June 30, 2020: https://supremecourt.nebraska.gov/self-help/small-claims (Nebraska)

[8] The Special Civil Part, like the small claims court but with more procedures, has a limit of $15,000. See https://njcourts.gov/courts/civil/specialcivil.html; www.judiciary.state.nj.us/civil/civ-03.htm. (New Jersey)

[9] Corporations and partnerships cannot sue in small claims court, but may appear as defendants. (Does not apply to municipal and public benefit corporations and school districts.) Instead, they can bring commercial claims, which have similar rules to small claims courts but are subject to these additional restrictions: (1) Same limits and procedures as regular small claims except claim is brought by corporation, partnership, or association. Business must have principal office in N.Y. state; Defendant must reside, be employed, or have a business office in the county where suit is brought. (New York)

Small Claims Court Limits (continued)

State	Statutes	Dollar Limit	Can Hear Eviction Suits?	Court Website
North Carolina	N. C. Gen. Stat. §§ 7A-210 to 7A-232; 42-29	Varies from $5,000 to $10,000. Call clerk of court in your county to find out limit.	Yes	www.nccourts.gov/courts/small-claims-court
North Dakota [10]	N. D. Cent. Code §§ 27-08.1-01 to 27-08.1-08	$15,000	No	www.ndcourts.gov/legal-self-help/small-claims
Ohio	Ohio Rev. Code Ann. §§ 1925.01 to 1925.18	$6,000	No	www.supremecourt.ohio.gov/JudSystem/trialCourts
Oklahoma [11]	Okla. Stat. Ann. tit. 12, §§ 131 to 141; 1751 to 1773	$10,000	Yes	https://oklacountyjudges.org/small-claims
Oregon	Or. Rev. Stat. §§ 46.405 to 46.570; 55.011 to 55.140	$10,000	No	www.courts.oregon.gov/forms/Pages/small-claims.aspx
Pennsylvania	42 Pa. Cons. Stat. Ann. §§ 1123; 1515	$12,000	Yes	www.pacourts.us/courts/minor-courts
Rhode Island	R.I. Gen. Laws §§ 10-16-1 to 10-16-16; 9-4-3; 9-4-4; 9-12-10 (appeals)	$2,500	No	www.courts.ri.gov/Self%20Help%20Center/Pages/default.aspx
South Carolina	S.C. Code Ann. §§ 22-3-10 to 22-3-320; 15-7-30; 18-7-10 to 18-7-30	$7,500	Yes	www.sccourts.org/selfHelp
South Dakota	S.D. Codified Laws Ann. §§ 15-39-45 to 15-39-78; 16-12B-6; 16-12B-12; 16-12B-16; 16-12C-8; 16-12C-13 to 16-12C-15	$12,000	No	http://ujs.sd.gov/Small_Claims
Tennessee [12]	Tenn. Code Ann. §§ 16-15-501 to 16-15-505; 16-15-710 to 16-15-735; 16-15-901 to 16-15-905; 20-4-101; 20-4-103	$25,000. No limit in eviction suits or suits to recover personal property.	Yes	http://tncourts.gov/programs/self-help-center
Texas	Tex. Govt. Code Ann. § 27.060	$20,000	Separate small claims courts have been abolished as of August 2013; both small claims cases and evictions are heard in Justice Court. Evictions cases are governed by Rules 500-507 and 510 of Part V of the Rules of Civil Procedure.	https://guides.sll.texas.gov/small-claims

[10] Plaintiff may not discontinue once small claims process is begun; if plaintiff seeks to discontinue, claim will be dismissed with prejudice (plaintiff cannot refile claim). (North Dakota)

[11] Collection agencies may not sue in small claims court. (Oklahoma)

[12] Tennessee has no actual small claims system, but trials in General Sessions Court are normally conducted with informal rules. (Tennessee)

Small Claims Court Limits (continued)

State	Statutes	Dollar Limit	Can Hear Eviction Suits?	Court Website
Utah	Utah Code Ann. §§ 78A-8-101 to 78A-8-109	$11,000	No	www.utcourts.gov/howto/smallclaims
Vermont	Vt. Stat. Ann. tit. 12, §§ 5531 to 5541; 402	$5,000	No	www.vermontjudiciary.org/self-help/debt-collection-small-claims
Virginia [13]	Va. Code Ann. §§ 8.01-262; 16.1-76; 16.1-77; 16.1-106; 16.1-113; 16.1-122.1 to 16.1-122.7	$5,000	No	www.courts.state.va.us/resources/small_claims_court_procedures.pdf; www.courts.state.va.us/courts/gd/home.html
Washington	Wash. Rev. Code Ann. §§ 12.36.010 to 12.40.120; 3.66.040	$10,000 if brought by natural person; $5,000 all other cases.	No	www.courts.wa.gov/newsinfo/resources/?fa=newsinfo_jury.scc&altMenu=smal
West Virginia	W.Va. Code §§ 50-2-1 to 50-6-3; 56-1-1	$10,000	Yes	www.courtswv.gov/lower-courts
Wisconsin	Wis. Stat. §§ 799.01 to 799.445; 421.401; 801.50; 808.03	$10,000. No limit in eviction suits.	Yes	www.wicourts.gov/services/public/selfhelp/smallclaims.htm
Wyoming	Wyo. Stat. Ann. §§ 1-21-201 to 1-21-205; 5-9-128; 5-9-136	$6,000	No	www.courts.state.wy.us/court_rule/rules-and-forms-governing-small-claims-cases

[13] General district courts, similar to small claims court but with more procedures, have exclusive jurisdiction of cases where the claim doesn't exceed $4,500, and it shares jurisdiction with the circuit courts for cases where $4,500 to $25,000 is in controversy. (See Va. Code Ann. §§ 16.1-77 to 16.1-80.) (Virginia)

Landlord's Duty to Rerent

State	Legal authority	Must make reasonable efforts to rerent	Has no duty to look for or rent to a new tenant	Law is unclear or courts are divided on the issue
Alabama	Ala. Code §§ 35-9A-105, 35-9A-423	✓ [1]		
Alaska	Alaska Stat. § 34.03.230(c)	✓		
Arizona	Ariz. Rev. Stat. § 33-1370	✓		
Arkansas	*Grayson v. Mixon*, 5 S.W.2d 312 (Ark. 1928)		✓	
California	Cal. Civ. Code §§ 1951.2, 1951.4	✓	✓ [2]	
Colorado	*Schneiker v. Gordon*, 732 P.2d 603 (Colo. 1987)	✓ [3]		
Connecticut	Conn. Gen. Stat. Ann. § 47a-11a	✓		
Delaware	25 Del. Code Ann. § 5507(d)(2)	✓		
District of Columbia	D.C. Code Ann. § 42-3505.52	✓		
Florida	Fla. Stat. Ann. § 83.595		✓ [4]	
Georgia	Ga. Code Ann. § 44-7-34; *Peterson v. Midas Realty Corp.*, 287 S.E.2d 61 (Ga. Ct. App. 1981)		✓	✓ [5]
Hawaii	Haw. Rev. Stat. § 521-70(d)	✓ [6]		
Idaho	*Consol. Ag v. Rangen, Inc.*, 128 Idaho 228 (Idaho 1996)	✓		
Illinois	735 Ill. Comp. Stat. § 5/9-213.1	✓		
Indiana	*Nylen v. Park Doral Apartments*, 535 N.E.2d 178 (Ind. Ct. App. 1989)	✓		
Iowa	Iowa Code § 562A.29(3)	✓		
Kansas	Kan. Stat. Ann. § 58-2565(c)	✓		
Kentucky	Ky. Rev. Stat. Ann. § 383.670	✓		
Louisiana	La. Civ. Code § 2002; *Easterling v. Halter Marine, Inc.*, 470 So.2d 221 (La. Ct. App. 4 1985); *Gray v. Kanavel*, 508 So.2d 970 (La. Ct. App. 1987)	✓		✓
Maine	Me. Rev. Stat. Ann. tit. 14, § 6010-A	✓		
Maryland	Md. Code Ann., [Real Prop.], § 8-207	✓		

[1] Landlord can prioritize renting other vacant units first. (Alabama)

[2] Landlord must make reasonable efforts to rerent. However, landlord may keep the lease in effect and recover rent as it becomes due provided possession is not retaken and the lease states the tenant has the right to sublet or assign, subject only to landlord's reasonable limitations. (California)

[3] Case law favors mitigation. (Colorado)

[4] Landlord can re-rent; do nothing (tenant remains liable for rent as it comes due); or invoke any liquidated damages or early termination provision(s). The latter two remedies are available only if the lease includes a liquidated damages addendum, or addition, that provides for no more than two months' damages and requires tenant to give no more than 60 days' notice. Liquidated damages provision must substantially include the language specified in Fla. Stat. Ann. § 83.595. (Florida)

[5] Ga. Code Ann. § 44-7-34 states that nothing precludes landlords from retaining the security deposit for rent and other damages provided the landlord attempts to mitigate the actual damages. However, a Georgia court has held that a landlord could keep the rental vacant and sue for rent as it becomes due in spite of this statute. *Kimber v. Towne Hills Dev. Co.*, 274 S.E.2d 620 (Ga. Ct. App. 1980). (Georgia)

[6] The statute implies that the landlord has a duty to rerent: When a tenant breaks the lease, the landlord is entitled to the lesser of (1) the entire rent due for the remainder of the term, or (2) the amount of rent accrued during the period reasonably necessary to re-rent at a fair rent plus the difference between fair rent and the rent under the lease, as well as a commission for the renting of the unit. The landlord is entitled to the lesser of these two even if the landlord doesn't actually re-rent the unit. (Hawaii)

Landlord's Duty to Rerent (continued)

State	Legal authority	Must make reasonable efforts to rerent	Has no duty to look for or rent to a new tenant	Law is unclear or courts are divided on the issue
Massachusetts	*Edmands v. Rust & Richardson Drug Co.*, 191 Mass. 123, 128 (1906)	✓ [7]		✓ [8]
Michigan	*Fox v. Roethlisberger*, 85 N.W.2d 73 (Mich. 1957)	✓		
Minnesota	*Control Data Corp. v. Metro Office Parks Co.*, 296 Minn. 302 (Minn. 1973)		✓	
Mississippi	*Alsup v. Banks*, 9 So. 895 (Miss. 1891)		✓ [9]	
Missouri	*Rhoden Inv. Co. v. Sears, Roebuck & Co.*, 499 S.W.2d 375 (Mo. 1973); Mo. Rev. Stat. § 535.300	✓ [10]		
Montana	Mont. Code Ann. § 70-24-426	✓		
Nebraska	Neb. Rev. Stat. § 76-1432	✓		
Nevada	Nev. Rev. Stat. Ann. § 118.175	✓		
New Hampshire	*Wen v. Arlen's, Inc.*, 103 A.2d 86 (N.H. 1954); *Modular Mfg., Inc. v. Dernham Co.*, 65 B.R. 856 (Bankr. D.N.H. 1986)			✓
New Jersey	*Sommer v. Kridel*, 378 A.2d 767 (N.J. 1977)	✓		
New Mexico	N.M. Stat. Ann. § 47-8-6	✓		
New York	N.Y. Real Prop. Law § 227-e	✓		
North Carolina	*Isbey v. Crews*, 284 S.E.2d 534 (N.C. Ct. App. 1981)	✓		
North Dakota	N.D. Cent. Code § 47-16-13.5	✓		
Ohio	*Stern v. Taft*, 361 N.E.2d 279 (Ct. App. 1976)	✓ [11]		
Oklahoma	Okla. Stat. Ann. tit. 41, § 129	✓		
Oregon	Or. Rev. Stat. § 90.410	✓		
Pennsylvania	*Stonehedge Square Ltd. P'ship v. Movie Merchs.*, 715 A.2d 1082 (Pa. 1998)		✓	
Rhode Island	R.I. Gen. Laws § 34-18-40	✓		
South Carolina	S.C. Code Ann. § 27-40-730(c)	✓		
South Dakota	No cases or statutes in South Dakota discuss this issue.			✓ [12]

[7] From www.masslegalhelp.org/housing/lt1-chapter-11-moving-out.pdf: For various statements of the landlord's requirement to mitigate damages, see *Edmands v. Rust & Richardson Drug Co.*, 191 Mass. 123, 128 (1906). The Massachusetts Supreme Court found that the "[landlord] owed to the [tenant] the duty to use reasonable diligence and to make the loss or damage to the [tenant] as light as [the landlord] reasonably could." (*Woodbury v. Sparrell Print*, 198 Mass. 1, 8 (1908).) See also *Loitherstein v. International Business Mach. Corp.*, 11 Mass. App. Ct. 91, 95 and n. 3 (1980), rev. denied 441 N.E.2d 1042 (1981)); *Cantor v. Van Noorden Co.*, 4 Mass. App Ct. 819 (1976). But see *Fifty Assocs. v. Berger Dry Goods Co. Inc.*, 275 Mass. 509, 514 (1931). Note that the Boston Housing Court has at least twice found a clear obligation to mitigate. *Bridges v. Palmer*, Boston Housing Court, 07326 (May 24, 1979); *Grumman v. Barres*, Boston Housing Court, 06334 (March 1, 1979). See also *Gagne v. Kreinest*, Hampden Housing Court, 91SC1569 (December 6, 1991), where the judge found that a landlord who did not advertise a vacant unit in the newspaper had not mitigated her damages. (Massachusetts)

[8] Although case law seems to accept a duty to mitigate, there is no definitive statement of the law and the issue remains unsettled. (Massachusetts)

[9] Many attorneys believe this old case is not sound authority, and that a trial judge would find a duty to mitigate in spite of it. (Mississippi)

[10] Landlord must mitigate only if intending to use tenant's security deposit to cover future unpaid rent. (Missouri)

[11] Duty to mitigate applies in absence of any clause that purports to relieve the landlord of this duty (courts must enforce this clause). (Ohio)

[12] However, it is likely that a S.D. court would require a landlord to mitigate damages. The S.D. Supreme Court has found that "[t]he breaching party has the burden of proving damages would have been lessened by the exercise of reasonable diligence on the part of the non-breaching party." *Ducheneaux v. Miller*, 488 N.W.2d 902, 918 (S.D. Sup. Ct. 1992) (South Dakota)

		Landlord's Duty to Rerent (continued)		
State	**Legal authority**	**Must make reasonable efforts to rerent**	**Has no duty to look for or rent to a new tenant**	**Law is unclear or courts are divided on the issue**
Tennessee	Tenn. Code Ann. § 66-28-507(c)	✓ [13]		
Texas	Tex. Prop. Code Ann. § 91.006	✓		
Utah	Utah Code Ann. § 78B-6-816, *Reid v. Mutual of Omaha Ins. Co.,* 776 P.2d 896 (Utah 1989)	✓		
Vermont	9 Vt. Stat. Ann. § 4462		✓	
Virginia	Va. Code Ann. § 55.1-1251	✓		
Washington	Wash. Rev. Code Ann. §§ 59.18.310, 59.18.595	✓ [14]		
West Virginia	W.Va. Code § 37-6-7, *Teller v. McCoy,* 253 S.E.2d 114 (W.Va. 1978)	✓		
Wisconsin	Wis. Stat. Ann. § 704.29	✓		
Wyoming	*Goodwin v. Upper Crust, Inc.,* 624 P.2d 1192 (1981)	✓		

[13] Applies only to counties having a population of more than 75,000, according to the 2010 federal census or any subsequent federal census. (See Tenn. Code Ann. § 66-28-102). (Tennessee)

[14] Detailed procedures must be followed when premises are vacant due to tenant's death. (See Wash. Rev. Code Ann. § 59.18.595.) (Washington)

Consequences of Self-Help Evictions

State	Amount Tenant Can Sue For	Statute Provides for Tenant's Court Costs & Attorneys' Fees	Statute Gives Tenant the Right to Stay	Statute or Legal Authority
Alabama	Three months' rent or actual damages, whichever is greater. If tenant elects to terminate the lease, landlord must return entire security deposit and all unearned prepaid rent.	Yes	Yes	Ala.Code § 35-9A-407
Alaska	One-and-one-half times the actual damages. If tenant elects to terminate the lease, landlord must return all prepaid rent and security deposits. Tenant can sue for attorneys' fees but not court costs.	Yes	Yes	Alaska Stat. §§ 34.03.210; 34.03.350
Arizona	Two months' rent or twice the actual damages, whichever is greater. If tenant elects to terminate the lease, landlord must return all security deposit and prepaid rent.	Yes	Yes	Ariz. Rev. Stat. §§ 33-1364(2)(D); 33-1367
Arkansas	Self-help evictions are not allowed, but it's up to the court to determine damages.	N/A	N/A	*Gorman v. Ratliff*, 712 S.W. 2d 888 (1986)
California	Actual damages plus $100 per day of violation ($250 minimum). Tenant may ask for an injunction prohibiting any further violation during the court action.	Yes	Yes	Cal. Civ. Code § 789.3
Colorado	Tenant may bring a civil action to prevent further violations and to recover damages, costs, and reasonable attorneys' fees. If a violation is found, the tenant will receive an award of their actual damages, costs, and attorneys' fees, plus the higher amount of either 3 times the monthly rent or $5,000.	Yes	Yes	Colo. Rev. Stat. § 38-12-510
Connecticut	Double actual damages. Landlord may also be prosecuted for a misdemeanor.	Yes	Yes	Conn. Gen. Stat. Ann. §§ 47a-43, 47a-46, 53a-214
Delaware	Triple damages or three times per diem rent for time excluded, whichever is greater. Tenant may recover court costs, but not attorneys' fees.	Yes	Yes	Del. Code Ann. tit. 25, § 5313
District of Columbia	Actual and punitive damages.	N/A	N/A	*Mendes v. Johnson*, 389 A.2d 781 (D.C. 1978)
Florida	Actual damages or three months' rent, whichever is greater.	Yes	No	Fla. Stat. Ann. § 83.67
Georgia	Landlord may not resort to self-help evictions. Damages are determined by the court.	N/A	N/A	*Forrest v. Peacock*, 363 S.E. 2d 581 (1987), reversed on other grounds, 368 S.E.2d 519 (1988)
Hawaii	Two months' rent or free occupancy for two months (tenant must have been excluded "overnight"). Court may order landlord to stop illegal conduct.	Yes	Yes	Haw. Rev. Stat. § 521-63(c)

Consequences of Self-Help Evictions (continued)				
State	**Amount Tenant Can Sue For**	**Statute Provides for Tenant's Court Costs & Attorneys' Fees**	**Statute Gives Tenant the Right to Stay**	**Statute or Legal Authority**
Idaho	Three times the amount of actual damages.	Yes	N/A	*Schlegel v. Hansen*, 570 P.2d 292 (Idaho Sup. Ct. 1977); *Riverside Dev. Co. v. Ritchie*, 650 P.2d 657 (Idaho Sup. Ct. 1982); Idaho Code Ann. §§ 6-301 to 6-324
Illinois	One month's rent for every month without utility service (partial months prorated), plus consequential damages. If termination resulted from deliberate or reckless indifference or disregard for tenant's rights, or bad faith, court may award each tenant $300 or (when multiple tenants have been affected), the sum of $5,000 divided by the number of affected tenants, whichever is less.	No	Yes	735 Ill. Comp. Stat. Ann. §§ 1.4, 2.1; *U.S. v. White*, 541 F.Supp. 1181 (N.D. Ill. 1982) (held that a tenant who has been subject to a self-help eviction remains entitled to possession of the premises).
Indiana	Statute doesn't specify damages.	No	No	Ind. Code Ann. § 32-31-5-6
Iowa	Actual damages, plus punitive damages up to twice the monthly rent and attorneys' fees. If tenant elects to terminate the lease, landlord must return all prepaid rent and security deposits..	Yes	Yes	Iowa Code § 562A.26
Kansas	Actual damages or one-and-one-half months' rent, whichever is greater. If the rental agreement is terminated, the tenant is entitled to the return of security deposit.	No	Yes	Kan. Stat. Ann. § 58-2563
Kentucky	Three months' rent. Tenant may also recover reasonable attorneys' fees. If tenancy is terminated, the landlord must return prepaid rent.	Yes	Yes	Ky. Rev. Stat. Ann. § 383.655
Louisiana	Landlord may not resort to self-help evictions. Damages are determined by the court.	N/A	N/A	*Weber v. McMillan*, 285 So.2d 349 (1973)
Maine	Actual damages or $250, whichever is greater. The court may award costs and fees to landlord if it finds that the tenant brought a frivolous court lawsuit or one intended to harass.	Yes	No	Me. Rev. Stat. Ann. tit. 14, § 6014
Maryland	Actual damages, reasonable attorneys' fees and costs.	Yes	No	Md. Code Ann. [Real Prop.], § 8-216
Massachusetts	Three months' rent or three times the actual damages.	Yes	Yes	Mass. Gen. Laws ch. 186, § 15F
Michigan	Up to three times actual damages or $200, whichever is greater.	No	Yes	Mich. Comp. Laws § 600.2918

Consequences of Self-Help Evictions (continued)

State	Amount Tenant Can Sue For	Statute Provides for Tenant's Court Costs & Attorneys' Fees	Statute Gives Tenant the Right to Stay	Statute or Legal Authority
Minnesota	Treble damages or $500, whichever is greater, and reasonable attorneys' fees. Landlord might also be found guilty of a misdemeanor.	Yes	Yes	Minn. Stat. Ann. §§ 504B.225; 504B.231; 504B.375
Mississippi	Landlord may not resort to self-help evictions unless lease gives landlord the right to remove the tenant and take possession of the premises without notice.	N/A	N/A	*Bender v. North Meridian Mobile Home Park*, 636 So.2d 385 (Miss. Sup. Ct. 1994)
Missouri	A landlord who wrongfully removes a tenant or tenant's property from rental, or who changes the locks, is guilty of forcible entry and detainer. Court will determine damages.	N/A	N/A	*Steinke v. Leight*, 235 S.W.2d 115 (1950), Mo. Stat. Ann § 441.233
Montana	Three months' rent or three times the actual damages, whichever is greater, along with all security deposits and prepaid rent recoverable.	Yes	Yes	Mont. Code Ann. §§ 70-24-411; 70-24-442
Nebraska	Up to three months' rent and reasonable attorneys' fees. If tenancy is terminated landlord shall return all recoverable security deposit and prepaid rent.	Yes	Yes	Neb. Rev. Stat. § 76-1430
Nevada	Actual damages, an amount up to $2,500 to be fixed by the court, or both. If tenant elects to terminate rental agreement or lease, landlord must return all prepaid rent and any security deposit that is recoverable under law. Tenant might be entitled to court costs.	Yes	Yes	Nev. Rev. Stat. Ann. § 118A.390
New Hampshire	Actual damages or $1,000, whichever is greater; if court finds that landlord knowingly or willingly broke the law, two to three times this amount. (Amount might also vary depending on the situation.) Each day that a violation continues is a separate violation. Court may order a tenant who brings a frivolous suit or one intended to harass to pay landlord's costs and fees.	Yes	Yes	N.H. Rev. Stat. Ann. §§ 540-A:3, 540-A:4, 358-A:10
New Jersey	Self-help in prohibited, and landlord who engages in self-help is a "disorderly person," a criminal offense that subjects the landlord to up to six months in jail.	No	No	N.J. Stat. Ann. §§ 2A:39-1, 2C:43-8
New Mexico	A prorated share of the rent for each day of violation, actual damages, and civil penalty of twice the monthly rent.	Yes	Yes	N.M. Stat. Ann. § 47-8-36
New York	Three times the actual damages. Violations are misdemeanors, and landlords are subject to civil penalties of $1,000 to up to $10,000.	No	Yes	N.Y. Real Prop. Acts. Law §§ 768, 853

Consequences of Self-Help Evictions (continued)

State	Amount Tenant Can Sue For	Statute Provides for Tenant's Court Costs & Attorneys' Fees	Statute Gives Tenant the Right to Stay	Statute or Legal Authority
North Carolina	Actual damages.	No	Yes	N.C. Gen. Stat. § 42-25.9
North Dakota	Triple damages.	No	No	N.D. Cent. Code § 32-03-29
Ohio	Actual damages. Tenant can sue for attorneys' fees but not court costs.	Yes	No	Ohio Rev. Code Ann. § 5321.15
Oklahoma	Twice the average monthly rental or twice the actual damages, whichever is greater.	No	Yes	Okla. Stat. tit. 41, § 123
Oregon	Two months' rent or twice the actual damages, whichever is greater. If the rental agreement is terminated, the landlord shall return all security deposits and prepaid rent recoverable under the state security deposit law.	No	Yes	Or. Rev. Stat. § 90.375
Pennsylvania	Self-help evictions are not allowed, but no specific penalties are provided (it's up to the court to determine damages).	N/A	N/A	*Wofford v. Vavreck*, 22 Pa. D. & C.3d 444 (1981); *Kuriger v. Cramer*, 498 A.2d 1331 (1985)
Rhode Island	Three months' rent or three times the actual damages, whichever is greater. Tenant can sue for attorneys' fees but not court costs. If the rental agreement is terminated the landlord must return all prepaid rent and security deposit recoverable under state security deposit law.	Yes	Yes	R.I. Gen. Laws § 34-18-34
South Carolina	Three months' rent or twice the actual damages, whichever is greater. Tenant can sue for attorneys' fees but not court costs.	Yes	Yes	S.C. Code Ann. § 27-40-660
South Dakota	Two months' rent. If tenant elects to terminate the lease, landlord must return entire security deposit.	No	Yes	S.D. Codified Laws Ann. § 43-32-6
Tennessee	Actual and punitive damages. If tenant elects to terminate the lease, landlord must return entire security deposit. Tenant can sue for attorneys' fees but not court costs.	Yes	Yes	Tenn. Code Ann. § 66-28-504
Texas	A civil penalty of one month's rent plus $1,000, actual damages, court costs, and reasonable attorneys' fees .	Yes	Yes	Tex. Prop. Code §§ 92.008, 92.0081, 92.009
Utah	Self-help evictions are not allowed, but no specific penalties are provided.	No	No	Utah Code Ann. § 78B-6-814
Vermont	Unspecified damages, plus court costs and attorneys' fees. Court may award costs and attorneys' fees to landlord if the court finds that the tenant brought a frivolous lawsuit or one intended to harass.	Yes	Yes	Vt. Stat. Ann. tit. 9, §§ 4463, 4464

Consequences of Self-Help Evictions (continued)

State	Amount Tenant Can Sue For	Statute Provides for Tenant's Court Costs & Attorneys' Fees	Statute Gives Tenant the Right to Stay	Statute or Legal Authority
Virginia	Actual damages, reasonable attorneys' fees, and the greater of either $5,000 or 4 months rent.	Yes	Yes	Va. Code Ann. § 55.1-1243.1
Washington	Actual damages. For utility shut-offs only, actual damages and up to $100 per day of no service. Court may award costs and fees to the prevailing party.	Yes	Yes	Wash. Rev. Code Ann. §§ 59.18.290, 59.18.300
West Virginia				
Wisconsin	Self-help evictions are prohibited. The court will determine damages.	No	No	Wis. Adm. Code ATCP § 134.09(7)
Wyoming				

How to Use the Downloadable Forms on the Nolo Website

This book comes with forms that you can download online at:

www.nolo.com/back-of-book/ELLI.html

To use the files, your computer must have specific software programs installed. Here is a list of types of files provided by this book, as well as the software programs you'll need to access them:

- **RTF.** You can open, edit, print, and save these form files with most word processing programs such as Microsoft *Word*, Windows *WordPad*, and recent versions of *WordPerfect*. On a Macintosh computer, you can use Apple *TextEdit* or Apple *Pages*. You can also work with the forms through a word processing app such as Google Docs (www.docs.google.com).

- **PDF.** You can view these files with Adobe *Reader*, free software from Adobe.com. Unless you have a pdf editing tool or software, you must print out our PDFs and complete them by hand.

Editing RTFs

Here are some general instructions about editing RTF forms in your word processing program. Refer to the form instructions in this book for help about what should go in each blank.

- **Underlines.** Underlines indicate where to enter information. After filling in the needed text,

delete the underline. In most word processing programs you can do this by highlighting the underlined portion and typing CTRL-U.

- **Bracketed and italicized text.** Bracketed and italicized text indicates instructions. Be sure to remove all instructional text before you finalize your document.

- **Optional text.** Optional text gives you the choice to include or exclude it. Delete any optional text you don't want to use. Renumber numbered items, if necessary.

- **Alternative text.** Alternative text gives you the choice between two or more text options. Delete those options you don't want to use. Renumber numbered items, if necessary.

- **Signature lines.** Signature lines should appear on a page with at least some text from the document itself.

Every word processing program uses its own commands to open, format, save, and print documents, so refer to your software's help documents for help using your program. Nolo cannot provide technical support for questions about how to use your computer or your software.

 CAUTION

In accordance with U.S. copyright laws, the forms provided by this book are for your personal use only.

List of Forms Available on the Nolo Website

Go to: **www.nolo.com/back-of-book/ELLI.html**

Forms in RTF Format	
File Title	**File Name**
Agreement for Delayed or Partial Rent Payments	Delay.rtf
Agreement Regarding Tenant Alterations to Rental Unit	Alteration.rtf
Amendment to Lease or Rental Agreement	Amendment.rtf
Consent to Assignment of Lease	AssignConsent.rtf
Consent to Contact References and Perform Credit Check	CheckConsent.rtf
Cosigner Agreement	Cosigner.rtf
Fixed-Term Residential Lease	FixedLease.rtf
Fixed-Term Residential Lease (Spanish Version)	PlazoFijo.rtf
Indemnification of Landlord	Indemnification.rtf
Landlord-Tenant Checklist	Checklist.rtf
Landlord-Tenant Agreement to Terminate Lease	Terminate.rtf
Letter for Returning Entire Security Deposit	DepositReturn.rtf
Letter to Original Tenant and New Cotenant	TenantLetter.rtf
Month-to-Month Residential Rental Agreement	MonthToMonth.rtf
Month-to-Month Residential Rental Agreement (Spanish version)	Mensual.rtf
Move-In Letter	MoveIn.rtf
Move-Out Letter	MoveOut.rtf
Notice of Conditional Acceptance Based on Credit Report or Other Information	Acceptance.rtf
Notice of Denial Based on Credit Report or Other Information	Denial.rtf
Notice of Intent to Enter Dwelling Unit	EntryNotice.rtf
Property Manager Agreement	Manager.rtf

Forms in RTF Format	
File Title	**File Name**
Receipt and Holding Deposit Agreement	Receipt.rtf
Rental Application	Application.rtf
Resident's Maintenance/Repair Request	RepairRequest.rtf
Security Deposit Itemization (Deductions for Repairs and Cleaning)	Itemization1.rtf
Security Deposit Itemization (Deductions for Repairs, Cleaning, and Unpaid Rent)	Itemization2.rtf
Semiannual Safety and Maintenance Update	SafetyUpdate.rtf
Tenant's Notice of Intent to Move Out	MoveNotice.rtf
Tenant References	References.rtf
Time Estimate for Repair	Repair.rtf
Verification of Disabled Status	StatusVerification.rtf
Warning Letter for Lease or Rental Agreement Violation	Warning.rtf

Forms in Adobe Acrobat PDF Format	
File Title	**File Name**
Disclosure of Information on Lead-Based Paint or Lead-Based Paint Hazards (English version)	lesr_eng.pdf
Disclosure of Information on Lead-Based Paint or Lead-Based Paint Hazards (Spanish version)	spanless.pdf
Protect Your Family From Lead in Your Home	leadpdfe.pdf
Protect Your Family From Lead in Your Home (Spanish version)	leadpdfs.pdf
Rental Application	Application.pdf
Resident's Maintenance/Repair Request	RepairRequest.pdf
Tenant's Notice of Intent to Move Out	MoveNotice.pdf

Index

More from Nolo

Nolo.com offers a large library of legal solutions and forms, created by Nolo's in-house legal editors. These reliable documents can be prepared in minutes.

Create a Document Online

Incorporation. Incorporate your business in any state.

LLC Formation. Gain asset protection and pass-through tax status in any state.

Will. Nolo has helped people make over 2 million wills. Is it time to make or revise yours?

Living Trust (avoid probate). Plan now to save your family the cost, delays, and hassle of probate.

Provisional Patent. Preserve your right to obtain a patent by claiming "patent pending" status.

Download Useful Legal Forms

Nolo.com has hundreds of top quality legal forms available for download:

- bill of sale
- promissory note
- nondisclosure agreement
- LLC operating agreement
- corporate minutes
- commercial lease and sublease
- motor vehicle bill of sale
- consignment agreement
- and many more.

Nolo's Bestselling Books

Every Landlord's Tax Deduction Guide

Every Landlord's Guide to Finding Great Tenants

Leases & Rental Agreements

Neighbor Law
Fences, Trees, Boundaries & Noise

Every Landlord's Guide to Managing Property
Best Practices, From Move-In to Move-Out

Every Nolo title is available in print and for download at Nolo.com.

www.nolo.com

 **NOLO** *Save 15%* off your next order

Register your Nolo purchase, and we'll send you a **coupon for 15% off** your next Nolo.com order!

Nolo.com/customer-support/productregistration

On Nolo.com you'll also find:

Books & Software

Nolo publishes hundreds of great books and software programs for consumers and business owners. Order a copy, or download an ebook version instantly, at Nolo.com.

Online Forms

You can quickly and easily make a will or living trust, form an LLC or corporation, apply for a provisional patent, or make hundreds of other forms—online.

Free Legal Information

Thousands of articles answer common questions about everyday legal issues, including wills, bankruptcy, small business formation, divorce, patents, employment, and much more.

Plain-English Legal Dictionary

Stumped by jargon? Look it up in America's most up-to-date source for definitions of legal terms, free at Nolo.com.

Lawyer Directory

Nolo's consumer-friendly lawyer directory provides in-depth profiles of lawyers all over America. You'll find information you need to choose the right lawyer.

ELLI16